Byron Farwell served as an officer in the North African and Italian campaigns in the Second World War and also in the Korean War. Since then he has lived in Switzerland, England and in the United States, where he was mayor of the town of Hillsboro, Virginia, for five years. He has travelled in more than one hundred countries, from Borneo to Timbuktu and from Lapland to the upper reaches of the Orinoco. He is the author of ten books, histories and biographies, including *The Man Who Presumed, Prisoner of the Mahdi, Queen Victoria's Little Wars, For Queen and Country, The Great War in Africa, The Gurkhas, Eminent Victorians* and *The Armies of the Raj*. He is a Fellow of the Royal Geographical Society and of the Royal Society of Literature.

BYRON FARWELL

BURTON

A BIOGRAPHY OF
SIR RICHARD FRANCIS
BURTON

PENGUIN BOOKS

PENGUIN BOOKS

Published by the Penguin Group
27 Wrights Lane, London W8 5TZ, England
Viking Penguin Inc., 40 West 23rd Street, New York, New York 10010, USA
Penguin Books Australia Ltd, Ringwood, Victoria, Australia
Penguin Books Canada Ltd, 2801 John Street, Markham, Ontario, Canada L3R 1B4
Penguin Books (NZ) Ltd, 182–190 Wairau Road, Auckland 10, New Zealand

Penguin Books Ltd, Registered Offices: Harmondsworth, Middlesex, England

First published by Longmans, Green and Co. 1963
This edition first published by Viking 1988
Published in Penguin Books 1990
1 3 5 7 9 10 8 6 4 2

Made and printed in Great Britain by
Richard Clay Ltd, Bungay, Suffolk

TO JOHN N. SAXBY

my father-in-law

CONTENTS

ILLUSTRATIONS — ix

FOREWORD TO FIRST EDITION — xi

FOREWORD TO SECOND EDITION — xv

INTRODUCTION — 1

1. Boyhood and Early Youth 1821–40 — 7
2. The Unscholarly Scholar 1840–2 — 21
3. Sin in Sind 1842–8 — 29
4. Books, Swords and a Lady 1848–53 — 49
5. The Haj Begins 1853 — 63
6. Medina and Mecca 1853 — 77
7. To Savage Harar 1854–5 — 98
8. Incident at Berbera 1855 — 121
9. Cavalryman in the Crimea 1855–6 — 127
10. Africa – The Little Trip 1857 — 137
11. Discovery of Lake Tanganyika 1857–8 — 146
12. The Great Mistake 1858–9 — 159
13. Sick Leave in Salt Lake City 1859–60 — 174
14. Marriage 1861 — 194
15. West African Consul 1861–3 — 206
16. Mission to Dahomey 1863–4 — 225
17. Bitter Brazil 1864–9 — 247
18. Damascus 1869–71 — 266
19. An Exile at Home 1871–2 — 289
20. Trieste 1872–5 — 307
21. India Revisited 1875–6 — 320
22. Gold in Midian 1876–80 — 327
23. Literature and Last Expeditions 1880–5 — 346
24. The Arabian Nights 1885–8 — 364
25. The Coming of the Camel 1885–90 — 383
26. Marble Tent and Burned Papers 1890–6 — 398

APPENDIX — 408

BIBLIOGRAPHY — 410

INDEX — 419

ILLUSTRATIONS

Following page 112

Burton, about 1855 (*Royal Geographical Society*)

Toda family and village, from *Goa and the Blue Mountains*, 1851

The cathedral of Goa, from *Goa and the Blue Mountains*, 1851

Burton outside his tent, *c*. 1859 (*Camberwell Public Libraries, on loan to Orleans House Gallery*)

Going to cover, from *Falconry in the Valley of the Indus*, 1852

Al-Madinah, from *Pilgrimage to Al-Madinah and Meccah*, 1855

The takhtrawan or Grandee's litter, from *Pilgrimage to Al-Madinah and Meccah*, 1855

Harar from the Coffe Stream, from *First Footsteps in East Africa, or, An Exploration of Harar*, 1856

Richard Burton dressed as 'Sheik Abdullah', his disguise in Arabia (*Topham*)

Isabel and Richard Burton at the time of their marriage. After the portraits by Louis Desanges (*Camberwell Public Libraries, on loan to Orleans House Gallery*)

John Hanning Speke (*BBC Hulton Picture Library*)

General Sir Charles Napier (*BBC Hulton Picture Library*)

Explorers in East Africa; A Ladies' Smoking Party; The Wazaramo Tribe, from *Lake Regions of Central Africa*, 1860

Following page 304

Richard Burton (*Topham*)

The Juju, or sacrifice house, Grand Bonny River, from *Wanderings in West Africa*, 1863

The King's Victims; The Amazon, from *A Mission to Gelele, King of Dahome*, 1864

The Paulo Affonso, from *The Highlands of Brazil*, 1869

Frontispiece to *The Battlefields of Paraguay*, 1870

Illustrations by Ernest Griset in *Vikram and the Vampire*, 1870

Burton's house in Damascus, by Lord Leighton (*Camberwell Public Libraries, on loan to Orleans House Gallery*)

Illustrations

Isabel and Richard Burton in their garden and dining-room in Trieste
(*Camberwell Public Libraries, on loan to Orleans House Gallery*)

Daneu's Inn, Opicina, about 1880, the retreat where Burton did much of his
work on *The Arabian Nights* (*The Life of Sir Richard Burton*, by Isabel
Burton, 1893)

Richard Burton on his death-bed (*Camberwell Public Libraries, on loan to
Orleans House Gallery*)

Richard Burton's tomb, Mortlake (*Geoff Howard*)

MAPS

Pilgrimage to Mecca	*Page* 66
Somalia	103
The Search for the Sea of Ujiji	143
West coast of Africa	209
The land of Midian	329

FOREWORD

As I drove my car up the winding road above Trieste I felt that sense of quiet excitement all searchers know when they hope at any moment to find the object of a quest. It was no great discovery that I hoped for. To be quite honest, perhaps I did hope for something big, but I did not expect to find anything important and my expectations were unfortunately realized. But I did experience one of those personal feelings of intimacy with an era now past and a man now dead, one of those rare moments when dead men come to life and seem to make the biographer's questing life worthwhile.

As we neared the crest of the ridge we looked around each bend for signs of the village of Opicina. In my mind was graven (to use a favourite word of Burton's) the image on a photograph taken in 1872 of the inn where Richard Burton had written much, if not most, of his *Arabian Nights*. It came as a surprise when we saw the inn before we reached the village. We, my wife and I, recognized the place immediately. It had changed remarkably little in the past eighty-seven years: a bit of roof altered here and there, some trees grown tall in front, a stretch of fence added – but it was undoubtedly the place, and, if any doubt had remained, there was the same monument across the now paved road. I parked the car and looked. The café, an adjunct of the main building, appeared new, but it had only been refurbished, I knew, for it was plainly shown on the old photograph.

Hoping for records, papers, the lucky bit of fact or legend that gives joy to the biographer, I talked with the owner of the inn in a combination of bad French and worse Italian. No, there was nothing: no plaque, no papers, no memory. Neither he nor the curious group of coffee drinkers who joined us had ever heard of Sir Richard Francis Burton. His name meant nothing to them. He was an *inconnu*. Strings of pink and green crêpe paper garlanded the café, a reminder that this was the last day of the year 1959 and that in a few hours hence a part of Opicina would here celebrate New Year's Eve. Would anyone raise a toast to Sir Richard? Would anyone remember stories from their grandfathers: how the Burtons here entertained the officers of the visiting British squadron; how the party was soaked by the rain and in the confusion the villagers got to the wine and drank it all. It is doubtful. Perhaps someone would idly mention the American who had stopped at the inn that morning to ask about someone long dead. . . . What was his name?

It has been my good fortune to have visited in the past twenty years most of those places where Burton lived, worked, wrote, thought, dreamed and explored. Seldom have I found any physical trace of his once having been there: his name on a wooden sign in Zanzibar saying he had visited a now ruined palace of the sultan; his name, with that of other gold medallists, on the wall of the Royal Geographical Society; a simple plaque at Bagamoyo; his picture (a gift of his wife) on a wall of the British Consulate in Trieste; his curious tomb in an obscure Catholic cemetery on the outskirts of London. There is little else. The house where he died is just now being torn down; São Paulo is a bustling modern city with little time to remember foreigners who lived there a hundred years ago; Bludan in Syria now has a public address system and phonograph record to give the muezzin's call, so it is perhaps best he has been forgotten there; and India is trying to forget all the thousands of Englishmen who ruled her for so long. Even his wax image at Madame Tussaud's has long since been destroyed.

Yet Burton made his mark upon the world. Perhaps it would be better to say his 'marks', for we can find traces of his influences in many spheres of activities from zoology to erotic literature. As J. S. Catton, one-time editor of *Academy*, said of Burton, 'His insatiable curiosity led him to explore almost every path of learning, especially the bypaths.' His accomplishments were often so unrelated that it is difficult for anyone unfamiliar with the total fabric of his life to imagine that the man who was one of the pioneers in Central African exploration, the discoverer of Lake Tanganyika, was the same man who made the brilliant translation of *The Arabian Nights*, or that the poet of *The Kasîdah* and the translator of the great Portuguese poet Camoens was the same man who made the adventurous pilgrimage to Mecca in disguise. Burton was one of those rare personalities who was both a man of action and a scholar, and he made significant contributions to the world in both science and literature. Unfortunately, there were quirks in this personality that thrust his claims to fame into obscurity.

Burton's character was complex. It would be an easy task to assemble an impressive body of evidence to show that he was cruel, dirty-minded, stupid, pretentious and basically evil. But it also would be easy to collect an equally impressive array of evidence (as was done by his wife) to show that he was kind, scholarly, brave, brilliant and badly neglected by the nation he devotedly served. In reality, Burton was all of these things. The man who carefully nursed Speke in the wilds of Africa was the same man who within a few weeks of his death launched a vicious attack on his character and all of the ideals and ideas Speke held most dear. The man who translated *The Arabian Nights* was the same man who translated the pure (if that is the right adjective) pornography of *The Perfumed Garden*. The man who stood in the dark with only a naked sword to face a crowd of wild Somalis intent on his blood was the same man who was afraid of losing his job and pension by being seen in a restaurant outside of his work area. A man of advanced scientific ideas, he was childishly superstitious; an expert on religions, he could find none for himself; a loving husband, he advocated polygamy. Richard Burton was a man who defies pigeon-hole classification and I have

Foreword

made no attempt to label him. He was a unique phenomenon and I have tried to show him as he was within the limits of available knowledge.

In this instance, the amount of available material has been stupendous and I have often felt that it would be an easier task to write a ten-volume biography of Burton than to compress the material into one. P. N. Penzer, one of the great authorities on Burton, once said, 'It would take more than one man to write Burton's life. It takes a genius to write and understand the life of a genius. . . .' I can only hope Mr Penzer will forgive my presumption. Still, there were aspects of Burton's life which until now have been hidden or misinterpreted. I have included new material and corrections, but I have tried to do so without disrupting the narrative by intrusive scholarship. For this reason I have avoided that crutch of poor writers and the device so abused by my subject: the footnote.

The spelling of words from languages using non-Roman alphabets always presents a problem. I have chosen the most familiar form wherever possible, even though this is not always the most exact: thus 'shaykh' is more phonetically correct than 'sheik', but I have used the more popular spelling. For most place names I have accepted the spelling of Webster's *Geographical Dictionary* or, if not listed, those on maps of the National Geographic Society. In some cases where neither of these sources could be used I have employed Burton's spellings. For the nouns used to describe inhabitants of present-day political entities in Africa I have used those recommended by G. Etzel Pearcy, Geographer of the United States Department of State.

BYRON FARWELL

Les Courtils
Petit-Saconnex
Geneva, Switzerland
1 December 1962

FOREWORD TO THE SECOND EDITION

Twenty-eight years have passed since I visited the inn at Opicina, the Slovenian village above Trieste where Burton translated so much of *Alf Laylah Wa Laylah*, commonly called *The Arabian Nights*, and found that the name of Burton was then unknown to the owner and to his customers.

An Italian sea-captain on reading the original preface thought it a shame that his countrymen were unaware of the great man who had once lived among them, so he raised money for a handsome plaque that includes a bas-relief of Burton's head. This was installed at a ceremony attended by the British ambassador to Italy, Italian officials, other dignitaries, an Italian television crew and, of course, local people.

I was invited to take part in the ceremony and I regretted deeply then and often since that I was unable to be present, for my work at that time took me to South Africa. I regret even more, and I am properly ashamed, that I no longer remember the captain's name. He kindly sent me copies of the speeches that were made and described the ceremony to me. Sadly, all papers and correspondence relating to the event have been lost in the course of too many moves over the intervening years.

Reading over what I wrote of Sir Richard Francis Burton, I have found nothing to change. Subsequent biographers have tried to stretch the man out on a psychologist's couch and to apply the science of Freud, but I do not favour such guesswork. I have found no reason to alter the interpretation of Burton which I derived from his known actions and his surviving words.

Interest in Burton has remained high, aided no doubt by television accounts of his exploits. I note, however, the changes in social mores since I was researching his life. A quarter of a century ago I experienced considerable difficulty in purchasing erotica such as the *Kama Sutra* and *The Perfumed Garden*, and in convincing librarians that my interest in such works was scholarly. Today, of course, these are to be found on open library shelves and on many news-stands.

I am grateful to Ms Eleo Gordon, my English editor, and to Ms Susan Rose-Smith, Viking's illustrations editor, for the many illustrations which ornament this new edition.

Hillsboro, Virginia
1987

ACKNOWLEDGEMENTS

I AM deeply indebted to a number of individuals and institutions who have been most helpful to me in the preparation of this biography.

Individuals: Carl A. Malouf of New York; Miss B. J. Kirkpatrick, Librarian of the Royal Anthropological Institute of Great Britain and Ireland; Alfred Schwartz of Washington, D.C.; Dr Sauro Pesante, Biblioteca Civica, Trieste; Robert T. Hatt, Director of the Cranbrook Institute of Science; John S. Mayfield of Bethesda, Maryland; Paul H. Gebhard, Executive Director of the Institute of Sex Research; Franklin P. Johnson, University of Chicago; Charles R. Schmitter, Fencing Coach of the University of Michigan; Charles M. Morhardt, Associate Director of the Detroit Public Library; N. M. Penzer of Fairwarp, Uckfield, Sussex; Mrs Lois Fohl, Michigan State Library; Richard H. Dillon, Librarian of the Sutro Branch, California State Library; Miss G. Johnson, Chief Librarian of Dulwich Library, Camberwell; J. J. Gelb, Oriental Institute, University of Chicago; Mrs G. A. Langdon, Archivist of the Royal Geographical Society; David L. Harrison of Sevenoaks, Kent; W. B. Neville-Terry, British Consul in Trieste; Gordon H. Fairbanks, Deccan College, Poona; N. Abbott, University of Chicago; John Brinton, Beirut, Lebanon; Lewis E. Hatch, University of Texas; the Hon. Sir Harold Nicolson; Brig. M. Jephson of Mallow Castle, Co. Cork; Ruth S. Farwell, the author's understanding wife.

Institutions: India Office Library; New York Public Library; Huntington Library; Public Records Office; Detroit Public Library; Library of Congress; California State Library; Camberwell Public Libraries; Cherer & Co.; Royal Geographical Society; Royal Anthropological Institute of Great Britain and Ireland.

In addition to these individuals and institutions, I would like to express my special gratitude to those dozens of used-book dealers in the United Kingdom, Canada and the United States who have searched for and found out-of-print books and even manuscripts for me.

I am grateful to the following for permission to include copyright material: the Trustees of the Fitzwilliam Museum, Cambridge, for extracts from *My Diaries* by Wilfrid Scawen Blunt, and Hutchinson & Co. Ltd. for extracts from *Memoirs* by Lord Redesdale.

INTRODUCTION

No man can be all things at once, no matter how hard he tries, but no man tried harder than Richard Francis Burton. He made significant contributions to the world in the field of literature and geography. He was also a poet, traveller, soldier, diplomat, inventor, author, explorer, archaeologist, linguist, anthropologist, student of religions and more besides.

Above all, however, Burton was an adventurer, in the purest sense of that word; and adventurers, and more specifically that breed of adventurers who travel and explore, have always held a fascination for most people. Although modern man rarely questions the value of exploration, the explorer pursues a course of activity that seems, logically, at variance with man's basic strivings for the good life, the best obtainable in food, shelter, and all those other physical, mental and spiritual comforts that characterize civilized life. The explorer deliberately turns his back on civilization and its pleasures simply to go and see unknown lands. Yet the explorer is always a civilized man; exploration is an advanced intellectual concept. The primitive or half-civilized man may move into new lands for food, protection or trade, but he is always driven there by necessity or greed and rarely troubles to record what he has seen. The true explorer goes only to see and to tell others what he has seen. It seems incredible, considering the hardships and dangers, that men would willingly do this. I speak of men rather than women because the spirit of adventure that leads to exploration is primarily a masculine trait; women, being more sensible and their curiosity being confined to more personal and realistic matters nearer home, are less afflicted by the desire to see what lies beyond the seas and mountain ranges. But this spirit lurks in all men, I would guess, to a greater or lesser degree. In some it is weak and easily satisfied by novels or television; in others it is a ruling passion that thrusts them to the remote corners of the globe.

What makes men risk life and health and willingly endure great hardships simply to travel in lands where no civilized man has ever been before? Explorers and great travellers always have been faced with this question, if not in its general form, at least in its particular, as it applies to them. One way or another they have been asked or have asked themselves, 'Why do you do it?' The answers they have given are interesting, and the kind of answer has varied with the era. Until modern times – say, until the end of the eighteenth century – the pragmatic answer sufficed. If some useful purpose could be found for the trip – to seek a north-west passage, to find a new route to the Indies, to found a colony – these kinds of answers were given and accepted as entirely satisfactory. If individual motives were needed, simple and selfish reasons were easily found and readily accepted. Many an honest adventurer could more or less repeat the words of Ponce de Léon who set off 'to do something to gain honour and increase estate'. In the last century such motives as patriotism, science and the desire to improve the lot of unenlightened heathens were readily accepted as valid excuses for men to wander and explore.

It is only in recent years that we have looked closely at the character of the individual explorer to ask what made this man launch himself into the unknown. Today, while travellers still use the old pragmatic reasons – with such modern touches as the need for, or profit from, films, or in the cause of some of the newer sciences – they find the deeper questions more difficult to answer and sometimes even confess their inability to explain, expressing their irritation with those who demand explanations – as in the famous but fatuous answer to the question of why men climb mountains: 'Because they are there.'

Romantic concepts are difficult to explain, and there is usually some romantic, even mystic, element in any great adventurer. Adventurers are perforce dreamers and those in whom this element is dominant have been described by Wilfred Noyce as the 'lodestone seekers'. They are those who, like De Soto seeking El Dorado, Columbus searching for the fabulous Indies in the Atlantic and Burton, with the host who preceded him, seeking the mysterious source of the Nile, look for – and sometimes find – the truly fabulous. Their particular goal becomes a spiritual, mystic, all-consuming intellectual and physical concept in their minds. They want to solve a mystery, but a mystery so seeped in myth or legend, so surrounded by romanticism, that they are forced to rise above themselves even to make the search for its solution. The daydreams of youth die slowly and romantic notions are bound to be imbedded in every adventurer. Such essentially adolescent dreams in the minds of men who are also imaginative, active and brilliant have sometimes given the world great discoveries and advanced social progress.

Still, many explorers and other adventurers sincerely believe that they are doing what they are doing entirely for the interest of their country, or for science, or for the sake of humanity. Their magnificent results often make these appear quite plausible, for frequently they do add to man's scientific knowledge, they do improve the lot of humanity or they do advance the interests of their country, and sometimes even of an entire civilization. But for such men, sincere though they may be, their avowed purposes, although serving well as an excuse for the world and even for themselves – seldom, however, for their wives – only cover reasons often unstated and unreasoned but nevertheless present and felt in the breasts of the adventurers themselves.

The fascination of exploration lies as much in the character of the explorers as in the deeds they do and the successes they achieve. Probably most men want to conquer something, if only a garden plot or a bureau. The strongest often work to conquer themselves, suffering a compulsion to overcome some real or imagined weakness or handicap. Adventurers usually attempt to conquer, in one way or another, masses of land or masses of people: a mountain or a nation; a desert or a passion. And this trait, too, is essentially masculine; women are generally content to conquer the conqueror.

Most men also feel the desire to escape from something. When they compare the romantic conceptions they harbour with the comparatively dull surroundings of a comfortable, civilized life, they develop a compulsion to escape. It is fashionable to call adventurers escapists. Most of them are, to some degree at least. But to say that a man leaves behind him the pleasures and comforts of modern civilization *only* to escape them is to put the matter too strongly. The common sensation of wanting to get away from it all rarely leads further than the local pub or a vacation. By itself, the escape motive is rarely compelling enough, but it exists in the heart of every true adventurer nonetheless. Certainly it was a factor in Burton's life; one among many.

In vigorous societies, the new and the different have always been attractive. For some people, the desire to see strange lands, unusual customs, and have different everyday experiences is as strong as the ties to home and hearth. Indeed, the two feelings are not inconsistent. Witness the large number of people who travel abroad every year for no other purpose than to experience the sensation of being in different surroundings, to see new sights, and marvel at the customs of those whose lives are apparently so different from their own; yet they are always happy to return to their own land, people and home. In Burton, the lure of strange lands was strong and he might well have repeated the words of a character from *The Arabian Nights*: 'Allah afflicted me with a love of travel.'

Burton's public excuses for his travels were always scientific or commercial; his personal reasons were like Ponce de Léon's: to seek fame or fortune, usually the former. The desire for fame was still an acceptable reason in the last century; today adventurers are expected to be more modest and altruistic. But fame doubtless seems a desirable ambition for many men. However, it is in reality, only a by-product of accomplishment; it does not explain the almost lemming-like instinct that takes men from their homes, families and native countries to live a life of hardship and danger in the remote corners of the world.

For Burton, and many other adventurers, the hardships he endured and the dangers he faced were enjoyable in themselves. He complained of mere discomforts, but he relished real hardships. On his pilgrimage to Mecca, for example, he wailed of the discomforts of life on the tame canal boat from Alexandria to Cairo, but shortly after was delighted by the far more uncomfortable dash across the desert to Suez because this was a genuine hardship, a test of his endurance. The sheer physical pleasure of stretching muscle and trying flesh was an attraction for him.

For a great many men, and Burton was certainly one of them, danger itself is thrilling, exciting the mind and the spirit. This is another of those elements in men which women find so difficult to understand, and their persistent ignorance has resulted in many an explorer dying at home in his bed. In Isabel Arundell, Burton was fortunate to find a woman who, if she did not completely understand this feeling, at least tried to.

In spite of the social or personal reasons, in spite of the hardships and dangers explorers often find attractive, it is difficult to escape the conclusion that these reasons are not completely sufficient, that there is something deeper that drives men forth into the world's wildernesses. Not even a man's desire to prove himself (although this is often a compelling force) nor his dedication to an ideal (and this can accomplish much) seem adequate explanations for the voluntary acceptance of privation, the exposure to unwholesome climates and to diseases, the terrors of the unknown, and the strain on mind and nerves to which explorers so often knowingly subject themselves.

There must be something else, something more than mere intellectual reasoning and logical excuses, that sends that one-man-in-ten-million away from his own kind to seek the mythical and find he knows not what beyond the reaches of his own kind, that makes him set his face away from the mass of mankind and go out into the desert or jungle, the ice cap or the steaming swamp. There must be some inner compulsion, an instinct, a drive, a force – who knows its proper name? – that compels men to seek that which is not known. Perhaps scientists will one day find it among the genes, for certainly it belongs on any list of those qualities which distinguish man from the other animals. And this highly developed quality in one individual such as Richard Burton is an unknown and indescribable but nonetheless potent factor in making him do what he did and become what he became.

So much for the physical. The questing spirit of Burton was in this sense no different from that of dozens of other explorers who have made their mark on history and on the map of the world. What made him different from most others, certainly from those explorers of his own era, was that he extended his exploration to the realms of the intellect and the spirit. He was avidly and actively interested in the entire range of the physical, biological and social sciences as well as the humanities. He wrote books or published papers on mining, archaeology, poetry, anthropology, military science, commerce, engineering, geography, mountain-climbing, religion, abnormal sexual practices, reptiles, ethnology, slavery, medicine, politics and a host of other subjects, all of more than passing interest to him. His conclusions and theories were frequently bizarre, heretical or erroneous, but his mind was capable of moving beyond the thoughts of other men. He dared to think and believe what other brave men would have shrunk from contemplating. He was an adventurer in the intellectual and the spiritual as well as the physical world and it was this combination of interests, actively followed, which made him unique, one of the rarest personalities ever seen on earth.

Chapter 1

Boyhood and Early Youth
1821 – 40

In 1820 Lieutenant-Colonel Joseph Netterville Burton, with a gallant but insubordinate gesture, threw away his career. Of English stock, he was born and raised in Ireland, where his father was Rector of Tuam, in Galway. He was a handsome man of moderate height with dark hair, sallow skin, a high nose and piercing black eyes. Joining the army at an early age, he saw service in Sicily under Sir John Moore. He had been serving in Genoa when Queen Caroline, the unwanted wife of George IV, visited the town with her travelling court of fancy ladies and amorous men. Whatever her morals or the opinions of society, she was gracious to the officers of the garrison and won their loyalty and devotion. Later, when she was called before the House of Lords on charges of adultery with an Italian named Bartolomeo Bergami, Colonel Burton was summoned to appear as a witness against her. He refused. Consequently, he was dismissed from his post and thrown on half-pay by order of the Duke of Wellington himself.

Colonel Burton was a gentleman; he was little else, but this was apparently enough; his children regarded him as the most honourable man they had ever known. In his youth he had once fought a duel with a brother officer and shot him through the chest. This was part of the code of being a gentleman, although it was his own kind-heartedness that led him to nurse his antagonist back to life – only to shoot him down again in a second duel later on. A gentleman he certainly was, but Colonel Burton was also noted as a man who spoke his mind plainly and bluntly. Once when a drawing-room conversation turned to a discussion of a woman said to be unfaithful to her husband, the colonel forthrightly called her 'an adultress', shocking the sensibilities of those present and causing his own wife to blush.

Shortly before his enforced retirement from active service Colonel Burton had married Martha Baker, a thin, delicate woman of good family – she believed herself a descendant of an illegitimate son of Louis XIV. Her elder sister, Sarah, later married Colonel Burton's youngest brother, Francis Burton. She came well dowered, but her father, who opposed the marriage, tied up her £30,000 inheritance in such a way that it came to her in the form of an allowance rather than in a lump sum. As Colonel Burton was frequently enthusiastic over various speculations which invariably cost him his investment, it was just as well that he did not have access to his wife's capital.

At 9.30 on the evening of 19 March 1821, at Barham House in Herefordshire, the home of Richard Baker, his maternal grandfather, Richard Francis Burton was born – or so the mature Burton believed; the Elstree baptismal record says it was Torquay, not Barham House, but no matter. The baby with red hair, blue eyes and fair complexion was to grow into a dark, broad-shouldered man with what his era called gypsy eyes.

Except for his mother's strong feeling of sibship and an unfortunate accident, Richard might have been a wealthy man. The heir to the Baker fortune was Martha's half-brother, also called Richard Baker, a lawyer who refused a judgeship in Australia and died a soap boiler. His father had little use for his son and wanted to settle his wealth on his grandson. Martha Burton, who was most attached to the wild young man, protested vigorously and for some time deterred her father. The old man was determined, however, and one day set out to keep an appointment with his solicitor and change his will in favour of young Richard. He had one foot in his carriage when he died of a heart attack. And so at the age of three Richard Burton lost a fortune. His uncle was soon parted from his inheritance by Baron de Thierry, one of the most notorious swindlers of his day, who bilked young Baker of £80,000.

A few months after Richard's birth, the family moved to the medieval city of Tours in France, and settled down in the Château Beauséjour on the right bank of the Loire. Colonel Burton decided on Tours because it was cheap, healthy, the hunting was good and, incidentally, there were educational facilities for British children. The family increased: Richard was followed into the world two years later by a sister, Maria Catherine Eliza, and in another year by a brother, Edward Joseph Netterville. Richard and Edward, in spite of the three years' difference in their ages, were to grow up as very close companions.

Childhood in Tours was delightful for the Burton children. They ate grapes from the garden, collected small shells and cowslips, played with the hunting dogs, climbed up the tails of the colonel's horses and teased their nurse. In those days, Englishmen, if not mad dogs, avoided the direct rays of the sun, but Richard's aunt, Georgina Baker, used to tell how he would lie on his back in the boiling sunshine and exclaim, 'How I love a bright, burning sun!'

At three, Richard's desultory education began with the study of Latin. The following year he started to learn Greek. At six, Richard and his three-year-old younger brother were enrolled in a school run by a lame Irish schoolmaster. When a few months later the school closed down, all three children were turned over to John Gilchrist, a Scots pedagogue who taught them dancing, drawing, French and music. Richard liked the drawing and French; hated the music and dancing. Both Richard and Edward were more interested in playing soldiers than in becoming scholars. When five years old, Richard's great ambition was to kill the family porter because he laughed at their wooden swords.

Gilchrist did not do much to discourage such bloodthirsty ideas. As a school treat, he once took his pupils to see an execution. The condemned prisoner, a woman who had poisoned her family, had been sentenced to the guillotine. As the children were piously told to cover their eyes when the knife fell, they naturally stood on tiptoe and avidly watched every bit of it. For days afterwards, the favourite game at school was one called guillotine. Strangely, no one was injured seriously.

When the boys deserted school to play Robinson Crusoe in the woods, their hands were well flailed with a ruler. Another favourite but forbidden pastime was fighting with the sons of the French peasants; sticks, stones, snowballs (in season) and fists were all fair weapons.

Richard felt the compulsion of all boys to test his manhood. Courage came easily to him from an early age, but self-control was a quality he never really mastered. His conception of this attribute was unique. Throughout his life he seems to have defined it in terms of a trial he devised for himself as a child. Taking sugar and cream – both being highly desired but forbidden items – from the kitchen, he set them out ceremoniously before him and asked himself solemnly, 'Have I the courage not to touch them?' The moment he felt sure he had mastered the temptation, he joyfully rewarded himself and greedily emptied both pitcher and bowl. He emerged each time from the trial in the best of moods – full of cream, sugar and confidence in his self-control.

Like many imaginative young boys, he was a resolute and unblushing liar. He scoffed at the idea of honour being in any way connected with telling the truth, although he would not lie simply to avoid unpleasant consequences and he never lied to shift the blame to others. Neither the colonel nor his wife appears to have taken any effective steps to guide their children. Through ignorance or disinterest, discipline in the home was almost entirely in the hands of a series of nurse-maids and, later, tutors, all of whom led unenviable lives in the Burton household. At one time a strapping, broad-shouldered Norman girl was given the task of attempting to maintain order among the Burton brood. During a decorous stroll through the town soon after, all three children suddenly attacked her and sent her sprawling across the cobblestones. Then they jumped on her. The defeated nurse, pursued by hooting children, ran home with red eyes and a torn cap, screaming that the whole lot would end on the guillotine.

Even when they tried, the children's parents were no better at managing their wild offspring. It is doubtful if Mrs Burton ever heard of the eighth-century Arab scholar and saint, Malik bin Dinar, who, when passing through the bazaar and seeing something he wanted, would say to himself, 'O soul, take patience, for I will not give you what you desire!', but she would undoubtedly have approved of his principles, for she tried to inspire a similar restraint in her ungovernable offspring. Taking Richard, Edward and Maria to a pastry shop, she told them to look through the window at all of the delicacies displayed there. Then blandly saying, 'Now, my dears, let us go away. It is so good for little children to restrain themselves', she started to walk on. Outraged, the young Burtons broke the window with their fists, clawed out a tray of apple-puffs and bolted, leaving their mother to pay the damages.

By the age of nine Richard was looking for more scope. He joined a gang of other young ruffians of good family and graduated to ogling the girls and raiding shops. He filched his father's gun, shot at the monuments in the graveyard and broke the fine old stained-glass windows of the church. Long before the term was invented, he had become the model of a juvenile delinquent.

Happily, there was another side to him. When he threw a stone that cut open his sister's forehead, he ran to her, threw his arms around her neck and fell into a paroxysm of uncontrollable sobs and tears. He loved animals and spent hours watching over sick pets or nursing birds that had broken wings or legs. Along with a tough exterior and a compulsion to make himself appear a devil, Richard Burton always retained a strong streak of sentimentality. To his family, Richard seemed the roughest, kindest, most vexing and most charming boy in the world. Although Colonel Burton and his wife certainly had little understanding of or influence over their children, Richard loved them both and in later life he once commented fondly, 'Nice to be able to feel proud of one's parents.'

He must have been about ten years old when Colonel Burton decided to take his family back to England. The French penchant for violent political upheavals had not only toppled Charles X from his throne, but it had now created a decidedly unfriendly climate for Englishmen. More and more often the cry of '*A bas les Anglais!*' was heard in the streets, and in Tours an English gentleman was actually threatened with prison for the mere riding down of an old lady with his horse. Besides, the colonel noticed that several of his friends' sons who had been raised in France were turning out badly and he could detect few signs in the behaviour of his own which encouraged him to believe that Richard and Edward would be any different.

Auctioning off the household goods and packing their personal belongings, the Burtons set off in their coach for Paris, then Dieppe, and finally across the channel to England where, for the first time in their memories, the Burton children saw their homeland. They were unimpressed. They sniffed the soot-filled air and shuddered under the cold grey sky. They were even more dismayed by the food served them at their hotel. The bread was too soft and had too little crust; the boiled potatoes and the huge joints of meat convinced them that they had fallen among savages; accustomed to the good red wine of France, they regarded the beer, sherry and port of England as undrinkable.

These impressions were not changed in the days ahead. Not only did Richard not like English weather and English food, he also disliked Englishmen, particularly 'the whole lower-class society' which seemed to him to be governed by the fist: men punched their wives, mothers punched their children, big children punched little ones and little children punched each other.

Colonel Burton originally had some idea of entering his sons for Eton to prepare them for Oxford and Cambridge. Unfortunately, he took the advice of a meddlesome friend and enrolled them in a school at Richmond run by Rev. Charles Delafosse, whose chief recommendation seems to have been that he was the chaplain to the Duke of Cumberland. The schoolmaster was a bluff, portly man who took in great quantities of snuff through his long aquiline nose and drank more port than was good for him. He was a favourite with the boys because he seldom beat them, but, as Burton later said, 'He was no more fit to be a schoolmaster than the Grand Cham of Tartary.'

At Delafosse's school, Richard managed to forget some of his excellent French and to acquire considerable dexterity with his fists. In his first fight, Richard concentrated on getting his opponent off his feet. When he finally had him on the ground, he happily jumped on him and proceeded to hammer his head on the floor, using the boy's ears as handles. It was at this point that he was introduced to English standards of fair play. The bystanders tried to pull him off and allow his enemy to regain his feet. 'Stand up!' cried Richard indignantly. 'After all the trouble I've had getting the fellow down!'

For Richard, school life consisted of one fight after another. Edward fought too, but not being as proud and sensitive as his older brother, he had fewer quarrels. At one point, Richard had no less than thirty-two affairs of honour to settle. The bouts took place after classes among the hacked benches and ink-stained desks of the schoolroom with the older boys sitting in judgement. The fighting went on daily until Richard was hammered into a thin, black and blue, feverish stripling.

The school food was hardly sufficient to keep up his strength. Although he had thought English hotel food terrible, he was appalled by the meagre rations doled out by Mr. Delafosse's thin-lipped wife. Breakfast consisted of a mug of very blue milk and a wedge of bread with a thin glazing of butter. The epicures among the students scraped the bread until they had collected enough butter at one end to make at least one decent bite. Dinner, served at 1 p.m., began with a pudding known as 'stickjaw' and ended with a piece of gristly, sinewy and badly cooked meat; potatoes like bullets; and an unwanted, hateful carrot. Supper was like breakfast, and Richard usually went to bed hungry after a hard day's fighting.

Meanwhile, Colonel Burton had settled in a house in Maids of Honour Row, Richmond. The cramped English houses seemed stuffy and mean after the châteaux of the Loire, but he was prepared to suffer it out for the sake of his sons. But Richard and Edward had been in school less than a year when measles broke out and spread among the students. Several of the boys died and the survivors were dispersed to their homes. Richard took sick – measles was the only childhood disease he ever had – and was cared for by Mrs Baker. When he recovered, Colonel Burton was ready to return to the Continent; for he longed to return to his boar-hunting in France. Still vaguely mindful of his responsibility for his children's education, he acquired a governess and a tutor before leaving England. A stout, red-faced girl named Miss Ruxton was selected to be Maria's governess, and a Mr H. R. Du Pre, an Oxford undergraduate and son of a clergyman who was later to become a clergyman himself, was chosen to teach Richard and Edward.

When the Burton family boarded ship and sailed for Boulogne, no one was happier than Richard and his brother. They whooped and yelled and danced up and down on the deck, shaking their fists at the white cliffs of Dover. They made jokes about England, 'the land where the sun never sets – nor rises!' and swore they would never return. When France came in sight they cheered.

By the time the Burtons reached Paris, Du Pre and Miss Ruxton had seen the need for discipline and were determined to exercise it. Taking their charges for a walk on the boulevards, they decided to march them in single file like other schoolchildren. They had gone some distance from the hotel in this fashion when suddenly the children broke ranks and fled, leading their guardians a wild chase until they lost them. Knowing Paris well from previous visits, the children easily retraced their steps to the hotel and blandly announced that their governess and tutor had unfortunately been run over by an omnibus. Richard thoroughly enjoyed the excitement that followed until the foot-sore victims finally found their way back.

Perhaps it was superstition that led Colonel Burton to look everywhere but Tours for a new home. He had been very happy there, but he would not return. He tried Orléans, but decided it smelled of 'goose and gutter' and drifted off to Blois. Here Miss Ruxton concluded that her job was impossible and left. Du Pre bravely remained, but his lot did not improve. He was a peculiar-looking man with a narrow forehead, close-set eyes and thick lips, and his appearance led Richard to exercise his drawing talents in making endless caricatures of him. He also made a sketch of Du Pre's tomb on which he wrote the following epitaph:

> Stand, passenger! hang down thy head and weep,
> A young man from Exeter here doth sleep;
> If any one ask who that young man be,
> 'Tis the Devil's dear friend and companion – Du Pre.

Commenting on this bit of verse later in life, Burton said he did not think much of the poetry, but the sentiment showed 'a fine sense of independence'.

In spite of his charges, Du Pre stuck firmly to his post. A schoolroom was set up in the house and several local teachers were called in to help. There was a dancing master, a professor of Latin and Greek, and a fencing master. It was the latter, an old soldier who had lost a thumb in the wars, who delighted the boys. There were real foils now instead of the wooden swords which had amused the gate-keeper, and the youngsters spent every spare minute exchanging thrusts. It was not until Richard rammed his foil down Edward's throat and nearly tore off his uvula that they learned the necessity of masks. This incident caused Richard considerable grief, but it did not deter either of them from continuing the sport. Richard also became interested in the medieval art of falconry and tried to train his own kestrel, but he subjected it to an over-rigorous regime and the bird died of starvation.

Life in Blois lasted only a year. Colonel Burton suffered from asthma, 'an honest and respectable kind of complaint', as his eldest son later called it, which served as a ready excuse for changing climates when he wanted to move on. Colonel Burton wanted to move now, although his wife hated travelling and was sick. Mrs Baker came over from England to dissuade him, but in spite of all objections and his mother-in-law's dire prediction – 'You'll kill your wife, sir!' – Colonel Burton decided to move to Italy. This was the last straw for Mrs Baker and, after dredging up some old stories of how the colonel's pay had once been turned over to a Sicilian girl to keep off claims, she flounced back to England and the Burton family moved to Pisa.

In Italy, a violin master and an Italian teacher were added to the list of tutors. Edward liked the violin, worked very hard at it, and became a proficient player; for Richard it was a form of torture. Apparently, Richard's playing was no less so for the violin master. One day, driven to madness by the sour notes, he screamed, 'All pupils are beasts, but you are an arch-beast!' It was the 'arch-' that did it. Richard broke his violin over the teacher's head.

After a cold and uncomfortable winter in Pisa, Colonel Burton moved his family to Siena for the summer of 1832. This city, too, he found unsatisfactory, for the hospitality of the natives was limited to an inscription of welcome over the city gate and the English colony consisted principally of men who had run off with their friends' purses or their wives.

In Siena the boys found a brace of duelling pistols in a little shop and set their hearts on owning them. They already possessed an old single-barrelled Menton which had been converted from flint to percussion and they were occasionally allowed to go hunting with it. Mrs Burton, not surprisingly, since the boys were only eight and eleven years old, feared an accident. She used to provoke quarrels with the boys in order to forbid the use of the weapon as a punishment. The duelling pistols would have to be bought and used secretly, they knew. They hoarded their own allowances, borrowed little Maria's savings, and at last scraped together enough money to buy the pistols and smuggle them home. Colonel Burton found them almost immediately and ordered them to be returned to the shop at once. The boys were so outraged that they ran away from home – but they were promptly returned by the police.

As the colonel's solution to every crisis was to move, the family again packed their bags and possessions. Although the Burtons belonged to the Church of England, it was decided they should pass Holy Week in Rome. Loaded into a four-wheeled trap pulled by a vicious nag they set out from Siena and, after a breakdown that the children found a delightful respite, they arrived in Rome and at once proclaimed it 'a piggery'. Indeed, Rome was then but a shadow of its former grandeur: the Forum was a level piece of ground broken only by bits of ruins sticking up here and there; the Palatine hill was unexcavated and the Colosseum was only a wreck; the Tiber frequently overflowed its banks; most of the city was overgrown with brush and it was believed that fatal fevers would result if the ground was dug up. Nevertheless, the Burtons 'did the curiosities' and watched with Protestant amusement the religious ceremonies of Holy Week at the Vatican.

From Rome, they wandered over Italy for several years, going to Naples, Sorrento, Florence, Capua. It was at Naples, where they had taken a house, that Colonel Burton, being a restless man with an active mind and absolutely nothing to do, suddenly became unpleasantly chemical. He bought a book of formulae entitled *A Chemical Catechism* by S. Parker which contained, as its sub-title pointed out, 'A Vocabulary and a Chapter of Amusing Experiments'. It is not known if the colonel mastered the vocabulary or read the poems that were sprinkled through the book, but he did enjoy the 'Amusing Experiments'. He concocted a horrible substance he insisted was soap; he spoiled thousands of lemons to make citric acid; and he filled the house with strange and terrible smells. When this fit was over, he took up chess. Perhaps to keep the colonel from returning to his chemistry, the entire family joined in with gusto and most of their days were taken up with the game. Richard enjoyed it immensely and soon became so expert that he could play two games simultaneously while blindfolded.

At Naples Colonel Burton took his sons to Pompeii, Herculaneum and to the top of Mount Vesuvius where, with difficulty, he managed to prevent them from descending into the crater. Other expeditions included a visit to a cockfight, the boys being accompanied by Du Pre. At Naples, too, the education of Richard Burton continued. An artist was engaged to teach oil painting but he and the boys spent their time making pencil caricatures of all the people they knew. Of real interest to both Richard and Edward was the new fencing master, a celebrated foil named Cavalli who was one of the leading exponents of the Neapolitan school of fighting. The boys took their fencing seriously and worked very hard at it. Richard, at fifteen, even conceived a plan for combining the Neapolitan and the French schools of swordsmanship so as to produce a school that would incorporate the best features of both systems.

As though following the Burtons, the cholera had gone through France and down the coast of Italy, striking Siena, Rome and now Naples. Richard and Edward had seen the plague before, but it held no terrors for them; it only excited their curiosity. They arranged with an Italian servant to obtain suitably shabby clothes and spent a night going the rounds with the dead carts, helping to pick up the bodies and dispose of them. On a plain just outside Naples, pits had been constructed to serve as graves for the infected corpses. Each pit was lined with stone and had an opening just large enough for a body to go through it. When the stone cover was rolled back and Richard and Edward stuffed the black and rigid corpses into the fleshpot, Richard, looking into the pit, thought he saw 'a kind of lambent blue flame about the sides of the pit' which lit up the mass of human corruption piled in festering heaps.

There were escapades of a very different kind. Near enough to the Burton home to be visible from the terrace was a brothel, and it was not long before Richard had established communications through signs with one of the prostitutes. One evening the boys stuffed carving knives into their belts and their savings into their pockets and paid the girls a visit. What the prostitutes thought of the young innocents is not known, but as far as the boys were concerned it was love, and – no adolescent love affair being complete without letters – they soon worked up a passionate correspondence with two of the girls. The boys' letters were filled with pure love; those of the prostitutes with extreme debauchery. Unfortunately for Richard and Edward, the letters from the girls were found by their mother. A family scene ensued. The boys were now too old to be spanked, but the colonel grimly brought out a horsewhip. A delighted Du Pre was prepared to assist with the punishment, but the boys took to the roof-tops and, climbing to the top of a chimney, refused to come down until they were forgiven.

This affair disgusted Colonel Burton and, of course, he decided to solve this problem by moving to what he hoped would be a purer moral climate. And so it was that in the spring of 1838 the Burton family again assembled their possessions into a mountain of boxes, bags and bundles and loaded them onto an English steamer bound for Marseilles. Customs were no problem as the word of an English gentleman that his belongings contained no contraband was accepted at face value. On landing they moved inland to a small village and settled down to what Colonel Burton hoped would be a peaceful life.

Provence was pleasant, but the people were not. In any argument with an Englishman, a Frenchman could always win by calling loudly, 'These are *les misérables* who poisoned Napoleon at St Helena!' and an angry crowd was soon ready to take his part. The Burtons moved on to Pau, the former capital of Béarn at the foot of the Pyrenees.

Pau was a delightful resort town, but as they arrived in the heat of summer they soon took themselves to the nearby mountains, settling in a village on the Gave de Pau until the heat subsided. It was here that Richard and Edward took up with a band of smugglers who seemed to them to lead a most romantic existence. Arriving at the hotel with their mules laden with chocolate, tobacco and *aguardiente* from Spain, they would call in the young girls, bawl for wine and bring out their guitars. These were gay evenings, occasionally enlivened by a shooting or a knife fight, and the boys joined the fun. They wanted to become *contrabandistes* themselves.

Returning to Pau at the end of the hot season, the Burtons joined the society of the local band of English. Edward and Richard now started to take an interest in social life and began a series of love affairs with various pairs of sisters. The first of these were the beautiful daughters of Baron de Meydell, who roared with laughter at the antics of the love-sick young men and discreetly carried his daughters away from Pau.

Besides love, there were other experiments to be made in manhood. The boys started smoking, took boxing lessons from the Irish groom of a family friend, and endeavoured to impress the soldiers at the local garrison with their ability to drink cognac. One day, filled with a potent punch and the smoke of strong cigars, Richard reeled home with the pale face and staring eyes of a young man about to be very sick. Startled by his odd appearance, his frightened mother put him to bed. His strange symptoms puzzled her and she called in his father. Colonel Burton examined his son carefully for a minute and then declared, 'The beast's in liquor!' With that he turned on his heel and left the room while his wife sobbed. The next day she extracted from her son a promise to be good, advised him not to read Lord Chesterfield's *Letters to His Son* and gave him a five-franc piece—which he promptly spent on brandy.

Although the hated Du Pre was still with them, the colonel continued the practice of bringing in other tutors for special subjects. At Pau it was a professor of mathematics, who offended the aristocratic nature of the boys by expounding his democratic principles. Richard thought him 'a red republican of the reddest'. But Richard did not need a tutor to teach him the local dialect, a charming combination of French, Spanish and Provencal. Béarnais also contained a number of appealing folk songs which he tried to learn. Unfortunately, although he always had a good speaking voice, he never learned to sing properly or to read and write musical notes.

Colonel Burton's asthma and restlessness prompted him to move his family back to Pisa, where they found a house on the south side of the Arno owned by a widow named Pini who possessed two of the most beautiful daughters the boys had ever seen. The eldest was Caterina Pini; she was tall, slim and dark, and Richard fell madly in love with her. Edward followed his lead and was no less in love with her younger sister Antonia. Marriage was proposed and accepted. Parental consent being out of the question, they considered standing up before the church congregation during the elevation of the Host and declaring themselves man and wife, it being a popular belief in Italy that this constituted a legal and binding marriage. A few inquiries revealed that young couples who tried this were promptly put in jail – and in separate cells. It was evident that the whole situation was impossible.

Love for the Pini sisters did not prevent the brothers from knowing other girls. Colonel Burton, walking through town with his sons one day, was appalled by the number of young women who ran to their windows to call out affectionate greetings to the young men. 'O! s'or Riccardo!' they trilled.

In Pisa, Richard and Edward took up with a group of riotous Italian medical students. One winter evening they acquired some Jamaica gin which, with lemons and sugar, they made into a hot punch. When well liquored, they sallied into the streets to shout, sing and hustle innocent pedestrians. It was not long before the watch came up on the double and grabbed those they could reach. Richard's long legs carried him safely from the scene, but Edward was caught. The following morning, a polite Italian policeman called on Colonel Burton to tell him that his son had been housed for the night at the government's expense. Marching to the jail, the colonel found his youngest son entertaining his fellow prisoners with the help of a pocket flask. This was the end.

The family packed their bags, the boys said tearful good-byes to Caterina and Antonia, and the Burtons were off to the baths of Lucca. But it was obvious that the family was about to dissolve. Colonel Burton could no longer thrash his boys, but he shouted at them continually. It did no good. Richard and Edward shot pistols in all directions, took up with a Swiss and practised yodelling all over town, experimented with eating and smoking opium, and cornered every stray fencing master to give them points. They had completely mastered their tutor and had once beaten him up. If he tried to give them lessons they threw their books out of the window and returned to their Italian novels. Everyone agreed they were impossible.

In the early summer of 1840, Colonel Burton decided it was time his sons went off to the university. With Du Pre, and the two young men, they started north for England. There was a six-week delay for Richard while he took a cure for a skin eruption at the Schinznach-Bad sulphur baths in Switzerland, before joining his brother, father, Mrs Baker and two of his aunts, Sarah and Georgina, at Hampstead. Richard did not find England any better than last time. Everything appeared small and mean to him. From the outside, English houses seemed prim, priggish and inartistic; the insides were cut up into little rooms like ship's cabins and filled with fragile tables heaped with bric-à-brac. The only agreeable part of their present situation, as far as Richard and Edward were concerned, was the presence of a pair of 'nice little girl cousins', Sarah and Eliza, the daughters of their aunt Sarah Burton.

Soon the two brothers, being considered a bad influence on each other, were separated and forbidden even to correspond. Edward was sent away and placed under the guidance of a country rector; Richard was put under a professor and the quality of his education tested. The professor was horrified. Nevertheless, Colonel Burton was determined that his sons must go to the university and it is indicative of his lack of understanding of their characters that he wanted them to become clergymen. A more preposterous profession for these two could hardly have been considered. Colonel Burton himself had had very little schooling before leaving Ireland at the age of seventeen to become an army officer, and, like many men of little formal education, he had an exaggerated opinion of its virtues. He had done the best he knew to provide for his sons' education and perhaps he should not be severely blamed for the fact that it was inadequate. He was in no position to judge of the extent of his sons' intellectual accomplishments or the depth of their ignorance; he only knew that he himself was determined that Richard and Edward should attend the finest universities in Britain. So in the autumn of 1840 Richard was enrolled at Trinity College, Oxford.

Chapter 2

The Unscholarly Scholar
1840 – 2

IN 1840 Queen Victoria married Prince Albert, Richard Henry Dana published *Two Years Before the Mast*, an incandescent lamp was demonstrated by Sir William Robert Grove and Samuel Cunard established a transatlantic steamship line. Men were clean-shaven, duelling had nearly passed out of fashion, and conformity to respectability was the order of the era. One autumn day of that year, Richard Burton, now a tall, dark, muscular young man of nineteen who carried a fierce, drooping moustache, strode defiantly through the gates of Trinity College, Oxford, for the first time. Two passing undergraduates looked at him with amazement and one made a remark about the unusual, un-British moustache. At once Burton turned on them. He presented his card with a flourish and announced fiercely that his seconds would call upon them to arrange the details. The astonished young man politely apologized and went off, wondering what manner of beast had been let loose in the university.

Although he possessed some remarkable skills, Burton's previous haphazard education was not likely to make him a success at the Oxford of his day. He spoke French and Italian fluently and had considerable knowledge of Béarnais and Provençal, but he was deficient in Latin and Greek. He could play chess blindfolded, but he knew hardly anything of religion and could not even recite the Apostles' Creed. English born, but bred on the Continent, he did not regard England as his home. He was already dissatisfied with the little he had seen of Oxford. He hated it from the beginning. He scorned the unfamiliar countryside. A kindly old porter warned him that second- and third-year men were in the habit of playing tricks on 'fresh young gentlemen' and advised him to keep the door to his room well locked. Characteristically, Richard left his door wide open but put a poker in the fire to make a warm reception for intruders. If he had fallen among barbarians, at least he knew how to protect himself.

He was a youth who had as yet tasted neither success nor failure, and he was untroubled by apprehensions. Oxford held no terrors for him, physical or intellectual. He had the supreme confidence of youth and an overweening faith in his own individuality – a faith he never lost.

Daily life at Oxford began with chapel, during which most students studied, and was followed by a large breakfast of ham, mutton chops and what Richard regarded as 'undigestible muffins'. There were a couple of lectures, which he considered 'time completely thrown away', and after these the students were free to do whatever they liked until dinner in hall. Young Burton was horrified to discover that wine was forbidden and that most students drank beer. After tasting the offensive haunches of meat, the plain boiled vegetables, the stodgy pudding and the waxy cheese, he decided to take his foreign stomach into town where he could find food and drink more suited to his continental tastes.

In his free time he took walks, rowed on the river, fenced and boxed. Along with a group that included Tom Hughes, later to earn fame as the author of *Tom Brown's School Days*, he took boxing lessons from stray pugilists that came to town. But it was in the fencing rooms of Archibald Maclaren, a man who wrote a little book on swordsmanship and even a volume of poetry called *Songs of the Sword*, that Richard made most of his friends, among them, Alfred Bates Richards, later editor of the *Morning Advertiser*, who described Burton at this period as 'brilliant, rather wild, and very popular'.

Although he called the fencing room 'the great solace of my life', young Burton also found occasional solace in other places. His walks at this time usually led him to Bagley Wood where a pretty gypsy girl named Selina waited for him. Burton had an affinity for gypsies. Throughout his life people were to see in his appearance and in his actions many resemblances to them. Most of these comments were from people who had only a romantic concept of gypsies and little real knowledge of them, but the *Gypsy Lore Journal* once said of him that 'he had the peculiar eye, which looked you through, glazed over and saw something behind, and is the only man, not a gypsy, with that peculiarity'. Perhaps it was from the beautiful Selina that he first began to learn the Romany tongue and the gypsy ways.

He also made a few friends outside the university and outside of the woods, and sometimes he was invited to dinner in town. On one such occasion he met the future Cardinal Newman, then still Anglican Vicar of St Mary's, and Matthew Arnold. He was disappointed in their conversation for they talked only of the size of the statues in St Peter's in Rome.

At another dinner in town he met a Spanish Arabic scholar, Pascual de Gayangos y Arce. Tiring of Greek and Latin, Richard had picked up an Arabic grammar and had started to teach himself Arabic. He had not progressed far, however, for he was writing his words in the conventional Western fashion instead of from right to left. Gayangos laughed when he saw him do this and taught him the alphabet. Later, learning there was a Regius Professor of Arabic at Oxford, Richard called on him for help, but was told curtly that a professor's job was to teach a class, not an individual, and that an Oxford don had no time to waste on a single student. But there were no classes in Arabic and Richard was incensed by the thought that although the British Empire contained the largest Moslem population of any nation in the world, Arabic was not taught at Britain's most famous university. It seemed equally disgraceful to him that there was not a single course in the original languages of the British Isles: Gaelic, Cornish, Irish and Welsh —a cause which Matthew Arnold was to champion a few years later.

Richard regarded his time at Oxford as wasted; the education worthless. He was intelligent – in some ways, brilliant even – and full of information, but intelligence was not enough and the kinds of information he possessed were not of the sort to win honours for him at Oxford. He would never admit it, but his exposure to higher education did arouse his intellectual faculties and, while creating in him a desire to excel, it taught him the difficulties of succeeding against formidable competition. He tried to obtain two scholarships and failed. Languages were his forte, but he was full of theories of his own and alienated his professors by obstinately holding to them. He spoke Latin in the Italian manner and refused to use the English pronunciation. In this he had a point. In Chaucer's time the Italian pronunciation was used, but in Spencer's day it began to take on a more English inflection. Later, to emphasize the breach with Rome, the English pronunciation was encouraged. Then for a hundred years England had two ways of speaking Latin, distinguished as 'Protestant' and 'Catholic'. In Burton's day, the Protestant pronunciation was the accepted form and Latin was spoken in England as nowhere else in the world.

Burton had another theory which annoyed his professors: he disapproved of the cognate German pronunciation of *j* in words of semitic origin. Thus he pronounced, and attempted to persuade others to pronounce, Yericho for Jericho, Yob for Job, Yakoob for Jacob, Yerusalem for Jerusalem. Here again, while technically correct, he was in no position to change a pronunciation hallowed on custom.

At the end of the autumn term, Richard went to London to stay with Mrs Baker, and his aunts Sarah and Georgina. Edward joined him, but they found a house full of elderly women dull; besides, Richard was now a heavy smoker and he was forbidden to smoke except under the stairway. The young men decided to move out. They took lodgings in Maddox Street and dedicated themselves to becoming 'men about town'. Richard took up gambling, playing whist, écarté, piquet and that complicated ancestor of craps: hazard. At first he had good luck at the public tables, but he did not have the instincts of a gambler. He started each evening with a fixed sum in his pocket; when this was lost, he quit. When he was winning, though, he plunged boldly ahead, not stopping until his luck turned against him. 'But hazard is a terrible game,' he concluded. 'It takes a man years to learn it well, and by that time he has lost all the luck with which he begins.' Gambling never became a vice with him.

The vacation was all too short and soon he had to return to his 'frowsy rooms' at Trinity. The spring term was no more successful than the previous one. Although he surprised his tutor by learning Adam's *Antiquities* by heart, he was beaten in a Greek competition by a student who turned a chorus of Aeschylus into doggerel verse. Time passed slowly for him until at last the term ended and the 'long vacation' began. Then Richard and Edward made for Wiesbaden where they were to meet their parents and Maria. Colonel Burton had assigned the young men to escort an aunt, Mrs D'Aguilar, and two of her daughters who were to join the Burton family in Germany. All went well until a stop of one day in Antwerp when the proper Mrs D'Aguilar was scandalized to discover her nephews romping with a pretty hotel maid. The girl was defending herself very nicely, however. Her hands were protecting her lips and red cheeks while her short petticoat enabled her to deliver a series of sharp kicks at the shins of the laughing young English gentlemen.

At last they reached Wiesbaden, which Burton later described as a summer resort for middle-class Germans, and joined their parents and sister. But Wiesbaden was only an assembly point for them; from here they set out to move about Germany before settling for a while in Heidelberg. For Richard and Edward, the town's chief amusement was again the fencing room. They tried to gain admission to one of the many duelling societies on the basis of their skill with the foil, but they were rejected. The Germans preferred the pointless, razor-edged *schläger*. In this type of play, the body was heavily padded with only the chest and face exposed. Although it was possible to cut into a lung, the grand thing was to walk off with the tip of an adversary's nose and there were many stories of German duels involving lost noses. One concerned a doctor attending a duel who picked up a sliced-off nose, popped it into his mouth to keep it warm, and then skilfully sewed it back on when the duel ended. More terrible was the tale of the handsome young man who engaged in a duel with a brutally ugly antagonist and lost the tip of his nose. Perhaps remembering the story of the skilful surgeon, he immediately ran to retrieve it. But his opponent deliberately stamped on it and ground it shapeless. The Burton boys, with their handsome noses, could not see the fun in this sport.

While at Heidelberg, Richard tried to convince his father that Oxford was unsuitable for him. He pleaded for permission to join the Army or to be allowed to emigrate to Canada or Australia – anything not to be made to return to the hated university. Edward, who was destined for Cambridge, assailed his father with the same arguments, swearing he would rather be a private in the infantry than a fellow at Cambridge. Richard even threatened to run off and join the Foreign Legion, but Colonel Burton was inexorable. Both boys returned to their studies.

Having a little time left before the new term began, Richard went to Ramsgate where Mrs Baker was staying and found some pretty girls with whom to amuse himself. Then he wandered about the country, visiting Margate, where 'the tone of society was perfectly marvellous', and adjacent bathing places. But all too soon he had to return, unwillingly, to Oxford.

Burton once wrote, 'I was always of the opinion that a man proves his valour by doing what he likes.' By this standard he was a brave man at Oxford. Unfortunately, what he liked was to bait the university authorities. In addition to pranks such as transplanting a don's flower bed with wild flowers, he used his drawing skills to make caricatures and his literary talents to compose mock epitaphs of the local dignitaries. As the results of his work were usually exhibited at wine and supper parties, his verses and his drawings were soon well known, making him popular at parties but doing nothing to promote his character with the dons.

At Cambridge, Edward, who complained that he had fallen among grocers, was cutting out a similar reputation for himself, but he did not last as long as his brother. When it was noted by his tutor that he never appeared for chapel, he was sent for and reprimanded.

'My dear sir,' Edward said, 'no party of pleasure ever gets me out of bed before ten o'clock, and do you *really, really* think that I am going to be in chapel at eight o'clock?'

'Are you joking,' asked the tutor, 'or is that your mature decision?'

'My very ripest decision,' said Edward, and out of the university he went to join the army and to become a surgeon.

Richard's undoing came about soon after. There was to be a horse-race at Oxford and a popular steeplechaser known as Oliver the Irish-man was to ride. The college authorities had forbidden the students to go to the race and, to make sure they obeyed the order, every student was required to attend the college lecture at the hour when the race was to be run. Burton and some of his friends decided to disobey the edict and see the race.

The next morning, all the culprits were summoned and given a lecture on the enormity of their crime. Richard made himself a hero in the eyes of his companions by daring to argue. He gave quite a speech. Attending a race did not involve moral turpitude, he said, and further-more the college had treated them like children rather than grown men. He offered some good advice to the effect that 'trust begets trust' and urged the authorities to heed the axiom that 'they who trust us, elevate us'. This was too much for the dons.

All of the boys who had disobeyed the order were rusticated, but young Burton was singled out by being sent down for good. Richard thought this was unjust. He wanted to be rusticated, but this was a dis-grace. He told the dons hotly that he hoped the 'caution money' de-posited by his father would be honestly returned. The dignitaries rose in anger, but Richard made them a courtly Austrian bow from the waist and left the room. He felt he had scored a point.

He quickly packed his bags and stowed them into a tandem drawn by high-trotting horses. Driving his horses over the flower beds and blowing on a long tin horn, he drove away from Oxford, waving to his friends and throwing kisses to the shop girls.

When he arrived unexpectedly in London at the home of his aston-ished aunts, explanations were necessary. Richard told them he had been given a special vacation for taking 'a double First with the very highest honours'. The gullible aunts were delighted, and to celebrate the grand accomplishments of their nephew a large dinner party was given. Unfortunately, one of the dinner guests, an old friend of the family, wiser or more outspoken than the others, grinned at Richard and ejaculated, 'Rusticated, eh?'

As Burton later remembered it, 'The aunts said nothing at the time, but they made inquiries, the result of which was a tableau.' Asked what he intended to do, Richard said he wanted to go into the Army but preferred the Indian Service. The family surrendered. The Directors of the Honourable East India Company were not allowed to sell commissions, but £500 changed hands and Richard Burton became an officer in the Bombay Native Infantry.

While waiting for the arrangements to be completed, Burton determined to have as good a time as possible. He took boxing lessons at Owen Swift's and fenced at Angelo's fencing room. He took up with a number of odd characters, including John Varley, an artist who was a student of alchemy and astrology and had written a book called *Zodiacal Physiognomy* which attempted to prove that everyone resembled the sign of the zodiac under which he was born. Burton was interested. Varley predicted he would become a great astrologer, so he studied all the books he could find on 'dark spells and devilish enginery'. Unfortunately, when Burton 'prognosticated' the reverse usually occurred.

It must have dawned upon him, though, that life was beginning in earnest. He finally gave up boxing and astrology and began the study of Hindustani under the remarkable Duncan Forbes, a Scotsman who smoked a huge meerschaum pipe, never took a bath, played chess with a passion and spoke a variety of oriental languages with a well-burred Scots accent. Forbes was raised in a small village in Scotland and did not learn English until he was thirteen. Yet, at seventeen he was the village schoolmaster, at twenty he entered grammar school, and at twenty-five he obtained his MA from the University of St Andrews. After three years in India he returned to London to teach Hindustani. He was forty-three and Professor of Oriental languages at King's College, London, when Burton met him. He was known as a superb teacher and doubtless he stimulated Burton's interest in Eastern languages.

At last the time came for him to be sworn in at the famous offices of the Honourable East India Company in Leadenhall Street. A gorgeously arrayed porter stood outside, while inside were the stuffy, gloomy rooms where Charles Lamb had worked. Here he found a group of other young men waiting to be sworn in, and Burton looked around him in dismay. Many of his future comrades and brother officers appeared to have come fresh from the country and he noticed that some did not even have gloves. A British army had recently been crushed in Afghanistan and the Honourable Company needed fresh bodies.

On 18 June 1842, Ensign Burton sailed from Gravesend on the barque *John Knox* bound for India, carrying with him a book of army regulations, Mill's *History of India*, several Hindustani dictionaries and grammars, a box-headed, pink-faced bull terrier, and a kit consisting of dozens of white jackets and trousers, guns, swords and saddles. He also brought with him an item that was not generally considered standard equipment: a wig. He needed this for social occasions, since he had decided it would be cooler if he shaved his head. As he retained his long and drooping moustache he must have presented an odd picture of a twenty-one-year-old Englishman.

During the four months' voyage around the Cape, Burton amused himself by boxing with the ship's captain and knocking him flat; making love to the women passengers and thrashing the first mate when he tried to interfere; coaxing three Indian servants on board to help him learn Hindustani; shooting sea birds from the deck rail; attempting to teach the other army officers on board to use their swords and himself to play the flute.

When, on 28 October, the long voyage was over and the *John Knox* sailed into the harbour of Bombay, all of the young ensigns on board were eager for news and excited by the prospect of almost immediate battle. When the government pilot came aboard they crowded about him to ask anxiously, 'What's doing in Afghanistan?' The disappointing answer was that the war was over: Lord Ellenborough had led an avenging army into the wild country, Ghazni had fallen the month before, the English prisoners had been released, and the victorious army was on its way back through the Khyber Pass. For the moment, India was at peace; there seemed no hope for a short cut to fame through military gallantry for Richard Burton.

Chapter 3

Sin in Sind
1842 – 8

In 1842 Bombay was a highly cosmopolitan city, filled with the races and creeds of half the Orient. In the centre of the town was the colourful Bhendi Bazaar where nearly anything could be bought for a price. It was a picturesque place, but Burton was unimpressed: 'The landing in a wretched shore-boat at the unclean Apollo Bunder, an absurd classicism for Palawa Bunder, was a complete disenchanter.' Going through the ancient Portuguese fort, described as 'dingy old fortifications', he made his way to the British Hotel. There he had his first view of an Indian soldier, a sepoy dressed in a faded scarlet coat and blue dungarees who had, said Burton, a 'dingy face', greasy hair, arms like broomsticks, and a body like a mummy.

The hotel itself he regarded as 'an abomination'; the whole place reeked of tea and curry; the rooms were loose boxes with thin cloth partitions so low that drunken brother officers could stand on chairs and peer into neighbouring rooms – an intrusion of privacy that made Burton 'sick with rage'. However, thanks to the kindness of Dr J. W. 'Paddy' Ryan, who bore the titles of Assistant Garrison Surgeon, Deputy Medical Storekeeper and Acting Surgeon in charge of Police, he was soon permitted to move from the detested hotel to what was called the sanatorium. But Burton was unappreciative. He thought the quarters unfit to house an Englishman's dog, complained of the lizards and bandicoot rats, and objected to the smell of 'roast Hindu' from the funeral pyres which burned continually at the back of the bungalows. Nevertheless, he stayed.

The inmates of the sanatorium were, in theory, invalids, but for the most part they were a collection of racketing, healthy young officers. Some of them introduced Burton into society – both English and native. The former proved stuffy, and his experience with the latter seems to have been confined to prostitutes. There was one bright spot in his life, however: he found a 'munshi', or language teacher, to help him along with his Hindustani, start him on Gujarati, and give him the beginnings of Persian. His name was Dosabhai Sohrabji, and he and Burton were to remain friends until the munshi's death many years later. Sohrabji said Burton was the only pupil he ever had who could 'learn a language running'.

Burton, with his extraordinary memory, had already developed his own system for teaching himself languages and boasted that he could learn to speak any language within two months. First he bought a simple grammar and vocabulary and underlined the words and rules he felt should be memorized. Putting these books in his pocket, he studied them at every spare moment during the day, never working more than fifteen minutes at a time. By this method he was able to learn 300 words a week. When he had acquired a basic vocabulary, he chose a simple story book and read it, marking with a pencil any new words he wanted to remember and going over these at least once a day. Then he went on to a more difficult book, at the same time learning the finer points of the grammar. When he came across a new sound not found in any of the other languages he knew, he trained his tongue by repeating it hundreds of times a day. When listening to someone talking in the new language, he silently repeated the words after him to perfect his pronunciation and accent. He was particularly attracted to alphabets that did not use Latin letters: Arabic, Hebrew, Chinese, Syriac and Sanscrit. He was seldom content simply to understand and to make himself understood; he wanted to talk like a native. When native teachers were available, he claimed that he always learned the 'swear words' first and laughingly said that after that the rest of the language was easy.

Perhaps it was this fascination with the languages of India that caused him to give up a scheme for quitting the East India Company, returning to Italy, and joining the Duke of Lucca's Guards. In any case, he seemed reconciled to his lot when, after six weeks at the sanatorium, he received orders to join his regiment, the 18th Regiment of Bombay Native Infantry, at Baroda, 244 miles north of Bombay. He bought a horse, picked up an additional dog, hired a number of servants – no English subaltern in India ever had less than a dozen – and made his way to his regiment.

His first night at the officers' mess he shocked superiors and fellow-ensigns alike by his refusal to drink beer, then the staple drink of the British soldier in India. Paddy Ryan in Bombay had told him that the best cure for fever was port. Reasoning that what would cure fevers would also prevent them, Ensign Burton had brought along a good stock. Besides, he hated beer.

At first, the new officer set about adjusting himself to his new life in a reasonably normal manner. He found the drill easy, and was amused by such new 'Hindi' words as 'Fiz Bag-net' (fix bayonets) and 'Tandalees' (stand at ease). Sword exercise was no problem, for he was already an expert. He studied Indian swordsmanship, but had little respect for it as only the blade was used, never the point. Wrestling was another matter. In spite of his broad shoulders and strong arms, he was frequently defeated by his slightly-built Indian soldiers. This led him to study the art and to begin an Indian training schedule that included a diet consisting of balls of unrefined sugar washed down with well-spiced hot milk. He soon gave up wrestling.

He had greater success with cockfighting. His favourite bird was named Bhujang (meaning 'Dragon') and Burton described him as 'about as dunghill and "low caste" a bird as ever used a spur, but a strong spiteful thing, a sharp riser, and a clean hitter withal'. Even many years later, he was fond of recounting how the dunghill Bhujang defeated a thoroughbred cock owned by a rich Indian. When Bhujang died, Burton gave the bird an elaborate funeral and made a special grave for him near his bungalow, giving rise to a rumour that he had buried a baby there.

Besides cockfighting, there were other amusements. He practised pig-sticking from horseback by riding down mongrel dogs – a practice he was much ashamed of later in life. He learned the Indian style of riding and won the regimental horse-race. Although he had always been squeamish about snakes, he studied the technique of handling them under a professional snake charmer until he had mastered the art, but finally decided it was too dangerous a pastime. Sometimes he borrowed elephants and hunting leopards from the local native prince and went on a tiger hunt, and occasionally he witnessed His Highness the Gaekwar's favourite sport – a fight between a tiger and a buffalo, or between two bull elephants with cut tusks.

In spite of such diversions, on most days he spent twelve hours on his language studies. He kept up his Arabic and worked hard at his Hindustani. He employed native teachers, but soon found a more effective kind of munshi in that invaluable aide to the anthropologist, the linguist and the lonely soldier: a native mistress. He was conforming to custom. English women being scarce, there was hardly an officer in the Indian Army without his *bubu*. One officer in Burton's regiment always referred to himself in the feminine gender when speaking Hindustani because he had learned all he knew of the language from his mistresses.

Burton's *bubu* kept house for him, controlled the servants, nursed him when he was sick, and taught him the syntax of Indian life as well as its grammar. Besides these virtues, *bubus* agreeably made contracts with their young officers dissolving the affair, should unwanted and embarrassing children become extant. But Burton maintained they had 'an infallible recipe to prevent maternity'.

Meanwhile, history was being made in another part of the Indian peninsula. On 17 February 1843, Sir Charles Napier with only 2,000 British troops achieved a brilliant victory by defeating a force of 20,000 Beluchis at Miani. A month later, the battle of Hyderabad was fought and Sind, 48,000 square miles in the valley of the Indus, fell into the hands of the British. According to *Punch*, Napier was alleged to have sent back from Sind a one-word announcement of his victory: '*Peccavi*' (I have sinned). It was more than a pun: he had Sind but he had indeed sinned. A treaty had been violated by the attack. This bit of inexcusable aggression was to have an important effect on Burton's life, but now he was far from the scene of action, buried deep in his study of Indian life.

Burton's interest in the languages of India led him to an interest in many other aspects of native life. He studied Hinduism with such thoroughness that soon he was as familiar with the religion as any foreigner could be. He read everything he could find and studied diligently under a Nagar Brahman named Him Chand. Eventually his teacher granted him the official right to wear the *Janeo*, or Brahminical thread of the twice born, and his messmates damned him as the 'White Nigger'.

Equally disconcerting to his associates were his experiments with Western religions. He now refused to attend the Church of England services, preferring instead to go to Mass at the local Catholic chapel of a half-caste Goanese priest who held services for the Catholic camp servants. Burton thought Catholicism 'a terrible religion for a man of the world to live in, but a good one to die in'.

In April, he obtained leave to take the official examination in Hindustani at Bombay. Although in India scarcely six months, he passed the tests, the best of twelve contestants. It was the first time he had ever won. Returning to his regiment, he plunged enthusiastically into the study of Gujarati and Sanscrit. On 26 June he was officially appointed regimental interpreter with a slight pay increase of thirty rupees a month. In October, only five months after passing his first language examination, he was back in Bombay to take an examination in Gujarati. The tests were not easy. They consisted of translating two books, reading a handwritten letter, carrying on a conversation and writing a paper in the language. But again he was placed first.

Although Burton never mentioned it and perhaps was unaware of the fact, one of the other successful candidates for a certificate in Gujarati at this time was Lieutenant Christopher Palmer Rigby, a most remarkable man and one whom Burton was to encounter again in his career under somewhat disagreeable circumstances. Although only twenty-three years old, Rigby was already considered the most outstanding linguist in the Indian Army. Gujarati was the fourth Indian language he had mastered and he was the first officer in the Bombay army to pass the examinations for official interpreter in so many languages. He had also studied Somali and Amharic during four years' service at Aden and a paper he wrote on the Somali language for the Geographical Society of Bombay was later to prove helpful to Burton. To surpass Rigby was an accomplishment.

Returning to Baroda in November, Burton found his regiment under orders to move to freshly conquered Sind. On New Year's Day of 1844, the 18th Regiment of Bombay Native Infantry (and one lone, unidentifiable woman) boarded HEIC *Semiramis* and set sail for Karachi, today the capital of Pakistan. On board the ship Burton made friends with Captain (later General) Walter Scott of the Bombay Engineers, a nephew of the famous Sir Walter. Scott, who was interested in history, was delighted to find someone familiar with Holinshed and Froissart; he was trying to learn Italian and Burton offered to help. Later in life, Burton spoke of Scott as 'a truly fine character' and as one who 'never said a disagreeable word or did an ungraceful deed'. Captain Scott had been detailed to make a survey of Lower Sind, a project which interested Burton very much. Although ignorant of surveying, the prospect of escaping the regimental mess and roaming the country with his new friend was inviting. Scott promised to do all he could to help him get an appointment as one of his assistants.

After a four-day voyage, the *Semiramis* sailed past Manora Head, anchored off the small village of Karachi, and discharged its passengers, drowning a sepoy in the process. No traveller ever complained more about his surroundings, wherever he was, than did Burton. Karachi was no exception. He described it several times, but always with disgust: 'Streets there were none; every house looked like a small fort, and they almost met over the narrow lanes that formed the only thoroughfares. The bazaar, a long line of miserable shops, covered over with rude matting of date leaves, was the only place comparatively open. Nothing could exceed the filthiness of the town; sewers there were none. And the deodorization was effected by the dust.' He also complained of the discomforts of camp life, the dust storms and the brackish water. Five thousand troops, British and Indian, were stationed in Karachi, which was the headquarters of Sir Charles Napier.

The 18th did not stay long at Karachi. They moved forty miles south to Bandar Gharra, described by Burton as 'that unhappy hole' and 'a desolate bit of rock and clay' and as a 'dirty heap of mud-and-mat hovels'. The hillocks which dotted the countryside he called 'warts upon the foul face of the landscape'.

It had been predicted that there would be ten years of guerrilla warfare before Sind was completely subjugated, but Napier made the country the safest province in India within a year. A Beluchi said the country was so peaceful that 'if you catch a wasp in your hand it will not sting'. Nevertheless, Sir Charles passed some strange laws and his ideas of justice seemed peculiar to the inhabitants of Sind. He liberated the African slaves and thus turned them out to starve; unfamiliar with the native custom of buying a poor man as a proxy to suffer the law's penalties, he once scandalized his civilian Judge Advocate by hanging the real criminal; and when he sent a husband to the gallows for killing his unfaithful wife, he turned the morals of the country so upside down that a deputation of Hyderabad prostitutes came to complain that the competition of married women was taking the bread from their mouths.

But Burton had no part in the policies of his Commander-in-Chief. He was only a junior officer in a native regiment of the Honourable East India Company whose board of directors Napier had scornfully called 'the twenty-four kings of Leadenhall Street'. Unable to afford the construction of a bungalow, he sweltered in a tent when temperatures reached $125°$. Nevertheless, lying under a camp table with a wet cloth thrown over it, he plunged into the study of Marathi (or Maratti) and in September he again made the trip to Bombay to take the official language examinations. Again he out-distanced all other candidates.

On his return, Burton was delighted to find himself assigned as one of Captain Scott's four assistants on the Sind Survey. It took him only a few days to master the mysteries of compass, theodolite and spirit level, and on 10 December 1844, he was sent out with six camels and a team of men to survey the Guni River and several canals. He did his work well, even receiving an official commendation, but he also found time to work on his Persian, which he regarded as the 'richest and most charming of Eastern languages', and to become something of an expert in the art of Indian falconry.

Returning to the headquarters of the Survey at Karachi in April 1845, he plunged deeper into Indian life. He even opened three small shops where, disguised as a native, he sold cloth, tobacco and other small items in exchange for a few rupees and a wealth of information. Always more interested in men's vices than their virtues, he became fascinated with the sexual practices of the Orient. What he learned he put down in his notebooks – and he learned a lot. He also made notes on folk tales, religions, magic, native cures, aphrodisiacs and talismans; weapons, armour, soldiers and methods of fighting; tribes, races, castes and trades; weddings, funerals, festivals and courtship. He learned and recorded that Karachi contained seven procuresses, three Hindu and four Moslem, and he noted the details of their operating methods. He paid careful attention to every item of clothing, including underclothing, worn by the Sindi women, and he made comparative notes on the shapes of their breasts.

It was at this time that Burton made his report on pederasty in Karachi for Sir Charles Napier. This was to prove ruinous to his reputation and to his career in the Indian Army. He said later that he was 'asked indirectly to make inquiries and to report upon the subject'. Just how he was 'asked indirectly' to make the report is not known. Perhaps it was no more than an overheard remark by Napier to the effect that he wished he knew what went on. In any case, Burton appears to have done a thorough job.

Staining himself with henna and donning native dress, Burton, posing as Mirza Abdullah of Bushire, disappeared into the back streets of Karachi with his munshi and friend Mirza Mohammed Hosayn of Shiraz. He found what he was seeking. There were three brothels in which eunuchs and boys were for hire. Burton was intrigued. He went back evening after evening until he had learned all, including such details as the fact that the price of boys was double the price of eunuchs because their scrota 'could be used as a kind of bridle for directing the movements of the animal'. His report, designed for the eyes of Napier only, was submitted with the full details.

In November 1845, his explorations into the inner life of Karachi were interrupted when, with Captain Scott, he set off on a long tour of northern Sind. They had reached Larkana, only 200 miles from Karachi, when Scott received a letter from Napier's headquarters saying that any of his assistants could return to their regiment if they were willing to resign their appointments on the Survey. The first Sikh War, which was to add the Punjab to British India, was about to begin. Burton begged to go, but his application was refused. Then an order came from Bengal to the effect that all members of the Survey must post bonds. Burton promptly wrote an official letter stating that no man would go bond for him, and back to his regiment he went.

Eager for action, he rejoined his regiment at Rohri on the Indus River, 240 miles north-east of Karachi. Rohri was a sacred spot for Hindus, 'but its sanctity is worn out, decrepit, broken down with years', Burton maintained. Here an army was being assembled to march on Moltan, then held by the Sikhs. It was bustling with activity and filled with excited officers and men. Burton found the camp 'a most picturesque spectacle'. It was a 'town of glittering white tents, laid out in mathematical streets and squares, thronged with gay uniforms and suburbed by guards and pickets. . . . Orderlies were continually galloping up and down the lines, battalions manoeuvring, and squadrons moving in all possible directions; the very river was covered with crazy boats, pontoons and dhundhis laden with stores. Every step was bustling, every face had a joyful *quid nunc* in it.'

On 23 February 1846, the 18th Bombay Native Infantry, along with the rest of the army, moved out of camp by brigades of three regiments each. Bugles blew, officers shouted, camels grunted and the men chattered with excitement in the ranks. The army marched off through the dust and heat, followed by the camp followers, servants, baggage and the inevitable army dogs.

The officers' hopes of winning honour and distinction in combat were fated to be disappointed. After two weeks' marching they reached Bahawalpur, only about sixty miles from Multan, where they unexpectedly received orders to return to Rohri. The war had been won by others. Angry and disappointed, they turned around and marched back. After only a few days' halt at Rohri, the 18th marched south to their regimental headquarters at Mohammed Khan Ka Tanda on the Fulayli River. Burton felt particularly dismal: not only had he seen no action, but he had lost his berth on the Sind Survey. He took out his chagrin on his fellow-officers and got into trouble with his superiors. Again it was his talent for doggerel rhymes that had so offended his tutor and the Oxford dons. This time it was his newly appointed Commanding Officer, Henry Corsellis, whose epitaph he wrote:

Here lieth the body of Colonel Corsellis,
The rest of the fellow, I fancy, in hell is.

The colonel was not pleased.

Deciding that monkeys were preferable to his messmates, Burton collected about forty of various breeds and proceeded to live with them – but in a civilized manner, of course. He assigned them ranks and titles and formed his own mess. He taught them to sit at the table and had the servants wait on them. Beside him sat a tiny, pretty, silky-looking monkey he called his wife. As a final touch he put pearls in her ears. The monkeys became involved in his language studies and he began to form a simian vocabulary. Using his usual system, he repeated the sounds of the monkeys until he could imitate them and claimed to have collected about sixty 'leading words'.

But natives were more interesting than monkeys and he spent considerable time among them. So skilful did he become in disguising himself as an Indian that he frequently passed his Commanding Officer without being recognized. He found most of his friends among the local inhabitants, but he did make the acquaintance of one European who took almost as great an interest in orientalia as he did. This was Dr John Frederick Steinhaeuser, a civil surgeon. He was to remain a close friend of Burton's all his life.

He also came to know his Commander-in-Chief through his duties as interpreter. Sir Charles Napier was a soldier so forthright and blunt that he struck even the tactless Burton as being 'utterly deficient in prudence'. He publicly referred to Sir James Hogg, Chairman of the Court of Directors of the East India Company, as 'that hog' and to a distinguished newspaper editor as a 'blatant beast'. According to Burton, 'he did not care a fig how many enemies he made, and his tongue was like a scorpion's sting'. Being a man who liked direct answers, Napier took a liking to his bright young interpreter. Once he asked Burton how many bricks there were in a newly made bridge. Unhesitatingly Burton replied, '229,010, Sir Charles.'

Another time, Napier scheduled a review on a grand scale to impress a group of visiting Indian rajas. Turning to his interpreter, he said, 'Lieutenant Burton, be pleased to inform these gentlemen that I propose to form these men into line, then to break into echelon by the right, and to form square on the centre battalion . . .' and went on at length briskly describing in detail the complicated manoeuvres he intended to order.

'Yes, sir,' said Burton, saluting.

Turning to the rajas, he said smoothly, 'O chiefs! Our great man is going to show you the way we fight, and you must be attentive to the rules.' He then saluted Napier as a sign that the translation was completed.

'Have you explained all?' asked Napier incredulously.

'Everything, sir.'

'A most concentrated language that must be,' muttered Sir Charles, riding off.

Associations, pleasant and unpleasant, were broken when, in early July 1846, Burton took sick with cholera. By September he was in serious condition and had to be sent to a hospital in Bombay. His recovery was slow, and he was at last given two years' sick leave to convalesce in the Nilgiri Hills (known as 'Neillgherry' to Anglo-Indians), a 7,000-foot plateau in South Madras. On 20 February 1847, he hired a *pattimar*, a lumbering native craft with a lateen sail, and set out for the sanatorium by way of the tiny Portuguese possession of Goa.

There was much to interest Burton in Goa. First of all there were the historical associations: Vasco da Gama had been here; here St Francis Xavier had won fame for his missionary work; and, most interesting of all to Burton, the famous sixteenth-century Portuguese poet Camões (or Camoens, in the old spelling) had lived here and had written about the country in his *Lusiads*. Burton had a great deal in common with Camões: both men were soldiers, both were poets (of different qualities, it must be added), both had a passionate love of travel, and both had served in India. Also of interest at Goa was the opportunity to study Portuguese, an easy task for a man of Burton's linguistic abilities who was already fluent in French and Italian and was familiar with Spanish. But there was another, unexpected, interest which Burton found in Goa.

Visiting the ruined churches, the scenes of the Inquisition, the tomb of St Francis Xavier and the places mentioned by Camões, Burton came across an old convent called Caza da Misericordia, still in use. His interest in religions extended to the nuns. Under the pretext of looking for a suitable convent for his young sister and the assurance that he could provide a large monthly allowance, the good prioress showed the young officer around the convent and introduced him to some of the nuns who would tutor his 'sister'. It was the Latin teacher who caught Burton's eyes: 'a very pretty white girl, with large blue eyes, a modest smile, and a darling of a figure'.

The difficulties of carrying on an affair with a nun were formidable. She hardly dared look at him and was always accompanied by a grim-faced elderly sister. Additional obstacles were the prioress, an ugly and forbidding sub-prioress, and guards and the convent's thick walls. Nevertheless, he laid an elaborate plot to carry her off to British territory where he fancied she would be happier. The lady had contrived to gain as her companion a half-blind and partially deaf sister and Burton was able to exchange enough glances and whispered words to lead him to believe she would co-operate in the project. He was right.

A Goanese servant was carefully corrupted and coached. Then he was sent to the convent with a bottle of cognac for the prioress – useful as medicine, of course – and presents for many of the other nuns. To the pretty Latin teacher went a nosegay with a little pink note concealed in a large jessamine blossom. As he knew they would, the nuns questioned the servant regarding his age, rank, parentage, education, travels, religion and prospects. To all of which the servant answered with the lies Burton had coached him to say, extolling his master's gallantry in action, his chastity, temperance, and devotion to the Catholic Church. As the servant told the nuns that Burton was sick and unable to come himself, the good nuns sent him a number of small presents, including a book on St Augustine from the Latin teacher, perhaps with an interesting, if unrelated, gloss.

After a fortnight of intrigue, a fast-sailing *pattimar* was obtained and tied to the wharf near the convent. Servants and baggage were put on board and the ship made ready for sea. About eleven o'clock one night, Burton in disguise, with his Moslem servant Allahdad, made his way to the convent. There were long knives up their sleeves and dark lanterns in their hands. At exactly midnight, the two men slipped through the door leading into the back garden. The guards were asleep, having been drugged by the addition of some datura to their evening tobacco. Forcing the lock to the convent with their daggers, they made their way through the cloisters towards the cell of the Latin teacher. Unfortunately, Burton made a wrong turn and ended up in the room of the ugly sub-prioress, who was raised, embraced and borne off before she could recover her senses. Once outside, Burton paused to look at his prize. Then the lady recovered from her terror sufficiently to scream.

'We have eaten filth!' exclaimed Burton to Allahdad as he gagged the poor sub-prioress. Then they fled.

Burton did not make a second attempt as in the future the convent

was guarded like a fortress. Besides, he had had excitement enough for
a convalescent and it seemed best to leave Goa, its charms and charm-
ers. But sitting on the deck of his pattimar waiting for the tindal, or
captain, and the crew to come aboard and hoist the anchor, he felt sad
and sentimental, so he composed a doggerel of farewell:

> *Adieu, fair land, deep silence reigns*
> *O'er hills and dales and fertile plains. . . .*
> *Whilst gazing on the lovely view,*
> *How grating sounds the word 'adieu!'*

When the tindal and his crew appeared they were roaring drunk and
in no mood to listen to poetry or work the ship. Burton coaxed and
cursed; then he kicked. Exasperated, he lashed out with his fists at the
shaven head of the captain and knocked him down. Struggling to his
feet, the tindal lurched towards him with drunken ferocity and
jumped – or fell – or was pushed – overboard. The tide was too strong
for swimming, at least while drunk, and he screamed for help, thrashing futilely in the water. The crew shouted sympathetically and did
nothing. The sentinels on shore bawled for the guard. The harbour
master, the collector of customs, the police, an army detachment, and
finally even the Portuguese governor himself (grandly styled 'Governor of All the Indies') appeared on the scene. It was perhaps as well for
Burton that the nun was not on board. Hauled from the water, the
tindal stoutly maintained that Burton had attempted to murder both
him and the crew. The police ended the uproar by throwing the tindal
in the guardhouse to sober up. The crowd dispersed, the crew fell
asleep on the deck, and Burton was left alone to fume at the delay.

The next day, when all were sober again, friendly relations were
restored. The tindal came on board, he and the crew devoutly said
their prayers, the sails were set, and they put to sea. St Ignatius was the
patron saint of the ship and his statue was firmly fixed to the cabin
wall, where a pot of oil with a lighted wick burned before it. But even
St Ignatius found life with the tindal difficult. Burton, the student of
religions, was surprised to find, one squally evening, that the saint's
lamp was not lit and asked why.

'Why?' said the tindal indignantly. 'If that fellow can't keep the sky
clear, he shall have neither oil nor wick from me, damn him!'

'But I should have supposed that in the hour of danger you would
have paid him more than usual attention,' said Burton.

'The fact is, Sahib, I have found out that the fellow is not worth his salt. The last time we had an infernal squall with him on board, and if he doesn't keep this one off, I'll just throw him overboard and take to Santa Caterina. Hang me if I don't!'

Travelling by sea and by land, Burton at last reached Ootacamund, known to Anglo-Indians as 'Ooty', in the Nilgiri Highlands. Although the *Bombay Almanac and Directory* of 1843 described the scenery as being 'exceedingly beautiful and of the grandest and most romantic description in the world', and it is considered today to have the finest climate in southern India, Burton complained that 'nothing could be duller or more disagreeable'. He even blamed the change of climate from hot, dry Sind to the 'damp, cold mountains' for an attack of 'rheumatic ophthalmia', an eye infection which remained with him for two years. But he could not remain idle, and immediately plunged into the study of the Dravidian languages of Telugu and Toda and continued his work on Arabic and Persian; he became excited by what he believed to be evidences of ancient gold mining; he conducted desultory archaeological excavations; and he studied the customs, history and religion of the natives of the area.

Had he been simply a scholar, the two years of sick leave could have been spent happily enough with his languages and other studies, but he was too eager for action to spend that long in quiet occupations. After only four months he convinced the doctors that he was cured and ready for duty. On 1 September 1847, he left the Nilgiri Hills and, after a few days spent in Calicut, he arrived in Bombay. There, on 15 October, he passed the official examination in Persian. About thirty men took the test, but Burton was again placed first; he received a compliment from the examiners and an honorarium of 1,000 rupees from the Court of Directors of the East India Company.

His luck continued. Instead of returning to his regiment, he managed to get another appointment to the Sind Survey. Boarding the steamship *Dwarka* of the Bombay Steam Navigation Company, he sailed for Karachi. It was discovered, however, that the captain had set out without a single able seaman among the crew. When both captain and mate turned up drunk as they were about to enter the dangerous waters near the port, Burton took command of the ship and safely brought her into the harbour. A nice trick for a twenty-six-year-old infantry officer.

His return to the Survey was hardly a boon to his friends. He suffered so much from his diseased eyes that he was unable to work regularly and the other officers had to carry his share. In spite of his weak eyesight, he continued his studies of languages and religions. He plunged into Sindhi, Jatki and Punjabi and, with the help of an Arab munshi named Sheik Hashim whom he had imported from Bombay, he continued his Arabic. Under Hashim, he also began the study of Islam. This was to have an important effect on his life. He learned the prayers and studied the Koran, even memorizing about 50,000 words, a quarter of that Bible of Islam.

Of the various schools of Islamic thought, the most attractive to Burton was Sufism, the elaborate symbolism of which was the favourite device of Arabic and Persian poets. He conscientiously did the exercises and the fasting to gain knowledge of the godhead through ecstasy and contemplation; all of which, incidentally, 'proved rather over-exciting to the brain'. He tried once to explain its mysticism:

Tasawwuf [Sufism] then may be defined to be the religion of beauty, whose leading principle is that of earthly, the imperfect type of heavenly, love. Its high priests are Anacreontic poets, its rites wine, music, and dancing, spiritually considered, and its places of worship meadows and gardens, where the perfume of the rose and the song of the nightingale, by charming the heart, are supposed to improve the mind of the listener. This is thorough Epicurism in the midst of one of the most gloomy faiths: the contrast is striking. . . .

Burton was charmed by the poetry of the Sufis. The Sufi poet, he found, was generally 'a profound student of the different branches of language and metaphysics' – as was Burton himself. Advancing in his studies of Sufism, he finally became a Kamil, or Master Sufi.

When overstrung from too intense a study of Sufism, he 'relieved his nerves' by studying the Sikh religion, that monotheistic Hindu faith without idols or caste. Never content simply to know, but always seeking to share and to experience, Burton was, in due course, solemnly initiated into Sikhism by an old priest in the presence of the swinging *Granth* (Nana Shah's scripture). Thus, it would have been possible at this time to assemble at least five people in the world, each of whom would have sworn Richard Burton belonged to a different religious persuasion: Hindu, Protestant, Moslem, Catholic and Sikh. And if Burton himself were included, perhaps a sixth could have been found who would have said that this man of many faiths was really the possessor of none. Yet, as he himself so immodestly, but quite correctly, stated, 'My experience of Eastern faiths became phenomenal.'

Burton's range of interests and activities was rapidly expanding. Always fascinated by gold, he took up alchemy and tried his hand at producing gold from baser metals. He learned '*mantih*', or eastern logic, in order to train his mind to think as an oriental. He mixed with Jat camel men, studying their language and way of life. In spite of his emaciated condition and the pain of his ophthalmia, he spent twelve to fourteen hours a day at his studies, believing that 'the more sluggish became my sight, the more active became my brain'.

When his health permitted, he resumed his practice of roaming the country in disguise. 'The European official in India,' he maintained, 'seldom, if ever, sees anything in its real light, so dense is the veil which the fearfulness, the duplicity, the prejudice, and the superstitions of the natives hang before his eyes. And the white man lives a life so distinct from the black, that hundreds of the former serve through what they call their "term of exile" without once being present at a circumcision feast, a wedding, or a funeral.' Burton went behind the veil.

After experimenting with various disguises, he found the easiest to assume was the character of a half-Arab, half-Persian. This guise concealed the defects in his pronunciation; there were thousands of such people, speaking in a wide variety of accents, along the northern shore of the Persian Gulf. With his hair falling down to his shoulders (the shaven head and wig were now gone), his skin stained with a thin coat of henna, and wearing a long beard, he posed as Mirza Abdullah from Bushire, Persia. He once explained why he had adopted the name Abdullah, which he assumed on many occasions throughout his life: 'Abdullah . . . is a kind of neutral name, neither Jewish, Moslem nor Christian.' On arriving in a new town he would open a shop and sit amid the flies and gossip of the bazaar before his trays of clammy dates, ginger, tobacco, rancid oil and strong-smelling sweetmeats. The prettiest girls were made steady customers of the Persian merchant by his polite manners and handsome face as well as his generous portions. They did not mind his questions.

Although he sometimes posed as a vendor of fine linens, calicoes, and muslins, he only sold his goods when he had to; mostly, he bragged of his merchandise and asked a thousand questions concerning the market and the local customs. Such men were occasionally allowed within the harem, and the broad-shouldered young merchant with the flashing eyes probably caught the heart of more than one poor Indian girl. In one of his early books (*Scinde; or, the Unhappy Valley*) he describes in a light-hearted manner a flirtation with 'one of the prettiest girls ever seen'. She was the daughter of a Persian noble, 'A****a

43

Khan', and Burton met her while halting on a march. She was being taken to her father's house near Karachi. He thought her 'a charming girl, with features carved in marble like a Greek's, the noble, thoughtful, Italian brow, eyes deep and lustrous as an Andalusian's, and the airy, graceful, kind of figure with which Mohammed, according to our poets, peopled his man's paradise'.

Burton made friends with a twelve-year-old slave in the party of Persians, and, pressing a rupee into the boy's hand, gave him a love letter to pass on to the young lady. The letter is like the fervent love notes found in *The Arabian Nights*:

The rose-bud of my heart hath opened and bloomed under the rays of those sunny eyes, and the fine linen of my soul receiveth with ecstasy the lustres which pour from that moon-like brow. But woe is me! the garden lacketh its songster, and the simooms of desire have dispersed the frail mist of hope. Such this servant knows to be his destiny; as the poet sings –

> 'Why, oh! why, was such heavenly beauty given
> To a stone from the flint rock's surface riven?'

Even so the hapless inditer of this lament remarketh that –

> 'The diamond's throne is the pure red gold;
> Shall the Almas [diamond] rest on the vile black mould?'

And he kisseth the shaft which the bow of Fate discharged at the bosom of his bliss. And he looketh forward to the grave which is immediately to receive him and his miseries. For haply thy foot may pass over his senseless clay; the sweet influence of thy presence may shed light over that dark abode.

Folding the letter and sealing it with wax, Burton hoped to add credulity to his improbable sentiments by writing a poem with an unsteady hand, making crooked and heart-broken characters:

The marks on this sheet are not the stains of smoke [i.e. ink], but the black pupils of my eyes dissolved by scalding tears. Ask of my heart what its fate is – it will tell thee that when tears are exhausted, its blood will begin to flow.

The slave delivered the letter and then returned to report. How had the lady received the letter? Did she ask to see its author? No, she merely asked if the stranger was 'learned in physic' and had any European remedies with him. Burton thought he had just the answer. Taking a bottle of coarse gin, he flavoured it with eau-de-Cologne and sent it off to the Persian beauty with a note saying he was a famous doctor who could cure all her ills if admitted to her presence. He then waited impatiently for her to summon him. As he later told the story, the summons never came. The Persians packed up and left, taking the girl with them, presumably never to be seen again. But according to a story told by his sister, Maria Stisted, and passed on by her daughter, Georgiana, Burton fell seriously in love with a Persian girl while in India. Little is known of this affair. Even the girl's name is lost, but she was said to have been of noble birth, intelligent and of rare beauty. According to the family story, Burton wanted to marry her and take her to England, but she died before he could carry out his plan.

In any event, love did not prevent him from plunging ever deeper into the swirl of native life. Finding that a 'clean turban and a polite bow' were as good as an invitation, he would boldly walk through the door of a house filled with music and guests, and would generally be welcomed. He spent many evenings in the mosques, listening to the ragged students, stretched full length on their stomachs in the dust, thumbing the soiled and tattered pages of theology books by the dim light of a hanging oil lamp. He sat for hours debating the finer points of the faith with the local *mullah*, or religious teacher, and played chess in the coffee houses. He made friends with the hemp-drinkers, the opium-eaters, the prostitutes and the marriage-makers. From each and all he gathered the private histories and domestic scandals that could be pieced together to tell the way of life of the races of Sind.

Believing that 'the knowledge of one mind is that of a million – after a fashion', he took particular pains to probe the mind of a poor tailor friend: 'and many an hour of tough thought it took me before I had mastered its truly Oriental peculiarities, its regular irregularities of deduction, and its strange monotonous one-idea'dness'.

For all his curiosity and probing, his living the native life and his intense interest in Indian *mores*, Burton remained a Victorian Englishman, and there was never a thought of seriously going native. In fact, he had nothing but contempt for the Sindhi: 'He is idle and apathetic, unclean in his person, and addicted to intoxication; notoriously cowardly in times of danger, and proportionately insolent when he has nothing to fear; he has no idea of truth or probity, and only wants more talent to be a model of treachery.' So much for the man. He had even greater contempt for Sindhi women. He approved of the Moslem prejudice against educating females, thinking them 'quite bad and cunning enough without putting such weapons as pens in their hands'. Sindhi women, he found, were fond of gambling and 'can cheat with formidable dexterity. . . . Sindhi women are most indecent in their language, especially in abuse; they have very few expressions peculiar to their sex, but deliberately select the worst words used by the men. They are fond of drinking liqueurs and the different preparations of hemp: intoxication is always the purpose of their potations. Many of them take snuff and almost all smoke Sukho [tobacco] in the Hookah. Their other amusements are dressmaking, the toilette, visits and intrigues.'

As to the relationship between Europeans and Indians, he became 'convinced that the natives of India cannot respect a European who mixes with them familiarly, or especially imitates their customs, manners and dress.' He believed the Englishman with his authoritative voice, nonchalant manners and broken Hindústani dealt with such people properly in a way 'which learning and honesty, which wit and courage, have not. This is to them the master's attitude: they bend to it.' As for himself: 'Even the experiment of associating with them is almost too hard to bear.'

Burton thought of his examination of native life as a scientific pursuit, and certainly he had the good scientist's faculty of careful observation. His notebooks bulged with valuable anthropological material and he thought of publication. In 1847, probably while recuperating at Ootacamund, he had made a literal translation of a book of Hindu ethics copied on ordinary notepaper and bound up to resemble a book. He even made a title-page:

AKHLAK I HINDI

or

A Translation of the Hindústání Version

of

Pilpay's Fables

———

BY R. F. BURTON, LT.

18th Regt. Bombay N.I.

———

With explanatory notes, and appendix

by the translator

———

[here an inscription in Arabic characters]

———

Bombay

Printed at

For

———

1847

The manuscript is short, consisting of only fifty leaves (100 pages in all) with the translation on the right-hand pages and his notes on the left. The work was never printed.

The earliest published works by Burton are two reports sent to the Bombay Government. The first one, submitted on 31 December 1847, is entitled: 'Notes relative to the population of Sind; and the customs, language, and literature of the people, etc.'. The contents of the report were taken from his notebooks, the results of his studies and his wanderings in disguise among the native population. This material was later expanded into a book: *Sindh, and the Races that Inhabit the Valley of the Indus.* The report contained a hodge-podge of facts and figures together with homely bits of gossip: 'It is not unusual for the husband to return home after a long sojourn in foreign lands and find his wife with a small family of her own. The offended party seldom allows these incidents to interfere with the domestic tie and after inflicting a meed chastisement thinks no more about it and treats the fatherless offspring with a truly paternal kindness.'

The second report was written by Burton and Assistant Surgeon J. Ellerton Stocks of the Bombay Medical Establishment, who was detailed as Vaccinator in Sind. Submitted on 2 March 1848, it deals with 'Brief Notes relative to the division of time, and articles of cultivation in Sind, to which are appended remarks on the modes of intoxication in that province'. Most of the report appears to have been written by Stocks, but the final bit on intoxication was obviously by Burton. He discussed in detail the kinds of wines, liqueurs, 'alcohols' and narcotics used in Sind and the methods used to manufacture them. He spoke with authority, as well he might, personally having tried most, if not all, of the intoxicants mentioned.

About this time he must also have written two reports for the Bombay Branch of the Royal Asiatic Society which were published in 1849: 'Critical Remarks on Dr Dorn's Chrestomathy of Pushtoo or Afghan Dialect' and 'A Grammar on Jataki or Belochi Dialect'.

In May 1848, the Second Sikh War broke out and Burton longed to see action. Having just passed his official examination in Punjabi before the only other officer in the Army who knew it, he now possessed interpreter certificates for six Indian languages and he had studied many others, including Multani, the language of the enemy. In the most suppliant terms, he applied for the post of interpreter for the army marching to Multan. His application was refused. The appointment was given to another officer who knew only Hindustani.

Unfortunately for Burton, his earlier report on pederasty in Karachi, although unpublished, had come to the attention of the authorities of the Bombay Government. Napier left Sind in 1847 and Burton's report had been forwarded to Bombay where its pornographic details horrified the officials who read it. This was the work of an English officer and gentleman! The 'White Nigger' was socially ostracized and it was even proposed that he be dismissed from the service. In the end he was allowed to remain in the army, but all roads to future advancement were now blocked.

Burton was heartbroken. He had worked hard and had found within himself a talent which he hoped would lead him to distinction. But now, although he was only twenty-eight years old, he looked upon his career as ruined, himself as a failure, and his nearly seven years in India as wasted. Still weak from his bout with cholera, tormented by his diseased eyes, he had no trouble convincing a medical board of his unfitness for Indian service. He was granted an extended sick leave and allowed to return to England. Sick, discouraged, and with tears of rage in his ophthalmious eyes, he said good-bye to his friends of the Sind Survey. When he reached Bombay he became so ill that he had to be carried on board the *Eliza*, a sixty-year-old brig bound for Britain.

Chapter 4

Books, Swords and a Lady
1848 – 53

THANKS to the sea air and the careful nursing of his servant, Allahdad, who accompanied him, Burton arrived in England with his health much improved. It was two o'clock in the morning when he energetically pounded on the door of his Aunt Georgina Baker's home in London. Mrs Baker had died in 1846 at the age of seventy-four; his parents were in Italy, as was his sister, who had married Henry Stisted (later General Sir Henry Stisted). But Burton was glad to see his aunts and, for the moment, to be in England, although his mother country held few attractions for him and he did not stay long. He toyed with the idea of returning to Oxford and taking his degree, but he was a scholar who now had no need for the crutch of an educational institution and he was unwilling to submit to its discipline. After a brief flirtation with a pair of pretty cousins, Sarah and Eliza Burton, he decamped for Italy and a joyous reunion with his family at Pisa. He found his mother ill and his father in his usual excellent state of poor health – no better and no worse than he had always been.

Maria now had two children, Georgiana and Maria, and these quickly became the favourites of Allahdad who, with his turban and baggy pants, appeared to them a character out of *The Arabian Nights*. At first Allahdad seemed to adapt himself very well to his new surroundings, even learning a few words of Italian, but before long he grew homesick and sulky. When Sabbatino, the Italian cook, teased the Moslem by showing him a ham boiling in a pot, Allahdad, his religious feelings outraged, seized the cook and tried to roast him on the charcoal fire. From that point on he was impossible. Mustering all his language skill, he compounded a simple phrase to express his feelings: 'God damn Italy!' This expression, repeated on all occasions to every Italian he met, resulted in a continuing series of engagements with the local citizens. When the Burtons moved to England, Allahdad was shipped back to India.

The elder Burtons had continued their restless life, roving about Europe as they had always done. It was almost like old times now that they were together again. Only Edward was missing. He had been serving as a surgeon in the 36th Regiment stationed in Ceylon, and although the two brothers had made many plans for meeting in India, they had somehow never been able to arrange it. Now they were separated forever. Edward Burton, while on an elephant hunt, had been beaten by natives. The beating was so brutal, particularly about the head, that the brain injury he suffered had reduced the wild, carefree young man to a human vegetable. Tragically, he lived on for forty years in this state without ever speaking. He died in 1895.

Most of Burton's second year of sick leave was spent in England between Leamington and Dover, with occasional trips to the mineral springs at Malvern in Worcestershire where he took the 'hydropathic cure'. Medicine being one of his many interests, he felt qualified to modify the treatment to suit his own ideas. He claimed success, and certainly his energy proved he was recovering rapidly. About the end of 1851 he moved to Boulogne where he was soon joined by the rest of the Burton family.

He now began his career as an author. Digging into his notebooks, he whipped out three books in one year. The first was *Goa, and the Blue Mountains: or Six Months of Sick Leave*, a rambling account of personal experiences, folklore, complaints about the government, bits and pieces of ethnology, etymology and history together with descriptions of religious customs, races, places and people. He also exposed a fine array of personal prejudices. Condemned or spoken of disparagingly were Freemasons, Jews, Christians, (and Catholics in particular), 'niggers' (by which he meant all non-whites), servants, antiquaries, several cities in Europe and Asia, and various categories of men and women in Indian society. He found fault with the Portuguese Army and this led him to the deficiencies of the British Army and, in particular, the failure of the British properly to instruct their soldiers in the use of the bayonet. *Goa and the Blue Mountains* is much like a personal letter of a traveller to a friend, written with the self-consciousness of one who is certain his letters will be published in the local newspaper.

The attempted abduction of the nun was too good a yarn to be left out, but he put the story into the mouth of a Goanese and implied that the deed was done by another officer. His description of this 'other officer' is interesting as it shows Burton's idea of what others thought of him: This 'Lieut. —, of the — Regt.' was 'a very clever gentleman, who knew everything. He could talk to each man of a multitude in his own language, and all of them would appear equally surprised by, and delighted with him. Besides, his faith was every man's faith. . . . Moreover, he chaunted the Koran, and the circumcised dogs considered him a kind of saint. The Hindoos also respected him, because he always ate his beef in secret, spoke religiously of the cow, and had a devil, (i.e. some heathen image) in an inner room. At Cochin he went to the Jewish place of worship, and read a large book, just like a priest. Ah! he was a clever Sahib that!' So does Burton have the Goanese describe the officer who tried to abduct the nun.

The reviewer of *Goa* in *Athenaeum*, a prominent English literary magazine of the time, said:

He should never have trusted himself to write a book. He has become too advanced a person to submit to the didactic restraints of composition. . . . The book before us is a curious piece of patch-work made up of the most heterogenous materials. Here and there the slang and the persiflage are carried to an extreme which borders on the offensive. . . . It is to be regretted that Lieut. Burton has acquired so much experience of the world that he did not think it necessary to obtain some competent opinion on the merits of the book before he printed it. A judicious friend would very likely have burnt one-third of the manuscript, and ordered him to re-write most of the rest.

Burton never took advice unless it coincided with his own ideas, which was seldom, and he certainly did not heed the *Athenaeum*. *Goa, and the Blue Mountains* was followed soon after by two books on Sind: *Scinde: or The Unhappy Valley*, in two volumes dedicated to his friend Walter Scott, and *Sindh, and the Races that Inhabit the Valley of the Indus*. (In all, he was to publish three books on Sind and the name of the region was spelled differently in the title of each of them.) In *Goa* and *Scinde* Burton had tried to write in a popular style; in *Sindh* he tried to be scholarly. None was a commercial success. The weaknesses of these books – and of most of those that followed – were serious ones. All were written too hastily and the material from his voluminous notebooks was not properly digested.

Of his first two dozen books it may be said that he often wrote a well-turned phrase, occasionally a good sentence, rarely a fine paragraph, and never a good book. Some very quotable lines can be found in *Scinde*: speaking of prevailing thought in the region, he says that in Sind 'opinions are heirlooms'. Of Sehwan, a town on the Indus river where he was continually importuned by beggars, he says, 'the very babies look impatient to begin begging'. And he mentions a 'deserted mosque having been desecrated into utility'.

His passion for language included an interest in grammar, etymology, and unusual words. Unfortunately, he was not always content with existing words and developed an incurable habit, which grew steadily worse, of coining new ones. Few of them were fortunate: 'conversationizing', 're-became', and 'us-wards', are some early examples. He was also fond of esoteric, archaic and foreign words, and he used 'natation' for swimming, 'piscation' for fishing, and, once, 'quadruped creation' for horse. Even *Goa*, supposedly written for popular consumption, contains words, phrases and quotations in Portuguese, Hindustani, Arabic, French, Latin, Persian, Greek, Italian and Sanscrit.

Above all, Burton loved footnotes. He always seemed to write more comfortably in them, and many of his most interesting and best written sentences lie buried in the fine print at the bottom of his pages. Some of his works contain almost as many words in the footnotes as are included in the text.

Footnotes were also useful for self-congratulation, as in this one from *Scinde*:

At a distance, Yellow Jack, earthquakes, the Cuchillo [a volcanic mountain in the Canary Islands], and similar strange enemies to human life, look terrible because indistinct: the heart does beat a little quicker when we fix thought upon it. But as soon as you find yourself amongst the dangers, you forget to fear them, and a little habit makes them, generally speaking, contemptible: your expected giants you find pigmies. Besides, I have been fortunate in opportunity of training, being brought up, as it were, to think lightly of such things in youth. And every one who thinks becomes, by some means or other, a fatalist on a small scale, after a few years in the East.

Certainly, one reason for Burton's lack of literary success was his unfortunate habit of expressing undisguised contempt for his readers. *Scinde* purports to take a Mr John Bull (that is, the reader) on a tour of the valley of the Indus: 'Yes, Mr Bull, we are now in Scinde, sir. . . .' Since Mr Bull is made to appear both naïve and stupid, it is little wonder the book failed to find enthusiastic admirers. The style, which was apparently meant to be colloquial, too often appears that of an undergraduate:

Here we are, Mr Bull, still sitting within our sundried brick box, on high backed arm-chairs of reed, with our feet *more Indico* upon the table, and glasses of pale ale *more Scindico* (it is 10 a.m.) placed within reach, on a floor freshly composted with one of the five venerable proceeds of the cow.

Characteristically, 'proceeds of the cow' is followed by an asterisk and the coy footnote to which it refers says, 'The Panjagaviya, as the Hindoos call them; if you want to know what they are, consult a Hindustanee dictionary.'

As with most of his travel books, the contents of his bulging notebooks were simply dumped into his manuscripts with no apparent editing. Encyclopedias aside, there are few books that cover such a wide range of subject matter: narcotics, courtship, poetry, politics, topography, obscure oriental literature, fornication, slavery, religions, education, history, Hindu mythology, exotic customs, personal experiences, and a miscellaneous collection of other topics are taken up with little regard to order or appropriateness. He scoffs at the hypocrisy of the British in their attempt to justify their colonial wars and offers much gratuitous advice to the British Government – a habit which also grew on him and did him little good. Nor did the Honourable East India Company escape his criticisms. Unable to cram all his complaints into his three books, he found time in the same year to send 'John Company' an impolitic essay 'upon the subject of Anglo-Indian misrule'. The young lieutenant's report was not kindly received.

Burton used these three books, and many of those that followed, as spring-boards for his own unconventional notions and to present a rare collection of opinions and prejudices that were certainly not 'heirlooms'. He admired nose rings on women, defended the use of opium, and deplored the use of the side-saddle for women. 'The natives of Central Asia are to be controlled only by strange and terrible punishments,' he contended, and he suggested such measures as flaying men alive, chopping them in two vertically, stoning them to death, impaling them and cutting off their limbs. He also favoured flogging instead of imprisonment. He thought acquisitiveness was 'the mainspring of human action' and that 'in all sacred places and holy cities from Rome to Mecca, the inhabitants are a very disreputable race' (although he had not yet visited Mecca). He also gave passing insults to various races, nationalities and religions: He refers to 'the Belochies, the Welsh, and other semi-barbarous races'; to the Banyans as being as skilful in forgery 'as a London Jew at manufacturing a Guido'; and to the Sindis as being like the Irish: lazy and ungrateful.

For all his knowledge and supposed sophistication, Burton was often naïve. He took a serious interest in alchemy and spiritualism and he was very superstitious. He believed in the evil effects of sleeping in the moonlight and claimed he had learned by experience how dangerous it was to sleep under a tamarind tree (he caught an ague when he tried it, thus confirming, he said, the native superstition). One of his pet theories, which he acquired in India and maintained throughout his life, was that women are more passionate than men in hot damp climates and that the reverse is true in cold, dry climates – a belief, incidentally, without scientific foundation; the differences, if they exist, being more cultural than climatic.

In *Sindh* he mentions his plan to write 'a detailed account of the principal works on the study of language and scholastic science in use throughout the tribes of Islam', an ambitious project he never completed. This, too, was characteristic. Throughout his life, in book after book, he was to speak of other books he planned to write but never did.

Amid all the literary and philosophical rubbish in these early books, there was at least one pearl. Unfortunately, it was not recognized as such when the opinion was published in 1851 nor has he ever been credited with it by *romane raia*. In Sind Burton had taken a keen interest in the Jats, a people of unknown antecedents, and concluded from philological evidence and their customs that the gypsies of Europe were descended from them. Now no one can say for certain where the gypsies originally came from, but it is a widely accepted theory today that they did indeed come from the valley of the Indus, and there is support from other than philological evidence that they may have once been Jats. Burton was probably unfamiliar with Potts' two-volume study of gypsies, *Die Zigeuner in Europa und Asien*, published six years before, in which it was first seriously suggested that the gypsies of Europe came from India; the first recognition of even their Indian origin in English literature (aside from Burton) was by John Beamer (*A Comparative Grammar of the Modern Aryan Languages of India*), nearly twenty-five years after Burton published his opinion. Neither does it appear that Burton knew the story related by Hamza of Isfahan, a tenth-century Arabic historian, who said that people called Zatts were brought into Persia from India by King Bahram V about A.D. 420. However, 'Zatt' is Arabic for Jat and the word is used even today to designate gypsies in Syria.

In 1852 Burton brought out *Falconry in the Valley of the Indus*. This sport (he called it an art) had interested him since, as a boy, he had starved a hawk to death trying to train it. He had studied the literature on the subject while at Oxford and he had practised falconry in Sind. But more than falconry was included in the thin (107 pages) volume. Burton added a brief autobiography and an interesting postscript, in which he deplored the low taste of the British reader (his first three books had not sold) and he told how he had been cautioned (he did not say by whom, but it was the gentle critic of *Athenaeum* in his review of *Scinde*) against 'extreme opinions' and condemned for his 'disregard of those well-established rules of moderation which no one can transgress with impunity': advice he never took. The criticized critic of *Athenaeum* replied, 'It would seem that Asiatic habits and a sporting vocabulary are not propitious to the growth of a logical faculty – at all events not in Mr. Burton.'

Five hundred copies of *Falconry* were printed and twenty-five years later his publishers reported to him that 257 were still unsold. Curiously enough, the book was never remaindered and nearly sixty years after its publication (and twenty years after Burton's death) it could still be procured from the successors of the publisher.

In 1853 he brought out his next book – a small booklet, actually. This was *A Complete System of Bayonet Exercise*, illustrated with drawings of soldiers carrying bayonets as though they were fragile glass rods. Strange to say, it was this seemingly inoffensive booklet which brought down upon him an official reprimand administered by Colonel William Sykes. Although bayonet drill was standard in the United States and in most European armies of that era, the British Army clung to the notion that knowledge of the proper handling of the bayonet would make the men unsteady in the ranks and that its only use was in the orderly charge. Therefore, the British soldier was taught only how to fix and unfix his bayonet. In close combat he was forced through ignorance to use his rifle as a club.

Some years later, after the Crimean War, Burton's manual, with only minor changes, was adopted by the British Army, but the only recognition its author ever received was a document entitling him to draw one shilling from the Treasury, thereby allowing the government to use his copyrighted material. Burton went to the trouble of drawing the shilling, going determinedly from office to office with papers and forms, to the amazement of the government clerks, until he got it. As he was coming out of the War Office, a beggar approached him. Burton threw him the shilling.

'Lord love yer, sir,' said the beggar.

'No, my man,' said Burton, 'I don't exactly expect Him to do *that*. But I dare say you want a drink.'

By the time the bayonet manual was published, Burton had emptied his notebooks and aired in print his prejudices, theories and opinions, most of which he continued to hold to the day of his death. Although few people bought his books, they were talked about. The opinions expressed in them were shocking to many people and added to his unsavoury reputation. His actions and his conversation did nothing to diminish his notoriety. His family shuddered; for them he was still the lovable *enfant terrible*.

An Arab proverb says, 'Conceal thy travels, thy tenets and thy treasures.' Burton was familiar with the saying, but knowledge of wisdom does not make a man wise. He boasted of his travels, proclaimed his heretical tenets to all who would listen, and openly displayed the only treasure he possessed: his well-filled mind. He took a childish delight in offending the innocently pompous, telling wild stories of how he had eaten a child or promiscuously killed a man, or praising the virtues of strange religions to bigoted Christians. This curious habit of making himself out to be worse than he was persisted to the end of his life. At Boulogne, where the Burtons moved about the end of 1851, his sister Maria tried to curb him, but he was not a man easily curbed. In consequence, some members of the English society at Boulogne crossed the road when they saw him, and one elderly matron flatly stated 'she would not and could not sit in the room with that fellow Burton'. Even his friends called him 'Ruffian Dick'.

Such a reputation had advantages and disadvantages for a young bachelor. It made him attractive to impressionable young girls; a horror to their mothers. One mother sent him a polite but imperious note, requesting that he call upon her. His friend Steinhaeuser was in town and went with him to the appointment. After a few formal preliminaries, the lady got down to business. 'I sent for you, Captain Burton, because I think it my duty to ask what your intentions are with regard to my daughter.'

'Your duty, madame?' Burton asked with a perplexed expression. Then, with a smile he said, 'Alas! madame, strictly dishonourable! I regret to say, strictly dishonourable.'

With this, he and the poker-faced Steinhaeuser bowed themselves out. When next he saw the daughter, he told her, 'Look here, young woman, if I talk to you, you must arrange that I do not have "mamma's duty" flung at my head any more.'

More serious was his attempt to marry one of his pretty cousins. He proposed; the girl's mother refused. She had wealth; he was only a poor subaltern of the Honourable Company – with a bad reputation and no prospects.

Burton's financial situation was more than a little worrisome. He was on half-pay, he had not made money on his books, and his ageing and ailing parents could give him very little. For a man of his expansive temperament, he found the want of cash most confining. He craved books, foils, women and companionship, but he found them costly. Lack of funds did not stop him from flirting, however. One August day while walking on the ramparts, he encountered a pretty, blonde and buxom young girl who was walking with one of her sisters. Burton, who had taken up hypnotism, threw her one of his magnetic glances. The girl, her face flushed with excitement, turned to her sister. 'That man will marry me,' she said.

The next day they met again on the ramparts. This time he scrawled a note on the wall: 'May I speak to you?' The blonde young girl picked up the chalk he had left and wrote, 'No, mother will be angry.' Mother found the notes on the wall and she was, indeed, angry.

The girl, Isabel Arundell, did not even know the name of the man who had captured her heart so easily. She saw only a muscular man standing five feet eleven inches tall, but looking shorter because of his broad shoulders and small waist. His hair was jet black, his features straight, his complexion brown and weather-beaten, and his mouth and chin nearly obscured by an enormous black moustache. It was said that he had 'the brow of a god, the jaw of a devil'. But the most noticeable feature was his eyes with their long, dark lashes. Black and flashing, they seemed to look through the young girl, thrilling and chilling her. 'He had a fierce, proud, melancholy expression, and when he smiled, he smiled as though it hurt him, and looked with impatient contempt at things generally,' she recorded. When she saw him this first time, he was wearing a black, shaggy coat and carrying a short, thick stick over his shoulder as if it were a rifle.

Of the society at Boulogne, the Arundells were, as Isabel said, 'the *crème*, who did not mix with the general "smart people"', which included Richard Burton. The name of Arundell is woven through English history from the days of William the Conqueror, and Isabel's godfather, her father's cousin, was Lord Arundell of Wardour. Throughout the family's long history, they had always remained devout Roman Catholics, and Isabel followed this tradition. She was born in London on 20 March 1831 and missed being exactly ten years younger than Burton by only one day.

Isabel was one of eleven children, of whom she was the eldest, and her childhood was much like that of any other child of a well-to-do

English family of that period. It was filled with life in the nursery, genteel rides in the park, nannies, and somewhat formal relations with her parents. A few years before her début at Almack's (where everyone who was anyone, put his daughters on the marriage block), the Arundells retired to a country-house in Essex to save their money for the great event. Isabel, at sixteen, found the freedom of the countryside delightful. In the near-by woods one day she discovered an encampment of gypsies. She was enchanted by them. It was in the gypsy camp that an old crone named Hagar Burton (Burton being a common name among English gypsies) told her fortune and wrote it out for her in Romany:

You will cross the sea, and be in the same town with your Destiny, and know it not. Every obstacle will rise up against you, and such a combination of circumstances, that it will require all your courage and energy and intelligence to meet them. Your life will be like one always swimming against big waves, but God will always be with you, so you will always win. You will fix your eye on your polar star, and you will go for that without looking right or left. You will bear the name of our tribe, and be right proud of it. You will be as we are, but far greater than we. Your life is all wandering, change, and adventure. One soul in two bodies, in life or death; never long apart. Show this to the man you take for your husband.

This was heady stuff for a prim Victorian miss who had never strayed more than a few yards from nursery and nanny. Moreover, about this time Isabel first read Disraeli's *Tancred, or the New Crusade*, which had recently been published. Later, her mother unwittingly abetted her daughter's restlessness by giving her a copy on her twenty-third birthday. This novel tells the romantic tale of a duke's son who refuses a seat in Parliament to seek a direct communication from God in the Holy Land. At Sinai he falls into a trance, receives a message from God to promote 'theocratic equality', becomes involved in a series of intrigues with Lebanese Druses and Maronites, is disillusioned and falls in love with a beautiful Jewess. Isabel thought this the most wonderful book she had ever read – next to the Bible. But even now she had an adolescent's craving to fly away from all that was familiar to her. She longed for 'Gypsies, Bedouin Arabs and everything Eastern and mystic; and especially a wild and lawless life'.

This was hardly a fit preparation for a début at Almack's. Her mother fretted and worried – and with reason. Thanks to her beauty and the influence of noble relatives, such as the Duchess of Norfolk, the début itself was a great success. Only Isabel did not find any

Bedouins or gypsies among the waltzing young men at Almack's. Although flattered by the attention she received, she did not find her ideal man – a being she created in her diary and whom she later found to bear a striking resemblance to Richard Burton. But Isabel loved society from her first taste of it. There were balls, operas (she heard Jenny Lind), sight-seeing, shopping and teas in London. The polka was just becoming popular and eighteen-year-old Isabel loved to dance. Then, too, society was snobbish, and Isabel was a snob. Of this period in her life she later said, 'At Almack's every one knew every one else; for society in those days was not a mob, but small and select. People did not struggle to get on as people do now, and we were there by right, and to resume our position in our circle. There is much more heart in the world than many people give it credit for – at any rate in the world of the gentle by birth and breeding.' And in her diary she wrote, 'I am never better pleased than when I watch this huge game of chess, Life, being played on that extensive chessboard, Society.' When the season ended without a match, the Arundells returned to Boulogne, to live in frugal and dull respectability in the English colony. It was there, walking on the ramparts with her sister Blanche, that she met Richard Burton.

There is no evidence to indicate that Burton felt any particular attraction for Isabel beyond his normal reaction to a pretty face and a fine figure. He had his own oriental ideas of what a woman should be. For himself, he said, he required only two things of a woman: beauty and affection. Besides, he was then engaged in a more serious affair with an acquaintance and distant cousin of Isabel's, a girl who shortly became Mrs Louisa Segrave. It was through her that Isabel was formally introduced to her idol and learned for the first time that he bore the name of the tribe of Hagar Burton. Now she was certain. This was her man. 'I was struck with the shaft of Destiny,' she exclaimed.

She made frequent walks on the ramparts to catch sight of him, to overhear the sound of his deep voice. When she did, she would turn hot and cold, dizzy and faint, sick and trembling. Her mother called in a doctor who prescribed pills, but Isabel threw the medicine in the fire. She prayed for Richard Burton every morning; she bought all his books and read them avidly, being particularly interested in Burton's theory that the Jats in Sind were the progenitors of the European gypsies. Burton became her gypsy Tancred.

One night Louisa gave a tea party and dance to which both Isabel and Burton were invited. He actually spoke to her 'several times', and then, wonder of wonders, he waltzed with her. When the great evening was over, Isabel carefully put away her gloves and the sash which his hand had pressed when he held her waist. She never wore them again.

But Burton had other things to do besides flirt with pretty girls. There was his writing, of course, and there was fencing, which he studied hard and seriously. He invented two new strokes: the 'Burton *une-deux*' and a '*manchette*', an upward cut of the sabre that disables the sword arm of an opponent. He earned the right to call himself *Maître d'Armes*, a title which then and now has almost the status of a university degree in France.

A fellow-officer and rake, Arthur Shuldham, once accompanied Burton to a fencing match at Boulogne and recorded the event. The bout was with a French sergeant of Hussars who was a celebrated fencer. The sergeant put on his mask and leather fencing-jacket, but Burton only took off his coat and rolled up his shirt-sleeves. Shuldham tried to prevent this reckless bit of bravado, but Burton shook him off. There was the customary salute and the two men squared off. After a brief bit of sparring, Burton, with a rapid swing of his arm, brought his weapon down hard on his opponent's sword, disarming him. There were seven bouts in all, and Burton performed the same disarming operation each time, receiving only one prod in the neck himself. The sergeant refused to continue, saying his wrist was nearly dislocated by the force of Burton's blows. 'To me,' Shuldham wrote, 'it was a marvellous display of fencing skill and the strange magnetic power that he seemed to possess over everybody present was equally surprising.'

Fencing, dancing, writing and flirting were all pleasant pastimes but they were still not demanding enough to satisfy his restless temperament and the pricks of ambition. He was impatient to be on the move. He was a wanderer and he had to rove; he was an adventurer and he needed new worlds to conquer. He wrote:

The thorough-bred wanderer's idiosyncrasy I presume to be a composition of what phrenologists call 'inhabitiveness' and 'locality' equally and largely developed. After a long and toilsome march, weary of the way, he drops into the nearest place of rest to become the most domestic of men. For awhile he smokes the 'pipe of permanence' with an infinite zest. . . . But soon the passive fit has passed away; again a paroxysm of ennui . . . he walks about his room all night, he yawns at conversations, and a book acts upon him as a narcotic. The man wants to wander, and he must do so, or he shall die.

To avoid dying of ennui, Burton planned a great exploit. Back in London in the autumn of 1852, he offered his services to the Royal Geographical Society of London 'for the purpose of removing that opprobrium to modern adventure, the huge white blot which in our maps still notes the Eastern and Central regions of Arabia'. The Geographical Society was interested, but first it was necessary to obtain the approval of the Court of Directors of the East India Company, for Burton was technically still on sick leave. A personal interview was arranged with its chairman, Sir James Hogg, but that gentleman refused to sanction an expedition across the Arabian peninsula, maintaining that it was too dangerous an undertaking. However, Hogg did grant him one year of leave to study Arabic 'in lands where the language is best learned'. Burton thought the best way to do this was by pursuing his original objective, although one year left him little time.

His original plan was to travel disguised as a Moslem either directly across Arabia, passing through Medina to Masqat, or diagonally through Mecca to the Indian Ocean. His secondary objectives were to determine where a market for stud horses could be opened in Central Arabia to supply the Indian market; to obtain information on the Rub al Khali, 300,000 square miles of sandy waste that is to this day virtually unexplored and unknown; to inquire into the hydrography of the Hejaz; and to see if in the population of the vast peninsula there existed enough physiological differences to controvert the theory regarding the common origin of the Arab race. Such were his avowed purposes. Actually, being more interested in people and religions than geography, his great object was to visit the holy and forbidden cities of Al Islam: Mecca and Medina. And that is what he did.

Mecca was the birthplace of Mohammed, the site of the Great Mosque with the Kaaba and sacred Black Stone. Medina contained the tomb of Mohammed and other holy places. Burton would not be the first European to visit these cities, but there were only eleven known Europeans who had been there before him – and lived to tell of it.

The first and only Englishman to see Mecca before him was Joseph Pitts, a sailor captured by pirates off the coast of Spain, who was sold as a slave in Algiers and carried to Mecca in 1680. Of the other Europeans, only two had brought out important information. The greatest of these was John Ludwig Burckhart (1784 – 1816). Born at Kirchgarten and educated at the universities of Leipzig and Gottingen, he reported with German thoroughness all that he saw during his stay in the holy cities in 1814 – 15. He was twenty-five years old before he learned English, but afterwards he always wrote in that language. Burton carefully studied his *Travels in Arabia* which had been published in London in 1829.

The second European scholar-adventurer who had made the pilgrimage was George Augustus Wallin (1811–52) who was born on the Abvenanmaa Islands (then a part of Russia and now Finnish) and educated in Finland. The danger of making notes during his visit to Mecca and Medina in 1845 deterred Wallin from being as thorough as Burckhart, and he did not write a book of his travels, but confined himself to a series of long papers in English for the Royal Geographical Society. Burton wrote to him in Finland, asking hundreds of questions, but his queries were never answered. Wallin was dead before the letter reached him.

To prepare for the trip, Burton made notes on every contingency he thought might face him and took elaborate steps to ready himself for his great adventure. Among other things, he apprenticed himself to a blacksmith and learned to make horseshoes and to shoe a horse. Such a skill might be needed, he thought.

At last all was ready. Burton, who hated to say good-bye, did not reveal his plans to his family, but left a letter to his mother which was found after he was gone. The letter outlined what he proposed to do and contained instructions for the disposition of his effects should he be killed: the 'small stock of valuables' was to be divided between mother and sister.

There was no word for Isabel, now forgotten. In her diary she wrote, 'I should love Richard's wild, roving, vagabond life; and as I am young, strong, and hardy, with good nerves, and no fine notions, I should be just the girl for him.' But now she was left to console herself as best she could, remembering their brief meetings, reading his books, and perhaps recalling the lines from *Scinde* which said, 'The meetings of this world are in the street of separation. And truly said the poet that the draught of friendly union is ever followed by the bitter waters of parting.' If she did not pause to ponder over these words, she should have.

On the night of 3 April 1853, a bearded Burton assumed the disguise he had used so often in India (he had brought back with him several bottles of henna stain), and, as Mirza Abdullah, he boarded the new screw steamer *Bengal* with his 'English Interpreter', a Bengal Lancer named Captain Henry Grindlay. Their destination was Alexandria.

Chapter 5

The Haj Begins
1853

ABOUT the year A.D. 610 a forty-year-old grain merchant in the city of Mecca concluded that he was God's prophet. The results of his conviction have had the most profound effects upon the history of the world. The man's name was Mohammed (Muhammed, Mahomet) and with the ever-popular appeals of religious reform and nationalism he set about the political and religious unification of Arabia.

Prophets, as everyone knows, are little regarded in their own countries. Mohammed was forced to leave Mecca in July 622, and fled to Medina. It is from the year of this flight, or *Hegira*, that his followers dated their calendar. In the year 6 A.H. (A.D. 629) Mohammed returned home to Mecca at the head of a host of armed converts. The city was his. He overthrew the pagan gods, proclaimed there were no other gods but Allah, with himself as His true prophet, and ordained that no unbeliever should henceforth set foot in the city. The prohibition was well kept, and many are the tales of Christians caught there and tortured to death. So it was with good reason that Burton took pains to see that his disguise would not be pierced.

More than an Eastern costume and a fluency in Arabic was necessary to prevent discovery. He had to sit, walk, gesture, pray and think as a Moslem who had grown up in the faith and in Eastern society. There were even new pleasures to be acquired as an oriental: *kayf*, for example. Burton describes this as

the savouring of animal existence; the passive enjoyment of mere sense; the pleasant languor, the dreamy tranquillity, the airy castle building, which in Asia stands in lieu of the vigorous, intensive, passionate life of Europe. . . . In the East, man wants but rest and shade: upon the banks of a bubbling stream, or under the cool shelter of a perfumed tree, he is perfectly happy, smoking a pipe, or sipping a cup of coffee, or drinking a glass of sherbert, but above all things deranging body and mind as little as possible; the trouble of conversations, the displeasures of memory, and the vanity of thought being the most unpleasant interruptions to his *Kayf*.

63

During the voyage to Alexandria, Burton, a careful observer and an excellent mimic, practised his role. Also on board was a friend, John Wingfield Larking, who knew Burton's secret and had offered to help him in Egypt. Larking was sitting on deck just before the boat sailed, talking with a fellow passenger, an officer of the Indian Army. The latter caught sight of Burton and stared. 'What on earth is he up to now dressed like that?' he exclaimed.

'What is who doing?' asked Larking innocently.

'Burton. What's he doing now?'

'I don't know who you are talking about. The individual standing there?'

'Well of course. Anyone can see it is Burton.'

'I don't know what you are talking about,' said Larking.

The officer got up from his chair and walked over to Burton. 'Hello Burton, what are you up to?' He received a cold stare for a reply and there was no sign of recognition on Burton's face. 'Stop it,' said the officer, 'I know quite well who you are.'

Burton continued to look blank. The officer returned to his seat beside Larking. 'Silly ass,' he muttered. 'As if I do not know someone when we've served together for years.'

Several days later, the officer again sat down beside Larking and confided, 'You know, it's a curious thing. I could have sworn that Persian prince was Burton, but now I've looked at him again and again and I do notice small differences. Curious thing, isn't it, how one can be taken in.'

'Very curious,' replied Larking.

When he stepped off the ship in Alexandria, Burton also deceived the Egyptians. By brushing off the beggars in true oriental fashion, he 'convinced the bystanders that the sheep-skin covered a real sheep'.

From the dock he travelled by donkey to the home of John Thurburn, Larking's father-in-law. Thurburn put him up in one of the outbuildings of his home where he could continue to perfect his disguise and to assemble the material he would need for his *haj* or pilgrimage to Mecca. He visited the mosques, read the Koran, went to the public baths and coffee houses, practised the prayers and ablutions, and set himself up as a combination of doctor, dervish, magician and fakir. As a doctor, he soon had quite a clientele. Burton enjoyed the opportunity this adopted profession gave him for seeing large numbers of men, women and children on an intimate basis – particularly the young women.

Although he had always been a 'dabbler in medical and mystical study', his words of medical wisdom hardly establish confidence: 'What simplifies extremely the treatment of the sick in these parts is the undoubted periodicity of disease, reducing almost all to one type – ague.'

In making his preparations for the *haj*, Burton discovered that he had neglected to provide himself with a passport. In 1853 this was not an unusual mistake. Burton, never a good prophet, spoke of the passport system as 'now dying out in Europe'. It took the influence of his friend Larking to get him the necessary papers certifying that he was an Indo-British subject named Abdullah. It is probably well that no Eastern saw him pay the five shillings for his passport, for he reacted with British indignation. 'That mighty Britain – the mistress of the seas – the ruler of one-sixth of mankind – should charge five shillings to pay for the shadow of her protecting wing! – O the meanness of our magnificence! the littleness of our greatness!'

To his disgust, the passport by itself was not enough; it had to be countersigned by the police magistrate, he was told at the British Consulate. For three hours Mirza Abdullah squatted at the gate of the police magistrate until a haughty clerk finally informed him that he must apply at the Egyptian Foreign Office. Taking himself to the palace, he found a policeman coiled in the shade enjoying his *kayf*. When Burton asked how to get a visa, the policeman irritably snapped, 'Don't know', and hoped he would go away. It was evident that he considered the matter settled, but Burton was persistent and kept repeating his questions until the officer, his repose spoiled, cursed him roundly and shouted, 'Go, O dog!' Burton left then, fearing he would receive a lash from the man's hippopotamus-hide whip, and, as he said, 'British flesh and blood could never have stood *that*.'

It was several days before he finally bribed a soldier to take him by the hand and lead him from office to office until he at last received the proper papers. Now he was ready to begin his journey. He packed up his belongings: a wooden comb, a toothpick, a goat-skin waterbag, a coarse Persian rug, a cotton-stuffed chintz pillow, a blanket and sheet, a housewife given him by Elizabeth Stisted, a dagger, a brass inkstand and penholder, his twenty-five sovereigns in gold concealed in a leather money-belt, a pair of saddle-bags, and a pea-green box with red and yellow flowers painted on it for a medicine chest. He also had several changes of clothes, believing that 'throughout the East a badly dressed man is a pauper, and, as in England, a pauper – unless he belongs to an order having a right to be poor – is a scoundrel'. Burton wanted no one to think him a pauper. To his costume he attached a star sapphire to elicit 'reverential awe' from those around him. Besides these articles, there were some others which were later to prove embarrassing to him.

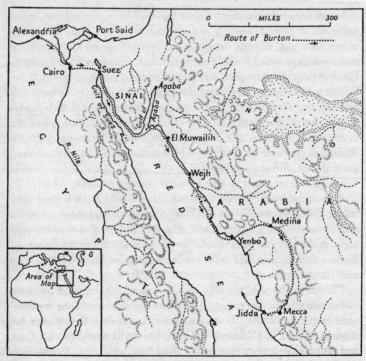

1. Pilgrimage to Mecca

Burton, his baggage and an Indian servant named Nur, then boarded a tiny Nile steamer and sailed third-class to Cairo. Although he was now parted from friends and fairly launched on his journey, he was not to be aroused to enthusiasm. The quarters were cramped and uncomfortable, the cooking was abominable, and even the scenery was 'nothing but muddy waters, dusty banks, a sand mist, a milky sky, and a glaring sun'. The people, reminding him of the Indians, were uninteresting. He did not even have a kind thought for the animals – 'gaunt, mange-stained camels, muddy buffaloes, scurvied donkeys, sneaking jackals and fox-like dogs'.

The passengers were a hodge-podge of Europeans and orientals, but included one pretty Spanish woman who seemed out of place in these surroundings, 'a rose in a field of thistles', thought Burton. More important to his mission, however, was the acquisition of two friends. One, an Indian from Lahore named Miyan Khudabakhsh Namdar, had a 'fleshy stomach, fat legs, round back' and a face with 'abundant rascality, an eternal smile and treacherous eyes'. He was a shawl merchant who had lived in London and Paris for two years and had acquired the worst habits of occidental life as well as a contempt for Europeans in general and Englishmen in particular.

The second friend was Haji Wali al-Din, a man of about forty-five with a close-shaven head, a bull neck and a thin red beard. Seeing Burton sitting alone one day on the deck, he sat down beside him and began a conversation. Burton liked him at once. He found that Haji Wali had a curious dry humour and delighted in teasing in a solemn, quiet and quaint way. A merchant in Alexandria, he was accompanying Khudabakhsh to Cairo in a matter of a lawsuit.

Also on board were two English officers of the Indian Army who talked only to each other. When Burton accidently brushed against the arm of one of them, the man turned and cursed the lowly native who had dared to be so incautious. 'He was a man of my own service,' Burton said. 'I pardoned him in consideration of the compliment he paid to my disguise.'

The discomforts of the Nile voyage were soon over and he found himself sipping pomegranate syrup at the Cairo home of the treacherous-eyed Khudabakhsh. It was a pleasant change from the steamer, but Burton disliked and distrusted his host, he had become too civilized, and sat on chairs, ate with a fork, talked European politics and cursed the British. Nevertheless, Burton stayed here ten days until he could find a room at a crowded khan, or native hotel.

Cairo was jammed with pilgrims who, like himself, were planning to make the *haj* to Mecca. He was finally forced to take two 'comfortless rooms' at the Jamaliyah Wakalah, an unfashionable khan in the Greek quarter 'swarming with drunken Christians' where he had to pay the exorbitant price of fourpence a day. It was here he again encountered his friend Haji Wali. The Haji (a title of one who has made the *haj*, or pilgrimage) offered him some sound advice regarding his disguise: because most Persians are Shi'as, and thus are members of a sect unpopular in Islam, they were not highly regarded in Arabia. 'If you persist in being a Persian,' Haji Wali told him, 'you will get yourself in trouble. In Egypt you will be cursed; in Arabia you will be beaten because you are a heretic; you will pay the treble of what other travellers do, and if you fall sick you may die by the roadside.'

Such advice did not imply that Burton's disguise had been penetrated. Many men travelled in disguise on the pilgrimage, pretending to be poor when rich, or seeking to escape justice, or to conceal unpopular heresies. Burton, after considering the various nationalities he might adopt, decided to become a wandering Pathan from Afghanistan; at the same time, he retained his pose as a doctor and a dervish. To support the character required a knowledge of Persian, Hindustani and Arabic – all familiar tongues to Burton. Any slips he might make could be covered, he felt, by pretending to a long residence in Rangoon. It is most curious that in his disguises Burton always pretended to be from a place such as Bushire, Rangoon or Afghanistan that he had never visited.

He was on safer grounds in his choice of a profession. 'Call yourself a religious wanderer if you like,' advised Haji Wali, 'and let those who ask of your peregrinations know that you are under a vow to visit all the holy places of Al-Islam. Thus you will persuade them that you are a man of rank under a cloud, and you will receive much more civility than perhaps you deserve.'

As an Afghan doctor, Burton was even more of a success in Cairo than he had been in Alexandria. His first great coup was in the khan itself. Living opposite him was an Arab slave-dealer whose Abyssinian slave-girls were constantly falling sick from consumption, dysentery, varicose veins and a variety of other ailments. Burton was called on to doctor the girls. He had great success with one in particular whom he cured by hypnosis of the price-lowering habit of snoring. As she was worth nearly fifty dollars (un-snoring), her owner was delighted. Burton was delighted too. He found the girls to be 'broad-shouldered, thin-flanked, fine-limbed, and with haunches of a prodigious size . . . there was something pretty in the brow, eyes, and upper part of the nose, coarse and sensual in the pendent lips, large jowl and projecting mouth, whilst the whole had a combination of piquancy with sweetness'. And they flirted with him outrageously.

He also had time to visit the tomb of Burckhart and to explore the native life of Cairo, making comparisons between Arab and European customs and institutions. He was there in June when the Mohammedan month of Ramadan came to the Islamic world and all good Moslems fasted from sunrise to sunset. Burton noted that 'like the Italian, the

Anglo-Catholic, and the Greek fasts, the chief effect of the "blessed month" upon True Believers is to darken their tempers into positive gloom'. He attended lectures at the great collegiate mosque, Al Azhar, where he found that 'as the attending of lectures is not compulsory, the result is that the lecturer is worth listening to'.

The political situation in the Middle East at this time being in its usual chaotic state, Cairo was alive with rumours: 'Report of war with Russia, with France, with England, who was going to land three million men at Suez, and the city of Mars [Cairo] became unusually martial.

There was an ordinance in Cairo that anyone out after dark without a lantern was to be picked up and forced to spend the night in jail. Burton was caught in this predicament. When the patrol tried to arrest him, he resisted, clouting three or four of them before he was at last overpowered and hustled off to jail. On the way, he tried to bribe one of his guards, who obligingly took the money and then gave him the end of a rifle butt in his buttock for his impertinence. At the jail, he was led before the pasha of the guard who recommended a bastinado. Burton protested loudly, showing his British passport and claiming he was under the protection of the British Government. The pasha asked the guards what his offence had been and all swore by Allah that he had been found dead-drunk, beating respectable people, breaking into houses, and invading harems. Burton raged and cursed the policemen as liars. The pasha ordered one of the guards to smell his breath. Sticking his nose to Burton's lips, he swore he smelled liquor. The pasha smiled complacently and sentenced him to a night in the lice-infested jail. When he was released next morning, he made straight for the *hamman*, or public baths, reflecting that a European in the same situation would have been instantly released.

Among the many acquaintances he made in Cairo was an eighteen-year-old boy from Mecca named Mohammed al-Basyuni, from whom he bought an *Ihram* (a special pilgrim's dress) and a *kafan*, or shroud, with which the good Moslem usually starts on his *haj*. Burton describes him as 'chocolate-brown, with high features and a bold profile. . . . His figure is short and broad, with a tendency to be obese, the result of a strong stomach and the power of sleeping at discretion. He can read a little, write his name, and is uncommonly clever at a bargain.' He was also 'eloquent in abuse' and 'profound at prayer'. Mohammed wanted to be Burton's companion on the way to Mecca, but Burton was afraid of him: for 'he showed signs of over-wisdom'. He had been in India and had been around Englishmen too much. Burton refused Mohammed's offer.

Burton's decision to quit Cairo and be on his way was hastened by what he termed 'an accident': this being the loss of his good reputation. There was not much that could be called accidental in the affair. He had been on his good behaviour too long.

In Haji Wali's room at the khan he met an Albanian captain of irregulars called Ali Agha. This was a tall, bony, broad-shouldered mountaineer with thin lips, fierce eyes, lean jaws and 'peaky chin'. He wore long tapering moustaches while the rest of his head was clean-shaven. He walked with a swagger, spoke with an affectedly gruff voice, continually wore a sneer, and was rarely sober. Burton was showing Haji Wali his pistols when the Albanian captain walked in. 'What business have *you* with weapons?' he said, snatching the pistols from Burton's hands.

Burton wrenched the pistols away from him. There was every in-dication of an impending brawl as the two men glared at each other. The captain cocked his hat; Burton twirled his moustaches. For-tunately, the Albanian was not armed and the little affair blew over. A couple of days later the captain called on Burton very politely and sat down to smoke and drink a cup of coffee.

There was a touchy moment when Ali Agha demanded liquor and was told there was none, but this passed away. He had come to ask for a little poison to take care of an enemy, and Burton gave him some calomel. Then he proposed a wrestling match, and Burton threw him on the floor with a 'cross-buttock'. The soldier took his defeat in good humour, and patted Burton's head affectionately, proposing that he come and drink with him that evening. Burton could not resist.

Among Moslems, drinking liquor is a sin. Devout Moslems will not touch it, but for many – in the Middle East, at least – drinking is con-sidered 'a funny and pleasant sort of sin'. Until now, however, Burton had made every pretence of being very devout. Yet, about nine o'clock that evening, he took his pipe, tobacco pouch and dagger and made his way to Ali Agha's room. The Albanian had made ample preparations for an evening's carousal. There was food as well as liquor, and four wax candles lit up the room. Ali sat on the floor and Burton sat down beside him. Taking his dagger from his belt, Ali casually threw it into a handy corner and his guest followed his example. Picking up a tumbler, the Albanian captain wiped it with his forefinger, filled it to the brim with raki (a kind of brandy made from distilled dates, grapes or grain), and handed it to his guest with a bow. Bowing in turn, Burton drained the glass and turned it upside down in front of his host. Taking turns in this manner they made fast inroads on sobriety.

Occasionally, Ali stopped drinking long enough to throw a handful of strong perfume into his guest's face, and Burton, with some satisfaction, did the same to him. The party was orderly enough until Ali hit upon the idea of enticing the staid and sober Haji Wali into the room and forcing him to drink with them. Burton thought this was a good idea, too. He jumped to his feet and reeled out to fetch his friend. When he returned with the good man he found that Ali had stuck a green twig in the dirt floor, turned over a water jug so that it trickled below the branch, and was sitting with moist eyes gazing at the fertile land he had created.

The appearance of Haji Wali changed his mood from dreamy wonder to a desire for more boisterous pleasures. Seizing Haji Wali, he made him sit down before the liquor and was 'ecstasied by the old man's horror at the scene'. Filling the glass, Ali tried to force Haji Wali to drink. The Haji refused. Burton and Ali Agha persisted. In vain Haji Wali begged and pleaded, quoting the Koran, promising to drink with them tomorrow, and finally threatening to call the police; they would not leave him alone. At last he jumped up and darted out of the door, leaving his fez, slippers and pipe. Ali stood up and staggered after him, but it was too much effort. He stopped at the door and turned back. After solemnly sprinkling Haji Wali's abandoned belongings with raki, he sat down again beside Burton to eat their supper.

Presently, Ali rose majestically and said they must have dancing girls. Burton advised him that such women were forbidden in the khans.

With calm ferocity, Ali asked, 'Who has forbidden it?'

'The pasha,' replied Burton.

Ali moved towards the door, proclaiming he would get the pasha himself to dance for him. Burton foresaw trouble and knew that the wisest course at this point would be to return quietly to his room, bolt the door and go to sleep. But he was too drunk for discretion. He followed after Ali and tried to persuade him to return to his room. Instead, the Albanian went wild. He knocked down the first person he met, broke down a door with his shoulder and reeled into a room where two old women were sleeping, cursed all Egyptians, assaulted the porter and vowed he would drink his blood, and soon had the entire khan in an uproar. At last, through the combined efforts of four or five men, the great Albanian was subdued and carried off to his quarters, still cursing the Egyptians as a race of dogs.

The next morning the khan was buzzing with gossip of the wickedness of the Albanian captain and the hypocrisy of the Afghan dervish. Haji Wali wisely suggested it might be best if Abdullah started on his pilgrimage at once. Burton agreed.

Packing his belongings, he quickly said good-bye to his friends, telling them he intended to go to Mecca by way of Jidda. He then hired two camels, together with a camel driver named Nassar and his brother, and departed for Medina by way of Suez and Yenbo.

Wishing to see if he had become soft during his four years in Europe, he set out on an eighty-four-mile ride across the Suez desert in mid-summer mounted on a moody camel with a hard wooden saddle. Nassar immediately proposed a race, and with the wind like the blast of a furnace, they dashed into the flaming desert. For once, Burton found the surroundings compatible with his temperament:

It is strange how the mind can be amused by scenery that presents so few objects to occupy it. . . . Above, through a terrible sky in its stainless beauty, and the splendours of a pitiless blinding glare, the Samún caresses you like a lion with flaming breath. Around lie drifted sand-heaps, upon which each puff of wind leaves its trace in solid waves, flayed rocks, the very skeletons of mountains, and hard unbroken plains, over which he who rides is spurred by the idea that the bursting of a water-skin, or the pricking of a camel's hoof, would be a certain death of torture, – a haggard land infested with wild beasts, and wilder men, – a region whose very fountains murmur the warning words 'Drink and away!' What can be more exciting? What more sublime? Man's heart bounds in his breast at the thought of measuring his puny force with Nature's might, and of emerging triumphant from the trial. . . . In the Desert, even more than upon the ocean, there is present death: hardship is there, and piracies, and shipwreck, solitary, not in crowds, where, as the Persians say, 'Death is a festival'; – and this sense of danger, never absent, invests the scene of travel with an interest not its own.

This was the hard and dangerous life he loved; it was the kind of romantic setting in which he loved to picture himself. Like all men of action, he thrilled to danger rather than feared it – even when, as here on the comparatively well-travelled caravan route between Cairo and Suez, the dangers were partly imaginary. It was with real feeling that he wrote, 'And believe me, when once your tastes have conformed to the tranquillity of such travel, you will suffer real pain in returning to the turmoil of civilization.'

At sunset, Burton and his guide turned off the road to say their evening prayers and eat their supper. Suddenly a figure loomed up and greeted them with effusive joy. It was the over-wise young Mohammed. He seized the halter of Burton's camel and forced it to kneel; led the astonished Burton to a carpet spread on the sand and took off his slippers; gave him water for his ablution and urged him to have supper with him. He would not take no for an answer. When Burton had refused to take the boy with him on his pilgrimage, he had considered the matter settled, but he had not reckoned on Mohammed's tenacity. Now the boy would take no excuses. He was determined to go with Burton, and for good reason – he was penniless.

Although Mohammed needed Burton, he suspected him. When they prayed the evening prayer, the Meccan boy shrewdly knelt behind him to watch his every movement. After prayer, he fixed Burton a pipe and then proceeded to examine the contents of his saddle bag, drawing out dates, rolls, boiled eggs and melons. Nassar and his brother were aghast at his impudence, but the boy only laughed and made fun of them.

After an hour's halt, the march was resumed, the smug Mohammed riding with them. With forced marches and little sleep, Suez was reached on the following night. Burton had sent Nur, his Indian servant, on ahead of him with the baggage and was now faced with the problem of finding him. With aching bones and skin raw from sunburn, he searched the thirty-six khans of Suez. At last he found his goods locked in a room and discovered that Nur had gone out to friends in the harbour, showing every sign of decamping with his master's belongings the next day. It was a tired and dispirited Burton who stretched out on the floor of an empty room at the khan.

The next morning he was up early and set about obtaining his goods. The porter at the khan would not open the door for him so he applied to the local governor. But in the meantime Nur appeared, looking as if he both merited and expected a beating. Burton forgave him in his relief.

While waiting for a boat at Suez, Burton fell in with a group of four men from Mecca and Medina who were returning home. In contrast to his own concern about money – he had obtained additional sums while at Cairo from his friend Thurburn and from Sam Shepheard, owner of Shepheard's Hotel – these true orientals were preparing for a long hard journey with scarcely two dollars of ready money among them, although their boxes were crammed with valuables they were taking home with them. Burton made each of them, and Mohammed, a loan and became a man of consequence by so doing. He saw an advantage in having Moslem friends with whom he could travel and with whom he could live while in Medina and Mecca.

One of these men was Omar Effendi, a plump, soft-featured young man of about twenty-eight with the manners of a student. His father had wanted him to marry, but he had fled to Cairo, becoming a student at Al Azhar. His relatives had sent a 'confidential man' to bring him home and this was now being done. It was Omar who told Burton (when much later they met by accident in Cairo) how narrowly he had escaped detection in Suez. Burton's new friends lost no time in examining his belongings. There was no protest he could make without arousing suspicion, but among his possessions was a sextant. Nothing was said at the time, but as soon as Burton left the room Mohammed declared his belief that this Abdullah was an infidel. The case was discussed. Omar Effendi, who had previously talked religion with Burton, felt himself well qualified to judge. He announced that Mohammed was wrong.

Another member of the group, Hamid al-Samman, sitting upon a box of presents for his wife, stated his opinion. Hamid, according to Burton, was 'a perfect specimen of the town Arab'. He was barefoot, dirty, and reluctant to pray because he did not want to take clean clothes from his box. 'He can sing all manner of songs, slaughter a sheep with dexterity, deliver a grand call to prayer, shave, cook, fight; and he excels in the science of vituperation.' Hamid, who looked forward to the lucrative task of being Burton's guide in Medina, agreed with the verdict of Omar.

In the end, Mohammed was damned and abused for impugning the faith of such a good Moslem and advised to 'fear Allah'. Burton knew none of this until later, but his quick eye had detected the puzzled expression on the faces of his friends when they saw the sextant. With the Eastern distrust of the mechanical, they wondered what any true believer was doing with such an instrument. He reluctantly decided to leave the sextant behind and he prayed fervently five times a day to dispel suspicion.

After more passport difficulties, Burton and his friends finally secured passage on a ship called *Silk al-Zahab* ('The Golden Wire'), leaving Suez for Yenbo. Ninety-seven pilgrims, including fifteen women and children, were crowded on a small, fifty-ton Arab dhow designed to carry sixty. Of his fellow-passengers, Burton said, 'They were all barefoot, bare-headed, dirty, ferocious and armed.' That he and his friends were able to secure positions on the ship at all was due to the exertions of one Sa'ad, called Sa'ad al-Jinni ('the Demon'). This was the 'confidential man' sent to bring Omar back to his parents. A freed negro slave, Burton described him as 'the pure African, noisily merry at one moment, at another silently sulky; affectionate and abusive, brave and boastful, reckless and crafty, exceedingly quarrelsome, and unscrupulous to the last degree. The bright side of his character is his love and respect for his young master, Omar Effendi.' His box was filled with presents for his three wives in Medina and his greatest concern was for the safety of this box.

Amid confusion, shouts, curses, yells and laments, the *Silk al-Zahab* hoisted sail at 10 a.m. on 6 July 1853 and ran down the channel to the roadstead to anchor. On board, the crowd of pilgrims shoved and pushed to make places for themselves. Burton and his friends had purchased space on the narrow poop deck, but this cramped area was also occupied by a group of Maghribis from the desert regions near Tripoli and Tunis who, for a while, ruled with a wild upper hand, pushing the other pilgrims about and nearly felling Nur with a blow from a palm stick. Then Sa'ad the Demon arrived on the scene. With his help, the poop deck was cleared of Maghribis by the process of throwing them off. This left three Syrians, the *rais* (captain of the ship), a Turk with his family, Burton and his friends – a total of eighteen persons – to settle down as comfortably as they could on the tiny poop deck.

But the Maghribis started a row on the deck below. When one of the Syrians on the poop deck enthusiastically jumped down to help out a fellow-countryman, he sank into the seething living mass. When he was finally fished out, his forehead was cut, half his beard was missing, and he bore the imprint of a fine set of sharp Maghribi teeth on his leg. Eventually the fighting subsided; five men were completely disabled from wounds and most were cut up in some manner.

It was finally agreed to send a deputation to Ali Murad, the owner of the ship, to complain of their over-crowded condition. Ali came alongside in a rowing boat, but he was careful to keep a respectful distance and too wise to come on board. He listened patiently to their complaints, and then offered to return the fare of anyone who wanted to leave. Since no one was willing to give up his place, Ali Murad rowed away with some parting advice to the effect that they should all be good and not fight and trust in Allah who would make all things easy for them.

The departure of the owner was a signal for a second fight, the Maghribis attempting to storm the poop deck under the leadership of their *maula* who somehow reminded Burton of Rev. Charles Delafosse of the Richmond school. Sa'ad the Demon provided a number of clubs, thick as a man's wrist and about six feet long. 'Defend yourselves,' shouted Sa'ad, 'if you don't want to be the meat of the Maghribis!'

At first Burton did not use all his strength for fear of killing his opponents, but he soon found the Maghribis' heads to be hard; it required solid blows to stop them. Burton's group was badly outnumbered, but they had the tactical advantage of being on the poop deck, about four feet higher than the deck below. In the midst of the battle, Burton hit upon an idea. On the edge of the poop deck stood a huge water jug which, with its heavy wooden frame, weighed about a hundred pounds. A smart push with his shoulder sent the jug crashing down on the heads of the Maghribis. This ended the fight.

Peace was made, the Maghribis sat down to lick their wounds, and about three o'clock in the afternoon the *Silk al-Zahab* let out its sail to belly in the favourable breeze. Burton described the ship as a sambuk with 'no means of reefing, no compass, no log, no sounding lines, no spare ropes, not even the suspicion of a chart'. The *rais* was 'an old fool' who did nothing but recite the Koran and beg for baksheesh. As they sailed out of the harbour, Burton could not resist a wistful backward look at the British flag flying over the Suez consulate. But there could be no turning back now. His *haj* had begun in earnest.

Chapter 6

Medina and Mecca

1853

THE custom of an annual pilgrimage to Mecca, spiritual centre of the Moslem world, is centuries old. No one knows when it began, but it was in existence long before the foundation of Islam. Prior to the birth of Mohammed's new religion, the Arabs came annually to Mecca to worship the idols in the sacred Kaaba. The Prophet wisely kept the pilgrimage as an institution, with all its economic, social and political benefits, while destroying the idols and introducing his monotheistic doctrine.

There are five fundamentals of Islam: recitation of the creed ('There is no God but Allah and Mohammed is his prophet'), prayer, fasting during certain times, the giving of alms and the pilgrimage to Mecca at least once in a lifetime for all those with the means to do so. Those who make the *haj*, or pilgrimage, are then styled *hajis*. The time of the pilgrimage is fixed for the final month of the Moslem year, but as the Islamic calendar is a lunar one, the month recedes thirteen days annually. It was to wait for this month that Burton tarried so long at Alexandria and Cairo.

Before the days of the railroad, a number of pilgrim caravans formed in various parts of the Islamic world to make the sacred journey. The two most important of these were the Syrian, or Damascus, caravan which started at Constantinople and came by way of Damascus, and the Egyptian caravan, which brought with it from Cairo a new covering for the Kaaba. Other caravans brought Moors, Persians, Turks, Indians, Tartars, Chinese, Africans, Malays, Javanese and dozens of other races and nationalities. These annual mass movements still continue today in spite of wars, plagues and depressions.

The pilgrimage can be a dangerous thing – not only to the pilgrims themselves, but to their countrymen as well. When the caravans carry deadly and infectious germs, the results can be, and often have been, catastrophic. In 1865 – twelve years after Burton's *haj* – the plague ran through the caravans and the pilgrims carried death back with them to their homes. It is estimated that in Egypt alone 60,000 people died of the disease. Over the seas it spread to every part of the world, and there were even cases in New York. It finally burned out in 1874, only to strike the crowded streets of Mecca again in 1893 and still again in 1902. The danger was always there and none knew when it might erupt.

To the Moslem, Mecca is the most holy of cities, but Medina is almost, if not quite, its equal as a sacred place. It was to Medina that Mohammed fled when forced by his enemies to leave his native Mecca and make his famous *Hegira*. From here he began his military campaigns to establish the Caliphate of Islam. Here, too, Mohammed died and is buried. To visit Medina is not a duty of Moslems, but it is considered a most devout and meritorious act. It was to Medina that Burton planned to go first, and the *Silk al-Zahab* was bound for Yenbo, Medina's port 120 miles away on the Red Sea. Its route took them down the Gulf of Suez, around the southern tip of Sinai, across the Gulf of Aqaba, and down the eastern shore of the Red Sea. Rocks, reefs and shoals abound in this area, so the Arab dhows carrying pilgrims did not travel after dark but dropped anchor each evening in some convenient cove.

It was a slow voyage – made slower, Burton noted, by the 'insufferable splendour' of the blazing sun, which caused the crew to crouch in the shade of the sail instead of working it to take advantage of the available wind. Except when crossing the mouth of the Gulf of Aqaba, the ship always anchored just off shore to allow the passengers to spend the night on land. The gruelling trip across the Gulf of Aqaba, however, took thirty-six hours and began about dawn on 11 July. Burton spent his time stretched out on deck 'in contemplation of the web of my umbrella' and making notes on the weather: 'The wind, reverberated by the glowing hills is like the blast of a lime-kiln. All colour melts away like the canescence from above. The sky is dead milk-white and the mirror-like sea so reflects the tint that you can scarcely distinguish the line of the horizon. After noon the wind sleeps upon the reeking shore; there is a deep stillness; the only sound heard is the melancholy flapping of the sail. Men are not so much sleeping as half-senseless; they feel as if a few more degrees of heat would be death.'

Omar Effendi managed to say his prayers, but the heat melted the boy Mohammed, rendering him incapable, for once, of exercising his disagreeable habits of complaining, teasing, scolding and making mischief. A Turkish mother held her dying baby in her arms; it was too enervated even to cry. The other pilgrims, for all their barbarity and roughness, vied with each other in giving the child their choicest bits of food. As usual, Burton compared this oriental tenderness with the aloof conduct he had seen exhibited by his own countrymen, concluding that 'the sons of Great Britain are model barbarians'.

Late in the evening, a cool wind brought life back to the ship: songs were sung, stories were told, prayers were said; Mohammed became impertinent again, the Maghribis fought with the *rais*, and the normal life on board the sambuk was resumed. The mouth of the Gulf of Aqaba was finally passed and on the morning of the following day the little dhow came into the harbour of Wejh where the weary pilgrims could at last stretch their legs and buy supplies. Burton bought some fresh food and an ounce of opium in the bazaar and then relaxed at the coffee house, watching with amusement a fight between Sa'ad the Demon and the owner that was stopped when Omar fired a pistol into the coffee cans.

At eight o'clock on the morning of 14 July, the *Silk al-Zahab* left Wejh on the last lap of its voyage to Yenbo. The frail sambuk was now sailing through dangerous waters filled with razor-sharp coral reefs. Near sunset the *Silk al-Zahab* dropped anchor beside another dhow loaded with Persian pilgrims. Unfortunately, their anchor rope was not long enough to allow the anchor to touch bottom and they drifted steadily towards a particularly dangerous reef. The crew scurried about, looking for a non-existent extra piece of rope, while the passengers cursed and yelled. They were finally saved by the *rais* of the dhow carrying the Persians who threw them a rope and towed them to safety. The passengers of the *Silk al-Zahab* then turned to the satisfying task of beating their *rais* – and 'richly had he deserved it', thought Burton.

On the evening of the following day, as the pilgrims waded to shore to spend the night on the beach, they found the bottom covered with sharp rocks that cut their feet. Burton suddenly felt an unusually sharp pain in his toe. Examining the wound, he pulled out what appeared to be a bit of thorn and tramped on. He later guessed that he had kicked a spiked sea urchin, but at the time he thought little of it. He had the true traveller's contempt for physical hardships. Once when the threat of a storm delayed the ship for a day, Burton, in spite of an outbreak of boils on his buttock, rode without stirrups on a mule equipped with only a hard pack-saddle in order to explore the countryside.

While spending the night on the beach next to the Persians who had rescued them, he learned the wisdom of the advice he had been given by Haji Wali regarding his disguise and was thankful he had changed from a Persian to a Pathan. Here as elsewhere on his pilgrimage, he found the Persians abused for practising their own brand of Islam. Like Christianity, Islam is divided into a number of sects, the points of difference being primarily concerned with the caliphate. The Sunnites comprise the largest sect and are generally considered the most orthodox; the Shi'ites (or Shi'ahs), who are mostly Persians, are considered unorthodox and are scorned by the adherents of other sects because they disclaim the first three caliphs: Abu Bakr, Omar, and Osman. Burton joined his friends in calling them 'slippers of Ali and dogs of Omar'.

Two days later, the *Silk al-Zahab* entered the harbour at Yenbo, ending the tiresome twelve-day voyage. Burton might have avoided this discomfort by hiring a boat for himself, but he wished to experience life on a pilgrim ship. It was a painful journey and he still had not paid the full price: his foot was now swollen, sore and aching. In spite of his pain, Burton, leaning on the shoulder of his servant Nur, set out to explore the town, to bargain for camels to take them to Medina, and to pick up the local gossip concerning the route.

He hired two camels and also a *shugduf*: a litter 'composed of two corded cots five feet long, slung horizontally, about half-way down, and parallel with the camel's sides. . . . Thick twigs inserted in the ends and the outer long sides of the framework, are bent over the top, bower-fashion, to support matting, carpets, and any other protection against the sun. There is an opening in this kind of wicker-work in front (towards the camel's head), through which you creep; and a similar one behind creates a draught of wind.' Generally these litters were used to carry women, children, and old men, but Burton pleaded lameness as an excuse for using one. Its greatest virtue, aside from being less painful for his injured foot, was the concealment it offered him for his note-taking. He had made elaborate preparations for taking the most careful notes. In Cairo he had ordered a long thin notebook made up for him that he could carry concealed in his breast pocket. In the beginning, he made his notes in Arabic, but finding he could easily make them without being detected, he soon switched to English. Sketches, however, were cut into tiny squares, numbered and hidden in canisters tucked away in his pea-green medicine chest – the one with the painted red and yellow flowers.

In spite of the rumour that the wild Hazimi tribe was out raiding and that pilgrims had had to fight every day, Burton and his friends set off on their 120-mile journey across the desert to Medina at seven o'clock on the evening of 18 July 1853, with a caravan of twelve camels. Early the next morning they joined a larger caravan of about two hundred beasts guarded by seven irregular Turkish cavalrymen.

Most desert travelling was done at night and days were spent under canvas in 'perspiration and semi-lethargy'. Shortly after sunset of the second night, the cry of 'Thieves!' rang through the caravan. The robbers turned out to be only a half-dozen ill-armed Bedouins who were soon driven off, but dread of robbers grew worse as each village and passing caravan added its stock of rumours. At last, fear forced the caravan to a halt at the little village of Al-Hamra. Burton was eager to be on, but the main caravan stayed in its tents.

Then, on 21 July, a caravan from Mecca bound for Medina arrived at Al-Hamra. As Meccans and Medinans were more respected than strangers in these parts and this caravan carried a two-hundred-man escort of Turkish soldiers, they had less fear of robbers and were proceeding on their way. Burton, with Omar, Hamid, Nur, Sa'ad and Mohammed, quickly seized the opportunity of moving on by attaching themselves to the Meccan caravan. Shortly after nightfall, however, they were halted by a band of Bedouins. Learning that the caravan was composed of 'Sons of the Holy Cities', they permitted them to pass, provided that the Turkish soldiers left them and returned to the coast. On hearing this, the two-hundred-man escort promptly wheeled and vanished. Perhaps wisely, for the next day, when they stopped at Bir Abbas, a caravan that had been following them came in with two dead bodies, one a Turkish soldier shot by a Bedouin.

As he wobbled in his *shugduf* across the sandy wasteland towards Medina, Burton must have wondered if he would be able to go to all of the places he wanted to visit once he had reached his goal; his swollen and infected foot was growing worse every day and the onion-skin dressing in which it was encased did not seem to be helping it. He tried cool, wet bandages, although his companions swore that water would poison the wound; nothing he did seemed to help. In spite of his pain, it never occurred to him to think of turning back.

Early on the morning of 24 July, the caravan approached a gorge known as Shaub al-Hajj ('Pilgrimage Pass'). Silence fell over the column as they apprehensively marched towards a natural ambush. Sure enough, wisps of blue smoke were seen curling from the rocks above them, followed by the crack of the Bedouins' matchlocks. A number of Arabs were seen 'swarming like hornets over the crests of the hills'. Burton, whose bravery was always a bit too elaborate, calmly asked one of his companions for a piece of rope to repair his *shugduf* during the halt, then laughed at the man's surprise.

While the Bedouins were enjoying themselves taking potshots at the pilgrims, the dignified old sheiks of the caravan squatted in council, lit their pipes, and proceeded to discuss the situation. The result of their calm deliberation under fire was the conclusion that 'as the robbers would probably turn a deaf ear to their words, they had better spare themselves the trouble of speaking'. Mounting their camels, they stoically led the caravan through the gorge, leaving behind twelve dead men and a number of camels and donkeys.

On 24 July, the boy Mohammed abused Burton's camel men so outrageously that they decamped, leaving Abdullah and his friends to tend their own camels. Shortly after dawn of the following day, there was a general hurrying of the caravan and all conversation ceased. Burton could not understand what was happening. 'Are there robbers in sight?' he asked.

'No', said Mohammed, 'they are walking with their eyes. They will soon see their homes!'

They passed through a dry wadi and presently came to a huge flight of steps roughly cut in a broad line of black basalt. They were now on holy ground, for the Prophet Mohammed had praised this passageway to Medina. At the top of the steps they passed down a road of dark lava with steep banks on both sides. Then, quite suddenly, they came upon a full view of Medina only two miles below them. Although no word of command had been given to the camels, the caravan shuffled to a halt. 'All of us descended, in imitation of the pious of old,' Burton recorded, 'and sat down, jaded and hungry as we were, to feast our eyes with a view of the Holy City.'

All around him he heard the pious and passionate exclamations of his Moslem companions. Burton too was carried away, and he later wrote, 'In all the fair view before us nothing was more striking, after the desolation through which we had passed, than the gardens and orchards about the town. It was impossible not to enter into the spirit of my companions, and truly I believe that for some minutes my enthusiasm rose as high as theirs.' After eight days in the desert, the sight of this oasis, marking the first goal of his journey, made him appreciate the phrase in the Moslem ritual that says, when the eyes of the pilgrim 'fall upon the trees of al-Medina, let him raise his voice and bless the Apostle with the choicest of blessings'.

But Burton the traveller soon replaced Abdullah the pilgrim and he quickly made a rough sketch of the town and then plied his companions with questions about it while they remounted and rode slowly towards the gate of the city. As the caravan contained many from Medina, they found a crowd of relatives and friends waiting to greet them. Hamid, who had invited Burton to stay with him, had gone ahead to greet his family and prepare for his guest.

When Burton arrived and Hamid walked out of his house to welcome him, he appeared a completely different man. The dirty and unkempt Hamid in his tattered clothes held together with a rope was transformed into the picture of an Arab gentleman. He wore a fine shirt of cotton and silk, a light pink outer cloak, a plaid sash, pantaloons with 'tasteful edgings about the ankles', and lemon-coloured slippers of the most fashionable Constantinople cut. In one hand he held a mother-of-pearl rosary and in the other a pipe with a jasmine stick and amber mouthpiece. He was clean and his beard was neatly trimmed. In a short time, Burton discovered that all his friends had undergone a similar transformation. He noted that 'as men of sense they appeared in tatters where they were, or when they wished to be, unknown, and in fine linen where and when the world judged their prosperity by their attire'.

Hamid's manners had changed with his clothes. The vulgar and boisterous man had now developed 'a certain staid courtesy'. He led Burton, Nur and Mohammed into his house where pipes were filled and coffee was boiling. It was the custom for friends and relations of a traveller to call on him the day of his return. Consequently, Burton had scarcely seated himself on a cool windowsill when the guests started arriving, bringing scores of children with them. Burton, forgetting what he himself had been as a boy, found these Arab children worse than a plague: 'they rushed in *en masse*, treading upon our toes, making the noise of a nursery of madlings, pulling to pieces everything they could lay their hands upon, and using language that would have alarmed an old man-o'-war's-man'. A three-year-old perched upon his wounded foot, a boy of six picked up his pipe and started to smoke it, while a third child seized one of his loaded pistols and clapped it to another boy's head – 'fortunately, it was on half-cock, and the trigger was stiff'.

At last he could stand no more. Breaking the laws of Arab etiquette, he told Hamid he was hungry, thirsty, sleepy and tired of company. His host at once threw out the children, brought him breakfast, lit a pipe for him, darkened the room, spread a bed, and left him to the society he most desired – his own.

Burton spent several weeks in Hamid's house and found it 'quiet, but not disagreeable'. Although there were women in the house, he said, 'I never once set eyes upon the face of a woman, unless the African slave girls be allowed the title. Even these at first attempted to draw their ragged veils over their sable charms, and would not answer the simplest question.'

Hamid was his guide and mentor as well as his host during the stay in Medina. They spent their mornings visiting the mosques and holy places. Then, 'at the primitive hour of 11 a.m.' dinner was served. After dinner, Burton would usually plead melancholia (a complaint common to Arabs and eliciting their sympathy and understanding) and retire to a rug spread in a dark passage. There he would strip off his clothes and spend the hottest part of the day in reading, smoking, dozing and writing. After sunset there were visits to and from friends, trips to coffee houses, story telling and conversation. It was a peaceful life – as long as he maintained his disguise.

The first holy place visited was the Prophet's Mosque, which Burton thought 'mean and tawdry'. To him, the holy mosque, one of the most revered in Islam, resembled 'a museum of second-rate art, an old Curiosity-shop, full of ornaments that are not accessories, and decorated with pauper splendour'. They went to see the tomb of Mohammed (although Burton doubted the Prophet was actually buried there), the tombs of the Caliphs Omar and Abu Bakr (where he noted the vigilance with which the guards watched the much-abused Persians who sometimes tried to defile the tombs) and the grave of Mohammed's favourite daughter, Fatima. Other visits were made to the Gate of Salvation, the five minarets, the three holy pillars, the Mosque of Kuba, and finally holy Mount Ohod, scene of a famous battle, where the graves of some 10,000 martyrs and saints were located. Here they visited the principal graves: Mohammed's son-in-law, the Caliph Othman; Halima, Mohammed's wet nurse; and about fourteen of Mohammed's wives and ten of his daughters. On the wall of a building at Ohod, Burton, like millions of tourists the world over, could not resist writing his name. Although he thought it a 'vulgar habit', he reconciled his action by the thought that 'the practice is both classical and oriental'. With a pencil he wrote in Arabic: 'Abdullah, the servant of Allah', and then the Moslem date: '1269'.

In continual pain from his swollen and infected foot, he still visited every point of any possible interest, not neglecting a well famous because Mohammed had once been seen to spit in it. Wherever he went there were special prayers and special rituals. Burton carefully remembered them all. He made a particular effort to learn those things which his European predecessors had neglected and to see the places they had been unable to see. He asked countless questions and acquired considerable information outside his main interest in Moslem rites and holy places. He was curious about the eunuchs who guarded and maintained the mosques, learning that they were generally regarded as honourable men, that they were fairly well paid, and that most of them were married, some even having three or four wives. He visited the slave market and noted the prices and condition of the merchandise: a black slave-girl for housework cost from 40 to 50 dollars, but 'neat-handedness, propriety of demeanour, and skill in feminine accomplishment' might raise her price to 100 dollars; mothers were less than 40 dollars; eunuchs were quite expensive; boys were sold, but there were few male adults on the market; Abyssinian girls were prized because 'their skins are always cool in the hottest weather' and they sold for between 80 and 240 dollars; white slave-girls were seldom on the market, their price being from 400 to 1,600 dollars he was told. All such information was written into his carefully kept notebooks together with notes on diseases and their treatment, magic, architecture, family life, the character and physical features of the people, the prices of dozens of articles of food, popular sayings, the status of agriculture and a host of other subjects.

On 30 August the streets of Medina were filled with Bedouins, match locks over their shoulders, hurrying to join a tribal fight that had broken out in the hills. Although it did not seem to be much of a war, Burton later wrote: 'This quarrel put an end to any lingering possibility of my prosecuting my journey to Maskat.' The feat of crossing Arabia from coast to coast was not accomplished until H. St J. Philby made the trip in 1917, sixty-four years after Burton abandoned his trip. But Burton seems to have had no real desire to go from Medina to Masqat. He wanted to visit Mecca, and the means for doing so were at hand. Two days earlier the Damascus caravan had arrived in Medina carrying about 7,000 people.

That morning, Hamid had returned hurriedly from the bazaar exclaiming, 'You must make ready at once, Effendi! All *hajis* start tomorrow. Allah will make it easy for you! Have you your water skins in order? You are to travel down the Darb al-Sharki where you will not see water for three days!'

Burton was delighted. No European had ever taken this route

through the Nejd Desert, but it was a route made famous by Caliph Harun al-Rashid and his chief wife, Zubaydah, mentioned so often in *The Arabian Nights*. No time could be lost if they were to leave with the caravan. Burton patched water skins, Nur was sent to purchase supplies for fourteen days, Mohammed worked at repairing the *shugduf*, and Hamid set off to find camel men.

In the afternoon, Hamid produced some wild camel men led by a sheik named Mas'ud; Omar Effendi and other friends dropped by to say good-bye; and Burton, as a final grand gesture, forgave all of his friends' debts. Although advised to make the 'farewell visitation' to the mosque, Burton, with his usual hatred of farewells, decided that this could be skipped. At nine o'clock on the morning of 31 August 1853, Burton, with Nur and Mohammed, had packed and mounted camels at the gate of the city. Here he was forced to part with all the friends he had made thus far on his pilgrimage except Mohammed. He was glad when the caravan at last began to move. He was on his way to Mecca.

The Damascus caravan was a colourful sight, composed as it was of people of all classes and a wide variety of nationalities. Burton classified the pilgrims into eight grades, ranging from the wealthy and noble who travelled on fine camels and carried with them an elaborate array of equipment to the lowly Takruri who hobbled on staves and carried only a bowl with which to beg water and food. Even during the first day's march the Takruri were forced to fight with the vultures for the carcases of dead camels, horses and asses. 'The heat was dreadful, the climate dangerous, and the beasts died in numbers,' Burton recorded.

The pilgrims were from every part of the Moslem world and it seemed as if no two were dressed alike. Guarding the caravan were about 2,000 irregular cavalry, bashi-bazouks, each armed as he pleased, 'exceedingly dirty, picturesque-looking, brave, and in such a country of no use whatever'.

To Burton's disgust, much of the travelling was again done by night. 'I can scarcely find words to express the weary horrors of the long dark march, during which the hapless traveller, fuming, if a European, with disappointment in his hopes of "seeing the country", is compelled to sit upon the back of a creeping camel.'

The route led the caravan over rough country, rocky and hilly. 'Nowhere had I seen a land in which the Earth's anatomy lies so barren, or one richer in volcanic and primary formations,' Burton said. He thought there might be gold in the rocks and picked up some samples to bring back with him.

The best part of the trip was the friendship he made with his came sheik, old Mas'ud, who had nicknamed him Abu Shawarib ('Father of Moustaches'). The name pleased Burton, who was always proud of his enormous moustaches. Since most of his intimate contacts had been with town Arabs, he was eager to learn first hand about the Bedouin (or 'Bedawin', as he called them). He questioned Mas'ud at every opportunity and the old sheik obliged him by telling 'his genealogy, his battles and his family affairs'. Burton found much to admire in these desert men, concluding that their character 'is a truly noble compound of determination, gentleness, and generosity. Usually they are a mixture of worldly cunning and great simplicity, sensitive to touchiness, good-tempered souls, solemn and dignified withal, fond of a jest, yet of a grave turn of mind, easily managed by a laugh and a soft word, and placable after passion, though madly revengeful after injury.'

Burton endeared himself to the Bedouins by singing for them the song said to have been sung by Maysuna, the beautiful Bedouin wife of the Caliph Muawiya, to her husband:

> *Oh, take these purple robes away,*
> *Give back my cloak of camel's hair*
> *And bear me from this towering pile*
> *To where the black tents flap the air.*
> *The camel's colt with faltering tread*
> *The dog that bays at all but me*
> *Delight me more than ambling mules,*
> *And every art of minstrelsy;*
> *And any cousin, poor but free,*
> *Might take me, fatted ass, from thee.*

This was a song to delight old Mas'ud who, like every Bedouin, had only contempt for the town Arab, whether beggar or caliph.

As the caravan plodded slowly but steadily forward, night after night, patience faded and tempers grew sharp. A Turk who quarrelled with an Arab camel man had his stomach ripped open and was left to die in the desert. A Wahabi who made fun of Burton's *shugduf* was insulted in turn: he drew his knife, but quickly sheathed it again in the face of Burton's cocked pistols. The Damascus caravan met the Bagdad caravan, and there was continual friction between the two as to precedence on the march.

They were drawing close to Mecca now, and on 9 September they performed the ceremony of *Al-Ihram*, which involved shaving the head, cutting the finger-nails, bathing, perfuming, and then donning the *Ihram*, or pilgrim's clothes, consisting of two cotton cloths, white with narrow red stripes, which were wrapped about the body in toga fashion. So prepared and costumed they said special prayers and performed special rituals. It was forbidden now for them to cut their nails or to have sexual intercourse until the ceremonies of the pilgrimage were completed. As they marched along on this final lap of their journey, they cried out from time to time, '*Labbayk!* – Here am I!' as though reminding their god of their existence and calling his attention to the religious rites they were about to perform.

Like a river gathering in small streams, the great caravan began to pick up smaller bands of pilgrims. Burton and his friends were thrown together with a group of Wahabis, those warrior puritans of Islam who since Burton's time, when they were a comparatively small sect, have gained control over most of the Arabian Peninsula. When they saw Burton or any of his party smoking, they cursed them roundly and damned them for infidels and idolaters. They were a wild group, with wilder camels that delighted in breaking loose and crashing among the files of the caravan. A dust storm added to the confusion as the 10,000 pilgrims pushed forward over the last few miles separating them from Mecca.

About five o'clock in the afternoon, the caravan moved down a dry river bed between precipitous walls of rocks. It seemed such a natural place for an ambush that an apprehension came over the caravan. As the cries of 'Here am I!' could be heard by bandits as well as Allah, they were gradually stilled. Soon all was silent except for the sounds of the moving feet of men and beasts. Then, high on a cliff on the right side, Burton saw a curl of smoke, 'like a lady's ringlet', and the echoing crack of a matchlock. A high-trotting dromedary just in front of him suddenly collapsed, its heart split by a bullet; its rider was thrown five or six yards in a somersault.

The caravan panicked. Women screamed, children cried, and men cursed. Animals were pounded savagely to drive them out of this death trap, but the road was so narrow that it was soon clogged into an immovable mass. The bashi-bazouks galloped up and down over the stones, shouting orders at each other, but they were useless. The pasha of the caravan spread his rug by the left-hand cliff, lit his pipe and debated with his officers as to what should be done. No one suggested attacking the robbers.

Then the wild Wahabis rode up on their camels, their hair in elf-locks flowing behind them. One body began a covering fire while about 200 dismounted and, led by their *sherif*, began to scale the cliffs. The robbers fled.

When the firing first broke out, Burton had primed his pistols and prepared to defend himself. But seeing that the Wahabis would take care of the affair in short order and 'wishing to make an impression', he called loudly for his supper. Nur was too petrified with fear to move, Mohammed groaned, and an Arab beside him exclaimed in disgust, 'By Allah, he eats!'

The only person amused by this bit of bravado was a dignified Meccan sheik named Abdullah with whom Burton had become friendly during the trip. From his camel behind Burton's he called, 'Are these Afghan manners, Effendim?'

'Yes,' called Abdullah Burton, 'in my country we always dine before an attack of robbers, because that gentry is in the habit of sending men to bed supperless.'

Sheik Abdullah laughed, but those around them seemed more offended than impressed.

With the robbers cleared by the Wahabis, the caravan continued its march. All night long they travelled. Although both men and beasts were becoming worn out by their exertions, still they kept on. By six o'clock the following evening they were almost at Mecca. Burton strained his eyes to see the holy city, but he could not. About one o'clock in the morning, however, he was aroused by cries of 'Mecca! Mecca!' Excitement swept through the entire weary caravan. Some called 'The Sanctuary! The Sanctuary!' and others began again the cry of '*Labbayk!*' Looking out of his *shugduf* Burton could see by the light of the desert stars the dim outlines of the city just ahead of them. An hour later they were in Mecca, 'the mother of towns', and drew up before the home of the boy Mohammed, with whom Burton was to stay.

Mohammed was to play the part Hamid had played at Medina. Like Hamid, he too underwent a distinct change in manner: from the boisterous and jaunty, he became grave and attentively courteous – Burton was his guest. Food was soon served and, after only a couple of hours' sleep, they began the round of ceremonies demanded of the pilgrim.

In the early morning light Burton saw for the first time what few Europeans had ever seen before him: the Kaaba, the Sanctuary – the 'navel of the world', as Ibn Haukal called it. This above all else symbolized the object of his mission, his goal, his great desire, his success.

His sense of exhilaration on reaching it was nearly as great as that of the true Moslem pilgrim who morning, noon and night during every day of his life had faced towards this one spot to say his prayers. This, above all else, was the most holy spot in Islam.

Stripped of its associations, the Kaaba is an unusual but unimpressive structure standing by itself in the centre of a large courtyard. It is simply a square, windowless, stone building with a door inconveniently located seven feet above the ground. The outer walls of the building are covered with a huge black hanging, embroidered with inscriptions from the Koran, called a 'kiswa' which is made by an hereditary family of weavers in Cairo. A new covering is provided each year, and brought to Mecca by the Egyptian caravan; the old kiswa is cut into small pieces and sold to pilgrims. Set into the south-east corner of the Kaaba is the 'Black Stone', believed to have been given to Abraham by the Angel Gabriel. Actually, the stone was the most revered of all the relics and idols that existed long before Mohammed when the Kaaba was a pantheon of heathen gods and saints. It is reliably reported that when Mohammed, in A.D. 630, threw out the old gods, there was even a painting of Jesus and the Virgin Mary on the inner walls of the Kaaba. The Sanctuary Burton saw was not the one Mohammed reformed; the building had been rebuilt several times since then, but always in the same shape, and always with the same Black Stone in the corner.

Moslems who come to Mecca for the first time look with fear and awe upon this most holy building and it is a Meccan joke that pilgrims often ask the direction for prayer, for this is the only spot in Islam where Moslems can pray facing any point of the compass by simply moving around the Kaaba.

Burton was as awed as any Moslem peasant:

I may truly say that, of all the worshippers who clung weeping to the curtain, or who pressed their beating hearts to the stone, none felt for the moment a deeper emotion than did the Haji from the far-north. It was as if the poetical legends of the Arab spoke truth, and that the waving wings of angels, not the sweet breeze of morning, were agitating and swelling the black covering of the shrine. But, to confess humbling truth, theirs was the high feeling of religious enthusiasm, mine was the ecstasy of gratified pride.

At this moment, Burton, the man of all faiths and of none, seems to have regretted his own lack of belief. He could imitate the feelings of others, but he knew it was not the same. Much as he might want to

share this emotional experience, he could not. For all his vast knowledge of religions, he was, and always would be, an outsider, one of
those for whom there exists no formal religion. Moslem Sufism came
closest to being a faith he could believe in; he was intrigued by its
mysticism and moved by its poetry, but in his heart there dwelt no
gods.

As Burton and Mohammed stepped from under the colonnades of
the great mosque into the spacious area containing the dark Kaaba,
Burton tried to shake off his feeling of awe and to regain his critical
faculties, his powers of observation: 'There were no giant fragments of
hoar antiquity as in Egypt, no remains of graceful and harmonious
beauty as in Greece and Italy, no barbarous gorgeousness as in the
buildings of India; yet the view was strange, unique. . . .'

Mohammed led him first of all to the holy well called Zemzem which
tradition says was used by Hagar to draw water for her son Ishmael.
The water from this well is used only for drinking and religious purposes. Burton drank from the well and, like many other pilgrims, filled
several bottles to take home with him. He noted that the water had a
'salt-bitter' flavour as though mixed with Epsom salts. It also had a
similar effect, for he found that 'it is apt to cause diarrhoea'.

They then proceeded to the south-east corner and, facing the Black
Stone, repeated the prayer:

There is no god but Allah alone, Whose Covenant is Truth, and Whose
Servant is Victorious. There is no god but Allah, without Sharer; His is the
Kingdom, to Him be Praise, and He over all things is potent.

Burton wanted to touch the stone, but was unable to do so at this
time because of the crowd of excited pilgrims around it.

He then began the *Tawaf*, or walk around the Kaaba counter-clock-
wise seven times repeating certain prayers. This done, he again
attempted to kiss, or at least touch, the Black Stone. The crowd was
still there, but Mohammed organized a gang of his Meccan friends and
cleared a space for him. By this means Burton managed to monopolize
the holy stone for ten minutes despite the indignant and impatient cries
of the other pilgrims. While kissing the stone and rubbing his forehead
on it, he was able to make a careful examination of the famous relic.

The stone is an irregular oval about seven inches in diameter set in
the wall about four or five feet above the ground. It appeared to Burton
as though it had been broken at some time and then stuck back together
again. He found it difficult to determine the quality of the stone because

it had been handled and kissed by so many millions, but it appeared to be of lava with small amounts of extraneous matter embedded in it. Its colour, according to him, is a deep reddish-brown, almost black. He came away persuaded that it was a meteorite.

The duties of the pilgrim to Mecca are somewhat arduous. After leaving the Black Stone, Burton made several other required prayers, took another drink of Zemzem water and had some of it poured over him to wash away his sins; then there were still more prayers to be said before he could return to Mohammed's house to snatch a few hours' rest before nightfall.

That evening, Burton and Mohammed, followed by Nur with a lantern, went again to the Kaaba. Burton was impressed with the number of nationalities, each with their different costumes and manners, that crowded the streets of Mecca. In the oval courtyard around the Kaaba he found Bedouin women with long black robes, an Indian woman in 'wrinkled tights', fair-skinned Turks, a negro in a religious frenzy shaking his head from side to side like a chained elephant, groups of pilgrims with guides, a corpse on a wooden shell supported by four bearers being carried around the Kaaba, and 'some poor wretch, with arms thrown on high, so that every part of his person might touch the Kaaba, was clinging to the curtain and sobbing as though his heart would break'.

Burton and his companions sat watching the spectacle. It was late in the night before he had an opportunity to make the prescribed two prostrations over the grave of Ishmael. When Nur and Mohammed dropped off to sleep and the crowd thinned, he walked around the Kaaba seeking a chance to steal a bit of the kiswa, which after a year's use was ragged and frayed at the edges, but the guards were too vigilant. He was able to make a rough survey of the area, however, pacing off in a discreet manner the various things he wanted to measure so as to make a sketch. About two o'clock in the morning, he awakened his companions and they stumbled home for a short sleep before the important events to come.

At ten o'clock the next morning, Burton, again dressed in his *Ihram*, mounted his *shugduf* and, with Mohammed and his nephew, Mas'ud and his camels, set out for Mount Arafat, fifteen miles south-east of Mecca, for the ceremonies of *Yaum Al-Tarwiyah*. This was the final ceremony, the climax of all the travel and hardship, the reward for the effort and expense. In spite of the short distance, Burton saw no less than five men die on the road of exhaustion and perhaps sickness. He met and talked with an Indian family consisting of an old man, his wife, and a young boy who had left India with only about fifty dollars. Although they were now destitute, they planned to go to Medina after the ceremonies at Mecca, begging their way. Burton thought they had little chance of ever reaching their home again.

In mid-afternoon they arrived at their destination and camped with 50,000 other pilgrims on the slopes of Mount Arafat. This one-night encampment was chaos. Families became separated, Bedouins sought out old enemies with the hope of knifing them unseen in the confusion, thieves were plentiful, and the whole crowded camp smelled so vilely that Mas'ud, accustomed to the clean desert air, sat holding his nose. To cheer up the old camel sheik, Burton sang him the song about the beautiful Bedouin girl who wanted to flee from her caliph husband. Old Mas'ud laughed and clapped Burton's shoulder, promising to take this 'Father of Moustaches' back to his own black tents in the desert. When a group of grave-diggers appeared and tried to bury a pile of fresh corpses near their tent, Burton and his friends drove them off. Such hastily dug graves were always shallow; the sun was hot; fresh corpses stink. When night fell, they lay down on their rugs to sleep, but, tired as they were, sleep was impossible. Near them an old man recited prayers throughout the night; there were loud shouts of laughter from some Egyptian hemp-drinkers; and the sounds of wild Arab music accompanied by clapping hands could be heard all night long.

At dawn a cannon banged loudly to announce the beginning of the day that would give the title of *haji* to all who had made the pilgrimage. During the day, Burton walked around the camp and visited the holy places near by. Late in the afternoon a sermon was preached from the hilltop by an Imam mounted on a camel. This was to be the principal event of the pilgrimage ceremonies and Burton was prepared with concealed paper and pencil to record the highlights of what was said. But he did not hear a word of it.

Since the carouse with the Albanian captain in Cairo, Burton had been careful to be on his best behaviour; he had also been most conscientious in observing and recording and visiting all the holy places, learning all that he could. Now, at the most important event of his entire journey, he tripped. Close by them he discovered a beautiful girl of about eighteen 'with regular features, a skin somewhat citrine-coloured, but soft and clear, symmetrical eyebrows, the most beautiful eyes, and a figure all grace. There was no head thrown back, no straightened back, no flat shoulders, no toes turned out – in fact, no "elegant" barbarisms: the shape was what the Arabs love, soft, bending and relaxed, as a figure ought to be.'

Instead of the usual veil, the girl wore a 'yashmak', a kind of double veil of transparent muslin. She looked with admiration at a red cash-mere shawl Mohammed had loaned him and Burton looked deep into her eyes. She then made 'the usual coquettish gesture' and threw back an inch or two of head-veil, revealing jet-black hair; then part of the face veil, showing a beautiful oval face, dimpled mouth and a rounded chin. Burton, to use his own words, 'was in ecstasy'.

During the sermon, seeing that his companions were occupied with their devotions and that the girl's mother was either unsuspicious or complaisant, he occupied himself with the girl, continuing the flirtation until the ceremony was nearly over and he and the girl had come 'to a good understanding'. Unfortunately – or perhaps fortunately – Burton's plans were thwarted by an old pilgrimage custom known as the 'Hurry from Arafat'.

The moment the sermon was over, which occurred just at sundown, all 50,000 people made a rush for the valley leading to the little village of Muzdalifah. Many new *hajis* have been crushed to death in this mad flight. Every man urged his camel or donkey forward although the ground bristled with tent pegs for men and beasts to fall over. Pedes-trians were run down, and camels toppled over; there were numerous fights, and general confusion. Burton had given Mas'ud a dollar and instructions to keep track of the girl. An old acquaintance from the caravan named Ali had taken up with their party, however, and com-plained bitterly about the rush. He persisted in demanding that Mas'ud stop or slow down; Burton tried to hurry the camels on even faster. The pretty face from the litter grew dimmer. A string of camels crossed their path. The face was gone. Burton, his sense of scholarly duty returning, halted his camel and made a quick sketch of Mount Arafat. Then he revenged himself on Ali by eating the old man's supper.

They were three hours on the road before reaching Muzdalifah where they spent the night. Before going to sleep, they followed custom by collecting seven small stones for stoning the devil on the morrow.

The next morning the seven stones were washed in seven waters and they proceeded to the narrow pass containing the pillar where tradition demands that each pilgrim throw his stones and curse the devil before sundown of that day. Burton had heard of the crush of people at this narrow spot on the road and had provided himself with a hidden dagger.

Mohammed had procured donkeys and when they came to the pillar called the 'Great Devil', they tried to ride into the throng to get close enough to throw their stones. No sooner had Burton entered the crowd of pilgrims than his donkey was overthrown by a dromedary. Burton found himself under the belly of the stamping, roaring beast. He scrambled free of the animal's legs and, whipping out his knife, fought his way out of the mob. Mohammed, with a bloody nose, also emerged unsuccessful from the mass of men and animals. They decided to wait patiently for an opening, and at last their chance came. Holding each stone with the prescribed thumb and forefinger, they threw it at the pillar crying, 'In the name of Allah, and Allah is almighty! (I do this) in hatred of the Fiend and to his shame.'

This done, they waited their turn at the barber's booth and had their beards trimmed. They were now free to cover their sunburned heads, put on their normal clothes, stroke their beards, and have intercourse with their women (if they had any).

Returning now to Mecca, the new *haji* was still not allowed to rest. Mohammed bustled him off to the Kaaba even before he had a chance to take off his travel-stained *Ihram*. There was a crowd about the high door of the Kaaba, but Mohammed made a path for him by crying out in an authoritative voice, 'Open a path for the *Haji* who would enter the House!'

Two stout Meccans stood below and hoisted Burton up the seven feet to the door-sill where a third man hauled him inside. At the entrance were several officials who questioned him concerning his name, nation and other particulars. Then Mohammed was told to show him about the building. Looking at the windowless walls and the officials at the door, Burton reflected on the kind of death he could expect, should his real character be suspected. In the eyes of true Moslems, he was polluting the Sanctuary. One false step, a slip of the tongue, a mistake in the prayers, and he would have been torn to shreds. Wallin had not dared to take a single note while in Mecca, but Burton now had the audacity actually to make a rough sketch of the interior of the Kaaba with a pencil on his *Ihram*. He did this during the long prayers under the very nose of the suspicious Mohammed. No single act of daring he had done before was fraught with such terrible consequences. There is no doubt that had he been caught making this sketch suspicion would have been instantly aroused, and, among a people for whom suspicion and condemnation were virtually synonymous, he would not have left the Kaaba alive.

Returning again to Mohammed's house, Burton was at last permitted to wash and change clothes. Then, late in the afternoon, they mounted on asses and rode out to nearby Muna to watch the sacrifices. Strictly speaking, Burton should have bought a sheep and sacrificed it immediately after stoning the devil, but he contented himself with simply watching others perform the rite. Already he was becoming bored by the seemingly endless ceremonies which had no real religious significance for him. Nevertheless, in the interests of scholarship and fame, he proceeded to participate in or to witness the remaining rites.

Camp was pitched and Burton, Nur, and Mohammed spent three days at Muna. It was not the most healthy environment. 'Literally, the land stank,' Burton reported. Well it might, for between five and six thousand sheep, oxen, and camels had been slaughtered and dismembered in a small valley with no attempt made to keep the area clean.

Returning to Mecca, they hurried to the great oval containing the Kaaba. It was filled with worshippers sitting on the ground facing the cloth-covered stone building. On a tall, pointed pulpit, gilded so as to flame in the sun, sat the venerable Imam who was to deliver the sermon. Presently he stood up, leaned on a short staff, and called down Allah's blessings on the audience. Then the muezzin, standing at the foot of the pulpit, gave the call to prayer. When he finished, the dignified old religious Imam preached a sermon that was punctuated at intervals by a general '*Amin*' from the audience. Towards the end of the sermon, nearly every third word was so answered by the crowd below him. Burton was quite moved by this simple ceremony. He later wrote, 'I have seen the religious ceremonies of many lands, but never – nowhere – aught so solemn, so impressive as this.'

During his remaining few days in Mecca, Burton visited the tomb of Mohammed's mother, the sacred cemetery of Mecca, and other holy places in and about the city. But he had accomplished his mission, the heat was 'simply unendurable', and he was anxious to return to his own brand of civilization. In spite of Mas'ud's advice that, because of tribal wars and the unrest in the country, he should remain in Mecca for a few more months, Burton resolved to return to Egypt by way of Jidda. Since Meccans were 'as fond of little presents as are nuns', Burton distributed gifts to all his friends. That done, he hired camels and set out with Mohammed and Nur for the coast. In seventeen hours of hard riding they reached Jidda.

Burton's funds were now exhausted and his camel men were clamouring for their pay. He still had the little piece of paper that constituted a draft for money from the Royal Geographical Society. This could be cashed at the British Vice-Consulate located at Jidda. Applying there and asking to see Charles Cole, the Vice-Consul, he was told by the dragoman at the door that Cole was 'not at home'. Since it was still not safe to reveal himself, Haji Abdullah squatted at the gate until he could obtain an audience. When at last he was admitted, he handed Cole a slip of paper on which he had written, 'Don't recognize me; I am Dick Burton, but I am not safe yet. Give me some money which will be returned from London and don't take any notice of me.' Cole complied, but they met in the evening and Burton was once more able to enjoy a bit of English society.

He used the money to purchase a costume so elaborate that he was generally mistaken for the Pasha of Medina and to live on a grander scale than he had enjoyed in the desert. After a ten day wait, the English ship *Dwarka* came into port and he booked a first-class passage to Suez. He was now so close to the end of his adventure that he apparently relaxed the disguise he had maintained throughout his *haj*. This was revealed to him when one day Mohammed coldly said goodbye and disappeared. Later, Nur told him that after a visit to the ship when Burton was making his final arrangements Mohammed had said to him, 'Now I understand. Your master is a sahib from India. He hath laughed in our beards.' In some unknown way Burton had at last confirmed the original suspicions of the shrewd young man.

On 26 September, Burton, still in Arab dress, boarded the *Dwarka*. While on his way down to his cabin an English officer gave him a kick and snarled, 'Get out of the way, you dirty nigger!'

And so the pilgrimage ended.

Chapter 7

To Savage Harar

1854 – 5

HAD Richard Burton hurried to England after his Meccan pilgrimage, the fame he sought might possibly have found him. It was the kind of daring exploit that excites admiration and wonder at all times, but in vigorous, aggressive Victorian Britain, then rising to the height of its great empire, it was sensational. It was, indeed, a milestone in the history of adventure for adventure's sake – in spite of its proclaimed practical aims. Had he told his story in person and speedily brought out his book, there doubtless would have been some greater reward from distinguished societies or Government. Men have been knighted for less. As explorers, soldiers and simple adventurers have learned before and since, there is much to be gained by being on hand to receive congratulations when those who can give them are in the mood to do so immediately after the deed is done. Not only did Burton fail to do this, but he failed to learn from the experience.

For several weeks he lounged about Cairo, recovering his health and working over his notes. He had talked of making a second excursion across Arabia by way of Al-Muwailih, a port sixty-five miles south-east of the entrance to the Gulf of Aqaba, but he did not. He gave as his excuse that he needed to recover from his ailments. However, one cannot help suspecting that he felt he had done enough and had earned his fame. This attitude, which kept him from pushing on after he had accomplished what he regarded as his main task, was a weakness of character that was to prevent him from achieving the degree of fame to which he ever aspired. Now he was content to remain in Egypt until the balance of his leave had been expended.

For no apparent reason other than his love for disguises, he continued to go about in native dress, although he was staying at Shepheard's Hotel, the favourite resort of Europeans in Egypt. One evening when he saw a friend standing with a group of officers in front of the hotel, he paraded up and down before them, taking, as he always did, a childish delight in being unrecognized. He walked closer and closer until his burnous brushed the arm of his friend.

'Damn that nigger's impudence!' exclaimed the officer in true Empire style. 'If he does that again, I'll kick him.'

'Well, damn it, Hawkins, that's a nice way to welcome a fellow after two years' absence.'

'By God, it's Ruffian Dick!' cried Hawkins.

Burton even wore his Arab costume on board the ship that took him to Bombay. James Grant Lumsden, senior member of the Bombay Council, was also on board and, seeing Burton, he remarked to a friend, 'What a clever, intellectual face that Arab has!' Burton, delighted, spoke to Lumsden in English and thus began a friendship.

When they arrived in Bombay, Burton stayed at Lumsden's house and there he wrote his three-volume *Personal Narrative of a Pilgrimage to Al-Madinah and Meccah*, which was published in 1855 – 6. The book proved popular in spite of Burton's style, the long footnotes, the ostentatious scholarship, and the fact that nearly a quarter of the book was taken up with appendices. The work passed through several editions – picking up more footnotes and appendices with each new issue – and inspired a rash of travels by Englishmen to 'forbidden cities' from China to Morocco.

A considerable portion of the book is devoted to detailed descriptions of Moslem prayers, rituals and holy places; Burton played down the danger. There are also a number of ethnological notes on tribes, races and nationalities, particular attention being given to the Bedouins, 'in all the dignity of pride and dirt', for whom Burton had developed an affection. As usual, though, he found opportunities for including a considerable amount of extraneous matter in the form of unrelated ideas, opinions and prejudices: the Dutch school of painting he called 'dirty picturesque'; he declared that no Eastern language had a single term for the English word 'gratitude' and 'none but Germans have ideas unexplainable by words'; he included a little lecture on the proper use of cavalry with a long footnote on his favourite military subject: the use of the bayonet in the British Army; he ventured the opinion that 'he who renders warfare fatal to all engaged in it will be the greatest benefactor the world has yet known'; he stoutly defended the use of the veil by Eastern women, believing it to be 'the most coquettish article in women's attire. . . . It conceals coarse skins, fleshy noses, wide mouths and vanishing chins, whilst it sets off to best advantage what in these lands is most lustrous and liquid – the eye. Who has not remarked this at a masquerade ball?'; he talked of ghosts, holy miracles, clairvoyance and similar 'spiritual' happenings, which, he said, were believed even in 'hard-headed America', adding in a footnote, 'In fairness I must confess to believing in the reality of these phenomena, but not in their "spiritual" origin'; and he added an interesting note on the use of sunglasses in the desert: 'It is Prince Pückler Muskau, if I recollect rightly, who mentions that in his case a pair of dark spectacles produced a marked difference of apparent temperature, whilst travelling over the sultry sand of the desert. I have often remarked the same phenomenon.'

It would appear that the original manuscript included a great deal of additional information of the sort which Burton called 'anthropological', i.e. sexual. Stanley Lane-Poole, who wrote an introduction to one of the later editions of the *Pilgrimage*, said that the manuscript had been entrusted to Sir John Gardner Wilkinson (1797–1875), the famous traveller and Egyptologist, to see through the press. Wilkinson took it upon himself to eliminate from the work a vast amount of 'unpleasant garbage' which, if left in, he believed would make the book 'unfit for publication'.

Among the many scenes described by Burton was one of the principal slave market of Mecca:

It is a large street roofed with matting, and full of coffee houses. The merchandise sat in rows, parallel with the walls. The prettiest girls occupied the highest benches, below were the plainer sort, and lowest of all the boys. They were all gaily dressed in pink and other light-coloured muslins, with transparent veils over their heads; and, whether from the effect of such unusual splendour, or from the reaction succeeding to their terrible land-journey and sea-voyage, they appeared perfectly happy, laughing loudly, talking unknown tongues, and quizzing purchasers, even during the delicate operation of purchasing. There were some pretty Gallas, douce-looking Abyssinians, and Africans of various degrees of hideousness.... The highest price of which I could hear was £60.

This matter-of-fact description is immediately followed by a remarkable vow and some ambitious day-dreaming:

And here I matured a resolve to strike, if favoured by fortune, a death-blow at a trade which is eating into the vitals of industry in Eastern Africa. The reflection was pleasant, – the idea that the humble Haji, contemplating the scene from his donkey, might become the instrument of the total abolition of this pernicious traffic. What would have become of that pilgrim had the crowd in the slave-market guessed his intentions?

Now that he was back in Bombay, fated to return to his regiment and the routine of a junior officer on garrison duty, there seemed little opportunity for accomplishing such grand objectives. But he was still full of ideas and plans. It was at this time that he probably began a book titled *El Islam; or, The Rank of Muhammadanism among the Religions of the World*. This work was never completed, but the fragment that remains is interesting. Its avowed purpose was to 'touch briefly upon the points wherein due measure of justice has not yet been dealt by philosophic and learned Europe to the merits and value of El Islam'. In doing this, he lauded the superiority of Islam over Christianity in many areas, some of them basic:

But this I claim for El Islam ... Christianity says we are fallen beings, fallen not through our own fault; condemned to eternal death, not by our own demerits; ransomed by a Divine Being, not through our own merits. El Islam, on the contrary, raised men from this debased status, and with the sound good sense which characterizes the creed, inspired and raised him in the scale of creation by teaching him the dignity of human nature. Thus modern Spiritualism is giving a shock to Christianity, whereas El Islam has power to resist it.

While not actually condemning Christianity, he did point out some of its shortcomings, including 'that poverty of invention and puerility of imagination that distinguish the religious rhymsters of Christianity'. In contrast, he pointed to the great Arabic religious poetry, of which he was always a great admirer.

He even came to the defence of some of those aspects of Islam generally criticized by Christians. Polygamy, for example, he defended as necessary in 'hot and enervating climates', for 'monogamy, polygamy, and polyandry are an affair of geography', he said. The weather also excused soft living: 'Self-mortification and religious penances soon degenerate a race, especially in hot climates, where a moderate indulgence in the comforts, the luxuries and the pleasures of life strengthens the body and with it the mind of man.'

Burton briefly traced the rise of religion from 'absolute ignorance of any God' to the rise of Islam. He spoke with admiration of Moses, 'a man of angry temper, as are all who accomplish wonderful actions', but he believed the great defect in his scheme was the substitution of a system of temporal rewards for a future paradise. Burton himself did not believe in any kind of life after death, although he thought that the belief, like veneration of sacred animals or objects, was 'implanted by nature in the very heart and soul of man'.

Jesus Christ, he said, 'preached a creed in conformity with his circumstances'. He believed his tenets to be those of the Essene, whom he described as 'the Sufis, the Spiritualists, and the Gnostics of Judaism', and that Christ gave 'an impetus to the progress of mankind by systematizing a religion of the highest moral loveliness'.

Of religion in general, he said, 'It is the race of man that exalts the faith in proportion to man's moral and material excellence. The faith fails, on the other hand, to raise a degraded race.'

Burton had his own ideas on how a religion could be made: 'From the literature of the Hindus and Persians, the Egyptians and the Arabs, it would be easy to collect a code of morality and a law of benevolence as pure and amiable as ever entered the heart of man.' An interesting statement since this is essentially what he attempted in his philosophical poem *Kasîdah*, which he may also have started about this time.

It was perhaps during his stay with Lumsden that Burton met F. F. (Foster Fitzgerald) Arbuthnot of the Bombay Civil Service. In 1853 Arbuthnot was only twenty years old and had been in India only a year, but already he was enchanted by oriental literature. Burton, now thirty-two, took a great liking to the young man and they formed a friendship that lasted for as long as Burton lived. Temperamentally they had little in common. Arbuthnot was quiet and amiable and was never heard to say an evil word of anyone. His friends spoke of his 'sweetness and serenity' – qualities no one ever associated with Burton, not even the infatuated Isabel Arundell.

Back in England, she wrote in her diary, 'Richard has come back with flying colours from Mecca; but instead of coming home he has gone to Bombay to rejoin his regiment. I glory in his glory. God be thanked!' But Burton had no desire to return to regimental routine. While writing up his adventures in Arabia, composing poetry, working on a history of Islam, and making new friends, he also had time to mature a plan for another expedition. This time his goal was to reach the legendary walled city of Harar in Somalia (today in Ethiopia) and to explore parts of East Africa.

The idea of travelling into the interior of Somalia was not new. In May 1849, a proposal for an expedition to discover the productive resources of Somalia had been made to the East India Company by the President of the Royal Geographical Society and the Superintendent of the Indian Navy. The Directors of the East India Company gave their usual cautious reply to this suggestion by saying that if a 'fit and proper person volunteer to travel in the Somali country', he would have to go at his own risk and without government protection, but that an officer of the Company who obtained permission to go would be given full pay, instruments, expenses and transportation. Several schemes were discussed, but the expedition had never got under way. The project was lying dormant when Burton applied for the assignment.

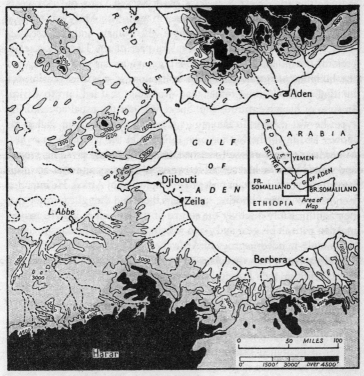

2. Somalia

Thanks to the influence of his new friend Lumsden, the venture was speedily approved and Burton was again given leave to go adventuring. His initial plan was to go inland from Berbera as far as Harar and then swing in a south-easterly direction across the Somali Peninsula, ending up in Zanzibar. He selected three officers to accompany him: Lieutenant William Stroyan of the Indian Navy, a companion of Burton's on the Sind Survey; Lieutenant G. E. Herne of the 1st Bombay European Infantry, a man 'skilful in surveying, photography, and mechanics'; and Assistant Surgeon J. E. Stocks with whom Burton had once written a report on Sind for the Bombay Government. Unfortunately, Stocks died of apoplexy just before he was due to leave.

Burton, Herne and Stroyan arrived in Aden on 1 October 1854, and there Stocks's place in the expedition was taken by a remarkable young man: Lieutenant John Hanning Speke of the 46th Regiment of Bengal Native Infantry. Speke was only twenty-seven years old (six years younger than Burton), but he had been in the Indian Army since he was seventeen, had served in campaigns in the Punjab, and had used his leave for the last five years to explore part of the Himalayas, even crossing the mountains into Tibet. His great interests were hunting and the building of a natural history collection; it was this passion for hunting and collecting, rather than exploring, that led him to Africa. In spite of his adventurous life, Speke was not the usual adventuring type: he was cold and calculating; much concerned about saving his money and in furthering his own interests in the world; he was also somewhat priggish and self-satisfied. Patiently, he had saved his money and waited until he had served ten years in the army and thus accumulated three years' leave, in order to go exploring in Africa. He intended to spend two years shooting specimens there and thought vaguely that he might possibly discover the source of the Nile en route. He arrived in Aden with all his gear and £390 worth of beads and trinkets to tempt the 'simple-minded negroes of Africa'.

Unfortunately for the plans of both Speke and Burton, Colonel James Outram, then Political Resident at Aden, was violently opposed to both their projects. The interior of Africa was too dangerous and the very presence of the young officers might arouse the latent hostility of the Somalis. He was at last persuaded to allow Burton to make some tentative explorations of the coastal areas and Speke was permitted to go too if he joined Burton, whose grand plans for geographical exploration were once more reduced to an attempt to visit a forbidden city: Harar.

Herne was sent to Berbera with instructions to inquire into the state of commerce, the slave trade and the caravan lines; to visit the maritime mountains, sketch all the places of possible interest and make notes on the weather; he was also to pave the way for a friendly reception for Burton when he emerged from the interior after visiting Harar. Herne was joined by Stroyan in January. Speke was to land near a small harbour known as Arz Al-Aman on the Somali coast and explore the Wadi Nogal where it was rumoured that gold dust had been found. For himself, Burton reserved the most dangerous, and also the most interesting part of the venture: a journey in disguise from Zeila on the coast to Harar. It is doubtful if Outram knew or would have approved of this plan.

While in Aden preparing for this expedition, Burton set about learning as much as he could of the language and customs of the country he was to visit. There were a few Somalis living in Aden, including a number of prostitutes from whom he learned that the Somalis had some peculiar sexual practices, interesting from an anthropological point of view: The prostitutes had 'the labiae and clitoris excised and the skin showing the scars of coarse sewing. The moral effect of female circumcision [*sic*] is peculiar. While it diminishes the heat of passion it increases licentiousness, and breeds a debauchery of mind far worse than bodily unchastity, because accompanied by a peculiar cold cruelty and a taste for artificial stimulants to "luxury". It is the sexlessness of a spayed canine imitated by the suggestive brain of humanity.' It was all most interesting.

There was also time while at Aden to have long talks with his friend John Steinhaeuser, now stationed here as a civil surgeon. They talked at great length about that remarkable collection of Arabic folklore commonly known as *The Arabian Nights*. Some of the tales, much expurgated, were quite well known in England, being considered suitable reading for children. But both Burton and Steinhaeuser had read and heard many of the stories in Arabic and knew what they contained. 'The most familiar book in England next to the Bible,' Burton wrote, 'it is the least known, the reason being that about one-fifth is utterly unfit for translation, and the most sanguine Orientalist would not dare to render more than three-quarters of the remainder.' Still, Burton and Steinhaeuser toyed with the idea of making a 'full, complete, unvarnished, uncastrated, copy of the great original' with Burton translating the poetry and Steinhaeuser the prose.

They also dreamed the occasional dream of all active men: of retiring to some quiet place where, without books or papers, worries or careers, they could lie in hammocks and enjoy the quiet life. Burton thought he knew just the place in the south of France. Neither included women in their retreat; and it is quite certain that Burton gave no thought to the young girl with whom he had flirted briefly in Boulogne. But she thought of him. In fact, she thought of little else. In her diary she wrote, 'Now Richard has gone off to Harar, a deadly expedition or a most dangerous one and I am full of forebodings. Will he never come home? How strange it all is, and how I still trust in Fate! The Crimean War is declared, and troops begin to go out.'

Harar, Burton's destination, although only about 150 miles from the coast, had never been entered by a European. Attempts had been made by a number of explorers and missionaries in the past, but all had failed. Africans and Arabs who had been to Harar told of a bigoted and despotic ruler presiding over a barbarous people. There was a superstition that Harar would prosper only until the first Frank entered the city. For this reason, great care was taken to exclude Europeans, and all strangers of whatever nationality or race were suspect.

On Sunday, 29 October 1854, Burton, disguised as an Arab merchant, left Aden for the coast of Africa. Steinhaeuser, following an old Arab custom, threw the slipper of blessing at his back. With him Burton took three servants, all originally of the Habr Girhajis tribe of Somaliland. The chief of these was Mohammed Mahmud, generally called Al-Hammal ('the Porter'). This was an Aden police sergeant whom Burton described as 'a bull-necked, round-headed fellow of lymphatic temperament, with a lamp-black skin, regular features, and a pulpy figure'. He had run away from home at an early age to become a coal trimmer on an Indian warship. He had a 'prodigious inventiveness and a habit of perpetual intrigue', but he suffered, according to Burton, from the Somali weakness of showing in his face all that passed through his mind.

The second servant was Gulad, another Aden policeman. He was described as 'one of those long, live skeletons, common among the Somali: his shoulders are parallel with his ears, his ribs are straight as a mummy's, his face has not an ounce of flesh upon it'. Long Gulad, as he was called, had also run away from home as a small boy. Still a young man, he had risen in life from servant to policeman.

The third retainer was Burton's favourite. His name was Abdi Abokr, but Burton nicknamed him 'End of Time', an Arabic joke referring to the prophesied corruption of Moslems in the last days of the world. He had acquired a smattering of learning in the form of a great collection of popular sayings and clichés. Burton found him 'an admirable buffoon, skilful in filling pipes and smoking them . . . an individual of "many words and little work", infinite intrigue, cowardice, cupidity, and endowed with a truly evil tongue'. He was about forty years old with small, deep-set eyes, a hook nose, scattered teeth and a short, scant beard.

On 31 October 1854, Burton and his men landed at Zeila on the

Somaliland coast. They were met by a tall, black spearman who led them to Al-Hajj Sharmarkay bin Ali Salih, the governor of the town. Sharmarkay (the name means 'one who sees no harm') was a remarkable man who had raised himself from captain of a small native boat to chief of his tribe. This was done principally through British influence; and he was considered a friend of the English, having once been wounded in the arm defending the life of an English sea captain whose ship had been attacked and plundered by the natives. Burton had met Sharmarkay in Aden where the latter had received instructions from the authorities to take care of him. Now, however, it was necessary to pretend they had never met, and the pulpy Hammal solemnly introduced them.

Sharmarkay received him kindly and installed him in a substantial two-storied mud house well furnished with Persian rugs, silk cushions and bats. Burton stayed twenty-six 'quiet, similar, uninteresting days' in Zeila, then a town of about 1,500 people. Because of a shortage of water, not a single horse, mule or dog was found, and vegetables were unknown. He spent his time smoking pipes, drinking coffee, talking with the natives about religion, politics and customs, and, when Arabs were present, reading aloud tales from *The Arabian Nights*. Meanwhile, guides were hired, camels bought, mules were sent for, and all the preparations made for the trek inland.

Burton, being an amateur barbarian himself, did not seem to mind the delay. He studied the Somali weapons and took as great a delight as the savages in exercising with their spears, knobsticks and eighteen-inch daggers. He considered their spear a 'puerile weapon' easily countered by a steady man in a day time fight, but, as he was to learn, it was a terrible weapon in a night attack when it could be hurled unseen. Burton soon acquired the reputation of being the strongest man in Zeila. This, he said, was 'the easiest way of winning respect from a barbarous people, who honour body, and degrade mind to mere cunning'.

The Somali women were rather pretty, he thought, except that, like the men, they always wore a deep scowl. This was all they wore, but for Burton, 'a black skin always appears a garb'. However, one girl, at least, seems to have fallen madly in love with him. She followed him about everywhere sighing, '*Wa wanaksan! – O fine!*' It was very flattering – even if she was only four years old.

About the end of November, five camels were obtained, two women cooks and a fourth servant were hired, an Isa *abban*, or guide, was engaged, and 'affairs began to wear the semblance of departure'. But at Zeila, as at Aden, no one believed he would return alive. Even the *abban* warned of danger and thought Burton must be tired of life to undertake such a journey. Zeila itself was hardly safe. Six or seven murders were committed in the small town during Burton's short stay and around the outskirts ominous nomadic tribesmen could be seen leaning on their spears, their great shocks of hair dyed red and dripping with rancid butter; many wore the ostrich feather to show they had proved their manhood by killing a man. But Burton was determined to start, even though he still did not have enough animals to carry all his baggage. Then, on 26 November, a boat landed and disgorged four fine mules for the expedition. It seemed a miracle.

The next day, he set out from Zeila. His route led south through the Isa country and then south-west through the lands of the Gudabirsi and Girhi tribes to the outskirts of Harar. His disguise of a well-to-do Moslem merchant enabled him to pose as an oriental, though a foreigner. Once again he was Haji Abdullah, the pious Moslem.

For his trading stock, he carried bales of American sheeting, Cutch canvas, coarse Surat tobacco, beads, earrings, watches and other trinkets. His servants from Aden returned to their native costume and greased their hair, oiled and blackened their spears, and carried new shields covered with canvas. They stowed their guns in the camels' packs, feeling that while such tools might be useful in Aden, they were effeminate in Somaliland.

His first night out, Burton slept with his rifle beside him but with 'none of that apprehension which even the most stout-hearted traveller knows before the start. . . . He who feels a thrill of fear before engaging in a peril, exchanges it for a throb of exultation when he finds himself hand to hand with the danger.'

The next morning they reached the kraal of their Isa guide, Raghi. The *abban* disappeared and they were at once surrounded by the tribesmen, who leaned on their spears and inspected them carefully while they muttered uncomplimentary remarks about foreigners and derided the merchant's weapons. Burton thought it necessary to make an impression. Seeing a bare-necked vulture about fifty feet away, he took aim and shot it. The Isa tribesmen were properly astonished. He then loaded with swan shot and brought down a second vulture on the wing. This feat brought satisfying cries of wonder from the crowd, one woman exclaiming, 'Lo, he brings down the birds from heaven.' When Burton distributed a bit of tobacco, they were all on good terms.

The tribe was about to migrate, so Burton, who wanted to see the spectacle, went with them. The next day the tribe moved out with about 150 spearmen and their families, 200 cows, 7,000 camels and 11,000 sheep and goats. On the following day, however, Burton told his *abban* that he wanted to move south-west across the desert. At Zeila, Raghi had promised to provide twenty of his tribesmen as an escort across the desert, but now only five or six paupers appeared. Burton turned them away, insisting that Raghi at least provide three of his relatives. After considerable argument, this was arranged and, about six o'clock in the evening, they set out across the desert towards a thin, blue strip of hills on the far horizon.

Burton's little expedition now consisted of the *abban* and his three kinsmen, the lumpy Hammal, the gaunt Long Gulad, the knavish End of Time, a one-eyed youth Burton called the Kalendar (from the story of the one-eyed kalendars in *The Arabian Nights*) and two buxom cooks who were given the classical names of Shahrazad and Dunyazad, after the teller of the tales in *The Arabian Nights* and her sister who encouraged her. Of the women Burton said, 'They look each like three average women rolled into one, and emphatically belong to that race for which the feminine attire called, I believe, a "bussle" [*sic*] would be quite superfluous.'

He was pleased to find that, unlike many primitive people, none of his party was afraid of the dark, although they were concerned about snakes, scorpions and plundering parties – and with good reason. Even Burton wore twists of black wool around his ankles to protect him from snakes and scorpions and he carried pistols and rifles to keep off bandits. The first night's march was anything but pleasant. They crossed a plain covered with the holes of field rats, ground squirrels, lizards and snakes. Shahrazad almost stepped on a viper. Hyenas howled and jackals barked. They moved rapidly and silently, but it was necessary to stop almost every fifteen minutes to adjust the slipping loads of the camels.

About 11 p.m. Burton called a halt and, in spite of the *abban's* warning against fires lest they be seen by marauders, Burton lit his pipe. They had travelled about twelve miles. A night wind from the hills chilled them through and Long Gulad became 'stiff as a mummy' from cold. They slept on the ground until 5 a.m., then resumed their march until 10 a.m. when the sun became too oppressive. They halted and slept until 3 p.m., then went on until evening.

Just before dark they came upon the fresh tracks of about 200 horsemen of the Habr Awal, a tribe with a deserved reputation as brigands. Terror seized the party. Their fear angered Burton, but the End of Time, impervious to his fuming, supplied the appropriate cliché: 'Verily, O pilgrim, who so seeth the track, seeth the foe!' and he quoted what Burton called 'those dreary lines':

> *Man is but a handful of dust,*
> *And life is a violent storm.*

They pressed on for another hour until the camels threw themselves on the ground from exhaustion and the women were lamed by thorns. A bivouac was made and the march was not resumed until six the next morning. They then continued on over rough, stony ground until they came upon an Isa kraal where they were hospitably received. Camp was made and they remained here until the middle of the following day when two Gudabirsi tribesmen appeared to escort them to the village of their *abban*.

Slowly, painfully, but safely, they marched over the Zeila Hills to the Marar plains. Villages became more numerous and Burton had ample opportunity to study the customs of the Somalis. Haji Abdullah's disguise was a failure, however. Here the natives could not tell a Turk from an Englishman and because he was not black he was marked only as an alien. He was mistaken for 'the ruler of Aden, the chief of Zayla . . . a boy, an old woman, a man painted white, a warrior in silver armour, a merchant, a pilgrim, a hedge priest, Ahmad the Indian, a Turk, an Egyptian, a Frenchman, a Banyan, a shariff, and lastly a Calamity sent down from heaven to weary out the lives of the Somal'.

At each kraal they were stopped and asked for news. Crowds would gather and listen intently to even the most trivial information. Burton recorded an example of a Somali imparting the news that he had been to the well: The headman of a kraal asks 'What is the news?' The new arrival gravely dismounts, places his spears before him, looks around, takes out his quid of coarse tobacco and puts it behind his ear, spits, squats on his heels and replies, 'It is good news, if Allah please!'

'*Wa sidda!* – Even so!' answer the crowd of listeners as they squat behind their shields and spears in a semicircle.

'I mounted mule this morning,' says the tale-teller.

'Even so!' reply the listeners.

'I departed from you riding.'

'Even so!'

'I threaded the wood.'

'Even so!'

'I traversed the sands.'

'Even so!'

'I feared nothing!'

'Even so!'

'At last I came upon cattle tracks.'

'Hoo! hoo! hoo!!' cries the crowd in astonishment.

The speaker makes an impressive pause and then says, 'They were fresh.'

'Even so!'

'So were the earths.'

'Even so!'

'I distinguished the feet of women.'

'Even so!'

'But there were no camels.'

'Even so!'

'At last I saw sticks.'

'Even so!'

'Stones.'

'Even so!'

'Water.'

'Even so!'

'A well!!'

Although tired by such courteous palavers at every stop, the custom enabled Burton to make friends with the various Somali clans and tribes and so learn much of their customs and language. As usual, he paid particular attention to the young women, noting that 'some of the girls have fine figures with piquant, if not pretty, features'. On 6 December, however, he saw his 'first really pretty face' in Somaliland. She had a well formed head, long thin neck, 'an arch look in the eyes', and a skin that was a 'warm, rich nut-brown'. She was graceful in her movements and wore a cloth that imperfectly covered her breasts. He gave her some cloth, tobacco, and a bit of his precious salt. Her husband was standing near at hand, but he showed neither anger nor jealousy at Burton's attentions. The girl expressed her gratitude by bringing him milk and helping to pack his gear the next morning.

On 10 December, Burton became ill. Bad water, bad food and temperature changes ranging from 107° at midday to 51° at night, had all affected his health. The next day the End of Time tried a local remedy. Making a fire by rubbing two sticks together, he proceeded vigorously to cauterize Burton's stomach, quoting an old adage: 'The end of physic is fire.' It did not help.

In spite of the pain in his bowels, Burton insisted on going forward. He was met by the sons of Ali Addah, a noted chief, and escorted by them to his village, several days' march away. As they drew closer and closer to Harar, they heard more and more tales of the terrors that awaited them at their destination. Burton was told, 'They will spoil that white skin of thine at Harar!' But he marched on.

There was much talk of lions and the Somalis had a great fear of them, but they only saw one. During a night march when Burton was riding in the rear, his mule pricked up its ears and uneasily tried to turn its head. Looking back, Burton saw the form of a huge lion stealthily following them. There was not enough moonlight for good shooting, but he frightened him off with a rifle shot.

In one kraal a bridle for one of the mules was stolen. This was the only case of theft Burton encountered in the course of the entire trip and he commented, 'I have travelled through most civilized lands, and have lost more.'

Christmas of 1854 came and went unnoticed. The desert was behind them now. Nomadic tribes were replaced by little settlements where land was cultivated and the kraals were replaced by villages of bell-shaped huts. On 27 December they entered the straggling village of Wilensi, home of the Jirad, or chief, of this area. They were well received and Burton, Long Gulad and the End of Time were lodged at the house of the Jirad's prettiest wife. Here the final arrangements were made for the visit to Harar, now only a few short marches away.

Smallpox was reported to be raging at Harar, so Shahrazad and Dunyazad, fearing for their complexions, begged to be left behind. Burton consented, deciding to leave them, along with most of his baggage, in charge of the Kalendar. Taking only what could be carried in leather saddle-bags on one mule, Burton, Long Gulad, Al-Hammal, the End of Time and an *abban* called Said Wal set off on the morning of 29 December for the last lap of the trip.

They travelled about fifteen miles under clumps of shady trees, over rocky dry river-beds, and down paths through tall cacti. On both sides of them were deep clefts and ravines. Late in the afternoon they reached the village of Sagharrah where they were received by Jirad Adan bin Kaushan, 'one of those cunning idiots so peculiarly difficult to deal with'. Burton had hoped the Jirad would himself take them to Harar.

Burton, about 1855

Toda family and village, from Goa and the Blue Mountains

The cathedral of Goa, from Goa and the Blue Mountains

Burton outside his tent, c. 1859

Going to cover, from Falconry in the Valley of the Indus

Al-Madinah, from Pilgrimage to Al-Madinah and Meccah

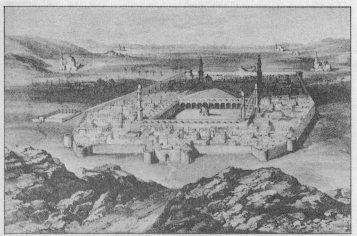

The takhtrawan or Grandee's litter, from Pilgrimage to Al-Madinah and Meccah

Harar from the Coffe Stream, from First Footsteps in East Africa, or, An Exploration of Harar

Richard Burton dressed as 'Sheik Abdullah', his disguise in Arabia

*Isabel and
Richard Burton
at the time
of their marriage*

John Hanning Speke (above) *and General Sir Charles Napier*

Explorers in East Africa;

A Ladies' Smoking Party;

The Wazaramo Tribe;
from Lake Regions of Central Africa

As presents, he gave him a sword, a Koran, a turban, a gaudy satin waistcoat and many cloths. The Jirad was powerful and reputed to be brave, but he preferred walking into the mouth of a crocodile to entering the walls of Harar.

At this crucial stage in his journey, Burton again fell violently ill with pains in his stomach. Everyone in Sagharrah was most sympathetic. Two of the Jirad's daughters sacrificed a sheep, two sons insisted on burning his stomach, and the Jirad sent for millet beer. Burton, who did not like any kind of beer anyway, found the mixture detestable. 'The taste is sour, and it flies directly to the head,' he complained. Crowds of people flocked to see him and wept at the evil fate that had led him so far from his homeland to die under a tree. He did indeed seem close to death. But the thought that the dashing Captain Burton should 'expire of an ignoble colic' was too much for him. He made a firm resolution to live, and he did.

On 1 January 1855, he felt well enough to dress in his Arab best and have another palaver with the Jirad. He read him a letter from Haji Sharmarkay asking for his co-operation and he again entreated the chief to assist him in reaching Harar safely. While they were talking, five strangers rode up: two were citizens of Harar and three were of the Habr Awal, a tribe of plunderers that stood high in the confidence of the Amir of Harar. These men regarded Burton with keen-eyed suspicion, and questioned him closely concerning his business and his intentions. When Burton left, they told the Jirad that the Arab *haji* was not really a merchant at all, but a spy sent to inspect the wealth of the land. They suggested to the Jirad that he make Burton and his whole party prisoners and send them to the Amir of Harar in their custody. The Jirad refused, telling them they were wrong to think such thoughts and advising them to 'throw far those words'. Unconvinced, the five departed for Harar late in the afternoon. When they had gone, Burton asked the Jirad point-blank to accompany him to Harar. The Jirad as pointedly refused. There was nothing to do, Burton decided, 'but *payer d'audace*, and, throwing all forethought to the dogs, to rely upon what has made many a small man great, the good star'.

Burton now proposed to throw off his Arab disguise and to enter Harar boldly as an Englishman. He had two reasons for this decision: 'All the races amongst whom my travels lay, hold him niddering who hides his origin in places of danger; and secondly, my white face had converted me into a Turk, a nation more hated and suspected than any European, without our prestige.' The first reason was a strange one for

Burton to offer; undoubtedly it was the second which was really valid. As an excuse for his visit, he forged both a letter purporting to be from the Political Agent at Aden to the Amir of Harar and instructions for himself to deliver it in person.

The End of Time, who was petrified with fear, was left behind with more of the baggage. Taking only a change of clothes, a few biscuits, guns and ammunition, a couple of books, some tobacco and presents for the Amir, Burton set out for Harar on the morning of 2 January, accompanied only by Long Gulad, Al-Hammal and two Girhi tribesmen. That evening they were hospitably received in a village in spite of the presence of the two men from Harar who had accused him to the Jirad and had arrived before them at the village. These men threatened the villagers with the wrath of the Amir if they so much as gave food to the strangers.

Setting out early the following morning, Burton, accompanied now only by his two servants, hurried on over the last lap of his journey. At two o'clock in the afternoon he pulled up under a spreading tree for his first view of the city of Harar, visible about two miles away on the crest of a hill. Burton recorded his impressions of the sight: 'The spectacle, materially speaking, was a disappointment: nothing conspicuous appeared but two grey minarets of rude shape: many would have grudged exposing three lives to win so paltry a prize. But of all that have attempted, none ever succeeded in entering that pile of stone: the thorough-bred traveller . . . will understand my exultation, although my two companions exhanged glances of wonder.'

An hour's ride brought them to the gates of the city. There they were halted by a surly guard. Through him Burton sent a message to the Amir saying that he came from Aden with a letter for him and requested the privilege of an audience. While waiting for an answer, Burton, Long Gulad and Al-Hammal squatted beside a round bastion where they were 'scrutinized, derided, and catechized by the curious of both sexes'. The three Habr Awal tribesmen who had seen him at the Jirad Adan's village came up to Burton with scowls on their faces and demanded to know why he had not told them of his intention to enter the city. Burton did not reply.

After a half-hour's wait, the guard returned and led them down the main street of Harar. When they were about a hundred yards from a gate of halcus stalks, the guard shouted at them angrily in Harari, which they did not understand, and made signs for them to dismount. Burton and his companions dismounted. The guard then broke into a trot and motioned for them to run behind him. Burton refused. Instead, he led his mule leisurely forward. Passing through the gate, they entered an irregularly shaped courtyard about eighty yards long and thirty feet wide, surrounded by low buildings, and filled with Galla tribesmen. The angry-voiced guard placed them under a tree in a corner of the courtyard beside a low building of rough stone. From inside the building came the ominous sounds of clanking fetters that told them this was a prison.

The guard disappeared, but presently returned and motioned for them to follow him. About twelve feet from the door of the central building they were made to take off their slippers and give up some of their weapons. Burton obstinately refused to part with his daggers and revolver. The guard then led them to a doorway and raised a curtain. Burton passed through to find himself in the presence of Sultan Ahmad bin Abu Bakr, the dreaded Amir of Harar.

Burton regarded the Amir closely. He found him to be 'an etiolated youth twenty-four or twenty-five years old, plain and thin-bearded, with a yellow complexion, wrinkled brows and protruding eyes'. He was dressed in a long red robe edged with white fur and he wore a narrow white turban wrapped around a tall, conical hat of red velvet. He was reclining on a small cot, resting his elbow on a pillow, under which was a Cutch sabre. In two lines in front of the Amir stood his relatives and advisers. Around the walls of the room hung rusty matchlocks and polished fetters.

When he entered the throne room Burton called out loudly in Arabic, 'Peace be upon you!' The Amir replied by extending his bony, yellow hand and snapping his fingers. Two court officials stepped forward and, holding his forearms, assisted Burton in bending low over the fingers. He could not bring himself to kiss the hand, 'being naturally adverse to performing that operation upon any but a woman's hand'.

After Long Gulad and Al-Hammal had also been presented, they were led to a mat in front of the Amir and seated. Burton began the conversation by polite inquiries into the state of the Amir's health, but these questions were quickly brushed aside and he was asked directly why he had come. Burton took his letter from his pocket and a court official carried it to the Amir. The ruler glanced at it, saw it was written in English, laid it aside, and demanded further explanation. Burton launched into a little speech about how he had come from the Governor of Aden to see the Amir and bring him the friendship of the English people. The speech was larded with many compliments, and it was greeted with a gracious smile. Inwardly, Burton sighed with relief. It was the first sign he had received that he would not be killed.

The audience over, Burton and his men were shown to a room in another house belonging to the Amir. There they were served a dinner consisting of holcus cakes soaked in sour milk and covered with a thick coating of red pepper. When they had eaten, the Amir's treasurer, an ugly man with coarse features, a pug nose, angry eyes and a stubby beard, appeared with a command from the Amir that they call upon Jirad Mohammed, the wazir, or prime minister. Burton hastened to comply and was led to the house of that powerful official.

Burton had heard many reports of the evil nature of Jirad Mohammed, so he was surprised to find him a venerable old man with a kindly face. He was seated on a carpeted stone bench surrounded by reeds, inkstands and the whitewashed boards that were used for paper. The wazir asked in excellent Arabic why he had come to Harar and Burton replied with the same speech he had made to the Amir, concluding with the wish that the English people could establish friendly relations and commercial intercourse with the people of Harar.

'*Khayr Inshallah!* – it is well, if Allah please!' exclaimed the Jirad.

With a low bow, Burton left and returned to his assigned quarters. He then sent a present of a six-barrelled revolver to the Amir, saw that his mules were watered and fed, and lay down on a bed of pillows, exhausted by fatigue and nervous tension. He had accomplished his mission and had passed his first test. So far, he had been lucky, but he was well aware of his precarious position: 'I was under the roof of a bigoted prince whose least word was death; amongst a people who detest foreigners; the only European who had ever passed over their inhospitable threshold, and the fated instrument of their future downfall.'

After a day of rest, he was again summoned to appear before Jirad Mohammed. He received a cordial reception and was seated beside the wazir on his mat. With him were a number of elders, one of whom read a long *Dua*, or Blessing upon the Prophet. During this exercise Burton had an opportunity to distinguish himself by displaying his Islamic learning. The reader of the Dua misread a line as 'Angels, Men and Jinnis'. The Jirad took the book from the old man and read it correctly as 'Men, Angels and Jinnis'. This started a discussion as to which were the higher order of beings, men or angels. Opinions among the elders were divided when Burton interposed his explanation that men were higher than angels because prophets, saints and apostles were men, whereas angels were merely a connection between the Creator and the created. This theology won general approval and Burton was regarded with greater respect by the elders.

The discussion was interrupted by a call from the Amir and both Burton and the wazir hastened to attend him. After a few preliminary remarks, the Amir suddenly produced Burton's letter, looked at it suspiciously and demanded to know what it said. Burton explained. The Amir then asked if he intended to buy and sell at Harar. Burton answered, 'We are no buyers nor sellers. We have become your guests to pay our respects to the Amir – whom may Allah preserve! – and that the friendship between the two powers may endure.'

This reply seemed to be satisfactory, so Burton entered upon another topic that was already beginning to concern him. When would the Amir give him an answer to take back to Aden and allow him to depart in peace? The air of Harar was too dry for his lungs, he said, and his attendants were in danger of the smallpox then raging in the town. The only answer he received was that he would be given a reply. He was not told when. This was not very satisfactory, but the Amir signalled that the interview was ended.

Having expended considerable effort getting into Harar, Burton now began to devote his time to the business of getting out. He directed most of his efforts towards the influential Jirad Mohammed. The wazir had an ailment, which Burton diagnosed as chronic bronchitis and promised to send remedies from Aden just as soon as he returned there. By this tactic he hoped to enlist the support of the wazir in his efforts to obtain the Amir's permission to depart. To attempt an escape without permission would have been suicide, he knew.

In the meantime, he took every opportunity to look about him and to learn as much as possible about the town and its citizens. The town itself was unimpressive. It was about a mile long and a half-mile wide, surrounded by an irregular wall with five gates. The only large building was the main mosque, 'a long barn of poverty-stricken appearance, with two broken-down gates, and two white-washed minarets'.

He found the men of Harar quite ugly with coarse and debauched features. Many were disfigured by smallpox, scrofula and other diseases. The women, by contrast, appeared beautiful to him: 'They have small heads, regular profiles, straight noses, large eyes, mouths approaching the Caucasian type, and light yellow complexions.' But they also tattooed their breasts with stars, dyed their eyebrows, fringed their eyes with kohl, and stained their hands and feet with henna.

According to Burton, 'both sexes are celebrated for laxity of morals' and occasionally it was necessary to flog a woman. Describing this operation, he said that a few gourds of cold water were first poured over the woman's head and shoulders and then a single-thonged whip was vigorously applied. He compared this with the custom in more modest Persia, where women were whipped inside a tent with their hands thrust through a hole in the tent wall and tied to a pole outside.

While Burton was so closely watched in Harar that he found it impossible to make notes or sketches, he learned all he could of the Harari language, a tongue spoken only by the 8,000 citizens of Harar. He believed the language to be more closely related to Amharic than to Arabic and maintained that the citizens of Harar were 'a distinct race'.

Burton was interested in Harar and the Harari, but he could never for a moment be at ease. Although free to wander about as he pleased, he knew that one false step would be the end for him. It was the most threatening position he had ever been in. But at last the day came when he was summoned before the Amir, given a letter to deliver to the Political Agent in Aden, and granted permission to leave the city.

He wanted to decamp at once, but the escape of a mule, bad weather and the words of a sheik that it was bad to leave on a Friday, the Moslem Sabbath, delayed their departure for a day. But before dawn on 13 January the mules were loaded, breakfast was hurriedly eaten, and Burton and his two attendants were ready to leave Harar. They had been in the city for ten anxious days. As they passed through the city gate, loudly salaaming the guards crouching over their fire, Burton had a feeling of intense relief. 'A weight of care and anxiety fell from me like a cloak of lead,' he said later.

Returning by the route that had brought them to Harar, they soon reached Wilensi. Here they halted for a week to rest, make plans and gather provisions for the return trip. The halt also gave Burton time to write up his notes and compile a vocabulary of Harari words. Instead of returning to the coast by the way they had come, Burton, although suffering from dysentery, wanted to make for Berbera. To do this, however, meant travelling through the land of the wild Habr Awal unless they attempted to skirt the Habr Awal country by going through the desert. This Burton decided to try.

The baggage, the women and the Kalendar were sent back to Zeila. Burton, with Long Gulad, the End of Time, and Al-Hammal prepared to make a mad dash across the desert. They had only one bottle of water among them and Burton took only a few limes, five biscuits, some sugar, and his arms and ammunition. This was not a caravan route. Any accident to the mules or their one water-bottle meant a terrible death, and Burton knew it.

It was a gruelling five day march:

The demon of Thirst rode like Care behind us – for twenty-four hours we did not taste water, the sun parched our brains, the mirage mocked us at every turn, and the effect was a species of monomania. As I jogged along with eyes closed against the fiery air, no image unconnected with the want suggested itself. Water ever lay before me, water lying in the shady well, water in streams bubbling icy from the rock, water in pellucid lakes inviting me to plunge and revel in its treasures. . . . I opened my eyes to a heat-reeking plain, and a sky of that eternal metallic blue so lovely to painter and poet, so blank and death-like to us. . . . I tried to talk – it was in vain; to sing – in vain; vainly to think, every idea was bound up in one subject – water.

Normally twenty-four to thirty hours without water in the desert will kill a man, but at one point Burton and his party went for thirty-six hours without water. They were close to death when Burton saw a 'katta' (apparently *tair el qata*, Arabic for sand-grouse). It was early evening, and the observant Burton had seen sand-grouse at this time of day drinking and carrying water in their bills to their young. 'See the katta! The katta!' he cried. They followed eagerly after the bird. It was, as Burton had hoped, going to a spring. Falling from their saddles, they plunged their heads into the water, the mules drinking with them. Grateful to the sand-grouse, Burton later wrote, 'I have never since shot a katta.'

Throughout this desert trip they had avoided all kraals for fear of the Habr Awal. On the night of 29 January, hearing the waves on the coast and thinking themselves among friendly tribes, they stopped to ask for water at a kraal. The inhabitants, however, turned out to be Ayyal Shirdon, deadly enemies of the Habr Girhajis, the tribe of Burton's attendants. Beating a retreat, they pushed on to the next kraal, hoping they would be among other tribes, but wherever they stopped that night they found the people in the kraals suspicious and in-hospitable; not one would give them a drop of water. It was not until early morning that they found some holes filled with bitter water. After fifteen hours of thirst, it tasted delicious.

At dawn on 30 January they came to Bulhar. Although today a

coastal settlement of about 7,000 souls, it was at this time a deserted ruin with only a heap of bleached bones to tell that it had once been inhabited.

Twenty-four hours more of flogging weary beasts and struggling with exhaustion brought them at last to Berbera. Burton was again safe among friends. Herne and Stroyan were waiting for him. He fell down on a cot to sleep, 'conscious of having performed a feat which, like a certain ride to York, will live in local annals for many and many a year'. Today, as far as can be determined, no one remembers.

Chapter 8

Incident at Berbera

1855

IT had been a neat exploit, the trip to Harar. It had taken courage, determination and endurance, and Burton had proved that he had these precious qualities in abundance. Now he wanted to follow up his success with a more ambitious expedition: a trek to the Nile from the Somaliland coast by way of Harar. How he overcame the objections and apprehensions of Colonel Outram is not known, but it is doubtful that he told him his true intentions.

By the time he reached Aden, on 12 February 1855, the other three officers had completed their missions. Herne and Stroyan had been successful on the coast and in Berbera. Speke, due to the treachery of his guide, had failed and returned to Aden in January. All three were to go with Burton on this new expedition.

Burton spent two months in Aden making his preparations. It was at this time that he learned of the death of his mother on 18 December 1854, but he did not pause. When the arrangements were complete, men, animals and baggage were transported to the mainland and assembled at Berbera. Burton was now in command of a party that included forty-two men of assorted races and nationalities and sufficient camels, horses and mules to move inland. Following a Moslem custom, he carried in his baggage his own shroud, the one he had bought from the boy Mohammed just before making the pilgrimage. In Berbera he almost had need of it.

On 7 April camp was made just outside Berbera on a rocky ridge under the protection of the East India Company Schooner *Mahi*, the small gunboat which had brought the expedition from Aden. The tents were pitched in a line with Stroyan on the right, Speke on the left, and Burton and Herne in the centre. The baggage was placed between the tents of Burton and Speke. The fifty-six camels were tethered in a sandy bed below the ridge in front of the tents and the mules and horses behind. At night, two sentries were posted, regularly relieved and periodically checked.

As Burton later wrote, 'We saw no grounds for apprehension. During thirty years, not an Englishman of the many that had visited it had been molested at Berberah, and apparently there was as little to fear in it as within the fortifications of Aden.' The local chiefs had listened respectfully to a letter from the British Political Agent at Aden asking them to treat Burton and his party with 'consideration and respect'. Besides, a great annual market, where inland tribes brought to the coast their slaves, gum, cattle, ivory and rhinoceros horns to be traded for cloth, beads, rice and dates, was just coming to an end. It was a peaceful, if primitive, setting.

Burton delayed the departure of his expedition from the coast in the hope of soon receiving an expected load of instruments and supplies from Europe. His eagerness to start was also tempered by his desire to see the end of the local fair. He had urged the captain of the *Mahi* to stay until they were on their way, but the gunboat had to relieve another ship on blockade duty and could not wait.

On 9 April an electric storm opened the Somali monsoon season and this acted as the signal for the end of the fair. Throughout Berbera, mats were taken from their frameworks, camels were loaded, and thousands of people set out for the long march to their inland homes. Except for the camp of the expedition, Berbera was nearly deserted by 15 April.

On 18 April a small craft entered the harbour with about a dozen Somali passengers who asked to accompany the expedition for some distance inland. Fortunately, Burton delayed the boat by feasting the captain and his crew with rice and dates so that it stayed off shore for an extra day.

At sunset, several musket shots were heard behind the tents. Investigating, Burton discovered that the sentries had fired over the heads of three horsemen to frighten them away from the camp. Burton reprimanded his men for this 'act of folly', ordering them to save their ammunition until it was needed. But the horsemen held their ground, not at all frightened by the shots of the sentries. Since it was possible they were scouts for a raiding party, Burton invited them to come closer so he could interrogate them. They complied and answered his questions readily enough. Their replies convinced him they meant no harm. That night the camp went to sleep with no thought of imminent danger.

Between two and three o'clock in the morning, Burton was awakened by a wild cry that the enemy was upon them. Leaping from his cot, he called for his sabre and ordered Lieutenant Herne to find out what was happening. They could hear the sound of moving men, cries of alarm and the noise of violence to the left and rear of the camp. Herne seized his Colt revolver and set out with some of the guard in the general direction of the disturbance. He had not gone far when a crowd of Somali tribesmen rushed towards him. Herne fired two shots into the crowd, then found himself alone. His own men had deserted him; the enemy had rushed on. He turned to go back to the tents, but in the dark he tripped over a rope and fell to the ground. As he struggled to his feet, he found standing over him a Somali with raised club, ready to bring it down on his head. Herne quickly fired and killed him, then ran to the tents.

Here he found Burton with Speke and Stroyan. Now the enemy was all around them and all but one of their own men had disappeared. The remaining man, called Al-Balyuz, was to prove more of a handicap than a help. Herne joined the group clustered in front of Burton's tent. Shortly after, they found that Stroyan – there a moment ago – was missing. Speke and Herne had pistols, but Burton stood between them with only his naked sabre.

As Speke stood hesitantly in front of the tent, he was hit by several stones from one side. He moved back under the fly. Burton snapped at him, 'Don't step back or they will think we are retiring.' Speke was piqued. Describing the incident later, he said, 'Chagrined by this rebuke at my management in fighting, and imagining by the remark that I was expected to defend the camp, I stepped boldly to the front, and fired at close quarters into the first man before me.' Filled with his personal grievance, he kept on walking straight into the camp and within minutes was separated from his companions.

The three men left were forced back into the tent. Herne fired from its shelter with good effect, but his ammunition was soon exhausted. He crawled out to find more bullets or at least to get some spears he had tied to his tent pole. Outside, he spied a man trying to worm through the back of Burton's tent. He crawled back to warn his companions of the danger.

The attacking Somalis tried to cut the tent ropes and entangle them in the folds of the tent. Burton gave the order for a sally and led the way out. There appeared to be about twenty men immediately in front of the tent and beyond them could be heard others, screaming war cries and driving off the expedition's animals.

Skilfully wielding his sabre, Burton cut his way through the mob before him. Thinking he saw Stroyan lying on the sand, he hacked his

way towards him through a dozen club-swinging Somalis. He was
handicapped, however, by Al-Balyuz, sheltering behind him, who
kept pushing him forward, spoiling his strokes. Once Burton mistook
him for an enemy Somali and turned to cut him down. The man cried
out in alarm and Burton, hearing the familiar voice, hesitated. At that
moment a Somali tribesman stepped forward and drove a javelin
through Burton's cheek, knocking out four back teeth and ripping
his palate. Burton reeled and staggered away.

Another of his own men appeared on the scene, Golab of the Yusuf
tribe, and Burton sent him to search for the boat. Golab set off while
Burton continued to stumble about in the dark looking in vain for his
companions. Almost fainting from the pain of his wound, he was forced
to lie down on the ground from time to time to keep his senses. Dawn
found him staggering towards the head of a little creek that ran into
the sea. There he was picked up by members of the crew of the little
ship whom he had feasted the night before.

Had the ship sailed earlier, Burton would not have survived. In spite
of his weakness, pain and fatigue, he was able to persuade the captain to
arm his men and return to the camp to look for Speke and Stroyan.
Lieutenant Herne was already on board. Following Burton in the sally
from the tent, he had used the butt of his revolver on the heads around
him until he was clear of the mêlée. Searching in the dark for his friends,
he passed through a dozen Somalis who were loudly calling, 'Kill the
Franks!' but they had allowed him to pass unmolested. At last he, too,
had made his way towards the ship and, with only some bad bruises,
had reached it shortly before Burton.

The search party sent out by the ship soon came upon Speke. He had
not been as fortunate as Herne, but he was lucky to be alive. Shortly
after leaving the tent, he had been knocked to the ground by a blow
from a war club on his chest. Two or three men had instantly jumped
on him and pinioned his arms. After searching him and tying his hands,
one of the Somalis pulled him away from the fighting. Instead of being
killed as he expected, he was actually defended by his captor from the
other Somalis and was even given a drink of water. Speke lay upon the
ground until morning, witnessing the victory celebration of the savage
Somalis as they marched around the tents and the booty, singing with
their deep voices a solemn song. A little further away, he could see in
the grey light of early dawn several badly wounded Somalis on the
ground. They were being tended by their kinsmen or friends who
kneaded their limbs, poured water on their wounds, and put dates in

their stiffening hands – if a fallen Somali lacked the strength to eat this delicacy, he was considered as good as dead.

With morning came the division of the spoils. The victors quarrelled loudly among themselves for the cloth, animals and weapons. Speke's captor left him to get his own share of the loot. Another Somali came to where Speke was lying on the ground and asked if he was a Moslem or a Nazarene, adding that if he was not a Moslem he would kill him. Speke answered that he was a Christian and the savage might as well kill him. The Somali laughed and left him.

A second tribesman then approached him. Swinging a sword menacingly above his head, he twice pretended to make the fatal stroke that would behead the helpless prisoner, but he also left without doing him any injury. Then a third man came upon him and brought down his spear to run him through the breast. By this time, however, Speke had managed to untie his hands. Grabbing the spear, he turned it away from his heart. But the savage also had a club and he smashed it against Speke's arm, temporarily paralysing it. Then, wrenching his spear free, the savage jabbed furiously at Speke, wounding him on the hand, back, right shoulder and left thigh. Jumping quickly to the other side of the wounded man, he drove his spear through his right leg.

Gathering all his remaining energy, Speke leaped to his feet. The astonished Somali fled. Speke, running as fast as he was able, stumbled towards the sea. Fortunately, he looked back as he ran and was able to dodge a spear thrown at his back. Sinking behind a sandhill, he recovered his breath and tried to keep himself from fainting, for he had lost much blood. Staggering into the village of Berbera, he was directed by some old women in the direction of the boat. With eleven wounds, two of them in his thighs, he walked and ran three miles before he was picked up by the search party.

The camp site was deserted when the search party reached it, except for the corpses of several Somalis and the body of Lieutenant William Stroyan, stark and cold. A spear had passed through his heart and another had been stuck into his abdomen; there was a great gash on his forehead and his body showed signs of having been frightfully beaten after his death.

Burton tried to preserve the corpse for burial at Aden, but it decomposed too rapidly and they were forced to bury Stroyan at sea the following day. Lieutenant Herne read the burial service.

A Somali named Ao Ali was later seen wearing the ostrich feather to proclaim his murder of young Stroyan.

The reasons for the attack are unknown; probably the motive was simply a desire for loot. Burton never attempted an explanation, but – much later – Speke placed most of the blame on Burton for his failure to employ native *abbans*. Speke was sensitive to slights and he held secret grudges. He kept his antagonism and his unfavourable opinions of his chief to himself until he was ready to use them as ammunition for his revenge. Unfortunately for Burton, he knew nothing of these traits in his subordinate until it was too late.

Chapter 9

Cavalryman in the Crimea
1855 – 6

WHEN Burton returned to England after success and failure in Somaliland, he found that his exploits had attracted little attention. Britain was preoccupied with the Crimean War, which had already been in progress for a year. Even Isabel's thoughts had been briefly diverted by the war, and she wrote in her journal:

It has been an awful winter in the Crimea. I have given up reading *The Times*; it makes me so miserable, and one is so impotent. I have made three struggles to be allowed to join Florence Nightingale. How I envy the women who are allowed to go out as nurses! I have written again and again to Florence Nightingale; but the superintendent has answered me that I am too young and inexperienced, and will not do.

So Isabel organized a girls' club 'to do good at home amongst the destitute families of soldiers away in the Crimea'.

Burton, after reading a paper on his exploits to the Royal Geographical Society, asked for leave to volunteer for active service in the Crimea. After the disaster at Berbera, the war seemed an 'opportunity of recovering my spirits'. Obtaining the necessary permission, he armed himself with letters of introduction to various senior officers and set off for Balaclava via Marseilles and Constantinople. On arrival he found that while there was much talk of actively resuming the campaign, the bulk of the fighting was over. The Light Brigade had made its famous charge while Burton was riding his mule to Harar; the battles of Sevastopol and the Alma were finished; and now that spring had arrived, even the horrors of winter were over. Had Burton known Lord Raglan's attitude towards officers of the Bengal and Bombay armies he would have known how unlikely were his chances of obtaining an important post – or even an unimportant one. Lord Raglan, the Commander-in-Chief of the British forces in the Crimea, had an enormous contempt for 'Indian officers' and early in the war had issued instructions that such officers were to be discouraged from participating in the campaign. He preferred to rely upon blue blood and bravery rather than brains and experience. Since Indian Army officers were practically the only men with recent battle experience, his antipathy towards them was one of the reasons for the Crimean War being the most ill-managed military campaign in British history.

Before the Russians shut themselves up in Sevastopol and the Allied armies laid siege to them, it had been realized that the Crimea was excellent cavalry country. But owing to sickness in the ranks and to some incredibly stupid logistical arrangements, Lord Raglan's cavalry division, composed of one brigade of light cavalry and one of heavy, with some units of horse artillery, was too weak physically and in numbers to exploit the advantages of the terrain properly. It was suggested that a corps of Turkish irregular cavalry be raised to increase their strength. A very able officer, Colonel W. F. Beatson, was available to take command of such a unit. He had joined the Bengal Army at the age of sixteen and was now a most experienced cavalry officer. He had commanded a regiment during the Carlist war in Spain in 1835; he had been in command of the cavalry of the Nizam of Hyderabad; and he had been commended no less than fourteen times by the Government of India for his exploits. Colonel Beatson placed himself at the disposal of Lord Raglan.

The very thought of irregular horsemen, bashi-bazouks, mixed with his splendid and elegant British cavalry filled Lord Raglan with horror. It was unthinkable. As for Colonel Beatson, he was an 'Indian officer'. Lord Raglan would neither give him a command nor put him on his staff.

Beatson then applied to Lord Lucan, who commanded the cavalry division, but Lucan would not have him either. He tried Lord Cardigan, commander of the Light Brigade, and was again refused. Finally, General James Scarlett of the Heavy Brigade took him on his staff, although in doing so he was braving the disapproval of his superiors. It was Scarlett who, with Beatson's help, a few hours before the famous charge of the Light Brigade before Balaclava, launched the equally heroic and far more creditable charge of the Heavy Brigade, where 500 British troopers broke and scattered a body of more than 3,000 Russian cavalry while Lord Cardigan with his Light Brigade sat watching only 300 yards from the Russian flank.

Like Beatson, Burton made the rounds of the generals with his letters of introduction and offered his services. Naturally, he was refused. Had he arrived in the Crimea earlier, he would probably have given up in disgust and left. However, in June 1855, Lord Raglan died and his place was taken by General James Simpson who had served in India and was more open-minded about officers of the Indian Army. Beatson was promoted and given permission to raise a contingent of Turkish irregular cavalry that became known as 'Beatson's Horse'. Burton, who had met General Beatson in Boulogne, was appointed Chief of Staff.

Returning to Constantinople, he purchased the gaudy uniform, blazing with gold, of the bashi-bazouks. 'I was gorgeous,' said Burton. After enjoying the embassy society at Constantinople and seeing all the sights, he boarded an Austrian Lloyd steamer and went down the Dardanelles, to near Gallipoli, where his unit was stationed. There General Beatson with his wife and two daughters and a corps of Turkish cavalry was ensconced on a hillside.

Captain Burton immediately became embroiled in the local military and civil squabbles that centred around the corps. They were a wild, undisciplined lot of men who doubtless would have followed Beatson on the most reckless of charges, but they were not content to sit peacefully in a camp. Naturally there was constant friction between the bashi-bazouks, the civilian population and the other bodies of troops, mainly Turkish and French, in the area.

Burton later defended the corps, maintaining that they were not as bad as they were reported to be. He admitted there was a considerable amount of duelling among the half-civilized soldiery. The custom was for the two duellists to stand quite close to each other with cocked pistols in their right hands and glasses of fierce raki in their left. At a given signal they began to drink, and the one who finished first blazed away at his opponent. Burton did not discourage the practice; he only insisted on fair play. He maintained that the corps did not commit nearly as many outrages on the civil population as was reported: 'Only one woman was insulted and robbery with violence was exceptionally rare.' The periodic mutinies among the troops were brushed off by Burton as 'mere sky-larking'.

There was friction at all levels. Beatson was honest; the Turkish officials and local Europeans were not. Beatson denounced their skulduggery and threatened to hang the Military Pasha of the Dardanelles. They, in turn, reported the misdeeds of Beatson's men, through official channels and in the newspapers in Constantinople. On two separate occasions, investigators were sent down from Constantinople: the first was a civilian named Skene whom Beatson later sued for libel and the second was a Brigadier T. G. Neil whom Burton described as 'a universal unfavourite with Beatson's Horse'. Beatson quarrelled with both of them. Burton blamed the local Greeks, the Jews, the Turkish authorities, some German engineers, and the officers of French units stationed in the area for spreading the rumours.

In spite of the official quarrelling, some troop training was begun. Burton set about forming a riding school as some of the infantry officers assigned to the corps were insecure in their saddles, and he began a school of arms to train officers and men in the use of the sabre. He also had time to mature grand battle plans and even went to Constantinople with a project for the relief of Kars, which the Russian Army was then besieging. Lord Stratford de Redcliffe, the British Ambassador, to whom Burton set forth his proposal, was enraged that a mere subaltern of the Bombay Army should dare attempt to meddle with high strategy, and called him 'the most impudent man in the Bombay Army, Sir!' ending his tirade with, 'Of course you'll dine with us today?' Burton's conclusion was that the politicians had deliberately made a deal with the Russians to let them capture Kars.

Perhaps to compensate him for the rejection of his plan to save Kars, Burton was indirectly sounded concerning a project to send him through the Russian lines to make contact with Shamyl, the Caucasian leader of the Dagestan tribes who was waging his long and futile war for independence from Russia. As Shamyl was known as a ruffian who flogged women prisoners and Lord Stratford was a gentleman who disapproved of such actions, Burton was somewhat surprised. Nevertheless, he began to turn the plan over in his mind and at last took the matter up with Lord Stratford. He asked him exactly what his mission was to be and what he should say to Shamyl when asked why he had come. Lord Stratford was vague. 'Oh, say you were sent to report to me.'

'But, my lord,' replied Burton, 'Shamyl will expect money, arms, and possibly troops, and what am I to reply if he asks me about it? Otherwise he will infallibly set me down for a spy, and my chances of returning to Constantinople will be uncommonly small.'

As Lord Stratford could not see it that way, the project was abandoned.

Burton returned to his corps where there was trouble enough to occupy him. The bashi-bazouks had clashed with French soldiers stationed in the area and the authorities feared serious consequences. On the morning of 26 September 1855, the corps found itself virtually besieged, not by the enemy but by its own side. Turkish regulars were drawn up in battle array supported by artillery, cavalry and three gun-boats. The inhabitants of the town had closed their shops and the British Consulate was deserted. General Beatson was furious, but he ordered his men to remain in camp 'till the Turkish authorities have recovered from their panic and housed their guns'.

No shots were fired and the regulars were removed, but two days later an order removed Beatson from his command and ordered him to turn over his troops to Major-General Richard Smith. Burton, with a delegation of other officers, protested to General Smith that the troops were well disciplined and under control, but to no avail. Consequently, Burton, feeling he could 'no longer serve with self respect', resigned his post. He and Beatson left the Dardanelles and after unsuccessfully pleading their case in Constantinople, returned to London where Beatson set about suing the vice-consul whom he felt had sent in the most libellous reports about him.

Burton wanted to do all he could to help his chief, but he feared that a lawsuit would keep him too long in London. At first he tried to disguise the fact that he was there at all. He stuffed a pillow over his stomach and donned sun-glasses. Revealing himself to a friend, he was asked, 'Are you really Burton?'

'I shall be,' he said, 'but just now I'm a Greek doctor.'

In the end, Burton did testify at the trial, treating his examiners with great contempt. Mr (later Sir) William Bovill (who later, as Chief Justice of the Common Pleas, presided over the civil trial of the famous Tichborne Claimant) cross-examined Burton: 'In what regiment did you serve under the plaintiff?' he was asked.

'Eh?'

'In what regiment, I say. . . .'

'In no regiment.'

Eventually, Burton condescended to inform Bovill that he had served in a 'corps'.

In this trial Burton was doing more than giving evidence for Beatson. He himself was implicated. The defendant charged that:

When General Smith arrived at the Dardanelles, General Beatson assembled the commanding officers of the regiments and actually endeavoured to persuade them to make a mutiny in the regiments against General Smith and against the authority of [General] Vivian. Two of these commanding officers then left the room, saying they were soldiers and they could not listen to language they thought most improper. . . . General Beatson subsequently had a sort of round robin prepared by the chief interpreter and sent round to the different officers in the hope that they would sign it, refusing to serve under any other general than himself. Both of these mutinous attempts are said to have originated from Captain Burton. . . .

Although Beatson came off well in the press, he lost his case. While this was taking place, Burton was writing a series of letters to *The Times* proposing that a large force of Kurdish irregular cavalry be raised to assist Circassia and to attack Georgia. The end of the war brought an end to Burton's letters, and to his military schemes and ambitions as well.

He now tried to form a company for helping pilgrims reach Mecca. The company was to be called The Hajilik, or Pilgrimage to Mecca Syndicate, Limited, and was to have had a capital of £10,000 in 100 shares of £100 each. A prospectus was drawn up, but nothing ever came of the scheme.

In spite of his abortive adventure in Somaliland, Burton still had his heart set on the 'unveiling of Isis', i.e. discovering the source of the Nile. This feat, if it could be brought off, would bring him real and lasting fame. It was all very well to be a first-rate swordsman, speak a dozen languages and exhibit one's courage in Arabia and Somaliland, but it would be a different matter to discover the fountain-head of the historic Nile. In April 1856, he resolved to make the attempt.

In the nineteenth century, interest in physical geography was high, much as interest in space exploration is today. Then there were vast areas of the world unexplored and Europe was curious and aggressive. The day of the lone explorer who was little more than a wanderer returning with strange tales of adventure was passing. Exploration required money, equipment and organizations or associations to supply them. There were dozens of geographical societies, and nearly every European country had at least one. They encouraged and financed explorers and adventurers to search the unknown paths of the world, the white spaces on the maps. The sextant, chronometer, camera and the application of the rudiments of scientific method all contributed to making exploration more trustworthy and valuable; explorers were sent out to Asia, Australia, the Arctic, South America and Africa. Probably the oldest and most classic of the geographical problems, and certainly the one which generated the most public interest, was the riddle of the source of the Nile, the great river flowing north from the depths of an unknown continent, the source of its bounty a mystery. It was Burton's plan to lead an expedition into Africa from the east coast and, with luck, to discover the answer to this problem which had perplexed geographers and historians since Herodotus. He spent the summer of 1856 in London maturing his plans and seeking support.

During this period he also transformed his notes into a book about his Harar exploit: *First Footsteps in East Africa*; 'a curious record of a curious enterprise' said the *Athenaeum*. As usual, it was as full of footnotes as footsteps and one third of the entire work was taken up with appendices. Even so, one appendix was omitted. It dealt with infibulation, i.e. the practice of fastening a ring or clasp on the female genital organs in such a manner as to prevent coition. The publishers thought this essay a bit exotic for their taste and 'found it necessary' to leave it out. It is now lost.

One appendix was Speke's account, re-written by Burton, of his unsuccessful attempt to reach the Wadi Nogal. Burton considered Speke's own version 'unfit for publication': he objected to the style, to certain sentiments, and to his geographical assertions. He did not treat Speke's exploit as seriously as he did his own and he said in his concluding remarks that 'though he [Speke] was delayed, persecuted . . . and threatened with war, danger, and destruction, his life was never in real peril'. Burton also patronized his companion under the pretence of making excuses for him: Speke, he said, did not know Arabic or Somali, he was 'ignorant of the Moslem faith', and, as he did not wear a disguise, he was recognized everywhere as 'a servant of Government'. As the leader of the Somali expedition, Burton felt himself justified in taking liberties with the report of his subordinate.

Of course Burton included in his book much extraneous material and many unsupported theories. But anyone with as many theories and opinions as Burton was bound to be right sometimes, and in this book he put forth his opinion that the mosquito causes malaria.

Until the last few years of his life Burton felt that his activities were cramped by a lack of money. He had no interest in those activities by which money could be acquired, but this did not prevent him from feeling its want. In the disaster at Berbera he had lost all of his gear and kit and he felt the loss keenly. He thought the East India Company should make good his losses and he made vigorous efforts while in London to obtain compensation. He was most bitter when the Honourable Company refused.

Although occupied with his writing and his daring plans for the future, Burton was not so busy that he did not have time for his other interests. One August day he went strolling through the Botanical Gardens with a friend, Louisa Segrave, later described by his wife as a 'gorgeous creature of Boulogne – then married'. There they met Isabel Arundell, the gorgeous creature's cousin, walking with her sister and a girl friend. They stopped and shook hands, exchanging polite conversation. It had been four years since their last meeting. Isabel recorded that 'all the old Boulogne memories and feelings which had laid dormant, but not extinct, returned to me'. Burton asked Isabel if she came often to the botanical gardens.

'Oh yes,' replied Isabel, 'we always come and read and study here from eleven to one because it is so much nicer than staying in the hot rooms at this season.'

'That's right,' said Burton. 'What are you studying?'

The book Isabel clutched to her bosom was hardly one Burton would have thought of 'studying'. But it was Isabel's favourite: Disraeli's *Tancred*.

They talked for nearly an hour and then separated. As they moved off, Burton said to his companion, 'Do you know that your cousin has grown charming? I would not have believed that the little schoolgirl of Boulogne would have become such a sweet girl.'

'Ugh!' replied the gorgeous creature.

Having taken care to let Burton know the precise hours she frequented the park, Isabel was rewarded by finding him there on the following day. He was alone and composing poetry. Of course they had a long talk, and of course there were other meetings – daily.

It only took a fortnight. With Richard thinking of himself as the pursuer and Isabel intent on catching him, the result was inevitable. Burton put his arm around her waist, laid his cheek against hers, and began with some qualifying ifs. If he could obtain the consulate at Damascus and if Isabel 'could dream of doing anything so sickly as to give up civilization', would she go with him?

Isabel was struck dumb – not with surprise, but with relief and joy. Burton stumbled on, 'Don't give me your answer now, because it will mean a very serious step for you – no less than giving up your people and all that you are used to and living the sort of life that Lady Hester Stanhope led. I see the capabilities in you, but you must think it over.'

As Isabel remained silent he added, 'Forgive me! I ought not to have asked so much.'

Isabel found her voice. 'I don't want to "think it over". I have been thinking it over for six years, ever since I saw you at Boulogne on the ramparts. I have prayed for you every day, morning and night. I have followed your career minutely. I have read every word you ever wrote, and I would rather have a crust and a tent with *you* than be queen of all the world. And so I say now, Yes! YES! YES!'

Burton was caught, but he said, 'Your people will not give you to me.'

She answered, 'I know that, but I belong to myself – I give myself away.'

After this, he began calling on Isabel at her home – as an acquaintance of the family. Mrs Arundell found him shocking, but Isabel wrote that Burton 'completely magnetized' her father.

The romance blossomed. Isabel showed Burton the horoscope Hagar Burton had made for her in Romany when she was a girl. Only two months before encountering him in the Botanical Gardens, Isabel had again met the old gypsy at Ascot.

'Are you Daisy Burton yet?' the old woman had asked.

'Would to God I were,' Isabel had replied.

'Patience, it is just coming,' Hagar told her.

Now it had come – almost.

Already Isabel was concerned over the lack of true religious faith in her fiancé. It was the only thing which prevented him from being perfect. She arranged for Burton to meet Cardinal Wiseman, a friend of the family, at the Arundell home. Probably through Isabel's influence the cardinal was persuaded to give Burton special papers recommending him to Catholic missions in remote parts of the world.

Isabel's own faith, though ardent, was hardly orthodox. She was very superstitious and believed in magic spirits and dreams. One October night she dreamed that Burton came into her room on a current of warm air and, standing by her bed, said 'Good-bye, my poor child. My time is up and I have gone, but do not grieve. I shall be back in less than three years, and I am your destiny. Good-bye.' Then he held up a letter, looked long at her and went slowly out, shutting the door.

Isabel sprang out of bed and ran out into the hall. There was no one there. She ran into the room of one of her brothers who tried to learn what had happened to his distraught sister. 'Richard is gone to Africa and I shall not see him for three years,' she cried.

'Nonsense,' he replied, 'you have only got a nightmare. You told me he was coming at four in the afternoon.'

'So I did, but I have seen him and he told me this. If you will wait until the post comes in, you will see I have told you truly.'

All night long Isabel sat in her brother's armchair. At eight o'clock in the morning the mail arrived. Sure enough, Burton had written, but not to her. Instead there was a note to Blanche Pigott, her married sister, asking her to break the news to Isabel that he had gone.

The talk of a consulate in Damascus would have to wait; the exploration of Central Africa was more exciting. He carried with him a medal of the Blessed Virgin which Isabel had hung round his neck on their last afternoon together, but he rejected the gold chain that came with it – 'They will cut my throat for it out there,' he explained. He left to an unhappy Isabel the difficult task of breaking the news of their engagement to her parents and a little love poem – not to Isabel, but to Fame.

The poem was hardly designed to console her.

> *I wore thine image, Fame,*
> *Within a heart well fit to be thy shrine!*
> *Others a thousand boons may gain,*
>   *One wish was mine –*
>
> *The hope to gain one smile,*
> *To dwell one moment cradled on thy breast,*
> *Then close my eyes, bid life farewell*
>   *And take my rest!*
>
>   *   *   *
>
> *She pointed to a grisly land*
> *Where all breathes death – earth, sea, and air!*
> *Her glorious accents sound once more:*
>   *'Go, meet me there!'*

He sent a copy to Louisa Segrave too, but naturally he did not tell Isabel.

Chapter 10

Africa – The Little Trip

1857

MEN have lived along the banks of the Nile for more than 5,000 years and some of the world's greatest cultures have been nourished by its waters. Yet, until little more than a century ago, its sources remained a mystery. But there had never been a lack of theories as to its origin. One of the most persistent was that set forth by a second-century Alexandrian geographer named Ptolemy, or Claudius Ptolemaeus, who said the Nile flowed from certain lakes in the heart of Africa. He placed these lakes approximately ten degrees south of the Equator – about the latitude of the northern end of Lake Nyasa. Al-Idrisi (1100 – 66), an Arab geographer and cartographer, made a fairly detailed map of Africa and even wrote a description of the Central African lakes based on Arab sources. Still, their exact location and even their actual existence remained a matter of conjecture.

Burton believed these lakes to exist and he intended to apply to the Royal Geographical Society for funds to enable him to find them. A wise letter from Heinrich Barth, the famous German explorer (1821 – 65), warned him that no prudent man would pledge himself to discover the source of the Nile, so he contented himself with simply volunteering to lead an expedition into the heart of Africa in search of the 'Sea of Ujiji', a name Arab slave- and ivory-traders had used in speaking of an inland African lake. To consider the project, the Geographical Society formed a distinguished committee that included Francis Galton, Monckton Milnes (later Lord Houghton), Sir Roderick Murchison, John Arrowsmith and Colonel William Henry Sykes, Chairman of the Court of Directors of the East India Company.

In due course the committee approved the project and even persuaded the Earl of Clarendon, then Foreign Secretary, to give a government grant of £1,000. The East India Company was supposed to donate a like amount, but contented itself with granting Burton two years' leave with full pay.

Speke, who had also taken part in the Crimean War between expeditions, was in London and Burton tried to obtain permission from the

Court of Directors of the East India Company to take him along. They refused. Undaunted, Burton and Speke set off for Bombay where they rightly believed that Lord Elphinstone and Burton's friend James Grant Lumsden could obtain the necessary permission. Speke appears to have already hated Burton but he concealed his feelings and pretended to be Burton's friend in order to go on the expedition.

At Cairo Burton received orders to 'instantly return to London' to serve as a witness in what Burton described as 'some wretched court-martial' against an officer of Beatson's bashi-bazouks. He ignored the order and the two officers proceeded to Aden. From here Burton sent off a dispatch to the home branch of the Indian government through the Royal Geographical Society stating that he considered the Red Sea ports to be inadequately defended and recommending that two additional ships be detailed to protect British lives and property in this area. That the Bombay Government, then charged with responsibility for the Red Sea area, would not take kindly to this sort of advice, addressed to them by a junior officer of the Bombay Native Infantry and sent them through a private association, never occurred to him.

Arriving in Bombay on 23 November 1856, Burton soon obtained all he desired: an East India Company sloop-of-war to take him to Zanzibar; instruments and supplies; and permission to take with him both Speke and Dr Steinhaeuser, who was still staff surgeon at Aden. Unfortunately, the order did not reach Steinhaeuser in time; no ships were leaving Aden for Zanzibar when he did receive his permission; and, although he even attempted to join the expedition by marching overland down the coast of Africa, sickness forced him back and he had to be left behind. For Burton, the loss of Steinhaeuser was almost as unfortunate as the acquisition of Speke.

So smoothly did the preparations go in Bombay that by 2 December the expedition was packed and ready to sail. Lumsden saw them off and Burton wrote in his journal:

Of the gladdest moments in human life, methinks, is the departure upon a distant journey into unknown lands. Shaking off with one mighty effort the fetters of Habit, the leaden weight of Routine, the cloak of many Cares, and the slavery of Home, man feels once more happy. The blood flows with the fast circulation of childhood. Excitement lends unwonted vigour to the muscle, and the sudden sense of freedom adds a cubit to the mental stature. Afresh dawns the morn of life; again the bright world is beautiful to the eye, and the glorious face of nature gladdens the soul. A journey, in fact, appeals to Imagination, to Memory, to Hope – the sister Graces of our mortal being.

Reading these lines fourteen years later, Burton commented, 'Somewhat boisterous, but true.'

This departure was hardly one of the gladdest moments in Isabel's life – nor were his departures ever to be. Before reaching Africa Burton sent her two letters, but no sooner had he arrived in Zanzibar than he was caught in the embrace of his old mistress: Africa. Isabel was distressed by the absence of letters but she tried to be philosophical: 'My only desire is that he return safe to me with changed religious feelings, and that I may be his wife with my parents' consent.'

On 20 December the sloop carrying Burton and Speke entered the harbour of Zanzibar and fired off a salute. This was answered by a twenty-two-gun salute from a Muscat warship which, said Burton, 'curious to say, did not blow off a single gunner's arm'. They landed on a beach where dogs were often seen munching human flesh and gnawing human bones: the washed-up bodies of sick slaves, thrown overboard by slavers just before landing to avoid paying the Sultan's head tax on poor or valueless merchandise.

All was not well at Zanzibar. Sayid Said, a sultan friendly to Britain, had recently died, leaving the island in a state of near anarchy; Lieutenant-Colonel Atkins Hamerton, the British Consul and agent of the East India Company since 1841, was so sick he could hardly move. It was soon quite obvious to Burton that neither the local government nor the British Consul, upon whom he had counted for support, was in a position to aid the expedition. In fact, Hamerton told him he ought to turn back. 'But rather than return to Bombay,' said Burton afterwards, 'I would have gone to Hades.'

In spite of his comment that 'what with bad water and worse liquor, the Briton finds it hard to live at Zanzibar', Burton himself lingered on the island and the coast of the mainland for some time – long enough, in fact, to compile notes for two volumes of more than 1,000 pages. He did the sights of the town, including the prison: 'to see its curio, a poor devil cateran who had beaten the death-drum whilst his headman was torturing M. Maizan'. Looking at the prisoner Burton may have wondered if he himself would be the unwilling cause of a similar imprisonment, for the unfortunate Lieutenant Maizan, a twenty-six-year-old French naval officer, had been the last European to attempt an inland march from the East African coast. He had been taken prisoner by Mazungera tribesmen and bound to a calabash tree. After cutting off various parts of his body, a savage with a double-edged knife proceeded to cut the victim's throat. In the process of cutting he had found his blade too dull and stopped to whet its edge. Only then did he slice through the throat and wrench off the head.

But there were other sights of a less morbid nature and much that was new and interesting to Burton. Disdaining 'mere geography', he collected proverbs, reviewed the political history of Zanzibar, studied the ethnological material of the island, compiled meteorological data, examined the commercial history and potential of Zanzibar, and made notes on the flora and fauna. Of course he was also learning Swahili, the lingua franca of East Africa, since he declared it to be a principle with him 'never to travel where the language is unknown to me'.

As usual, he filled his notebooks with his prejudices, opinions and comments on those aspects of native life which the ordinary British traveller of that day, no matter how scientific, would have considered outside his field of interest. He noted that doctors were unknown, urinary and genital diseases were prevalent, sickness seemed to follow 'turning up fresh soil', and 'gonorrhoea is so common that it is hardly considered a disease'. He also noted gleefully that 'in these lands a drunkard outlives a water-drinker'. Zanzibar was then a regular port of call for whalers in the Indian Ocean, particularly American ships, and Burton made notes on whaling. He stated as a fact that ambergris is taken from the rectum of the sperm whale and that its main virtue is its heavy price. He found few prostitutes on Zanzibar, discovered that white slave-girls were rare, found Swahili women ugly, and noted that most white residents kept Abyssinian or Galla concubines. Finding that dogs were eaten by the natives, he commented on the European 'prejudices and squeamishness' concerning dog meat and predicted that 'the day will come when "dog meat" will appear regularly in the market'. The beginnings of German influence in East Africa he found encouraging and welcomed 'this accession to power of a kindred people'. He found little good in the peoples of East Africa. The negroes he considered 'an undeveloped and not to be developed race' and had some acid comments on what he regarded as 'Negro insolence'. Even the Arabs, of whom Burton was quite fond, were here a debased people: 'wealth has done much to degenerate the breed, climate more, and slavery most'. Indolence – which Burton called 'Californian fever' – resulted, he said, in 'luxury and unbridled licentiousness'.

But in spite of all his activity, Burton was bored: 'All is wearisome monotony; there is no society, no pleasure; sporting is forbidden by the treacherous climate.' Besides, Hamerton warned him that his continual questioning and note-taking were being viewed with suspicion and were 'exciting ill will'.

So on 5 January 1857, Burton and his little party set off on what he described as a 'tentative expedition'. In addition to Speke, Burton had brought with him from Bombay two Portuguese boys from Goa: Valentino Rodrigues and Caetano Andrade. At Zanzibar he also engaged a number of Africans to accompany him. One of these was the *kirangozi*, or guide, a short, thin, delicate Arab half-caste who, before Burton engaged him, had probably never walked two consecutive miles. His name was Said bin Salim el Lamki. He was timid, nervous, and could not stand hunger, thirst, fatigue or loss of sleep. Burton had a knack for engaging unsuitable fellow-travellers.

The provisions and supplies for the expedition were slight. As presents for native chiefs Burton bought twenty strips of muslin for turbans, a score of embroidered caps, a broadcloth coat, a loincloth, two gaudy cotton shawls of yellow and scarlet, and thirty-five pounds of small white and pink Venetian beads. For food the little party carried only three bags of rice, a barrel of flour, a bag of dates, twenty pounds each of coffee and sugar, and a small supply of salt, pepper, onions, curry, oil, clarified butter, snuff and tobacco. Even including such items as soap, cords and candles, the total spent for supplies was less than £30. Explaining this meagre outfitting, Burton wrote, 'I must observe, however, that we travelled in humble guise, hired poor vessels, walked the whole way, and otherwise practised a somewhat rigid economy.' Wages were low: Said was paid little more than £5 a month and the two Goanese each received about £2 a month.

Among the equipment Burton had brought to Zanzibar with him was a special boat of galvanized iron, twenty feet long and divided into seven sections, each weighing just under forty pounds. It was named the *Louisa*, not *Isabel* – and was designed to be carried inland in sections and to be sailed on the great lakes he hoped to discover there. On this short trip, however, it was towed behind the Arab dhow and was an object of wonder to the natives. Near Mombasa it was lost in a storm, 'but an article so remarkable and so useless to any but ourselves was of course easily recovered'.

After a brief stop at Pemba, the island where Burton believed Captain Kidd buried his 'blood-stained hoard of precious stones and metal, the plunder of India and the further Orient', they proceeded to Mombasa, landing on 16 January. Leaving the servants to stow away the explorers' 'cockroach-gnawed luggage', Burton and Speke set out for the mission house of Johannes Rebmann (1820 – 76), the German missionary and explorer who, with Johann Krapf (1810 – 81) had discovered Kilimanjaro nine years earlier. The mission was located near the present town of Rabai, only a few miles from Mombasa.

Burton carried with him a letter from Rebmann's superiors of the Church Missionary Society in London authorizing the missionary to accompany the expedition should he choose to do so. Apparently he at first considered going, but changed his mind after meeting Burton. The expedition appeared to rely too much on its guns and too little on God. His instructions from his society read: 'The Committee have only to remark that they entirely confide in you, as one of their missionaries, that wherever you go you will maintain all the Christian principles by which you are guided . . . while you may also obtain access to religions and tribes where missionary enterprise may be hereafter carried on with renewed vigour.' He saw little chance of doing missionary work under Burton.

Nor was Burton impressed with the missionary: 'An honest and conscientious man, he had yet all the qualities which secure unsuccess,' he said. He feared the consequences of having as a member of his party a man who would try to convert every heathen tribe they encountered.

It had been Burton and Speke's original intention to march inland from Mombasa to Mt Kilimanjaro and the surrounding country. Had they done so, swinging around the north side of the great mountain and continuing in a westerly direction, they would have discovered the Victoria Nyanza, largest lake in Africa and the second largest body of fresh water in the world. Its only outlet: the Nile. But they decided against it. Indeed, conditions argued against this trip. There was famine in the country, the savage Masai tribesmen were plundering the area and *pagaẓis*, or porters, were unprocurable, since they were afraid to face the Masai raiders who had already made their appearance on the outskirts of Mombasa. Burton philosophized that 'the explorer can never be sure of finding a particular road practicable: a few murders will shut it for a generation'.

He was later accused of cowardice for failing to enter a country where missionaries had marched, 'weaponed only with their umbrellas'. The man who taunted Burton in this fashion was Augustus Petermann (1822 – 78), a famous German geographer who while promoting expeditions to Africa had never been on one.

So for this trial expedition, Burton contented himself with cruising down the coast and catching fever. After a week in Mombasa, they

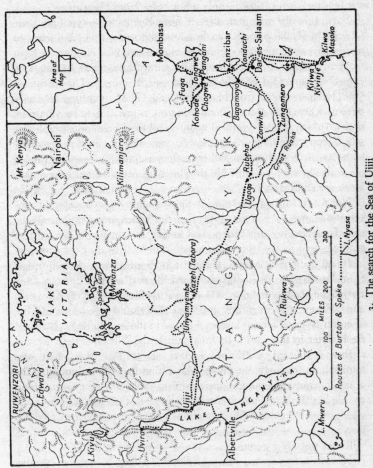

3. The search for the Sea of Ujiji

moved down to Tanga, then Pangani, and up the Pangani (or Ruvu) River. Leaving the boat, the party marched to Tongwe. On the second day out they were effectively discouraged by an attack of bulldog ants – a half-inch-long, black insect whose bite burns like a hot needle, they can literally eat a man alive. Even when its body has been torn from its head, the pincers remain embedded in the flesh, and it tends to concentrate its attack on the tenderest parts of the body.

At a Zanzibar outpost Burton managed to acquire a small escort of ragged soldiers. One of these deserves special mention. His name was Sidi Mubarak, but he called himself 'Bombay'. He had been sold as a slave at Kilwa in early youth and was carried to Cutch by a Banyan trader. He ran away from his master, however, and eventually enlisted as a soldier. 'His head is a triumph to phrenology,' Burton wrote, 'a high narrow cranium, denoted by arched and rounded crown, fuyant brow and broad base with full development of the moral region, deficiency of the reflectives, fine perceptives, and abundant animality.' Burton found him gay and hard working and arranged for him to 'take leave of soldiering' and accompany him on his major expedition where, because he spoke a little broken Hindustani, he became the servant and interpreter of Speke. Burton, who was ever scornful of his companion's linguistic deficiencies, pointed out that this was the only man beside himself with whom Speke was able to converse. Bombay later accompanied the expedition of Speke and Grant (1860 – 3) and in 1870, when Henry M. Stanley set off to find Dr David Livingstone, the indestructible Bombay was again a member of the expedition in charge of the bodyguard.

Reaching Korogwe they marched on towards Fuga along the banks of the Ruvu River. In one village they found the people eager to trade in female slaves. Burton found some of the girls 'rather comely, despite the tattoo that looked like boils'. But when the porters chaffed the girls, asking them how they would like to have the 'men in trousers' as lovers, they answered scornfully, 'Not at all!'

By the time they reached Fuga it was the middle of February and the rainy season had set in. Fearing fevers from the 'dense raw vapours that rose from the steamy ground', Burton decided to return to the coast. Neither of the white men escaped sickness, however, and they arrived back in Zanzibar on 6 March with fevers and stomach disorders.

It is impossible to understand the reason for this coastal expedition with the short inland trip to Fuga. It had no apparent objective, except to talk with Rebmann, and it accomplished nothing except to give the explorers a taste of the hardships awaiting them on the longer trip. Both officers were limited in the time they could be away from their regiments and Burton complained often enough of the meagre financial resources available to them. Both time and money were spent to gain a bit of experience that could have been acquired on the actual march to the lake.

Nevertheless, on 11 May, when Burton and Speke had recovered their health, they set out on still another coastal expedition to collect information upon certain subjects of interest to the secretary of the Bombay Geographical Society: coastal limestone formations and copal gathering. It is true that copal, which is used in making certain varnishes and lacquers, was becoming scarce and consequently expensive. The aforementioned secretary of the Bombay Geographical Society had said, 'Materially to reduce the price of coach-varnish would probably be considered to entitle Captain Burton to a larger share of the gratitude of his countrymen than the measurement of the elevation of the Mountains of the Moon or the Determination of the Sources of the Nile.' But Burton failed to win this claim to fame as he was unable to find a better or cheaper way of obtaining copal. He also failed to find any trace of a limestone band along the coast. The expedition returned again to Zanzibar.

When the rains ended on 5 June 1857, Burton and his party were still at Zanzibar. Now the moment for the actual departure could be postponed no longer. Six months had been spent on Zanzibar and the neighbouring coast. Incredibly, Burton wrote, 'Our preparations were hurriedly made'! He explained that 'delay, even for a week, might have been fatal to my project'. Colonel Hamerton was dying and local Zanzibar politics were becoming confused.

At long last, on 17 June, Burton left Zanzibar and crossed to the mainland to begin his search for the lakes. He landed at a place he called Kaol (no longer in existence) located just south of Bagamoyo. There he engaged thirty-six Unyamwezi natives as *pagazis* (porters) and bought thirty baggage asses. Ten days after landing, the expedition got under way and Burton was off on the most important journey of his life. It was to prove crucial to his entire career. His intention was first to discover the lakes and then to prove that the lakes were indeed the Nile's source by marching north down the Nile, emerging at Cairo as the man who had solved the most fascinating geographical riddle of the ages.

Chapter 11

Discovery of Lake Tanganyika
1857–8

THE route taken by Burton and Speke was no untrodden wilderness. It was, in fact, a rather well-worn path, being the way taken by Arab slavers who carried beads, cloth, gunpowder and other articles of trade into the interior and brought out slaves and ivory. It had originally been opened about 1825 by Sayf bin Said el Muameri, an Arab slaver, but Burton and Speke were the first Europeans to take the route (and return alive), and they were followed by Stanley when he went to find Livingstone twenty-four years later. Although taking an unbeaten path was more dangerous and difficult in nineteenth-century Africa, there were also disadvantages in following the caravan routes due to the tribute levied by every petty chief along the way and the ease with which *pagazis* could desert and find their way home.

The personnel of the expedition consisted of the two Englishmen, the two half-caste Goan boys, Bombay and a friend of his called Muinyi Mabruki, two native gun-bearers, thirteen 'Baloch' *askaris* (soldiers) supplied by the Sultan of Zanzibar and reinforced by ten gun-carrying slaves, five ass-drivers and thirty-six *pagazis*. But even with the addition of the asses, there were still not enough baggage carriers to transport all the loads.

Although he took great pains to prepare himself personally for his great expedition, Burton took remarkably little care in his selection of the men who were to go with him. Picking up the bulk of his personnel at the last moment, he simply hired those he found at hand willing to make the trip. The men who were to reinforce the Sultan's *askaris*, for example, were hired from a Banyan customs clerk in Zanzibar called Ramji. This rogue rented out ten slaves, whom he called his sons, at a price higher than Burton could have bought them himself in the slave market. Burton realized this, but nevertheless he took on the 'sons of Ramji'. After all, he was in a hurry. It is impossible to escape the conclusion that, had he devoted the six months spent in wandering up and down the coast to selecting properly the all-important members of his expedition, the difficulties he was to face would have been considerably lessened. Although a professional soldier, Burton had little experience in the command of organized bodies of men and he had a curious disregard for the talents required. Unaware, however, of any deficiencies in this regard he was full of self-confidence, apparently convinced that his own considerable abilities would offset any deficiencies in those serving under him. He was a lone wolf who now found himself leading a very assorted pack of animals.

On the backs of men and asses were all the supplies necessary for a long expedition. The most important of these, perhaps, were the long, narrow bags of beads, conical bundles of cloth and coils of brass wire that served in the African interior as copper, silver and gold respectively. Then there were the provisions: salt, pepper, pickles, soap, vinegar and oil, twenty pounds of sugar, five boxes of tea, one box of cigars, five dozen bottles of brandy, seven canisters of snuff and a supply of 'Warburg drops', a patent medicine recommended to him by Colonel Hamerton. Well armed, the expedition carried two smooth bores, three rifles, a Colt carbine, three revolvers, the muskets of the bodyguard, and three swords, besides 140 pounds of gunpowder, caps, wadding, and flints. Camp furniture included one small and one large tent, a table and two chairs, silverware and cooking utensils, two large cotton pillows (for stuffing birds), an air pillow, two ordinary pillows, a cork bed, eight blankets, three solid leather suitcases and three mats for carpets.

Scientific instruments were considered essential and included a lever watch, two chronometers, two prismatic compasses, a pocket thermometer, a sundial, a rain gauge, an evaporating dish, two sextants, a mountain barometer, measuring tape, two boiling thermometers, telescope, pocket pedometer and a box of 'mathematical instruments'.

A great supply of stationery was necessary for the ever-writing Burton: paper, blank books, diaries, memo pads, notebooks, pencils, ink, pens and sealing-wax. Then there were maps, Nautical Almanacs, and a table of stars. A considerable supply of practical books was carried, including volumes on surveying, navigation and Swahili; there was Jackson's *What to Observe*, Galton's *Art of Travel*, and Prichard's *History of Man*. In these days before the camera became practical and portable it was also considered essential to have a complete artist's kit for both sketching and painting.

A tool-box was taken along, together with seventy pounds of nails; clothing, largely of flannel, plus turbans and thick felt caps; and a miscellaneous assortment of other items, such as four umbrellas, two thousand fish-hooks, several lanterns, two dozen pen-knives, a cigar case and a Union Jack.

Due to the shortage of carriers most of the ammunition and a considerable amount of cloth, beads and wire – in all, twenty-two loads – had to be left behind with a Hindu merchant who promised to forward them up country as soon as *pagazis* became available. It was nearly eleven months before they saw these supplies again.

The day before his departure, Burton overheard a conversation between the rascal Ramji and Ladha, the respectable collector of customs. Burton had insisted that he must take enough native currency to enable him to buy a boat when he reached the 'Sea of Ujiji' since the steel boat which had been specially built to sail the expected lakes would have to be left behind for lack of transport.

'Will he ever reach it?' Ladha asked Ramji, speaking in a Hindi dialect which he assumed Burton did not understand.

'Of course not,' Ramji replied. 'What is he that he should pass through Ugogo?' he added rhetorically – Ugogo being a particularly dangerous stretch of country through which the expedition must pass.

In the evening Burton took the opportunity of informing Ladha that not only had he understood what had been said but that he intended to pass through Ugogo and to sail on the Sea of Ujiji. To do so, he would need the supplies of cloth, wire and beads he was insisting on carrying. While they were talking, a loud wail was heard outside, quickly followed by other cries of sorrow. News had just been received of the death of the only son of a local dignitary. He had been killed by a hippopotamus while going up the Kingami River.

'Be honest!' said Ladha to Burton. 'Admit that this is the first calamity which you have brought upon the country by your presence.'

Burton could only reply with the commonplaces of European logic. When Ladha left him, he gave himself up to despair. In the darkness and solitude of his hut, he reviewed his troubles. 'I felt myself the plaything of misfortune,' he said later. He could find no blame in himself, but much in the malice and ignorance of others and in circumstance. He thought of the trip ahead with dread, for he was entering an unknown land at the fatal season when the rains were over and the malarial season would begin, and he regretted the absence of his friend Surgeon Steinhaeuser. But it was too late to retreat now. Indeed, this thought did not occur to him. He had started and he would finish what he had begun. Already Speke was on the road, driving the loaded asses and *pagazis* before him. In the morning he, too, would start the long trek into the interior.

The first journey – by tradition a short march – was not one to re-assure him. He had bought three more asses that morning, loaded them with additional supplies, and set off after Speke with Valentine, his Goanese servant, three Beluchis, and two slaves. The asses reared, plunged, bucked, kicked and refused to go forward. Once started, they rushed into the bush, ran into each other, bolted, shied and threw their loads. About sunset, one ass sank girth-deep in a patch of boggy mire and the three Beluchi soldiers ran away. Said Burton, 'This little event had a particular significance to one about to command a party composed principally of asses and Baloch.'

His troubles were increased when he joined the main party. And even after a week on the road, he still complained of the difficulty of getting men and animals to move forward. There was, for example, the usual daily squabble in which a Beluchi drew his dagger on a slave who, in turn, pointed his loaded Tower musket at the Beluchi. Burton com-pared his labours with trying to drive a herd of wild cattle. 'At length, by ejecting skulkers from their huts, by dint of promises and threats, of gentleness and violence, of soft words and hard words, occasionally backed by a smart application of the "bakur" – the local "cat" – by sitting in the sun, in fact by incessant worry and fidget from 6 a.m. to 3 p.m., the sluggish and unwieldy body acquired some momentum.'

Their route led them slowly and painfully through the fetid vegeta-tion of a stretch of dense jungle. Although a much used path, this was not a road. They passed several 'down-caravans' bringing slaves from the interior, the merchandise being tied together by ropes around their necks.

By 5 July, three of the asses had been lost and Speke was sick with fever. Five days later, Burton awoke weak and depressed, with aching head, burning eyes, and trembling legs. Of this day he wrote, 'The new life, the alternations of damp heat and wet cold, the useless fatigue of walking, the sorry labour of waiting and reloading asses, the exposure to sun and dew, and last, but not least, of morbific influences, the wear and tear of mind at the prospect of imminent failure, all were beginning to tell heavily on me.' The trip had scarcely begun.

On 14 July Burton derived some comfort from the fact that in eighteen days he had marched his caravan 118 statute miles – some of them in the right direction. But he was seriously ill and so weak he could no longer walk. When sick, Burton, through hope or curiosity, was always willing to try native remedies, uncomfortable and even painful though they might be. Now he submitted to being placed on a stool, covered with hair blankets and smoked with coals and herbs. Like most of the other remedies he had tried in Arabia and Somaliland, this was ineffectual. Warburg drops did not help either. On 18 July, when the caravan had to cross three bogs, one of them a mile wide, he had to be supported on an ass by the mire-covered porters.

On 21 July, with swimming head and trembling hands, Burton wrote a report for the Royal Geographical Society to be sent back to the coast. Then, after three days of rest, he again pushed forward. They were in true jungle now, hideous and grotesque. From the rain-drenched, black, glassy ground sprang spear grass, twelve and thirteen feet high with each blade as wide as a man's finger; there were tall trees completely covered with moss and fungi, and creepers and climbers stretching from tree to tree across the footpath to trip the unwary and the tired. The stench of rotten vegetation added to the horrors. The intense humidity corroded everything. Metal clasps and springs snapped, paper turned into soppy pulp, guns rusted, clothes mildewed, matches refused to light, and food turned into paste.

Of the people who lived in this disagreeable land, Burton said, 'Filthy heaps of the rudest hovels, built in holes in the jungle, sheltered the few miserable inhabitants, whose frames are lean with constant intoxication, and whose limbs, distorted by ulcerous sores, attest the hostility of Nature to mankind. Such a revolting scene is East Africa from Central K'hutu to the base of the Usagara Mountains.'

When they reached the slave caravan station which Burton called Zungomero (probably the present town of Morogoro in Tanganyika), a halt was made for nine days to rest and secure porters. Although Burton was no better and Speke was so weak he could hardly walk, they marched out on 7 August 1857, towards the Usagara Hills.

Every day had its difficulties. Unable to control their men, Burton and Speke had trouble each morning in getting their caravan organized. There were constant quarrels among the men, and each *pagazi* ran off with the lightest bundle or the most compliant ass. Burton was not an administrator and commanding a caravan demanded some administrative skill. Had he assigned a specific load to each *pagazi*; noted its contents and made each man responsible for it, his troubles would have been lessened. On the march, asses were lost, men straggled and supplies were uncared for and often ruined. Once when their men thought it too much bother to unload the asses for a stream crossing, all the salt and sugar melted away and tea, soap, cigars and dried vegetables were spoiled. The Beluchis, the 'sons of Ramji', the Goanese boys and the porters hated each other and quarrelled incessantly. All stole goods from the loads.

Smallpox was upon the land and beside the path were the vulture-picked bones of fallen porters and sometimes swollen corpses of fresh victims. The second day out of Zungomero they encountered a large caravan that had already lost fifty from the disease. It was a terrible sight:

Men staggering on blinded by disease, and mothers carrying on their backs infants as loathsome objects as themselves. The wretches would not leave the path, every step in their state of failing strength was precious; he who once fell would never rise again; no village would admit death into its precincts, no relation nor friend would return for them, and they would lie till their agony was ended by the raven and vulture, the fisi and the fox. Near every khambi or kraal I remarked detached tents which, according to the guides, were set apart for those seized with the fell disease. Under these circumstances, as might be expected, several of our party caught the infection; they lagged behind, and probably threw themselves into some jungle, for the path when revisited showed no signs of them.

Most of the scientific instruments were broken, and when Speke accidently broke their only remaining boiling-point thermometer it seemed the last straw. The expedition appeared to be fast disintegrating. Burton spent a sleepless night 'watching each star as it sank and set in its turn, piercing with a last twinkle the thin silhouette of tall trees that fringed the hilly rim of the horizon, and in admiring the hardiness of the bull-headed Mabruki, as he lay half-roasted by the fire and half-frozen by the cold southern gale'.

Foul weather, desertions, and a shortage of food completed their misery. The high point of the expedition's difficulties came at the little village of Zonhwe. Here Burton ordered the loads to be repacked and adjusted. The Beluchi soldiers refused to obey. The one-eyed *jemadar*, leader of the Beluchis, had hot words with Burton, who was almost prostrated by fever, and accused him of starving them. Burton told him not to eat abominations. The *jemadar* dramatically clapped his hand to his sword and dared him to repeat the words. Burton contemptuously repeated them a half-dozen times. In a rage, the *jemadar* retired to confer with the other Beluchis. They clustered around him, talking arrogantly at the top of their voices so that Burton would be sure to hear: one threatened to 'take that man's life'; another declared sententiously that 'in all Nazarenes there is no good'; and all complained they were not given enough food, particularly meat. These men, who in Zanzibar probably did not see meat more often than once a year, now sent a deputation to Burton demanding that in the future they be given a sheep a day. This demand being refused, they then said they should have three cloths a day instead of one. Since food was indeed scarce, and thus expensive, Burton agreed to allow them two cloths. The Beluchis jeered at this offer and marched away in a body, saying they would leave the next day for Zanzibar.

The next day, as the asses were being loaded, the *jemadar* and two of his men came up to Burton and begged for a paper of dismissal to 'cover their shame'. Far from deserting him, he was deserting them, the *jemadar* said. Burton, sick and disgusted, did not reply, but mounted his ass and rode off. Later in the day the whole lot rejoined the caravan and implored forgiveness.

As soldiers, the thirteen Beluchis were of doubtful value except to frighten off natives who did not know them. They were cowardly; they did not know how to shoot properly, and they could not be trusted with ammunition because they either wasted it in shooting at small birds, or sold it. Burton had the lowest opinion of them:

Like the lower races of Orientals, they were ever attempting to intrude, to thrust themselves forward, to take an ell when an inch was offered. They considered all but themselves fools, ready to be imposed upon by the flimsiest lie, by the shallowest artifices. Gratitude they ignored; with them a favour granted was but an earnest of favours to come, and one refusal obliterated the trace of a hundred largesses. Their objects in life seemed to be eating and buying slaves; their pleasures, drinking and intrigue. Insatiable beggars were they; noisy, boisterous, foul-mouthed knaves; swearers 'with voices like cannons'; rude and forward in manner; low and abusive in language; so slanderous that, for want of other subjects, they would calumniate one another, and requiring a periodical check to their presumption.

Burton was no amateur vituperator himself. But the above quoted lines are from a report written at the end of the expedition when Burton had to answer an official complaint against him forwarded to the Bombay Government by Captain C. P. Rigby, Colonel Hamerton's successor at Zanzibar. The Beluchis had complained to the new consul that Burton had failed to reward them properly. Rigby's report stressed the injustice shown them, considering 'the hardships they endured, and the fidelity and perseverance they showed'.

The caravan marched on, over rivers and bogs, desert and savannah. Through carelessness and theft, the dissolution of their supplies continued. Burton and Speke were apparently incapable of preventing it. 'The fact is,' Burton wrote, 'we were physically and morally incapacitated for any exertion beyond balancing ourselves upon the donkeys.' But the asses were giving out. By 4 September only one weak riding-ass remained. Fortunately, they now came to a country where, for the first time, they were able to procure milk, honey and butter. Also, they met up with a slave caravan and were able to trade cloth for two asses and some salt, rice and snuff.

It was here that Burton purchased a female slave who added to the trials of the expedition. Her name was Sikujui ('Don't Know'), and she was a true virago. Her herculean proportions had raised her price to six cloths and a large coil of brass wire. Her morals were frightful. To make her an honest woman, she was married to the sturdiest of the *pagazis*, but she treated him with sublime contempt and gave him a dozen rivals. She threw the caravan into even greater disorder by her irregularities, and, as the easiest method of lightening her load, she broke every article entrusted to her. When she was finally sold for a few measures of rice in Unyanyembe, her new owner appeared the following morning with a cracked head.

On 10 September they steeled themselves for the arduous ascent of the Ruhebo Mountains of the Usagara range. The path was too steep to ride the asses and Burton was so weak he had to be supported the entire way. Speke was also ailing and required a man on each side to help him along. Crossing a bushy bit of jungle they found themselves facing a steep hill of loose white soil and rolling stones up which the *pagazis* were scrambling like monkeys with the asses stumbling behind. Burton and Speke painfully followed. At last they were compelled to fall to the ground, coughing from the chalky dust, consumed by thirst, and half-dead from fatigue. Suddenly they heard the war cry of the savage Wahumba and soon they saw the hills swarming with black files of warriors moving down to plunder the villages in the valley. Burton's men were terrified. One proposed they flee and leave the white men to their deserved fate. One of the Beluchis fell to the ground and pretended to be sick, crying like a girl. The remainder made for the rear. Fortunately, the Wahumba, their hearts set on the cattle of the villagers, did not molest the expedition.

After six hours of climbing, resting every few yards and clinging to their supporters, Burton and Speke reached the top and passed into a mountain valley. By the time they stopped, Speke was almost in a coma; he had advanced mechanically and now could hardly talk. During the night he had two attacks of fever and was so violently delirious that his weapons had to be removed. Burton believed the attack had a 'permanent cerebral effect'. By morning, the look of death was on his face. All day long the Beluchis and the sons of Ramji clamoured to go on, saying the cold disagreed with them.

By the following day Speke was better but he could not march. While discussing the matter, the drum signal for departure was sounded without Burton's order and the caravan began to move out with unaccustomed speed. Burton tried to recall them, but they replied that it was a principle with them never to return when once started. He observed that this was 'a well-sounding principle against which they never offended except to serve their own ends'. There was nothing to do but hurriedly contrive a hammock and have Speke carried in it by the porters – the Beluchis and the sons of Ramji refused to assist.

Two days later Burton, who had himself been sick, was well enough to make an inspection of the loads. Of the supplies intended to last for a year, half were gone, and they had been only three months on the march. He discussed his anxiety with Said bin Salim. Said was not disturbed. He said they had enough to last them until they reached Unyanyembe where they would be joined by the twenty-two porters who were bringing up the remaining loads from the coast.

'But how do you know that?' Burton asked.

'Allah is all knowing,' replied Said, 'but the caravan *will* come.'

Fatalism has an infectious quality about it in times of stress. Burton ceased to worry.

On 18 September they left the mountains and marched out into the plains of Ugogo. Speke still had to be carried in the hammock, but now the *pagazis* refused to carry him and the task was left to Bombay and Mabruki. On the trip over the mountain a case containing Speke's store of boots, the table and a chair were lost. Burton considered the table and chair indispensable and sent a party of Beluchi *askaris* and slaves back to find them. After spending a pleasant day lounging by the nearest well, they returned with a tale of how they had been unable to recover the missing items because they had been chased by a war party of Wasagara. The missing articles were later found by another caravan and returned to their owner – for a price – at Unyanyembe.

On the plains of Ugogo Burton called a three-day halt. Here both he and Speke rapidly recovered their health and Speke even did some hunting. By a stroke of luck, Burton was able to acquire fifteen Wanyamwezi porters who had deserted from another caravan. On 22 September they continued the march over grassy plains and broom jungle. It was easy travelling and the explorers were now in reasonably good health. The only disaster was an attack by a swarm of bees during which one of the new porters lost his box. Unfortunately, this was the case containing the Nautical Almanac for 1865 and most of the writing material. Burton was furious.

They were entering dangerous country. One evening Kidogo, leader of the sons of Ramji, bawled, '*Maneno! Maneno!* – Words! Words!', and he called everyone around him to hear a solemn speech: 'Listen, O you whites! and you children of Sayyidi Majidi! and you sons of Ramji! Hearken to my words, O you offspring of the night! The journey enters Ugogo – Ugogo! Beware, and again beware. You do not know the Wagogo. . . . Speak not to those washenzi pagans. Enter not into their houses. Have no dealings with them; show no cloth, wire nor beads. Eat not with them, drink not with them, and make not love to their women. Kirangozi of the Wanyamwezi, restrain your sons! Suffer them not to stray into the villages to buy salt out of camp, to rob provisions, to debauch with beer, or to sit by the wells . . .' For nearly half an hour Kidogo poured out his wisdom. It went unheeded.

Up to this point, the native chiefs encountered had been content with small presents, but in Ugogo the system of *honga*, or tribute, was extracted with a vengeance as the tribes were strong enough physically to force payment. Porters were terrified of them and would refuse to go on unless each chief was satisfied. Along the path they were taking there were four main chiefs to be appeased. On 2 October 1857, they encountered the first. He was the least powerful of the four, but he demanded, and got, ten cloths – four white and six blue – and a handsome cotton and silk loincloth. But this was cheap compared with the others, one of whom began by demanding six porter-loads and settled only for twenty cloths, thirty strings of coral beads, six feet of red broadcloth and a coil of brass wire.

At this price Ugogo was safely crossed and the caravan marched on into Unyamwezi, where Burton discovered that the women were 'well disposed toward strangers of fair complexion, apparently with the permission of their husbands'. The box of books and writing material was found by an 'up caravan' and returned, but four boxes of ammunition and all the bullet moulds were lost. The quarrels among the various elements of the expedition continued and all remained undisciplined: one of the sons of Ramji even tried to steal a slave-girl from an Arab caravan camp. They suffered the usual annoyances from swarms of insects, but escaped injury from the many wild animals in the region.

On 7 November 1857, 134 days after leaving the coast, the expedition marched into Tabora, then, as now, the principal inland city of Tanganyika. Burton was now 450 direct miles from his starting point, but he estimated he had marched 600 miles. Curiously, Burton, who always paid close attention to the names of places and had a phenomenal grasp of languages, called the town Kazeh. After Burton and Speke, the next European to reach this place was Stanley, who in June 1871 arrived here on his search for Livingstone. But the town was then called Tabora – as it is today – and Stanley was unable to find anyone who had ever heard of 'Kazeh'.

Tabora was then the capital of the Arab slave- and ivory-traders, many of whom had built homes for themselves there. The water supply was good, many trade routes converged here, and, with the slave trade at the zenith of its prosperity, as many as a half a million caravan *pagazis* passed through the town in a year. Here Burton had to halt and reorganize as this was the end of the line for the *pagazis* from the coast and new porters would have to be recruited for the onward journey. He soon made friends with the Arab slavers: 'striking, indeed, was the contrast between the open-handed hospitality and the hearty good-will of this truly noble race, and the niggardness of the savage and selfish African – it was heart of flesh after heart of stone'. In particular, he was impressed by the kindness shown him by an Omani slaver named Snay bin Amir who helped him warehouse his goods, hired new porters for the remainder of the trip, provided him with a house, gave him food, and imparted much valuable information.

Burton remained at Tabora for five weeks, enjoying the hospitality of the Arabs, quarrelling with the sons of Ramji, haggling over the price of *pagazis*, and resting from his hardships. On 14 December he started out on the last lap of his trip to Ujiji and the shores of the expected lake, now 200 miles away in a direct line. After a month of marching, plagued by desertions, theft and continual troubles with Kidogo and the sons of Ramji, he finally dismissed the armed slaves and sent them back.

On the afternoon of 18 January 1858, Burton was stricken with a horrible sickness. He shivered with a cold paroxysm and his feet and legs began to burn and swell. In a few hours he was palsied and powerless to move either his arms or legs. Except for a throbbing and tingling sensation that felt as though he were pricked by countless needles, his feet lost all sensation. The attack spread upward from his feet and even his ribs felt compressed. He thought he was going to die. But after a halt of only three days, he persuaded four *pagazis* to carry him in a hammock and he ordered the march to Ujiji continued. The muscles of his legs were now contracted both above and below the knee and he could not put his weight on them. It was to be a year before he would be able to walk any distance and even longer before the numbness in his hands and feet left him.

Less than a week later, Speke was afflicted with an eye inflammation. He had first been blinded by ophthalmia when a child and his eyesight had never been good since. Even reading was always 'a very painful task,' he said. In India, he had experienced snow blindness while crossing the Himalaya. Now he suffered 'an almost total blindness, rendering every object enclouded as by a misty veil'. One of the Goanese servants was stricken with the same disease and Burton, too, had a similar ailment to a lesser degree. Throughout the trip, Burton and Speke, while technically the leaders of the caravan, had been more or less carried along by their own followers. Now that both were incapacitated, they became even more dependent upon the whims of their employees. But in spite of their bad health and miserable condition, neither gave a thought to turning back. Throughout the trip they had been sustained by their desire to reach the lake. Now that they were drawing close to their objective, this determination was all the more firm in their minds. Speke, sitting blind and in great pain on his donkey, had to be led and Burton, his legs almost useless, had to be carried in a hammock, but they faced the west, the direction of the lake, and they pressed on, through rain, over rugged terrain, across rivers. Everything seemed to combine to make their life miserable, including the loss of Burton's bedding and tent. On 13 February they passed through tall grass to a steep and stony hill sparsely clad with thorn trees. As they struggled up, Speke's ass collapsed and died.

Halting to rest at the top, Burton saw something shining below them. Turning to Bombay, he asked, 'What is that streak of light that lies below?'

'I am of the opinion,' said Bombay solemnly, 'that that is *the* water.'

Burton stared with his still weak eyes into the valley below. What he saw made him sick with disappointment. Through the veil of trees all he could see was what appeared to be a very small lake indeed. Was it for this he had risked his life and health? It seemed a poor prize. He thought of immediately returning to Tabora. Perhaps the other lake he had heard of to the north could be explored instead. But these thoughts were premature.

Advancing only a few yards further, the entire view was soon open to him and he stared with 'admiration, wonder and delight'. It was Lake Tanganyika, spread out as though lying in the lap of the mountains, shimmering in the gorgeous tropical sunshine. Burton was in raptures: 'Forgetting toils, dangers, and the doubtfulness of return, I felt willing to endure double what I had endured; and all the party seemed to join with me in joy.' All, that is, except poor Speke who could only see a dim blob of light:

Here you may picture to yourself my bitter disappointment when, after toiling through so many miles of savage life, all the time emaciated by divers sicknesses and weakened by great privations of food and rest, I found, on approaching the zenith of my ambition, the Great Lake in question nothing but mist and glare before my eyes. From the summit of the eastern horn the lovely Tanganyika lake could be seen in all its glory by everybody but myself.

The sick and weary explorers had reached their goal at last: Lake Tanganyika, symbol of their success.

Chapter 12

The Great Mistake
1858 – 9

AT last Burton was on the edge of fame. This was no wild adventure for adventure's sake, no journey in fancy disguise to a religious capital, no mad dash across a stretch of wild country to a forbidden city: this time there appeared the possibility of solid geographical discovery, an important contribution to knowledge. Already he had found and proved the existence of Lake Tanganyika; now he had only to exploit his discovery, learn everything he could about it, and report his findings to the world. Of particular interest would be knowledge of the rivers that flowed into and out of this great lake. What if the river at the north end of the lake proved to be an affluent, flowing northward? Would he not then have discovered the source of the Nile? It was an exhilarating prospect.

On 14 February 1858, they entered Ujiji – later to become famous as the meeting place of Livingstone and Stanley. The trip had taken them seven and a half months, of which a hundred days had been spent in marching. Ujiji was a trading centre for slaves and ivory; Burton and Speke found themselves under suspicion because, as they had no desire to trade, their presence here seemed unaccountable. The chief, named Kannena, was particularly disturbed since he levied a tax upon each slave and tusk of ivory sold. Burton further alienated the chief by ejecting him from his quarters when he arrived unannounced and unrecognized. In the end, Burton was forced to pay dearly for the animosity he had created in the breast of the savage Kannena. Thieves stole all the clothes of the *jemadar* and the bull-headed Mabruki; the asses were repeatedly wounded by spears; the price of milk became so exorbitant it could no longer be bought; the white men were accused of bewitching the cows; and Kannena levied a heavy tax because the white men did *not* trade.

Having had difficulty getting his men to leave Tabora, Burton had promised extra pay if they would go on with him. He was now forced to keep his promise and to make a distribution of cloth. 'Moreover,' Burton explained, 'most of the party had behaved badly, and in these exceptional lands bad behaviour always expects a reward. In the first place . . . no man misconducts himself unless he has power to offend you and you are powerless to punish him.' The cloths he doled out were at once spent by his men for slaves, most of whom promptly deserted, 'leaving the unhappy ex-proprietor tantalized by all the torments of ungratified acquisitiveness'.

Burton's main concern was to obtain a boat large enough to enable him to explore the north end of the lake. This was not easy. None could be had locally, so he sent Speke across the lake in a canoe to try to get a dhow from an Arab slaver who was said to possess one. Speke was suffering terribly from his eye disease and he had a strange distortion of his face that forced him to chew sideways, but he went off in search of the dhow.

The dispatch of Speke gave Burton twenty-seven days of solitude which was 'chiefly spent in eating and drinking, smoking and dozing'. Burton enjoyed the solitude, for he and Speke were getting on each other's nerves. To be free of the constant presence of his companion and not to work was a tremendous luxury. Every afternoon he lay on his cot, 'smoking almost uninterruptedly, dreaming of things past, and visioning things present, and sometimes indulging . . . in a few lines of reading and writing'. Did he think of Isabel? If he spared her a thought during his entire stay in Africa, he did not record the fact, and in the thousands of pages he wrote, not one line was directed to her.

Speke returned on 29 March. He was in rough shape. Having been caught in the monsoon rains, he was soaked through; his clothes were mildewed and his guns were covered with rust. But the worst disaster was caused by a tiny bug. On an island in the lake one night his camp was struck by a violent storm; the wind and rain whipped his tent so hard that its pegs were torn out and the tent pole had to be held upright by force. When the wind died down and the tent could be set up again, Speke lit a candle to rearrange his gear. Almost instantly the tent was filled with thousands of black beetles. He tried to brush them off his bedding and clothes, but there were so many and they were so persistent that at length he gave up and went to bed. Although the bugs were crawling over his body and even in his hair, he was thoroughly exhausted and soon fell asleep. He was awakened by one of the tiny beetles entering his ear. In trying to get the insect out, he pushed it further in and could soon feel it begin, 'with exceeding vigour, like a rabbit at a hole, to dig violently away at my tympanum'. Speke did everything he could think of to dislodge the creature. Tobacco smoke, oil and melted butter all failed. In desperation, he tried a pen-knife. He killed the beetle, but he also injured his ear and the insect's body remained inside.

By the time he returned to Ujiji he was in great pain, his ear was inflamed and pus was running from it. All of the facial muscles from his ear to his shoulder became contorted and drawn on one side and his glands were so swollen he was unable even to open his mouth and had to feed on broth alone. 'For many months the tumour made me almost deaf,' Speke reported, 'and ate a hole between that orifice and the nose, so that when I blew it, my ear whistled so audibly that those who heard it laughed. Six or seven months after this accident happened, bits of the beetle, a leg, a wing, or parts of the body, came away with the wax.'

Burton was not sympathetic. He was, in fact, furious that Speke had been unable to procure the dhow. 'He had done literally nothing,' he said. 'When my companion had somewhat recovered from his wetness, and from the effects of punching in with a pen-knife a beetle which had visited his tympanum, I began seriously to seek some means of exploring the northern head of the Tanganyika.'

Speke had been told by an Arab slave who claimed he had visited the north end of the lake that the influence of a large river draining the water northwards could be felt in a boat. Burton had talked with a man who claimed to have seen the river. He, too, mentioned that the water flowed *out* of the lake – to the north. 'When we compared statements, we saw what was before us – a prize for which wealth, health, and life were to be risked. . . . I trusted, therefore, to fate, and resolved that at all costs, even if reduced to actual want, we should visit this mysterious stream,' Burton wrote.

He now opened negotiations with Kannena for two canoes, one sixty feet long and the other about forty. Eventually the price was agreed upon and Burton paid 33 coiled bracelets and 803 strings of beads. The crew was paid 80 cloths and 210 strings of beads, including 40 strings of white and blue porcelains that locally were three times more valuable than the more ordinary whites and greens. The interpreter was given eight cloths and twenty-seven pounds of the valuable white and blue porcelains. In addition, Burton promised a fine reward to Kannena if he kept his promise to take him to the river, throwing six feet of red broadcloth over the chief's shoulders to prove that he meant it.

On 10 April they set out in the two canoes with horns braying, gongs clanging, drums booming and drunken crewmen singing.

Although they had paid a high price for the use of the men and canoes, Burton and Speke were not the leaders of the little nautical expedition, only passengers. They moved or halted at the convenience of the crew, and often when Burton wanted to stop at a likely looking spot for collecting shells or rocks the paddlers could not be persuaded to land. They travelled up the eastern side of the lake for about seventy-five miles and then crossed over to what Burton believed to be a large island (actually it is a long narrow peninsula) and then up the western shore to Uvira, arriving on 26 April. They were now at the furthest limit of the area covered by the slave-dealers. The tribes to the north were considered warlike and unfriendly.

The explorers spent nine frustrating days at Uvira. The crew refused to go further north and the natives would hardly stir out of their villages. So terrible were the tales of the ferocious tribes to the north that even Bombay and Mabruki turned mutinous. Although they did not know it, they were only twenty miles from the mouth of the Ruzizi River at the northern end of the lake. Burton did his best to procure an escort to take him there, but he could not persuade a single person to go with him. In the end he was silenced by an ulcerated tongue that left him unable to speak. 'It is characteristic of African travel,' he philosophized, 'that the explorer may be arrested at the very bourn of his journey, on the very threshold of success, by a single stage, as effectually as if all the waves of the Atlantic or the sands of Arabia lay between.' Making the trip unaccompanied in a small canoe does not appear to have been considered as a possibility. As to the Ruzizi, all the natives at Uvira agreed that the river flowed into, not out of, the lake. This was subsequently proved to be the case when, twelve years later, Stanley and Livingstone examined the mouth.

To Burton and Speke it now seemed that it only remained for them to turn back. The return trip to Ujiji was not without its incidents, including a storm that nearly swamped the canoes and a fight with some local inhabitants of the lake shores. While camped by a village one night, Burton was awakened by Mabruki, who rushed into his tent and gave Burton his sword and the news that they were about to leave. Outside, all was confusion, but Burton could see the crews hurriedly loading the boats. There was an argument going on round Kannena and a badly-wounded man was being carried into a boat. Fearing he might be left behind, Burton, too, quickly stowed his gear in the canoes. After they had pushed out from shore and still no enemy had appeared, Kannena was persuaded to return.

Here is Burton's version of what had happened:

During our sleep a drunken man . . . had rushed from the crowd of Warundi, and, knobstick in hand, had commenced dealing blows in all directions. Ensued a general mêlée. Bombay, when struck, called to the crews to arm. The Goanese, Valentine, being fear-crazed, seized my large 'Colt' and probably fired it into the crowd; at all events, the cone struck one of our own men below the right pap, and came out two inches to the right of the backbone. Fortunately for us he was a slave, otherwise the situation would have become desperate. As it was, the crowd became violently excited; one man drew his dagger upon Valentine, and with difficulty I persuaded Kannena from killing him. As the crew had ever an eye to the 'main chance', food, they at once confiscated three goats, our store for the return voyage, cut their throats, and spitted the meat upon their spears: thus the lamb died and the wolf dined, and the innocent suffered and the plunderer was joyed, the strong showed his strength and the weak his weakness, according to the usual formula of this sub-lunary world.

On 13 May they arrived back at Ujiji. In spite of the miserable weather they had encountered throughout the trip and the discomfort of squatting in a narrow canoe for days on end, both Burton and Speke were improved in health. Speke was almost recovered from his blindness, although he was still deaf and in pain from his ear. Burton's tongue, which had been swollen for seventeen days, was now back to its normal size and his hands and feet were somewhat better.

They now prepared for the return march. Their supplies were much reduced and they had hardly enough left to get them to Tabora. Quite unexpectedly, however, a caravan arrived and Burton found himself surrounded by bales, boxes and porters. Here at last were the long awaited supplies from the coast – fifteen porter-loads brought up with the caravan of an Arab merchant. There were also letters and papers from India, Europe and Zanzibar, the first news they had received in eleven months. They told of the Indian Mutiny, of supplies sent but not received, and of the death of Colonel Hamerton.

The boxes and bales proved to be something of a disappointment. Of the fifteen loads, twelve contained ammunition that was not needed in addition to some food supplies that were. The remaining three loads contained cheap cloth, coral bracelets and white beads: 'All were the refuse of their kind: the good Hindoos at Zanzibar had seized this opportunity to dispose of their flimsy, damaged, and unsaleable articles. I saw, however, with regret that it was wholly inadequate for the purpose of exploring the two southern thirds of the Tanganyika Lake, much less for returning to Zanzibar *via* the Nyassa or Maravi Lake and Kilwa, as I had once dreamed.'

Had Burton visited the southern end of the lake he would have learned what a really important discovery he had made, for Lake Tanganyika is the longest fresh water lake in the world. Burton estimated the width to be from 30 to 35 miles across, and this is correct, but he estimated the length of the lake to be only about 250 miles, covering an area of 5,000 square miles. Actually, the lake is 400 miles long and covers an area of 12,355 square miles. It was also unfortunate that he could not make soundings. He might then have discovered that Lake Tanganyika is, except for Lake Baikal, the deepest lake in the world, soundings of 4,708 feet having been recorded. It is ironical that the curious Burton, greedy for information and impatient for fame, did not learn the two most important facts about the lake he had reached. Consequently, he underestimated the magnitude of his discovery.

Both Burton and Speke made a curious mistake in determining the height of the lake above sea level. Speke said it was 'only 1,800 feet' and on Burton's map it is shown as being 1,844 feet. The true level is 2,534 feet. Had Burton been closer to the real elevation, it would have given him tremendous theoretical support for his claim that the lake was a source of the Nile.

Burton's expedition did not make an indelible impression on Africa. There is no mountain, lake, river, island, city or village that bears his name. Nor is his great exploit much remembered by the rest of the world. But among the shells Burton and Speke picked up along the shores of the Tanganyika was one of a species of fresh water clam found only in this lake; it was originally named *Unio burtoni* after Burton and is known today as *Grandidiera burtoni*. Such is fate and fame.

On 28 May 1858, Burton and Speke left Ujiji for Tabora in Unyanyembe. Because all of Burton's men had invested their money in slaves which they were fearful of losing, the march resembled a rout, each man anxious to get his newly acquired property out of the country. The slaves complicated the march. The *jemadar* almost lost his mind when three of his six slaves deserted him. The *kirangozi* from Unyamwezi lagged behind because his slave-girl developed sore feet and could not keep up. Finding the sore feet getting worse rather than better, he cut off her head so that no one else would benefit from his loss. The bull-headed Mabruki had a six-year-old boy whom he carefully tended until the novelty wore off, and then he abused him so badly that Burton insisted on his being entrusted to Bombay.

On 18 June they met an Arab caravan containing seven more loads for Burton. As six of the loads contained cloth, it was most welcome. Two days later they reached Tabora. There Burton found an additional supply and was able to recover the table and chair which had been lost months earlier and had been found by an up caravan. At Tabora, too, were the dismissed sons of Ramji, who begged to be rehired. Burton turned them away.

At Tabora it was obvious that all needed rest. The Beluchis were suffering from malaria, Speke was still deaf and his vision was so dim he could not read or write; neither, according to Burton, could he observe correctly. Again Burton suffered from the swelling and numbness of his hands and feet. There was also the relaxation from many months of nervous tension.

But under the influence of narcotics, tonics, and stimulants, we presently progressed toward convalescence, and stronger than any physical relief, in my case, was the moral effect of success, and the cessation of the ghastly doubts and cares, and of the terrible wear and tear of mind which, from the coast to Uvira, had never been absent. I felt the proud consciousness of having done my best, under conditions from beginning to end the worst and the most unpromising, and that whatever future evils Fate might have in store for me, it could not rob me of the meed won by the hardships and sufferings of the past.

During the first halt at Tabora, Burton and Speke had heard from the Arabs of another lake lying to the north that was said to be larger than Lake Tanganyika. Although Burton had maintained that they did not have enough supplies to enable them to explore the southern end of Lake Tanganyika, still a sub-expedition under Speke was launched to find the northern lake. According to Speke, the whole idea was his. Burton he said, was 'most unfortunately quite done up, but most graciously consented to wait with the Arabs and recruit health'. According to Burton, this was 'far from the fact'. In the book Speke wrote on this expedition he quoted a letter Burton had written at this time to the Royal Geographical Society: 'Captain Speke has volunteered to visit the Ukerewe Lake, of which the Arabs give grand accounts.' The quotation, while not quite accurate, was close enough, and Burton, when he encountered this passage in Speke's book, wrote in the margin, 'To get rid of him.' Since Speke was unable to talk the language of the Arabs and since Burton deemed it necessary to gather information from them and to prepare for the trip back, he maintained that he *sent* Speke to find the lake. Perhaps the truth is somewhere in between. Undoubtedly they discussed the matter between them and probably both agreed that Speke should go. Whatever the case, at the moment he sent Speke, or agreed to let him go, Burton made the greatest mistake of his life. With this one slip he threw away his chance of taking his place with Livingstone and Stanley among the great explorers of Central Africa. Burton had always talked much of life's 'main chance'. This was it, but he did not take it. In effect, he gave it away.

On 9 July, Speke set out northward to make one of the greatest, if not the greatest, of all African discoveries. Burton, meanwhile, stayed in the comparative comfort of Tabora and talked with his Arab friends. They gave him much information, and some of it was accurate. They told him of peoples and tribes, native wars, rivers and mountains. They told him of Mtesa, the fabulous king of Uganda, who ruled not a tribe, but a whole nation. They spoke of the Nyanza, which curiously Burton thought to be the name of a lake (the word 'Nyanza' means 'lake'), that Speke was now marching towards. And they helped Burton to compile vocabularies of native tongues. In general, he enjoyed himself and was again, as at Ujiji, happy to be separated from his companion.

Basically, there are four reasons, great and small, why Burton made his great mistake. First of all, he did not believe Speke would make a discovery of any importance. Secondly, he wanted to be freed of his associate and to spend his time enjoyably and, he believed, profitably by gathering information from the Arabs at Tabora. Thirdly, he wanted to regain his health and make plans for the return trip *via* Kilwa. But the most important reason was that Burton felt he had already accomplished what he had set out to do; he had already achieved success. He did not feel it was necessary to do more. Geography was a means to an end, fame; and exploration carried many pleasures for a man of his temperament, but he did not possess that overpowering desire to see what was on the other side of the mountain that has led other explorers on to great discoveries. The great discoveries of Livingstone, Stanley, Cameron, Speke and Grant were in the future. Burton was first in the field and many of the geographical finds of those who came after him could have been made by him. He failed to grasp his opportunity – the 'main chance' – because he was never truly smitten by that irresistible desire to make great discoveries that crowded out Livingstone's missionary zeal, made Stanley an empire builder instead of a newspaper reporter, and raised Speke, in most ways a lesser man, from an adventurer to a great explorer. In Burton's mind there were too many other things that seemed more important than 'mere geography'. Having discovered Lake Tanganyika, he had achieved his objective and simply lacked the desire to push on into the unknown. His desire to visit Kilwa, which was known, rather than Lake Victoria, which was not, marks Burton as the great traveller, which he was, rather than the very great explorer, which he just failed to be.

While Burton was lounging in Tabora, Speke made his way north until, on 3 August 1858, he reached a lake. He at once concluded that this was the source of the Nile. 'I no longer felt any doubt,' he said later, 'that the lake at my feet gave birth to that interesting river, the source of which has been the object of so many explorers.' He did not attempt to explore the lake, but returned to Tabora, arriving on 25 August. He waited until breakfast was served to announce almost casually that he was sorry Burton had not been with him as 'I felt quite certain in my mind that I had discovered the source of the Nile.' One can imagine Burton's feelings on hearing this news. Fortunately, there must have seemed to Burton abundant reasons for doubting the statement. Speke knew nothing of the extent of the lake, but he had questioned the inhabitants living on its shores: 'On my inquiries about the lake's length, the man (the greatest traveller in the place) faced the north, and began nodding his head to it; at the same time he kept throwing forward his hand, and making repeated snaps of his fingers endeavoured to indicate something immeasurable; and added that nobody knew, but he thought it probably extended to the end of the world.' Burton's sarcastic comment was: 'Strongly impressed by this valuable statistical information, my companion therefore placed the northern limit about $4 – 5°$ north lat.' Burton was always impressed with information he himself received from natives; rarely by information so received by anyone else. It was true Speke's only method of communication was in Hindustani through Bombay, whose Hindustani, according to Burton, was 'an even more debased dialect than that of his master', and it must have been difficult indeed for Speke to gather information from the local inhabitants.

In theory, it seemed highly improbable that Speke had found so great a lake and that it was indeed the source of the Nile. He certainly based his belief more on faith than on any available facts he had collected or anything he had seen for himself. But Speke was convinced that he had discovered, as he said, the 'solution of a problem, which it has been the first geographical desideratum of many thousand years to ascertain, and the ambition of the first monarchs of the world to unravel'.

Against all probability – and all Burton's logic – Speke was essentially right. He *had* found the second largest body of fresh water in the world and the largest lake in Africa, being 250 miles long, 200 miles wide and covering an area of 26,828 square miles. Even more importantly, it constitutes the major source of the mighty Nile. It was indeed a magnificent geographical find. Speke named it Lake Victoria, after his queen, and in the south-east corner is a major indentation known today as Speke Gulf.

As Speke had seen only a small portion of the southern shore of his lake, Burton found it impossible to believe in either its magnitude or its importance. He also objected to giving English names to African places. The breach between the two men was now wide. Burton later wrote this unflattering description of his companion:

Even at the beginning of our long absence from civilized life I could not but perceive that his former alacrity had vanished: he was habitually discontented with what was done; he left to me the whole work of management, and then he complained of not being consulted. He had violent quarrels with the Baloch, and on one occasion the Jemadar returned to him an insult which, if he had not wanted the man, he would have noticed with a sword-cut. Unaccustomed to sickness, he could not endure it himself nor feel for it in others; and he seemed to enjoy pleasure in saying unpleasant things. . . . Much of the change he explained to me by confessing that he could not take an interest in an exploration of which he was not the commander. On the other hand, he taught himself the use of the sextant and other instruments, with a resolution and a pertinacity which formed his characteristic merits. . . . The few books – Shakespeare, Euclid and so forth – which composed my scant library, we read together again and again: he learned from me to sketch the scenery, and he practised writing a diary and accounts of adventure, which he used to bring for correction.

One cannot but feel that many of the faults which Burton saw in Speke were, unfortunately, his own. Burton himself would have been a poor subordinate on an expedition; there was obviously little management done, as Burton was unable to control his people adequately; surely no one had more quarrels with the Beluchis than Burton himself; Burton was a master of the unpleasant word; and, considering the amount of sickness and physical pain that both had to endure, his comments on this score seem most unfair.

Speke was as tired of Burton as Burton was of him. Writing to the Secretary of the Royal Geographical Society he once said, 'B. is one of those men who never *can* be wrong, and will never acknowledge an error so that when only two are together talking becomes more of a bore than a pleasure.' Now, however, for better or worse, Burton and Speke, like an ill-matched married couple who stay together for the sake of the children, had to be together and work together and take care of each other during the long march back to the coast. For the sake of peace, the word 'Nile' was deemed unmentionable. It must have been an unhappy march indeed: a brooding Burton with swollen limbs carried in a hammock; a resentful Speke stumbling along with diseased eyes and painful ear.

Re-engaging the sons of Ramji and hiring porters to carry them only from district to district, they started on their way. There were the usual troubles, but Burton finally exerted a strong hand and managed to infuse enough discipline to give him some command over the expedition he was supposed to be leading. Perhaps his irritation with Speke made him more forceful with the Africans. In any case, the expedition now proceeded in a somewhat more orderly fashion.

Less than two weeks after leaving Tabora, Speke was again struck down by a serious illness. It began with a burning sensation in the chest and then extended towards the heart. On 10 October, just before dawn, he woke up screaming from a nightmare in which tigers, leopards and other beasts, harnessed with a network of iron hooks, were dragging him over the ground. Bombay ran to help him and eased him to a sitting position as it was impossible for him to lie down. Shortly after, he had a second spasm, but it was not so severe. Then the next morning he had a third attack which, according to Burton, 'more closely resembled hydrophobia than aught I had ever witnessed'. He was again haunted by demons who were wrenching and stripping the sinews and tendons of his legs. The handsome young man now appeared a most hideous creature, 'with limbs racked by cramps, features drawn and ghastly, frame fixed and ridged, eyes glazed and glassy, he began to utter a barking noise, and a peculiar chopping motion of the mouth and tongue, with lips protruding – the effect of difficulty of breathing – which so altered his appearance that he was hardly recognizable, and completed the terror of the beholders'.

When he recovered from this seizure, Speke called for pen and paper to write a farewell letter to his family. But the worst was now over, and with the nursing of Burton and Bombay – or perhaps in spite of it – he slowly improved. During this illness Speke, perhaps unconsciously, revealed his anger over Burton's rewriting of his Somaliland diary.

During the enforced halt caused by Speke's breakdown, Burton improved his position as leader by numbering and registering the loads, flogging two disorderly sons of Ramji, dismissing Said bin Salim as headman and appointing Bombay in his place. When the march was resumed – now with both Burton and Speke carried in hammocks – Burton found a most effective way of enforcing his orders by refusing rations to those who would not carry loads. Why he did not do all this earlier remains a mystery. The caravan now numbered 152 people, including the slaves who had been purchased by various members of the expedition and had been unable to escape.

On 5 or 6 December (Burton says 5th in one place and 6th in another) they met an up caravan carrying a packet of letters for the expedition. According to Burton, it was at this time that he received a letter addressed to 'Captain R. F. Burton, 18th Regiment Bombay N.I.' from the Secretary to the Bombay Government and dated 23 July 1857. It was an official reprimand for his letter of 15 December 1856, in which he had given his own views on the situation in the Red Sea area and the mismanagement of the Government in not providing more warships for the protection of British interests in that region. The letter stated:

I am directed by the Right Honourable the Governor in Council to state, your want of discretion, and the due respect for the authorities to whom you are subordinate, has been regarded with displeasure by Government.

With the same packet of mail, Burton said, was a copy of the Overland Summary of the Bombay *Telegraph Courier* of 4 August 1858. It contained an account of a massacre at Jidda that included among its victims the British and French Consuls; the article ended with the fear that a similar event might occur at Suez. Thus, in a tragic way, his advice was vindicated.

Burton was bitter:

But an Englishman in these days must be proud, very proud of his nation, and withal somewhat regretful that he was not born of some mighty mother of men – such as Russia and America – who has not become old and careless enough to leave her bairns unprotected, or cold and crusty enough to reward a little word of wisdom from her babes and sucklings with a scolding or a buffet.

It made a fine story with a neat touch of irony to say that the letter of reprimand came in the same packet with the newspaper account of the massacre – and Burton told the story many times. Unfortunately for the tale, an examination of the documents and a comparison of dates make it evident that such could not have been the case. Burton's reply to the Bombay Government was dated 'Unyanyembe, Central Africa, 24th June, 1858' – in other words, before the massacre at Jidda was committed: His reply to the letter did not mention the Jidda massacre and was humble in tone:

I beg to express my regret that it should have contained any passages offensive to the authorities to whom I am subordinate; and to assure the Right Honourable the Governor in Council that nothing was further from my intentions than to displease a Government to whose kind consideration I have been, and am still, so much indebted.

Most probably, Burton received the 'wigging', as he called it, with the loads he had received from an up caravan on 18 June and replied from Tabora, which he reached a few days later. By 5 December he was out of Unyanyembe and almost through Ugogo. Undoubtedly, it was then that he received the newspaper account of the events at Jidda. He simply made a good story by altering the date.

Burton's newly-found understanding of how to run his expedition is well illustrated by an event that took place on 15 December. The caravan was quietly preparing to break camp and march when suddenly a rope was snatched, a sword flashed, a bow was strung, and the whole expedition was in an uproar. Instead of rushing in to settle the argument, Burton, who was now well enough to ride, mounted his ass and rode off with Speke and some of the sons of Ramji. Soon after, Said bin Salim came running up to announce that the *jemadar* had struck a *pagazi* who, in turn, had stoned the *jemadar*; now the Beluchis had drawn their swords and were about to massacre the porters. Being now experienced in these matters, Burton calmly sent back word that he would not be delayed and that unless the *pagazis* brought up their loads at once he would hire new porters at the next village. The combatants soon rejoined their leader and the caravan continued on its way.

On 14 January 1859, they received from an up caravan the drugs and medical supplies Burton had requested by letter in July 1857. On 30 January the Zanzibaris screamed with delight at the sight of the familiar mango tree, an indication that they were nearly home. On 2 February Burton and Speke sighted the Indian Ocean and 'as Britons will do on such occasions' took off their caps and gave three cheers. The next day they arrived at the coastal village of Kunduchi, about ten miles north of present-day Dar es Salaam.

They were now again on the edge of civilization; but instead of returning to Zanzibar and then to England, Burton sent back the Beluchis and the sons of Ramji with an order for a boat and supplies to take them to Kilwa Kisiwani, 150 miles south, where he had wanted to finish his expedition. Nine days later Burton and Speke began still another coastal expedition.

Kilwa, located on a little island that hugs the coast, was the Quiloa of Da Gama, and it was undoubtedly the associations of the Portuguese explorer, described by the great poet Camoens, which explain Burton's interest in this coastal area. When they arrived at Kilwa they found that cholera was sweeping the island and had, in the previous two weeks, wiped out half the population of the town.

Burton had seen cholera before in Italy and had experienced it in India, but he had never seen anything to compare with the horrors of Kilwa. The very soil and air seemed polluted and a great stench hung over the town. In the bay were corpses that had been thrown there: 'black and brown when freshly thrown in, patched, mottled and particoloured when in a state of half pickle, and ghastly white, like scalded pig, when the pigmentum nigrum had become thoroughly macerated. The males lay prone upon the surface, diving as it were, head downwards, when the retiring swell left them in shallow water; the women floated prostrate with puffed and swollen breasts. . . . Limbs were scattered in all directions, and heads lay like pebbles upon the beach.' Burton later collected twenty-four of the skulls and sent them to the museum of the Royal College of Surgeons.

Apart from the cholera, there was little of interest at Kilwa, so after inspecting the near-by Portuguese and Arab ruins, Burton and Speke returned to Zanzibar, arriving on 4 March 1859.

The two men had gone where no other Europeans had ever gone before; they had suffered much and accomplished great things. In general terms, the expedition had been a success: it had set out to find the lake regions of Central Africa and in the face of immense difficulties had discovered two important lakes. Burton later boasted, 'My labours rendered easy the ingress of future expeditions, which had only to tread in my steps.' The unfortunate part is that, measured in terms of what it might have accomplished, the expedition was something of a failure. Had Burton not wasted time and resources on the coastal expeditions; had he taken a firmer hold on his expedition from the start and exercised greater control of its expenditures of cloth, beads and wire; and had he been firmer in his purpose to make geographical discoveries rather than dispersing his energies in botanical, zoological, anthropological and other interests, the expedition might well have explored Lake Tanganyika more thoroughly and even have followed the northern route round Lake Victoria and gone down the Nile to Egypt. To have done so would have made Burton the foremost explorer of his generation and earned him a greater place in the history of exploration. This had been his main chance. He would never get another.

Chapter 13

Sick Leave in Salt Lake City
1859 – 60

ZANZIBAR was in a turmoil when Burton and Speke arrived there. The Sultan's elder brother was preparing an invasion fleet at Musqat and the Sultan was trying to raise an army to repel him. Cholera was sweeping the island; there had been some 30,000 deaths in recent weeks and the death rate was still 250 a day. Colonel Hamerton had been replaced by Captain (later General) C. P. Rigby, the man Burton had beaten to first place in the Gujarati examination sixteen years earlier. Rigby and Burton took an immediate and intense dislike to each other. In the difference of opinion between Burton and Speke, Rigby sided with Speke. In a letter to his friend J. Miles, Rigby said, 'Speke is a right good, jolly, resolute fellow. Burton is not fit to hold a candle to him and has done nothing in comparison with what Speke has, but Speke is a modest, unassuming man, not very ready with his pen. Burton will blow his trumpet very loud and get all the credit of the discoveries. Speke works. Burton lies on his back all day and picks other people's brains.' Later, when the expedition's personnel complained that they had not been paid enough, Rigby wrote an official letter of complaint against Burton. He also felt that Burton, who was a favourite of the Sultan, was taking too great an interest in the internal politics of the island and was intruding on his own sphere of responsibility. He did not conceal his desire to have Burton off the island.

Although he had requested additional leave and funds for further exploration, Burton decided to leave Zanzibar on 22 March, taking a ship for Aden. He and Speke arrived there on 16 April and were greeted by Burton's old friend John Steinhaeuser. When HMS *Furious* came into port a few days later, the two explorers were offered transportation back to England. Speke left, but once again Burton failed to hurry back for his reward. He pleaded illness, although Aden was certainly not the place for recuperation and a sea voyage generally had a good effect upon his health. Undoubtedly, the truth was that he simply wanted to be free of the companionship of Speke and to stay awhile with his friend Steinhaeuser.

According to Burton, the following conversation was the last he ever had with Speke:

Burton: 'I shall hurry up, Jack, as soon as I can.'

Speke: 'Good-bye, old fellow. You may be quite sure I shall not go up to the Royal Geographical Society until you come to the fore and we appear together. Make your mind easy about that.'

Speke arrived in England on 8 May and on the following day he was showing his maps and explaining his own theories to Sir Roderick Murchison, President of the Royal Geographical Society. Here are Speke's words:

Sir Roderick, I need only say, at once accepted my views; and, knowing my ardent desire to prove to the world, by actual inspection of the exit, that the Victoria N'yanza was the source of the Nile, seized the enlightened view that such a discovery should not be lost to the glory of England and the society of which he was president; and said to me 'Speke, we must send you there again.' I was then officially directed, much against my own inclination, to lecture at the Royal Geographical Society on the geography of Africa, which I had, as the sole surveyor of the second expedition, laid down on our maps. A council of the Geographical Society was now convened to ascertain what projects I had in view for making good my discovery by connecting the lake with the Nile, as also what assistance I should want for that purpose.

Speke's unsupported announcement that he had discovered the source of the Nile created a sensation, both in scientific circles and in the popular press. Burton reached London on 21 May 1859, thirteen days after Speke, but he was too late. He found, he said, 'the ground completely cut from under my feet'. Speke was the hero of the hour, Burton had been forgotten.

But there was one person who was ready to greet Burton like a conquering hero: Isabel Arundell had waited for three years without the encouragement of a single letter. She was thinking of becoming a nun when she received from Zanzibar a short, six-line poem written in a familiar hand entitled 'To Isabel'. That was all. No letter. No news. On the day Burton reached England Isabel wrote in her diary, 'I feel strange, frightened, sick, stupefied, dying to see him, and yet inclined to run away, lest, after all I have suffered and longed for, I should have to bear more.' During his long absence she had spent part of her time taking a continental tour with her sister Blanche Pigott and her husband who were on their honeymoon. Throughout the trip her thoughts were constantly of Richard Burton. In Genoa his picture was stolen and she offered a large reward for its return, even ordering posters to be printed. She was in agony until it was at last returned. It was here that she received a letter from Burton's sister telling her that he would return in June 1858. (He appears to have written to all of his relatives and friends except Isabel during the course of his African expedition.) That New Year's Eve Isabel's one thought was, 'This year I shall see Richard!' (She did not, of course.) In Pisa she climbed the Leaning Tower to find where he had carved his name as a boy, and she chiselled her name beside his. In Lausanne she sat beside the Lake of Geneva and prayed for Richard 'in that far-away swamp in Central Africa'. She wondered if he was thinking of her and thought she heard 'an angelic whisper' tell her 'yes'. But she was haunted by dreams in which he returned home but would not speak to her. She was delighted with Venice and for the first time on the trip she seemed to enjoy herself, but even here she was tormented by her dreams and wrote in her diary, 'Not a night passes here that I do not dream that Richard has come home and will not speak to me.' In Geneva she was proposed to by a rich American who had made a fortune in California and by a dashing Russian officer who serenaded her with his violin at six o'clock in the morning. In Geneva, too, a large fire threatened to destroy the Hôtel des Bergues where she was staying. Abandoning her money and clothes, she fled the hotel with her pet bullfinch and Richard's picture.

At twenty-six Isabel's passion for Burton was as complete, unquestioning and romantic as if she were still sixteen. Near Chamonix, on the slopes of Mont Blanc, she came across a desolate bit of snow-covered table-land swept by winds and canopied with dark clouds. It made her think of 'an exile in Siberia or Dante's Damned Soul in a Hell of Snow'.

Dramatically she asked herself, 'If an angel from heaven came from Almighty God, and told you that Richard was condemned to be chained on that plateau for a hundred years in expiation of his sins before he could enter heaven, and gave you the choice between sharing his exile with him or a throne in the world beneath, which would you choose?' She did not hesitate to give herself an answer: 'A throne would be exile *without him*, and exile *with him* a home!'

The day after he landed in England, Burton stopped at the home of a mutual friend to inquire about Isabel's whereabouts and by co-incidence he found her there seeking news of him. He at once took her away with him in a cab and Isabel's happiness knew no bounds:

I felt like one stunned; I only knew that he put me in and told the cabman to drive. I felt like a person coming to after a fainting fit or in a dream. It was acute pain, and for the first half-hour I found no relief. I would have given worlds for tears or breath; neither came, but it was absolute content, which I fancy people must feel the first few moments after the soul is quit of the body.

Her lover was no longer a handsome, dashing young man. He was still suffering from partial paralysis and the effects of his twenty-one attacks of fever. 'He was a mere skeleton,' Isabel recorded, 'with brown-yellow skin hanging in bags, his eyes protruding, and his lips drawn away from his teeth.'

Burton had need of love, understanding and comfort, and Isabel had all these to give. During his first weeks in England, misfortunes poured on him. He was in poor health; his manuscript on Zanzibar and his coastal expeditions had unaccountably been lost; at thirty-eight he was only a brevet captain in the Indian Army and without much in the way of additional funds; his request to be reimbursed for the supplies and equipment he had lost during the attack at Berbera was denied by the government; he was feuding with Captain Rigby and the Bombay Government; and, worst of all, though he was given the gold medal of the Royal Geographical Society, the command of the next expedition to Africa had been given to Speke, his own theories were disputed and those of Speke were being promoted.

Speke saw what was happening to Burton and gloated in a letter to Rigby, 'Burton has got the dumps, and is cutting himself at every turn.' Speke was delighted by Rigby's charges that Burton failed to give adequate payment to the porters and supported him in every way. He told Rigby, 'They listen at India House with great pride when I tell them the way in which you govern at Zanzibar – defeating the French Consul and carrying everything before you – that you are the father of Zanzibar and the Sultan your eldest son.' Rigby was not immune to such flattery. Later in the year, when Speke was back in the African interior, he was still writing to Rigby about Burton. One of these letters, written on 6 October 1860, is of particular interest:

I am sure everybody at Zanzibar knows it, that I was the leader and Burton the second of the Expedition. Had I not been with him he never could have undergone the journey, and so confident was old Col. H. of this that at one time when I had reason to ask him confidentially if I could leave Burton with propriety . . . he said, no for God's sake do not, or you will hazard the success of the Expedition. – I wished indeed then to forsake Burton and go to the

Nyassa, and the old Colonel was the only man who prevented me from doing it. The last words the poor old Colonel said to Burton, and he cannot deny it, for he told me so himself, was, that he, the Colonel, was sorry he was going, although he had been accessory to it, for he felt certain from what he had already seen that he, Burton, would fail, but at the same time he said, 'I must say you are lucky in having Speke with you, and I hope you will get on well together.' At the same time that he said this to Burton, he said to me 'Speke, I am sorry to part with you, for I fear this Expedition will fail. Do you know I would not myself go with that man Burton on any condition.' . . . Burton thought I never would write because I had been soft enough to give him up my Somali diaries, or he never would have asked me to go with him.

The letter goes on, describing in detail his relations with Burton prior to the expedition and complaining of Burton's selfishness and egotism. He then continues:

After coming home from the Crimea at Burton's invite . . . I told him I would not go again with him if I should be led into such expenses as I was at Berbera, so little did I care about acting second fiddle to him whom I have always thought I could show the way to better than he me. But he pressed me to do so and even gave a money order for my passage out to Bombay rather than *lose my services*. Oh what humbug!!! . . . I cannot tell you how much obliged I shall be to you for writing to my Mother. She will love you for it.

Both Rigby and Grant have testified to Speke's modesty, but from his actions and his letters he certainly appears the reverse. The more one learns of Speke's character, the less wholesome it is revealed. It is difficult to escape the conclusion that the discoverer of the major source of the Nile and the largest lake in Africa was a cad.

Speke's disloyalty undoubtedly hurt Burton, financially, in terms of his honour and reputation, and perhaps most importantly by the very fact that a man with whom he had been more intimately associated than any other person since his youth had turned on him so violently in such an underhanded manner. It is against this background that his courtship of Isabel – or her courtship of him – must be viewed.

There is no doubt that Isabel's whole-hearted love and her sympathy touched him deeply. He would have been less than human if it had not. He wanted to marry her, but even here he was thwarted by Isabel's mother, who objected to her daughter marrying a penniless man without prospects and with a bad reputation. Burton and Isabel now spent much time together and Burton often visited her home, trying as best he could to win over her family. He had succeeded with her father, but her mother remained adamant.

Isabel described her mother as 'a worldly woman of strong brain, of hasty temper, bigoted, and a Spartan with the elder half of her brood', but she desperately wanted her blessing. In October she wrote her mother a long letter describing her own feelings towards Burton and attempting to answer the objections to the marriage:

My Dearest Mother,

I feel quite grateful to you for inviting my confidence. It is the first time you have ever done so, and the occasion shall not be neglected. . . . I am rather ashamed to tell you that I fell in love with Captain Burton at Boulogne. . . . The moment I saw his brigand-daredevil look, I set him up as an idol, and determined that he was the only man I would ever marry. . . . When I came home one day and told you that I had found the Man and the Life I longed for, that I clung to them with all my soul, and that nothing would turn me, and that all other men were his inferiors, what did you answer me? 'That he was the *only* man you would not consent to my marrying; that you would rather see me in my coffin.' Did you know that you were flying in the face of God? Did you know it was my destiny? Do you not realize that, because it is not *your* ideal, you want to dash mine from me? . . . It surprises me that you should consider mine an infatuation. . . . Look at his military services – India and the Crimea! Look at his writings, his travels, his poetry, his languages and dialects! Now Mezzofanti is dead he stands first in Europe; he is the best horseman, swordsman, and pistol shot. He has been presented with the gold medal, he is an F.R.G.S. . . . There is not a particle of pettiness or snobbery in him; he is far superior to any man I ever met; he has the brain, pluck, and manliness of any hundred of those I have seen, united to exceeding sensitiveness, gentleness, delicacy, generosity, and good pride. He is the only one who awes me into respect, and to whose command I bow my head. . . . I want to '*Live*'. I hate the artificial existence of London; I hate the life of a vegetable in the country; I want a wild, roving, vagabond life . . . you will certainly repent it, if you keep me tied up. . . . He appears to me as something so unique and romantic. . . . He is proud, fiery, satirical, ambitious; how could I help looking up to him with fear and admiration? . . . I wish I were a man. If I were, I would be Richard Burton; but, being a woman, I would be Richard Burton's wife. . . . Whatever the world may condemn of lawless or strong opinions, whatever he is to the world, he is perfect to me, and I would not have him otherwise than he is.

You have said that 'you do not know who he is, that you do not meet him anywhere.' I don't like to hear you say the first, because it makes you illiterate . . . but as to your not meeting him, considering the particular sort of society which you seek with a view to marry your daughters, you are not likely to meet him there, because it bores him, and it is quite out of his line. In these matters he is like a noble, simple savage, and has lived too much in the desert to comprehend the snobberies of our little circle in London. . . . The next subject is religion. With regard to this he *appears* to disbelieve, pretends to self-reliance, quizzes good, and fears no evil. *At present* he is following no form; at least, none that he *owns* to. He says there is nothing between Agnosticism and Catholicity.

Do not accuse me of deception, because I shall see him and write to him whenever I get a chance, and if you drive me to it I shall marry him in defiance, because he is by far my first object in life, and the day he (if ever) gives me up I will go straight into a convent. . . . If I choose to live out of the 'World' that forms your *happiness*, what is it to you? how does it hurt you? I have got to live with him night and day, for all my life. The man you would choose I should loathe. . . . Do not embitter my whole future life, for God's sake. I would rather die a thousand times than go through again what I have borne for the last five years. . . . Remember that day will come when you will forgive and repent, and you will feel quite hurt to find that the 'World' does *not* forgive, that it remembers all you said when you were angry, and that you have debarred your own children from many pleasant things in this life. . . . Parents hold so much power to bless or curse the future. What will you do for me? Let it be a blessing! I look upon him as my future husband; I only wait a kind word from you, the appointment, and Cardinal Wiseman's protection. Do write to me, dearest mother, but write not with *your* views, but entering into *mine*.

Your fondly attached child,
ISABEL ARUNDELL

As might be imagined, such a letter was hardly pleasing to Mrs Arundell, and Isabel received 'an awful long and solemn sermon' for her pains. But Isabel and her mother were a pair of stubborn women. Burton said that both of them were gifted with 'the noble firmness of the mule'.

Although Burton scorned 'society', he had many friends, some of whom were influential. One of the most important, certainly, was that extraordinary catalytic character, Richard Monckton Milnes, later Lord Houghton: poet, politician and a Maecenas of the age. It is not known exactly when Burton and Milnes first met, but apparently they became intimately acquainted during the summer of 1859, for it was in August that Burton paid his first visit to Milnes' home at Fryston. Milnes, now fifty years old, was not yet a peer, but he had a tremendous reputation as a friend of the eminent in literature. He also had a more private reputation among his intimates for his collection of erotica. The man who procured most of this for him was an unusual person named Frederick Hankey, whom Milnes probably introduced to Burton this year in London.

In February 1860, Burton was in Boulogne working on his *Lake Regions of Central Africa*, the story of his African adventures and misadventures. While there he corresponded with, if he did not actually meet, Fred Hankey. This man was about Burton's age, from a good family, exquisitely polite, and noted for his gentle, almost sweet manner. Obviously, the ideal place to find erotica, then as now, was Paris, and it was here that Hankey lived, but he made frequent trips to England to see Milnes and to seek out those particular kinds of pleasures he fancied. There was, for example, a place in London known to him where one could whip young girls – and even stick pins in them. One of the Goncourt brothers visited Hankey's apartment at 2 Rue Laffitte and described his experience. Hankey showed his visitor his unusual library, including a book on flagellation with some remarkable stamps on the binding. He had had difficulty getting them made. It had been necessary to corrupt the mind of the man who made the stamps, develop in him a taste for young girls, and to wreck his marriage – but he obtained the stamps. He also showed Goncourt an unbound book, saying that the human skin being prepared for the binding was not ready yet. This was just an ordinary skin, he explained, but he had been promised by Burton (this was in April 1862) the skin of a negress stripped from her while she was still alive. '*Moi, j'ai les goûts cruels,*' he explained. Burton thought Hankey a very amusing person. In the future, writing to Milnes, he would often ask, 'What of poor old Hankey?'

On 10 April, after, as usual, only one 'revise', Burton sent off the long manuscript on his African expedition. He had intended to publish it earlier, he said, but 'the impairment of my health, the depression of spirits, and, worse still, the annoyance of official correspondence, which to me have been the sole results of African explorations, may be admitted as valid reasons for the delay'.

Opinions regarding the value of Burton's *Lake Regions of Central Africa* vary. Most modern writers praise its accuracy, but this can only be gauged by those who came immediately after. Verney Lovett Cameron, following roughly the same trail in 1873, said, 'Going over ground which he explored with his *Lake Regions of Central Africa* in my hand, I was astonished at the acuteness of his perception and the correctness of his descriptions.' Henry M. Stanley, who went over the ground two years before Cameron, thought the book 'wonderfully clever and truthful' but complained that he acquired many 'eccentric ideas' as a result of reading it and that Burton had left many blank spaces on his map which he had found spotted with villages. In *How I Found Livingstone* Stanley wrote:

Shall I inform you, reader, what *The Lake Regions of Central Africa*, and subsequently the reports of European merchants of Zanzibar, caused me to imagine the interior was like? It was that of an immense swamp, curtained round about with the fever. . . . In this swamp, which extended over two hundred miles into the interior, sported an immense number of hippopotami, crocodiles, alligators, lizards, tortoises, and toads; and the miasma rising from this vast cataclysm of mud, corruption, and putrescence, was as thick and sorely depressing as the gloomy and suicidal fog of London. Ever in my mind in the foreground were the figures of poor Burton and Speke, 'the former a confirmed invalid, and the other permanently affected' in the brain by this fever. The wormwood and fever tone of Capt Burton's book I regarded as the result of African disease. But ever since my arrival on the mainland, day by day the pall-like curtain had been clearing away. . . . We had been now two months on the East African soil, and not one of my men had been sick.

In Burton's lengthy two-volume work, the name of Speke is not mentioned. He is referred to only as 'my companion'. In the preface, however, Burton gave vent to his feelings:

The history of our companionship is simply this: – As he had suffered with me in purse and person at Berberah, in 1855, I thought it but just to offer him the opportunity of renewing an attempt to penetrate into Africa. I had no other reasons. I could not expect much from his assistance; he was not a linguist – French and Arabic being equally unknown to him – nor a man of science, nor an accurate astronomical observer. The Court of Directors officially refused him leave of absence; I obtained it for him by an application to the local authorities at Bombay. During the expedition he acted in a subordinate capacity; and, as may be imagined, among a party of Arabs, Baloch, and Africans, whose languages he ignored, he was unfit for any other but a subordinate capacity. Can I then feel otherwise than indignant, when I find that, after preceding me from Aden to England, with the spontaneous offer, on his part, of not appearing before the society that originated the expedition until my return, he had lost no time in taking measures to secure for himself the right of working the field which I had opened, and from that day he has placed himself *en evidence* as the *primum mobile* of an expedition in which he signed himself 'surveyor' – *cujus pars minima fuit*?

As Burton's indignation sputtered off into Latin, Speke was preparing to depart from England for Lake Victoria, taking with him Captain (later Colonel) James A. Grant, whom he was careful not to send off on important independent missions. Speke and Grant left for Africa on 27 April 1860. In that same month, Burton, too, left England.

Isabel, never at a loss for a premonition, was talking with two friends when she suddenly clasped her hand to her heart and said, 'I am not going to see Richard for some time.'

'Why, you will see him tomorrow,' said her friend.

'No, I shall not. I don't know what is the matter.'

Soon after there was a knock on the door and Isabel was handed a note. Of course it was from Burton, who always hated to say good-bye in person. The note told Isabel that her lover had gone to America and that he hoped when he came back she would have made up her mind to choose between him and her mother. Isabel collapsed and was put to bed with her heartache while her mother futilely called a doctor.

There is no record of Burton's movements after he reached North America. He is known to have been in Canada, to have visited Washington, D.C., and he possibly travelled in some of the Southern States.

On 7 August Burton mounted a stage-coach at St Joseph, Mo., for a long ride to the Wild West of the United States. His first destination: Salt Lake City, Utah. He was armed with a book entitled *The Prairie Traveller* by Captain Randolph B. Marcy of the United States Army (when the next edition of this book was issued in 1863 it carried Burton's footnotes), Warren's *Explorations of Nebraska*, and Bartlett's *Dictionary of Americanisms*. He also carried a silk hat in a hat-box; an umbrella; an English tweed shooting-jacket; a pocket-sextant; a telescope that later proved worthless; some tea, sugar, cigars, cognac and opium; a 'broad leather belt for "six shooter" and for "Arkansas toothpick"'; and two revolvers, for 'from the moment of leaving St. Jo. to the time of reaching Placerville or Sacramento the pistol should never be absent from a man's right side – remember it is handier there than the other – nor the bowie from his left.'

Burton's travelling companions included a federal judge, a state marshal and Lieutenant James Jackson Dana, an artillery officer travelling with his wife Thesta and their two-year-old daughter May. All had paid $175 ($5 = £1) for the trip and were assembled at 8.30 in the morning in front of Patee House to load their allotted twenty-five pounds of baggage and mount their 'Concord coach'. The driver dropped a hat-box – not Burton's – and was soundly cursed with many a 'God Damn' which, Burton explained, 'in these lands changes from its expletive or chrysalis form to an adjectival development'. An hour later all was properly stowed and Burton and his companions were rolling through the dusty streets towards the west.

Ostensibly, Burton's purpose was to add Great Salt Lake City to the list of other holy cities he had seen – Rome, Mecca, Jerusalem, Benares – and to learn about the Mormons. He also had 'the mundane desire of enjoying a little skirmishing with the savages, who in the days of Harrison and Jackson had given the pale faces tough work to do'. In actual fact, he wished simply to flee England and its problems and humiliations, and to do this he resorted to a device he had used before and would use many times again: sick leave. Burton's idea of convalescence was hardly the usual rest and light exercise. With his interest in religions and in primitive peoples, a trip across the plains to Salt Lake City and its colony of Latter Day Saints with the opportunity of studying the American Indian along the way seemed the ideal solution. He was probably right, for he appears to have enjoyed this trip immensely. He was no longer an explorer, merely a traveller.

Burton the linguist was fascinated by the American idiom and by Western jargon in particular. He took pains to learn the local dialects and could soon talk of a 'neck o' the woods', of 'criks', of having a 'high old time of it', and of a lawyer who 'hung out his shingle'. He collected the names he found used for whisky, such as tarantula-juice, red-eye, strychnine, corn-juice, Jersey-lightning, leg-stretcher, and other 'hard and grotesque names'. He learned not only the phrase 'liquoring up', but quickly adopted the custom. He could soon explain to his English friends that cowboys' boots were 'cowhide Wellingtons'; that a 'drink' was any body of water, but that the 'big drink' was the Mississippi River; that corn was maize, crackers were biscuits and that 'doughnut' was untranslatable. He also learned that certain English expressions were unacceptable in the United States and that one should not use the phrase 'knocked up' (English for fatigued) in the presence of American women.

He disapproved of changing Indian place names into English ones, but he thought many of the American designations colourful. He found several places named after white men who had been killed by Indians, 'murder', he noted, 'being here, as in Central Africa, ever the principal source of nomenclature'. Burton's coach took him to Bleeding Kansas and on to Emigration Road. 'Passing through a few wretched shanties called Troy – last insult to the memory of hapless Pergamus – and Syracuse (here we are in the third, or classic stage of U.S. nomenclature), we made at 3 p.m., Cold Springs, the junction of the Leavenworth route.'

There were, of course, new sights to see, such as the covered wagon, 'those ships of the great American Sahara which, gathering in fleets at certain seasons, conduct the traffic between the eastern and western shores of a waste which is everywhere like a sea and which presently will become salt. . . . They are not unpicturesque from afar, these long winding trains, in early morning like lines of white cranes trooping slowly over the prairie.' He also saw the Pony Express, which had come into operation only five months earlier, and made a note on his first sight of a coyote.

Like Englishmen before and since, Burton was appalled by the hearty American breakfast, 'the eternal eggs and bacon'. The man who had suffered in silence the primitive fare of India, Arabia and Central Africa, now wailed loudly at the thick rashers of bacon and vile coffee. But it was characteristic of Burton to suffer real hardships without complaint and to grumble unceasingly at minor discomforts.

At Fort Kearny his hopes of seeing active service against the Indians with the United States Cavalry were dashed. Before leaving for the west, he had stopped off in Washington and had called on John B. Floyd, former Governor of Virginia who was serving his last days in office as Secretary of War under Buchanan. Floyd was polite to this wild Englishman who volunteered to kill Indians for him and gave him letters of introduction to the commanders of the military departments, or districts, in the west. At Fort Kearny Burton learned that a successful action had just been fought by six companies of the 1st Cavalry and was told that a considerable body of Comanches, Kiowas and Cheyennes had been dispersed. Although disappointed by the news that there would be no new campaign until the Indians gathered their strength and their courage again, Burton still took hope that he might be attacked on the road, reflecting that 'fifty or sixty miles is a flea-bite to a mounted war party, and disappointed Indians upon the war path are especially dangerous – even the most friendly cannot be trusted when they have lost, or have not succeeded in taking a few scalps'.

Throughout his trip, Burton compared the sights with those he had seen in other exotic lands and he 'could not but meditate upon the difference between travel in the pure prairie air, despite an occasional "chill", and the perspiring miseries of an East Indian dawk, or of a trudge in the miasmatic and pestilential regions of Central Africa'. The bows and arrows of the Indians reminded him 'of those in use amongst the Bedouins of El Hejaz'; a station-house on the way was 'not unlike an Egyptian Fellah's hut'; and the buttes made him think of the City of Brass, fabled city of magic in *The Arabian Nights*.

The ever-curious Burton talked with everyone and made copious notes on many things which he himself was not fortunate enough to see first-hand: scalping, for example. Burton was most interested in this custom. Near Alkali Lake there was an encampment of Sioux and he tried to persuade a brave to show him in pantomime how the operation was performed. The Sioux refused. 'A glass of whisky would doubtless have changed his mind,' he reflected, 'but I was unwilling to break through the wholesome law that prohibits it.' Nevertheless, he learned enough from others to describe the details; his description, in fact, reads like directions for a do-it-yourself scalping kit:

In the good old times braves scrupulously waited for the wounded man's death before they 'raised his hair'; in the laxity of modern days, however, this humane custom is too often disregarded. . . . When the Indian sees his enemy fall he draws his scalp-knife . . . and twisting the scalp-lock, which is left long for that purpose, and boastfully braided or decorated with some gaudy ribbon or with the war-eagle's plume, round his left hand, makes with the right two semicircular incisions, with and against the sun, about the part to be removed. The skin is next loosened with the knife point. . . . The operator then sits on the ground, places his feet against the shoulders by way of leverage, and holding the scalp-lock with both hands he applies a strain which soon brings off the spoils with a sound which, I am told, is not unlike 'flop'. . . . A few cunning men have surprised their adversaries with wigs. The operation of scalping must be exceedingly painful; the sufferer turns, wriggles and 'squirms' upon the ground like a scotched snake.

He speaks like an expert and warns the curio hunter that only one scalp can come off one head.

This knowledge is the more needful as the western men are in the habit of manufacturing half a dozen cut from different parts on the head; they sell readily for $50 each, but the transaction is not considered reputable. The connoisseur, however, readily distinguishes the real article from 'false scalping' by the unusual thickness of the cutis, which is more like that of a donkey than of a man.

If he bought a scalp for his friend Hankey, it is not recorded.

Burton wrote equally authoritatively of the buffalo, although he was one of the few people to cross the plains at this period without seeing a single one. He did not encounter a hostile Indian either, but he prepared for the encounter by learning Indian sign language. In *The City of the Saints*, Burton's inevitable book on his trip, he tells of some of the signs which he says 'will be found useful upon the prairie in case of meeting a suspected band': he gives a description of the 'words': 'Halt!' 'I don't know you!' 'I am angry!' 'Are you friendly?' He also gives instructions for communicating with friendly Indians. '*Love!* – Fold the hands crosswise over the breast, as if embracing the object, assuming at the same time a look expressing the desire to carry out the operation. This gesture will be understood by the dullest squaw.'

Another danger Burton was prepared for was snake-bite. The favourite remedy in the United States, he said, was the 'whisky cure'. One almost has the feeling that Burton would have welcomed a snake-bite for the pleasure of the cure: 'It has the advantage of being a palatable medicine; it must also be taken in large quantities a couple of bottles sometimes producing little effect.'

But Burton did not really need the help of a snake. He 'liquored up' at every station along the route and drank along the way as well. Perhaps it was the whisky that reconciled him to travelling with a two-year-old child, but he became very fond of the entire Dana family, attempting to obtain the best bed at each stop for Mrs Dana and talking for hours with Lt. Dana. Thesta Dana was apparently a perceptive woman with a keen sense of humour who enjoyed Burton's company as much as he enjoyed hers. The memory of her trip with her husband, her baby and Burton has been passed down even to her great-nephew.

On 19 August the coach reached Three Crossings where the station house was kept by a stout, active, middle-aged matron called 'Miss' Moore who provided excellent food in clean surroundings. Even her children were clean, Burton noted. This, he said, was the third novel sensation he had experienced in America. 'The first is to feel (practically) that all men are equal; that you are no man's superior, and that no man is yours.' The second was the novel sight of negroes dressed in European clothes. The third was 'meeting in the Rocky Mountains with this refreshing specimen of that far old world, where, on the whole, society still lies in strata, as originally deposited, distinct, sharply defined and rarely displaced, except by some violent upheaval from below, which, however, never succeeds long in producing total inversion'. Miss Moore's husband is described as 'a decent appendage'. But it was Thesta Dana who pointed out 'one sign of demoralisation on the part of Miss Moore. It was so microscopic that only a woman's eye could detect it. Miss Moore was teaching her children to say "Yes surr!" to every driver.'

They were now entering Mormon country and were on the route normally taken by emigrants to Salt Lake City. Being near the end of their journey, the emigrants were in their worst condition: 'We passed several families and parties of women and children trudging wearily along: most of the children were in rags or half nude, and all showed gratitude when we threw them provisions.'

At last, after nineteen days in the stage coach, they caught sight of Salt Lake City. As when he first saw Mecca, Burton looked on the scene with emotion. Here was another holy city at the end of a long journey. He thought that from a distance it had an oriental aspect and also in some points resembled modern Athens – without the Acropolis, of course.

He spent twenty-four days at Salt Lake City and the bulk of *The City of the Saints* is devoted to his accurate, quite comprehensive, and sympathetic account of the Church of Jesus Christ of the Latter Day Saints and the men and women who braved so much to practise their unpopular faith. He talked with everyone: the Governor of the Territory (Utah was not yet a State); Brigham Young, the prophet, president and leader of the church; many of the apostles, bishops and other dignitaries; new emigrants and old settlers; saints and gentiles.

From here he sent a letter to his friend Norton Shaw, Secretary of the Royal Geographical Society:

> Salt Lake City, Deseret, Utah Territory,
> September 7.

My Dear Shaw,

You'll see my whereabouts by the envelope; I reached this place about a week ago, and am living in the odour of sanctity, – a pretty strong one it is too, – apostles, prophets, *et hoc genus omne*. In about another week I expect to start for Carson Valley and San Francisco. The road is full of Indians and other scoundrels, but I've had my hair cropped so short that my scalp is not worth having. I hope to be in San Francisco in October, and in England sometime in November next. Can you put my whereabouts in some paper or other, and thus save me the bother of writing to all my friends? Mind, I'm travelling for my health, which has suffered in Africa, enjoying the pure air of the prairies, and expecting to return in a state of renovation and perfectly ready to leave a card on Muata Yanoo, or any other tyrant of that kind.

> Meanwhile, ever yours,
> R. F. BURTON.

Shaw read the letter to the Royal Geographical Society on 13 November. At the same meeting a letter was read from Speke saying that he had reached the Cape of Good Hope and that the governor of the colony had supplied him with a guard of twelve Hottentot soldiers and an additional £300. A warship was now taking them to Zanzibar. The President also announced at the meeting that a subscription was being taken to send boats up the Nile to meet Speke and Grant when they came out that way.

Burton walked the streets of Salt Lake City and was impressed with the results of Mormon industry he found reflected there – although he doubted that the temple would ever be completed. With unusual humbleness and his usual tolerance, he wrote, 'I would not willingly make light in others of certain finer sentiments – veneration and conscientiousness – which Nature has perhaps debarred me from ever enjoying; nor is it in my mind to console myself for the privation by debasing the gift in those gifted with it.'

It had been only twelve years earlier that Brigham Young had led the advance guard of picked emigrants into the valley of the Great Salt Lake. There, against all probability, they were prospering in spite of government harassment and the abuse heaped on them by an indignant world. The story of the Mormons was known (usually in some distorted fashion), not only in the United States but throughout Europe. The most prominent feature of the sect to the outside world was the controversial and exotic practice of polygamy, or, as the Mormons preferred to call it, 'plural marriage'.

Burton's excellent account of Mormon life was, and is, one of the best unbiased accounts of the religion. Being himself a man of all religions and of none, Burton was able to view polygamy with an Olympian detachment :

To the unprejudiced traveller it appears that polygamy is the rule where population is required. . . . The other motive for polygamy in Utah is economy. Servants are rare and costly; it is cheaper and more comfortable to marry them. . . . The consent of the first wife to a rival is seldom refused, and a *ménage à trois*, in the Mormon sense of the phrase, is fatal to the development of that tender tie which must be confined to two. In its stead there is household comfort, affection, circumspect friendship, and domestic discipline.

He had not been long in town before he contrived to meet Brigham Young. To Burton he looked like 'a gentleman farmer in New England', and he noted with approval that the prophet's hands were 'not disfigured by rings'. The interview lasted for about an hour: 'His manner is at once affable and impressive, simple and courteous: his want of pretension contrasts favourably with certain pseudo-prophets that I have seen. . . . He shows no signs of dogmatism, bigotry, or fanaticism, and never once entered – with me at least – upon the subject of religion.'

This version of the interview is in conflict with one which Isabel later related: 'He asked Brigham Young if he would admit him as a Mormon, but Brigham Young shook his head, and said, "No, Captain, I think you have done that sort of thing once before." Richard laughed, and told him he was perfectly right.' Undoubtedly the first version is the correct one, and undoubtedly the second is the one Burton often told for his own and his friends' amusement.

Actually, he did not even ask Brigham Young how many wives he had, being 'unwilling to add to the number of those who had annoyed the Prophet by domestic allusions'. When the interview was over, Burton was left with the impression that 'the Prophet is no common man, and that he has none of the weaknesses and vanity which characterise the common uncommon man'.

At the end of three weeks, after seeing the sights and learning all he could about Mormonism, Burton became bored with the monotony and decorum of life in Salt Lake City. Although the saints were interesting, he found the society of sinning soldiers at near-by Camp Floyd more to his taste. Drinking with the officers, he sympathized with their problems and compared them with those in the British Army. The American officers complained that enlistments were too short (five years), desertion was too easy and frequent, that they were misunderstood by the public and ruled by a civilian Secretary of War. Burton sympathized. In general, these are the complaints of all professional soldiers in peace time. Burton also found some faults of his own with the American Army:

The Federal uniform consists of a brigand-like and bizarre sombrero . . . and a blue broad-cloth tunic, imitated from the old Kentuckian hunter's surtout or wrapper, with terminations sometimes made to match, at other times too dark and dingy to please the eye. Its principal merit is a severe republican plainness, very consistent with the prepossessions of the people, highly inconsistent with the customs of military nations.

Burton also had some gratuitous recommendations to make. He suggested the United States Army form a camel corps to use in the

Far West (an experiment that was later tried, incidentally), that they organize regiments of friendly Indians like the sepoys, and that they abandon the outpost system for a more centralized army. But it was only a matter of a few months now before the army and the nation would be split apart by civil war.

He spent five days at Camp Floyd before setting out on 27 September with a miscellaneous collection of other people for San Francisco. As this was considered a particularly dangerous stretch of country, he had his hair cropped short so his scalp would not be a temptation to hostile Indians and regretted he had not brought his wigs with him. It was rugged country, and Burton, with his usual lack of correct prophecy, predicted that 'a paying railroad through this country is as likely as a profitable canal through the Isthmus of Suez'.

At one of the stations they encountered a young woman who was on her way east from San Francisco. Members of Burton's party who asked her about various girls they knew in San Francisco, were usually told that the girls in question had 'got to git up and git'. Most of her sentences ended with 'you *bet*', even, Burton noted, 'under circumstances where such operations would have been quite uncalled for'.

There was much talk of Indians on the war-path and they met with an army patrol that had recently had a fight. Burton noted that the weather was fine for an Indian attack; the ground being covered with snow, small parties could be easily tracked down. All were on the alert. On 5 October they were making their way through a canyon that seemed made for an ambush when suddenly Burton spotted two fires half-way up on the hillside on their left. In a moment they were quenched, probably with snow. As they all expected instantly to be attacked, the horses were whipped forward as fast as they could go. Luckily, there was no attack and they were soon out of the canyon. They were not comforted, however, to find that the next station-house had been reduced to a chimney-stack and a few charred posts. The Indians had been there but two or three days before. The wolves had been at the corpses and parts of bodies were strewn about, one arm sticking up grotesquely from the snow. There was nothing to be done. Burton and his party rode on. Except for the coach overturning and breaking all the whisky bottles, they proceeded without further incident to Carson City, arriving on 19 October.

Carson City in 1860 was wild and woolly. During his three days there, Burton 'heard of' three murders. He also heard of western justice and was impressed with the story of a man who asked bystanders to

'Stoop down while I shoot this son of a bitch.' When brought to court, his words were used against him, but were turned in his favour by his lawyer who maintained that the man was obviously trying to shoot a dog and so the murder was accidental. The man was acquitted.

From Carson City he went to Virginia City (Mark Twain was to join the newspaper there two years later) to inspect the silver mines; then on he went to San Francisco by way of Sacramento. He spent ten days in San Francisco. 'Temptingly near' were Yosemite, the great sequoia forests, Los Angeles, and Vancouver Island, but Burton was tired of it all: 'My eyes were full of sight-seeing, my pockets empty, and my brain stuffed with all manner of useful knowledge. It was far more grateful to *flâner* about the stirring streets, to admire the charming faces, to enjoy the delicious climate, and to pay quiet visits like a "ladies' man", than to front wind and rain, muddy roads, *arrieros*, and rough teamsters.'

He soothed his conscience by saying that he wanted to see with his own eyes a presidential election and the workings of a system he had heard called 'universal suffering and vote by bullet'. It was an uncommonly interesting election this year. Out of four and a half million votes cast, Abraham Lincoln received less than two million, yet he was elected President of the United States and his election precipitated a war that was perhaps inevitable. But Burton did not stay. On 15 November he boarded the *Golden Age*, a model steamer with a cuisine that featured terrapin soup and devilled crabs à la Baltimore. Speke this day made a forced march over semi-desert table-land in Usagara; there was famine in the land and the natives would not sell him food.

Exactly one month later Burton debarked at Panama. The place was filthy and reminded him of a native hotel in Bombay, but he hated to leave. He had met 'a charming country-woman, whose fascinating society made me regret that my stay could not be protracted'.

Isabel read in a newspaper that a Captain Burton had been murdered. Even her mother pitied her and took her to the post office to learn the details. There a clerk informed her that it was true a Captain Burton had been killed by his crew on board his ship. The clerk was astonished that such macabre news should delight her so.

On 18 December Burton took the train across the Isthmus to Colón (then called Aspinwall), where he was delighted by the discovery of a certain muscatel cognac called 'Italia'. He would have liked to have lingered and was sorry when the ship arrived to take him back to England.

On Christmas Day, 1860, Isabel was at the country home of Sir Clifford and Lady Constable in Yorkshire together with twenty-four relatives and close friends of the family. They were singing and someone propped up the music with a copy of *The Times*. Isabel's eyes strayed from the music to the newspaper. The first announcement that caught her eye told her that 'Captain R. F. Burton had arrived from America.'

Chapter 14

Marriage
1861

BURTON had been left £1,500 by his father, but his patrimony and his Army pay combined brought him an income of only £350 a year. Knowing that she was going to marry a relatively poor man, Isabel had been preparing herself for the hardships she expected to endure, although her ideas of what these might be were somewhat naïve. She arranged to spend some time on a farm where she learned 'every imaginable thing' so that 'if we had *no* servants, or if servants were sick or mutinous, we should be perfectly independent'. She asked a friend, Dr George Bird, to give her fencing lessons in order, she said, to be able to defend Richard if attacked – perhaps by the mutinous servants. Richard, of course, being one of the finest swordsmen of his day.

Isabel was an unusually determined and single-purposed young woman. Finding herself in the camp of the enemies of love (her relatives), and her lover in London, she proved that, where Burton was concerned, she could be quite resourceful. Although nine miles from the railroad station and with the roads blocked with snow, she somehow managed within twelve hours to have a sham telegram sent to her which ordered her to go to London and then to actually catch the train. 'What a triumph it is to a woman's heart,' she wrote, 'when she has patiently and courageously worked and prayed, and suffered, and the moment is realized that was the goal of her ambition!'

It is unfortunate that while we have very detailed records by Burton of his thoughts, opinions, and actions even on routine trips and the most minor adventures, there is no record of his feelings or thoughts regarding his courtship of and marriage to Isabel. But Isabel wrote and, from the accounts of her contemporaries, apparently talked about little else except Burton and her relationship with him. It is only from Isabel, then, that we learn of her meeting with him following his return from America.

According to her, Burton made the following speech:

'I have waited for five years. The first three were inevitable on account of my journey to Africa, but the last two were not. Our lives are being spoiled by your mother, and it is for you to consider whether you have not already done your duty in sacrificing two of the best years of your life out of respect to her. If *once* you *really* let me go, mind I shall never come back, because I shall know you have not got the strength of character which *my* wife must have. Now, you must make up your mind to choose between your mother and me. If you choose me, we marry, and I stay; if not, I go back to India and on other explorations, and I return no more. Is your answer ready?'

'Quite,' said Isabel. 'I marry you this day three weeks, let who will say nay.'

The words hardly sound like Burton's, but the sentiments are undoubtedly his. The date of the marriage was not quite so easily arranged when they consulted a calendar. Both were superstitious and Wednesdays and Fridays being unlucky days for them, they settled for a Tuesday: 22 January 1861.

Isabel consulted her father. Would he agree to the marriage? 'I consent with all my heart – if your mother consents,' he answered.

Mrs Arundell said, '*Never!*'

Isabel now turned to Nicholas, Cardinal Wiseman. This wise and famous prelate, who had been influential in the Oxford Movement and had confirmed Newman, was a family friend and he offered to help. From Burton he extracted written promises to allow Isabel to practise her faith freely, to raise any children as Catholics, and to be married in the Catholic Church. He obtained a special dispensation from Rome and intended to marry the pair himself. It was to be a quiet affair with only a few intimate friends, and Burton was pleased that it was so, for he considered a large wedding 'a most barbarous and indelicate exhibition'.

In her devotional book Isabel wrote, 'The principal and leading features of my future life are going to be: Marriage with Richard. My parents' blessing and pardon. A man-child. An appointment. Money earned by literature and publishing. A little society. Doing a great deal of good. Much travelling.'

Many wives lay down rules of conduct for their husbands; fewer make rules for themselves. The most remarkable document Isabel ever wrote was the list of rules she set down as a guide for her marriage to Burton. It would be difficult to find an assemblage of rules better designed to suit a husband – particularly if that husband was Richard Burton. They deserve to be quoted in full, not only because they illustrate an important aspect of Isabel's character and the depth of her devotion, but also because they indicate her understanding of some of the less amiable aspects of his nature and the character of the marriage itself, for Isabel tried steadfastly to adhere to them for more than thirty years.

RULES FOR MY GUIDANCE AS A WIFE

1. Let your husband find in you a companion, friend, and adviser, and *confidante*, that he may miss nothing at home; and let him find in the wife what he and many other men fancy is only to be found in a mistress, that he may seek nothing out of his home.

2. Be a careful nurse when he is ailing, that he may never be in low spirits about his health without a serious cause.

3. Make his home snug. If it be ever so small and poor, there can always be a certain *chic* about it. Men are always ashamed of a poverty-stricken home, and therefore prefer the Club. Attend much to his creature comforts; allow smoking or anything else; for if you do not, *somebody else will*. Make it yourself cheerful and attractive, and draw relations and intimates about him, and the style of society (*literati*) that suits him, marking who are real friends to him and who are not.

4. Improve and educate yourself in every way, that you may enter into his pursuits and keep pace with the times, that he may not weary of you.

5. Be prepared at any moment to follow him at an hour's notice and rough it like a man.

6. Do not try to hide your affection for him, but let him see and feel it in every action. Never refuse anything he asks. Observe a certain amount of reserve and delicacy before him. Keep up the honeymoon romance, whether at home or in the desert. At the same time do not make prudish bothers, which only disgust, and are not true modesty. Do not make the mistake of neglecting your personal appearance, but try to look well and dress well to please his eye.

7. Perpetually work up his interests with the world, whether for publishing or for appointments. Let him feel, when he has to go away, that he leaves a second self in charge of his affairs at home; so that if sometimes he is obliged to leave you behind, he may have nothing of anxiety on his mind. Take an interest in everything that interests him. To be companionable, a woman must learn what interests her husband; and if it is only planting turnips, she must try to understand turnips.

8. Never confide your domestic affairs to your female friends.

9. Hide his faults from *every one*, and back him up through every difficulty and trouble; but with his peculiar temperament advocate peace whenever it is consistent with his honour before the world.

10. Never permit any one to speak disrespectfully of him before you; and if any one does, no matter how difficult, leave the room. Never permit any one to tell you anything about him, especially of his conduct with regard to other

women. Never hurt his feelings by a rude remark or jest. Never answer when he finds fault; and never reproach him when he is in the wrong, *especially when he tells you of it*, nor take advantage of it when you are angry; always keep his heart up when he has made a failure.

11. Keep all disagreements for your own room, and never let others find them out.

12. Never ask him *not* to do anything – for instance, with regard to visiting other women, or any one you particularly dislike; trust him, and tell him everything except another person's secret.

13. Do not bother him with religious talk, be religious yourself and give good example, take life seriously and earnestly, pray for and procure prayers for him, and do all you can for him without his knowing it, and let all your life be something that will win mercy from God for him. You might *try* to say a little prayer *with* him every night before laying down to sleep, and gently draw him to be good to the poor and more gentle and forbearing to others.

14. Cultivate your own good health, spirits, and nerves, to counteract his naturally melancholy turn, and to enable you to carry out your mission.

15. Never open his letters, nor appear inquisitive about anything he does not volunteer to tell you.

16. Never interfere between him and his family; encourage their being with him, and forward everything he wishes to do for them, and treat them in every respect (as far as they will let you) as if they were your own.

17. Keep everything going, and let nothing be at a standstill: nothing would weary him like stagnation.

Isabel's conception of her marriage to Burton was one of high and constant service – mixed with a little missionary work – and it was this concept that made it necessary for her to dramatize herself, her husband and their marriage. After Burton's death, Isabel, reflecting on this period just before her marriage, wrote, 'I began to feel, what I have always felt since, that he was a glorious, stately ship in full sail, commanding all attention and admiration, and sometimes, if the wind drops, she still sails gallantly, and no one sees the humble little steam-tug hidden on the other side, with her strong heart and faithful arms working forth, and glorying in her proud and stately ship.'

A tug with both heart and arms is hardly a neat conceit, particularly when the adjectives applied to them appear to be reversed, but Isabel, the faithful tug, perhaps instinctively felt that the arms might be needed to hold the stately ship in case it should fill its sails and cruise off without her.

It was a trembling Isabel who dressed that morning of her wedding in a fawn-coloured dress, a black lace cloak and a white bonnet. She first went in to receive the blessings of her mother and father, who thought she was going to the country to visit friends. Then, with tears running down her cheeks, she went out the door of her parents' home. She turned to kiss the outside of the door, and then entered the waiting cab that took her to the home of Dr George Bird. From there she and Dr Bird went to the church of Our Lady of the Assumption, generally called the Bavarian Catholic Church because it had been the chapel of the Bavarian Embassy, in Warwick Street.

Burton was waiting for her by the entrance. As they stepped inside, he ostentatiously took holy water from the small font by the door and made a very large sign of the cross. He could be as good a Catholic as he had been a Moslem, Hindu and Sikh if the part called for it. The small party was led into the sacristy. There they learned that Cardinal Wiseman had been taken ill and could not perform the ceremony but that his vicar-general had been deputed to act in his place. The marriage was soon performed. Burton was nearly forty years old; his bride not quite thirty.

After the ceremony they all went to Dr Bird's house for the wedding breakfast. Dr Bird, a physician, began to tease Burton about some of his exploits. 'Now, Burton, tell me: how do you feel when you have killed a man?'

Burton looked up quizzically and drawled, 'Oh, quite jolly. How do you?'

At last Burton carried off his bride to his bachelor lodgings: a bedroom, dressing-room and sitting-room. For Isabel it was heaven. 'To say that I was happy would be to say nothing; a repose came over me that I had never known. I felt that it was for Eternity, an immortal repose, and I was in a bewilderment of wonder at the goodness of God, who had almost worked miracles for me.'

Exactly what Burton felt is not recorded, but he was embarrassed and annoyed at being pointed out as a bridegroom and he told everyone that they had been married for 'a couple of years'.

Two of Isabel's aunts saw her entering what they took to be bachelors' quarters and immediately reported the scandal to her parents. But by this time they already knew. The day after the marriage, Burton scrawled a note to Isabel's father on writing-paper with the word 'Allah' in Arabic printed in the upper left-hand corner:

My dear Father

I have committed a highway robbery by marrying your daughter Isabel at Warwick St. Chapel and before the registrar – the details she is writing to her mother.

It only remains for me to say that I have no ties or liaisons of any kind, that the marriage was perfectly legal and 'respectable'. I want no money with Isabel; I can work, and it will be my care that Time shall bring you nothing to regret.

I am

Yours Sincerely
RICHARD F. BURTON

It was not long before Isabel and her husband were received by both parents and Mrs Arundell spent the rest of her life in self-mortification for the wrong she had done her daughter. Much credit for this change of attitude must go to Burton himself. The great hater of 'Mrs Grundy' did everything he could to make himself appear a respectable husband. It was an admirable deception.

Their first dinner at the Arundells' was, not unnaturally, a tense affair. The entire Arundell clan was present. For the most part, all sat in restrained silence. The younger children were allowed to come down for dessert and, on special occasions – and this was certainly special – they were permitted to have a small glass of wine. But Burton, when the wine went around, forgot to pass the bottle. Finally, a youngster from the foot of the table called out, 'I say, old bottle stopper – pass the wine!'

This broke the ice and child-hating Burton laughed heartily. When Mrs Arundell ordered the boy to go without wine as punishment for his brashness, Burton looked at her sweetly and said, 'Oh *Mother*, not on my first night at *home*!'

The Burtons now plunged into an active social life which Isabel described as 'seven months of uninterrupted bliss', although they may have been something less than that for her husband. 'We had a glorious season,' she said, 'and took up our new position in Society.' Monckton Milnes, the master manipulator, arranged for Lord Palmerston, the Prime Minister, to give a party at which Isabel was the guest of honour. Lady Russell presented her at court 'on her marriage', an important event for Isabel as Queen Victoria did not receive ladies who had made 'run-away marriages' and there was some doubt as to Isabel's position in this regard. Then there were parties in London and in the country. There were also interesting weekends at Milnes' place, Fryston. But this was Isabel's kind of life, not Burton's.

He did acquire one remarkable friend during this period, however. On 5 June he had breakfast with Monckton Milnes at his London house in Upper Brook Street. There he met a small, delicate, red-headed, hero-worshipping young man of twenty-four who interested him very much. His name was Algernon Charles Swinburne, and Houghton thought he had some promise as a poet. The swarthy and muscular Burton and the delicate, pale Swinburne apparently took an immediate liking to each other. For Swinburne, Burton must have seemed the living prototype of all literature's adventurers, a hero in real life who had actually done what he himself could only dream of doing. It is more difficult to guess what the first attraction of the older man to the young poet could have been. Perhaps he simply enjoyed being worshipped; on the other hand, the versifying Burton may have recognized in Swinburne the spirit of the true romantic poet. Both were romantics who, according to their own fashions, lived their romanticism. Both were interested in erotic literature, as was their host. Both, too, had an exceptionally great love of poetry. Perhaps they discussed *The Rubaiyat of Omar Khayyam*, adapted by Edward Fitzgerald, seventy-five quatrains of which had been published anonymously only two years before. These verses had made a tremendous impression on them both. In any case, the friendship between the two continued for as long as Burton lived.

While Burton was winning the heart of his mother-in-law, talking poetry and going to parties, his former comrade was striving for greater things in Africa. Speke had now reached Tabora in Unyanyembe with the loss of one man, three donkeys and twelve mules dead; he had been forced to discharge seven men; 123 men had deserted; and half of his property had been stolen. One would imagine that he would have had enough to concern him with his present expedition, but he was full of his hatred for his former chief and he poured out his feelings in a long letter to Rigby from Tabora on 12 May 1861:

All my letters are open for your use. . . . The one to Blackwood I wish you and all the good folks of Zanzibar to read, and if you would all sign it, so much the better. I hope its publication may have the effect of reforming Burton: at any rate it will check his scribbling mania, and may save his soul the burthen of many lies. . . . One of Burton's unpaid orders has just been presented to me, but I have written across it referring the matter to you that Burton may be prosecuted to teach him better. . . . Unyanyembe has gone untimely to the dogs through the bad example of the traders and of such as Burton is.

Only a few days before his marriage Burton was shown by his friend Norton Shaw, Secretary of the Royal Geographical Society, a letter he had received from Rigby in which Burton's book was denounced as a pack of lies, and which complained of the injustice done to his own character and that of the Zanzibar medical officer whom Burton blamed for the loss of the manuscript of his book on Zanzibar. Burton at once sent off a letter to Rigby that was the most angry he had ever written:

14 St. James Square, London
16th January

Sir, – I have been indebted to the kindness and consideration of my friend Dr. Shaw for a sight of your letter addressed to him the 10th of October last from Zanzibar. I shall not attempt to characterize it in the terms that best befit it. To do so, indeed, I should be compelled to resort to language 'vile' and unseemly as your own. Nor can there be any necessity for this. A person who could act as you have acted must be held by everyone to be beneath the notice of any honourable man. You have addressed a virulent attack on me to a quarter in which you had hoped it would prove deeply injurious to me; and this not in the discharge of any public duty, but for the gratification of a long standing private pique. You sent me no copy of this attack, you gave me no opportunity of meeting it; the slander was propagated, as slanders generally are, in secret and behind my back. You took a method of disseminating it which made the ordinary mode of dealing with such libels impossible, while your distance from England puts you in a position to be perfectly secure from any consequences of a personal nature to yourself. Such being the case, there remains to me but one manner of treating your letter, and that is with the contempt it merits. My qualifications as a traveller are, I hope, sufficiently established to render your criticism innocuous, and the medals of the English and French Geographical Societies may console me for the non-appreciation of my labours by so eminent an authority as yourself. . . . I have only to add . . . that I shall at all times, in all companies, even in print if it suits me, use the same freedom in discussing your character and conduct that you have presumed to exercise in discussing mine.

I am, Sir, your obedient servant,
RICHARD F. BURTON

The day after writing this, Burton received a letter from the India Office censuring him for not settling the claims of the porters and implying that Speke and Rigby were believed and he was not; he was also threatened with an order to repay the government for the money Rigby had turned over to the porters to settle their claim. In his reply Burton said, 'I venture to express my surprise that all my labours and long service in the cause of African exploration should have won me no other reward than the prospect of being mulcted in a pecuniary liability incurred by my late lamented friend, Lieut.-Colonel Hamerton, and settled without reference to me by his successor, Captain Rigby.'

It was about this time, too, that he suffered a great material loss. All of his most valuable possessions were destroyed in a fire that burned down the warehouse of his agents, Grindlay and Co., in which he had stored them. Lost were most of his books, Persian and Arabic manuscripts, a collection of costumes, and many of his own manuscripts and notes – including the simian dictionary. It was as though his past life had been literally burned behind him. He accepted the loss philosophically enough. Thinking perhaps of the erotic nature of some of the literature that had been destroyed, he said, 'Well, it is a great bore, but I dare say that the world will be none the worse for some of those manuscripts having been burnt.'

More serious for Burton was the loss of his sinecure in the Indian Army. For nineteen years he had been carried on the rolls of the 18th Regiment of Bombay Native Infantry, although he had actually been with his regiment for less than a quarter of that time. In 1858 the Honourable East India Company's administration of India ceased. The Company's European troops became part of the regular British Army, while the remaining Indian troops, greatly reduced in strength, were retained under the three presidencies of Bombay, Madras and Bengal. Officers such as Burton, who were continually engaged in non-military activities and always appeared to be in official difficulties, could hardly have been considered valuable additions to the officer corps. The Bombay Army must have been waiting for an excuse to eliminate the troublesome Captain Richard Burton from its rolls. He soon gave them one.

Burton desperately wanted to obtain the position of consul in Damascus. Isabel did all she could through her family connections to get it for him. All efforts failed to obtain the desired appointment, but Lord John Russell, then Foreign Secretary, did offer the consulship on the tiny island of Fernando Po at a salary of £700 a year. It was hardly a choice post and had a reputation for being the 'Foreign Office grave'. Nevertheless, on 27 March 1861, Burton wrote to the Foreign Office accepting the post, adding however, that he did not want to lose his position in the army: 'My connection with H.M.'s Indian army has now lasted upward of nineteen years, and I am unwilling to retire without pension or selling out of my corps. If, therefore, my name could be retained upon the list of my regiment – as, for instance, is the case with H.M.'s Consul at Zanzibar – I should feel deeply indebted.' Burton's request was forwarded to the Bombay Government. Soon after, he read that another officer had been gazetted to replace him.

Burton picked up his pen to try to save his sword. It was 'an act of injustice on the part of the Bombay Government' to remove him. They were treating him 'as a man who had been idling away his time and shirking duty'. He offered to prove that 'every hour' had been spent for his country's benefit. He waxed rhetorical: 'Are my wounds and fevers, and perpetual risk of health and life, not to speak of personal losses, to go for nothing?' and then he maintained that the government was 'unjustly prejudiced' against him because of the '*private piques* of a certain half-dozen individuals'. It was particularly galling, of course, that Rigby should retain his rank in the Indian Army while serving as consul, whereas he was denied the privilege. The difference, however, as Burton should have known, was that Zanzibar, where Rigby served, came under the jurisdiction of the Bombay Government, while Fernando Po did not.

But all his words were wasted. At the age of forty, without financial reserves or the prospect of a pension, he was now compelled to begin a new career at the bottom rung of the diplomatic ladder. And the post of Her Majesty's Consul for Fernando Po and the Bight of Biafra seems indeed to have been close to the bottom.

The mountainous little island of Fernando Po (or Fernando Poo), comprising only 800 square miles, lies twenty miles off the west coast of Africa less than four degrees above the Equator. It has a curious political history. Discovered in the last half of the fifteenth century by a Portuguese navigator whose name it bears, it was ceded to Spain in 1778. Because of the unhealthy climate, Spain's first attempts to develop the island failed and Spain allowed Great Britain to take over the administration in 1827. Seventeen years later Spain again assumed control, but appointed a British governor. In 1858 a Spanish governor was sent from Spain and some attempt was made to administer the island until fourteen years after Burton left, when Spain again abandoned the unhealthy place. In Burton's day, the one and principal town, called Santa Isabel by the Spanish and Clarence by the British, swarmed with mosquitoes; malaria killed off the Europeans almost as fast as they arrived. Even today, the island is considered unhealthy and supports a population of less than 27,000, including the stone-age Bube natives.

But Burton's jurisdiction extended to the Bight of Biafra, that wide-mouthed bay in the Gulf of Guinea that touches on the southern Nigerian coastline and the coast of the Cameroons. Here was a bit of Africa proper for him to explore. It was not much, but Burton was to stretch that bit of coastline 5,000 miles until it reached from Dahomey to Angola. It had never before nor has it since assumed such proportions.

Before leaving London, Burton checked in at the Foreign Office to learn about his new duties. It was in the Slave Trade Department that he met the future Lord Redesdale (Algernon Bertram Freeman-Mitford, 1837 – 1916), then a young clerk of twenty-four. Burton, he later recorded, was 'a man possessed of a great power of awakening enthusiasm'. He persuaded Freeman-Mitford that he should go with him. Perhaps they would find a gorilla, that animal concerning whose existence there was then so much dispute, for no European had ever seen one alive. The young man was ready to go, but 'happily my father put his foot down, and I remained in Downing Street'.

Fernando Po and the Bight of Biafra were a long way from Arabia, but the position paid more than his former captain's salary and Burton was grateful. Isabel was to be left behind. She was willing and eager to go, but her master said no. She hated to see him leave and she had the loving wife's fearfulness for the safety of her husband. Knowing how close his new post lay to the intriguing continent of Africa, she was 'in constant agitation for fear of his doing more of those Explorations into unknown lands'. Doubtless she would have been even more fearful had she known that he was thinking of returning from his post by way of Central Africa.

On 24 August 1861, Isabel went down to see him off. She complained:

There were about eighteen men (West African merchants), and everybody took him away from me. He had made me promise that I would not cry and unman him. It was blowing hard and raining; there was one man who was inconsiderate enough to accompany and stick to us the whole time, so that we could not exchange a word (how I hated him!). I went down below and unpacked his things and settled his cabin, and saw to the arrangement of his luggage. My whole life and soul was in that good-bye. . . .

Burton wrote:

A heart-wrench – and all is over. . . . The day was a day to make the Englander leave England without a sigh. . . . If Britannia chills with tears and sighs the hearts of her sons home-returning, at any rate, with the same tenderness she consoles them under departure. Who ever landed at Southampton in other but the worst weather? Who ever left Dover on a fine clear morning? . . . However, on this occasion, thus distinguished from many others, I did not lose either box or bag. . . . My connection with my beloved native land concluded with a further demand of 6£ 2s. for baggage.

And thus were thoughts of Isabel overwhelmed by the traveller's concern for weather, baggage and expenses. He was off for new adventures. Isabel returned to live with her parents.

Chapter 15

West African Consul
1861 – 3

THE steamer that took Burton to his first consular post boasted a 120-horse-power engine and the captain made five per cent on all the coal he could save; consequently, he was in no hurry. The cruise lasted more than a month and stopped off at twenty-four ports before arriving at Fernando Po. Burton complained that the wine on board was expensive and execrable; he also found the ship's screw 'painfully noisy'. Nevertheless, he enjoyed the ship and plunged vigorously into sight-seeing, questioning of residents and note-taking at every port. He also liked the frequent opportunities to liquor up – an expression he no longer put in quotes; it had become a part of his vocabulary and was rapidly becoming a part of his way of life.

The first stop was Madeira, where he complained that the food was bad, tobacco was too expensive, and there were no pretty faces. The latter situation was remedied at the second stop, Tenerife, where, after inspecting the cathedral, he 'wandered about the streets seeking *l'aventure*. . . . For those who admire black anywhere except "in the skin", there is nothing more enchanting than the women of Tenerife. . . . I will confess that one soon wearies of black eyes and black hair, and that after a course of such charms, one falls back with pleasure upon brown, yellow, or, what is better than all, red-auburn locks and eyes of soft limpid blue.' Exactly what his course of dark charms consisted of can only be guessed, but Isabel had the locks and eyes of the proper colour for falling back on – if that was a consolation.

At last they stopped at Bathurst, Gambia, and Burton once more set foot on the mainland of Africa: 'It felt like a return to *dulce domum*,' he said. But the west coast was a different Africa from that he had known before. At Sierra Leone he offered a native sixpence to carry his bag. The man demanded an extra sixpence because, the day being Sunday, he would be 'breaking the Sabbath'. 'I gave it readily,' said Burton sarcastically, 'and was pleased to find that the labours of our missionaries had not been in vain.' And he reflected on 'how much better is the heart of Africa than its epidermis'.

Several thousands of miles south-east of Bathurst, in the heart of Africa he had in mind, Speke was having his difficulties with the Africans whom Burton was extolling. He and Grant were separated and his porters refused to go on. A few weeks later, Grant's camp was attacked and plundered.

Burton filled his notebooks with comments on the flora, fauna, tribes, customs, agriculture, languages, topography, history and even the trivial local gossip of each port, as though such long-established towns as Sierra Leone, Monrovia, Cape Palmas, Accra, Lagos and Bonny were unexplored territory. He bought local curios, went to stare at an albino negro in Accra, was incensed to learn that it was against the law to call an African 'nigger', and found a special delight in telling two Americans he encountered at Cape Palmas the news of the Federal Army's defeat at Bull Run: 'perhaps the most remarkable style of "taking ground to the rear" that history has ever had to chronicle'.

His greatest shock, and a source of continual irritation to him throughout the trip was what he termed the 'insolence' of the West Coast negro. This part of the African coast north of the Equator had been exposed to European influence – if not civilization – for more than three hundred years. It had been, until quite recently, the very centre of the slave supply for European nations and the United States. That many should have adopted European manners and attitudes, and some not always the best, was the source of great annoyance to Burton, who was a hard-headed conservative in matters of class and race distinction.

It is curious but characteristic that Burton, the professed lover of Africa, should have had such an antipathy to its principal inhabitants. He set forth his views in no uncertain terms:

I believe the European to be the brains, the Asiatic the heart, the American and African the arms, and the Australian the feet, of the man figure. I also . . . opine that, in the various degrees of intellectuality, the Negro ranks between the Australian and the Indian – popularly called red – who is above him. From humbly aspiring to be owned as a man, our black friend now boldly advances his claims to *égalité* and *fraternité*, as if there could be brotherhood between the crown and the clown! The being who 'invents nothing, improves nothing, who can only cook, nurse, and fiddle'; who has neither energy nor industry, save in rare cases that prove the rule! – the self-constituted thrall, that delights in subjection to and imitation of the superior races. . . . And yet we – in these days – read such nonsense pure and simple as 'Africa for the Africans'.

It was not just the port towns and the talk of the European residents that kept Burton in a continual fit of peeve. Several Africans rode as first-class passengers between ports and Burton, who had eaten many a meal with negroes in the African interior, was incensed that they should eat with him in the main cabin. 'It is a political as well as a social mistake to permit these men to dine in the main cabin which they will end by monopolizing,' he complained. 'A ruling race cannot be too particular about these small matters.'

Equal to his wrath over civilized Africans was his contempt for the philanthropists who were working to raise their standards of living. Perhaps the fact that his enemy Rigby was among this group helped to shape his attitude.

But in spite of all his complaints, Burton seems to have thoroughly enjoyed the voyage. Certainly he was sorry to see it end at Fernando Po, 'the very abomination of desolation', on 27 September 1861. He felt 'uncommonly suicidal through that first night on Fernando Po'. But he did not stay long at his post. In a week he was off to inspect the delta of the Niger, then known as the Oil Rivers.

He returned to Fernando Po on 2 October and remained there exactly one week – he described it as 'a long, long, a very long week' – and then he was off to Nigeria and the Cameroons. The opportunity for this escape came when the commodore of the West African squadron on HMS *Arrogant* put into Fernando Po and offered Burton a lift to Lagos (in the Bight of Benin) for the purpose of acquiring 'certain necessaries', such as a cook, a carpenter, and a *dewan* or steward. Five days later, Burton was in Lagos. But here he simply transferred himself to HMS *Prometheus*. While still anchored in the roadstead of Lagos, the ship was struck by lightning, missing by only three feet the two tons of explosives stored in the powder magazine. Burton took a piece of the lightning-splintered foremast and made a paper-knife for Isabel.

Burton moved himself ashore for five days, and acquired a servant named Selim Aga who had once been a slave of his friend Robert Thurburn in Alexandria. He had lamp-black skin and semitic features; he could speak Scotch, make an excellent turtle soup, stuff birds and keep accounts. An admirable employee was Selim Aga. He was killed in Liberia in 1875 during the Grebo War.

On the morning of 29 October 1861, Burton left with Commander Bedingfield, captain of the *Prometheus*, in a small boat for Abeokuta, where the captain had orders to get the signature, or mark, of the

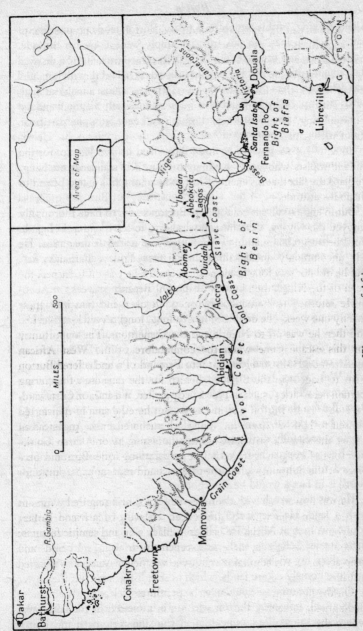

Dakar
Bathurst
R. Gambia
Conakry
Freetown
Monrovia
Grain Coast
Ivory Coast
Abidjan
Gold Coast
Accra
Slave Coast
Ouidah
Abomey
Volta
Bight of Benin
Lagos
Abeokuta
Ibadan
Niger
Brass
Fernando Po
Santa Isabel
Bight of
Biafra
Victoria
Douala
Cameroons
GABON
Libreville

Area of Map

MILES
500

4. West coast of Africa

Akale, or king, of this region on a treaty. Burton made no pretence of having any business on this trip; he simply went along for the ride. Naturally, he and the captain had their disagreements. Burton disliked the captain's dog, which the captain insisted on bringing with him, and was delighted when the animal was lost: 'He was a most amiable animal; when tied up, he barked and howled most musically all the way, and when loose he insisted upon springing overboard, stopping the boat, and exciting different emotions amongst those in it. A St. Helena pointer – he even pointed at butterflies – and he was just recovering from mange. Of course we made on the way down all inquiries for so pleasant a companion, but we had to mourn his loss.' The captain, for his part, complained of the 'size and obstinacy' of Burton's umbrella which, he declared, slowed down the progress of the boat.

Landing near the barbarian capital, they transferred from the boat to horses. Burton had a bad fall when his horse reared at the gate of the city. He considered it a bad omen, but as it was Friday, an unlucky day, he felt he had been let off easily.

Burton, with the captain and his party, spent three weeks at Abeokuta – at least this was implied in his account of the trip; as will appear later, he probably visited Dahomey during this time, although he had reason to conceal his visit. Without responsibilities of his own, Burton made fun of those of the missionaries and the captain. He had little use for the missionaries and blamed them for much of what he found wrong with West Africa. Inside the mission grounds at Abeokuta there was a compound which the missionaries had labelled Wasimi, or Come-and-Rest. Burton thought it a bit of contemporary Alabama in Africa: 'As might be expected from that mortal energy which the Anglo-Saxon has so successfully distributed about the world, poor African Come-and-Rest is approached by all the preparations for severe and protracted toil, gins, saws, cotton-presses and what not. "Come-and-Rest" is in fact a would be workhouse.'

He was also wroth with the missionaries for bringing their wives to such a land. He felt 'truly grieved at the sight of my poor pretty countrywomen at Abeokuta'. He thought it 'a crying shame to expose these tender beings to such rude, unworthy trials. . . . I could only leave them my wishes, my vain hopes, that they may soon be restored to those homely decent lands, which no Englishwoman – if the power of ukase were mine – should ever be permitted to leave.'

As usual, however, Burton was more interested in the anthropological aspects of life around him than in the diplomatic mission of

Commander Bedingfield or the efforts of the missionaries to bring spiritual enlightenment and material progress to a savage land. He found that here, as elsewhere in Africa and Asia, polygamy was the 'foundation-stone of Yoruban society'. This, of course, was an institution of which he heartily approved. Being a respectably married man did not change his view that monogamy is 'the most curious delimitation of human liberty ever forced upon mankind'. He was also pleased to find that a kind of caste system was used by the Egbas. Caste, in Burton's opinion, being 'one of the most enlightened inventions of the civilized East'. But this was a race 'worseted and spoiled . . . by its own folly and want of a proper despotism'.

Burton and party left Abeokuta on 8 November, another Friday, and he again had a mishap with a horse. When a 'wild beast of a Yoruba pony' charged down on him, he tried to defend himself with his umbrella and almost put out his own eye with this weapon in the process. 'Considering, however, that it was Friday, I congratulated myself upon a very pretty escape,' he recorded.

Back in their boat again they sailed downstream towards Lagos. In the evening they stopped off at the village of Baragu where they spent 'a right merry evening', according to Burton. The natives gave a party for them and there was singing, feasting and dancing. Burton was taken by the fine figures ('*superbae formae*') of the women. Of this evening he wrote, 'Our hosts were perfectly civil and obliging, and so were our hostesses – rather too much so I could prove, if privileged to whisper into the reader's ear. But what would Mrs Grundy say?' More to the point, what did Isabel say? No one knows, unfortunately, but Isabel did develop a decidedly jealous attitude towards her naked African sisters. Burton, who had done little but complain throughout the entire trip, now concluded on this 'soft and balmy' evening that 'upon the whole, our trip was decidedly "jolly"'.

No sooner was this excursion completed than Burton embarked on another trip, leaving Lagos on 21 November 1861, aboard HMS *Bloodhound* for the Brass and Bonny Rivers and the coast opposite Fernando Po near the Cameroon Mountains. Landing at Victoria, Nigeria, then but a missionary station, Burton met Gustav Mann, the young botanist known as the 'Kew collector'. Mann was making plans to ascend the Cameroon Mountains, having failed in an earlier attempt. As this was exactly what Burton had in mind, he urged Mann to wait awhile and they would scale the peak together. Mann promised to do this, but instead he set out to do it alone. Burton, meanwhile, visited the

Cameroon River and then returned to Fernando Po, staying just long enough to prepare for his mountain-climbing venture. He also induced an acquaintance, Atilano Calvo Iturburu, a Spanish assistant judge on Fernando Po, to come along with him. By 11 December, Iturburu, Burton and Selim Aga were back at Victoria. There they picked up Rev. Alfred Saker, the founder of the missionary station, with several Krumen and set off towards the Cameroon Mountains.

On the way they met Mann, who announced that he had just returned from scaling the summit of Elephant Mountain. This caused Burton to 'tie a face', but he soon concluded that 'considering the distance and height, it was some mistake on his part; and this it proved to be. The enterprising botanist, so far from having scaled the summit, had never even seen it.' Burton, who had a perfect knack for starting quarrels, now began one with Gustav Mann. Writing to Sir Joseph Dalton Hooker, then Assistant Director of Kew Gardens, Mann affirmed that he had indeed been the first to climb the mountain, but that he was not going to make a fuss about it: 'As to having a quarrel with Burton, we all know what it is to touch pitch,' he said bitterly. Now, however, Mann joined the party and turned back with them towards the mountains.

Between the coast and the mountains they had to pass through the territory of a native chief who caused them some difficulty until appeased with gifts. Saker knew the language, but Burton was pleased by the progress he was able to make using the sign language he had learned from the American Indians. He decided that if he ever got back to Europe and had the time he would develop a system of signs useful to anyone dealing with people who spoke a completely foreign tongue. 'A hundred words easily learned in a week, 200 signs, and a little facility in sketching, would enable, I believe, a traveller to make his way through any country, even China, a few days after arrival.'

The forty-year-old Burton was no match for the young botanist, who outwalked the entire party. Burton noted, however, that 'he subsequently suffered severely for this evidence of superior vigour'. Burton was also pleased when Mann despaired of finding water and the talented Selim Aga solved the problem by squeezing out half a gallon from moss.

At last they reached the spot for their base camp and Burton, who had been placed at his own request in charge of the natives, erected a whipping post in the middle of the camp. The entire party now went in for mountain-naming: first, of course, the two highest peaks were called Victoria and Albert (they were, naturally, unaware that Prince Albert had died only two days before). Burton named three peaks: Mount Isabel, Mount Selim and Mount Milnes; Saker also named three: Helen (his wife), Arthur and Leopold; and poor Mann was lucky to stake his claim to a Mount Dorothy. Unfortunately for the mountain-namers, none of these designations has survived. Since Burton had made some strong statements against those who gave new places European names instead of native ones, he felt it necessary to justify his actions: 'Even strict geographers cannot blame the act,' he maintained, 'in a place which has absolutely no terminology.'

From their base camp they made excursions to the various peaks in various combinations. Burton and the Spanish judge climbed Mount Milnes. 'We were the first Europeans certainly, perhaps the first men, who have ever stood within gunshot of that tall solitary pile. We made eternal silence vocal with a cheer, – there was no one to deride our demonstrativeness.'

They then decided to scale the tallest peak, Mount Victoria. The judge sprained his ankle and had to stop, but Burton pushed on. This was the mountain Mann claimed to have ascended, and Burton confessed that there was 'perhaps a bit of "*malice*"' in his desire to reach the top first: 'To be first in such matters is everything; to be second, nothing.' At the top he made a cairn of stones and put some pages of *Punch* inside it.

It was after dark before Burton regained the base camp. He was so exhausted that he went immediately to bed, not bothering even to remove his boots, but he spent a wakeful night, tortured by cramps and spasmodic contractions of his legs. The next morning, when he took off his boots, he discovered that his feet were in a sad state due to his having made the climb in waterproof boots that were too loose for him. He soon developed 'a little ague and fever' and spent the next month sitting around the camp. He enjoyed himself hugely, studying the Kru tongue, collecting plants and small animals, and flogging the Krumen at his whipping post whenever they were found derelict in their duties (thirty-six lashes being the greatest number recorded).

Perhaps there was also a bit of malice in Burton's botanizing; a desire to beat Mann at his own business. He succeeded in obtaining a number of small animals, birds and plants that were subsequently named after him or, at his request, Isabel. One of the rats he collected, *Otamyr burtoni*, was not officially classified until 1918 when Oldfield Thomas named it in honour of Burton.

While Burton was contentedly collecting specimens on the mountainside and was pleased with the prospect of small fame, Speke was negotiating the western shores of Lake Victoria, working his way northward to the Nile.

On 22 January there was a violent electrical storm on the mountain and Burton found that 'the tonic of oxygen developed by the storm' caused him to recover from his illnesses. Mann, who had been suffering from dysentery, recovered a few days later in spite of his diet of iron rust burned in brandy and cold arrowroot mixed with chalk and he resumed his collecting of plants, even generously naming one after Burton, *Senecio burtoni*.

With the whole party healthy again, they made together a final ascent of the peak they had named Victoria. At the top Selim hoisted a Union Jack, they drank a bottle of champagne, and then they wrote their names on a slip of sheet-lead and put it in an empty bottle with two sixpences. Sir Harry Johnston, who climbed the peak in 1886, found several bottles inside a cairn, including the one Burton and his party had left.

At the end of January 1862, the party broke up and Burton ended what he described as his 'Christmas holidays'; they had lasted six weeks. On 4 February, he sailed from Victoria across the narrow bit of water to Fernando Po. He had thoroughly enjoyed himself and waxed very poetic as he pulled away: 'Farewell, Cameroons! Farewell beautiful heights! where so many calm and quiet days have sped without sandflies, or mosquitoes, or prickly heat. Adieu! happy rustic wilds! where I have spent so many pleasant weeks, even in West Africa. Adieu! . . .'

Back in his consulate, Burton wrote a report advocating that the coal depot and the consulate of Fernando Po be moved over to Victoria on the mainland and that the Cameroon Mountains be made into a sanatorium for Europeans on the West African coast. A year later he wrote to *The Times*, advocating the Cameroons as an excellent place for a convict station. None of his suggestions was adopted – fortunately, for an immense amount of rain falls in the area and, in more recent times, an annual rainfall of forty *feet* has been recorded.

Burton, to his disgust, now found it necessary to remain longer than a week on Fernando Po. He hated the place. His statement that here 'man found it hard to live, but uncommonly easy to die' was not an exaggeration. In the month following his return to the island, yellow fever broke out, killing 78 of a total of 250 white men. The consulate was located 'unpleasantly near a military hospital: breakfast and dinner were frequently enlivened by the spectacle of a something covered with a blanket being carried in, and after due time a something within a deal box being borne out on four ghastly men's shoulders'.

Although he spoke much of the unhealthy climate of Fernando Po, Burton himself was never ill for a day while on the island. But then, he spent little time there. He was back for less than six weeks from his Cameroons 'holiday' when he left to look for gorillas in the Gaboon. So far, his trips had been confined mostly to the coastal area around the Bight of Biafra, within his consular area. Now, however, early in his career as a consul, he began that habit of leaving his post and neglecting his consular duties to indulge his appetite for travel. Certainly it would be stretching a point to call the Gaboon (also spelled Gabon or Gabun) territory within the Bight of Biafra; yet, on 17 March 1862, Burton was in a ship anchored opposite Libreville.

Two days later, with Selim and some hunting dogs, he was in a borrowed boat with a borrowed crew in the Gaboon river, his craft stocked with candles, bread, sugar, cocoa, potatoes, preserved meats, soups and, of course, plenty of cognac and claret. Crossing the wide mouth of the Gaboon, the boat was nearly swamped by a tornado, but, though old and rotting, it somehow managed to stay afloat and they reached Denis. Here Burton hired the services of the local king's son, a French-speaking boy named Paul, as a guide and set off up the river. More storms caused them to put in for the night on an unpromising river bank. Burton made himself as comfortable as he could in his wet clothes, but the mosquitoes were soon upon them in great swarms. Prince Paul suddenly proposed that he go get some fire from *l'habitation*.

'What habitation?'

'Oh, a little village belonging to papa.'

'And why the hell didn't you mention it?' exclaimed Burton.

'Ah! this is Mpombinda, and you know you are bound for Mbata,' said the boy blandly.

Four hundred yards away was a neat village containing warm fires, cigars, tea, quinine and meat.

The next day, after a short canoe ride and a long tramp through the wet jungle, they reached Mbata. For all their difficulty in reaching the place, they were only about six miles from Libreville. Prince Paul introduced Burton to all his relatives, including a pretty, bare-bosomed young sister whom Paul informed him would be his wife *pro tem*. But

Burton was more interested in talking with a man called Forteune, the village hunter who would be his guide on the gorilla hunt.

Had Burton been able to find a gorilla and capture him, he would have achieved a greater degree of current fame than he had by his discovery of Lake Tanganyika. Prior to 1847 when two skulls were sent to England, the gorilla was only a legendary creature; the first complete skeleton was only found in 1851. Interest in the gorilla was high. Recently, Paul Du Chaillu (1831 – 1903) had published his *Explorations and Adventures in Equatorial Africa* and had taken back to the United States the first gorilla skin, but it is doubtful if even Du Chaillu had actually seen one of the shy creatures.

Burton showed the villagers the pictures in Du Chaillu's book and offered a big reward to anyone who could show him a gorilla, double the amount if they could capture one alive. It had been said that the gorillas built houses for themselves, so Burton asked the villagers about this. They showed him a few branches fastened up in a tree. He concluded that the gorilla was simply 'a vulgar nest-building ape'.

Burton continued to explore the region. With Forteune, he spent twelve days in the jungle and on the river. He did not find a gorilla, although he claimed he had caught a glimpse of one, but he did have a remarkable experience with lightning:

Selim and I stood close together, trying to light a match, when a sheet of white fire seemed to be let down from the black sky, passing between us with a simultaneous thundering crash and rattle and a sulphureous smell as if a battery had been discharged. I saw my factotum struck down, while in the act of staggering and falling myself; we lay still for a few moments, when a mutual inquiry showed that both were alive, only a little shaken and stunned; the sensation was simply the shock of an electrical machine and the discharge of a Woolwich infant – greatly exaggerated.

The failure to find a gorilla was a great disappointment. Forteune said it was because Burton cast a spell over the place that would be broken as soon as he left and that he would send him a gorilla later. Burton did not believe a word of it, but he was discouraged and returned to Libreville. No sooner had he reached the coast than Forteune sent him a dead gorilla he had shot the day after Burton left. It was a fine specimen: 'When placed in an arm chair he ludicrously suggested a pot-bellied and patriarchal negro considerably the worse for liquor. From crown to sole he measured 4 feet $\frac{3}{4}$ inches, and from finger tip to finger tip 6 feet 1 inch.' Burton ordered the gorilla skinned and sent to the British Museum. Unfortunately, the taxidermist did not know his business and when Burton later saw him stuffed in the museum he was no longer the 'broad-chested, square-framed, pot bellied and portly old bully-boy of the woods', but instead he was only a caricature of his real self, pigeon-breasted, lean-flanked and shrunken-limbed.

Burton now set out on a second expedition up the Gaboon River in a twenty-ton schooner with a crew of six. His purpose was to visit the Fan, or Fang (also called Fanwe, Fahouin and Pangwe), a cannibal tribe that had been described by Du Chaillu. Burton inquired diligently into the custom of eating human flesh and concluded that there was really very little cannibalism, the practice being confined mostly to certain quasi-religious ceremonies. He inquired also into the practice of tanning human skins (perhaps thinking of his friend Fred Hankey), but learned that most of the hides believed to be human were made from wild cows.

The Fans were nevertheless a barbarous race: 'Prisoners are tortured with all the horrible barbarity of that human wild beast which is happily being extirpated, the North American Indian, and children may be seen greedily licking the blood from the ground.' The Fans also murdered infant twins and buried criminals alive.

Burton spent less than a week with the Fans, returning to the coast on 17 April. A week later he was back in Fernando Po.

In August he was off to visit Benin City in Nigeria. It had once been the capital of a flourishing negro kingdom before the arrival of the Portuguese in 1485. Now it had lost much of its power, but retained many of its ancient customs. On the night of Burton's arrival, a negro slave was crucified in his honour and the following morning a second slave was killed and placed in his doorway. His lodgings overlooked the principal square, which was strewn with human bones. Benin was not in his consular area, but he could hardly be expected to overlook such an interesting place.

Until now, Burton had been fortunate in escaping from his consulate, thanks to the squadron of ships Britain maintained on the African west coast in an effort to curtail the slave trade. Now the ships did not call as often and he would sometimes be confined to the island of Fernando Po for as long as two months. Naturally he did not stay at his consulate in Clarence, but made expeditions around the island, climbing the mountain, studying the Bube natives, and collecting flora and fauna. He also wrote letters full of instructions and complaints to his wife. Sometimes, however, without telling the Foreign Office, he would slip away on a merchant ship to meet Isabel in the Canary Islands.

During his absence, Burton left Isabel little time for idleness. On his orders she tried unsuccessfully to have him reinstated in the Indian Army; she attempted to have a gunboat assigned to Fernando Po (what wonderful opportunities for exploring this would have given him!); she handled all the arrangements for bringing out his book on the Mormons, *The City of the Saints* (a splendid job for a bride, much of it consisting of a long defence of polygamy); and she made a special trip to Paris to see the Emperor and Empress of the French. It must have been a very discouraging time for Isabel, since she was successful only in bringing out the book.

The trip to Paris was particularly humiliating. Burton's uncle, Francis Burton, had been one of the officers stationed on the Island of St Helena at the time of Napoleon's exile. When Napoleon died, Francis Burton had made a sketch of the dead man and had collected a few locks of his hair. Sketch and hair (preserved in a watch-case) had been in the Burton family for forty years. On instructions from her husband, Isabel had the locks made into a ring, decorated with a wreath of laurels and the Bonaparte bees. Then, taking the ring, the death sketch, and a specially bound set of Burton's books, she went to Paris to present the lot to the French Emperor and Empress. It was a most naïve expedition. She had no friends in Paris and was ignorant of the way to proceed. She was not granted an audience and ended by leaving the gifts at the Tuileries, returning home without even an acknowledgement. What her husband thought is not recorded, but the rest of the Burton family were furious with her. They had entertained no love for her in the first place, since she was a Catholic, but now she had made a fool of herself and had lost their treasured relics. To a friend, Isabel remarked, 'I never felt so snubbed in my life, and I shall never like Paris again.'

Burton's reasons for sending his wife on this mission are obscure, but they probably relate to his belief that he was the great-great-great-grandson of Louis XIV by a morganatic marriage. Later in life he was discussing this matter quite seriously with Sir Bernard Burke one day during a visit to Dublin. Sir Bernard said to him, 'I wonder, Captain Burton, that you, who have such good Northern and Scottish blood in your veins, and are connected with so many of the best families, should trouble about what can only be a morganatic connection at best.'

Burton, hands in pockets, leaning against a bookcase, replied, 'Why!

I would rather be the bastard of a King, than the son of an honest man.'

Isabel's unhappiness during this period of her husband's absence was further increased by an attack of diphtheria and even more by the malicious rumours retailed to her by her acquaintances. In addition to the usual stories that circulated about Burton, there was a new one to the effect that he was 'keeping a seraglio' at Fernando Po. Isabel refused to believe these tales, but her loneliness and misery took her, in October 1862, to the Foreign Office. There, in the office of Sir Austen Henry Layard (a man who was a rare combination of diplomat and archaeologist), Isabel broke down and cried as she begged him to send her husband home. Layard excused himself for a few minutes and returned with permission to give Burton four months' leave. The dispatch was sent out the same afternoon.

Two months later, Burton was in England. A radiantly happy Isabel was in Liverpool to meet him. Christmas was spent at a large Arundell family gathering at Wardour Castle; then they were off to Garswood near St Helens in Lancashire, the home of Isabel's uncle Gerard; and a round of other country-houses, including Monckton Milnes' place at Fryston.

There were several unusual features about Fryston Hall – quite apart from its proprietor and his collection of friends: it lacked a billiard-room and it contained a large and remarkable library. There were books all over the house. Robert Lowe, later Lord Sherbrooke, compared it to 'one of those amorphous animals which have their brains all over their bodies'. The thousands of books reflected Milnes' primary interests: English poetry, the French Revolution, theology, magic and witchcraft, executions and punishments, and erotica. Since five out of these six subjects were those in which Burton was also interested (he had little interest in the French Revolution; he merely disapproved of it), it is no wonder that it was Burton's favourite country-house to visit. He never returned to England without going there.

Since Burton and Milnes had last met, Milnes had written a favourable review of *City of the Saints* and Burton had named an African mountain peak after Milnes. On this occasion, Burton again met Swinburne, who was then making one of his many extended stays at Fryston. Although the bringing together of Swinburne and Burton by Milnes has been described (by Humphrey Hare, a biographer of Swinburne) as 'a piece of calculated corruption', it is doubtful if Milnes had any evil thoughts in view when he introduced them. Perhaps he was as surprised as any by the passionate friendship that developed. At Fryston, Burton and Swinburne would go off by themselves in a corner and whisper together. The rest of the company would hear only the murmur of excited talk and an occasional shriek of laughter from Swinburne. Burton's corrupting influence is said to have consisted in urging the young poet to drink more than was good for him and in encouraging his interests in erotic literature. Most likely, however, Burton was simply one friend who did not disapprove of Swinburne's interests in liquor and pornography – an attitude Swinburne undoubtedly found refreshing.

Through the Burtons, Swinburne met George Bird, who became one of his close friends, and also the Arundell family. One day Swinburne shocked Mrs Arundell into saying, 'Young sir, if you talk like that you will die like a dog!' To which Swinburne replied, 'Oh, don't say "like a dog" – do say, "like a cat".'

Burton did not spend all his time visiting friends, however. Back in London he formed, on 6 January 1863, the Anthropological Society of London (today the Royal Anthropological Institute of Great Britain and Ireland) together with Dr James Hunt, a man whose scientific capabilities were called into doubt by Huxley. Hunt became the first president and Burton was named vice-president. Burton had felt the need for a suitable organ in which to publish some of the material he had collected which the journals of more prudish learned societies would not print: 'As a traveller and writer of travels, I have found it impossible to publish those questions of social economy and those physiological observations, always interesting to our common humanity, and at times so valuable,' he wrote. The *Anthropological Review*, organ of the society, provided this outlet. Eight volumes of this magazine were published over a seven-year period. The first volume was entitled *Transactions of the Anthropological Society of London* and the other seven volumes were labelled *Journal of the Anthropological Society of London*. Burton contributed articles for all except Volumes V and VIII.

An adjunct of the Anthropological Society was a less formal organization called the Cannibal Club, of which Hunt was also president. The club met for dinner between the afternoon and evening meetings of the Anthropological Society at a restaurant called Bertolini's near Leicester Square, close to the meeting rooms of the society at 4 St Martin's Place. Revolt against conventionality was the bond of those who met there. Swinburne joined this club in 1865, probably being introduced to it by Burton, and even wrote a poem, 'The Cannibal Catechism', which was later 'printed for private circulation'. The Italian food they ate on these occasions was frequently the subject of anthropological jokes which have been described as 'more witty than delicate'.

In the month Burton remained in England he not only managed to visit all his friends and help found the Anthropological Society, but he also put two new books out to be printed: *Wanderings in West Africa* and *Abeokuta and the Cameroons Mountains*. The former is a remarkable work in many respects. It consists of two volumes, 598 pages, simply describing his trip from London to Fernando Po. The book is dedicated to 'The True Friends of Africa – not to the "philanthropist" or to Exeter Hall'. Even more than was usual with him, Burton used this book as a springboard for expressing his opinions, his complaints and what might loosely be called his ideas. Burton was an acute observer, but he was not an original thinker. This never prevented him from acquiring opinions and prejudices in what appears to be a wholesale manner. *Wanderings in West Africa* contains information animal, mineral, vegetable and abstract on each of the territories his ship touched on its trip down the coast. It also discussed gold and gold mining, the treatment for dysentery, the tsetse fly, circumcision, sharks, narcotics, slavery, cannibalism, punishments, use of the toothpick (he favoured it), colonial salaries, negro education (he was against it), and geographical exploration. One of Burton's ideas, however, has since become a reality. He included considerable information on the Kola nut telling how it is thought to be an aphrodisiac, how taken with a glass of lime juice it causes abortions, how travellers use it to obviate thirst, and detailing its other virtues. He describes the taste of the nut when taken with water and says it makes a fine tonic: 'I am not aware of an extract having been made of it: if not, it would be as well to try.' Since there is no record that Burton ever made the experiment, he can not be credited with inventing Coca-Cola.

The book also contains much gratuitous advice on how to make India pay, how to run a colony, how to improve port facilities, and similar suggestions. He registers his disapproval of old men who dance, philanthropists, mistakes in history books, and he includes scathing criticisms of several books written about life in West Africa. He also has nasty references to Jews, Americans, Irishmen, negroes and missionaries of any nationality or faith. His antipathy to the Irish is curious considering that his father, whom he admired, was born and raised in Ireland and was described by Burton as being 'In mind . . . a thorough Irishman'. He never explained this prejudice, but unkind remarks concerning them are to be found in many of his books.

In this book he first attacks W. D. Cooley, an otherwise un-note-worthy geographer. Burton's first reference to this man was in his *Lake Regions of Central Africa*. He carried at least one of Cooley's books with him on his expedition and spoke well of him after. But Cooley made the mistake of criticizing Burton and he was never forgiven. From this point on, there was scarcely a book in which Cooley is not castigated in a footnote.

Burton may have felt even more free than usual to flay his enemies and display his prejudices and hatreds since he published the book anonymously. The book is signed merely by 'a F.R.G.S.' (Fellow of the Royal Geographical Society). Naturally he speaks of himself, but in the third person: 'I landed with the consul of Fernando Po' and 'the consul at once recognized a species different from that which he had found at Zanzibar and in Central Africa'. He even has a footnote praising his own book: 'Captain Burton has, I think, well explained this absorbing peculiarity of the South African dialects in the *Lake Regions of Central Africa*.'

Burton's writing was, as always, undisciplined. He usually asked his readers to forgive 'minor blemishes' on the grounds that there was time for only 'a single revise'. A gun is the 'hot mouthed weapon', gold is 'vile yellow clay', the sun is 'Dan Phoebus', freed slaves are 'pets of philanthropy', the buttock is the 'caudal region', and a pig is 'Paddy's friend'. *Abeokuta and the Cameroons Mountains* abounds in similar expressions: blood is the 'curious juice', people are 'human bipeds' and women are 'the last created sex'.

Abeokuta also contains the usual enemy-making phrases, praises of his own books, and the expression of some unconventional ideas. He made fun of David Livingstone and maintained that 'he never made a Kafir convert'. He criticized a book by a Miss Tusker called *Abbeokuta; or Sunrise within the Tropics*, and is most bitter that although the author had never seen West Africa, her book had already gone through six editions; he wondered if his own would ever see a second edition. (It did not.) He maintained that liquor was essential in tropical climates and gleefully mentions a man who died of 'confirmed teetotalism'. He makes a case for polygamy again, maintaining that 'in these later days the claims of polygamy have been wholly neglected'. Polygamy, he says, is the 'instinctive law of nature' and Europeans are 'violating the order of natural creation' by failing to adopt it. Husbands, he felt, should not have intercourse with their wives when they are pregnant, so naturally husbands need more than one wife. The book was dedicated to 'my best friend, my wife'.

In addition to these two books of his own, Burton also made arrangements for bringing out Marcy's *The Prairie Traveller* with his own annotations based on his experience in the United States.

On 24 January 1863, the Burtons left England for the Canary Islands. Isabel had complained, 'One's husband in a place where I am not allowed to go, and I living with my mother like a girl. I am neither maid, nor wife, nor widow.' So Burton took her with him as far as Tenerife, where he planned to spend the rest of his vacation.

The first night out they ran into a heavy storm with waves that washed one man overboard, sent the captain into the scuppers with a sprained wrist, and stove in the doors of the main cabin. Isabel crawled trembling and sea-sick to her bunk while Burton helped man the pumps. Isabel was not left alone with her wretchedness. A drunken naval officer, who was also a passenger on board, stumbled against the door of her cabin, rolled in and collapsed on the floor. When Burton returned, he picked up the officer and kicked him down the deck. Then, shutting the door, he told her, 'The captain says we can't live more than two hours in such a sea as this.'

'Oh! thank God it will be over so soon,' moaned Isabel.

Burton was furious. She was not frightened and he gave her a lecture on how she should be.

But the ship weathered the storm and, on 2 February, landed at Funchal, Madeira. The Burtons disembarked here and spent a month climbing around the island. The boat that was to take them to Tenerife also brought letters from England, and Isabel received word that her mother had had an attack of paralysis. It was a blow to Isabel and nearly spoiled what was one of the happiest times of her life.

Once on Tenerife, Burton did not now go seeking *l'aventure*, but carried his wife off to a mountain village. The accommodations they were given at the inn were dismal, but Isabel soon set about cleaning and making over a deserted ballroom. 'I was delighted with my handiwork,' she wrote. 'We had arrived at seven, and at nine I went to fetch my philosophic husband, who had meanwhile got a book, and had quietly settled down, making up his mind for the worst. He was perfectly delighted with the fine old den, for we had good air, light, a splendid view, lots of room, and good water . . . and here we intended to pass a happy month – to read, write, study, chat, walk, make excursions, and enjoy ourselves.'

It was indeed a happy month for Isabel. She was with her husband in a strange land and they were roughing it, after a fashion. It was true this was not the desert, but they climbed the mountain, camped out, and made friends with the peasants. There was even a bit of danger in climbing the peak of Tenerife: they were the first people to make the ascent in winter since 1797.

Although much fatigued, Isabel made it to the top: 'At 6 a.m. the guides told us to turn around: a golden gleam was on the sea – the first of the sun; and gradually its edge appeared, and it rose majestically in pure golden glory; and we were hanging between heaven and earth – in solitude and silence – and were permitted to enjoy this beautiful moment. It was Sunday morning, March 22 – Passion Sunday.'

At the top of the peak, the guides suggested a *Gloria Patri*; Burton preferred a cigar. Isabel and the guides knelt to pray and Isabel prayed that 'the only unbeliever of our little party might one day receive the gift of faith'.

The above quotations come from an unpublished book which Isabel wrote on their experiences in the Canary Islands. Burton would not allow her to publish it, saying she needed more practice. So, copying him, she became a furious note-taker.

At last the happy time ended. Isabel had to return to England and Burton to Fernando Po. Until the last moment, Isabel hoped her husband would relent and allow her to go with him; she cried and begged, but he steadfastly refused. With a heavy heart she embarked for England.

Chapter 16

Mission to Dahomey
1863 – 4

AFTER four months Burton was thoroughly dispirited and looking for
some way to escape his hated consulate. At the end of July, relief came
in the form of another visit from a warship, HMS *Torch*. He scrambled
on board for a ride down the coast to Loango, about a hundred miles
north of the mouth of the Congo. From there he secured another ride
down to Luanda, in Angola. He was far from his consular duties, but
this did not disturb him. He even made a trip into the interior of
Angola.

On 22 August 1863, he left Luanda on still a third ship and sailed
into the mouth of the Congo River. Then, travelling overland and by
small boat, he made his way up the river as far as the first cataract,
delving into native customs, collecting plant samples (490 specimens)
and studying the local languages. He wrote up a long report on this
trip and sent it off to the Foreign Office, where his superiors must have
wondered what on earth their consul for Fernando Po was doing in the
Congo. He was preparing for another overland trip when word reached
him that he had been appointed Her Majesty's Commissioner to
Dahomey. Arriving at Banana Point at the mouth of the Congo on
27 September, he just had time to catch the ship that would take him
back to Fernando Po to make his preparations.

Here, for once, was a chance for the Foreign Office to utilize
Burton's peculiar talents to best advantage. Burton was delighted. Two
years earlier he had suggested that he make an official call on the ruler
of the savage kingdom of Dahomey, but his superiors had not then
deemed it advisable. Now they had decided to send him, and probably
they could not have found a better man in the government service for
such an outlandish mission.

It has been suggested that Burton was a man born out of his time,
that he should have been an Elizabethan or a Roman, but the fact is that
there has never been a right time for a man such as Burton. He would
have been a misfit in any age – one whose temperament, character and
vast range of interests, would have put him outside the main social

stream whatever the era. The Victorian period was as good as any for a restless man with an inexhaustible hunger for travel and excitement. He should have had independent means, for he was essentially unsuited for any sort of employment. Basically undisciplined, he was destined to spend his entire adult life under military or consular discipline without ever conforming to the patterns that make for success in those fields. Had Her Majesty's Government created the post of Roving Ambassador to Barbarians, Burton might have adequately filled the post, but unfortunately only a single opportunity was given him to perform in this capacity, and his diplomatic mission was an impossible one.

The Kingdom of Dahomey was founded in 1625 and first emerged as a powerful African state in the early part of the eighteenth century when it was raised to its greatest strength and influence by King Gezo who, ascending the throne in 1818, reigned for forty years. On his death, he was succeeded by his son, Gelele (or Glegle), who immediately began to attack neighbouring tribes, harass Christians, enliven the slave trade and engage in other activities that disturbed the English and French governments who were then competing for influence in this area.

There were two sociological aspects of life in the Dahomey Kingdom that made it highly interesting to Richard Burton: it had a well organized army composed of women warriors, and its people practised certain particularly cruel rites known as the 'Dahomey customs'. There were two kinds of 'customs': the yearly customs that resulted in the wanton killing of large numbers of men, women and children, often in the most terrible manner, and the grand custom which took place only when a king died and was a similar bloodbath carried out on a grander scale.

Burton's instructions from Lord John – now Earl – Russell stated that he was to attempt to dissuade the king from his slaving practices and 'to impress upon the King the importance which Her Majesty's Government attach to the cessation of this traffic'. But Lord Russell had little hope that Burton would be entirely successful; he only hoped that through his efforts the trade would at least be mitigated. Burton was also instructed to deliver certain presents to the king and to gain as much good will as possible for the British. In the previous year, King Gelele's troops had captured the town of Oshogbo and had carried away a number of prisoners, including some Christian converts. Burton was to do his best to secure the release of these prisoners, if any of them remained alive. Before proceeding to Abomey, the capital of the Dahomey kingdom, he was to attempt to persuade the king not to make any human sacrifices while he was visiting him. The presents which he was sent to deliver consisted of 'One forty feet circular crimson silk Damask Tent with Poles complete (contained in two boxes). One richly embossed silver Pipe with amber mouth-piece, in morocco case. Two richly embossed silver Belts with Lion and Crane in raised relief, in morocco cases. Two silver and partly gilt Waiters, in oak case. One Coat of Mail and Gauntlets.'

On 29 November 1863, all was ready and Burton boarded HMSS *Antelope* as the cannons boomed a seventeen-gun salute to Her Majesty's Commissioner to the Kingdom of Dahomey. On 5 December the ship anchored off Ouidah (also spelled Whydah or Wida) and Burton sent off a messenger to King Gelele announcing his intended visit. Receiving a favourable reply, he set off on 14 December for Kana (or Kama), the 'country capital', where King Gelele was then staying.

Accompanying Burton were Selim; John Cruikshank, a naval assistant surgeon; Rev. Peter W. Bernasko, described as a 'native assistant missionary'; forty-nine porters, thirty hammock men and sundry interpreters, cooks, flag carriers and others – a total of ninety-nine persons.

They had only a short way to go but were delayed by celebrations in their honour at each village. Burton referred to these as 'the usual infliction'. The region through which they passed was one of the most ruinous Burton had ever seen and he was struck by the scantiness of the population, particularly the lack of adult males. On 18 December they reached Kana, which he described as 'a well-less scatter of huts and houses, thickening as usual around the palace and market-places, and straggling over some three miles of ground'. He estimated its population to be about 4,000. The following day he prepared for 'the penance of reception'.

Burton was urged early in the morning to make ready, but knowing that such affairs rarely start before noon he delayed his appearance until 1 p.m. – and even then he was an hour early. As soon as he sat down, an old card table was put beside him and bottles of 'trade rum' were placed upon it. This same table was to follow him and to be set up whenever and wherever he appeared. After witnessing a procession and dancing, he was presented to King Gelele: 'He looks a king of (negro) men, without tenderness of heart or weakness of head. . . . His person is athletic, upwards of six feet high, lithe, agile, thin flanked and broad

shouldered. . . . His eyes are red, bleared and inflamed. . . . The only
vestige of tattoo is the usual Dahoman mark, three short parallel and
perpendicular lancet cuts, situated nearer the scalp than the eyebrows.'
Sitting behind the king in a semicircle was a group of women. Burton
was disappointed to find that none of them were pretty.

The king began a speech in which he complimented Burton upon
keeping his promise to return to Dahomey. In his book describing his
mission, Burton wrote, 'I had promised on a previous occasion to apply
for permission to revisit Dahome, and here to redeem a promise is a
thing unknown. The king frequently afterwards referred to this trifle,
attaching great importance to truth-telling, and assuring me that it
made me his good friend.' There is other evidence also to the fact that
Burton had been to Dahomey before: previous recognition of Kana
and references to the fact that he had previously been made an honorary
commander of a troop of women soldiers. Just when Burton made his
previous visit is unknown; the double visit appears to have escaped the
notice of previous biographers. Most probably it was in early November 1861, when he had been to near-by Abeokuta. He had sufficient
reason for concealing this first visit: he had applied for official permission at that time to go to Dahomey and his request had been
refused. Possibly he had made his application and completed the trip
before receiving a reply, and only learned on his return that he should
not have gone.

Now, however, Burton had returned in an official capacity and he
insisted upon all the honours due him. When a nine-gun salute was
fired, he objected; there had been eleven guns for Commodore Wilmot,
the last official visitor. Burton's interpreter, an ex-slave named John
Beecham who at Ouidah called himself a prince, was afraid to translate
the objection, but Burton insisted and the extra two salutes were fired.

On 20 December he moved on to Abomey, the Dahomean capital,
and the king and his suite followed the next day. Gelele was detained
at Kana because some 150 of his amazons were found to be pregnant –
'so difficult is chastity in the tropics', said Burton philosophically.

Passing through the gate to the city, Burton noted a human skull
set in the clay wall, with thigh bones and other human fragments
'hanging about'. On several doors he also saw skulls nailed up. He was
conducted to the large thatched hut that was to be his home during his
stay. He promptly knocked a hole in the back wall of the hut to let in
more air and made a shutter for it from a claret case.

The next day he visited the main palace. He did not see a courtyard strewn with bones, as he had been led to expect, but only a single skull nailed with a white flag to a tree. Riding in his hammock to the palace, however, he did pass a small market where women were selling food and he noticed a prisoner standing in front of a drummer. The man was gagged with a Y-shaped forked stick, the fork holding the tongue and the sharp end wedged in the palate so that the man's mouth was kept pried open but he was unable to speak. Burton was told that the man was a criminal due to be executed at the coming customs.

At the palace, he was kept waiting for three hours ('these people have no bowels of compassion', he groaned) until the ceremony began. Looking around him, he saw that the palace was not a grand affair but only a collection of fetish huts, scaffolding and thatched buildings. He amused himself by drinking the gin and rum provided on the old card table, supplemented by some liquor of his own that Paul Du Chaillu had sent him. He was gradually joined by other dignitaries: Buko-no, a fetish man who was also Burton's official host and landlord at Abomey, and Prince Chyudaton, a Dahomean noble who appeared riding side-saddle on a tiny horse, an umbrella over his head, and sucking a lettuce leaf.

At last, at 3.45 in the afternoon, a long line of flags and coloured umbrellas were seen coming in the gates of the palace. To the beating of drums, the braying of horns and firing of muskets, the procession began its parade around the courtyard. There were thirty-three different groups of caboceers, royal relatives, fetish men and other dignitaries. Last of all came King Gelele with 500 musketeers, a skull standard, many gorgeously coloured umbrellas, fetish sticks, coloured flags and a band of drums, rattles and horns. The king himself rode under four white umbrellas with three brightly coloured parasols waving and twisting over him as fans in a kind of brougham pulled by men. Behind him came a crowd of slaves carrying chairs, boxes, baskets and cowrie shells, bottles and other valuables. In the midst of din and dust Gelele was carried ten times around the yard – twice in a bath chair – while Gelele covered his mouth with a handkerchief to keep out the dust. Burton thought he looked wearied and cross, but reflected that this was 'an expression not unfrequent upon the brow of royalty in all lands'.

Then the male soldiers retired and the women soldiers took over the centre of the stage, parading, dancing, singing, and firing their muskets. They were accompanied not only by the usual coloured umbrellas and flags but also by platters of skulls, women carrying weapons like oversized straight razors, and rattles, cymbals and drums. Twelve of them proceeded to carry the king around in a hammock made of yellow silk slung on a long pole with red, blue and yellow umbrellas shielding him from the sun. It was a wild, colourful, barbaric spectacle, but Burton affected to be bored with it all. He retired from the row and riot, he said, 'with the usual finale to a Dahoman parade – a headache'.

The following day was appointed for Burton and his party to present the gifts they had brought for the king and various members of his court. In addition to the official presents, he had also brought along some presents of his own: a picture, a box of French perfumes, a case of liquor, one dozen coloured-glass tumblers, and several kinds of cloths. He had tried to find some children's toys on the coast, particularly a Noah's Ark, which he thought would be an excellent present for the king and suited to the level of his mentality, but he had been unable to find any.

The presentation of the gifts was not a success. Burton and his party had to pitch the crimson tent themselves. It was equipped with wooden pegs which, in a land swarming with white ants, was not practical. Although splendid to behold, Gelele thought it was too small and the only part of it admired was an ornamental lion on the top of the pole. The fancy pipe was never used; Gelele preferred his old red clay pipe with the wooden stem. The silver belts were a disappointment; Gelele wanted bracelets. The coat of mail was too heavy and the gauntlets were too small. What Gelele really wanted was a carriage complete with white horses. He had made this request to Commodore Wilmot and he had fully expected Burton to bring it. Over and over again Burton had to explain to Gelele and to his ministers why he had failed to provide them. 'On the present occasion, the king never even uttered an expression of gratitude,' Burton recorded. 'His disappointment soon pierced through his politeness, which was barely retained by a state of feeling best expressed in our popular adage, – "Better luck next time," especially in the matter of an English carriage and horses.'

Burton had hoped that when he distributed his presents he would have an opportunity to deliver the message from his government. His presents were carried away by the amazons, however, and he was presented with a decanter of rum – the signal that it was time for him to leave. He was told that his message would be heard at another time.

December 28 was the first day of the customs, but Burton lost no time in studying the language (before he left Dahomey he was able to carry on a conversation in Fon); prying the secrets of Afa divination from Buko-no, in whose house he was staying; learning the complex organization of the Dahomean government; studying the funeral, marriage and religious customs of the people; and, of course, learning all he could about the corps of amazons.

Burton thought the idea of having women soldiers was one that European nations might profitably adopt:

The warlike instinct, as the annals of the four quarters of the globe prove, is easily bred in the opposite sex. A sprinkling of youth and beauty amongst the European Amazons would make campaigning a pleasure to us; and the measure may be taken into consideration when our new-fangled rage for neutrality shall be succeeded by more honourable and less 'respectable' sentiments; and when the model Englishman shall be something better than a warm man of business, with a good ledger, and 'the dean's daughter' to wife.

Isabel had been delighted by the news of Richard's appointment, but she did not care for the idea of her husband being surrounded by an army of women. To reassure her, Burton sent a sketch of the fierce and exceedingly ugly captain of one of the amazonian companies. It would appear that Isabel had little to fear: 'As a rule the warrioresses begin to fatten when their dancing days are passed, and some are prodigies of obesity,' he said.

Burton estimated that there were about 2,500 women soldiers in Gelele's army. Although he commented on their ugliness, he did not believe that their appearance, their strict regimen, or their enforced celibacy caused them to be less womanly: 'All the passions are sisters. I believe that bloodshed causes these women to remember, not to forget, LOVE; at the same time that it gratifies the less barbarous, but, with barbarians, equally animal feeling.' Commenting on the much broken rule requiring celibacy, he said, 'Wherever the she-soldiery is, celibacy must be one of its rules, or the troops will be in a state of chronic disorder between the ages of fifteen and thirty-five.' Twenty-five years after his visit, he recorded that he had seen 'a corps of prostitutes for the use of the amazonian soldieresses' in Dahomey.

Life in the Dahomean capital was all very interesting, but, as usual, Burton found it almost unbearable to remain in one spot longer than a week. He wanted to move out and explore some of the country around the capital but he was prevented from doing so by the king who maintained the practice of keeping his guests as virtual prisoners until he saw fit to dismiss them. Burton had to remain in Abomey.

Early on the morning of the first day of the customs, there was a discharge of musketry at the palace and a messenger arrived to tell Burton that his presence was required. Shortly after noon he decided to mount his hammock and go. In the market place just outside the gate, the victim-shed was now completed. Burton compared its appearance to an English church, 'a barn and a tower'. It was about 100 feet long, 40 feet wide and about 60 feet high at its tallest point. The roof was covered with a tattered blood-red cloth, bisected by a broad blue stripe. Twenty victims were seated on stools in the shed and tied with neck-laces of rope to posts. All were dressed in calico shirts decorated around the neck and down the sleeves with red binding. A crimson patch was sewn on the left breast. On their heads were long white nightcaps with spirals of blue ribbon on them. The victims did not seem unhappy about their impending doom. They chattered among themselves and beat time to the music of a drum.

Burton entered the palace yard and took his seat by the card table with his notebook and sketch pad. Gelele, preceded by a corps of amazons, made his appearance soon after amid a barbaric din. Inside the palace yard was another victim-shed with two storeys. Burton exhibited a rare bit of compassion for these doomed men: 'I counted nine victims on the ground floor and ten above, lashed to nearly every second post of the front opposite the palace. They resembled in all points those of the market-shed, and looked wholly unconcerned, whilst their appearance did not attract the least attention. Yet I felt haunted by the presence of these *morituri*, with whose hard fate the dance, the song, the dole, and the noisy merriment of the thoughtless mob afforded the saddest contrast.'

Near the victims sat the chief fetish-men. Burton thought they looked at him with unfriendly eyes, but reflected that 'such is, perhaps, the custom of reverend men generally with respect to those not of their own persuasion'.

About 2,500 people were assembled in the palace yard to witness the first day of the customs. After some preliminary dancing, Gelele stepped forward and made a speech to the effect that it was a fine and pious old custom he was carrying out as his father had done before him and as he hoped his sons would do after him. The victims tied in the shed listened attentively.

Following this speech, the king retired behind a curtain to take a drink, it being forbidden for anyone to see the king eat or drink. Refreshed, he then emerged to sing and dance before his people:

'though the style is purely Dahoman and barbarous, the movements are comparatively kingly and dignified', Burton recorded. Gelele was assisted in his dancing by two 'leopard wives', the youngest and most beautiful of his harem, who were dressed in white waistcoats and striped loincloths. When finished, Gelele wiped the sweat from his forehead with his finger and scattered it with a jerk over the faces of his delighted subjects. He then retired to be wiped down with yellow silk cloths by his wives.

The king finally sat down to listen to praises of himself from his court dignitaries: 'All gave the ruler that full meed of flattery which his soul loves. He may be said to breathe an atmosphere of adulation, which intoxicates him. The wildest assertions, the falsest protestations, the most ridiculous compliments, the ultra-Hibernian "blarney" – all are swallowed in the bottomless pit of poor human vanity, and midnight will often see him engaged in what ought to be a very nauseous occupation.' To wit, the cutting-off of heads.

Whenever any of his subjects appeared before Gelele they crawled on the ground and shovelled dust on their heads. It is little wonder that Gelele had an exaggerated opinion of himself and his prowess. His chief goal in life at this time was to attack and destroy the city of Abeokuta. It was a constant theme in his speeches, and, of course, of his warrior captains (male and female), ministers and court followers. One and all boasted of the great and horrible deeds they would do when the day came to attack their enemies.

The dancing and speech-making went on until after sunset. Burton wrote, 'Nothing could be poorer than the display . . . any hill rajah in India could command more wealth and splendour. All was a barren barbarism, whose only "sensation" was produced by a score of men looking on and hearing that they are about to die.'

The next day Burton again sent a message to court saying that he officially objected to being present at any human sacrifice and suggesting that lower animals be substituted for men. He also stated that he would at once return to Ouidah if any death took place in his presence. All this was what he was expected to do in his official capacity, but privately he must have been hoping that if human sacrifices were to be made, he would get a chance to see the sight. To his friend Monckton Milnes he wrote:

At Benin . . . they crucified a fellow in honour of my coming – here nothing! And this is the Bloodstained Land of Dahome!! The 'monster' as your papers call the King is a jolly looking party about 45 with a pleasant face, a frank smile and a shake of the fist like a British shopkeeper. He made me Captain of his Corps of Amazons. About these individuals a fearful amount of bosh has been talked and written. I was looking forward with prodigious curiosity to see 5,000 African adult virgins, never yet having met with a single specimen. I found that most of them were women taken in adultery and given to the king as food for powder instead of being killed. They were mostly elderly and all of them hideous . . . I took up a few presents of cloth . . . and (keep this quiet) three very *dégagé* coloured prints of white women in a state of Eve-ical toilette. This charmed him and he inquired whether such articles are to be procured alive. I told (Heaven forgive me) a fearful fib and said that in my country the women are of a farouche chastity. . . . Disgusted with the tameness of this place.

In the same light vein, Burton had promised to send his friend Fred Hankey a human skin stripped from a living human victim, preferably a woman. But Burton was not actually to witness a human sacrifice, although he saw plenty of evidence of its having taken place. He was told that all of the intended victims were either criminals or captives taken in battle but that some of them would be released. For the first three days of the customs, however, there was no evidence of killing. The victims sat in their sheds and around them was the drinking, dancing, singing and speech-making that made up the bulk of the ceremonies.

On the second day of the customs Gelele took off most of his clothes in the presence of his subjects, stripping down to his shorts, satin with yellow flowers on them. He then performed a marathon of thirty-two dances and refreshed himself by drinking rum from brass-mounted skulls of former enemy chiefs. Burton was invited to drink from the skulls too. Of course he did.

On the third day the king distributed cowries to his people who fought savagely for them. Eyes were sometimes gouged out and noses torn off in the scuffle, and if anyone was killed, he was considered to have fallen while fighting for his king and the killer was forgiven. Burton saw a hand that had been bitten through by the sharp teeth of an enthusiast. The king invited Burton and his party to join the sport and they consented, scrambling like schoolboys for the shells.

Following this amusement, the king walked over to the victim-shed and chatted with the prisoners. He then came over to snap fingers with Burton and hint that some of the victims might be pardoned if he would intercede for them. This Burton did, adding a bit of flattery to the effect that mercy is the great prerogative of kings. Several of them were then untied and placed on all fours to hear the king pardon them.

By the fourth day of the customs, 1 January 1864, Burton was finding that 'the labour of pleasure in Dahome is somewhat hard'. Already he was weary of the spectacle. Nevertheless, he continued to make his notes on every aspect of the ceremonies. On this day he noticed that the vultures were beginning to gather on the tree above him. 'Can their sagacity extend to guessing that death is near?' he wondered.

That night was called the 'Evil Night'. Burton estimated that the 'butchery bill' was about twenty-three victims, but he did not think Britons should be too upset by the Dahomean customs: 'We can hardly find fault with putting criminals to death, when, in the year of grace 1864 we hung four murderers upon the same gibbet before 100,000 gaping souls at Liverpool, when we strung up five pirates in front of Newgate . . . and when our last but one Christian king killed a starving mother of seventeen, with an infant at her breast. A Daho-man visiting England but a few years ago would have witnessed customs almost quite as curious as those which raise our bile now.'

Since all who left their houses on this night were beheaded, Burton was unable actually to witness what took place. The next day he debated whether in his official capacity he should take part in the ceremonies. He decided that he should, and at eleven o'clock in the morning he proceeded to the palace. In the market place were four corpses, still dressed in their criminals' shirts and nightcaps, propped up on stools with their backs against posts. A little way further on were two more, and then a single one hanging by his heels from a gallows. Still further on were two more bodies hanging head down-ward from a cross-bar. These latter were entirely nude and the bodies had been mutilated – after death, Burton believed. At the palace gate were some small idols in front of which were a dozen fresh heads. Inside, all was prepared for another day of dancing, singing, speech-making and parading. The festivities this day lasted for seven hours, and when at last Burton and his party were free to leave, they hurried home past corpses already beginning to stink after an afternoon in the sun.

In Dahomey there was a 'double king': Gelele was the king of the city and Addo-kpon was the king of the country, but both were repre-sented in a single person. When Gelele's customs were completed, those of Addo-kpon's began. On 4 January, Burton and his people went to a village six miles from Abomey to take part in these customs. As they passed through the city they saw that the corpses had not been moved. The smell was terrible and the turkey buzzards were greedily picking at the rotting flesh.

The ceremonies had already started when they arrived. The king was about to distribute cowries again and Burton was once more invited to take part in the scramble. He pleaded a sprained wrist and asked to be excused. The king did not insist, but said he had admired his bravery and cunning on the previous occasion (he had rolled the Reverend Bernasco) and wanted to see him in action again.

The next day was terribly hot, so Burton postponed his appearance until the middle of the afternoon. This was the day the king had selected for Burton to dance for him. Burton agreed. Giving the beat to the band, he performed a 'Hindustani *pas seul* which elicited violent applause, especially from the king'. Then the Rev. Bernasco sang hymns and preached for half an hour. The king then suggested that Bernasco sing while Burton and Cruikshank danced. Burton said, 'It was almost too ridiculous, but we complied for a short time.' Burton then did a sword dance alone before his company of amazons, who all fired off their guns and cheered him. It must indeed have been a sight to cheer.

That night Gelele killed the remainder of his victims – bringing the total to seventy-eight or eighty according to Burton's estimate.

On the fifth day of the country customs Burton again danced for the king. This time he performed a *pas de deux* with the commander-in-chief of the amazons – 'with left shoulder forward, corresponding arm akimbo, and ditto leg in the air'.

Except for these occasional exercises, Burton's life at Abomey was fairly static. Forbidden to explore the countryside, he remained in town with little to do except learn and record what he could from the people he met and the scenes that passed before his eyes. He still had not delivered his message. 'Time slips easily away at Agbome,' he wrote. 'Rising with the dawn, we set out as soon as the hammock-men can be collected, and walk till nine a.m. Refection follows till eleven, and my lesson in Ffon outlasts the noon. If we visit the Komasi Palace, the rest of the day will be a blank; the brain becomes so weary that work in the evening is impossible. . . . The afternoon is an inverted copy of the forenoon.'

As in the case of every people with whom Burton came in contact, with the sole exception of the Bedouin, he found little to admire in the

Dahomeans and much to condemn. He summed up his opinion of King Gelele's subjects with these words: 'The modern Dahomans . . . are a mongrel breed, and a bad. They are Cretan liars, *cretins* at learning, cowardly and therefore cruel and bloodthirsty; gamblers, and consequently cheaters; brutal, noisy, boisterous, unvenerative, and disobedient, dipsas-bitten things who deem it a "duty to the gods to be drunk"; a "flatulent, self-conceited herd of barbarians", who endeavour to humiliate all those with whom they deal; in fact, a slave race – vermin with a soul apiece.'

But the Dahomeans had a far finer opinion of Burton – at least by his account. They thought him, he said, a great prodigy because he could sketch their likenesses, read and write, use a sword with dexterity, and, of course, perform exotic dances. Gelele himself thought him a good man but 'too angry'.

Time dripped away and Burton still had not accomplished what his government had sent him to do. He witnessed some interesting events – the ceremony of formally declaring war on Abeokuta; the return of a war party that had captured a small village, bringing with them a batch of miserable prisoners and some imperfectly cleaned skulls; the torture of small animals for fetish purposes to bring good luck; and the Dahomean funeral customs – but he was becoming most impatient to complete his mission and leave. This impatience was intensified by the receipt on 8 February of an official letter stating that a cruiser was waiting for him at Ouidah.

On 9 February, Burton ostentatiously packed up his gear in the compound and sent word to Gelele that, unless he granted him an audience and enabled him to deliver his message from Her Majesty's Government, he would leave the next day. The king sent him a letter of apology, blaming his ministers, whom he said he had beaten, and setting at last a date for the audience. Four days later, Burton presented himself at the palace.

The audience lasted four hours. Both Burton and the king were polite, but neither minced words. Burton began by complaining about his own treatment: he had not been allowed to mix with the visiting chiefs; and he had been made to wait in the sun almost every day of the customs. In reply, Gelele asked if his orders had said he was to explore the country (of course, the answer was no) and if it was true that Burton had beaten the slaves of Buko-no, his host (the answer was yes).

When personal grievances had been put aside, Burton finally read his official message. He did not expect complete success, but he did hope for some concessions on the part of the king. He received nothing but counter-demands from Gelele. The slave trade was an ancestral custom established by white men and he would continue it. Besides, if the captives taken in battle were not sold, they would be executed. Regarding the Christian prisoners taken at Oshogbo, Gelele said they were all dead, although Burton believed otherwise. The customs to which the English objected were part of his religion and he could not stop them if he tried. Gelele again complained about not receiving a carriage and horses and protested loudly against the practice of the British warships of seizing cargoes of slaves off the coast. In short, Burton accomplished nothing.

Although the failure to accomplish his mission was probably not due to any fault on his part, Burton was disappointed: 'The personal courtesies of the King compared badly with his stubborn resolve to ignore, even in the smallest matters, the wishes of Her Majesty's Government. Nothing appeared uppermost in his mind but an ignoble greed of presents.'

The next day Burton and his party set out for the coast. He described it as the most comfortless march he had ever made in Africa, although he appears to have encountered little more than the usual difficulties and inconveniences. On 18 February they reached Ouidah and found it a smouldering ruin. Three separate fires in three days had created havoc and an estimated sixty to eighty people had been killed. Burton did not tarry but boarded the waiting warship for a tour of the Oil Rivers.

A week after Burton's departure, the Dahomean army marched out to attack Abeokuta. They were completely defeated and the nation never again regained its former power. It remained an independent kingdom until a French army captured the city of Abomey in 1892; Dahomey was made a French colony two years later.

Burton received no acknowledgement of his services, but Isabel was sent a private note from Lord Russell that said, 'Tell Captain Burton that he has performed his Mission to my utmost and entire satisfaction.'

After his tour of the Oil Rivers, Burton returned to Fernando Po – and fell in love with the place he had so soundly damned! Of course he did not stay at his consulate at Santa Isabel, but in a sanatorium the Spanish governor had established on the mountainside: 'Nothing could be more genial and healthful than the place where I am now writing these lines. . . . The view from the balcony facing north is charming. . . . In front is a narrow ledge of cleared ground bearing rose trees . . . and a cacao, showing what the island would have been but for the curse of free labour.'

While Speke and Grant, having emerged from Central Africa by way of the Nile, were receiving the adulation of the world for their great exploit, Burton was settling down to a quiet life on his tiny island, content, for the moment, with his existence:

An hour of work in my garden at sunrise and sunset, when the scenery is equally beautiful, hard reading during the day, and after dark a pipe and a new book of travels, this is the '*fallentis semia vitæ*' which makes one shudder before plunging once more into the cold and swirling waters of society – of civilization. My 'niggers' are, as Krumen should be, employed all the day long in clearing, cutting, and planting – it is quite the counterpart of a land-owner's existence in the Southern States. Nothing will prevent them calling themselves my 'children', that is to say, my slaves; and indeed no white man who has lived long in the outer tropics can prevent feeling that he is *pro tempore* the lord, the master, and the proprietor of the black humanity placed under him. It is true that the fellows have no overseer, consequently there is no whip; punishment resolves itself into retrenching rum and tobacco; more-over, they come and go as they please. But if a little 'moral influence' were not applied to their lives, they would be dozing or quarrelling all day in their quarters, and twanging a native guitar half the night, much to their own dis-comfort and more to their owner's. Consequently I keep them to their work.

Isabel, meanwhile, was trying her best to destroy this idyllic existence by clamouring at the Foreign Office for a better appointment. Even though Burton had discovered that the Bubu natives of Fernando Po made the best palm toddy in western Africa, he could not long be content to remain in one place. In August 1864, he left his consulate for home leave in England. It was an eventful leave and it marked the end of his service in West Africa.

Oddly enough, one of the first activities of Burton and his wife was to shop for a cemetery plot. After looking at several burial grounds, they selected a very small one located in Mortlake, a London suburb.

Those whom Burton loved least were in London while he was there: James Hanning Speke and Christopher Palmer Rigby, now a general. Both were then at the height of their popularity. Speke and Grant had just returned from their African trip in which they had proved – to their own satisfaction, at least – the connection between Lake Victoria and the Nile; Rigby had achieved fame for his efforts to suppress the slave trade on the African east coast, having liberated eight thousand slaves in person. Rigby had been on hand to greet Speke and Grant when they landed in Southampton and had been with them almost daily since. It seemed that Burton had been forgotten. At the Royal Geographical Society he left his card with one of his undergraduate verses on it:

> *Two loves the Row of Savile haunt*
> *Who both by nature big be*
> *The fool is Colonel (Barren) Grant*
> *The rogue is General Rigby.*

Rigby later became a member of the Council of the Royal Geographical Society, and Burton, for a time, no longer submitted papers. He was alienated from the one organization that could have assisted him financially in worthwhile exploration and which had awarded him its highest honour.

In spite of Speke's truly magnificent achievement, Burton still violently disagreed with many of the more important geographical conclusions drawn by his former companion. The quarrel was fanned into a hot flame by Lawrence Oliphant and at last a showdown meeting was arranged. In mid-September, the British Association was meeting at Bath. Oliphant reported to Burton a statement he attributed to Speke to the effect that 'if Burton appeared on the platform at Bath, he would kick him'.

'Well, *that* settles it,' Burton retorted. 'By God, he *shall* kick me!'

A public airing of their quarrel was quickly arranged and Burton and his wife went down to Bath on 13 September. The Burton–Speke debate was scheduled for the 16th.

Africa was not discussed on the first day, but the disputants were both present on the platform. They eyed each other coldly. Isabel recorded her impression of Speke: 'I shall never forget his face. It was full of sorrow, of yearning, and perplexity. Then he seemed to turn to stone.'

Here were two men who had shared much danger and hardship together in Somalia and again in East Africa. They had nursed each other through strange and terrible sicknesses; they had struggled together over difficult and strange lands towards a common objective; they had once been friends. Now they met as strangers – worse, as enemies – and the cause of their disagreement was a question of theoretical geography: Speke maintained he had discovered the source of the Nile; Burton as stoutly maintained he had not. Burton later spoke of this affair as that 'unfortunate rivalry respecting the Nile

Sources [which] arose between us, and was fanned to a flame by the enmity and the ambition of "friends"'.

Now they stared at each other coldly before an eminent scientific gathering. Many were waiting eagerly for the following day's explosion when the two would confront each other on the platform.

Speke was uncomfortable and fidgeted in his seat. At last he said half-aloud, 'Oh, I can't stand this any longer', and rose.

'Shall you want your chair again, sir? May I have it? Shall you come back?' someone asked.

'I hope not,' said Speke and left the hall.

A large crowd was assembled for the debate on 16 September. All of the distinguished people present were behind the scenes together with the Council of the Association. All, that is, except Burton. He was left alone on the platform with Isabel, nervously fingering his notes. The meeting was twenty-five minutes late in starting. At last the Council and speakers filed in. It was announced that Speke was dead. He had shot himself accidentally.

Burton sank into a chair. 'I saw by the workings of his face the terrible emotion he was controlling,' Isabel wrote. 'When we got home he wept long and bitterly, and I was for many a day trying to comfort him.'

Burton was not so overcome that he could not carry on, however. He filled the gap in the following day's programme by reading a paper: 'On the Present State of Dahome.'

One may wonder whether Burton's tears on Speke's death were caused by grief or frustration. Yet there is little doubt that the two men had, at one time, been very close friends. Burton had once found much to admire in Speke's character and in his qualities as a man. Had he not, he would hardly have taken such trouble to have him as his companion on the African campaign after being with him in Somaliland. All this old feeling must have returned to him when it was announced that his former friend was dead. But he could never forgive an injury done to him; it was not in his nature to forgive. To Frank Wilson, a friend, he wrote, 'Nothing is known of Speke's death. I saw him at 1.30 p.m., and at 4 p.m. he was dead. The charitable say that he shot himself, the uncharitable that I shot him.'

The death of Speke at the age of thirty-seven was as perplexing as it was dramatic when one considers that he was an experienced shot. He had abruptly left the meeting and had at once set out on a shooting trip near by in Neston Park with his cousin and a gamekeeper. About

4 p.m. his cousin heard a shot and looking towards Speke he saw him fall from a low stone wall. When he reached him he discovered that he was wounded in the breast. 'Don't move me,' mumbled Speke. While his cousin ran off for help, Speke died. At the inquest the jury concluded that his gun had accidentally discharged close to his chest.

An article on Speke in *The Times* said, 'This unfortunate accident will put an end to the controversy which was to have amused the Geographers at Bath.' *The Times* was wrong. Speke was dead, but the controversy went on.

Burton had only contempt for Speke's ideas and theories and refused to value his discoveries at their true worth. In Burton's own copies of Speke's two books there are hundreds of annotations in the margins attesting to his disbelief in nearly everything Speke thought and to disapproval of everything he did: 'No', 'not true', 'a lie', 'stuff', 'not a line true', and Burton's favourite expression of contempt, 'Rot'.

Speke was not a good writer and certainly his books are rambling, sometimes contradictory, and frequently improbable. Describing his expedition with Burton he speaks of settling quarrels among the men, but this must have been difficult since, by his own admission, he did not speak any African language. He reports conversations with Arab chiefs that must have been with Burton as interpreter – and it is difficult to imagine Burton as a passive linguistic medium. Yet Speke says the Arab chiefs 'said to me' as though he were talking directly. When all is said and done, however, it *was* Speke who discovered the most important source of the Nile.

Although Speke was now dead, Burton saw no reason to discontinue his attacks upon him. Only two months after his death, on 14 November, Burton read before the Royal Geographical Society the talk he had apparently intended to give in his debate with Speke at the meeting of the British Association in Bath. This talk was later published as a small book entitled *The Nile Basin* which also included a most vicious and sarcastic attack on Speke by Burton's friend, James M'Queen. Although he speaks of Speke as 'my late lamented companion', he certainly does not spare his reputation.

In April of the preceeding year, Speke, writing from the Sudan, had sent word to the President of the Royal Geographical Society: 'The Nile is settled.' Burton did not feel it was settled at all. In his speech he pointed out the main objections to Speke's claim and his many inconsistencies. He and M'Queen made much of the fact that Speke travelled along the western shore of Lake Victoria without making sure that the lake was truly on his right. He actually touched the shore at very few points and left well over one hundred miles of the Nile untraced because he simply assumed that the Nile made a big bend and that the river he had been following and the one he later picked up were the same.

Nearly all of the criticisms of Speke's expedition given by Burton and M'Queen were valid ones. It might have been that the lake was not one lake, but several; it might have been that the river flowing out of Lake Victoria which he had imperfectly traced was not the Nile. The famous and respected Dr David Livingstone agreed with Burton. He thought Speke had 'turned his back upon the real sources of the Nile' and that the river Speke had seen flowing north from Lake Victoria at Ripon falls was 'not large enough for the Nile'. Nevertheless, Speke was right. He had indeed followed the shore of this mighty lake and the river was the Nile – and in spite of his own logic, Burton lived to see Speke's intuition proved right by Henry M. Stanley twelve years later.

It appears to have been a characteristic of nineteenth-century African explorers not to be shy in setting forth their own claims to fame and to express the utmost confidence in their own abilities. The only real exception to this rule was the gentle and gentlemanly Colonel James Grant – and the world has largely forgotten him. Speke claimed for himself the honour of having discovered *the* true source of the Nile and had plans for returning to Africa, crossing it from sea to sea, his object being 'nothing less than to regenerate Africa'. For years Burton had smarted under neglect. Now he lashed out with a tremendous blast on his own horn:

After so long a silence upon the subject I am, methinks, justified in drawing public attention to what was effected by the expedition of 1857 – 59, which was under my almost unaided direction. When wholly ignorant of the country, its language and trade, its manners and customs, preceded only by a French naval officer, who was murdered shortly after he landed on the coast, and but feebly supported by my late lamented friend Lieutenant-Colonel Hamerton, Her Majesty's Consul at Zanzibar, whom nearing death prevented from carrying out the best of intentions, I led the most disorderly of caravans into the heart of Eastern Africa, and discovered the Tanganyika and the Nyanza lakes. I brought home sufficient information to smooth the path for all who chose to follow me. . . . Dr. Beke has kindly found 'reason to call this emphatically a memorable expedition.' Except by a few esteemed friends it has hitherto either been ignored or forgotten.

The labours of the first expedition rendered the road easy for the second. The line had been opened by me to Englishmen, and they had but to tread in my steps.

But for Burton the Nile question and the promotion of his own claims for honours were only a part of his varied activities. Writing, of course, was a constant labour, as the stream of books attest: *Abeokuta and the Cameroons Mountains* was published in two volumes in 1863; *A Mission to Gelele, King of Dahome*, also in two volumes, came out the next year; and now he sent to the printer a new book, *Negro Wit and Wisdom*, a collection of proverbs and sayings, to be published in 1865. In all, he was to publish no less than nine volumes of material collected during his stay in West Africa – and even then he did not cover all of his activities and wanderings.

There was one other little book in blank verse which Burton published at this time under the name Frank Baker (Frank was for Francis, his middle name, and Baker was his mother's name). Isabel did not know about this book until one day on a train when Burton took it out of his pocket and handed it to her as though he had just bought it at the station bookstall. Isabel was delighted with it and kept reading out passages to him and laughing.

'Jemmy,' she said, using the affectionate nickname she had adopted for her unconventional idol, 'I wish you would not go about talking as you do. I am sure this man has been associating with you at the club, picked up all your ideas and written this book. And won't he just catch it!'

Isabel went on in this vein for some time until it finally struck her that her husband was the real author: 'You wrote it yourself, Jemmy, and nobody else!' she accused him.

'I did,' he confessed.

It was one thing to laugh at an indiscreet book written by a stranger; it was another matter to find that her Jemmy had written a book so likely to get him into trouble. Isabel showed the volume to Lord Houghton at the first opportunity, and he agreed that it would certainly not help Burton's promotion. Only 200 copies were printed and a publisher's statement extant shows that 128 were sent to the author; of these, thirty-three were sent to newspapers and magazines. Isabel made a determined effort to buy up all the copies she could and destroy them, so that very few were ever read.

The book, called *Stone Talk*, is an attempt at witty satire on England and its hypocrisy. The verses reflect not only Burton's usual brand of unorthodoxy, but the increasing bitterness he was feeling at his neglect by the government he served. The poem tells how Dr Polygott goes to dinner with a friend with whom he talks about India. They both get drunk and Dr Polygott wanders out in the street and falls in love with a beauty, but is repelled by the girl's mother, who is a Mrs Grundy. He then sits down on the street and is addressed by a paving stone. The stone proceeds to tell him all that is wrong with the world and presents the unhappy doctor with Burton's views of society, civilization and, in particular, his own countrymen. He takes up many of the themes of earlier books and a few new ones: there are anti-Christian, anti-Jew and anti-negro feelings expressed; Clive, Hastings and Napier are called bandits; the knighting of Indians, the government policies regarding Tasmania, Turkey and India, philanthropists, streetwalkers, Wilberforce, women's dresses and hair-styles, the practice of shaving and wearing rings, book reviewers, flesh-coloured tights, 'shopkeeperishness', liberals and white slavery – all are condemned. Medals are now cheap and easy to get; Britain is a land of traders; in England, 'to be poor is to be vile'; the Civil War in the United States ('Uncle Sham') could have been prevented by Britain; there would soon be a revolution in England; the Crimean War was a mistake; and British policy in general is hypocritical in the extreme – such are the thoughts expressed. Some of the couplets were obscene:

> *I felt as if a corking-pin*
> *Were thrust my os coccygis in.*

Many of the thoughts on religion were later rephrased in the *Kasîdah*:

> *Chance birth, chance teaching – these decide*
> *the faiths wherewith men feed their pride.*
>
> *   *   *
>
> *In fact, all to their faiths are true*
> *And in them good, save, Christians, you!*

Although a student of religions, Burton seldom mentioned his own attitude. It was at this period of life, however, that he spoke before the Anthropological Society of London and said, 'My religious opinion is of no importance to anybody but myself. No one knows what my religious views are. I object to confession, and will not confess. My standpoint is, and I hope ever will be, the Truth, as far as it is in me, known only to myself.'

Largely through Isabel's efforts – she haunted the Foreign Office, pleading for a better position for her husband – Burton did not return to Fernando Po but was given an appointment as consul at Santos in Brazil. Doubtless the order was given to find some distant post for Burton where his wife could go with him and thus free the Foreign Office for more important matters. Santos was hardly a choice post, although from Isabel's viewpoint, it was better than Fernando Po, but it was far from London, far from Africa, and far indeed from the Arabia of Burton's dreams.

Chapter 17

Bitter Brazil

1864 – 9

'Isn't a Consul a horrid creature that lives in a seaport, and worries merchant seamen, and imprisons people who have no passports? Papa always wrote to the Consul about getting our baggage through the Customs House, and when our servants quarrelled with the porters or hotel people, it was the Consul sent some of them to jail; but you are aware, darling, he isn't a creature we know. They are simply impossible, dear, impossible!' So speaks Lady Augusta, a character in a contemporary novel called *The Bramleighs of Bishop's Folly* by Charles James Lever, himself the British Consul in Trieste from 1867 until his death in 1872. Isabel often quoted these lines to illustrate that a man of her husband's qualities should be raised to a better position. She was forever dreaming that his abilities would suddenly be recognized and he would be given a higher and more important post, such as ambassador to Turkey or minister to Morocco, and she laboured unceasingly to bring this about. But now, for the moment, she was happy enough to have her husband sent as a consul to Santos. For the first time they would be able to live together in a home of their own, and, while it was hardly a lawless life in Arabia, it was, at least, exotic. She would be at his side to help him in his duties and to face the dangers and hardships she was sure awaited him.

Burton himself did not appear eager to reach Brazil. First he took Isabel on a holiday to Ireland, where they travelled over the country in an Irish car and fed their horse on hay and whisky. In Dublin they met a philanthropist with an enthusiasm for the rehabilitation of ex-criminals. He took the Burtons around the prisons and attempted to enlist Isabel's support for his pet project. Specifically, he wanted her to take on as a maid a woman who had just been released from prison after serving a sentence of fifteen years for murdering her own baby when she was only sixteen years old. 'Well, I would do anything to oblige you,' Isabel told him, 'but if I took her, I dare say I would often be left alone with her, and at thirty-four she might like larger game.'

Returning from Ireland, the Burtons set off on 10 May 1865, for two months' additional holiday in Portugal. On arriving at the Braganza Hotel in Lisbon, Isabel was horrified by the number and size of the cockroaches that cavorted over the whitewashed walls and the yellow satin curtains. Her reaction was to leap on a chair and scream. Burton was disgusted.

'A nice sort of traveller and companion you are going to make!' he exclaimed. 'I suppose you think you look very pretty and interesting, standing on that chair and howling at those innocent creatures.'

Isabel was hurt, but she 'made a meditation' and concluded that 'if I was going to live in a country always in contact with these and worse things, though I had a perfect horror of anything black and crawling, it would never do to go on like that'. She bravely climbed down from her chair, took a basin of water and a slipper and set to work. In two hours she killed ninety-seven.

Burton insisted on taking Isabel to a bullfight because, he said, she ought to see everything once. They went several times, actually. At first she shrank down and covered her eyes with her hands; then she began to peep through her fingers until she saw everything. 'It awed me so much that I was almost afraid to come out of our box, for fear we should meet a bull on the stairs.' Isabel was eventually able to justify the fighting to herself in spite of her great aversion to any sort of mal-treatment of animals.

The Burtons did not remain long in Lisbon; they wandered around Portugal, visiting Corregado, Sercal, Caldas, Pombal, Leiria, Coimbra and Oporto. Portugal was the home of Camoens and doubtless Burton did more work here on his translation of *The Lusiads*. Isabel began the study of Portuguese, the language she would need in Brazil.

Returning to Lisbon, Richard said good-bye to Isabel and sailed alone for South America in HMS *Serpent*. When the ship stopped for coal at St Vincent, Cape Verde Islands, he had an opportunity to examine an eight-year-old hermaphrodite. The examination was quite thorough: 'The penis is distinctly formed, about an inch and a quarter long, and proportionally thick, though not of the large African's size; the naked glans looks as if naturally circumcised. The orifice, instead of being at the top, is under the virga, thus constituting a clear case of hypospadias. The parents declare that he micturates from both organs, but less from the masculine. The urine, therefore, would pass through the frenum. No signs of testicles could be seen or felt.' Burton sent off a report on the child along with a detailed sketch to the Anthropolo-gical Society of London, of which he was then vice-president.

Isabel, on seeing Burton off in Lisbon, had promised him she would take the next ship for England. Since she believed in keeping her word literally, she boarded a tiny (428-ton) steamer only a few hours later. It took eight days to make the voyage and the ship ran aground in the Thames about fourteen miles east of London. The travel pattern set here was one that Isabel would soon know well. Burton would simply leave, while Isabel remained behind to 'pay, pack and follow'.

After winding up all the family loose threads in London, Isabel went into retreat for a week at Kensington Square Convent. Her devotional book of that period indicates that she now realized her husband was not the model of perfection her girlish dreams had made of him, although he was in her eyes still the most admirable man alive. She still tended to attribute godlike qualities to him and the conflict in her mind between the God of the Roman Catholic Church and the living god she had made of her husband caused her great anxiety. Her only solution was the vow to attempt to induce the living god to bow before the God of her church.

I am to bear *all* joyfully, as an atonement to save Richard [she wrote in her devotional book]. Let me not think that my lot is to be exempt from trials, nor shrink from them, but let me take pleasure and pain alike. Let me summon health and spirits and nerves to my aid, for I have asked and obtained a most difficult mission, and I must acquire patient endurance of suffering, resistance of evil, and take difficulties and pain with courage and even avidity. My mission and my religion must be uppermost. As I asked ardently for this mission – none other than to be Richard's wife – let me not forget to ask as ardently for grace to carry it out. . . . How I have bowed down before my husband's intellect! If I lost Richard, life would be worthless. Yet he and I and life are perishable, and will soon be over. . . .

The following week Isabel sailed for Brazil – and her mission – reaching Recife (then called Pernambuco) on 27 August 1865. Here she discovered all the letters she had written her husband since their separation. They had reached Brazil, but none had gone further than this. This caused Isabel to have 'a good boohoo in the moonlight'.

Moving down the coast Isabel was reunited with her husband at Rio de Janeiro and promptly had her first fever: It consisted of 'sickness and vomiting, colic, dizziness, fainting, shivering, heat and cold, delirium, thirst, disgust of food'. Naturally such a variety of symptoms called for a variety of treatments that included calomel, castor oil, hot baths, blankets, emetics, ice, starvation, quinine and hypnotism – the latter being Burton's cure for delirium.

When she recovered, they took ship for Santos, Burton's consulate two hundred miles further down the coast, arriving 9 October 1865. Isabel described Santos as being 'only a mangrove swamp', but Burton did not intend to live there; instead, he decided to make his home forty-five miles away (in a direct line) at São Paulo. He was later criticized for this, but Isabel, his defender, maintained that both places *required* a consul. The fact remains, however, that the British Government that employed him had ordered him to Santos. Fortunately for the government's business, there was a very capable vice-consul in Santos who dealt with all the day-to-day affairs of the consulate.

Isabel set to make a home out of an old convent (70 Rua do Carmo) which she rented, and hired slaves from their masters to help her redecorate. It was among the slaves and freed slaves that she found her own work. She made one room of her house into a chapel for them and set aside another as a place where they could be lodged, fed and given religious instruction. She taught them that 'not only had they souls, but that, although they were condemned by class and colour and custom to be slaves upon earth, just as it was in the Bible, once dead, they, and we, would stand equal before God'. For her personal servant and pet she acquired a negro dwarf named Chico, thirty-five years old and recently emancipated. Isabel described him as 'brimming full of intelligence'. There is, she said, 'something superior and refined in my dwarf, and I treat him with the same consideration as I would a white servant'. But from all accounts Chico appears to have been simply a first-class knave. Even Isabel must have had her doubts about him when she caught him trying to roast her favourite cat over the kitchen fire.

The chief feature of their new home was Burton's study, a room forty feet long where he continued his ceaseless writing, working on translations of Camoens' *The Lusiads*, verses in *The Arabian Nights*, and a collection of Hindu folk tales later published under the name of *Vikram and the Vampire*; he was also working on the last part of a series of four articles on his trip to South America for *Fraser's Magazine for Town and Country*.

Besides his writing, there were other outlets for Burton's restless mind and great energy. A simple recital of the multifarious activities of this man during his three years as consul in Brazil shows accomplishments and feats that would suffice the ordinary man for a lifetime. He wrote three books and worked on several others; he invented a carbine pistol; he explored São Paulo province; he made an expedition into

Minas Gerais province to inspect the diamond and gold mines there; he went down the São Francisco River for 1,300 miles in a raft; he visited the new republic of Argentina and the battlefields of Paraguay; he crossed the pampas and the Andes to visit Chile and Peru; he took out a concession for a lead mine and discovered rubies in Brazil. In addition, he kept up his old interests and acquired some new ones. Yet, this was the low point of his life. He made no geographical discoveries of note; his books were even duller and less popular than usual; and he appeared to be forgotten in a remote and unimportant consulate. There was no single great task at hand for him; he was forty-five years old, and his future seemed bleak.

Burton's acquisition of a lead-mine concession in São Paulo province got him into official trouble, since paid consuls were not allowed to engage in trade. Sir Edward Thornton, the British Ambassador to Brazil, was furious and wrote an official complaint to London. Fortunately, Lord Stanley, the Foreign Secretary, was an admirer of Burton's and took a broader view, saying that he hardly thought being interested in mineral production could be called trading.

On one trip in the neighbourhood of São Paulo, Burton washed some sand and came up with several small rubies. Not sure what he had really obtained, he sent his finds to William Crooker in London to be analysed. The answer came back: 'If you get any more, bigger than this, throw up the Consulate and stick to rubies.' Isabel implored him to buy up the land along the river bank, which was owned by an old woman who would have sold it for £50, but Burton would not do it, maintaining that it would be cheating the woman and besides no one could live on the site for more than three days without getting 'Brazilian fever'.

Isabel soon learned that although she was in the same country with her husband and had made a home for him, it was impossible to keep him with her for very long at a time. He was continually wandering off and leaving her with her big house, her chapel and her negro dwarf. She had all the discomforts and little of the romance of a foreign post and complained that she lived a 'farmhouse life'. In a letter home she wrote that she was now 'settled down in a place that my Irish maid calls the "end of God's speed", whatever that may be; but which I interpret that, after Providence made the world, being Saturday night, all the rubbish was thrown down here and forgotten'.

Scarcely had Isabel arrived than Burton was off for a month to look at some mines. Then he was gone for another nineteen days somewhere in the interior; then on an excursion along the coast for a fortnight. Occasionally, too, he had to put in an appearance at his consulate in Santos. Isabel saw little enough of him during her first ten months in Brazil. Her only escape from São Paulo was an occasional trip to Santos to take care of work he had neglected. But Santos was worse than São Paulo: 'I do hate Santos. The climate is beastly, the people fluffy. The stinks, the vermin, the food, the niggers are all of a piece.'

Battling alone against snakes, insects, fevers and boils, she was, understandably, often despondent. On 9 March 1866, when she had been in São Paulo about six months, she wrote to her mother, 'I got the same crying fit about you, dear mother, last week, as I did at Lisbon, starting up in the night and screaming out that you were dead; I find I do it whenever I am over-fatigued and weak.' Her mother, indeed, now became her confidante for the things she could not tell Richard. When Chico threw a bucket of slop over a neighbour, she told her mother but warned her, 'Richard would have killed him if he knew it; so you must none of you write back any of my jokes.'

Complaining of her hard life she wrote, 'I often think a *parvenue*, or half bred woman, would burst if she had to do as I do. But do not notice any of this writing back.' Once, while Burton was gone, a drunken sailor came to the house demanding a passport and other papers. Isabel gave him food and money, but had great difficulty making him leave. Writing of this adventure to her mother, she again begged, 'Do not mention about the drunken sailor writing back.'

Just how much Isabel was able to conceal from her husband is uncertain. Probably very little. He used to learn all her little secrets by hypnotizing her. He had started doing this when they were first married. Isabel did not like it and used to resist, but at last consented. She finally reached the stage where he had only to look at her and say, 'Sleep!' and she would immediately do so. If he said, 'Talk!' she would begin to tell him all she knew: 'I have often told him things that I would much rather keep to myself,' she confessed. He used to boast laughingly of his power over his wife, saying, 'It is the only way to get a woman to tell you the truth.'

In June 1866, Burton took Isabel with him to Rio de Janeiro and near-by Petropolis. Here Isabel found true society; a royal court, in fact, where the Emperor and Empress of Brazil were kind to them and made them feel they were still honoured people in a civilized world. A lady who knew the Burtons then spoke highly of Isabel: 'It was impossible to be dull with her, for she was a brilliant talker, and always had some witty anecdotes or tales of adventure to tell us. She was devoted to her husband and his interests, and was never tired of singing his praises. She was a great help to him in every way, for he by no means shared her popularity.'

Undoubtedly a part of Burton's unpopularity was due to the exceptional courtesies shown him by the Emperor, Don Pedro. Once there was a dinner given by the Emperor at a hotel following a reception at the palace. Following strict protocol, the ministers were shown into one room to wait for the dinner, while the inferior consuls were shown into another. But a messenger came to conduct Burton into the ministers' room. They all waited a long time. Then a second messenger came and all thought it was to announce dinner. As everyone in the room moved towards the door, the messenger called out that their Majesties wanted to see only Captain and Mrs Burton. Isabel wrote, 'The poor humble people [the Burtons] were exalted; their Majesties had sent for us to their private drawing-rooms, and gave us a long sitting-down audience.' Meanwhile, the ministers, including Sir Edward Thornton, Burton's superior, stood around waiting in their separate room. Such events do not lead to popularity.

Isabel said, 'The Emperor delighted in scientific men and the Empress liked good Catholics, so that we were frequently sent for.' Burton sometimes gave private lectures on his travels to the Emperor and Isabel became quite intimate with the Empress. She wrote to her mother, 'I told the Empress all about your paralysis, and how anxious I was about you; and she is so sympathetic and kind, and always asks what news I have of you.'

Isabel's happiness at being again in society was soon dampened by an outbreak of boils: 'I cannot sit or stand, walk or lie down, without a moan, and I am irritated and depressed beyond words. . . . I am very thin, and my nose is like a cut-water; and people who saw me on my arrival from England say I look very delicate.' So wrote Isabel to her mother on 8 July. Nevertheless, Burton left her four days later to go look for a sea serpent, said to be 160 feet long and reported to be on the coast. He was gone for a month. Isabel asked her mother not to speak of this junket as it might get her husband into trouble with the Foreign Office. She returned to Santos on 11 August and Burton was put ashore from a ship the following morning: his canoe had overturned and he had spent two days in the water before being picked up.

Among Burton's consular duties was that of marrying any English couple who asked for the ceremony. On 3 September he had his first opportunity. No one was more struck by the incongruity than Isabel: 'Richard has to marry them. It seems so strange. Fancy him doing parson!' They laughed and joked about it together, but it was obvious that Isabel had made no progress in her attempts to convert her husband. She did feel, though, that she had curbed him a bit. In a letter to her mother written on 15 September 1866, apparently in answer to a letter suggesting that she return to England for her health, she wrote, 'I should not feel justified, I think, in coming home for anything but *serious* illness. I have just domesticated and tamed Richard a little; and it would not do to give him an excuse for becoming a wandering vagabond again. He requires a comfortable and respectable home, and a tight hand upon his purse strings; and I feel that I have a mission which amply fills my hands.'

In December Isabel was in Rio de Janeiro again, trying to sell a book of Burton's and to obtain a concession for a gold mine he wanted. Burton was off on another trip into the interior. Isabel came down with a mild case of cholera. It struck her at three in the morning. Thinking she would surely die, she got up and went to her desk, settling all her worldly affairs. Then she dressed and went out to confession and communion. She did not die, however, but in a few days began to recover, attributing her resistance to the disease to her temperate and industrious habits.

In early June 1867, the Burtons left for Rio and a trip into the Minas Gerais province. Burton had obtained a three-month leave of absence, which meant he could do what he always did anyway for a longer period and without secrecy. But this time he took Isabel with him, a rare treat for her.

Burton described his long trip in a two-volume work, *The Highlands of Brazil*, undoubtedly the dullest of all his books and distinguished only by a most remarkable preface written by Isabel. Of this work, more later. The trip was in two parts: the first was a journey through the state of Minas Gerais; the second, a trip down the São Francisco River. Isabel accompanied her husband on only the first part of the journey; she had intened to go all the way, but she sprained her ankle so badly that she was unable to go down the river with him. Her brief account of the trip is far more interesting than his bulky tome.

Burton's primary interest in Minas Gerais was the gold mining that was being carried on there. In August, at Morro Velho (near present-day Belo Horizonte), he and Isabel descended the deepest mine in the province. Even Burton was impressed with the experience. Chico took one look at the hole and said that nothing could ever make him go into it. Burton said, 'He had lately been taught that he is a responsible being with an "immortal soul", and he was beginning to believe it in a rough theoretical way: this certainly did not look like a place "where the good niggers go".' They descended in a crude bucket that bumped and scraped against the sides of the pit, crashed against the sides of ascending buckets and tilted and tipped half over against a kibble-way drum.

Burton described the scene at the bottom:

The walls were either as black as the grave or reflected slender rays of light glancing from the polished watery surface, or were broken into monstrous projections, half revealing and half concealing the cavernous gloomy recesses. Despite the lamps, the night pressed upon us, as it were, with a weight, and the only measure of distance was a spark here and there, glimmering like a single star. Distinctly Dantesque was the gulf between the huge mountain sides apparently threatening every moment to fall. Everything, even the accents of a familiar voice, seemed changed; the ear was struck by the sharp click and dull thud of the hammer upon the boring-iron, and this upon the stone; each blow invariably struck was to keep time with the wild chants of the borer. . . .

Through this Inferno gnomes and kobolds glided about in ghostly fashion – half-naked figures muffled up by the mist. Here dark bodies, gleaming with beaded heat-drops, hung in what seemed frightful positions; there they swung like Leotard from place to place; there they moved up loose ropes like the Troglodytes; there they moved over scaffolds, which even to look at would make a nervous temperament dizzy. . . .

At length we reached another vaulted cavern. . . . It was lit up with torches, and the miners – all slaves, directed by white overseers – streamed with perspiration, and merrily sang their wild songs and chorus, keeping time with the strokes of hammer and drill. The heavy gloom, the fitful glare, and the savage chant, with the wall hanging like the stone of Cisyphus, like the sword of Damocles, suggested a sort of material Swedenborgian hell.

Isabel went down with Mrs Gordon, the wife of the mine superintendent, who, although she had been at Morro Velho for more than nine years, had never been able to screw up her courage to make the descent. Isabel thought the negro slaves looked healthy and she was impressed by the fact that they worked only eight hours a day in the mine. After two hours in the pit the visitors came out by the same bucket and Isabel found the ascent worse than the descent.

Disaster was soon to strike the Morro Velho mine. The very next day the chain that had lowered them down in the bucket broke, killing several miners. Isabel preserved the broken link as a souvenir. Six months after their visit, the mine was almost completely destroyed by fire. Tragedy also struck the family of the mine superintendent. As Isabel, *en passant*, tells it, 'poor Mrs Gordon died eventually from a horrible shock (her youngest and favourite son was caught in the machinery in an instant and ground to death – a subject too sad to dwell upon), I commenced my long ride home – a very pleasant ride.'

Shortly after this visit, Richard and Isabel parted, he to go down the São Francisco River on a raft and she to make her way back to Rio with Chico as an escort, the 'pleasant ride' referred to above.

Except for the usual discomforts of travel – which Burton generally regarded as pleasures – the 1,300-mile trip down the river was without adventure. There were plenty of settlers and much of interest to the curious Burton in the way of flora, fauna, minerals, and people. He was convinced that this river and this country were destined to become a centre of a great civilization and that his account of every farmhouse would some day be of great historical importance. So it may yet be, but great civilizations are made by great peoples, not alone by fertile land and mineral wealth, and Brazil has yet to achieve Burton's prophesied splendour.

It is perhaps this feeling that he was describing a land with a promising future that gives his account its dullness. Many pages, for example, are written on the town of Guaicui (Burton called it Guaicuhy), which he describes minutely, including his advice to the city fathers to widen their streets for the day when they will have streetcars: 'I shall ink more paper than enough for the present settlements; thus, when my forecast of their future greatness shall have been justified, the traveller may compare his Present with my Past, and therein find another standard for measuring the march of Progress as it advances, and must advance with giant strides, in the Land of the Southern Cross.'

Burton was wrong again. Progress with its giant strides appears to have left the village of Guaicui behind. It is smaller now than it was in Burton's day, and it takes a detailed map to find it at all. The nearest 'city' is Pirapora, twelve miles away, with a population, at last count, of 7,513 souls.

It was a delightful trip for Burton and he hated to return to civilization:

After a few days of traveller's life and liberty, of existence in the open air, of sleep under the soft blue skies, of days without neckties, the sensation of returning to 'Society' is by no means pleasant; all have felt, although, perhaps, all will not own the unamiable effort which it has cost them. The idea of entering a town after a spell of the Prairie or on the River, is distasteful to me as to any Bedouin of the purer breed, who must stuff his nostrils with cotton to exclude the noxious atmosphere.

Back in this atmosphere was Isabel, fretting at her husband's four months' absence. She had hardly reached Santos when she returned as far as Rio to wait for him to emerge. Like all worried wives, she had made a careful catalogue in her mind of all the evils which could have befallen her husband. If he did not return soon, she planned to go after him. To her mother she wrote:

I fear Richard is ill, or taken prisoner, or has his money stolen. He always would carry gigantic sums in his pockets, half hanging out; and he only has four slaves with him, and he has to sleep amongst them. I am not afraid of anything except the wild Indians, fever, ague, and a vicious fish that can easily be avoided; there are no other dangers. However, I trust that news may soon come. I cannot remain here so long as another month. I had a narrow escape bathing the day before yesterday. What I thought was a big piece of sea-weed was a ground shark a few yards from me; but it receded instead of coming at me.

The dreamy young girl was now a mature woman, but living her dreams. Reality was not quite as she had imagined it, but it was close enough, although filled with unthought-of responsibilities and the worries of adulthood. Wilfrid Scawen Blunt, the traveller, poet and writer of political exposé, met Isabel in Rio. He was then twenty-seven and on his way to a minor diplomatic post in Buenos Aires. Thirty-nine years later he wrote his impressions of her as he then saw her. They had met several years before at the home of Isabel's aunt, Lady Arundell: 'At that time she was a quiet girl enough, of the convent type – at least so I remember her – fair haired and rather pretty – very different from my recollection of her in later years.' He did not particularly care for the new Isabel he found in Rio: 'She had developed into a sociable and very talkative woman, clever, but at the same time foolish, overflowing with stories of which her husband was always the hero. Her devotion to him was real, and she was indeed entirely under his domination, an hypnotic domination Burton used to boast of.'

Isabel's devotion sent her down to the quay to meet every ship that came in – every ship but one, that is, and of course Burton was on it. He was most angry with her for not being on hand to greet him. At last Isabel had her husband back with her in their home at São Paulo. But her happiness was short-lived. In April 1868, Burton came down with a terrible illness. The doctor, when he arrived eight days after the first attack, said his pain was due to 'congestion of the liver, combined with inflammation of the lung, where they join'. Whatever the cause, Burton was unable to take a pain-free breath and he could not speak or eat without a paroxysm of pain that made him scream for a quarter of an hour. It must have been a terrible thing to hear a man like Burton scream.

Isabel and the doctor subjected him to every hopeful remedy; he was bled, blistered, and stuffed with powders, tonics and pills. Nothing eased the pain. After seventeen days Isabel thought he was dying. She told him, 'The doctor has tried all his remedies; now let me try one of mine.' She sprinkled some holy water on his head, prayed over him, and put scapulars around his neck. Isabel took his failure to protest as a silent consent. About an hour later Burton said, 'Zoo, I think I'm a little better.' From then on, according to Isabel, he slowly began to improve and, as she wrote to her mother several days later, he 'has never had a *bad* paroxysm since'.

At last he was able to take some chicken broth and then to sit up in a chair. Isabel described his condition: 'He is awfully thin and grey, and looks about sixty. He is quite gaunt, and it is sad to look at him. The worst of it is that I'm afraid that his lungs will never be quite right again. He can't get the affected lung well at all. His breathing is still impeded, and he has a twinge in it.'

Burton was now forty-seven years old, sick, and condemned to live as an obscure consul in an unimportant and remote post. Where was the promise of greatness he had shown in his youth? He had climbed the hill of success and entered the portals of fame, then he had turned and gone down again into obscurity. No one was more aware of his failure in life than Burton himself. It was a bitter pill for him.

In *The Battlefields of Paraguay* he wrote a description of a photograph of Dr José Gaspar Rodriguez de Francia, one-time dictator of Paraguay, that might well serve as a description of Burton himself at this period. Perhaps he had himself in mind as much as Francia when he wrote of 'that painful, distrusting, care-worn expression which belongs to men whom hope deferred has made sick, and who have risen to the height of their ambition only when Siren life has lost many of her charms'. Burton had not achieved the height of his ambitions, but already he feared that it was too late. There was still hope, but there was also bitterness, frustration and disappointment. He had almost reached the nadir of his life.

But life's day-to-day activities go on, and all participate: games are played by sons while battles are fought by their fathers; men talk of local news, interested, though their hearts ache; and whatever the conclusions men come to regarding life's main issues, the daily amusements continue to amuse. So when he had recovered sufficiently from his illness, Burton and his wife went down to Santos to see a regatta in which each nationality that could muster a crew was represented; there were nine or ten in all. The British boat came in last, much to their disgust. Burton and Isabel made their way back home to São Paulo, collecting butterflies along the way.

Isabel briefly described the climax of their Brazilian adventure:

When we got back to São Paulo, Richard told me that he could not stand it any longer; it had given him that illness, it was far away from the world, it was no advancement, it led to nothing. He was quite right. I felt very sorry, because up to the present it was the only home I had ever really had quietly with him, and we had had it for three years; but I soon sold up everything, and we came down to Santos, and embarked on the 24th of July, 1868. Here he applied for leave, as the doctors advised him not to go to England at once, but to go down to Buenos Ayres for a trip, and he asked me to go to England and see if I could not induce them to give him another post.

After dispatching his wife to cry in the Foreign Office for a better post for him, Burton set off on a journey for his health: a visit to the battle front of the sanguinary war raging between Paraguay and her neighbours!

The war he went to see was one of the most bitterly contested struggles in the annals of South American warfare. Paraguay had mustered all of its human resources: every able-bodied man was under arms and there were even battalions of women and regiments of boys from twelve to fifteen years of age. Paraguay fought the combined forces of Brazil, Argentina and Uruguay. In the five years of the war, from 1865 to 1870, the population of Paraguay was reduced from more than 1,337,000 to less than 250,000, and there were only 28,700 men among the survivors. Thus, four out of every five inhabitants of Paraguay died within a five-year period. The cause of all this bloodshed was a dispute over boundary lines.

Reading Burton's description of the war, it seems today to have been conducted in a most leisurely fashion, although it must be admitted that his account was almost entirely second-hand. He talked with generals and admirals and saw the sites of previous battles, but the closest he ever came to actual combat was to hear the sound of some cannon banging away in the distance and to see a few mouldy corpses by the riverside. He saw only the war in the south; he did not see the fierce fighting in the Mato Grosso and northern Paraguay. Also, he saw only one side of the war – the winning side. He did not visit the Paraguayan Army for fear of the official embarrassment he would create if he were imprisoned, a likely possibility as he would have been coming from the Allied side and his sympathies were with Brazil.

Leaving São Paulo, a place 'whose many charms had begun to pall on the traveller's palate', he arrived in Montevideo on 6 August 1868. He spent ten days here in spite of the fact that he felt duty bound not to stay in the city's best hotel: 'I would not lodge there, as during the cholera days it made the mistake of refusing to admit the wife of the British minister. . . . This barbarity cost the house much and should cost it more. The United States officers at once deserted the Oriental, despite its ready baths and marble courts. I regret to say that English gentlemen did not.'

Montevideo had a good deal of public spirit, he found, but it had no English Club. He was surprised that 'this first sign of civilization' had not appeared. Another surprise to him was that while Uruguay had only one man to every four women, 'marvellous to record, polygamy . . . has not been made the law of the land'.

On 16 August he crossed the river to Buenos Aires and the following day left to go up the Parana to Rosario, a town he predicted would presently become 'another Chicago' (present population: 500,000; Chicago: 3,650,000). He felt it his duty to make notes on everything he saw in this booming town, including detailed descriptions of the dogs. Burton liked almost everything about the place except the organ grinders and the local magazine. Of the former he said, 'With great theoretical respect for the subject's liberty, I practically would seize all such sturdy vagabonds and put them to honest labour.' He described the *South American Monthly*, a magazine edited by an American missionary, as 'a magazine suited to the most limited capacity, full of goody-goody talk, victorious polemic, and a few apocryphal conversions'.

At Rosario, Burton went to a circus. Except for the clowns, whom he found 'painfully dull', he enjoyed himself very much.

More amusing and of course more barbarous were the next two acts, when the dogs were loosed at various animals, especially at a pony and afterwards at a donkey. The latter was ridden by a pink-dressed monkey. . . . Some of the dogs preferred the rider and received tolerably severe scratches, others flew at the monture, and that maligned animal the ass was in all duels the cleverer by half; skilfully avoiding exposure of the throat ... it bit, it trampled, it kicked, it struck out with the forehand, all with the agility of the original zebra.

One wonders if this delight in the cruel sport with animals was not a reaction to Isabel, who loved all animals so dearly. Poor Isabel had failed so far to convert her husband to home, animals or God.

Although Burton stated that he spent a week at Rosario, he was actually there for only three days. Going on up the Parana River, he stopped at Humaita, Paraguay, the scene of one of the great battles of the war. He was close to the front now and he spent two weeks wandering in this area, talking with the officers and soldiers of the Allied armies. Making his way slowly back to Buenos Aires, he stopped off for a week at Corrientes. This was a dangerous and lawless town, according to Burton: 'A revolver at night is as necessary as shoes; and if an unknown ask you for a light, you stick your cigar in the barrel and politely offer it to him without offence being given or taken.'

By 20 September he was back in Buenos Aires and he took the time to look round the town. He saw little that pleased him. 'The streets are long, narrow, and ill ventilated. . . . There is absolutely no sewerage; a pit in the patio is dug by way of a cesspool. . . . Beyond the town, the unpaved lines become quagmires, impasses, and quaking bogs where horses and black cattle are hopelessly fixed . . . the wild Indians now ride up within a few leagues of the capital.' As for the people: 'A permanent gallows in the outskirts of the city would do a power of good for Buenos Aires. And yet, you know, I would abolish in civilized countries capital punishment.'

Burton was invited to a ball attended by all the best people in town – presumably those who were not the rogues fit for the gallows. 'The men are extensively "got up"; every cheek displays the handiwork of the *artiste*; every head has been subjected to the curling-irons; the dressing-room is crowded throughout the night. . . . Yet, with the exception of a foreigner or two, there are no figures worthy of atten-tion. . . . Young Buenos Aires is not given to affecting manliness.'

What a curious person Burton was. At the end of the chapter describing Buenos Aires and its people in such terms (*Battlefields of Paraguay*), he says, 'If I have written in this letter anything to offend Buenos Aires or the Buenos Aireans, you will, I am sure, allow me to withdraw it and beg pardon. Amongst the thousand places which store my cabinet of memory there is none that stands more favourably than the Platine capital. . . . The week that I passed at Buenos Aires will ever be remembered by me with that pleasure with which on a wintry day we recall to mind the sweet savour of perfumed spring.'

The young Wilfrid Scawen Blunt was in Buenos Aires at the same time and, although Burton never mentioned meeting him, he wrote later that they had spent much time together and had had many intimate discussions on religion, philosophy, travel and politics:

In his talk he affected an extreme brutality, and if one could have believed the whole of what he said, he had indulged in every vice and committed every crime. I soon found, however, that most of these recitals were indulged in *pour épater le bourgeois* and that his inhumanity was more pretended than real. Even the ferocity of his countenance gave place at times to more agreeable expressions, and I can just understand the infatuated fancy of his wife that in spite of his ugliness he was the most beautiful man alive. He had, however, a power of assuming the abominable which cannot be exaggerated. I remember once his insisting that I should allow him to try his mesmeric powers on me, and his expression as he gazed into my eyes was nothing less than atrocious. If I had submitted to his gaze for any length of time – and he held me by my thumbs – I have no doubt he would have succeeded in dominating me. But my will also is strong, and when I had met his eyes of a wild beast for a couple of minutes I broke away and would have no more.

On matters of religion and philosophy he was fond, too, of discoursing. . . . He was not really profound; and always at the bottom of his materialistic professions I found a groundwork of belief in the supernatural which refused to face thought's ultimate conclusions. I came at last to look upon him as less dangerous than he seemed, and even to be in certain aspects of his mind, a 'sheep in wolf's clothing'. The clothing, however, was a very complete disguise, and as I have said he was not a man to play with, sitting alone with him far into the night, especially in such an atmosphere of violence as Buenos Aires then could boast, when men were shot almost nightly in the streets. Burton was a grim being to be with at the end of his second bottle with a gaucho's navaja handy to his hand.

Blunt's recollections, written in 1906, long after Burton was dead, conclude with:

Such is my personal recollection of Burton when he must have been forty-eight years old [Close. He was forty-seven and a half], as I was twenty-eight. He seemed to me then already a broken man, physically, nor did he impress me very strongly on his intellectual side. For that reason, perhaps, I have never been able to rate him as highly as have done most of his contemporaries, the friends who knew him. I am aware that I saw him at his worst. . . . In his talks with me, and also in his books, he showed little true sympathy with the Arabs he had come to know so well. He would at any time, I am sure, have willingly betrayed them to further English, or his own professional interests.

As for Isabel:

She was indeed a very foolish woman, and did him at least as much harm in his career as good. . . . It is a fine trait in his character that he should have borne with her absurdities for the sake of her love so long.

Such was one man's opinion.

Just how long Burton remained in Buenos Aires this time is unknown. For here begins one of the most mysterious episodes in his life. From this period, sometime in September 1868, until 29 March 1869, very little is known of his activities. It was during this time that he made his only unrecorded trip. Only the bare outlines of his journey can be pieced together. With William Constable Maxwell, whom he had met on the ship going to Humaita, he set out overland across northern Argentina. They visited Cordoba and then, with a Major Ignacio Rickard, they explored the Sierra de San Luiz and visited the scene of the terrible earthquake that had virtually destroyed the town of Mendoza on 20 March 1861. Burton and Maxwell then crossed the Andes through the Uspallata Pass (La Cumbre) into Chile. According to testimony given by Burton at a trial three years later, 'the whole country was covered with plunderers, and it was an extremely dangerous journey'. A man named Luke Ionides, who claimed to be a friend, said Burton told him he had suffered four wounds and killed four men who attended him during this trip, but neither Burton nor his wife ever mentioned this. After resting in Santiago de Chili, they continued on to Valparaiso where they boarded a ship for Peru.

Sometime during this trip, or just before it began, at Buenos Aires, or Villa Nueva, or Villa Maria, Burton encountered a man whose name – or rather, the name by which he became known – was to become a household phrase in Britain and was to create a controversy equalled only by the Dreyfus case in France: the Tichborne Claimant. There is a mystery here. Although Burton was probably the most prolific autobiographer of his age, and although he met the Claimant in Argentina and later testified in the famous case of Tichborne *v.* Lushington, not a single word about the man from his pen ever appeared in print; not even in passing did he ever mention his name or imply that he knew him.

This entire episode makes a curious hiatus in Burton's life. But this was the nadir of his career.

Although Isabel would never have admitted it, it is most probable that she had no idea where her wandering husband had gone or where he would go next. Perhaps Burton himself had no clear idea of what he was about. There is evidence that he was drinking quite heavily throughout this Argentine–Pacific Coast period; drink and ceaseless wandering were his answers to what appeared to be a wrecked career. Then one day in a café in Lima, Peru, he was unexpectedly congratulated upon his appointment to the consular post at Damascus. How startled he must have been! So Isabel had been successful after all! He set out for Argentina (whether with or without his companion is not known), sailing around the horn through the Straits of Magellan.

He arrived back in Buenos Aires on 29 March 1869, although in his official letter accepting the post, which he wrote the next day, he stated that he had arrived only that day. This official letter was written in response to two communications (dated the previous December 3rd and 7th) from Lord Stanley, then serving his last months as Foreign Secretary. Thus, it must have been nearly six months after making the appointment before Stanley received Burton's acceptance and an additional four months before Burton arrived at his post.

It would seem, on the surface, to have been an ideal post for Burton. It was in Arabia, 'the land of my predilection', and he had long wanted this position. Isabel, too, was delighted. She was to go to the East, the desert, the land of Tancred. The post was well salaried: £700 a year plus an allowance of £300 for office expenses and £160 'for outfit'. Perhaps remembering Burton's mining interests in Brazil, Lord Stanley pointed out to him that he was 'restricted from engaging in commercial pursuits'. It appeared that his fortunes had taken a turn for the better at last.

Although he had been instructed by Lord Stanley in his letter of 7 December 1868, to 'at once proceed to his post', he claimed to have missed the Royal Mail and delayed his actual departure for England for another month in order again to visit the Battlefields of Paraguay.

During his absence, the allied armies of Brazil, Argentina and Uruguay had advanced and captured the Paraguayan capital of Asunción, and it was for Asunción that Burton embarked on 4 April, reaching his destination nine days later. He was here able to form his own estimation of the Paraguayan character: 'personally, I may state that in every transaction with Paraguayans – of course not the upper dozen – they invariably cheated or robbed me, and that in truthfulness they proved to be about on a par with the Hindu'. Of the Paraguayan woman he said, 'Love is with her as eating and sleeping – a purely corporeal necessity.' As for Asunción, 'nothing could be viler than the thoroughfares'. Naturally there were unkind words for the 'meddling and greedy Jesuits'. Burton even had bad words to say about the weather and the general unhealthiness of Paraguay, although he had gone there ostensibly for his health.

On 17 April he returned to Buenos Aires and embarked for England via Rio. Arriving in Southampton at four o'clock in the morning on 1 June 1869, he reported his arrival by letter to the Foreign Office two days later, saying he had 'arrived in England on this day'. Two more days of freedom. After having stretched a six weeks' sick leave into a ten-month adventure, one of his first actions on arriving in England was to complain of his hepatitis and request an additional six weeks' leave.

Chapter 18

Damascus

1869 – 71

SHORTLY after seeing her husband off for Buenos Aires in July 1868, Isabel herself started on the long trip back to England. She stopped briefly at Salvador (formerly São Salvador or Bahia), where she had dinner with Charles Williams, a friend of her husband's who possessed a garden stocked with wild beasts and a hall full of snake cages. After dinner, Williams insisted on showing her his rattlesnakes. In the process, he was bitten on the wrist. Throwing the snake back in its cage, he staggered against the wall.

Isabel had been taught by her husband to be ready for emergencies, but the only helpful thing she could find handy was a box of matches. Frantically lighting them, she jabbed them, one after the other, into the snake-bite on his wrist until she had made 'a regular little hole'. She bawled for the servants and sent them to fetch a bottle of whisky. After forcing him to drink the entire bottle, she and the servants walked him up and down for about three hours before letting him go to bed. Having survived the cure, the snake-bite must have seemed a scratch. Williams recovered and gave Isabel a silver-handled riding whip as a memento.

As soon as she arrived in England, Isabel set to work. Burton had given her plenty to do. Her primary mission, of course, was to obtain a better post for her husband, but she was also to try to form a company to work Burton's lead mine at Ipiranga (old spelling: Ypiranga; Isabel's spelling: Iporanga) in the state of São Paulo, Brazil; to patent a carbine pistol her husband had invented; and to arrange for the publication of a number of books, including *Explorations of the Highlands of Brazil*; *The Lands of Cazembe*; *Uruguay, Iraçema, or Honey-Lips*; *Manuel de Moraes the Convert*, and a third edition of *Pilgrimage to Mecca*. Amazingly, she succeeded in accomplishing almost half of this. Most importantly, she obtained the Damascus post for Burton, with the hope of its leading to even better posts in Cairo and Constantinople. She also patented his pistol and brought out *Highlands of Brazil*, a two-

266

volume work whose most interesting feature is a short preface Isabel herself decided to add.

With her husband wandering around in Argentina, and she knew not where else, while she was left to do his work in London, the quiet little tug pulling the big ship showed signs of being restive. 'Before the reader dives into the interior of Brazil with my husband as a medium, let me address two words to him,' begins Isabel in her own preface to Burton's *The Highlands of Brazil*:

It has been my privilege ... to have been his almost constant companion; and I consider that to travel, write, read, and study under such a master, is no small boon to any one desirous of seeing and learning. ...

As long as there is anything difficult to do, a risk to be incurred, or any chance of improving the mind, and of educating oneself, I am a very faithful disciple; but I now begin to feel, that while he and his readers are old friends, I am humbly standing unknown in the shadow of his glory. It is therefore time for me respectfully but firmly to assert, that, although I proudly accept of the trust confided to me, and pledge myself not to avail myself of my discretionary powers to alter one word of the original text, I protest vehemently against his religious and moral sentiments, which belie a good and chivalrous life. I point the finger of indignation particularly at what misrepresents our Holy Roman Catholic Church, and at what upholds that unnatural and repulsive law, Polygamy, which the author is careful not to practise himself, but from a high moral pedestal he preaches to the ignorant as a means of population in young countries.

I am compelled to differ with him on many other subjects; but, be it understood, not in the common spirit of domestic jar, but with a mutual agreement to differ and enjoy our differences. ...

Having now justified myself, and given a friendly warning to a *fair* or *gentle* reader, – I leave him or her to steer through these anthropological sand-banks and hidden rocks as best he or she may.

She would do the devil's work gladly, but she wanted the world to know that she did not approve of it. Burton thought the preface a great joke and laughed heartily.

With the other books Isabel was not so successful. She was unable to convince a publisher to bring out another edition of the *Pilgrimage*, nor did she succeed in publishing *The Lands of Cazembe or Lacerda's Journey to Cazembe in 1798*, a translation from the Portuguese of an eighteenth-century African expedition well annotated by Burton which was eventually published by the Royal Geographical Society in 1873. *Iraçema*, translated by Isabel, and *Manuel de Moraes*, translated by both Burtons, being works from the Portuguese, were finally published together in a paperback edition in 1886. *Uruguay*, Burton's translation of the epic poem in Portuguese by José Basilio da Gama, was never published, and the manuscript is now in the Huntington Library in San Marino, California.

But finally her Jemmy came home and Isabel was the first person to board the ship to welcome him. Apparently he had maintained the disreputable appearance Blunt had noticed in Buenos Aires. Isabel thought he looked as if he had just come from the mines. But she spruced him up and they began a round of calls and social engagements: parties at the Admiralty and the Foreign Office, a Literary Fund affair at which Burton made a speech, dinner with Sir Roderick Murchison, President of the Royal Geographical Society, and attendance at a meeting of the society itself where, according to Isabel, he '*was not satisfied with his reception*' (italics hers).

On 19 June 1869, Burton's sick leave was approved and he set out for Vichy. Isabel accompanied him as far as Boulogne, a city which evoked memories of their first meeting. But from there he sent her back to London, much against her will, to 'pay, pack and follow' to Damascus.

Burton went on to Vichy in the company of Swinburne. This was a combination that created an uneasy anxiety among their friends. Lord Houghton, who had brought them together in the first place, now felt that Burton was not a good influence on the young poet. When Burton left for Brazil, Swinburne assured Houghton, 'As my tempter and favourite audience has gone to Santos, I may hope to be a good boy again.' But now his tempter was back and he went off with him to Vichy. The two had corresponded even while Burton was in Brazil, chiefly about erotica. In a letter of 11 January 1867, Swinburne had written of a work he was then planning: 'I have in hand a scheme of mixed verse and prose – a sort of étude à la Balzac *plus* the poetry – which I flatter myself will be more offensive than anything I have yet done. You see I now have a character to keep up.' Both men had the same curious desire to shock and to make themselves out to be worse than they were. Swinburne's 'scheme' was a disjointed romance called *Lesbia Brandon*. It was ten years in manuscript and was not set in type until 1877. Swinburne finally decided to repress it, and the original manuscript is now lost, but Andrew Chatto, the publisher, kept a single galley proof of most of it.

In Vichy the pair were joined by Sir Frederick Leighton, the artist, and by Mrs Sartoris (*née* Adelaide Kemble, of the famous family of actors that included Sarah Siddons, her aunt). According to Swinburne, Mrs Sartoris, then fifty-five years old, had a voice that was still 'in the days of its glory', although after her marriage to a rich Italian she had given up her brief but brilliant career in opera.

It was an exceptionally pleasant time for this strangely assorted group. No one, Isabel excepted, enjoyed being with Burton more than Swinburne. He was fascinated and thrilled by 'the look of unspeakable horror in those eyes which gave him at times an almost unearthly appearance'. For Swinburne, this was perhaps the happiest time in his life. Both Leighton and Burton later had poems written in their honour based upon their time together at Vichy and Swinburne promised to dedicate a book of poems to Burton while pledging their friendship in a beaker of hot Vichy water. This promise he kept nine years later when he brought out *Poems and Ballads, Second Series* – although he almost forgot. The book was ready for the press with the dedication and a dedication poem to William Bell Scott, an artist. At the last minute he remembered his promise to Burton and changed the dedication to read: 'Inscribed to Richard F. Burton in redemption of an old pledge and in recognition of a friendship which I must always count among the highest honours of my life.' A poem was written to Burton and Vichy and, while entitled 'Dedication', was stuck in as the last poem of the book. This volume is considered by most critics as being the best Swinburne ever produced.

The thought of Burton enjoying himself in Vichy was too much for Isabel. For once, she rebelled. 'Soon after Richard had started to Vichy, I began to get unhappy, and wanted to join him, and I did not see why I could not have the month there with him and make up double-quick time after; so I just started off with J. J. Aubertin . . . who was also going there to join him.' Burton and Swinburne met them at the station. Now Isabel, too, could enjoy the brilliant company with her husband. Swinburne recited, Burton told of his adventures, Mrs Sartoris sang; there were excursions during the day and sparkling conversation in the evening. For Isabel, 'They were very happy days.' But all this was fiddling while Burton's career was starting to burn. The match was already lit. The explosion would come later.

Isabel had arrived in London from Brazil in the nick of time to obtain the coveted appointment. Lord Stanley, who then headed the Foreign Office, was an old friend of the Arundell family and thought kindly of the Burtons. But shortly after making the appointment, the government changed and the Earl of Clarendon replaced Lord Stanley as Foreign Secretary. As he was not at all friendly to the Burtons, Isabel would have had little success crying on his shoulder.

While Burton was on his way to London from South America, another ship was coming from the opposite direction carrying a letter from Sir Henry Elliot, British Ambassador at Constantinople. The letter reached London first. Dated 12 May, it stated that Burton's appointment was 'viewed with apprehension' in Damascus. Reasons, whether the real ones or not, were set forth by Sir Henry:

Damascus is probably the most fanatical town in the Empire, and the presence there, in the character of British Consul, of a person who had penetrated to the Prophet's shrine, is regarded as certain to cause exhibitions against him that may be productive of very undesirable consequences.

By the Mussulman population Captain Burton is regarded either as having insulted their religion by taking part as an unbeliever in their most sacred rites, or else as having, at that time, been a Mohomedan and having become a renegade.

Under either supposition he would be regarded with aversion by most, and with hatred by very many of the population, and it is my duty to draw your Lordship's attention to a consideration which was probably lost sight of when Captain Burton was selected for the post.

In London, Burton had had a talk with Lord Clarendon who warned him of the objections made to his appointment, though not of their source. Burton tried to reassure him, but Lord Clarendon doubtless remained uneasy for he wanted to have the matter put in black and white. On 19 June James Murray (on behalf of Lord Clarendon) wrote Burton to repeat what the Secretary had told him verbally: that 'very serious objections to your appointment at Damascus have reached him from official quarters, and that, although Lord Clarendon has allowed the appointment to go forward on receiving from you assurances that the objections were unfounded, his Lordship has warned you that if feeling stated to exist against you on the part of the authorities and people at that place should prevent the proper performance of your official duties, it would be his Lordship's duty immediately to recall you'.

Two days later Burton replied, expressing his 'gratitude for the sanction with which his Lordship has favoured me' and repeating his verbal promise to 'undertake to act with unusual prudence, and under all circumstances, to hold myself only answerable for all the consequences'. Again he assured Lord Clarendon that 'neither the authorities nor the people of Damascus will show for me any but the most friendly feeling'.

Undoubtedly, Burton felt confident in giving such assurances. He knew perfectly well that there would be no objections to his presence on the part of the Moslem population because of his journey to Mecca, but he did not know his real enemies or he would not have been so certain that the authorities would be friendly to him.

There were, of course, the missionaries, who made up a large percentage of the European population of Damascus then, and who were not anxious to see a man as outspoken against missionaries and Christianity as Burton come into their midst in an official capacity. But one of the real villains of the piece was one Mohammed Rashid Pasha, the Turkish Wali, or Viceroy, of Syria. He was a man so corrupt that even in that most corrupt and rotting empire of the Ottomans, he was so distinguished that he was eventually recalled and cast in chains. Rashid Pasha was a shrewd man. He had no objections to consuls as long as they did not mix too freely with his subjects, did not know the language, and stayed in their consulates. Burton, obviously, was not a man he wanted prying about in his pashalik.

Rashid Pasha's witting or unwitting ally was Sir Henry Elliot, British Ambassador to the Porte at Constantinople. Strangely enough, Burton seems never to have recognized Elliot as his enemy. Burton, and of course Isabel, while they soon became aware of Rashid Pasha's enmity, blamed much of their difficulty upon S. Jackson Eldridge, the Consul-General in Beirut and Burton's immediate superior. In his journal Burton wrote, 'Eldridge does nothing and is very proud of what he does.' Burton resented having to report to him and felt the consul at Damascus ought to report directly to the ambassador, never realizing that it was the ambassador himself who was his worst enemy.

On the morning of 5 July 1869, while Burton was enjoying himself in Vichy, a most unfortunate meeting took place in Constantinople. Sir Henry Elliot sat down for a talk with Rashid Pasha and they discussed the new consul to Damascus. He told him that while Lord Clarendon could not properly cancel the appointment made by his predecessor, he had nevertheless 'laid strict injunctions upon Captain Burton which he would not be likely to neglect'. He added that Burton had been warned to be 'extremely careful to avoid doing anything calculated to give offence, or to create susceptibility on the part of the people of Damascus'.

Nothing could have been said which would have done more to

undermine Burton's position. Rashid must have been delighted, but to Elliot he expressed great worry and covered his own future misdeeds by saying that 'a British Consul who would be regarded as a renegade Mussulman must necessarily find himself in a very difficult position'. Rashid now knew that whatever happened he had laid the groundwork well for blame to slide from his own shoulders to Burton's and that he could count on the British Ambassador as his ally.

Burton, confident of his own abilities and oblivious of danger, was not worried. With Isabel and young Swinburne, he set out from Vichy. Swinburne left them at Lyons to go to Paris; Isabel went on with him as far as Turin and then regretfully turned back to wind up affairs in London; Burton went to Brindisi to take ship for Beirut, arriving there on 1 October 1869, 'still full of the might and majesty of the Chilean Andes, and the grace and grandeur of Magellan's Straights – memories which fashionable Vichy and foul Brindisi had strengthened, not effaced'. Two days later he was at his consulate in Damascus.

Burton appears to have taken his work – such as he conceived it to be – quite seriously. Unfortunately, his distaste for routine duties, his naïveté in personal politics, and his incurable *wanderlust* worked against him. He had scarcely arrived in Damascus when he set out to climb the nearest mountain (Mount Hermon) with Captain Charles Warren, a young soldier and archaeologist. Six weeks later he was off into the desert east of Damascus to see some ruins in company with M. Poichard de la Boulerie, an entomologist. He simply could not resist going off exploring with every visitor that came to town. The watchful and suspicious Rashid Pasha looked for deeper motives; to him, it was inexplicable that a foreign official should go wandering about the desert and mountains just for the fun of it and to see old ruins; Burton was obviously up to no good and was probably plotting with the tribesmen against him. But since Burton had not yet committed any act with which he could be charged and since he encountered no overt resentment from the people, Rashid Pasha was forced to bide his time.

On 31 December 1869, Isabel arrived in Damascus with her English maid, five dogs (including a St Bernard), and a mountain of baggage; she expected to stay about ten years. She found her Jemmy sick, but not seriously, and decided that the first thing he needed was a home of his own. She found a big house in the Kurdish village of Salahiyyeh, now a suburb but then fifteen minutes' ride from the city walls of Damascus, and at once began to collect a managerie that eventually included a white Persian cat, three goats, fifty pariah dogs, a pet lamb, horses, chickens, turkeys, geese, ducks, guinea fowl, pigeons, a white donkey and a leopard that slept on her bed. Burton said it was like the house that Jack built: the fowls ate the seeds and flowers, the cat killed the birds, the dog worried the cat, the leopard not only ate the lamb but so harried the goats that one of them jumped into the river from sheer despair and was drowned.

'As soon as we had settled in our house,' Isabel said, 'I had to accustom myself to the honours of my position, which at first were rather irksome to me; but as they were all part of the business I had to put up with them.' She was in heaven.

For Isabel, this was the beginning of the happiest period of her life. Her husband's position as consul in Damascus was somehow not quite as low on the social ladder as it had been when he was a consul in South America: 'In the East . . . the consular service is still a gentlemanly profession. . . . In Damascus, a consul enjoys free life, Eastern life, and political life; and my husband was, therefore, quite *dans son assiette*. His beat extends from Bagdad on the east to Nablus on the south, and as far north as the Aleppo district.' Her only complaint was that it was a 'galling and chafing position' for him to report to Eldridge, when he should be the consul-general himself and report directly to Constantinople. 'He must do all the work, but he must never be heard of,' she complained; Eldridge, she maintained, was jealous of her husband.

Burton's duties do not appear to have been arduous. Although Beirut was only seventy miles away, letters and reports were sent off only once every fortnight. 'His day was divided into reading, writing, studying, and attending to his official work,' Isabel said. Although he got up at dawn, he did not arrive at his consulate before noon and he left between four and five in the afternoon. In other words, only four or five hours of work a day – when he was in town, which was not often. From June until November he occupied summer quarters in the village of Bludan, located on a hillside overlooking a pleasant green valley, some five hours' ride away in the Anti-Libanus, and visited his consulate only rarely. Even during the working months, he was seldom in Damascus. From April 1870, until his final departure in August 1871, he did not spend a single full month at his consulate or working at his official duties. While it is impossible to learn of all his wanderings and expeditions, it is possible to compile a list of fourteen separate trips taken during this period which in themselves total 183 days – and this does not include the months spent at Bludan.

It was in Bludan that Burton did most of his writing. In less than two years he finished *Vikram and the Vampire*, a collection of Hindu folk tales; *The Battlefields of Paraguay*; and *Proverbia Communia Syriaca*, a compilation of Syrian proverbs first published by the Royal Asiatic Society and later incorporated into *Unknown Syria*. Besides these completed works, he also made many notes on a wide variety of other subjects for future books, including many on the trips he took into the Syrian desert and the mountains of Lebanon.

It must be said that Burton's trips were interesting ones and often resulted in minor geographical or archaeological discoveries. His first long trip of which there is a record was to Palmyra. Taking Isabel with him, he left on 5 April and returned on 21 April 1870. At last Isabel was in the desert with her husband in the land of Tancred and her dreams. She was not disappointed. She lived with him in the black Arab tents and even participated in his talks with the Bedouin by disguising herself as a boy and pretending to be his son. She thought of herself as 'his companion, his private secretary, and his *aide de camp*'.

They travelled in some style to Palmyra. Their party consisted of the Russian Consul, the Vicomte de Perrochel (a French traveller) and an assortment of servants, dragomans, and kavasses; there were seventeen camels, twelve horses and a detachment of friendly Bedouin tribesmen. At Palmyra they hired forty-five men to make excavations in search of curios and skulls; in the evenings there were Arab feasts, complete with sword dances to the wild strains of barbaric music amid the remains of ancient and decaying grandeur. What more could a romantic woman ask for?

Although Isabel did not minimize her discomforts to her friends and relatives at home in England – 'no beef, no fish, no veal, no pork, no meat of any kind except the coarsest mutton; and who would drink anything save native wine, whose only strength is a flavour of goatskin, must get our *vin ordinaire* from France at great expense, and tea from England' – nevertheless, she enjoyed the strange life and worked hard to find a niche for herself that was in keeping with what she conceived to be the high position of her husband. She held a reception every Wednesday and reserved every Saturday for 'my poor'. She believed that she had a 'natural instinct about medicine' and undertook to doctor sick Syrians. Her methods hardly inspire confidence, however, for she believed that in dispensing medicine she must always 'multiply an English dose by four'. Burton swore she would kill somebody, but she nobly persisted.

Isabel also helped settle disputes, and for this she was later criticized for setting herself up as a judge. With her elementary knowledge of Arabic, one wonders if she was ever really able to get to the heart of complicated oriental arguments, but Isabel was a do-gooder who was not to be stopped by such obstacles. She also gave advice to the women in the harems on how to keep their husbands.

On one of her trips with her husband she visited a Protestant mission run by Miss Ellen Wilson at Zahle (about twenty-three miles east of Beirut). At Isabel's request, Miss Wilson turned over to her a beautiful Syrian girl of seventeen named Khamoor, 'The Moon', who became her maid. Isabel thought her charming and attempted to civilize her. This proved difficult, for, as the girl said, 'All the men want my lip and my breast.'

Although she always tried to abide by local customs, Isabel simply could not stand the normal maltreatment of animals that prevailed in Syria. She would rush out at the donkey boys and break their pointed sticks, so that they took to hiding them whenever they saw her. One day she found a sick dog under her window. Passers-by gave it kicks, boys teased it, and it was too feeble to crawl away. At last a crowd collected and began to torment the creature. Its screams were piteous. Isabel begged her husband to shoot it, but he knew perfectly well what the reaction of the people would be if he took the dog's life, and he wished to preserve his good reputation in this regard. She tried to get the Moslem servants to kill it. Of course, they would not. The Christian servants would not do it for fear of the Moslems. Isabel finally took her gun, threw open the window, and shot the dog dead. The crowd was horrified and called upon Allah to witness her sinfulness. All day long she could hear them telling of her cruelty and pointing to her window.

Isabel tried to emulate her husband and to mix with all classes and creeds. Although she took a strong dislike to certain Jews who tried to hurt her husband, she could not forget that Disraeli was a Jew and said, 'there *are* Jews who redeem the whole nation'. She seems to have got on well with the Jewish women and later commented that 'some of my dearest native friends at Damascus were of the Jewish religion'. The local Christians were disappointing: they had 'the same virtues and vices of the lower and middle class Irish'. But her favourite women companions were found among the Arab women. Like them, she learned to smoke the nagrilla, or Turkish water-pipe; Isabel enjoyed smoking, but felt that she had to justify the practice; this she did in one of her more snobbish statements: 'I am told that the middle classes imagine that if a woman smokes she must have all the other vices.'

Among their best friends in Damascus were two people famous in the Western world. One was Abd el Kadir, the Algerian sheik who had waged such a long war against the French and was now in exile in Syria. The other was the strange and romantic Jane Digby el Mezrab, formerly Lady Ellenborough, who after three husbands and countless lovers had finally found happiness and contentment in her fourth marriage to Medjuel el Mezrab, an Arab sheik. The life she led was a strange one: for six months of the year she lived as a European woman in Damascus; for the other six months she lived the life of all Bedouin wives in the desert. Jane's life was even more romantic than Isabel's. But Isabel could not quite condone the marriage: 'The contact with that black skin I could not understand. His skin was dark – darker than a Persian – much darker than an Arab generally is. All the same, he was a very intelligent charming man in any light but that of a husband. That made me shudder.' But Jane Digby el Mezrab had found her heart's ease in living the wild lawless life of her husband's tribe; Isabel could only play at it.

In what she regarded as part of her official duties, Isabel entertained Rashid Pasha, the Turkish Wali: 'He was very amiable and polite. He reminded me of an old tom-cat: he was dressed in furs; he was indolent and fat, and walked on his toes and purred. At first sight I thought him a kind-hearted old creature, not very intelligent and easily led.' How wrong she was! Rashid must have been perplexed by the behaviour of the Burtons and, like most people, he condemned what he did not understand, his suspicious mind construing evil intentions in each inexplicable action.

Behind the scenes, trouble was brewing. On 11 January 1871, Sir Henry Elliot passed on to Earl Granville, the successor of the late Earl of Clarendon as Foreign Secretary, a memorandum inspired by Rashid Pasha requesting Burton's recall. There had been no demonstrations against Burton, as Rashid and Elliot had darkly predicted, and no real reason could be given for demanding his recall; there were only vague forebodings of evil to come: '*La présence de cet Agent à Damas ne saurait se prolonger plus longtemps sans de graves inconvénients,*' Rashid said.

Four days later Elliot wrote a confidential letter to Granville enclosing a '*Note-Verbale*' from Rashid Pasha. Rashid still had no concrete facts upon which to base his charge. He spoke only of Burton's 'character and general proceedings', his long and frequent absences, and malicious rumours concerning Isabel. He pretended to be concerned about the dangers to which they exposed themselves in roaming about the desert, and it is obvious that he was most concerned about Burton's conversations with the Bedouin and his mixing with all classes of society. Rashid knew that here was a man who would soon learn all there was to know about the mismanagement and corruption within the pashalik. He felt it necessary to protect himself by saying that Burton had *'les relations les plus intimes avec les gens des plus malfamé dans le pays'*. Rashid also stooped to an outright lie: *'Malheureusement, M. Burton a, on ne sait pour quel motif, une aversion toute spéciale pour la nation Musulmane.'*

In his letter enclosing this slanderous memorandum, Sir Henry confessed that it was difficult 'to be accurately informed as to what is doing by our own agents at such a distant place as Damascus', but he also adumbrated evil to come and said he had been 'apprehensive that Captain Burton's proceedings were of a nature to give ground for anxiety, although it would have been impossible for me to bring forward one act sufficient to justify a recommendation of his removal from his Consulate'. He was also not above stating that he had heard 'vaguely and unofficially' that Isabel had horsewhipped someone for not showing her proper respect.

Rashid apparently grew more and more disturbed by Burton's wandering about the countryside. Anxiety about whom he was seeing, what he was learning, and what he was doing appears to have driven him nearly frantic. Given the devious and unscrupulous mind of Rashid Pasha, it must have been inconceivable that Burton was more interested in the anthropology, archaeology, geography and natural history of the country than in political scheming. A month later he sent off a telegram to his friend and superior, Aali Pasha, who promptly passed it on to Elliot. He still had nothing definite to complain of, only the rumour that Burton was reported to have said that there would be war with Russia and that Isabel, with her excessively exalted manner, had repeated this opinion. Elliot promptly passed this telegram along to Granville, saying that Burton's attitude was becoming more and more intolerable. Still, there was no incident on which to make a charge, no solid reason for demanding Burton's recall.

If Rashid Pasha could not provide good reasons for getting rid of Burton, Elliot, with the skill of a superior bureaucrat, conceived a scheme of his own. He told Granville that he thought Burton was overpaid and that his post should really be reduced to a vice-consulate. Obviously, Burton would not be able to accept a demotion. To confirm his opinion – and to give the appearance of official impartiality – it was decided to send an official from Cairo to investigate the matter.

The man sent on this mission was Mr C. M. Kennedy, referred to in Isabel's journals as simply 'Mr. K.' Isabel describes his visit and, although in her account she implies that her husband is also there, Burton was actually out wandering about the countryside with their snake-keeping friend from Brazil, Charles Williams. Isabel, however, did the best she could. She met Kennedy at the half-way station between Beirut and Damascus; took him to meet Abd el Kadir, showed him the tourist sights of the town, gave a large party in his honour to which she invited representatives of every race and creed in Damascus (including every one of the fourteen Christian sects), and she drove all the way back to Beirut with him. During his stay he was kept so busy by Isabel that he had only one morning to spend at the consulate.

While in Damascus, Kennedy stayed at the Burton home and Isabel even made certain he had a good night's sleep: a neighbour's squeaking gate kept Kennedy awake his first night. The next night the squeak was gone and he commented upon the absent gate and his quiet sleep. 'If you will look out the window,' Isabel said, 'you will see it in our courtyard. I sent two Kawasses to take it down yesterday at sunset.'

Kennedy put on an official face. 'Oh, but you really must not treat the people like that. Suppose that they knew these things at home?'

'Suppose they did,' said Isabel, laughing.

Although she had arranged for the gate to be replaced the next day and had paid off the woman to whom it belonged, she did not tell this to Kennedy. Doubtless he believed the reports that Isabel ruled like a princess in Damascus. There were many of these rumours, most of them so preposterous and out of character that they could not be true. She once wrote directly to Lord Granville to contradict a story that she had grossly insulted a Jewess. While her manner was indeed imperial and she once broke her riding whip across the face of an impudent servant, she was not cruel nor did she make it a practice deliberately to insult those among whom she lived.

Kennedy's report of his visit was forwarded directly to Earl Granville. He recommended exactly what Elliot wanted: 'Beyrout and Damascus are so near and communication between the two places by means of a good carriage road on which a daily coach runs, as well as by telegraph, is so easy, that in the abstract it would be better to station resident Vice-Consuls at those places [Aleppo, Jerusalem and Damascus], both to be under the direct superintendence of the Consul-General.' He also recommended that the salary and allowances for Damascus be halved.

Still Granville hesitated. He wrote to Elliot asking his opinion, although his views were already known to him. Elliot said, 'I have not been satisfied with the manner in which Her Majesty's Consulate at Damascus has been conducted. . . . I cannot withhold the opinion that he [Burton] is not well suited to the post which he occupies. . . . I consider . . . that his presence tends to unsettle the public mind at Damascus, and to keep alive a sentiment of insecurity, which may at any time become a source of danger, and that it would be very desirable that he should be removed whenever an opportunity for it might offer.'

Many a British consul in this era acted more like a proconsul and received the support of his superiors and his government. Burton, quite obviously, did not; his every act was viewed with suspicion by his superiors. The reasons for Elliot's antipathy to Burton are not clear. Whether he was simply duped by Rashid Pasha and Rashid's friends in Constantinople or whether he distrusted Burton because of his reputation is not known. There is no evidence that they ever met. But it is certain that Sir Henry Elliot, more than any other single person, was responsible for Burton's downfall. The Burtons never suspected him. He appears to have pretended to be their friend, for Isabel sometimes wrote him confidential letters. He had, she said, 'kindly expressed his willingness to hear from me when I had anything special to communicate'. Elliot never disclosed this correspondence with Isabel to his superiors; neither did he ever tell the Burtons directly of his dissatisfaction with them.

Although Burton spent many days away from his consulate, he was probably as good a consul as could be found for this unusual post with its wild array of creeds, colours and races. He appears to have made every effort to be impartial and just; he spoke many of the local languages and was familiar with most of the creeds. But his every act was turned against him. When he tried to save from imprisonment the followers of a new Christian creed, he was accused of prejudice against Islam. When he tried to protect Moslem villagers from the usurous practices of Lebanese Jews who claimed British protection, there were letters of protest filed by important Jews in England. Without official support, he could not win.

As far as Burton knew, he was officially safe and doing good work.

He enjoyed his life and he enjoyed the company of old friends and interesting strangers who came to Damascus to see the sights or to explore the countryside.

Among other visitors was Freeman-Mitford, the young man whom Burton had almost tempted to come with him to West Africa to look for gorillas. Redesdale put down his impressions of Burton and his wife as he then saw them:

The day after we arrived in Damascus Burton came to breakfast. He was excellent company, as of old, full of information and good stories of adventures and stirring scenes in which truth was so richly embroidered as almost to become fiction. One had to know one's Burton, for the thing which he loved above all others was to astonish, and for the sake of that he would not hesitate to violate the virtue of the pure maiden who dwells in a well. Take him with a grain of salt, which was what he expected, and he was the best of boon companions. . . . Burton had dared and done more almost than any man living; that, however, was not enough for him. He was compelled to invent more. But his little inventions were almost childlike in their transparent simplicity.

But Redesdale had no grains of salt to spare for Isabel:

Her manner with the Mohammedans among whom she lived, and whom it was her business to conciliate so far as in her lay, was detestable. On one occasion I was with her and one or two others in a very sacred mosque; a pious Moslem was prostrate before the tomb of a holy saint. She did not actually strike him with her riding crop, but she made as though she were going to do so, and insisted on the poor man making room for her to go up to the tomb. . . . I left the mosque in disgust. If actuated by no higher motive, she should have reflected upon her husband, to whom, to do her justice, she was entirely and most touchingly devoted. It is only fair to Burton's memory to show how heavily he was handicapped. He was not responsible for all the trouble that led to his removal a few months later from the romance of the Damascus that he loved. . . .

The controversial couple could not please everyone. But there was one person whom both Burtons liked very much indeed and who, in turn, liked them. This was Charles F. Tyrwhitt-Drake, a young man in his early twenties who appears to have shared many of Burton's ideas, beliefs, enthusiasms, virtues and failings. Drake first arrived in Syria in July 1870, in the company of Edward Henry Palmer, then a young man well on his way to becoming a distinguished oriental scholar. Both of these men were to die in the Middle East, Tyrwhitt-Drake only four years later. Together they had visited Baalbek and explored the Anti-

Libanus. On 25 March 1871, he was back in Syria and a few months later he and Burton were off to Palestine by an overland route, leaving Isabel to take the easier route by sea, for Burton had obtained that passport to adventure, a two-month sick leave.

Never were there more passionate sight-seers than Tyrwhitt-Drake and the Burtons. They were at it day and night. For Tyrwhitt-Drake and Burton it was an archaeological and anthropological feast; for Isabel it was a religious pilgrimage. By the end of Holy Week she was exhausted; she had not only attended the ceremonies of her own church but those of every other church as well. When the men suggested some cave explorations, Isabel went along, but she was too tired. Leaving them to explore a cave, she lay down outside, her head on a stone, and slept. She had a most remarkable dream. Isabel, for all her Christian piousness, was as superstitious as any peasant. 'There is hardly ever a contingency, or a situation, which to me is strange, and which I do not foresee; and I have known beforehand, places, people, books, and situations,' she averred. 'You may call it by what name you please, dreaming, instinct, electricity, or mesmerism, only you must not call it miracles, for those never come to people like me, only to the very good.'

Isabel recorded this particular dream in a two-volume work miscalled *The Inner Life of Syria, Palestine, and the Holy Land from my Private Journal* (London, 1876). Fifty pages are devoted to the dream, though she calls her account only a résumé of the principal scenes. It was, she said, 'a long, detailed, vivid dream, a *bonâ fide* honest dream'. Detailed it certainly was, for it was nothing less than the re-arrangement of heaven and earth to suit Isabel Burton. She arranged her account of the dream under such headings as, Heaven, A Bird's Eye View of Creation, The Royal Family, Church and State, Government at Home, Policy Abroad, General Reform – the Poorer Classes, Middle Classes, Moral Plague, Society, Richard Burton (this, naturally, was the longest part), I Arrange France, I Settle the Papal States, and The Priesthood. The dream also covered such subjects as the evils of the entire British Government, the handling of convicts, vivisection (she was against it), the rights of women, and the Tichborne case.

In her dream, Isabel died, but instead of going to purgatory God sent her out with a guardian angel to reform the world. The most important part of this reform, of course, was to remedy the neglect the world had shown for her husband. Isabel's talk with Queen Victoria gave her the chance to tell of all his great deeds: how 'he has never in all his life told a lie' and how in the service of his government he 'has toiled every hour and every minute for *thirty-two* years' (Isabel added four years in her printed account to bring his toiling up to date). She then went on to tell the Queen of his neglect and how she had tried to further her husband's interests:

Madam, all England knows that I have passed the whole of my married life in trying to obtain justice for him. It has been my one occupation. It is a thorn in my side to see the best and noblest and truest man that breathes never employed in a sphere or in a manner suitable to his merits and talents. I am an ambitious woman, Madam, but all my life bears upwards to noble ends. I fear I have been tiresome to many great and good people in your Majesty's various governments for the past fourteen years in this cause. . . . I shall cry like an eagle for justice till it comes – I shall cry for it, Madam, till I die.

When the Queen asked Isabel what she thought would be the proper position in the world for her husband, Isabel replied that he should be given a high military rank, created a Knight Commander of the Bath, and given the post of Envoy Extraordinary and Minister Pleni-potentiary to an Eastern court. Queen Victoria granted her wish.

In this ideal world Isabel created for herself, even the Pope sent Burton 'his blessings as one of God's elect'! Poor Isabel. The world of her dreams and life's realities were too far apart ever to meet. In her all inclusive dream there was even room for excuses for her husband's failure: 'Europe has become common-place, *parvenu*, and money-making, and she must have everything in keeping – brand new, tawdry, and fleeting. She has rushed into a feverish progression, and does not know that she is racing madly around in circles. Now I understand why there is no place for Richard Burton.'

Isabel later spoke of this recounting of her dream as 'the gem of my book, to which the rest is but the framework'. Although she maintained that 'I did not compose any part of my dream for the public; I really did dream it', still the dream is written entirely from the viewpoint of the situation as it existed four years after, at the time she published it. 'It is a very bitter thing,' she said, 'to sit as he is now doing by his distant fireside in a strange land, and read in the newspapers how England has forgotten him, and to know that men who have not done a tithe of his service will reap the credit and reward of his deeds.'

She was awakened by a goatherd. 'Pardon, *ya Sitti*,' he said, 'I thought you were dead.'

On Easter Sunday, Isabel attended two masses and received Holy Communion in the Sepulchre. Two days later some British warships put in at Jaffa and that night the solemn silence of Jerusalem rocked to the singing of 'Sally Come Up', 'Champagne Charlie' and 'We Won't Be Home Until Morning'. Isabel sent the sailors some liquor and asked them to sing 'Rule Britannia'.

On 24 April they started on their leisurely way back to Damascus. On 4 May they reached Nazareth, and here occurred an important incident. They camped near a Greek Orthodox church; there were four other groups also camped near by – two English, one American and one German – but the Burton–Drake camp was concealed from the others by a small hill.

May 5 was the feast of St George and the Greek church was opened for services. Just at dawn, a Copt tried to enter Isabel's tent. He may have intended to steal something, he may have wanted baksheesh, or he may have been simply curious. In any case, the Burton servants caught him and tried to drive him away. A fight developed in which the Copt, being one man against several, came out the loser and was getting a sound beating from the servants. Isabel's words, though they sound callous today, were probably true: 'A little affair of this sort amongst the people is such a common thing that nobody notices it.' Unfortunately, in this case it was not only noticed but resented. The Greeks, coming out of church from their early morning services, saw the fight and decided to take the Copt's part against the foreigners. The Copt fled, but the six servants and about 150 Greeks carried out an uneven struggle with stones as weapons. Burton and Drake ran out of their tent half-dressed and tried to calm the combatants. They were greeted with a shower of stones, some the size of melons. A well-dressed Greek shouted, 'Kill them all! Kill them all! I will pay the blood money.'

One of Burton's muleteers called out, 'Shame! Shame! This is the English Consul of Damascus, and on his own ground.'

'So much the worse for him!' yelled one of the Greeks.

Although a number of the stones hit him, Burton stood calmly by, marking the ringleaders. Isabel got dressed and ran out to give him his two six-shot revolvers, but he waved her back. Isabel stuck the pistols in her own belt, 'meaning to have twelve lives for his one if he were killed'.

Three of the servants were wounded. One lay on the ground and two Greeks started to stamp on his chest. Burton then pulled out a pistol from the belt of a servant beside him and fired into the air. Isabel took this as a signal to run for help. She ran over the hill to the other camps and came back with ten armed English and Americans. The fight ended.

The next five days were spent in nursing the wounded servants and efforts on Burton's part to punish the ringleaders, a difficult task. The head of the village was most reluctant to make arrests. He said he only had twelve policemen and that most of them were only young boys armed with canes. Also, out of a population of 7,000, 2,500 were Greeks. Burton sent to Acre (then called St Jean d'Acre) for soldiers and managed to have a dozen of the ringleaders arrested.

But the Greeks drew up counter-charges, forced their bishop to sign it on penalty of being ridden out of town, and sent off their report to Damascus. It reduced the mob of men to a group of children and stated that Burton and his men had fired on them. Carried away by their own inventions, they also swore that Burton had entered the Greek Orthodox church armed and had torn down pictures, broken lamps and shot a priest. Isabel, too, was reported to have entered the church in her nightgown, sword in hand, and to have helped in the wrecking.

To Rashid Pasha this document must have seemed an answer to his prayers. This was exactly the sort of incident for which he had been waiting. He gleefully endorsed the report and quickly sent it off to Constantinople, preceding the report with a telegram. Burton, who regarded the affair only as a village row, neglected to report the matter. Isabel, however, sent a complete account of the affair direct to Elliot. But on 5 June Elliot wrote Granville that he still had not received Burton's report on the Nazareth incident and on 14 June Odo Russell (called 'Oh Don't' behind his back and who later became Lord Ampthill) wrote on behalf of Lord Granville a stern letter to Burton demanding an explanation and informing him that the Foreign Office had received 'serious complaints in regard to your general proceedings'. On 23 June Russell again wrote Burton demanding an 'immediate explanation' of Burton's failure to report the affair.

On 8 June, more than a month after the incident, Burton sent Elliot a telegram stating, 'My servants unprovokedly attacked by Greek Orthodox at Nazareth on account of a slight quarrel with an insolent negro. Three of mine seriously hurt. Have applied to local authorities for redress. Great opposition, at first, from Greek clergy, who now own themselves mistaken, and wish for an amicable settlement. Details by post.' But eight days later Elliot wrote Granville that he had still received no explanation from Burton and the Porte had demanded his immediate recall.

Although Elliot and Rashid Pasha did not yet know it, their fight against Burton was practically won. On 25 May 1871, Granville had written to Elliot telling him he was at liberty to inform the Turkish Government that another post would be found for Burton.

Finally realizing that he was in serious official difficulties, Burton started to collect affidavits. But while he was preparing to defend himself, the wily Rashid Pasha was able to manufacture another charge. Burton, with Tyrwhitt-Drake, made an excursion into the desert to talk with some of the Druze tribesmen. This was the sort of expedition Burton loved. It could be construed as part of his official duties to make friends with the natives while at the same time it gave him the opportunity to explore the countryside and to study the customs of the Druzes. But Rashid Pasha sounded the alarm. Burton was now attempting to raise the Druze in revolt against Turkish rule, he claimed. Perhaps he really believed this. In any case, he sent out a party of Bedouins to murder him. Had they succeeded, Rashid Pasha would have had little difficulty explaining the event: he had often warned Burton and his superiors of the dangers of wandering about the desert. Thanks to a timely warning from Isabel, the two men were able to hide in some high rocks and watch the Bedouins searching for them in the desert below. But Rashid Pasha's best weapon was the official letter. He obtained a copy of Burton's invitation to the Druze chiefs to meet him, written in Arabic; and by mis-translating it into French he gave the appearance of substance to the charges he forwarded to Constantinople.

On 26 June 1871, Elliot wrote to Granville that the Nazareth affair seemed to be satisfactorily explained, but he brought up the meeting with the Druze; he said that Burton appeared to have set himself up as a governor and complained that there had been no trouble in Syria before Burton arrived on the scene. Politically, Elliot believed in letting sleeping beasts lie: 'That many abuses exist in the administration of the province may be fairly assumed; but Captain Burton, in his desire to remedy them, has not, as it appears to me, been sufficiently careful in avoiding just cause for umbrage on the part of those who are responsible for its tranquillity. . . . The knowledge that the British Consul is in direct opposition with the local authorities is liable to be taken by the restless populations of those countries as an encouragement to resist them.'

Ironically, Consul-General Eldridge, whom Burton called 'The F.O.'s most undistinguished servant' and whom he blamed for all the official misunderstandings, appears actually to have tried to clear them up and to help him. Writing directly to Granville, he said that Burton's letter to the Druze chiefs seemed to him 'to have been simply intended to give notice to those who might wish to see him', which indeed it was.

On 5 July, Elliot sent Granville a copy of Burton's explanation of the Nazareth incident (which had been written on 11 June). On the same date, Burton also wrote Granville a report of the persecution of Christian converts by the local authorities and complained of the lack of official support: 'As regards the apparent resolution at headquarters here to take my proceedings in ill part, and to regard all movements with suspicion, I expect to see the effects cease as soon as the cause shall be removed.' This remark proved to be ironic indeed. Three days before receiving this letter Granville took definite steps to remove what he believed to be the cause: Burton himself.

Examining the evidence now, there appears to have been no single instance of Burton overstepping the bounds of his authority. True, he spent little time in his consulate, but he was criticized for what he did do rather than what he failed to do. Yet, in all he did, he did right and within the confines of his responsibilities. A missionary at Damascus who had not, at first, been pleased by Burton's appointment confessed that 'shielding the weak from cruelty and protecting the poor from oppression, constituted Captain Burton's chief work at Damascus'. Had Burton neglected his duties completely and remained at home reading and writing books, he might have risen in the service to even higher posts. Eldridge said, 'If Burton had only walked in *my* way, he would have lived and died here.'

In his innocence of diplomatic ways, Burton did not realize until it was too late the seriousness of his official difficulties. Knowing that he had always acted in the right and had done nothing wrong, he naïvely assumed that all would turn out well in the end. He was wrong. On 8 July, he received an order direct from Granville commanding him to remain at the seat of his consulate, Damascus, until further notice. This was one order Burton refused to obey. He would not be confined. Pleading illness and the unhealthy climate of Damascus at this season, he moved to Bludan. With Tyrwhitt-Drake, he was soon off exploring a mountain range. He had been back from this trip only a few days when, on 16 August, Isabel reported that 'a bombshell fell in the midst of our happy life'.

The horses were saddled at the door and they were preparing to go out for a ride when Isabel saw a ragged messenger stop to drink at the spring and then advance towards the house. Isabel took the message, saw it was for her husband, and carried it in to him. The note was from Thomas Jago, the vice-consul at Beirut, stating that he had arrived in Damascus the day before and had taken charge of the consulate. Burton and Tyrwhitt-Drake were soon in their saddles. Isabel wanted to come too, but Burton told her to stay home.

In Damascus Burton learned the galling truth. Granville's letter, after reminding him of Clarendon's original warning, said, 'I regret to have now to inform you that the complaints which I have received from the Turkish Government in regard to your recent conduct and proceedings render it impossible that I should allow you to continue to perform any consular functions in Syria. . . . You will, therefore, make your preparations for returning to this country with as little delay as possible.'

Burton sent his wife a cryptic note: 'Don't be frightened – I am recalled. Pay, pack, and follow at convenience.' He then set out for Beirut. In his journal he wrote, 'August 18th – Left Damascus for ever; started at three a.m. in the dark, with a big lantern; all my men crying; alone in *coupé* of diligence, thanks to the pigs. Excitement of seeing all for the last time. All seemed sorry; a few groans. The sight of Bludan mountains in the distance at sunrise, where I have left my wife. *Ever again?* Felt soft. Dismissal ignominious, at the age of fifty, without a month's notice, or wages, or character.'

In Bludan that night, Isabel tried to sleep. But she had one of her dreams. 'I thought someone pulled me, and I awoke, sat up in bed, and I could still see it and feel it; and it said in a loud whisper, "Why do you lie there? Your husband wants you – get up and go to him!" I tried to lie down again, but it happened three successive times, and big drops were on my forehead with a sort of fear.'

The maid in the next room called out, 'Are you walking about and talking, madam?'

'No!' said Isabel, 'but somebody is. Are you?'

'No,' she replied, 'I have not stirred. But you are talking with somebody.'

Isabel jumped up, dressed, had her horse saddled, and rode with all her might through the night, heedless of rocks, bushes, hills and wandering tribesmen. Five hours later she reached the post house on the Beirut-Damascus road. The passengers had just finished their breakfast and had mounted the diligence. The driver had raised his whip and was about to start when he saw Isabel, hot, torn and covered with mud. He waited for her. She reached Beirut just twenty-four hours before her husband's ship sailed.

She found him walking alone down the street, looking sad and serious. 'It was a real emblem of the sick lion,' she wrote. 'But *I* was there (thank God!) in my place, and he was so surprised and glad when he saw me! We had twenty-four hours to take counsel and comfort together.'

Womanly wisdom and devotion are not incompatible with ridiculousness. Isabel was a gallant wife.

As Burton's ship pulled away from shore, a former servant was seen rushing to the water's edge. Finding he was too late to bid his master goodbye, he flung himself down on the quay and cried bitterly.

Chapter 19

An Exile at Home

1871 – 2

BURTON'S unexpected recall was a traumatic experience for him – probably the greatest shock of his life. Isabel said, 'It broke his career, it shattered his life, it embittered him on religion; he got neither Teheran, nor Marocco [*sic*], nor Constantinople.' It was not really as bad as all that, but perhaps it seemed so at the time. 'I may be wrong,' Isabel continued, 'but I have always imagined that he thought Christ would stand by him, and see him through his troubles, but he did not like to speak of it.' Isabel's hope that her husband would become a Christian was induced by his academic interest in a new Christian sect that had sprung up in Syria while he was there; it is doubtful indeed that he had any thought that 'Christ would stand by him'. But it was true enough that he was disheartened by the setback to his career, although it was Isabel who set out to defend him in official quarters.

Remaining in Syria to wind up their affairs, Isabel was left without money to get home or even to live. For this state of domestic economy she blamed the British Government, not her husband. She finally sent off a telegram to her uncle Lord Arundell who generously wired the Imperial Ottoman Bank to let Isabel have any money she needed.

Although left alone in a semi-barbarous country, she was surrounded by her husband's friends of all races and creeds. She had tempting offers from two of them: one, a Moslem, volunteered to shoot Rashid Pasha from behind a rock as he was passing in his carriage; another, a Jew, offered to put poison in his coffee. There were even flattering signs of mass demonstrations, as Moslems collected in the mosques to say prayers for Burton's return and groups met to discuss the matter in the cafés and coffee houses.

Isabel set to work breaking up her household, finding new homes for her many pet animals and collecting letters from friends testifying to her husband's good name and good deeds. In the midst of it all she became sick. Nevertheless, she struggled on, and when the work was done she tried to slip out of the city quietly to avoid being the centre of an anti-Rashid pro-Burton demonstration. Half-way to Beirut she became delirious with fever and had to be set down in a tiny village. It was ten days before she was well enough to go on. Even then, bad luck pursued her and she was involved in two ship collisions before she finally reached England on 14 October 1871.

In London she found her husband living in a small hotel. Although he had been back for a month, she was irritated to discover that instead of protesting against the injustices of Rashid Pasha and attempting to vindicate his conduct at the Foreign Office, he had spent his time railing at Speke, a book publisher, the Royal Asiatic Society, the Royal Geographical Society and other old enemies. There was so much in Burton's life that called forth his righteous indignation. It is perhaps understandable that his dismissal had brought to his mind earlier disappointments and frustrations. He lashed out at them all and hurt none.

In 1857 Burton had sent off from Zanzibar to Dr Norton Shaw, then Secretary of the Royal Geographical Society, the manuscript of his book on Zanzibar, the results of all his note-taking prior to the Tanganyika expedition. For some inexplicable reason, the manuscript ended up at the Bombay branch of the Royal Asiatic Society and remained there for five years before being forwarded to Shaw. This was not the only time Burton had lost a manuscript: his account of the trip to Kilwa at the end of his African expedition was also lost for many years. This manuscript had a most curious history. Burton had entrusted it to a ship's captain to take to England. The captain died and his widow sold the manuscript to a London bookseller. The bookseller marked it 'Burton Original MS. Diary in Africa' and sold it to an artillery officer. The officer left it by accident in a government office where it was found and finally returned to Burton. In a similar fashion, Burton's meteorological notes from his African expeditions were also mislaid for a number of years at the Foreign Office. But then there were so many manuscripts. . . .

Now Burton collected all this miscellaneous material, added an acid-filled chapter on Speke with some additional notes on why Lake Victoria was not a single lake, and sent it off to be published in two thick volumes (1,034 pages) as *Zanzibar*. He was writing the preface when Isabel arrived. It was a bitter preface, reflecting his frustrations and his never-dying hope that his African explorations would some day be honoured. The strange fate of his lost manuscript he described as 'typical of the fate of my East African Expedition, which, so long the victim of uncontrollable circumstances, appears now, after many weary years, likely to emerge from the shadow which overcast it, and to occupy the position which I ever desired to see it conquer'. This was a badly written book, reflecting the carelessness with which he handled his material. Burton frequently said the same thing in the same words in different books, but in *Zanzibar* he said the same thing in the same words in the same book. The harsh but just verdict of the London *Examiner* was: 'We are afraid that these two rambling, egotistical, and excessively bulky volumes will prove tiresome reading even to the most arduous student of African travel.'

Henry Morton Stanley, after following Burton's steps to Ujiji and the shores of Lake Tanganyika and finding Dr David Livingstone, was now on his way home. Few believed his story and the Royal Geographical Society was in the process of equipping an expedition of its own to accomplish the same purpose. There was considerable interest now in Central Africa. This interest was to grow, but recognition of Burton's accomplishments was not, unfortunately, a by-product.

Isabel, however, was not concerned about Africa. She was shocked to find that her husband had made so little defence of his conduct in Syria and she set about to defend him herself. Down to the Foreign Office she went. She argued and pleaded with more than a dozen people and even had an interview with Lord Granville himself. She wrote letters to all their influential friends and to those whom, like Sir Henry Elliot, she believed to be their friends. She put together a 'blue book' consisting of letters from a wide variety of people ranging from missionaries and patriarchs to Druse tribesmen and Bedouin chiefs as well as testimonials from fourteen villages near Damascus or Bludan. It was an impressive array of good evidence, even setting aside those who were personal friends of Burton and in no way connected with his official duties. Some of the documents make interesting reading for their own sake. Abd el Kadir's letter begins with a delightful oriental preface:

Allah favour the days of your far-famed learning and prosper the excellence of your writing, O wader of the seas of knowledge, O cistern of learning of our globe, exalted above his age, whose exaltation is above the mountains of increase and our rising place, opener by his books of night and day, traveller by ship and foot and horse, one whom none can equal in travel. To his Excellency Captain Burton. But afterwards, verily, we wondered at the suddenness of your departure. . . .

All of this material, together with a long review of his actions at Damascus, was sent by Burton to Granville shortly after Isabel's arrival in London. 'I confidently hope,' wrote Burton, 'from your Lordship's well known sense of justice, that it will be taken into consideration, and that my Consular career, especially at Damascus, will be found not undeserving of your approbation' This was hoping for too much. By this time, however, Rashid Pasha had himself been recalled (shortly after, to Burton's delight, he was murdered) and Granville finally sent Burton a letter which gave him as much vindication of his conduct as he was ever to receive. Ignoring the charges and counter-charges and, incidentally, the real reasons for his recall, Granville simply said:

I am willing to give you credit for having endeavoured, to the best of your ability and judgement, to carry on the duties which were entrusted to you. But, having come to the conclusion, on a review of the Consular establishments in Syria, that it was no longer necessary to maintain a full Consul at Damascus . . . your withdrawal from that residence necessarily followed on the appointment of an officer of lower rank and at a lower rate of salary, to perform the Consular duties in that place.

Burton was offered small posts, but he refused them. Of the post at Belém in northern Brazil, he remarked in his diary, 'Too small a berth for me after Damascus.' On 12 November he wrote to Granville, 'With respect to my own future employment, it only remains for me to place myself at your Lordship's commands, in the assured hope that such employment will be of a nature to mark that I have not forfeited the approbation of Her Majesty's Government.'

It was about this time that Burton was called to give testimony in the Tichborne case, the most famous trial of the century. This concerned one Arthur Orton, alias Thomas Castro, alias Sir Roger Tichborne. He was apparently an English sailor who had jumped ship in Australia and settled there as a butcher. His rise to fame, or at least notoriety, began when he claimed to be Roger Charles Tichborne, a rich baronet's heir lost at sea when the ship on which he was sailing as a passenger went down with all hands off the coast of South America in 1854. Roger Tichborne's mother refused to believe that her son had drowned and advertised widely for news of him, offering a liberal reward for information. When the Claimant appeared, years later, she felt sure she recognized in him her lost son. The rest of the Tichborne family thought differently. In 1871 the Claimant sued for possession of the title and estates to which Roger Tichborne would have been entitled and after a long trial of 102 days he lost his case. Nevertheless, the controversy continued and there were few Englishmen who did not take sides. In general, the split in opinion followed class lines, the lower classes championing the Claimant and the upper classes siding with the family. Three years after his unsuccessful suit, the Claimant was charged with perjury, and after a trial that lasted 188 days, the longest in British history, he was found guilty and sentenced to fourteen years in prison.

Just before his unsuccessful suit for the Tichborne title and estates, the Claimant went to South America, allegedly to gather material to support his case. There he was believed to be the genuine article by most people, including Wilfrid Scawen Blunt, and, apparently, by Burton as well. According to Blunt, Burton arrived in Buenos Aires in company with the Tichborne Claimant, 'with whom he chiefly consorted during his two months' stay in Buenos Aires'. The testimony offered at the long Tichborne trial of 1871 was taken down in shorthand by the firm of Cherer & Co., Shorthand Writers. The firm still exists and for ten guineas they consented to search through their unindexed notes for the words of Richard Burton. On 13 December 1871, the sixty-fourth day of the trial, Burton testified under oath, 'I met the plaintiff, not at Buenos Aires, but at a place called Villa Nueva. It is now called Villa Maria.' (Actually, Villa Nueva is a small place near the town of Villa Maria.)

Mr Serjeant Ballantine: 'What was he doing when you saw him? Where was he?'

Burton: 'He was returning to Buenos Aires.'

Ballantine: 'From the direction of the Pampas?'

'He had been at Cordova.'

'You heard from him he had been at Cordova?'

'I heard from him he had been at Cordova.'

'Did you see much of him?'

'We passed one evening together.'

'Had you an opportunity of ascertaining from your own observation the state of his health?'

'I distinctly remember his complaining of the state of his health to me, and to Mr William Constable Maxwell, who was my travelling companion.'

Under cross-examination by the Attorney-General, Burton was asked, 'Did you meet him there by appointment?'

'Almost by appointment,' Burton replied, 'that is to say, it was understood he was going over with us. He was tired of staying at

Cordova, where he waited, I believe, about twenty-five days, and returned to Buenos Aires.'

'You had not seen him before?'

'No.'

'I really do not understand exactly what you mean to say, that it had been almost agreed between you?'

'Not having met him at Buenos Aires, and personally agreed that we travelled together [*sic*], that he sent a message, through a friend, to say he would be happy to join Mr Maxwell, Major Rickards, and myself.'

'Then, if I understand you, he had left Cordova, when you met him?'

'Yes.'

'And was on his return?'

'Was on his return to England.'

'That was the first, and except for the purpose of seeing him in Court, perhaps the last interview you had with him?'

'The first and last.'

Re-examined by Ballantine, Burton spoke of the dangers of his crossing of the Andes.

'It was a very near thing?' Ballantine asked.

'It was a near thing,' Burton replied. 'We passed Christmas Day in a very disagreeable manner.'

'With the natives?'

'Not with them, fortunately; running away from them.'

The court was most concerned about the physical appearance of the Claimant and Burton testified that he was too fat: 'A man I should be sorry indeed to travel across the Andes with.'

The Attorney-General recalled Burton to ask him another question. 'I asked you if that was the only time you had seen him that evening; had you any conversation with the Claimant before that evening?'

'We passed about a couple of hours in conversation.'

'Did he tell you that he had received important letters from home, and the letters had recalled him and he must return?'

'He told me something about letters recalling him. As I mentioned before, I have my diary in my pocket, which I wrote out immediately on arriving at Cordova.'

'You may refresh your memory.'

'If you will allow me, I will read the passage concerning it.'

'Very well.'

'"We went to the 'Hotel Orientale' kept by a most extortionate

Pole. I there met Sir Roger Tichborne, who was returning from Cordova. After waiting a week he said he was sorry he could not join us, but had letters urging him to return to England.'''

There is much evidence to indicate that Burton's version of the affair is the correct one, although he probably saw the Claimant more often than he admitted in court. Blunt's diaries twice mention Burton and the Claimant together in Buenos Aires, but one entry was made twenty-one years after the event and the other thirty-nine years later. Blunt's recollection, however, appears to have been remarkably good. He even remembered a dinner given by Mrs Charles Russell (later Lady Russell) attended, according to Blunt, by Burton and the Tichborne Claimant. He also recollected that this took place in 'the autumn of 1868'. It is possible. Burton probably did not leave on his trip across the Andes until sometime in December 1868.

Blunt's recollection of the 'strange and disreputable couple' is more than a passing mention: 'With these two men I therefore spent much of my time during the next few weeks but naturally more with Burton. (I unfortunately kept no notes nor journals then.)' But the most interesting statement Blunt makes is this: 'His visit to the Pampas ended tamely enough in his crossing it with "The Claimant", the two inside the ordinary diligence, to Mendoza and thence on mules to the Pacific.'

Such are the conflicting stories of Burton and Blunt. Isabel gave a third version. According to her story, which she presumably got from her husband, Burton 'fell in with the Tichborne Claimant, and travelled with him for a week, and never having seen the real man, and as he appeared very gentlemanly, and when he gambled, lost his money and won it without any emotion, he concluded that he was the real thing until he came home'. Isabel wrote this about 1892.

One wonders how much Arundell family pressure and Burton's financial dependence upon Lord Arundell affected his testimony. It seems doubtful that Burton told all he knew at the trial. Two facts are certain: Burton believed the Claimant to be genuine when he knew him in South America; Lord Arundell, who was related to the Tichbornes, was personally and passionately involved in the case on the side of the Tichborne family against the Claimant. Later the Burtons were spectators at the trial during the testimony of Isabel's cousin, Katherine Radcliffe, whom the Claimant maintained he had seduced in his youth.

It was shortly after Burton gave his testimony that he and Isabel were invited by Lord Arundell to come and stay with them at Garswood, Lord Arundell paying their fare both ways. The Burtons were fast running out of money. When invited to Garswood they were down to their last £15. In the train Isabel dropped a sovereign on the floor and it rolled down a crack, reducing their fortune to £14. Isabel sat on the floor of the carriage and cried. Burton knelt beside her and, putting his arm around her, tried to comfort her.

The Burtons stayed at Garswood for about a month in December and January. When they left, Lord Arundell gave Isabel a present of £25. All his life Burton had complained of insufficient money for his needs, but he had never been so reduced as he was now. Tempted one day by some oysters, he regretfully turned away, 'They were three shillings a dozen – awful, forbidden luxury!' Out with Isabel one day he quoted, 'Lunch, one shilling, soup not filling.' It is doubtful that the Burtons actually went hungry, but he was certainly humiliated by his poverty. It was probably not long after this period that he wrote:

The chief bane of poverty is not so much that it renders man ridiculous, as that it brings him into contact with a life-form of which only Mr. *Punch* can make fun. I envy the *richard* in civilization only because the talk of the Vestibule does not reach the Peristyle: his wealth removes him from all knowledge of what is going on within a few yards of him, the mean jealousies, the causeless hatreds, the utter malice and uncharitableness which compose 'high life below stairs.'

The Burtons' poverty, although real enough to them, was nevertheless of the genteel variety. Isabel still had her Syrian maid, the young and beautiful Khamoor. Neither did their reduced financial position curtail their very active social life nor prevent Burton from continuing his membership in the Athenaeum and engaging in a wide range of intellectual activities. They paid visits to all their old friends and met new ones. They saw Monckton Milnes, Lord Strangford and the Duke and Duchess of Somerset; Winwood Reid, the famous war correspondent, and Charles Reade, the novelist and playwright; and they visited the Earl of Derby and planted a cedar of Lebanon in his park. Just how much of the 'high life below stairs' they encountered at these homes is unknown, but Burton was once much amused to hear one startled servant confide to another, 'Why, Captain Burton looks like an old gypsy.'

There is a suspicion that the Burtons were sometimes invited not for their own sake, but simply because they were socially acceptable curiosities. When Lady Marian Alford gave a party to open her new house at Prince's Gate and exhibit her fountain sculptured by Harriet Goodhue Hosmer, she invited the Burtons but asked that Richard come disguised as a Bedouin sheik. Burton complied, and even brought along Khamoor in oriental dress to complete the deception. He spoke Arabic to Khamoor and Isabel and broken English and French to the rest of the guests. The Prince of Wales and the Duke of Edinburgh were also there (although they were told of the deception in advance), and after dinner Khamoor entered with a tray of coffee on her head which she served, kneeling, to the royal pair. It was a great change. The disguise with which he had ferreted out oriental secrets and done great deeds was now only a parlour trick.

At a Foreign Office party Burton encountered Musurus Pasha, the Turkish Ambassador, who apologetically explained that his government had forced him to complain of Burton's actions in Syria. Burton replied seriously, 'Well, Pasha, I did not know that you had, but I can tell you that, though I never practically wish evil to my enemies, they all come to grief, and you are bound to have a bit of bad luck on my account.'

The following day Musurus Pasha fell and broke his arm.

Certainly one of the most curious facets of the Burtons' characters was the way Isabel's Catholicism and Burton's mysticism met on the ground of their mutual superstition. Isabel said, 'It is an absolute fact that everybody who did my husband an injury had some bad luck.' There is no indication, however, that ill luck attended Sir Henry Elliot as a result of his work against Burton.

Burton's vast intellectual interests remained unflagging. He visited coal mines, and alkali works, and the Surrey County Lunatic Asylum. He sent to the British Museum a collection of thirty-two species of plants he had collected in Syria, he continued his voluminous correspondence with scholars in various fields, and he visited the meetings of learned societies. He created quite a stir at one session of the Royal Geographical Society.

Hormuzd Rassam, the Turkish Assyriologist, stood up to make a comment regarding a native message to Dr David Livingstone. Burton's old enemy, Colonel Rigby, then a member of the Council of the Royal Geographical Society, contradicted Rassam on one point, whereupon Burton contradicted Rigby and a furious argument ensued. Burton described the scene that followed:

I made it very lively, for I was angry, and proved my point, showing that my opponents had spoken falsely. My wife laughed, because I moved from one side of the table to the other unconsciously, with the stick that points to the maps in my hand, and she said that the audience on the benches looked as if a tiger was going to spring in amongst them, or that I was going to use the stick like a spear upon my adversary, who stood up from the benches. To make the scene more lively, my wife's brothers and sisters were struggling in the corner to hold down their father, an old man, who had never been used to public speaking, and who slowly rose up in speechless indignation at hearing me accused of making a misstatement, and was going to address a long oration to the public about his son-in-law Richard Burton. As he was slow and very prolix he would never have sat down again, and God only knows what he *would* have said; they held on to his coat-tails, and were preparing, in event of failure, some to dive under the benches, and some to bolt out of the nearest door.

It was Burton's misfortune to have more than one enemy in the Royal Geographical Society. His quarrel with Speke had undoubtedly done much to diminish his popularity with many of the members. Although frequently angry with them, his own interests so clearly corresponded with those of the Society that he could never stay away from it for long; nor could he help being hurt by the slights he received from its officials. When Sir Roderick Murchison, as president, omitted his name in making an important address to the Society, Burton wrote in his journal, 'Why? Old Murchison hates me.'

No matter how he tried, Burton could never forgive – not even the dead. When Murchison died he wrote:

Sir R. I. Murchison has passed away, full of years and honours. I had not the melancholy satisfaction of seeing for the last time our revered Chief, one of whose latest actions was to oppose my reading a paper about the so-called Victoria Nyanza before the Royal Geographical Society; whilst another was to erase my name from the list of the Nile explorers when revising his own biography. But peace be to his manes! I respect the silence of a newly made grave.

At the less distinguished Anthropological Institute (not for many years yet would it become the Royal Anthropological Institute of Great Britain and Ireland) Burton was still a leading personality. He gave several lectures there, one of which, 'Stones and Bones of Haurán', appears to have been taken down verbatim. It gives an interesting glimpse of Burton's colloquial style when speaking about himself:

Since we last met in this room, I have had two years of service in Syria and Palestine: and I may assure you, gentlemen, that I have not found the Holy Land a bed of roses. Without entering into political or official matters, which would here be out of place, I may, in a few words, assure you that my post was one of great difficulty and of greater danger. I have been shot at by some forty men, who, fortunately, could not shoot straight; I have been wounded on another occasion; and lastly, my excellent friend and fellow-traveller Charles F. Tyrwhitt-Drake and I were pursued by a party of about three hundred Bedawin assassins, placed upon our track by a certain Rashid Pasha, late Wali or Governor-General of Syria. On the other hand, my friend and I have been able to explore the highly interesting volcanic region lying immediately to the east of Damascus, and to bring home a plan of the giant cave, which seems to have been mentioned by Strabo. We have also surveyed the whole of the Anti-Libanus, a region far less known than the heart of the Andes, the best proof being that upon the best maps the name of only one peak is given, and even that is given incorrectly. Our notes upon the subject are reserved for the Royal Geographical Society, whose actual president, the world-famed Sir Henry Rawlinson, has, in his opening address of Monday, November 13, made courteous allusion to our labours: it is sufficient for me here to state that our joint publication will alter the map of Northern Syria. And, neglecting all details concerning the peculiar circumstances which led to my leaving Syria, I may briefly assert, that the action taken by the authorities has led to a result which I hardly expected: it has made my name historical in the Holy Land. The Moslems of Damascus gathered in thousands at the great Amawi, or Cathedral Mosque, of that once imperial capital, and prayed publicly for my return; whilst Mrs. Burton was compelled to quit the city privately, in order to avoid a demonstration which might have been dangerous. You will excuse me if I have made these personal details too personal; but I feel it due to you and to myself that my unexpected appearance in this room should be honourably accounted for.

The above transcript was thrown into *Unexplored Syria* (two volumes, of course) which Burton tossed together during this period of unemployment. Burton described the work as 'a *pot-pourri*, a gathering of somewhat hetrogeneous materials – all, however, bearing, more or less upon the subject of Unexplored Syria'. The result was certainly a jumble: a miscellaneous collection of chapters and odd notes, it was written by Isabel and Tyrwhitt-Drake as well as by Burton, although Isabel is not listed as one of the authors. Whole passages were taken intact from Isabel's own manuscript and were used again in her *Inner Life of Syria, Palestine and the Holy Land*. The actual manuscript must have been in a deplorable condition, for Burton makes a point of thanking 'Messrs. Robson and Sons, my printers, for the prodigious trouble caused them by the state of a manuscript written on shipboard, and subjected to various corrections'. Even in this period it was certainly unusual for an author to tell his readers that he knows his book

is a mess but that he did not have time to make a good job of it. Yet
this is what Burton did. Of the 757 pages in the book, 281 are taken up
by appendices. Of these Burton said, 'The appendices which contribute
so much to swell the bulk of these volumes are simply necessary: an
endless succession of labour left me no time for working the material
into the text.' As was not unusual for Burton in his books, he announced the future publication of a book he had not written and never
found the time to write. In this case he promised his 'Personal Adventures in Syria and Palestine' which was, he said, to be published by
Tinsley Brothers. It might have been an interesting work if it had been
written.

In February 1871, Burton tried to revive the Cannibal Club, which
had dissolved early in 1869. He invited all the members to a 'can-
nibalistic gathering' and many came. Swinburne replied, 'I shall come
and bring my friend [Simeon] Solomon. Yours in the cannibal faith,
A. C. Swinburne.' They dined once more as of old, but then met no
more.

In April 1872, Sir Frederick Leighton began his painting of Burton
and found him quite vain. 'Don't make me ugly, don't, there's a good
fellow,' he begged, and he insisted that Leighton include his necktie
and pin. The portrait is an excellent one. The necktie, pin and coat
accentuate rather than soften the rugged head that sits above them. The
head is turned to show the great scar on his cheek, where it had been
pierced by the Somali spear. Shown in three-quarters profile, one
fierce, cruel eye dominates the face; the long moustaches do not quite
conceal the sensuous mouth; and a large nose and an ear bracket his
weather-worn features. But the hair is thinning a bit and there is the
hint of a man who, though unbroken, has suffered too many disappointments.

During all of this period of unemployment Burton and his wife
were doing everything they could to obtain another consular post.
They knew that Teheran was vacant but, as Isabel said, 'we also knew,
sub rosa, that Mr. (afterwards Sir Ronald) Thompson, a personal friend
in their youth of Mr. and Mrs. (afterwards Lord and Lady) Hammond,
of the Foreign Office, was to get it'. This must have been a great disappointment to Burton, who would have considered the post a promotion.

He was disgruntled and impatient. When called before a Consular
Committee, Burton, who was never known to forget a grievance, took
this opportunity to complain that the salary he had received at Santos

had been 'very inadequate' and that he had been forced to use his own capital to supplement his pay. When asked how his predecessor, a baronet, had managed on the same salary, he snapped, 'By living in one room over a shop and washing his own stockings.'

Although he had received some back pay and small sums came in from his writings (*Vikram and the Vampire* and *Battlefields of Paraguay* had been published in 1870), he was still worried about money and no acceptable consular post was in sight. Finally, he received a private offer to explore the sulphur-mining possibilities of Iceland. He accepted, although Isabel was somewhat bitter that her expenses were not included and she was forced to remain in England. In mid-May, 1872, he set off for Scotland and on 4 June he sailed for Iceland on the first commercial undertaking of his career.

After stopping briefly at the Orkneys and Shetland Islands, he landed in Reykjavik on 8 June. The capital of Iceland, according to a census that had been taken two years earlier, had a population of 2,024 and, according to Burton, reeked of decayed fish. The present population is twenty times larger than it was in Burton's day, but he maintained that Iceland in general was overcrowded and should encourage emigration.

Although he spent less than three months there, Burton wrote, three years after the event, two volumes of 794 pages on the country (*Ultima Thule; or A Summer in Iceland*) besides writing two long articles for the *Morning Standard* and articles in *The Mining Journal*. Later he also wrote another book on Iceland which was never published. Although he says his subject is 'to some extent . . . of the sensational type', there is certainly nothing sensational in his account. As a treatise on Iceland, the book may be of some interest to scholars; as a narrative of personal adventure, it is dull; but as an insight into Burton's character and attitude at this stage of his career, it is excellent.

In the preface to the book Burton says that 'a wanderer knowing only enough of the language to express his humble wants, whose travels have been limited to a single fine season, has little right *ex cathedrá* to pronounce, even in this scanty community, upon religion and politics, upon commerce and civilization; but he is fully justified in quoting as his own the judgements formed by consulting experts and authorities, upon whom his experience, and that "sixth sense" developed by the life-long habit of observation, have taught him to rely'. The first part of this sentence, while true, has been manifestly violated by Burton himself who commented upon everything. The second half of the statement makes Burton an avowed plagiarist, although some might question whether a plagiarist is a plagiarist if he proclaims himself one in the very book in which the plagiarism appears.

Nearly the whole of the first volume is taken up by scholarly gleanings, consisting of nine sections dealing with historical, political, geographical, anthropological, zoological and other aspects of the island's culture. Chapter One does not begin until page 267. One would imagine that it would be difficult to devise a more effective method for discouraging readers. The library copy used by the author had not been withdrawn since 1916 – and that withdrawal appears to have been the first. In addition, Burton included his usual liberal sprinkling of sentences and phrases in French, ancient Greek, Latin, Spanish, Hindi, Arabic, Italian, and German, plus some in Swedish and Danish. The main purpose of *Ultima Thule* appears to be a criticism and a debunking of all previous books written on Iceland.

Burton still had all of his usual energy, but the zest was gone. He saw little that was new to him; he had seen it all before. One of the defects of the book, of which he was himself aware but was apparently unable to control, gives us an interesting picture of the fifty-one-year-old Burton: 'Those who have seen much of the world make themselves unintelligible and unpleasant (myself, alas!) by drawing parallels between scenes unknown or unfamiliar to their Public, who resents the implied slight accordingly.' Eating habits were 'somewhat after the fashion of the Druses'; the flowers reminded him of those in Syria; a Danish boat was 'much like a gunboat on the West Coast of Africa'; the sheep were 'like their congeners of Somaliland'; he finds a patch of desert 'which might have been in the heart of Arabia Deserta'; the wild oat is 'like the *pasto fuerte* of the Argentine Republic'; the gnats are compared to the midges of Maine; there was an evening that 'might have been in Tuscany'; a southern wind is like the wind in Sind; dried meat is as at Sierra Leone; a night in the open beneath a mountain makes him exclaim, 'What a difference was my night in the open below Fernando Po peak!'; a mound is 'like a nest of African termites'; of the peasant chests he says, 'I could not but remember the pea-green and gamboge box which carried to Meccah the drugs of a certain "Haji Abdullah"'; and small trading boats reminded him of 'the banyans at Berberah and the trade boats on the Amazonas'. The impression surely is that he was writing only for himself rather than for his readers. At one point he describes a steeple-less chapel as being like the church in

Bludan. There were few even of his own friends who had seen that remote Syrian village.

Everything he sees in Iceland compares unfavourably with other sights he has seen. The hot springs only 'reminded me of Central African frog-pools'. Hekla, Iceland's famous volcano, is only 'a commonplace heap, half the height of Hermon, and a mere pygmy compared with the Andine peaks'. At Hekla, too, he found that 'everything was painfully tourist' and that 'even alpenstocks with rings and spikes are to be found at the farm house'. Burton presented a most unflattering view of the Icelandic people: 'Dawdling is worse in Iceland than in Peru' and 'more cases of open, shameless drunkenness may be seen during a day at Reykjavik than during a month in England'. There is also a reference to the 'couthless calibans from the country'. Guides and servants were singled out for special mention. Of the latter he says, 'This class in Iceland appears to me the worst in the world – practical communists with the rude equality of the negro, worse even than Irish help in the United States, or the servitor at Trieste, where the men are either louts or rogues, and the women are cheats, bacchanalians, or something worse.'

In this far northern land, Burton's thoughts remained in his beloved East. A rock formation reminds him of the head- and feet-stones of a Moslem grave and he puzzles how in this land of the midnight sun a Moslem would know the hours of prayer. Even the paths reminded him of the wooded areas of the Anti-Libanus. A mountain peak seen at sunset he found to be 'an affecting reminiscence of the Jebel al Mintar' in Syria. The tameness of it all impressed him unfavourably: 'There are no thieves in the Icelandic desert, in this point mightily different from that of Syria.'

He was no longer young, yet there remained in him the desire to repeat the feats of his youth: 'I went to my old quarters, well satisfied with having ridden from under the very shadow of Vatnajökull, in two days to the eastern coast.'

Neither in his book, nor in his newspaper articles, written 'for the benefit of intending tourists and explorers', is there any hint of the purpose of his trip to Iceland. True, he submitted a long report on sulphur mining, but this was mostly a compilation of what others had written and what he himself had been told. Although interested in mining, Burton was not an engineer and he had only the vaguest notions of the realities of profit and loss. During his three-month visit, only three days were spent inspecting the sulphur mines. An anonymous writer in *The Mining Journal* wrote, 'I have the greatest respect for Captain Burton as a traveller, but none whatever as an inspector of mining properties.'

Although in Iceland on business, he spent his time as the great traveller had always spent it. When not looking at ruins, studying the native customs, climbing mountains, throwing sod into geysers in efforts to make them erupt, inquiring into the whaling industry, or making wild rides across the countryside, he occupied himself leisurely enough in reading, writing and talking. His account of how he spent his days in Reykjavik certainly sounds unbusinesslike. In the mornings he slept until the children of the house where he was staying awakened him, then spent the entire forenoon reading and writing in his room. After lunch he made a call or two and went for a long walk. In the evening there was a short walk and more reading. 'The monotony,' he said, 'may be varied by picnics and excursions.'

On 1 September Burton sailed from Iceland and, after a brief stop for sight-seeing in the Faeroes, he arrived in England on the evening of 14 September. The summer interlude was over. Isabel had found a post for him.

It had been both a busy and a tragic summer for Isabel, full of successes and sadness. She had launched an appeal for funds with which to furnish impoverished Christian churches in Syria. This had been successful and she had sent off to Syria a fine supply of church furnishings. On 5 June, the day after Burton sailed for Iceland, Isabel's mother died. She felt the loss keenly. On 21 June *Unexplored Syria* was published and in July Isabel accepted a consular post for her husband. In August, Isabel's youngest brother Jack, thirty-one, a naval officer, died at sea. Then, in September, her husband returned to her. It had indeed been an eventful summer.

The transactions of the Foreign Office regarding the new post for Burton were curious. Lord Granville wrote to Isabel, not her husband, telling her that Charles Lever, the Anglo-Irish novelist-consul at Trieste, had died and asking her if she thought Burton would accept the post. He strongly advised her to urge her husband to accept, saying that it was unlikely that a better post would become available for some time. On 15 July she told Granville that Burton would accept. Later she said that they knew a post in 'a commercial town on £600 a year, and £100 office allowance, meant that his career was practically broken; but Richard and I could not afford to starve, and he said he would stick on as long as there was ever a hope of getting Marocco [*sic*]'.

Richard Burton

The Juju, or sacrifice house, Grand Bonny River, from Wanderings in West Africa

The King's Victims;

The Amazon;
from A Mission to Gelele, King of Dahome

The Paulo Affonso, from
The Highlands of Brazil

Frontispiece to The Battlefields of Paraguay

Illustrations by Ernest Griset
in Vikram and the
Vampire

Burton's house in Damascus, by Lord Leighton

Isabel and Richard Burton in their garden in Trieste

Isabel and Richard Burton in their dining-room in Trieste

Daneu's Inn, Opicina, about 1880, the retreat where Burton did much of his work on The Arabian Nights

Richard Burton on his death-bed

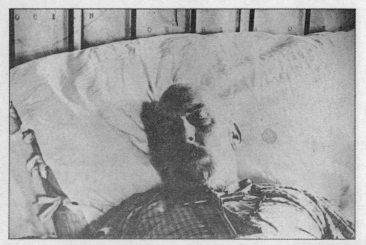

Richard Burton's tomb, Mortlake

Isabel, after talks with Granville, now felt that she knew the '*real cause of the recall*' from Damascus. It was, she said, because Granville had not understood a despatch of Burton's relating to protection for a new Christian sect that had arisen in Damascus. Burton's comment on this final explanation was: 'We won't have anything more to do with this subject until I am free from an enlightened and just-minded government in March 1891.' Already he was looking forward to the day of his retirement nearly twenty years ahead when he would be free to quarrel more openly with the Government.

Burton did not at once leave for his post but spent six more weeks in England. On the morning of 5 October he had a minor operation for what Isabel described as a 'tumour' on his back. Their old friend Dr Bird performed the operation of cutting it out while Burton sat astride a chair, smoking a cigar and chatting. That afternoon he in-sisted on going to Brighton alone. Isabel could not approve and was worried by what seemed to her rashness, but she went to the station with him, bought his ticket and secured him a place in the coupé.

While Burton was off buying his book and paper, Isabel found a train guard, tipped him half a crown, and asked him to look after her husband, explaining that he was not well. Eager to earn his tip and touched by her concern, the guard first singled out an aged man on crutches and then a consumptive boy as the most likely candidates for his charge, but Isabel pointed out the sick man when Burton, fierce and broad shouldered, came striding towards them.

As the train pulled out, Isabel heard her guard tell another, 'She would never ask me to take care of such a chap as that unless he was a raving lunatic. I'll take devilish good care I don't go near him. He would probably pitch me out of the carriage.'

About this time Burton met Verney Lovett Cameron, then a twenty-eight-year-old British naval officer, at a dinner at Clement Markham's. (Cameron said this was in November 1872, but he was mistaken; it was probably in October.) He was eager to pump Burton for information about Central Africa and later spoke of 'how kind and patient he was in answering my many inquiries, many of which must have seemed trivial and uninteresting to him'. What Cameron did not know was that Burton, like many men with great memories, always had difficulty in distinguishing the trivial from the important; this was one of the defects which kept him on the verge of greatness. He and Burton were later to become close friends, but now they parted, Cameron to Africa to lead the Royal Geographic expedition designed to aid Livingstone and then to cross Africa from east to west, and Burton to leave for Trieste, his last post.

Trieste, then a free port and a part of the Austrian crown land with a population of about 130,000, appears to have been considered by the Foreign Office as a good post for scribbling consuls. It must have seemed to them an ideal spot to send Burton. It was respectable, yet unimportant, and there seemed little opportunity for their consul there to get in trouble. Once in Trieste, he could be forgotten. It is doubtful if they ever even considered an Eastern post for the greatest orientalist alive. But with a faintly glowing ember of hope for the future, Burton sailed for his new post on 24 October 1872.

It was typical of Burton that in Southampton on the day of his departure he scribbled a long letter to the *Tablet* outlining a scheme for preventing the Tiber from overflowing its banks by providing it with a new channel.

Chapter 20

Trieste
1872 – 5

FOR all of his adult life Burton, the most undisciplined of men, lived under military or consular discipline. But in his own mind, no other possibilities were open to him. A born rebel and an expatriate by preference, he was at the same time a complete Tory in his social and political views. Although he continually lashed out against what he regarded as the stupidities and injustices of his government, he never questioned the creed of Queen, Empire and the code of the English gentleman. Both he and his wife were of 'good family' and adhered strictly to the code this distinction imposed on them in Victorian England. Being also without a family fortune, it was vitally important to him that he attach himself to a profession that 'has a right to be poor'. Thus, the number of occupations open to him was extremely limited. The Church was obviously not for him and he had not the temperament, interest nor the qualifications for law, politics or academic life. When, to his horror, he lost his commission in the Indian Army, there was no place left for him except in the Government service; his years and dignity limited this area of opportunity to the Consular Service. Initially he had hoped to rise to great heights in this late-found haven. These hopes had now dimmed, but there was nowhere else for him to turn.

Without private means, the Consular Service offered a living; Trieste seemed a dull place, but there was always the hope that he would yet be given the post in Morocco some day. And so, without enthusiasm, he turned towards Trieste, but he was in no hurry to get there and he so dawdled along the way that the trip took him more than a month. The result was that Isabel, who followed him by the faster overland route three weeks later, caught up with him unexpectedly in Venice. This gave rise to a story about them that circulated at the time. It was said that the Burtons, wandering separately around Europe, completely out of touch with each other, met by accident in the piazza at Venice, shook hands like a pair of brothers as though nothing extraordinary had occurred, walked off to a hotel, and immediately sat down to their writing. The actual event was not quite that way, but close enough. Isabel stopped in at the consulate in Venice and was led by the British Consul to her husband.

'Hallo!' said Burton, 'what the devil are you doing here?'

'Ditto,' replied Isabel, and they sat down to explanations. To the bewilderment of the consular staff, they had both been writing letters to each other and sending them to Trieste.

Their arrival in Trieste, at 5.15 on the afternoon of 6 December 1872, was also the source of some amusement to the British population and it was remarked that 'Captain and Mrs. Burton (the new Consul) took up their quarters at the Hôtel de la Ville, he walking along with his gamecock under his arm, and she with her bull-terrier.'

After living for six months in a hotel, the Burtons moved to an apartment on the fourth and top floor of a building covering an entire block. This was their home for ten years. They began with only six rooms, but Isabel kept extending their domain until eventually their flat occupied twenty-seven rooms and covered the entire floor. It became a joke in Trieste that Isabel would soon build a bridge to the next building and start acquiring rooms there too.

Five years after they had moved to Trieste, an article, entitled 'Celebrity at Home', appeared in the London *World*. Isabel said it was written by Alfred Bates Richard, an old newspaper friend of Burton's (they had met at Oxford), but it was actually written by a staffer on the *World* who was passing through Trieste and stopped off to do a feature. He presented an interesting picture of the Burton home:

Captain and Mrs. Burton are well, if airily, lodged in a flat composed of ten rooms, separated by a corridor adorned with a picture of our Saviour, a statuette of St. Joseph with a lamp, and a Madonna with another lamp burning before it. Thus far the belongings are all of the Cross; but no sooner are we landed in the little drawing-rooms than signs of the Crescent appear. Small but artistically arranged, the rooms, opening into one another, are bright with Oriental hangings, with trays and dishes of gold and silver, brass trays and goblets, chibouques with great amber mouthpieces, and all kinds of Eastern treasures mingled with family souvenirs. There is no carpet, but a Bedouin rug occupies the middle of the floor, and vies in brilliancy of colour with Persian enamels and bits of good old china. There are no sofas, but plenty of divans covered with Damascus stuffs. Thus far the interior is as Mussulman as the exterior is Christian; but a curious effect is produced among the Oriental *mise en scène* by the presence of a pianoforte and a compact library of well-chosen books.

Burton conducted his visitor through the apartment:

Leading the way from the drawing-rooms or divans, he takes us through bed-rooms and dressing-rooms, furnished in Spartan simplicity with little iron bedsteads covered with bearskins, and supplied with reading-tables and lamps, beside which repose the Bible, the Shakespeare, the Euclid and the Breviary, which go with Captain and Mrs. Burton on all their wanderings. . . . The little rooms are completely lined with rough deal shelves, contain-ing, perhaps, eight thousand or more volumes in every Western language, as well as in Arabic, Persian, and Hindustani. Every odd corner is piled with weapons, guns, pistols, boar-spears, swords of every shape and make, foils and masks, chronometers, barometers, and all kinds of scientific instruments. One cupboard is full of medicines necessary for Oriental expeditions or for Mrs. Burton's Trieste poor, and on it is written, 'The Pharmacy'. Idols are not wanting, for elephant-nosed Gunpati [Ganapati or Ganesa] is there cheek by jowl with Vishnu.

The most remarkable objects the journalist found in the rooms were the eleven rough deal tables that were scattered about. Each was covered with writing materials. Burton liked to have a separate table for each book on which he was working so that when he tired of one project he could move to another table and a new subject.

Asked why he lived on the fourth floor, Burton said, 'Why we live so high up may be easily explained. To begin with, we are in good condition, and run up and down the stairs like squirrels. We live on the fourth storey because there is no fifth.'

The visitor from the *World* also described how the Burtons spent their time:

The *ménage Burton* is conducted on the early-rising principle. About four or five o'clock our hosts are astir, and already in their 'den', drinking tea made over a spirit lamp, and eating bread and fruit, reading and studying languages. By noon the morning's work is got over, including the consumption of a cup of soup, the ablution without which no true believer is happy, and the obligations of Frankish toilette. Then comes a stroll to the fencing-school, kept by an excellent broadswordsman, and old German trooper. For an hour Captain and Mrs. Burton fence in the school, if the weather be cold; if it is warm, they make for the water, and often swim for a couple of hours.

Then comes a spell of work at the Consulate. 'I have my Consulate,' the Chief explains, 'in the heart of the town. I don't want my Jack-tar in my sanctum; and when he wants *me*, he has usually been on the spree and got into trouble.' While the husband is engaged in his official duties, the wife is abroad promoting a Society for the Prevention of Cruelty to Animals, a necessary institution in Southern countries, where – on the purely gratuitous hypothesis that the so-called lower animals have no soul – the uttermost brutality is shown in the treatment of them. 'You see,' remarks your host, 'that my wife and I are like an elder and younger brother living *en garçon*. We divide the work. I take all the hard and scientific part, and make her do all the rest. When we have worked all day, and said all we have to say to each other, we want relaxation. To that end we have formed a little "mess", with fifteen friends at the *table d'hôte* of the Hotel de la Ville, where we get a good dinner and a pint of country wine made on the hillside for a florin and a half. By this plan we escape the bore of housekeeping, and are relieved from the curse of domesticity, which we both hate. At dinner we hear the news, if any, take our coffee, cigarettes, and *kirsch* outside the hotel, then go homewards to read ourself to sleep; and tomorrow *da capo*.'

The interviewer commented on the tameness of this life compared to their former adventures, but Burton replied, 'The existence you deprecate is varied by excursions. We know every stick and stone for a hundred miles around, and all the pre-historic remains of the countryside. Our Austrian Governor-General, Baron Pino de Friedenthal, is a first-rate man, and often gives us a cruise in the Government yacht. It is, as you say, an odd place for me to be in; but recollect, it is not every place that would suit *me*.'

Although Burton now had a home, he was no more prone to remain in it than he had ever been. He had not been long at his new post when he discovered that strange race of people called Cici who live in the Val d'Arsa of Istria. Isabel described them as 'a very peculiar and wild race of men . . . called Cicci [*sic*]; they are Wallachians of the old Danube, and they dress in the Danube dress, and live in inner Istria. They are a wild people, and have their own breed of wild dogs, which are of a very savage nature.' Isabel suffered from a certain scholarly inaccuracy. In actual fact, the Cici are not Wallachians but a Ruman offshoot representing a fifteenth-century Morlach colony from the island of Veglia. Burton went off to live with them in their villages for a week, sleeping on the floor and eating their black bread and olives. It is unfortunate that he did not publish his experiences with this interesting race. Perhaps then they still spoke their native tongue (now abandoned), which was the last trace of the old Morlach language and formed a connecting link between Rumanian (or Daco-Roman) and the Macedo-Roman dialects.

One of the first things Burton always did at a new post was to find a place where he could get away from it. Isabel said he always looked for 'a sanitarium to which he might go for change in case of being seedy', but it was more than that. What Bludan was to Damascus and São Paulo to Santos, Opicina was to Trieste. Isabel described their retreat:

There is a Slav village, one hour and twelve hundred feet above Trieste, called Opçina. You can drive up by a good road by zigzag wooded ways in an hour, or you can climb also in an hour by five other different rugged paths up the cliff. Once arrived at the top, Trieste, the Adriatic, and all the separate points of land, with their villages, churches, towers, villas, and objects of interest, lies before you like a raised map. There are ranges of wooded hills, cliffs dotted with churches and villages, which seem to cling to them. . . . The house you inhabit is Daneu's old-fashioned rural country inn, on the edge of the declivity, and is an outpost to the village of Opçina; and its terrace commands all this lovely view.

The inn remains today, little changed, still an outpost of the village, and the view is still much as Isabel described it. Here the Burtons took permanent rooms and furnished them to their taste. It was, she said, 'our delight to come up alone, without servants, from Saturday to Monday, and get away from everything, wait upon ourselves more or less, and keep some literary work here. We sometimes stayed a fortnight or six weeks if we had a great work on hand.' It was here that Burton did much of his work on *The Arabian Nights*.

The Burtons' life together seems to have been happy if platonic. The visitor from the *World* quoted Burton as saying that they lived '*en garçon*', and Isabel remarked that 'we lived absolutely the jolly life of two bachelors, as it might be an elder and younger brother'. It seems a strange way to describe a marriage between such an essentially feminine creature as Isabel and such a masculine one as Burton, but the words 'bachelors' and 'brothers' was frequently used by them at this period. Early in her married life Isabel had greatly longed for children, particularly a son; now she wrote to a friend, 'Yes, I have twelve nephews and nieces, five boys and seven girls . . . quite enough. Thank God we have none.' Whatever the cause of her childlessness, she had come to terms with it.

A home in Trieste and a cosy retreat in Opicina were all very well, but Burton had to be on the move. He seems to have been constitutionally unable to remain in one spot for longer than a week or two, and this disease increased in virulence as he grew older. At first they visited the district around Trieste: Aquila, Prevald, San Bartolo, Lipizza, and made excursions around the bay of Trieste. By cart, foot and boat they explored the countryside and seashore for a hundred miles around. Then the trips began to range further afield, to the caves of San Canziano and to Pinguete; Venice became, according to Isabel, 'our happy hunting ground'. There was soon not even the pretence of remaining within the consular district. Burton took it into his head to make a pilgrimage to Loretto – holy places still fascinated him – and off they went. From Loretto they went on to Rome, where Burton showed his wife all the places he had known as a boy and Isabel came down with 'Roman fever'. From Rome they went to Florence; Ouida was staying there and they saw much of her. Then on they went to Bologna to explore the Etruscan remains and to collect enough material for a book, then back to Venice and finally Trieste.

They remained in Trieste only long enough to change baggage and then set off to see the Great Exhibition in Vienna, a fifteen-hour trip by express train. They remained three weeks in Vienna, taking in the exhibition, getting themselves invited to the court and entering into the dazzling social life. Although Isabel says they bought 'nothing but absolute necessaries', they spent £163 in three weeks – expensive indeed for a man whose salary was £600 a year.

While Isabel complained about the high prices, her husband complained of the small portions served in restaurants and engaged in that repartee with waiters he always enjoyed. Brought a *demi-tasse* of weak coffee, Burton looked at it and asked, 'What is that?'

'Coffee for one, sir,' replied the waiter.

'Oh, is it indeed,' said Burton, inspecting it with feigned curiosity. 'H'm, bring me coffee for ten.'

On another occasion, when Burton was served a very small piece of steak, he took up his fork and turned the morsel over to look at it from all sides. 'Yes, that's it,' he said after a careful examination. 'Bring me some more.'

The Burtons returned home – doubtless to the relief of the Viennese waiters – in time to greet Charles Tyrwhitt-Drake. This, of course, set them off on another round of trips, Burton and he exploring the countryside around Trieste as thoroughly as they had the Libanus in Syria. Isabel went with them on an excursion to the Adelsberg caves where a government fête was being held, climaxed by a ball in the cavern itself, illuminated by thousands of candles. Later, Burton returned to these caves and swam deep in the underground stream to see where it led, but he was seized by cramps and had to be hauled out. He had to be satisfied by catching some blind fish, which he sent off to the Zoological Gardens in London.

When it was time for Tyrwhitt-Drake to leave, the Burtons went with him to Venice and saw him off to Arabia on 4 July 1873. They were never to see him again. One year later they received a letter telling them that Charlie Drake had died in Jerusalem. He was only twenty-eight years old. When Burton read the letter, he fainted. Isabel later wrote, 'We had lost a true friend, perhaps a better than we should ever see again, and we felt it bitterly.'

In mid-February 1874 Dr Carter Blake read to the London Anthropological Society a paper Burton had written on his archaeological activities. The report of the meeting said that Burton had devoted 'the first holiday he had' to excavating the *castellieri*, or hill forts, of Istria. It described his paper as 'one of the most important contributions to prehistoric literature which has ever been published'. An overstatement, certainly.

The year 1874 was, in general, marred by sickness. That summer there was cholera in Trieste. At the height of the epidemic it killed an average of sixteen people a day. Isabel caught it. For fear of the quarantine, they told no one; Burton treated his wife and she recovered.

Returning from a mountain-climbing expedition, Burton took sick three days later and developed an inflammation in his groin. A tumour appeared and he suffered horribly for seventy-eight days. At last the tumour was cut out. He was put to sleep for the operation, but it took forty minutes and two bottles of chloroform to do it. Even so, he awoke before all the blood and mess of the operation could be cleared away. Isabel said, 'He was so brave, he smoked a cigar and drank a soda-and-brandy an hour after the operation.' The Burtons always attached some sort of mystic significance to the fact that on the day the tumour was cut out Charlie Tyrwhitt-Drake died – just as, in Brazil, Burton had thought it more than a coincidence that on the day his old friend Steinhaeuser died he had lost a tooth.

Burton was a long time recovering from the effects of his illness. By the end of July he was becoming despondent. He came to believe he would never be able to leave his sickroom and he turned quite nervous and irritable. Isabel, who could never stand to see her husband unhappy, developed a plan she was sure would help him. She went to Opicina and rented a suite of rooms on the ground floor of the inn. Then she arranged for a carriage with a bed in it and for an invalid chair to carry him down the steps of their apartment. Burton was told nothing of these arrangements. The next time he darkly predicted that he would probably never leave his bedroom again, Isabel, in command of the situation herself for once, delightedly told him that he would indeed, for she intended to move him out the next day. He told her flatly it was impossible; he could never be got down all those flights of stairs from their flat. It was true that even with Isabel's careful plan, the move promised to be an ordeal. Faced early the next morning with the invalid chair and the men who were to carry him, Burton, the man of iron, for the first and last time in his life, admitted that he was afraid. 'Do you know,' he confessed with a smile, 'I am absolutely sweating with funk.'

The men moved him gently into the chair and Isabel gave him a glass of port. There were 120 steps to go down, and Isabel gave him a drink at every landing. At last they reached the carriage, Burton was tucked inside and Isabel ordered the driver to walk his horses slowly. Isabel sat beside her husband and held his hand. After a few minutes Burton said, 'I am all right. Tell them to drive on.' An hour later he was lifted into a bed at the inn at Opicina. Burton said, 'I feel as if I had made a journey into Central Africa; but I shall get well now.'

Twelve days later Isabel took him to see a famous doctor at Padua. He recommended that Burton go to the baths at Battaglia, about eight miles away. Then, turning to Isabel, he said sternly, 'As for you, you've got gastric fever, and you will go to Recoaro for four weeks; and you will drink the waters, which are purgative and iron, take the baths and have a complete rest.'

They went first to Battaglia and, since for the Burtons rest meant travel, they made daily excursions to Arqua Petarca or Monselice. Sometimes they went further, to Monte Rua or Vicenza. Burton was getting much stronger now, but he remained grateful to Isabel for her ability to make him mobile: 'I have always been afraid of being paralysed, but I do not care in the least now, because I see that I could go about just the same.'

When Burton's cure was complete, they moved on to Recoaro for Isabel's treatment, which she described: 'The cure here is chiefly a sitz-bath of Fonte Reggia water once a day, from one to three ounce of Acqua Amara (bitter water) to drink per diem, a douche for the eyes twice, a douche for the back once, and cold compress at night.'

Returning to Trieste, Isabel, who now took to calling herself 'countess', a title of the Holy Roman Empire to which she was entitled, now began to take a more active part in those two activities, other than her husband, which constituted her main interests in life: religion and animals. She founded a society for the prevention of cruelty to animals and took over the leadership of a religious society called the Apostle-ship of Prayer, founded by ex-Queen Maria Theresa of Spain, which had as its aim simply to do good deeds. Isabel became president and ran the society for sixteen years, increasing its membership to 15,000.

Once Isabel's Italian Capuchin confessor proudly told her that he had converted a Protestant and asked her to be his godmother. Isabel agreed, although she did not like the look of the man. Burton jeered when, a month later, the man was arrested as the leader of a gang of burglars.

To Isabel's dismay, Burton one day presented her with several pages of instructions and told her she must go off to London. Isabel said, 'It made me exceedingly miserable; but whenever he put his foot down, I had to do it, whether I would or no.' So on 4 December 1874, Isabel and her dog 'Nip', set out for England. Burton was to follow at a later date.

There was plenty for Isabel to do in England. She was to 'study up the Iceland sulphur mine affair' and to try again to obtain a KCB for her husband, but her main concern was to find publishers for a wide variety of literary works. In spite of sickness and travel and consular work, Burton had managed to complete, after his fashion, a consider-able number of scholarly papers, magazine articles and books during the two years he had been stationed in Trieste.

His writing was the only socially acceptable activity which held out some hope of bringing him financial independence, but this hope must have seemed dim even to Burton. Up to this point in his life he had written or translated twenty-three books, but he had never earned more than pocket money from them. Yet he kept on writing, probably be-cause it brought him some degree of fame, it gave his wanderings and his myriad interests some semblance of purpose, and simply because by this time writing had become an enjoyable habit.

In an era noted for travels to out-of-the-way places, Burton had travelled to more than any of his contemporaries. No man of his age had been to so many interesting places, seen so much, or was more able than he, because of his peculiar linguistic abilities and anthropological interests, to give a fascinating insight into life in remote parts of the world. His books, mostly about himself and his travels, ought to have been popular; they could have been. Only Burton's heavy style and his inability to discard dull material prevented him from becoming a successful author. One cannot escape the conclusion that he badly needed a ruthless editor; he appears to have had none at all.

A year earlier his translation of *The Lands of Cazembe: Lacerda's*

Journey to Cazembe in 1798, well annotated by Burton, had been published by the Royal Geographical Society; shortly afterwards he had privately printed 'Supplementary Papers to the Mwátá Cazembe' in Trieste: this consisted of material which he had wanted to include in *The Lands of Cazembe*, such as a criticism of Henry M. Stanley's book on how he found Livingstone, but which the Royal Geographical Society had considered too controversial. Within the past year he had published his annotated version of a Translation by Albert Tootal of *The Captivity of Hans Stade, in A.D. 1547 – 1555, Among the Wild Tribes of Eastern Brazil.*

He now had a number of other books he was anxious to see in print: *Ultima Thule*; a small book called *A New System of Sword Exercise for Infantry*; a two-volume work on his experiences on the coast of West Africa: *Two Trips to Gorilla Land and the Cataracts of the Congo*; and the still unpublished and never to be published *Uruguay*. In her biography of Burton, written sixteen years later, Isabel said that at this period she also tried to publish *Etruscan Bologna*, but her memory was faulty, for Burton did not complete this until 15 February 1876. The publisher's contract for *Gorilla Land* is still extant and shows the financial arrangements between Burton and his publisher: the book was printed at the publisher's expense and any profit that accrued after expenses were made was divided equally between author and publisher.

In addition to these books, Burton also wrote a number of miscellaneous works during this period. Among these were: two articles on Rome that were published in *Macmillan's Magazine*; three articles for the *Journal of the Anthropological Society*: one on human remains he had brought back from Iceland, another on 'The Primordial Inhabitants of Minas Geraes, and the Occupations of the Present Inhabitants', and a third on 'The Long Wall of Salona and the Ruined Cities of Pharia and Gelsa di Lesina'; for the *Journal of the Royal Geographical Society* he wrote 'Geographical Notes on the Province of Minas Geraes'; an article in *Anthropologia* entitled 'Notes on the Kitchen-Middens of São Paulo, Brazil, and the Footprints of St. Thomas, alias Zomé'; a testimony on spiritualism for *The Spiritualist*; and 'The Port of Trieste, Ancient and Modern' which was eventually published in the *Journal of the Society of Arts*.

As yet, however, Burton had not found that genre for which his peculiar abilities were most suited. Although he now knew no less than twenty-nine languages plus nearly a dozen dialects, he had published only two books of translations. One of these was simply a loose collection of proverbs (*Wit and Wisdom from West Africa*, 1865) and the other was an adaptation-translation, *Vikram and the Vampire*. This latter work, originally published as a series of stories in *Fraser's Magazine* in 1868 – 9, is interesting both for its own sake and because it was an adumbration of what was to come, for the format and nature of these stories are similar to *The Arabian Nights*. Burton's true literary genius lay in the difficult art of being able to make translations and adaptations from obscure and difficult languages come vividly to life in English. The Foreign Office, by blighting Burton's diplomatic career, undoubtedly helped make a major contribution to literature. By attempting to confine Burton to a comparatively uninteresting post, the time necessary for the painstaking task of creating worthwhile literary translations was eventually forced upon him.

But this work was not yet begun in earnest. Isabel's job in London was primarily to get printed the odd assortment of manuscripts he had on hand. In addition to handling Burton's business in London, Isabel had a book of her own for publication: *The Inner Life of Syria, Palestine, and the Holy Land*. This was turned over to her publisher on Christmas Eve, 1874. It was her first book and she was so nervous about it that she took to her bed on publication day. Isabel's book was certainly more lively and readable than anything her husband had written up to this time. If it exhibited her foibles, prejudices, superficialities and follies, it also showed her charm, wit, devotion to her Jemmy, and a zest for the strange life she had chosen and never regretted. Isabel spent more than five months alone in London, working on her husband's business during the day and indulging in the society life, that she enjoyed so much, in the evenings.

On 1 March 1875, the *Scotsman* contained an item on Burton's death. Isabel read it with horror. She sent off a telegram to Trieste for confirmation, packed, and gathered her money to go back. But Burton quickly telegraphed, 'I am eating a very good dinner at *table d'hôte*.' On 12 May, he arrived in England.

As he grew older, Burton seemed to feel the lack of money more and more acutely. This led him into bizarre schemes for making his fortune. None of his schemes was more curious than his desire to market a concoction he intended to call 'Captain Burton's Tonic Bitters'. It was supposed to have been compounded by a Swedish physician in 1565 and given to a monastery; Burton got the formula from a Franciscan monk. One tablespoon was to be taken in a glass of sherry, water or diluted cognac and it was intended to stimulate digestion and to cure hangovers. Burton planned to put it in a 'pretty bottle' and to have his picture on the label. Isabel wistfully said later, 'Many people have made a fortune with less, but we were not knowing money-makers.'

As always when in England, the Burtons were swept up in such a round of social engagements that it is surprising they had time for anything else. They met the Queen of the Netherlands on several occasions and the Queen asked for a copy of one of Burton's books, which Isabel sent her. At one party Burton met Gladstone and the two talked together for hours. Some days the Burtons had two breakfasts and two lunches in order to meet all their social obligations. Finding one day that they had thirteen invitations for one evening, beginning with a dinner party, they made a bet with friends that they could make them all – and won their bet.

On one of the evenings Burton was mistaken for a waiter by a young swell. Isabel said, 'Richard was lounging at a supper-room door of a ball one night, when an impertinate young "masher" walked up to him and said, "Aw – are you one of the waitahs?" So Richard smiled and pulled his long moustache, and said with a quiet drawl, "No – are you? For you look a damned sight more like a waiter than I do, and I was in hopes you were, because I might have got something to drink."'

Burton waited upon the Sultan of Zanzibar at the Duchess of Sutherland's; he lectured before the Numismatic Society, the Anthropological Society, the Royal Geographical Society and made a speech at a dinner given by the Licensed Victuallers. Late one night, after a party of the Princess of Wales, Burton left for another trip to Iceland. He stayed only about six weeks, returning to England with lumbago and this was soon followed (all those invitations to meals!) by gout. The result of this trip was a manuscript of another book, *Iceland Revisited*, but although Burton corresponded with several publishers, the book was never published.

It was during this period that Isabel for the second time attempted to obtain a knighthood for her husband. She wrote to friends, acquaintances and the press. It appears somewhat strange that for all their friends in high places no official honours had been bestowed upon him. But Burton was paying for his reputation as the godless devil-of-a-fellow which he had always so carelessly cultivated. Nevertheless, in spite of his avowed disdain for honours, he felt their absence keenly. He chose to be unconventional, but he was never reconciled to paying the price society always exacts from those who flout her conventions.

In pressing the claims to fame of her husband, Isabel was able to say what Burton himself, in decency, could not, and she amplified the virtues of her husband which she had detailed in her similar attempt six years earlier:

Captain Burton deeply feels this want of appreciation of his services, for it is not only a neglect, it amounts to an imputation upon his career. . . . Most men who have done even average duty, military and civil, during thirty-two years, are acknowledged by some form of honour. To what, then, can the public at home and abroad attribute the cold shade thrown over exploits which are known and appreciated throughout Europe? . . . He hopes that he may be recommended to her Majesty's Government for honours no less than those received by Sir Samuel Baker, and which would have been conferred upon the other heroic travellers had they lived to receive them. In one word, he asks to be made a K.C.B.

The popular press responded to Isabel's plea, although the government did not. In the newspapers he was called 'the neglected Englishman'. Burton found this publicity very gratifying and wrote that 'the public is a fountain of honour which amply suffices all my aspirations. . . . With a general voice so loud and so unanimous in my favour, I can amply console myself for the absence of what the world calls "honours", which I have long done passing well without'. But he was unable to sustain this noble tone for more than a few sentences and ended with: 'It certainly is a sad sight to see perfectly private considerations and petty bias prevail against the claims of public service, and let us only hope for better things in future days.'

As soon as his lumbago permitted, Burton set off by himself for Vichy in the hopes that the water would be good for his gout. Naturally, this meant a tour of France: Rouen, Tours, Paray-le-Monial. He returned on 6 October and two months later he and Isabel set off for Trieste. After ten days in Paris they moved slowly towards home by way of Turin, Milan and Venice. At last, on Christmas Eve 1875, they reached Trieste. Burton had been away from his post on this occasion for more than seven months. Then, Isabel said, 'We embarked at once for India.'

Chapter 21

India Revisited
1875 – 6

'My husband, finding he had still six months' leave, asked me what I should like to do. I consulted my heart, and it answered, "India."' So said Isabel. How Burton managed to obtain a leave of fourteen months – if, indeed, he really was granted the leave – is unexplained. It was late in the season to be starting for India, as they could expect hot weather, but Isabel said, 'Consuls, as well as beggars, can't be choosers', and they embarked on 31 December 1875.

On board ship the Burtons kept busy. He started to dictate his biography (never finished) and Isabel took it down. Burton also worked on several articles, including one on 'The Partition of Turkey' which he sent to the *Daily Telegraph* from Jidda, and his book on Etruria. Isabel read *The Veiled Prophet of Khorassan* and *The Light of the Haram*, two of a series of four oriental tales written in verse and connected with a prose story by Thomas Moore; also, *The Adventures of Roderick Random* and *Memoirs of a Lady of Quality* by Tobias Smollet. Isabel said, 'I was told that this course of reading is supposed to be necessary to form one for novel writing, and so I took it on board to save time, in case I should ever wish to write a novel.' She never did.

In the nineteenth century ships appear to have collided with frightening frequency, although usually little damage was done. As they were sailing into Jidda, Isabel and her husband were standing on the bridge; he touched her arm and said, 'By Jove! We are going right into that ship.' Isabel thought it was only a 'beautiful bit of steering'. Then they crashed into the *Standard*, an English ironside.

They spent eight days at Jidda and Isabel thought it was 'the pleasantest eight days I ever remember'. They visited the khan where Burton had stayed, saw the mosque whose minaret he had sketched, rode to the Mecca gate and looked out over the route to Mecca. It was the beginning of a period of reminiscence, of emotional looking back upon scenes from a youth now gone. Isabel enjoyed it all, for it gave her an opportunity to share vicariously a part of her husband's life that she had only dreamed of at the time, and Burton appears to have enjoyed being her cicerone.

When their ship stopped at Aden for a few hours they inquired about the members of Burton's expedition to Somaliland. Hasan Ahmed, the boy, was now a grown man and a *havildar* (sergeant) of the Water Police of Aden; Al-Hammal and 'The End of Time' had died natural deaths; Yusuf, the one-eyed 'Kalendar', had been killed by an Isa tribesman; Long Gulad was alive and so were the two women, Shahrazad and Dunyazad, in Somaliland. Aden provoked sad memories for Burton. His friend Steinhaeuser, who had spent nearly twenty-five years here as a civil surgeon and had always been on hand to greet Burton, was now dead. Burton could not disassociate Aden from Steinhaeuser in his mind, and perhaps he thought of their many long talks together and of how they had planned to make an unexpurgated edition of *The Arabian Nights*.

The ship that took them from Jidda to Bombay was jammed with pilgrims returning from Mecca and Isabel had a close view of the frightful trials of pilgrimage for the poor. There were twenty-three deaths in the twenty-three days of the voyage. She wrote, 'They die not of disease, but of privation, fatigue, hunger, thirst, and opium, – die of vermin and misery.' For Isabel, who could not eat if she saw a dog looking wistfully at her food, it was a terrible time. She spent all her days staggering about on the rolling ship carrying food and medicine to the hungry and sick, her work made dishearteningly difficult by the frequent refusal of her patients to take the food she offered if they thought she had defiled it by touching it. On 31 January she wrote in her diary, 'A delightful day, without events, and nobody died.'

The pilgrims died quietly and Isabel wrote, 'What a contrast is this quiet dropping to sleep with the horrors of the English death-bed, with the barbarous predilection for prolonging the agony, with the atrocious boast that the moribund was enabled to keep his senses to the last!' She was to forget these words when the time came for her husband to die.

On 2 February 1876, the thirty-third day after leaving Trieste, they arrived in Bombay and put up at Watson's Esplanade Hotel. It was here that Burton finished *Etruscan Bologna* on which he had been working while Isabel cared for the sick and starving Indian hajis on shipboard.

They spent nineteen days in Bombay before exploring further. They visited temples, saw the grounds where corpses were burned, visited an animal hospital, and Isabel met one of Burton's old munshis, Mirza Ali

Akbar. But most of their time was spent in the company of F. F. Arbuthnot. The young man Burton had known when he was last in India was now an important personage, a collector, and he delighted in showing Isabel the sights and her husband the changes that had taken place since he had left. Burton found that he could look at the scenes of his youth with 'a certain amount of affection and interest' but added that he 'would not live here again for anything. The old recollection makes me sad and melancholy.'

Because smallpox was raging in Bombay, the Burtons made up a large party to be vaccinated. There were about 400 grouped around the cow at the hospital. Isabel's vaccination took and she had a sore arm for a long time, but Burton's did not.

At first Isabel remained unaffected by India. She enjoyed the sights but 'the populace struck me as being stupid and uninteresting'. She seems to have sought the mysticism of India and, like all who seriously seek this quality in the East, she found it. The Hindu religion with its animal worship had an appeal to Isabel. 'I admire immensely a religion that believes in animals having a kind of soul and a future,' she wrote. 'To me this is the missing link between Nature and Grace.' Then, catching herself, perhaps feeling how close she was to heresy, she wrote, 'Perhaps I had better not say what I do think about it.'

Isabel became obsessed by the cruelty to animals she saw every day in India. Once, riding alone in her carriage, she saw a group of men working on the road. One of them was twisting the tail of a bullock to make it move. Isabel flew from her carriage in a rage. The men huddled together like a covey of frightened partridges, but Isabel singled out her man, called a policeman and had the man taken to her carriage. On the way to the police station she reflected that she would have to swear that it was this particular man who had wrung the bullock's tail. She was tormented with the thought that possibly she had caught the wrong man. The policeman was English and when they reached the station she confided her doubts to him. In the end the man was let go after promising to stop pulling cow's tails.

In a land where cruelty to animals was so commonplace, Isabel was kept in a ferment. She wrote a letter to the *Bombay Gazette* complaining about the cruelty, particularly to carriage horses and snakes. She was continually berating the drivers of the carriages she rode in and often drove the horses herself, much to Burton's annoyance. She made herself miserable and everyone around her as well, including her dog. She was aware of this and once wrote:

I get so nervous, bully the driver, take his whip away, promise him bakshish if he won't do it, and then drive myself. Then the foolish things stand still when *I* have the reins, and will not go without the whip. Then my husband swears at the driver for being cruel, and scolds me for spoiling an excursion by my ridiculous tender sensibilities. On this occasion my fox terrier, 'Nip', tried to bite the coachman for beating the ponies; and not being allowed, she laid her head on my shoulder and went into hysterics.

The misfortunes of Nip in India undoubtedly aggravated matters. She acquired a disease that attacked her eyes and made her blind. The dog had been a constant companion for five years and Isabel, like many childless women, maintained she 'loved her as dearly as a child'. She twice told the story of Nip's end. In the first version she called in six doctors (one of whom was in Trieste at the time) and implied that she chloroformed the dog in India. In the second version there were only four doctors and the deed was done in Trieste. It seems clear that she was unable to screw up her courage to put the pain-racked and wretched dog out of its misery while in India and had carried it all the way back to Trieste. Poor Isabel. Poor Nip.

For Burton the trip to India was less of a sentimental journey than it was for Isabel. He inspected iron mines, made notes on the railroad system and prepared to write an article on diamonds as an undeveloped resource of India. He also took a lively interest in the state of the Indian Army and, like every ex-soldier that ever lived, he found that the army had deteriorated badly since he himself had left it: 'Truth compels me to own that the men are no longer what they were; for this decline the military authorities have only to thank their own folly.' If Isabel liked to see all the sites of her husband's youthful adventures, he did not: 'How small and mean are the dimensions which loom so large in the pictures stored within the brain. . . . How strange are the tricks of Memory, which, often hazy as a dream about the most important events of man's life, religiously preserves the merest trifles! And how very unpleasant to meet one's Self, one's "Dead Self" thirty years younger!'

The trip to India naturally called for a new book, and Burton duly produced *Sind Revisited*, but it was not, strictly speaking, a new book. It was simply an annotated reprint of *Scinde, or the Unhappy Valley* which was originally published in 1851. In that book, it will be recalled, he pretended to be taking 'Mr John Bull' on a tour of Sind. Although on this trip he was giving the tour to his wife, he continued the same fiction as his earlier book and did not even mention that Isabel was with him. To those more interested in Burton than in Sind, there is an interesting footnote in *Sind Revisited* relating to Charles Darwin. Darwin's *The Descent of Man* had been published in 1871 and in the great controversy provoked by Darwin Burton was one of his defenders. Burton's footnote says that 'almost the only point on which I dare to differ with the learned Dr. Darwin's theory of development' is the question of female beauty among the races of man; Burton maintained that only white women are beautiful and appear so to all races.

On the steamer from Bombay to Goa Burton entered into a discussion with a Catholic archbishop. 'My wife is the Jesuit of the family,' remarked Burton.

'What a capital thing for *you*!' said the archbishop.

They appear to have entered into a discussion of Darwin. Spotting some monkeys scampering about, the archbishop said, 'Well, Captain Burton, there are some of your ancestors.'

Burton pulled at his moustache and drawled, 'Well, my lord, I at least have made some progress. But what about your lordship, who is descended from the angels?'

According to Isabel, the archbishop roared with laughter.

From Bombay, the Burtons' first excursion was a visit to Matheran, a small hill-sanatorium thirty miles east of Bombay. Isabel found it unfashionable, being 'affected by the commercial classes from Saturday till Monday'. On 28 February 1876, they started for Hyderabad, the largest of the native states, where the husband of Charles Lever's sister was serving in the Nizam's army. Here they enjoyed dinner parties, military balls and ostrich-racing. Burton also enjoyed the cockfights, but Isabel could not stand this and left. Burton sympathized with his wife's feelings towards animals, but he did enjoy cockfighting – so Isabel defended the sport. 'I could never understand,' she said, 'why we have abolished the classical sport as barbarous, whilst we conserve our ignoble pigeon-shooting.'

They returned to Bombay in time to see the pomp surrounding the departure of the Prince of Wales after his visit to India, and then they set off for a brief tour of Sind. Back to Bombay, a few days in Mahabaleshwar (another sanatorium thirty miles south-east of Bombay), then on 22 April they caught the steamer for Goa.

Isabel had been looking forward to seeing Goa. It was, in a sense, a double pilgrimage: both Burton and her favourite saint had been there. Here was an enclave of Catholic Christendom in the vast wilderness of exotic Eastern religions. It had been established by Europeans and it was the scene of the labours of St Francis Xavier. She was disappointed by what she found: 'Of all the God-forsaken, deserted holes, one thousand years behind the rest of creation, I have never seen anything to equal Goa.' The only good thing she could find to say about it was that 'the manners of the lower classes are excellent', and this she attributed to the teachings of St Francis.

Isabel wrote a book about her visit to India, a more personal account than that of her husband. Although it dealt almost entirely with India, she entitled it *Arabia Egypt India*. She devoted a great deal of space in her book to Goa and told how they went out to visit the Convent of the Misericordia. She spoke of the orphan girls who were kept there until they received an offer of marriage: 'With a world full of nice, pretty girls, and love affairs that come spontaneously, who would think of going to the world's end to overhaul this cage of forgotten captives, kept there for the purpose of respectable *mariages de convenance*, and who would look upon any suitor as a deliverance from the house of bondage?' This was the convent where Burton had tried to abduct a nun, but Isabel made no mention of it. Also, although she managed to make reference to a great many of her husband's books, even including *The Highlands of Brazil*, she does not make any mention of Burton's *Goa*, although she uses as her excuse for writing so much about the country that 'there are actually no English books whatever upon it, or the few that are, are not worth reading'. Had she forgotten reading Burton's book as a love-sick young girl at Boulogne? It is doubtful. Many years later, after Burton's death, she again told of this visit to the convent and added, 'Richard gives a rather amusing account of his visit to this convent when he was a young lieutenant thirty years before.' In her book Isabel also avoided any mention of the Persian girl whom Burton was said to have loved in Sind, although she later confessed that he waxed sentimental at the place where 'he had a serious flirtation with a Persian girl'.

In fact, they did not actually visit the convent at Goa and saw only the outside walls. They arrived after five o'clock in the afternoon and the convent was locked up for the night. They were due to leave the next day. And Isabel was anxious to get away. The ship that was to take them from Goa did not stop there but simply passed by once a fortnight and would lay to, if there were passengers to be picked up. The steamer was to be off Goa at midnight and the Burtons, with Mr Major, their host at Goa, and his secretary got into a large open boat manned by four rowers and a coxswain. They rowed down the river, into the bay, and on into the open sea. They remained for some time rolling in the trough of the heavy sea. Then a violent storm came up and Mr Major proposed that they retreat to the walls of the fort at the mouth of the bay where there were some arches that would give them shelter. At the fort they all went to sleep, leaving Mr Major's secretary, a young Goan, to keep watch for the steamer.

About 1.30 Isabel heard a cannon boom across the water. She aroused the others and they looked for a light or some sign of the ship. Seeing nothing in the storm, they all went back to sleep – all, that is, except Isabel. She fidgeted for half an hour and then got up and went down to the water's edge. She called to the secretary to ask if he had seen any sign of the ship. He calmly replied that the ship had been laying to for three-quarters of an hour and that they ought to have put off when the gun sounded.

Isabel was frantic at the possibility of another fortnight in Goa. She sounded the alarm and they all set off for the ship. In the boat, Mr Major and Burton slept, or pretended to sleep. Isabel picked up a boat-hook and managed to prick their shins with it from time to time. 'Everybody except myself was behaving with Oriental calm and leaving it to Kismet,' Isabel said. She, on the other hand, shouted at the rowers, promised them baksheesh if they would hurry; made the secretary stand up and wave a lantern on a pole; and tried to get the good-natured Mr Major to shout 'Mails!' every minute.

When they finally reached the ship, the heavy seas made it difficult to catch the rope ladder. Isabel berated everyone on the boat and manned the boat-hook herself to hold them alongside. An English sailor threw her a rope. Isabel caught it and jumped for the rope ladder. Climbing over the side she said, 'Thanks! I'm the only man on the boat tonight.' Burton enjoyed the performance immensely and laughed loudly at Isabel's energy and officiousness. Isabel laughed too, when it was over, but she insisted that if it had not been for her they would have missed the ship for Bombay.

Now the visit was over and they boarded ship for Suez. They reached Aden on 19 May 1876 and from here Burton sent back to the *Times of India* his article urging the development of the diamond industry. A week later they were in Suez and the Burtons disembarked to spend sixteen days more in Egypt and to make a curious proposal to the Khedive.

Chapter 22

Gold in Midian

1876 – 80

ALL his life Burton had looked for gold: as a young student interested in alchemy, on convalescent leave in the Neilgiri Hills of India, in California and in Brazil. Gold never lost its fascination for him. Its allure increased as he grew older and this interest absorbed more and more of his time and energy.

The visit to India, a time of reminiscence and reflection, recalled an incident from his young manhood. Isabel's version, written after her husband's death, says that he found gold while on his pilgrimage to Mecca but that he paid little attention to it, being a young man more interested in fame than in wealth; seeing that Egypt was in serious financial straits, Burton at this time remembered the gold he had found and offered his discovery to the Khedive, acting as 'a second Joseph to the land of the Pharaoh'. The truth of the matter, easily pieced together from Burton's own writings, gives a different version of the affair and assigns more worldly motives to his efforts.

It was not Burton but his friend of the pilgrimage, Haji Wali, who had once found a rock containing gold in a wadi on the eastern shores of the Red Sea in the ancient land of Midian. Only in the Tauchnitz edition of the *Pilgrimage* had Burton mentioned this. Egypt at this time was indeed in serious need of money, and so was Burton; he saw no reason why he should not seek out the source of the gold Haji Wali had found and turn it to profit for Egypt and for himself. In May 1876, he sent a proposal to His Highness Ismail I, the Khedive of Egypt, suggesting that an expedition be sent into Midian to explore the possibilities of mining gold there. It does not appear that at this time he was actually granted an audience, but apparently he received some encouragement. He enlisted the support of his friends in Egypt and they began searching for Haji Wali to see if he was alive and could remember where he had found the gold. Having gone this far, he and Isabel returned home to what Isabel described as 'a quiet time in Trieste'.

Isabel plunged at once into her SPCA and religious work; made a retreat in a Dalmatian Jesuit asylum for the deaf and dumb; and attended spiritualist seances at the home of Jules Favre, brother of the famous Leon Favre. Burton resumed his writing and made a long trip through Austria, but his principal interest lay in planning an expedition to Midian. To promote this project, he maintained a steady barrage of letters to those whom he felt could help him. At last a summons arrived from the Khedive, asking him to explain his proposal in person and on 3 March 1877 he left Trieste for Egypt, confident that after a personal conference with the Khedive he would be able to start at once on his cherished expedition. Haji Wali had been found; Lord Arundell was willing to supply some money; and the Foreign Office had given him a month's sick leave on the basis of a severe winter in Trieste. Isabel, to her 'great annoyance', was left behind.

At first the Khedive seemed only mildly interested in the project. Burton was discouraged and prepared to return to Trieste. Then, on 25 March the Khedive changed his mind and gave Burton his approval and support. A government ship was promised for the 29th and was actually ready by the 31st. As soon as the Khedive had given his blessings, Burton left Cairo for Zagazig where his friends, Hugh Thurburn and the curiously named J. Charles J. Clarke, Director of Telegraphs, had rounded up old Haji Wali. Burton and Haji Wali had not seen each other for twenty-four years:

The lapse of so many years had affected him. The figure had become stouter and the face more leonine; but the change was not sufficient to prevent my recognizing at once the well-remembered features and the cheery smile. We embraced with effusion, and, in the few words of conversation which followed, it was pleasant to find that his memory, tenacious as of old, had not forgotten the least detail. This inspired me with a perfect confidence that he would lead us directly to the place where he had made the discovery.

These words were written before Burton learnt how completely unreliable his old friend really was.

For the moment, Burton was in the highest spirits. Three Egyptian officers and a French mining engineer, George Marie, were put under his command as well as soldiers and, of course, the necessary ship, the steamer *Sinnar*. The ship was loaded and they sailed into the Red Sea for the land of Midian. 'At last!' Burton exclaimed. 'Once more it is my fate to escape the prison-life of civilized Europe and to refresh body and mind by studying Nature in her noblest and most admirable form – the Nude. Again I am to enjoy a glimpse of the "glorious desert"; to inhale the sweet pure breath of translucent skies that show the red stars burning upon the very edge and verge of the horizon; and to strengthen myself by a short visit to the Wild Man and his old home.'

To find gold, yes; but to escape what he regarded as dreary routine, and again to ride into the desert – this was a pleasure worth as much as

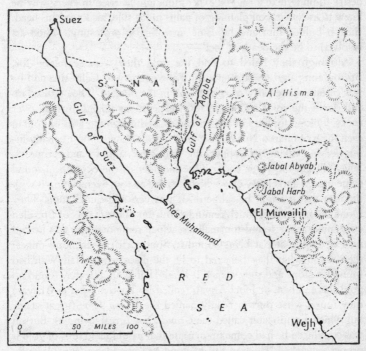

5. The land of Midian

gold to Burton. Once more he was at the head of his own expedition, but he thought less of his responsibilities and more of the opportunity it offered to plunge into that freedom in uncivilized lands which he craved. It was years since he had been so exhilarated. When they reached the bare, desolate coast on the east side of the Red Sea Burton wrote, 'The first aspect of Midian is majestic.' And when he and Marie set out on a reconnaissance in a native boat such as he had used on his pilgrimage, he was delighted: 'I felt thoroughly at home on board the sambuk.'

The expedition lasted less than three weeks. It was so short, Burton said, because they had started late in the season when it was too hot. It developed, however, that Haji Wali was not at all certain where he had found the piece of ore so many years earlier. He tried to draw a map at Burton's insistence, but he was ignorant of topography and nothing could be made of his results. Now an old man of eighty-two, he had no desire to undertake a rugged expedition, and he tried in every way he knew to escape it, complaining of pains in his side, his knees, his head. Burton bullied him and he came unwillingly, protesting, 'Thou art resolved to be the death of me!'

Although they failed to find the gold they were searching for, Burton compared the appearance of the country to California and he was certain that gold was to be found in the interior. They cruised up and down the coast and made short expeditions inland, turning over rocks, looking for sites of ancient mines, and imagining tons of gold in each mass of quartz. Not finding gold, they became almost equally interested in evidence of copper, tin, lead, zinc, sulphur and turquoise. They all had ore-fever badly. One member of the expedition found some brown and crusty clay which he tried to test, even tasting it with the idea that it might be saltpetre. It was very old camel dung. They found chloritic slate, which reminded Burton of the matrix of Brazilian gold mines; they found tourmalines, which reminded him that he had read of such material being found in South African diamond mines; they found what they believed to be the place where Haji Wali had found his stone and they named it Wadi Haji Wali, but they found no gold there. Then, at Jebel Abyab (called by Burton Jebel el-Abayaz) they found what Burton boldly named the *Grand Filon* (great vein), but which a critic later called the *Grand Filou* (great swindle). Burton was convinced he had come upon a site that would yield tons of gold if properly worked. He was full of hope and confidence and blissfully happy: 'Nothing could be more refreshing than the sense of complete freedom, of breathing boundless air, of feeling that the world lay open before one.'

Not even gold could completely distract him from his many other interests, however, and he spent much time examining ruins and ancient inscriptions, inquiring into local tribal customs, collecting botanical specimens, pickling reptiles and making collections of local insects and 'other creeping things'.

Returning to Egypt, Burton and his party brought back eight large boxes of stone, fourteen water bags full of gravel and twelve baskets of sand. None of this, as it later turned out, contained any gold to speak of, but Burton, on his arrival at Suez, promptly telegraphed the Khedive, announcing, '*Succès complet*'. He then hurried off to Cairo to report in person. Unfortunately, Russia declared war on Turkey the day he arrived and he found Cairo in 'a general confusion of excitement'. The Khedive had little time to talk with Burton, but he did grant him a brief audience the following day and expressed great interest in his charts and his scheme to open mines and work them with convict labour. Burton wanted immediately to prepare for a new expedition on a large scale, but because of the war these plans had to be deferred.

There was now nothing further to be done in Egypt, but Burton stayed to investigate the origin of some 'palm runes' he had found, to lecture at the Institute Egyptien and to be made an honorary member. Haji Wali turned up in Cairo. His friends had convinced him he was being cheated and that all the gold of Midian should be his. He caused Burton endless trouble until he was at last persuaded that he would receive his just share. Burton had planned to return to Trieste by way of Jaffa, Beirut and Constantinople, but the war forced him to change these plans and he took ship direct for Trieste. On board, he amused himself by examining an African dwarf that was being brought to Europe. On 12 May, having stretched one month's leave to two, he arrived back in Trieste 'restored to marvellous good health and spirits'.

Burton was tremendously excited by the possibilities of Midian. Fame and fortune were to be found there. 'Throughout the summer of 1877,' he wrote, 'I was haunted by memories of mysterious Midian. The Golden Region appeared to me in the glow of primaeval prosperity described by the Egyptian hieroglyphs.' He laughingly told Isabel that 'the only title he ever wished for' was to be called the Duke of Midian.

Viewed coldly, it is difficult not to see that Burton's dreams rested upon very infirm foundations. It was true he had found minerals that are frequently located with gold, but no mineral can be used as an infallible guide to gold; even if some gold was found, there was not a shred of evidence to indicate that it would be economically feasible to extract it. It is a curious fact that only a few years earlier there was more gold to be found in the crudely minted silver coins of the small German states than was to be obtained from the mines of Midian. When the German government melted down these coins, nine million dollars' worth of gold was extracted. But such a project would have had little interest for Burton even had he conceived of it. There are no deserts in Germany.

During this summer, when his thoughts were filled with visions of the gold of Midian he received an interesting and curious proposal from the famous General Charles 'Chinese' Gordon which, had he accepted, would have drastically changed the future course of his life. The two men had never met, but there had been some previous correspondence beginning with a letter from Gordon in July 1875, asking for information about Zanzibar and Lake Victoria. This letter had hit the right tone by speaking slightingly of Burton's old enemy Rigby. On 21 June 1877, Gordon, writing from Oomchanga in Darfur (140,000 square miles of land west of the central Sudan) said:

You now, I see, have £600 a year, a good climate, quiet life, good food, etc., and are engaged in literary inquiries, etc. etc. I have no doubt that you are comfortable, but I cannot think entirely satisfied with your present small sphere. I have therefore written to the Khedive to ask him to give you Darfur as Governor-General, with £1,600 a year, and a couple of secretaries at £300. . . . Now is the time for you to make your indelible mark in the world and in these countries. You will be remembered in Egypt as having made Darfur.

Before he received a reply to this proposal, Gordon wrote a second letter on 18 July, designed to whet Burton's appetite for the job:

You will find much to interest you here, for the Ulemas are well-read people, and know the old history. I found a lot of chain armour here, just like the armour of Saladin's people, time of the Crusades, with old helmets, some embossed with gold. . . . The people would delight in the interest you would take in them. . . . On the border are Niam-Niam, who circumcise. I suppose they took it from these Arab tribes. I only hope you will come up.

Had this offer come fifteen years earlier, Burton would probably have accepted it, but now his dare-devil days were over. He was fifty-five years old and, like every other civil servant, he valued his steady salary and the prospect of a pension. Besides, there was excitement enough in the wealth to be had in Midian. In his reply to Gordon he said, 'You and I are too much alike. I could not serve under you, nor you under me. I do not look upon the Soudan as a lasting thing. I have nothing to depend upon but my salary, and I have a wife, and you have not.'

Gordon was disappointed when he received Burton's reply and he wrote (19 October 1877), '£1,600, or indeed £16,000, would never compensate a man for a year spent actively in Darfur. But I considered you, from your independence, one of Nature's nobility, who did not serve for money. Excuse the mistake – if such it is.'

Burton was right, however. The two men would never have worked well together. Both were individualists who had little in common except that while alive they were both neglected by their government. Given Gordon's militant religious views, it is surprising he even considered a non-believer such as Burton. By refusing the post, Burton probably saved his own life. The vast province of Darfur fell to the Dervish army even before Gordon himself was killed in the destruction of Khartoum. Rudolf Slatin, the young Austrian officer who took the post that had been offered to Burton, was captured and made to serve for fourteen years as the personal slave of the Mahdi and his successor. Because he pretended to adopt Islam to save his life, Gordon refused to bargain for his release and held him in contempt. Although Slatin finally managed to escape and lived to assist the British Army in the reconquest of the Sudan, became an honorary major-general in the British Army, headed the Austrian Red Cross in World War I, and did not die until the age of eighty-five in 1932, it is doubtful if Burton would have been able to stand the restraint of close imprisonment, nor, not being a leader of men, would he have done better than young Slatin in holding back the forces of Mahdism.

In the five-month interval between expeditions to Midian, Burton wandered restlessly about southern Europe. He went to Verona to see a couple of Akka Pygmies Gessi Pasha had brought back from Central Africa; made a 'little trip of ten days' around the Adriatic coast; and, with Isabel, he went to Postojna (then called Adelsberg) and on to Styria in Austria. From Bertoldsten on 8 August he wrote to Swinburne, 'We are here, a charming place, on a short visit, after which Francis A. [Swinburne's name for Isabel] returns to Trieste and I run on to Karlsbad. We shall probably both pass the winter in Egypt, and if Providence does not put a spoke in the wheel we hope to see you in London about May next.' He also found time in these five months to experiment with dynamite, work up a long correspondence with learned friends on Midian, ransack the literature of the many languages he knew for information on mining in Arabia, and to dash off a 400-page book on his sixteen-day trip to Midian. The book, he said, 'should be considered a sequel and a continuation of my "Pilgrimage to El-Medinah and Meccah"'.

On 19 October 1877, Burton left Trieste for his second expedition to

Midian, leaving a reluctant Isabel behind to bring out his book. She was promised that she could join the expedition as soon as she had seen *The Gold Mines of Midian* through the press, but she did not make it.

Burton's second expedition was on a more elaborate scale and lasted from 19 December 1877 to 20 April 1878. To the infirmly seated Khedive Ismail it must have been an act of desperation. His country was all but insolvent and many officers and civil servants had not been paid their salaries for more than a year. Yet he managed to find the money and resources to send Burton again into the Midian desert in search of gold. And this in spite of the advice of all his advisers and ministers. Burton praised him as 'a prince whose superior intelligence is ever anxious to develop the resources of his country', but he had to admit that 'His Highness was perhaps the only man in his own dominions who, believing in the buried wealth of Midian, had the perspicacity to note the advantages offered by its exploration.' The Khedive promised him – verbally, unfortunately – either a concession or five per cent on the gross produce if he succeeded.

The expedition was supposed to have got under way on 15 November, but lack of funds delayed it for five weeks. The financial arrangements were rather loose. Burton paid for many expenses out of his own pocket and was expected to turn in bills at the end of the expedition. Nevertheless, there was a certain amount which the Khedive had to provide before the expedition could move, for Burton, even with his borrowed money, could not finance the entire venture. At last the Khedive scraped together two thousand napoleons and Burton left Cairo for Midian once more, picking up Haji Wali at Zagazig and a ship at Suez.

The second Midian expedition was unhappy from the start. Burton had been laid up with lumbago in Cairo (an illness he attributed to a fit of temperance during which he limited himself to a pint of claret a day), and he had neglected to attend to the details involved in organizing his expedition. The result was that much was forgotten. He had not even taken the time to select the proper instruments offered to him by General Charles Stone, the American Chief-of-Staff of the Egyptian Army.

Steaming out of Suez on 10 December, the expedition's ship, the *Mukhbir*, had to turn back to repair a faulty boiler. They set off again after a few days and despite a fire in the waste-room, more boiler troubles and a severe storm they finally made what Burton described as an 'unexpected safe arrival' at El Muwailih on 19 December. Two days later Burton, with about a hundred men, set out for Jebel Abyab 'with the most disorderly of caravans'. These words were identical to those he had used to describe his expedition into Central Africa twenty years earlier. Burton, who learned so much from nature and from his wide reading, never seemed to learn from experience. He never acquired the art of leading or managing men, nor did he ever seem to realize that such an art existed, blithely confessing his own deficiencies: 'The second march was as disorderly as the first,' he said. 'It reminded me of driving a train of unbroken mules over the Prairies; the men were as wild and unmanageable as their beasts.'

They made camp at the foot of Jebel Abyab where Burton for the first time began to have some doubts concerning the success of his expedition. 'I had an uncomfortable feeling,' he said, 'that the complication of the country called for an exploration of months and not hours.' Nevertheless, after only six days ('a se'nnight') they moved back to the coast with a ton of stone collected in a random fashion. The stone was crushed and washed, but it produced no gold. Burton still believed that gold was in the mountain, and he designed a tramway which he felt could easily be built to connect the great mine of his dreams with the coast.

So far, no new ground had been covered. The thirty quarrymen that had been brought along on the expedition had been used mostly on archaeological work, digging up graves and sites of ancient cities. Burton himself had also done some exploring of caves and discovered some interesting bats with fat at the root of their spiky tails. On 9 January 1878, the expedition finally moved off into new territory, looking now for sulphur, iron, basalt, copper, silver, coal, turquoise – any sign of a valuable mineral or metal.

Although small search-parties were sent off in all directions, nothing of any importance turned up and ill-luck dogged the expedition. Haji Wali deserted; Burton stepped on a snake, which he regarded as a bad sign, 'a clairvoyante having already warned me against serpents and scorpions'; and he lost his dog, a mongrel he had picked up in Cairo because he had 'a certain sneaking belief in metempsychosis'.

Although the expedition was in Midian for four months for the sole purpose of seeking evidence of gold ore and it had thirty quarrymen to dig for specimens, Burton at one point in his description of this expedition made a most remarkable statement: 'I must regret that here, as indeed throughout the exploration, all our specimens were taken from the surface: we had not time to dig even a couple of feet deep.'

On 17 February the expedition set out for Al Hisma, the region behind the coastal mountains in Midian, which Burton believed would prove to be an 'unworked California'. This was virtually unexplored country and they soon ran into trouble with unfriendly, or at least greedy, Arab tribesmen. When the tribesmen readily volunteered to supply the expedition with transport and sent out messengers in all directions to collect camels, Burton decided this looked like a summons of fighting men to join in the looting.

It was not pleasant to beat a retreat; but under the circumstances, what else could be done? No one was to be relied upon but the Europeans, and not all even of *them*. The black escort, emancipated slaves, would have run away at the first shot. . . . And when I told the officers assembled at mess that we should march back early next morning, the general joy showed how little they relished the prospect of an advance.

The next day, 25 February, was 'a day of humiliation'. The unfriendly sheiks of the local tribe were most angry when they heard of Burton's decision to turn back; the head sheik demanded two hundred dollars. Burton countered by an offer to pay one hundred. The sheik raged and Burton caved in and gave the blackmail. The sheik then demanded a handsome dress for himself or an additional twenty-five dollars for each of his headmen. Burton managed to escape by promising to send a robe from El Muwailih.

Of course he was convinced that had he been able to go on he would have found virgin ore in the unknown tracts of Al Hisma. 'Too bad to be thwarted in such a project by the exorbitant demands of a handful of thieves!' he said.

The expedition once more returned to the coast. At Burton's request, the unseaworthy *Mukhbir* was exchanged for the *Sinnar*, his ship of the first expedition. They cruised south and then made short excursions inland. They picked up what Burton described as 'very satisfactory' specimens of gold. Unfortunately, the geologists in Cairo were later to label the 'gold' carbonate of copper.

Lacking the single-purposed determination that has brought success and fame to so many explorers, Burton could not resist trying to satisfy his myriad interests. To ride by a pass that might contain ruins gave him a 'cold sweat'; he was delighted by a delay that enabled him to climb a mountain: 'I was anxious to collect specimens of botany and natural history from an altitude hitherto unreached by any traveller in western Arabia; and, lastly, there was geography as well as mineralogy to be done'; and, since he was now passing through country which he had traversed during his pilgrimage, he was eager to see the sights of his earlier triumph again, and to make corrections of his old geographical notes. At Wejh he 'resolved to pass a day at these old quarters of a certain Haji' Abdullah'.

The stay at Wejh gave him a chance to study a low-caste local tribe that interested him very much: the Hutaym or Hitaym. He thought they might be related to the gypsies of Europe. 'The men are unwashed and filthy; the women walk abroad unveiled, and never refuse themselves, I am told, to the higher blood.' Among the local folklore was the custom of wives feeding the brains of hyenas to jealous husbands. 'It acts as a sedative,' Burton reported.

On 29 March, with a caravan of fifty-eight camels, he again set out inland, following what is today (and probably was then) a caravan route towards Umm Harb. At a place he called Umm el Karayat he found a series of caves which, he was convinced, were the sites of ancient gold mines. He set the quarrymen to work, but did not supervise them. Not unnaturally, they picked up rocks off the ground – and as few of these as possible. Although he believed this to be 'the focus and centre of the southern mining region, even as the northern culminates in the Jebel el-Abyaz [Jebel Abyab]', yet he spent only one day here!

At Umm Harb they found what Burton described as 'an open mine, scientifically worked by the men of old'. He stated unequivocally, 'these are gold mines'. But he did not stay long here either. Satisfied that there was gold to be had here and pleased that he had found a new species of snake, he turned his caravan around and started back for Egypt.

On one of these last marches, he followed the advice given him by an experienced hand in Cairo: he marched his men in military order and himself brought up the rear to prevent straggling. It was, he said, 'the most unpleasant of our marches', but he had to admit that the system was also effective: 'The effect was excellent: never had there been so little straggling; never had the halting-places been reached in such good time and good order.' But he never repeated the experiment.

The twenty-four-day excursion into the southern part of the region ended on 10 April with the return to the coast. This was also Burton's last day in the ancient land of Midian. The specimens, animal, mineral and vegetable, were loaded aboard the *Sinnar* and they departed for Suez, arriving there on 20 April.

Isabel was waiting for him at Suez. As soon as she had finished with the last proof sheet of *The Gold Mines of Midian* she hurried off to Egypt, hoping to be able to catch up with the expedition. At Alexandria she found a letter from her husband that did not please her very much. She was instructed not to attempt to join the expedition unless she could do so 'in proper order'. Isabel thought it remained to be seen what 'proper order' meant. She made her way via Cairo and Zagazig to Suez and watched for a chance to cross over to Midian. She was offered passage on the *Sinnar*, but after much soul searching she finally refused as 'the accommodation was of too public a nature'. Also, for a woman to travel without her husband on an Egyptian man-of-war would 'lower *her* in *their* eyes, and hurt *his* dignity'. She considered taking a sambuk, but this, too, 'would have been dangerous to *me* and *infra dig.* for my husband's position'. And so she was forced to sit and wait.

In Cairo, she met Gordon, who told her he did not believe in the 'Midian Myth' and, through her, offered Burton £3,000 if he would join him in the Sudan. Isabel may have had her own doubts about Midian, but she loyally told Gordon that her husband would need that much money just to buy gloves once he had obtained the gold he was seeking.

On 1 June 1878, there was a letter in the *Home News* describing Burton's arrival:

I had occasion to be at Suez on the return of Haji Abdullah (Dick Burton) from Midian last month [*sic*], and I noted the sensation his arrival created. His name is as well known among the natives in Egypt as if he had passed all his days amongst them. Pashas and other great personages from Europe are continually passing to and fro almost unheeded. How different was the case when it became known that Haji Abdullah was leaving for Cairo! The platform was crowded with Europeans and natives. The rumour had got abroad that 'that wonderful man' was at Suez on his return from the exploring trip to Midian.

For Burton, however, 'the return to civilization was in nowise cheery'. Everything seemed to go wrong. His men disappeared, leaving him with the problem of getting several tons of rock to Cairo; when a special train was at last loaded it broke down several times on the way and caught fire three times in one morning; at the railroad station in Cairo the railroad employees quit work and went home, as did Burton's escort of soldiers. Burton was furious. 'We were detained at the station for three mortal hours, working with our own hands. If this be a fair specimen of European management in Egypt . . . the sooner we return to Egyptian mismanagement the better.'

But the next day things began to look better. He had an audience with the Khedive together with some of his ministers and other distinguished persons, including Ferdinand de Lesseps, builder of the Suez Canal. The Khedive appeared pleased and ordered that there should be an exhibition of the results of the expedition, after which the rocks would be sent to London for analysis. De Lesseps volunteered to send some pieces to the Parisian Académie des Sciences. Knowledge of Burton's activities had spread far and wide, and the Khedive said he had received requests for concessions from all over the world, but repeated his promise to give Burton either a concession or 'a royalty of five per cent. on the general produce of the mines' as his reward for the great discoveries he had made.

Work now began on the exhibition the Khedive had requested. Religious holidays, military reviews and court functions delayed the date when the Khedive would be free to open the show until 9 May. Characteristically, instead of using the time to supervise the setting up of the exhibits, Burton went off on a flint-hunting expedition on the left bank of the Nile. On the day the exhibition opened, Burton wanted the hall kept clear until after the Khedive's visit, but the hippodrome was crowded at an early hour. Tewfik Pasha, who was soon to become the next Khedive, was also present for the great event. Again, things went wrong. The maps were very imperfect, half-finished at the last minute and abounding in errors. This was a comparatively small matter. More important was the response given by M. Marie, the expedition's engineer, when asked by the Khedive if he was sure that certain specimens contained gold. Marie hedged. 'Midian is a fine mining country,' he replied. One of the courtiers whispered in Tewfik's ear, 'There can't be much gold there or *ces messieurs* would have said more about it.'

Nevertheless, the Khedive requested Burton to draw up a concise general description of the country, to give recommendations on what should be done to develop Midian, and personally to superintend the work of assaying. Charles Clarke was sent with the ore to England by boat and Burton and his wife left for Trieste. They did not stay long in Trieste. Clarke reached England on 20 June and the Burtons set off by sea on 7 July, Burton having again obtained leave – this time for two months. They reached Liverpool on 26 July. After nursing Burton's gout for two weeks in London, they went to Dublin where Burton gave several lectures on Midian. Two weeks later they were back in England, staying first with Isabel's father, then with Lords Arundell and Houghton. There was the usual social round, including a masquerade in which Burton went dressed as an Australian miner and Isabel as Carmen, and Burton wrote another book, *The Land of Midian Revisited*. He received another letter from Gordon dated 8 August 1878, begging him to come and work for him and offering £5,000 a year, but he refused.

Soon the work of assaying the rock specimens was completed. The results were not satisfactory. A few specks of gold were found, but certainly not enough to justify large-scale mining operations. In *Midian Revisited* Burton not only told the story of the second expedition (in two volumes, naturally), but he also gave all of his excuses for failure: the members of the expedition were lazy, Marie was incompetent, the local sheiks concealed information, and the Egyptian staff officers were disloyal. One sheik whom Burton had praised in the highest terms in his first book on Midian he as roundly damned in his second. Parts of the book were so dull they even bored Burton. He referred to one chapter as being 'dull reading as well as writing', and another he ends by saying, 'I conclude this unpopular chapter.' But it never occurred to him to leave anything out that could possibly be put in. His vast knowledge of many languages also kept getting in his way and he managed one twelve-word sentence which included words in four languages (French, Arabic, Italian and English).

On 21 February 1879, he was still in England on the 'two months' leave' he had obtained the previous July. On this date Isabel's book, *A.E.I.*, was published and they attended a dinner party given by the publisher which lasted until five in the morning. The earliest he could have been back in his consulate was in April but it was probably May as he took a three-week tour of Germany alone before returning to Trieste – and then he went at once to Opicina.

As Isabel was leaving her father's house in London for the trip back to Trieste a beggar woman approached her and Isabel gave her a shilling. 'God bless you,' said the woman, 'and may you reach your home without an accident.' In a Paris hotel on 30 April, Isabel slipped at the top of a flight of stairs. With her leg doubled under her and after striking her head and back on every step, she was picked up unconscious at the bottom of the stairs. The doctor said she must stay six weeks in bed, but she left the next day and continued her now painful trip back to Trieste. Her back and ankle were never the same, in spite of repeated 'shampooing and soap baths'. Isabel said, 'Strong health and nerves I had hitherto looked upon as a sort of right of nature, and supposed everybody had them, and had never felt grateful for them as a blessing; but I began to learn what suffering was from this date.'

They were a stout pair, the Burtons: she with her injured back and leg and he with his lumbago and gout; yet they still made excursions about the countryside and it was not long before they were off for a tour of Austria. Burton revived an old interest in bringing out a book on swords and in making a translation of the *Lusiads* of Camoens. He translated a German ghost story; both took a lively interest in spiritualism. Isabel in a letter written 26 December 1879 expressed her belief that 'Catholicism is the highest order of spiritualism', for, she said, 'nothing happens by luck or chance; but that we are moved by our good and our bad angels'. If Isabel confused Catholicism with superstition – her beliefs, basically simple and naïve, hardly differed from those of a southern Italian peasant – the beliefs of Richard Burton were somewhat more complex.

In October and November of 1876, after his return from the visit to India, Burton had engaged in a debate through the columns of *The Times* on the subject of spirits and spiritualism. Here he made it quite clear that while he believed in extrasensory perception and a sixth sense, he did not believe in ghosts. He described himself as 'a Spiritualist without the Spirits'. And, in another place, he stated that 'intellectual truth is eternally one: moral or sentimental truth is a geographical and chronological accident that varies with the individual'.

Seven years earlier (on 13 December 1872), he had addressed a meeting of the British National Association of Spiritualists in their London rooms at 38 Great Russell Street. The room was crowded and people stood on the stairs and in the street. What he had to say did not altogether please his audience, including Isabel: 'No man – positively, absolutely, no man – neither deity or devil – angel or spirit – ghost or goblin – has ever wandered beyond the narrow limits of this world – has ever brought us a single idea or notion which belongs to another and a different world – has ever eluded the cognizance of man's five wits.' He spoke of the soul and his own conception of it: 'Personally, I ignore the existence of soul and spirit, feeling no want of a self within a self, an I within an I. If it be a question of words, and my *ego*, or subject, as opposed to the *non-ego*, or object; or my individuality, the concourse of conditions which differentiates me from others, be called a soul, then I have a soul, but not a soul proper. For some years, however, I have managed to live without what is popularly called a soul; and it would be hard to find one violently thrust into the recusant body.' On this occasion, to Burton's great amusement, Isabel stood up in the meeting and announced to the audience that she did not agree with her husband's philosophy.

Burton's life-long interest in religions led him to reject all, but to take in a bit of each. He still thought that 'revealed religions consist of three parts, all more or less untrue. (1) A Cosmogony more or less absurd. (2) An historical sketch more or less falsified. (3) A system of morality more or less pure.' He believed in a creator, but not a God; he believed in a soul, but not in the usual sense of the word; and he believed in a spirit that was related to animal magnetism or 'zoo-electricity'. Above all he believed in a 'Higher Law of Humanity', a fuzzy concept he had developed as early as his Somaliland expedition and now set forth in a slender work called *The Kasîdah*.

In spite of his intense study of many religions and in spite of all he had written about himself, Burton had never actually put on paper his own religious belief. Now he set about doing this, infusing the whole with his own bitterness at life's lost opportunities and fate's hard blows. Perhaps because it revealed so much of his inner thoughts and beliefs, he published it anonymously – yet not really, for it was not difficult to deduce that Haji Abou was Haji Abdullah, the Arabic name of Burton himself, who pretended he was but the translator of the Arabic verses. There is little in the piece that is completely original; Burton was not an original thinker. What he did was essentially what Edward Fitzgerald had done in the *Rubaiyat of Omar Khayyam*. If we pass over *Stone Talk*, *The Kasîdah* was the only piece of original verse he ever published, yet much of his fame rests upon it. Of the more than forty books he was to write or translate, only this one has remained continuously in print and can be purchased today through any bookstore. Of the millions of words he wrote and published, only some verses from *The Kasîdah* are ever quoted and they can be found in Bartlett's *Familiar Quotations*. Yet, the first review of the book, which was privately printed, did not appear until twenty years after its first publication, and of the first edition less than one hundred copies were sold.

In *The Kasîdah* Burton expounds his belief in a creator, but at the same time denies the existence of a God:

Gold in Midian 1876 – 80

And still the Weaver plies his loom,
whose warp and woof is wretched Man
Weaving th' unpattern'd dark design,
so dark we doubt it owns a plan.

There is no God, no man-made God;
a bigger, stronger, crueller man;
Black phantom of our baby-fears,
ere Thought, the life of Life, began.

He talks of morality:

There is no Good, there is no Bad;
these be the whims of mortal will:
What works me weal that call I 'good,'
What harms and hurts I hold as 'ill':

And of faith:

All Faith is false, all Faith is true:
Truth is the shattered mirror shown
In myriad bits; while each believes
his little bit the whole to own.

Of souls and evolution:

The race of Be'ing from dawn of Life
in an unbroken course was run;
What men are pleased to call their Souls
was in the hog and dog begun:

Of how man's desire for life beyond death created religious institutions:

Hence came the despot's darling dream
a Church to rule and sway the state;
Hence sprang the train of countless griefs
in priestly sway and rule innate.

And then there was a bit of personal creed in a verse that constitutes the best known lines of Burton:

Do what thy manhood bids thee do,
from none but self expect applause;
He noblest lives and noblest dies
who makes and keeps his self-made laws.

In the last set of verses there is some preaching – odd in Burton, who, although he argued with everyone concerning intellectual

343

matters, never attempted to impose his religious beliefs on anyone, not even his wife. In these final verses he gives a mystical crystallization of his years of study of the world's religions:

> *Pluck the old woman from thy breast:*
> *be stout in woe, be stark in weal;*
> *Do good for Good is good to do;*
> *spurn bribe of Heav'en and threat of Hell.*

> *To seek the True, to glad the heart*
> *which is of life the* HIGHER LAW,
> *Whose differ'ence is the Man's degree,*
> *the Man of gold, the Man of straw.*

Although there is evidence that Burton began *The Kasîdah* many years earlier, he did not finish the work until November 1880. While polishing up *The Kasîdah* – and this piece, unlike most of his books, is indeed a polished work – he must have been, at the same time, carrying on his disappointing correspondence with Riaz Pasha, President of the Council of Ministers of Egypt, concerning his gold-mining concession in Midian.

Early in January 1880, Burton was once more in Egypt. Ismail had been forced to abdicate and Tewfik was the new Khedive. There were no more personal audiences. From Shepheard's Hotel he wrote to Riaz Pasha asking for a concession and authorization to form a company to exploit the gold he was still sure was to be found in great abundance in Midian. Thus began a correspondence in French, which lasted from 5 January until 27 February 1880. Riaz Pasha's reply was to ask for more specific details of the mines Burton proposed to exploit. Burton said he wanted the mining concession for a strip, twenty miles wide, extending from Aqaba to Wejh; he also asked Riaz Pasha to hurry as time was being wasted. Two weeks later Riaz Pasha replied that the Council of Ministers had refused his request. This was an unexpected blow. Burton was desperate. He sent off two more letters in which he tried to throw an official British government cloak over his personal venture. He reminded Riaz that the council's decision adversely affected '*les intérêts d'un sujet d'une Puissance Amie*' and that Ismail had engaged him with the consent of the British government. He also commented on the fact that he had not been reimbursed for many of his expenses on the two expeditions to Midian and that he was a man of some reputation in the world. But Riaz Pasha knew that Burton was not representing his own government in any way in this matter and he ignored the veiled threat of adverse publicity as well as the question of the expenses of the Midian expedition. There were more letters, but Riaz Pasha tired of the correspondence and refused to answer.

Writing from Lausanne in March 1880, Gordon told Burton he was not surprised he had 'failed with Tewfik' and he called Riaz Pasha a 'dancing boy'. But Burton was bitterly disappointed. All of his great golden dreams had ended in nothing. Perhaps it was at this time that he wrote in *The Kasîdah*:

> *How every high heroic Thought*
> > *that longed to breathe empyrean air,*
> *Failed of its feathers, fell to earth,*
> > *and perisht of a sheer despair;*

In *The Kasîdah* Burton gives a fictional biography of Haji Abou in which he described the author of the distichs: 'Briefly, his memory was well-stored; and he had every talent save that of using his talents.' Such was Burton's not unrealistic impression of himself.

Chapter 23

Literature and Last Expeditions
1880 – 5

BURTON appears to have stayed in Egypt until about May of 1880 before returning, defeated, to Trieste and his mountain retreat at Opicina. There is no substitute for a loving wife to help a man when he is licking his wounds and struggling to retain his self-confidence. Isabel's faith in her husband never wavered, and no one was better equipped to restore his spirits. She loved every minute of it. 'I can never remember to have had a more peaceful and happy time with Richard than in Opçina, where we led a Darby and Joan life. . . . We did all the six volumes of Camoens, he translating, I helping him and correcting.'

The astonishing versatility and energy of Burton is almost incredible. In good times and in bad, in sickness or good health, he was always on the move and yet he was always writing. Always there was some literary work at hand, the results of his travels or the putting together of his notes on one or another of the many subjects in which he was interested. In this last decade of his life he turned more and more to projects he had long considered writing but had never found the time to complete. *The Kasîdah*, the life and works of Camoens, *The Book of the Sword*, and *The Arabian Nights* were all books on which he had made notes for years, and had thought much about. All dealt with subjects in which he took a passionate interest. They stand in marked contrast to his hastily written travel books. They are also quite different in quality from those books which were concerned with subjects of more or less passing interests, such as *Etruscan Bologna* and *Wit and Wisdom from West Africa*, and controversial works such as *The Nile Basin*. These later works, the fruits of a well-stocked mind carefully considered, show very clearly what Burton might have achieved had he been more self-disciplined and less travelled. Certainly his popularity as an author, both in his own age and in ours, would have been considerably greater. But this is asking too much of any one man: it is too difficult to be both doer and teller. Few men indeed have

346

managed to achieve such successes as he in both the fields of action and scholarship in the course of one lifetime.

It is natural that Burton's one biography should be of a man whom he considered most like himself. Luis Vaz de Camoens (or 'Camões' in the modern spelling) was, like Burton, both a man of action and a scholar. But unlike Burton, Camoens did not achieve any notable success in the world of action; he discovered no Lake Tanganyika. By applying himself to poetry he became one of the greatest lyric poets of the sixteenth century, occupying a position in Portuguese literature comparable to that of Shakespeare in English literature.

Camoens was born about 1524, probably in Lisbon. He served two years in the army in North Africa, where he lost his right eye, and then enrolled as a student at Coimbra University. His love-life appears to have been spectacular; he wrote poems to many women of all classes, including one to a Chinese slave-girl. In 1552 he wounded a court official in a duel and was sent to prison for eight months. Three weeks after his release he again joined the army and set out for Goa. There he took part in Portuguese expeditions on the Malabar coast and in the Red Sea. In Goa, too, he began to write his great epic, *The Lusiads*. After serving in Macao in a civil position for a while, he returned to Goa, suffering shipwreck on the way. In 1567 the penniless Camoens left Goa for Mozambique. Three years later he returned to Lisbon, and in 1572 he published *The Lusiads*. Eight years later he died of the plague in a Lisbon hospital and was buried with other victims in a common grave. Bones believed to be his now rest beside those of his kinsman and hero, Vasco da Gama, in Jeronimos Convent at Belem.

Burton called Camoens 'my master' and it is perhaps significant that the only master he ever acknowledged had been dead for nearly three centuries. But there is an indisputable resemblance between the temperaments of the two men: both were adventurous, loved poetry and had a passion for travel. Both, too, were interested in literary and scientific knowledge and, to judge from *The Lusiads*, Camoens was as eclectic as his century would allow him in his religious inclinations.

Burton had long been interested in Camoens and may have begun his translation of *The Lusiads* as early as 1847. In a letter to his publisher (27 October 1880) he said, 'It is the work, off and on, of some twenty years!' The first edition of 1880 was followed by an enlarged edition in 1881 that included a biography of Camoens and in 1884 by a translation of *The Lyricks*. He was not the first to try his hand at putting the complex verses into English; Sir Richard Fenshawe had made the first English translation in 1665. Burton was aware of this edition, as he was of all the other translations of Camoens that had been made into European languages. The remains of his library show that he owned them all. Burton thought he could produce a better one.

The Lusiads is an epic poem modelled on the *Aeneid* describing a part of the voyage of Vasco da Gama. But it is more than a simple story; Camoens makes the poem a history of the Portuguese nation by blending the historical with the contemporary, the classic with the modern, realism with a neo-platonic mysticism, paganism with christianity. Much of this blending strikes the present-day reader as simply ludicrous. At one point in the epic the Greek god Bacchus, disguised as an Arab sheik in Mozambique, gives advice to a Moslem sultan who is angry with Da Gama because he is Christian.

Burton's translation does little if anything, to make the text clearer. On the title page of *The Lyricks* is written: 'Englished by Richard F. Burton.' The word 'Englished' is also used to describe the translation of *The Lusiads*. Burton chose to use this word instead of 'translated', so as to indicate that his was a literal translation, although 'Burtoned' might have been more apt: there is scarcely a line that does not contain an esoteric, archaic or coined word. Some are quite choice. Take, 'kye', 'eyen', 'commoved', 'surquedry' and 'stounds'. He also used obsolete spellings, such as 'syne' (for sin), 'Ladye' and 'musisk', just for the quaintness. For those who feel that poetry must be spoken to obtain the full beauty of the lines, there are such words as 'hope-lessest' and 'consentedst'. Camoens experimented with a wide variety of metrical forms in which Burton took great interest, often sacrificing sense for form. Isabel realized how difficult it would be for even an educated and widely read reader to make his way unaided through her husband's translation, so she compiled a glossary to go with it. Burton would not accept it: 'You are never going to insult the English public with that,' he said.

When *Camoens: His Life and His Lusiads* appeared, Swinburne wrote to Isabel saying:

Congratulations to Burton on having in that translation, as I think, matched Byron on his own chosen ground as a translator, and beaten him at his own weapon. The version of Pulci's 'Morgante', on which Byron prided himself so greatly as being, in his own words, the best translation that ever was or will be made, is an infinitely less important, and I should think less difficult attempt on exactly the same lines of work, and, certainly, to say the least, not more successful, as far as one can judge, without knowledge of Camoens in the original language.

Three years later when *The Lyricks* was published and dedicated to Swinburne, the poet wrote to Burton saying, 'The learning and research of your work are in many points beyond all praise of mine, but not more notable than the strength and skill that wield them.'

Swinburne was a better poet than he was a critic. Being a close friend of Burton he could not do otherwise than praise the work. The books are dull and as difficult to read as Spencer's *Faerie Queene*. But in justice it must be said that translations of poetry are always difficult and rarely can they approach the merit of the original. Camoens appears to present unusual difficulties and it may well be that Burton attempted the impossible. If Burton produced a bad translation, no one since has been able to produce a better one.

In the same year that the first books on Camoens appeared, Burton brought out a thin volume entitled *A Glance at the "Passion-Play"*. This was the result of his visit with Isabel to see the famous Passion Play at Oberammergau in 1880. Isabel wrote her version of the experience and the original idea was that the two versions should be published together as 'Ober-Ammergau as seen by four eyes'. Isabel said, 'He wrote the cynical and I the religious side, but as the man who printed them [W. H. Harrison] was too poor to produce the two, he published Richard's.'

In the year 1633 the Black Death entered the small Alpine village of Oberammergau. It was then the villagers vowed they would perform every decade a play based on the suffering of Christ if only God would deliver them from this calamity. As a result of keeping this promise, the village has been able to enjoy a period of intense prosperity and increasing fame every ten years. The last performance, in 1960, contained a cast with 125 speaking parts and gave eighty-five performances, each of which lasted for twelve hours, and was attended by nearly 100,000 people.

The Burtons made the pilgrimage in August 1880. Burton went, he said, 'neither to scoff nor to pray' but to see if he could 'trace some affinity between the survival of the Christian "Mystery" and the living scenes of El-Islam at Meccah'. Nevertheless, he appears to have been in a critical mood from the very beginning. Reduced now to lesser travels, he found much fault with minor discomforts: a habit that was to increase as he grew older and his trips became easier. Among his bits of advice to fellow-travellers is the warning: 'In Bavaria do not forget a hard pillow, unless you would rest your head upon a down bag which appears to have the consistency of custard.'

On the way there were the usual turmoils caused by Isabel's hatred of cruelty to animals. At one point she was 'told to mind her own business by a carter, with whom she remonstrated for ill-treating his beast'. When they reached Oberammergau, Burton was not particularly pleased by the place: 'I suspect that the climate is feverish. . . . In the village, of course, there is consumption.'

When the plays began, Burton was in no mood to enjoy them, and when they ended he wrote, 'I felt weary, with a brain oppressed by the manifold scenes of eight hours . . . and, as all know, nothing fatigues so much as sight-seeing, especially as picture-seeing.' He was not pleased by the drama: 'The utter absence of local colour and of chronological truth . . . revolts the traveller.' The amateur actors come in for very hard criticism: 'The large, surly-faced, coarse women require nothing but beards to make full-grown grenadiers.' He thought 'Moses is not what he should be' and that 'the Roman soldiers are triumphs of "anachronistic impropriety"'. No one recognized the Archangel Raphael, he said, because he did not have wings; he suggested that perhaps he had lately moulted. He also thought that 'the scourging is altogether without realism'.

Isabel's reaction, of course, was somewhat different: 'Suffice it to say, that the simplicity of a theatre in the open air was most realistic. . . . The men acted beautifully. . . . I can only say that I thanked God for having been allowed to see it. . . . I am not ashamed to say that I sobbed bitterly. . . . The penitent thief on the Cross, and Judas's despair, I shall never forget all my life. With all Richard's cynicism, he was right glad to have seen it.'

The Burtons returned to Trieste in time to greet a number of old friends who came to visit them, including J. J. Aubertin who had now apparently retired from India, and was himself preparing a translation of Camoens' sonnets. The first bound copy of the finished product, *Seventy Sonnets of Camoens* was presented by Aubertin to Burton on 5 March 1881. Back home, the Burtons gave a little party for the old vice-consul who was celebrating his fiftieth year at Trieste. Isabel and the wife of an English merchant in town went around collecting money for 'our dear old Vice-Consul Mr. Brock'. Isabel was able to present a purse of £170 to the man who did all the work for which her husband was paid. 'The dear old man was so much affected that I was afraid he would have a fit,' Isabel reported. 'He could not sign a Consular report for two hours after.'

It was old Brock who was left in charge of the consulate when Burton was away – which was most of the time. Earlier in this same year, when Burton was in Cairo carrying on his negotiations with Riaz Pasha about the gold mine concessions – and doing many other things, such as visiting Coptic convents and studying the still existing though illegal slave traffic – he made his only extant reference to Brock in a letter to Lord Granville written in May 1880, which indicated that he did pay the old man something for running the consulate for him.

The letter which mentions Brock is remarkable in many other respects as well. Burton was not altogether convinced that slavery was a bad institution. He had, in fact, frequently pointed out its virtues. Yet, we now find him recommending himself to his superior as the man to stamp out the slave trade in the Red Sea area:

The Ministry under Riaz Pasha is doing all it can to abolish Colonel Gordon's fine anti-slavery work for the last six years. They have sent up a certain Rauf Pasha, almost a black, who will have no weight whatever; and the Red Sea will be in a worse state than ever unless some measures are soon taken; and slave-trade is speedily reviving in the Soudan and the Red Sea. The Ministry wishes to drive out all foreigners, and this makes times in Egypt harder than ever.

I would like to have a temporary appointment in the Red Sea as Slave Commissioner. I want a salary of from £1600 to £2000 a year (£1600 would do if allowed to keep Trieste on half-pay, £350 per annum), the use of a gun-boat, and a roving commission, independent of the Consul-General of Egypt, but to act in concert with a Consul (such as young Wylde) appointed to the Soudan. It is a thing that has long been talked about as a great want in the Red Sea, *if slavery is really to be exterminated,* and Gordon's splendid work to be carried out on the coast. Gordon Pasha has long wished to recommend *me* for this work. As this last appointment would only be *temporary* – say for a couple of years – I would like to be allowed to keep Trieste to fall back upon when my work is done, and as a home for my wife when she can not be with me. Other men are allowed to retain their Indian appointments, and still to take temporary service in Egypt: for this there are several precedents. Mr. Brock, Vice-Consul at Trieste, who is thoroughly reliable, would act for me on half-pay, as he has done the last forty years. I guarantee that, placed in such a position, in *two years'* time the Red Sea *shall be as clear of slaves as if slavery had never existed.*

Here again Burton had no thought of his lack of ability to command. Fortunately for him, Lord Granville did not give him the opportunity to make good a promise he would never have been able to fulfil. But perhaps Burton really had something else besides slavery in mind when he proposed this commission for himself. If he had received the assignment on the terms he requested he would certainly have exerted an influence over what he regarded as 'the retrograde Ministry of Riaz Pasha'. The slave trade undoubtedly existed in the Red Sea area and Egypt undoubtedly did nothing to prevent it. Burton would have been able to make his headquarters in Midian, to cause no end of embarrassment to the Egyptian Government by reporting what he could easily learn of the trade, and, by being independent of the British Consul-General in Cairo, he would be, in effect, the virtual governor of the very area in which he sought a large gold-mining concession. He would have two years to explore the area and obtain a concession which he could work after the termination of his commission. Perhaps Lord Granville had this in mind as well when he rejected Burton's proposal.

In addition to mining, Burton also had other schemes for exploiting the wealth of Midian. It does not appear that he ever mentioned to the Khedive or the Egyptian Government the fact that he found oil in Midian, but he had sent samples of crude oil he found there to the firm of George Binnie & Co. in Glasgow and on 10 December 1879, he received back a most encouraging reply: 'We think if such crude oil can be had in sufficient quantities that it is certainly worth while to erect machinery to refine it on the spot and it ought to pay well if properly gone about.' Burton now began to think seriously of forming a company to exploit the oil and engaged in a long correspondence in 1880 – 1 with a Mr C. G. Cleminshaw regarding this scheme. But nothing came of it.

Strangely enough, it was silver Burton regarded as the metal for which he had a personal affinity. He believed that everyone had a particular metal which influenced him and that silver was his own metal. He would put silver florins on his eyes when they ached from too much reading, and he would bind them on his feet and legs when he had an attack of gout. But it was thoughts of gold which obsessed him, and his last expedition was to be another search for it.

It was at this time that an 'Anecdotal Photograph' of Burton appeared in a magazine called *Truth*. Isabel wrote to them to protest because they had said he had a bruise on his head instead of a spear wound on his cheek. She also claimed for Burton a virtue he did not possess: modesty. Of her husband, who had at this point written twenty-two books about himself and his adventures, she said, 'Captain Burton usually spares Society any allusion to his adventures.'

The year 1881 was spent with his writing and with fitful excursions about Europe, visiting a scientific congress in Salzburg, studying bees with a Father Pauletic at a deaf and dumb institute, examining prehistoric ruins in Istria, and visiting friends. He had to keep moving.

The Burtons were sitting down to dinner in a hotel restaurant in Vienna one day when they saw Rev. G. L. Johnson, Chaplain of the British Embassy at Vienna on the staff of Burton's immediate superior. Being absent without leave, as usual, Burton was afraid he would be seen and that the chaplain would report his unauthorized presence to his chief. In a fright, he bolted the table and went to his hotel room. Isabel, braver than her husband in such matters, took the bull by the horns and went up to him. When she explained the situation to Johnson, he laughed and said, 'My dear child, I am just doing exactly the same thing myself.' It was not quite the same since the Chaplain was at least in the town where he was stationed, but Isabel ran upstairs to bring back her worried husband. The position of consul was not much for a man of Burton's largeness of outlook, but it was all he had, he was near retirement, he would have found it difficult indeed to find another job that would allow him the leisure he was able to take in his present position, and he was thus in great fear of losing it. But nothing could prevent him from travelling.

Early in September 1881, the Burtons went from Vienna to Venice to attend a geographical congress. There, by accident or design, they met Captain Verney Lovett Cameron, RN, who since their last meeting had won the gold medal of the Royal Geographical Society for his explorations in Central Africa. Five years earlier Cameron had crossed the breadth of Africa from sea to sea, the first European to do so. Neither Burton nor Cameron had been asked to speak at the congress and both felt slighted. One day the Burtons and Cameron went on a picnic at the Lido and found that many of the most distinguished and stuffiest people from the geographical congress were also there. Under their noses, Cameron, age thirty-six, and Burton, age sixty, both took off their shoes and stockings and sat down to make mud pies. Burton pointed to his and called out to Isabel, 'Look, nurse, we have made such a beautiful pie.' And Cameron yelled, 'Please tell Dick not to touch my spade.'

At the congress itself Burton left his card on which he wrote:

We're Saville Row's selected few
Let all the rest be damned;
The pit is good enough for you,
We won't have boxes crammed.

He still loved to play the *enfant terrible*. A story is told that once in Trieste when Isabel was giving a tea attended by some of the town's best society Burton entered the room and casually put down a manuscript on which he had apparently been working. Society could not resist a look. The title page said: 'A History of Farting.'

Cameron and Burton had, or found, a more serious purpose for being together in Venice. Just how it came about that Cameron and Burton were sent to the Gold Coast (present-day Ghana) on behalf of the Guinea Coast Gold Mining Company is not clear, but the plans to do so were apparently developed in Venice. The patron of this expedition appears to have been James Irvine, a Liverpool merchant and director of the mining company, whom Burton had met on the Oil Rivers when he was consul at Fernando Po. On 24 September, when the Burtons returned to Trieste, Cameron went with them. They completed their plan and Cameron left for England to gather his equipment and arrange his affairs.

On 18 November 1881, Burton sailed from Trieste for the Gold Coast. His superiors had apparently resigned themselves to putting up with him and this meant giving him frequent leaves of absence in addition to the unauthorized leaves he took, undoubtedly with their knowledge. 'The Foreign Office liberally gave me leave to escape the winter of Trieste,' he wrote. As a matter of fact, he pleaded ill health, but, as someone once said to him, 'You are certainly the first that ever applied to seek health in the "genial and congenial climate" of the West African Coast.' It will be recalled that he complained loudly of the ill effects of that same climate when he was stationed in the area.

He stopped off for a week in Lisbon where he spent most of his time examining the collection of Camoens material in the Biblioteca Nacional. Then he went on to Madeira where Cameron joined him. They reached Axim on the Gold Coast on 25 January 1882. Burton had intended to do some exploring further inland, but they found so much of interest along the coast and upon the Ancobra River that they did not have time. By this time of life Burton was more interested in wealth than in exploration. As he said, 'Geography is good, but gold is better.' Besides, he came down with fever.

Burton was enthralled by the gold-mining prospects of this region which he described as 'far richer than the most glowing descriptions had presented it. Gold and other metals are there in abundance, and there are good signs of diamond, ruby, and sapphire.' Here at last was the untapped gold he had so long sought:

We are truly in the Land of Gold, in an Old New California. . . . Any one who has eyes to see can assure himself that Axim is the threshold of the Gold-region. It abounds in diorite, a rock usually associated with the best paying lodes. After heavy showers the naked eye can note spangles of the precious metal in the street-roads. You can pan it out of the wall-swish. . . . The whole land is impregnated with the precious metal. I found it richer in sedimentary gold than California was in 1859.

Burton also believed he knew the way to get at the gold and bring it out in large quantities: through hydraulic sluicing.

This time he was right. The land was indeed full of gold. Twenty years later it began to be brought out in great quantities and it was done by using the very methods he recommended. Also, as he suspected, there were diamonds to be found there as well. He sent in a glowing report to the Guinea Coast Gold Mining Company, but they decided to send out a consulting engineer to check his conclusions. The engineer disagreed with Burton and the company decided to believe the engineer.

Cameron and Burton appear to have done their work with thoroughness and enthusiasm. Cameron surveyed the concessions and Burton settled the legal claims, dealing with the local tribal chiefs. Burton remained in the area less than two months. On 4 March they both came down sick and returned to the coast. Cameron went back inland, but Burton decided that he had seen enough and went off on a visit to Fernando Po and the Oil Rivers and then on to Madeira to wait for his companion.

The literary result of this expedition was, of course, another two volume book: *To the Gold Coast for Gold*. The title not withstanding, only 162 of the 725 pages actually deal with Burton's experiences on the Gold Coast. Although both Burton and Cameron are listed as authors, Cameron actually appears to have written only sixty-eight pages. The bulk of the book consists of notes on Madeira, the Canary Islands and the coastal towns at which they stopped (sometimes for only a day) on their way to the Gold Coast. It is, in fact, much like *Wanderings in West Africa* and contains a number of notes made nearly twenty years earlier. Like the earlier book, this one was also full of Burton's opinions and prejudices. Most of them had changed very little.

The man who only a few months earlier had asked to be allowed to stamp out the slave trade in the Red Sea area now wrote, 'Serfdom, like cannibalism and polygamy, are the steps by which human society rose to its present status: to abuse them is ignorantly to kick down the ladder. The spirit of Christianity may tend to abolish servitude; but the letter distinctly admits it.'

During the American Civil War Burton's sympathies had been with the South and he was ever contemptuous of the Union, whose flag he referred to as the 'oysters and gridiron'. One evening he talked with some Liberians, whose country he called 'the Yankee-Doodle-niggery colony, peopled by citizens who are not "subjects"'. His opinions regarding the United States were tied up with his ideas concerning negroes and those of mixed blood: 'Had the Southern States of America deported all the products of "miscegenation", instead of keeping them in servitude, the "patriarchal institution" might have lasted to this day instead of being prematurely abolished.'

He was not above comparing peoples whose only similarity was in that they were both looked down upon by Richard Burton. 'The men are the usual curious compound of credulity and distrust, hope and fatalism, energy and inaction, which make the Negro so like the Irish character.'

At Bathurst, Gambia, his conservative instincts were outraged by the fact that the townspeople had 'organized "companies", the worst of trade unions, elected headmen, indulged in strikes'. For workers in the gold mines of his dreams he advocated the importation of Chinese coolies.

In whatever lands he visited, whether Iceland, England or Arabia, he found the most annoying members of any community to be the children. Isabel maintained that he liked children and that children adored him, but there is certainly no evidence of this in his own writings; quite the contrary, in fact. In Axim he wrote, 'The gorbellied children are the pests of the settlement. At early dawn they roar because they awake hungry and thirsty; they roar during the day when washed with cold water, and in the evening they roar because they are tired and sleepy. They are utterly spoiled. They fight like little Britons; they punch their mothers at three years of age; and, when strong enough, they "square up" to their fathers.' The reaction of a child to Burton is remembered by Sir Harold Nicolson who as a small boy met Burton and was terrified. 'I remember that he once seized me by the shoulders and thrust his dark face close to mine; I can still recall the glitter and the bristles of his eyes; I screamed and screamed until Lady Burton, large and benign in her dove-coloured silk frock, bundled out to rescue me.'

The failure of *To the Gold Coast for Gold*, like most of his other books, lies basically in the fact that, being more learned than wise, he never realized that knowledge alone is not wisdom, and that catalogues of fact and opinion do not, in themselves, constitute literature.

On 12 May 1882, Cameron arrived in Madeira and eight days later the two of them reached Liverpool where Isabel, who had arrived five days earlier from Trieste, and James Irvine were on hand to meet them. Isabel had not had an easy time of it during her husband's absence. She had been ill – with the beginning of the cancer that would kill her – and she had got into trouble with the Austrian authorities. She had received a summons one day telling her to appear before the tribunal. She replied that she was too sick to appear. She wondered what she could have done. When the tribunal came to see her she found out: they showed her a letter she had written to Arthur Evans, the British archaeologist who was later to become famous for his excavation of the palace of Knossos and his discovery of a pre-Phoenician script in Crete. At this time he was thirty-one years old and was studying the archaeology of the Balkan states and the ethnological conditions of their peoples. He became somewhat too involved with current political affairs, however, and, suspected of complicity in a Dalmatian rebellion, was in danger of being arrested by the Austrian authorities. Isabel had written to warn him of his danger, but the mail was slow between Trieste and Herzegovina and her letter arrived too late; Evans had already been arrested and her letter fell into the hands of the authorities who now wanted to know what part Isabel played in the conspiracy. Isabel could only reply, 'I only know that I heard some of the officers here saying that he was meddling in what did not concern him, and that, if they could catch him off civilized ground, they would hang him up to the first tree, and as I know his wife and her family, and they are my compatriots, I thought I would write and say to him, "What are you doing? Whatever it is, leave it off, as you are incurring ill will in Austria by it".' In those simpler days, Isabel's explanation was accepted and she was let off.

Burton's passion for gold mining was one of his interests that Isabel did not share, although she had taken pains to learn a great deal about it and had herself been involved in the paperwork since their days in Brazil. 'I was always sorry when he got on the mine track, because he always ended in one way,' she said. 'He did his work in his simple, gentlemanly, scientific way, fully knowing the value of the mine, but nothing about business.' She was not surprised when this latest hopeful venture collapsed, although the process took several years. In the meantime Burton proposed that the government appoint him governor of the Gold Coast, give him half a regiment of West Indian troops and not pry too closely into his affairs; the result he promised was vast quantities of gold for the coffers of Britain. No, no, said the Foreign Office.

Although Burton had requested leave to escape the hard Trieste winter, he stayed away through spring and summer as well, not returning to Trieste until September of 1882. The Burtons remained in England until mid-July, then they travelled about the Continent, taking various cures for their different ailments. Even the general public was beginning to wonder when Burton discharged his consular duties and *Vanity Fair* called him an 'Amateur Consul'. Writing from Bohemia to answer the charge, Isabel said:

It is true that Government has sometimes, but not often, spared him for a few months at a time to do larger works, which have been for more general public benefit and wider extended good; but all the journeys quoted in *Vanity Fair* have been undertaken *between* his various posts, when he has been out of employment, or during the usually *allowed* leave that *other* men spend in Pall Mall. On all other occasions when he has had 'leave' as above, he has gone *voluntarily* on half-pay those few months.

There is no evidence that Isabel ever told a lie concerning herself, but she did not hesitate to do so to defend her husband.

Burton now sat down to write a book for which he had voluminous notes and which he had considered writing for forty years: *The Book of the Sword*. It was planned as a three-volume work, but only the first volume was ever completed. It was a very scholarly work and experts today agree that had he completed his series it would be the definitive work on the subject. Unfortunately, the first small edition was unsuccessful and today copies are among the rarest of all Burton's books. In a letter to a friend he said, 'It has the high honour not only of being unread but also of being unreviewed – what articles have appeared are below contempt.' After his death, Burton's many notes for the other volumes were given to A. Forbes Sieveking to 'see through the press', but the notes were too disorganized and incomplete and he could do nothing with them.

On 27 October 1882, his work on *The Book of the Sword* was interrupted by an official telegram from London:

H.M. Government wish to avail themselves of your knowledge of Bedouins and the Sinai country to assist in search for Professor Palmer. There is a chance of his being still alive, though bodies of his companions, Charrington and Gill, have been found. Proceed at once to Ghazzeh. Place yourself in communication with Consul Moore who has gone from Jerusalem to institute inquiry.

This was the kind of summons for which Burton regarded himself as specially equipped to respond. Gout forgotten, he at once replied:

Ready to start by first steamer. Will draw £100. Want gunboat from Alexandria to Ghazzeh or Sinai. Letter follows.

Isabel gave him some wifely advice as she saw him off: 'Mind, if they are really dead, don't be put like a ferret into a hole to bring out the dead bodies. That won't be worth while.'

Burton said, 'If they are dead, no; but if there is a chance of saving dear old Palmer, I will go anywhere and do anything.'

If the British governments of the last century often neglected brilliant and capable men it was perhaps because there were so many of them. What most amazes anyone looking back at this constellation of talented men was the extraordinary versatility they displayed. In the ranks of such men was Edward Henry Palmer, a linguist, professor, journalist, explorer, draughtsman, conjurer, author, poet and more besides before he met violent death at the age of forty-two on a secret mission for his government in the Sinai desert.

Burton had first met Palmer in Syria twelve years before when Palmer had just come back from his first trip to the Sinai desert. Now Burton was off to search for him or his bones in that same desert. What Palmer was doing is still something of a mystery. There had been a revolt in Egypt and he had first been sent to keep the Bedouin tribes from joining the rebels and to prevent them from attacking the Suez Canal. In this he was apparently successful. Returning to Egypt, he was appointed chief interpreter for the British forces. Then, with Captain William John Gill and Flag Lieutenant Harold Charrington, he was sent back into the desert to procure camels and, apparently, to attempt to buy the allegiance of a number of other Bedouin tribes. Probably the large amount of money they carried with them caused their deaths.

Burton was prepared for a dramatic expedition, but he did not get past Egypt. Charles Warren, another extraordinary Briton, was in the field before him. Although Warren did not find Palmer's bones, he did find enough evidence (including an old truss of Palmer's and a stocking of Charrington's containing part of his foot) to indicate that the entire party had been waylaid; the chances of Palmer being alive were too remote to be considered. Burton, his services not needed, returned to Trieste on 10 December, only six weeks after his departure. He wrote an article about the trip which told of the Palmer expedition and Warren's work but dealt mostly with the problems of Egypt and his own ideas on how they should be solved – including a proposal that 3,000 London 'bobbies' should be sent to keep order in Egyptian cities. The article was not published.

Back in Trieste, Burton found fault with the large apartment Isabel had created and said they should move. Isabel did not want to move, but she complied. They took a large house where Burton insisted on taking the biggest room for his bedroom, which he divided into four areas: one for sleeping, one for dressing, one for writing and another for breakfasting. It was four years before Isabel could dislodge him from this room, which she considered too drafty, and get him into the second largest room in the house.

Old age and the effects of an exceptionally active life were beginning to make themselves felt. He received a letter from Gordon written on 3 June 1883, saying, 'Sorry, that £.s.d. keep you away from the East, for there is much to interest here in every way, and you would be useful to me as an encyclopaedia of oriental lore.' But it was not money that now kept Burton chained to civilization. His gout was worse; he had to give up fencing and swimming; and he had become increasingly irritable. From now on he was forced to lead a life of comparative stability, kept close to home by gout, wife and government.

Isabel said that Burton was 'not only the best husband that ever lived, but the pleasantest man to live with and the easiest'. She undoubtedly believed this, but it took a unique character to be Mrs Burton. It seems doubtful that any other woman but Isabel could have made a happy marriage with him. She bowed to his desires and was proud of her submission. 'I am glad to say there was only *one* will in the house, and that was *his*,' she said. On his part, he undoubtedly loved her and appreciated her, but it was not in his nature to pay her compliments. He had a number of minor eccentricities that must have made living with him difficult at times. There was a streak of asceticism in him. If anyone brought a bouquet of flowers into the house, he threw them out, although he would sometimes himself bring in a single wild flower or a weed and put it in a vase of water. If Isabel put something she considered pretty in his room, he would move it out in the hall. He liked new clothes, but insisted on wearing old, shabby hats. He bought dozens of greatcoats, but seldom wore any of them as he wanted to 'keep hardy'. He had a great love of boots and once owned a hundred pairs. For eighteen years he carried around a single fencing-shoe, the mate to which he had lost, and he would ask cobblers all over the world to make him a shoe to match. As there is a superstition among some cobblers about this – apparently more common in Burton's day than now – he was amused to find that no cobbler would do it. He always ate the local food when he travelled, but at home his favourite foods were cod and sauerkraut. Isabel objected because they made the house smell, but she served them. The only food he would not eat was honey. He was one of those people who could exist with very little sleep. Isabel said that 'for the first twenty-two years of my married life, I made our early tea at any time from three to half-past five (and if I happened to go to a ball I did not find it worth while to go to bed)'.

Isabel kept all the money in the family and Burton never knew how much he had or how much he owed. Isabel once said, 'He was born to be rich, and he liked to be thought rich.' But he would sometimes joke to his friends that his wife sent him out with only half a crown. Sometimes when he made a little profit from a book or an article he would hide the money away; it was usually lost or stolen.

In his early life he always carried about heavy objects – a thick, heavy stick; an elephant gun that weighed twenty-four pounds, a pipe that held a quarter of a pound of tobacco – but in his old age he took to buying small, dainty things: 'more fit for a doll's house than for a man', according to Isabel. His handwriting also became smaller and smaller as he grew older.

His health grew worse as he was beset by unrecognized diseases, but his condition would alternate between periods of good health and sickness. When he was well he insisted on acting as he had always acted and refused to take care of himself. It was very difficult for him to realize that he was becoming an invalid. Isabel said, 'Foreign doctors do not understand English constitutions', and, in spite of her own poor health, she nursed him tenderly. On 4 February 1884, Burton temporarily lost the use of his legs. Now his tremendous energies could be directed in only one direction: writing. On 18 April he began to put together for publication his translation of the *Book of the Thousand Nights and a Night*, popularly called *The Arabian Nights*.

He had first begun work on the *Nights* thirty-two years earlier when

he and John Steinhaeuser had agreed to collaborate on a joint translation, Burton translating the poetry and Steinhaeuser the prose. They
corresponded on the subject for years, but when Steinhaeuser died his
papers were dispersed and very little of his work came into Burton's
hands. Burton continued to work on the translation alone, off and on,
until 1881 when he saw in a magazine that John Payne (1842–1916) had
also been working on a translation and was about to publish. Neither
man had until then been aware of the activities of the other. In November 1881, Burton wrote to Payne, giving him precedence and clear
possession of the field. He did this because there still burned within him
the coal of professional ambition and he felt that 'literary labours, unpopular with the vulgar and the half-educated, are not likely to help a
man up the ladder of promotion.'

He knew now, at last and alas, that there would be no more expeditions; he knew now, although he refused to admit it, that he would
never climb higher on the professional ladder. On 6 December 1883, he
wrote in his diary in red ink, 'This day eleven years ago I came here.
What a shame!!!' He had to admit, 'I was not a success.' Pride caused
him to put this in the past rather than the present tense and he denied
that he should be ashamed of his failure, claiming that 'in our day we
live under a despotism of the lower "middle class"' and only medio-
crities succeeded. Burton was bitter, and now that he was nearing the
end of his career he took fewer pains to conceal his feelings. Speaking
of the Foreign Office that still employed him, he said, 'It is hard for an
outsider to realize how perfect is the monopoly of commonplace, and
to comprehend how fatal a stumbling-stone that man sets in the way of
his own advancement who dares to think for himself, or who knows
more or who does more than the mob of gentlemen-employés who
know very little and do even less.' He now felt that there existed no
reason why he should not bring out his own translation of *The Arabian
Nights* – none, except that he had given the field to Payne. Burton's
only justification for bringing out his work so soon after Payne's was
that Payne's edition was limited to 500 copies and Payne had not fully
annotated his translation; also, Burton wanted to make his version 'a
book whose speciality is anthropology'.

Since *The Arabian Nights* is actually a collection of anonymous folk
tales, there does not exist a single complete written source. In compiling
his version, Burton used no less than twenty-one other translations and
manuscripts to make his ten volume work, and still more manuscripts
to produce his six-volume supplement.

The method used by Burton to bring his greatest literary work into the world was in many respects peculiar. The title-page of the original edition says, 'Printed by the Kamashastra Society for Private Subscribers Only.' A word of explanation is necessary concerning the Kamashastra (or Kāma Shāstra) Society. It was a very select society indeed, consisting only of Burton and his friend F. F. Arbuthnot, who probably supplied the capital for the venture. The purpose of the 'society' was to publish translations of oriental literature of an erotic nature and it existed only from 1883 until Burton's death.

'Kama' is the Hindu god of love (described by Burton in *Vikram and the Vampire* as 'the Hindu Cupid') and is usually depicted in Hindu art as a handsome youth riding a parrot and surrounded by nymphs; his bow is of sugar cane with a bowstring of bees, and each arrow is tipped with a flower. 'Shastra' means simply scriptures. Besides *The Arabian Nights*, the society published five other works: *Kama Sūtra* (1883), *Ananga Ranga* (1885), *The Perfumed Garden* (1886), *Behāristān* (1887) and *Gulistān* (1888). The first three were probably translated by Burton and Arbuthnot, although their names do not appear on the title-page or cover; the latter two books, although generally believed to have been translated by Burton, were actually translated by Edward Rehatsek, a friend of both Burton and Arbuthnot who had spent most of his life in India. The idea of publishing this type of literature in English translation occurred to Burton and Arbuthnot many years earlier and they had made at least one early attempt to publish a book in this field. In 1873 the *Aranga Ranga* (96 pages) was printed under the generic title of *Kāma Shāstra*. The title-page reads: 'Kāma-Shāstra or The Hindoo Art of Love (Ars Amoris Indica) Translated from the Sanskrit, and Annotated by A.F.F. and B.F.R. For Private Use of the Translators Only in Connection With a Work on the Hindoo Religion, and on the Manners and Customs of the Hindoos.' The initials of the translators, of course, are those of Arbuthnot and Burton in reverse. This book was never actually published, however, and only the existence of four sets of proofs show that the work reached this stage. When the printer read the proofs he became alarmed at the nature of the book and refused to print the edition. Using a more liberal-minded printer and under the label of the Kamashastra Society, the first volume of *A Plain and Literal Translation of the Arabian Nights' Entertainments, Now Entitled [sic] The Book of the Thousand Nights and a Night* appeared on 12 September 1885, six months after the time promised in the prospectus. Volume I was dedicated to John Frederick Steinhaeuser.

Chapter 24

The Arabian Nights
1885 – 8

THE translation of *The Arabian Nights* was a labour of love. It had to be. Isabel said, 'He loved his work, and he was sorry when it was finished.' He undoubtedly was. In the *Nights* Burton found escape – escape from his routine consular duties (such as they were), escape from unpleasant or uncongenial surroundings, escape from his over-solicitous wife and comfortable home, escape from the thoughts of what he might have been and the position in which he now found himself.

In his Foreword to the *Nights* he told how his work had been a charm against ennui and despondency during his 'long years of official banishment' in West Africa and Brazil. It became 'impossible even to open the pages without a vision starting into view' and 'the Jinn bore me at once to the land of my predilection, Arabia'. Sinking into this escape world populated by medieval Arabs, he brought forth into the light of Victorian Britain a unique masterpiece. The value of the work lies not in the excellence of the translation – others have produced more technically accurate versions – but in the spiritual and intellectual qualities which he brought to the stories. The *Nights* enabled him to make use of the vast storehouse of knowledge tucked away in his retentive memory and his over-laden notebooks, providing him with a vehicle to carry his ideas, opinions, prejudices, facts, fancies and a curio chest of anthropological oddities to a public that received them with astonishment and delight.

Burton was not the first person to attempt a translation of that collection of tales known in Arabic as *Alf Laylah Wa Laylah*, but his ten-volume work with its six-volume supplement is the most complete and the most famous; no one has attempted to duplicate his efforts since its publication. The first man to bring these stories to the attention of the Western world was Antoine Galland who, between 1704 and 1717, published *Mille et Une Nuits, Contes Arabes Traduits en Français*. It was designed for popular consumption and it proved very popular indeed; Galland's translation was in turn translated into other languages, including English. The first original effort in English was by Henry Torrens in 1838, but he died before he could complete his work. The man who might have made a translation as complete as Burton's was Edward William Lane, for he had a vast and intimate knowledge of Arabic life. But he was too timid: his translation, published between 1839 and 1841, was designed for 'the drawing-room table' and he 'thought it right to omit such tales, anecdotes, &c., as are comparatively uninteresting or on any account objectionable'.

Burton's only serious competitor was John Payne, who published his translation in 1882 – 4 through the Villon Society. Although Burton dedicated Volume II to Payne ('to express my admiration of your magnum opus . . .'), it was only natural that given Burton's temperament and capacity for criticism some of his caustic and unkind comments should result in a scholarly rivalry between the two men and their separate translations. This rivalry continues to exist today among those who still read the *Nights*, and outraged defenders of Payne point accusing fingers at Burton, claiming that he plagiarized whole passages from Payne's book – which he did.

Burton's object was 'to show what "The Thousand Nights and a Night" really is'. He aimed to 'preserve intact, not only the spirit, but even the *mécanique*, the manner and matter'. The structure of the *Nights* is not unique in either occidental or oriental literature, but in a work of such vast proportions it is often confusing to a modern reader. The story that provides the frame encompassing all the other tales is the familiar account of how the beautiful Shahrazad, the daughter of the Wazir, encouraged by her sister Dunyazad, so amused and delighted King Shahryar for 1001 nights by her story-telling that each morning he refrained from cutting off her head in order that he might hear the end of the story or the telling of a new tale she had promised him. King Shahryar had embarked upon his programme of executing maidens after a single night in his bed because he and his brother were convinced of the worthlessness of women. Presumably, the nimble-witted Shahrazad succeeded in proving that women are of some value, for in the end the king married her and, we hope, since each night's tale was interrupted only by the dawn, allowed them both to get some sleep.

The work as a whole is divided both artificially by the nights and somewhat more naturally by the unrelated stories. The interruption of the dawn causes the reader almost as much annoyance as it did King Shahryar since, as in a soap opera, the end of the last tale is repeated at the beginning of the next night's episode. Some stories continue for many nights.

The confusing aspect of the work is caused by the stories within stories within stories, like those schoolboys' tablets that show a picture of a boy holding the tablet, which in turn shows a boy holding the tablet, which in turn. . . . We have, for example, Shahrazad telling the story of 'The Fisherman and the Jinni' in which is told the 'Tale of the Wazir and the Sage Duban' in which is told three other stories. The reader must keep all of these frames in mind if he is to work his way out (successfully) to the original story knowing who is telling what story to whom.

Most English- and French-speaking persons, if asked to name the best-known tales from *The Arabian Nights*, would probably name 'Aladdin' and 'Ali Baba and the Forty Thieves'. Yet, curiously enough, 'Aladdin' is not at all like the familiar children's story and the story of Ali Baba does not appear at all – at least, no known Eastern manuscript of the tale exists. The story of Ali Baba first became known through the French version of Galland. While Galland's repute as an honest scholar would make it appear unlikely that he invented the tale, his source for the story has never been found. From the French both stories made their way in their familiar innocent form into English and were well known to English-speaking children long before Burton's day. A cynical guess would be that Galland himself altered Aladdin and invented Ali.

The great charm of Burton's translation, viewed as literature, lies in the veil of romance and exoticism he cast over the entire work. He tried hard to retain the flavour of oriental quaintness and naïveté of the medieval Arab by writing 'as the Arab would have written in English'. The result is a work containing thousands of words and phrases of great beauty, and, to the Western ear, originality. Arabic, if we can trust Burton, contains the most beautifully phrased clichés of any tongue in the world.

The ideas and emotions displayed in the Nights are elemental ones, earthily expressed. The tales concern life's fundamentals: death, old age, marriage, anger, revenge, fear, pain, love, regret, loyalty, beauty, religious faith, temptation, sickness, delight, luck – the gamut of life's experiences and feelings. All are told in a simple, direct manner with little subtlety or sophistication: all black and white without shadings. Some are mere sex fantasies or gross day dreams of glittering wealth. There are no great ideas in the *Nights*; no thought-provoking theories or philosophies. There is only folk wisdom, sometimes crudely and often beautifully expressed.

'Man may not be trusted with woman, so long as eye glanceth and eyelid quivereth,' expresses the basic distrust of the medieval Arab. Here, too, is one of Burton's favourite quotations: 'Death in a crowd is as good as a feast.' Some of the adages might with little change be heard from a French peasant woman, an Aunt Jemima, or almost anybody's mother: 'Speak not of whatso concerneth thee not, lest thou hear what will please thee not.' Still others carry an atmosphere that seems so foreign and out of our time that it repels: 'Three things are better than other three; the day of death is better than the day of birth, a live dog is better than a dead lion, and the grave is better than want.'

For the most part, the thoughts of the characters in the tales are concerned with the practical matters of their everyday life – revenge, for example. Far from being an evil passion, revenge is one of life's sweet enjoyments: 'It is not for any save King Afridun to kill them, that he may gratify his wrath.' And this speech: 'Whoso would solace himself with seeing the beheading of Nur al Din bin al Fazl bin Khakan, let him repair to the palace! So followers and followed, great and small, will flock to the spectacle, and I shall heal my heart and harm my foe.' The deed of revenge is always described in some detail and when it is done there is no repentance nor mercy for the victim's soul: 'Then I took up a great stone from among the trees and coming up to him smote him therewith on the head with all my might and crushed in his skull as he lay dead drunk. Thereupon his flesh and fat and blood being in a pulp, he died and went to his deserts, The Fire, no mercy of Allah be upon him.' Nor is the enjoyment of revenge, no matter how ghastly the form, considered an unladylike entertainment. After a horrible description of the destruction of an enemy army by friendly demons we find: 'And this was high enjoyment for Janshah and his father and the Lady Shamsah.'

Anger, of course, is the concomitant of revenge, and they knew how to be angry in the land of *The Arabian Nights*. There was, for example, the woman who 'raged with exceeding rage and her body-hair stood on end like the bristles of a fretful hedgehog'. There were even some among the Arabs of the Nights who were permanently angry and one is described as 'a man of wrath and a shedder of blood'.

But anger was seldom so strong that it prevented elaborate vilification, particularly among women. Here is but a part of a speech by one young girl to another:

If one joke with thee, thou art angry; if one sport with thee, thou art sulky; if thou sleep, thou snorest; if thou walk, thou lollest out thy tongue! if thou eat, thou art never filled. Thou art heavier than mountains and fouler than corruption and crime. Thou hast in thee nor agility nor benedicite nor thinkest thou of aught save meat and sleep. When thou pissest thou swishest; if thou turd thou gruntest like a bursten wine-skin or an elephant transmogrified. If thou go to the water-closet, thou needest one to wash they gap and pluck out the hairs which overgrow it; and this is the extreme of sluggishness and the sign, outward and visible, of stupidity. In short, there is no good thing about thee, and indeed the poet saith of thee. . . .

And here follows a bit of poetry as vulgar as the preceding speech.

Death is a common enough occurrence in the *Nights* but it is nevertheless dreadful. Beautiful and terrible words such as these often provide the happy ending to a tale: 'And they led the most pleasurable of lives and the most delectable, till there came to them the Destroyer of delights and the Sunderer of societies and they became as they had never been.' When the Arabs of the *Nights* drained 'the cup of death' they were 'numbered among the folk of futurity and heirs of immortality'. Death came in many guises. Often it was a camel with a bell around its neck. Sometimes it was disguised in human form and spoke to its intended victim:

'Verily the Lord of the House sent me to thee, nor can any doorkeeper exclude me, nor need I have leave to come in to kings; for I reck not of Sultan's majesty neither of the multitude of his guards. I am he from whom no tyrant is at rest, nor can any man escape from my grasp: I am the Destroyer of delights and the Sunderer of societies.' Now when the king heard this a palsy crept over him and he fell on his face in a swoon; but presently coming to himself, he asked, 'Art thou then the Angel of Death?' and the stranger answered, 'Yes'.

It is this grim figure who caused the craven terror of even the noblest characters: 'We lost the power of thought and reason and were stupefied for the excess of our fear and horror,' says one hero. Sometimes the emotion is even more graphically described, as when it was said that 'fear fluttered the scrotum below his belly'.

When misfortune struck, whatever its form, none could grieve and despair as these folk. Usually the world grew black in their sight and sometimes they cried out, 'I am a lost man! Verily we are Allah's and to Allah we are returning' or 'What is the worth of mine eyes if they do not weep?' One man walked from a room with 'grief scattering from his body'. The causes of these laments vary, but once it was simply from 'eating too much of the world'.

But life had its sunny side as well, and it was as bright as the dark side was black. Then one could 'joy with exceeding joy', particularly if one was 'suckled at the breast of fond indulgence and was reared in the lap of happy fortune'. For even kings were happy in those days and of one it was said that 'his subjects joyed in him and all of his days were gladness'. Sometimes when friends or lovers met 'they embraced and fell to the ground senseless for excess of joy'. And a man was welcomed by being told that 'this thy day with us is white as milk'. There was wonder in the world then, too, and a man looked at a carved wooden horse and 'marvelled with exceeding marvel and was confounded at the beauty of its form', or he could see 'a mansion whose beauties would beggar the tongue'. And he would sometimes ask incredulously, 'And is all this in the world?'

Most of the beauty of the Arabs' world was to be found in women, of course, and they reserved their choicest expressions for them. They were frequently compared to 'the moon at its full' or to 'the rising full moon'. Some of the women had 'dewy lips sweeter than syrup' or 'a mole like a dot of ambergris on a downy site'. Princess Dunya was a typical beauty and she is perhaps best described by the effect she created: 'Taj al-Muluk looked upon her and fed his eyes on her beauty and loveliness (but she knew it not); and every time he gazed at her he fainted by reason of her passing charms.' Dunya, it will be noted, created this effect without even trying; others created a similar sensation by working at it. Shams al-Nahar, for example, walked into a room 'as she were the moon among the stars swaying from side to side, with luring gait and in beauty's pride'. And a slave-girl walked towards Ala-al-Din (Aladdin, of course, but presented by Burton in the unexpurgated tale as much more worldly and less wholesome) 'swinging her haunches and gracefully swaying a shape the handiwork of Him whose Boons are hidden; and each of them stole one glance of the eyes that cost them a thousand sighs'.

Much attention was given to the way in which a woman walked. There was a handmaiden who moved 'with the gait of a gazelle in flight and fit to damn a devotee, til she came to a chair, whereon she seated herself'; and another who went 'walking with a voluptuous gait and ravishing all beholders with her lithe and undulating pace'.

But perhaps the best single description of the ideal *Arabian Nights* girl is found in the four hundred and twenty-first and the four hundred and twenty-second nights where we find this passage:

The girl is soft of speech, fair of form like a branchlet of basil, with teeth like chamomile-petals and hair like halters wherefrom to hang hearts. Her cheeks are like blood-red anemones and her face like a pippin: she has lips like wine and breasts like pomegranates twain and a shape supple as a rattan-cane. Her body is well-formed with sloping shoulders dight; she hath a nose like the edge of a sword shining bright and a forehead brilliant white and eyebrows which unite and eyes stained by Nature's hand black as night. If she speak, fresh young pearls are scattered from her mouth forthright and all hearts are ravished by the daintiness of her sprite; when she smileth thou wouldst ween the moon shone out her lips between and when she eyes thee, sword-blades flash from the babes of her eyes. In her all beauties to conclusion come, and she is the centre of attraction to traveller and stay-at-home. She hath two lips of cramoisy, than cream smoother and of taste than honey sweeter. . . . And she hath a bosom, as it were a way between two hills which are a pair of breasts like globes of ivory sheen; likewise, a stomach right smooth, flanks soft as the palm-spathe and creased with folds and dimples which overlap one another, and liberal thighs, which like columns of pearl arise, and back parts which billow and beat together like seas of glass or mountains of glance, and two feet and hands of gracious mould like unto ingots of virgin gold.

Sometimes the sight of all these bulks of sex produced rather untidy results: it was said of one woman that 'all who looked on her bepissed their bag trousers, for the excess of her beauty and loveliness'.

Often one feature of a woman proved exceptionally pleasing. There was one young man who 'took her feet and kissed them and, finding them like fresh cream, pressed his face on them'. There was a woman who 'tucked up her sleeves from a forearm like fresh curd, which illuminated the whole place with its whiteness and Sharrkan was dazzled by it'. This particular hero was always impressed with hands and arms and Sharrkan once told a girl that 'my ecstacy cometh from the beauty of thy fingertips'. A large rump was much admired and picturesquely described: a woman 'tucked up her trousers and displayed two calves of alabaster carrying a mound of crystal'. The creator of all these fine parts of women's anatomy is not forgotten: Describing a breast that is 'a seduction to all that see it', an admirer adds, 'glory be to Him who fashioned it and finished it!'

One has the feeling in many passages that the teller of the tales or the character describing the charms of some 'high bosomed virgin' was often carried away with his own powers of description and that the girl herself comes off appearing rather ungainly. Try to imagine a creature with 'breasts like two globes of ivory, from whose brightness the moons borrow light, and a stomach with little waves as it were a figured cloth of the finest Egyptian linen made by the copts, with creases like folded scrolls, ending in a waist slender past all power of imagination; based upon back parts like a hillock of blown sand, that force her to sit when she would lief stand, and awaken her, when she would fain sleep'.

These women 'cool of eyes and broad of breast' were not unaware of their physical qualities and social accomplishments, nor were they above boasting of them. One heroine says modestly, 'If I sing and dance, I seduce, and if I dress and scent myself, I slay. In fine, I have reached a pitch of perfection such as can be estimated only by those of them who are firmly rooted in knowledge.' If they felt their charms were not sufficiently appreciated, they were capable of calling out, 'O man, dost thou not behold my beauty and loveliness and the fragrance of my breath; and knowest thou not the need women have of men and men of women?' They were often bold and brazen, these women from *The Arabian Nights*. Princess Budur, a well-brought-up young lady, awoke in the night to find a strange young man asleep beside her. She was quite taken with him and called out, 'My life on thee, harken to me; awake and up from thy sleep and look on the narcissus and the tender down thereon, and enjoy the sight of naked waist and navel; and touzle me and tumble me from this moment till break of day!' Perhaps many of these young girls received the unpuritan advice of one lovely who asked, 'And what is the medicine of passion, O nurse mine?' and is told, 'The medicine of passion is enjoyment.'

Not all women are beautiful, however, even in *The Arabian Nights*. There were a few – usually old ones, it is true – who were as ugly as others were beautiful: 'Now this accursed old woman was a witch of the witches, past mistress in sorcery and deception; wanton and wily, deboshed and deceptious; with foul breath, red eyelids, yellow cheeks, dull-brown face, eyes bleared, mangy body, hair grizzled, back humped, skin withered and wan and nostrils which ever ran.' This particular dame had morals to match her appearance and 'could not exist without sapphism or she went mad'.

But fortunately for the male characters in the *Nights*, most of the women were designed to love and be loved. Certainly no one ever experienced such violent reactions to love as did the men of these tales when 'delight got hold of them'. One confessed, 'I was drowned in the sea of her love, dazed in the desert of my passion for her.' And later he tells his love, 'If I offered my life for thy love, it were indeed but little.' Another proclaims, 'I will never part with thee, but will die under thy feet.' And still another announces, 'O mistress mine, I am thy slave and in the hollow of thy hand.' A youth describes how 'she took leave of me and went away and all my senses went with her'. The women respond in kind, however, with such sentences as, 'O my lord, my life hath been lived in vain for that I have not known the like of thee till the present.'

But the men seek 'that which men seek in women' and it is doubtful if world literature contains more graphic or more crude descriptions of coition. Sometimes it is stark and brutal as in this speech: 'O strumpet, I am the sharper Jawan the Kurd, of the band of Ahmad al-Danaf; we are forty sharpers, who will all piss our tallow into thy womb this night, from dusk to dawn.' More often, though, the act of love, if not always legal, is at least committed by two lovers. On a wedding night a bride 'did off her clothes' and the groom was happy to find her 'a pearl unpierced and a filly unridden'. But always the description of copulation itself is in the grossest terms – even irreverent – as in the story of Ali Shar and Zumurrud where Ali 'threw himself upon her as the lion upon the lamb. Then he sheathed his steel rod in her scabbard and ceased not to play the porter at her door and the preacher in her pulpit and the priest at her prayer-niche, whilst she with him ceased not from inclination and prostration and rising up and sitting down, accompanying her ejaculations of praise and of "Glory to Allah!" with passionate movements and wrigglings and claspings of his member and other amorous gestures . . .' And this is not the crudest passage to be found in the *Nights*.

If a man is denied the object of his passion, he sickens and often dies. This side of the story is usually quickly passed over when the man in question is not the hero of the tale, as when an unfortunate young man 'went out sore afflicted and sadly vexed and, returning home, felt sick, for his heart had received its death blow; so he presently died'. Tellers of the tales often find this a convenient way to rid themselves of characters no longer needed in their stories. Women, too, are often sick with longing, but they rarely die; they only lose sleep: 'she has not tasted sleep by reason of her heart being taken up with thee'.

When lovers finally meet, the meeting does not always seem satisfactory – at least by Western standards. Take the case of Ali bin Bakkar and Shams al-Nahar. Shams was 'burned with love-longing and desire;

and passion and transport consumed her'. Ali was in a similar state. Then, 'she rose from the sofa and came to the door of the alcove, where Ali met her and they embraced with arms round the neck, and fell down fainting in the doorway; whereupon the damsels came to them and carrying them into the alcove, sprinkled rose-water upon them both'.

But love is not quite everything in life. There is also friendship – between men, never women. For a friend, the *Nights* tell us, 'is not like a wife, whom one can divorce and re-marry: nay, his heart is like glass: once broken, it may not be mended'. Tired of love stories, King Shahyrar sometimes asked Shahrazad for tales of loyalty and friendship: 'Say me, hast thou any story bearing upon the beauty of true friendship and the observance of its duty in time of distress and rescuing from destruction?' She had indeed. In one tale a man says to his sick friend, 'Were thy healing at the price of my head, I would cut it off ere thou could ask me; and, could I ransom thee with my life, I had already laid it down for thee.' Caliph Harun al-Rashid has trouble getting to sleep one night and his faithful eunuch Mansur says to him, 'O my lord, strike off my head; haply that will dispel thine unease and do away the restlessness that is upon thee.'

Sinning or doing good, the Arab is always pious. Then, as now, religion played an important part in the daily life of bad Moslems as well as good ones and the name of Allah is frequently on their lips; they 'say the say that ne'er yet shamed the sayer, "There is no Majesty and there is no might save in Allah, the Glorious, the Great!"' Few Europeans ('Franks') or Christians ('Nazarenes') appear in the tales. When they do, they are inevitably villains. It is a Nazarene who, knowing the Arabs' greatest weakness, suggests the following plot to gain control over a Moslem enemy: 'I will tempt him to abjure his faith, and on this wise: we know that the Arabs are much addicted to women, and I have a daughter, a perfect beauty, whom when he sees, he will be seduced by her.' It is little wonder that no deed is proclaimed more virtuous than the killing of such abhorrent unbelievers.

After women and wine, it was poetry and song that most delighted the soul of the Arab in the *Nights*. '"Prose is a wordy thing, but verses," rejoined the Caliph, "are pearls on a string."' They quoted poetry when they were sad ('Needs must I recite somewhat of verse; haply it may quench the fire of my heart'), and when they were happy ('Oppression and depression left her and gladness took mastery of her, and she repeated these verses . . .'); and when 'tormented with the displeasures of memory'. Over-excitement inevitably stimulated poetry

('For excess of emotion he broke into verse'). But poetry and song also created violent emotion, as in this passage: 'Then she went on to sing . . . til our senses were bewitched and the very room danced with excess of delight and surprise at her sweet singing; and neither thought nor reason was left in us.' Sultan and peasant, they all recited or improvised verses and they often conversed in poetry: a fisherman, hearing a girl's sad love story 'wept and made moan and lamented; then, recalling what had betided him in the days of his youth, when love had mastery over him and longing and desire and distraction were sore upon him, and the fires of passion consumed him, replied with these couplets . . . .'

The verses themselves – at least as they appear in translation, and Burton's translations are no worse than others – seem poor things indeed to evoke so much emotion. Even Burton, fond as he was of Arabic poetry, confessed that much of it was bad. To one set of verses in the *Nights* he attached a footnote saying, 'It is sad doggerel.' They contribute nothing to the stories and, like songs in a bad operetta, are frequently introduced at inappropriate times. In his Terminal Essay, which covers a goodly portion of Volume X, Burton discusses the technical and historical details of the verses at great length. According to his count, there were 'no less than ten thousand lines' of poetry in the first ten volumes, plus uncounted thousands more in the six supplementary volumes. Sometimes, when poetic lines translated by Burton in one story are repeated in another, he used the translations of other scholars for variation. But, in general, one version is as bad as another. Rhymed and alliterative prose in the texts created another problem for the translator, but, as can be seen from some of the quotations used here, Burton was more successful in his handling of this type of material.

While Burton used a large number of coined and archaic words in his translation of the *Nights*, he did not overdo their use as he did in his translation of Camoens. There are still many words such as 'grievouser', and even 'grievousest', but some of his coined words are not unapt, as when he speaks of brigands who live by 'violenting' mankind. Most Arabic scholars declare that Burton was not as exact and literal in his translation as Payne, but he succeeded admirably in catching the spirit and conveying the expression rather than capturing the precise meaning of each word. Phrases such as 'she snorted and snarked' are certainly expressive, although Burton himself might have been hard put to define 'snarked', since in his usage it obviously does not mean snored and is redundant if it means snorted. One of the words he invented – or, more correctly, resurrected from Middle English – has become a part of the English language and can be found in most dictionaries: the word is 'ensorcel', meaning to bewitch or enchant. While he was still Victorian enough to avoid most of those four-letter words attributed to the Angles and Saxons, he sometimes used old variants of them, such as the old Norse word 'skite', and 'coynte'. 'I have carefully Englished the picturesque terms and novel expressions in all their outlandishness,' he said.

As much of Burton's fame as a translator is due to his remarkable footnotes as to his translation of the text. It is probably safe to assume that, in his published works as a whole, no man, not even the most scribbling college professor, ever wrote more footnotes than did Richard Burton. In the *Nights* his passion for footnotes reached full flower. Here, for once, it enhances and makes unique his literary efforts. Because he had lived among so many diverse kinds of people and had studied their customs so intimately, he was able to add a curious gloss to the text he was translating. These notes, written at the end of a long and active life, form, as he said, 'a repertory of Eastern knowledge in its esoteric phase'. He felt that he had a unique contribution to make. 'The accidents of my life, it may be said without presumption . . . have given me certain advantages over the average student, however deeply he may have studied.' The footnotes in the *Nights* are also illuminating footnotes on his own life, for they range far from the text and many are written in a very personal vein.

There is every type of footnote represented in the *Nights*, from scholarly comments on points of Arabic grammar to regular essays on subjects suggested by words or phrases in the text, but the most delightful perhaps are those ingenuous notes that act as a personal gloss on the stories, almost as though Burton himself was an Egyptian fellah listening to the story being told in the coffee house and believing every word he heard. He makes such asides as, 'My sympathies are all with the old woman who rightly punished the royal lecher', and 'The young man must have been a demon of chastity.' When a girl in the story strikes her husband Burton notes, 'Which probably would not be the last administered to him by the Amazonian young person, who after her mate feared to approach the dead blackamoor must have known him to be cowardly as Cairenes generally are.' He could also sigh, 'Poor human nature! How sad to compare its pretensions with its actualities.'

Sometimes Burton stands outside the story but gives his comments on the tales themselves. Of the 'Story of the Three Witches' in Volume VI he says, 'It is the grossest and most brutal satire on the sex, suggesting that a woman would prefer an additional inch of penis to anything this world or the next can offer her.' Of another story he says, probably with tongue in cheek, 'I remark with pleasure that the whole of this tale is told with commendable delicacy. O si sic omnia!' When a character called Abu Nowés makes his appearance in the tales, Burton issues a warning: 'All but anthropological students are advised to "skip" over anecdotes in which his name and abominations occur.' Abu Nowés, the story tells us, 'loved to sport and make merry with fair boys and cull the rose from every brightly blooming cheek'.

Some of the stories contain anecdotes so revolting that even Burton was repelled by them, although this did not prevent him from translating them and commenting upon them. In one tale, for example, a woman bakes bread from dough that had been used as a dressing for a 'corroding ulcer' on a man's spine. Burton had heard the story before and says, 'This nauseous Joe Miller has often been told in the hospitals of London and Paris. It is as old as the Hitopadesa [i.e. *'Pilpay's Fables'*, about the thirteenth century].'

Sometimes Burton comments on his own translation. 'The original is intensely prosaic – and so am I,' he says at one point. When he uses the versions of previous translators of the *Nights* he notes, 'I have borrowed from Mr. Payne', 'I give Torrens by way of specimen', or 'I quote Lane'. The other translators are sometimes praised for certain aspects of their work, but more often they are damned or scorned. Noting that Lane omitted a certain story, he says, 'probably he held a hearty laugh not respectable'.

Burton also used his footnotes to attack fellow authors and to get back at critics of his own earlier books, A book called *The Natural History of the Bible* is frequently scored and its author ridiculed for 'his painfully superficial book'. Andrew Lang, a critic who spoke unfavourably of his *Book of the Sword* in *Academy* is ticked off for an introduction he wrote to *Grimm's Household Tales*: 'It is curious that so biting and carping a critic, who will condescend to notice a misprint in another's book, should lay himself open to general animadversion by such a rambling farrago of half-digested knowledge as that which composes Mr. Andrew Lang's Introduction.'

There are many odd scraps of biographical material embedded in the footnotes, such as the fact that he believed in always wearing a nightcap 'however ridiculous', and that a eunuch's wife once told him how different kinds of eunuchs are made. There are many references to his own books and he takes advantage of the opportunity to correct mistakes he had made in some of them. He also lays to rest a story that had circulated about him for years: it was said that during his pilgrimage to Mecca he had once been caught urinating while standing up instead of squatting as is the practice of Arab males. To prevent disclosure, he was said to have killed the Arab who saw him. Not true, said Burton.

All his life Burton had been a keen observer of men and their manners, customs and perversions. That he did not always learn from what he saw does not detract from his merit as an observer and reporter. Some curious bits and pieces of things he had seen or experienced turn up in the footnotes. He noticed, for example, that women of the 'trading classes of Trieste' walk with 'a "wriggle" of their own'; that only occidentals say 'damn *it*' while 'damn *you*' is understood the world over; that Eastern women lie naked between sheets in hot weather; that 'the beauties of nature seem always to provoke hunger in Orientals, especially Turks, as good news in Englishmen'. Whether from experience or hearsay, he also records that 'the most terrible part of a *belle passion* in the East is that the beloved will not allow her lover leave of absence for an hour'. In addition, Burton also set down a number of statements as fact which there is little likelihood of his having observed directly but which are recorded as though he did; he says, for example, that in Egypt 'a favourite feminine mode of murdering men is by beating and bruising the testicles' and that 'apes are lustfully excited by the presence of women'.

Above all, the footnotes in the *Nights* serve as a vehicle for Burton's hatreds, prejudices and opinions. All of the races, nations, professions and classes of people he had vilified in books and articles over the previous forty years are again abused, often in the identical words he had used earlier. He sometimes adds unusual theories to account for the deficiencies he noted in other people as when he states that the 'mildness and effeminacy' of the Hindus is probably due to their habit of defecating twice a day. He believed that his own race was vastly superior to all others and that Englishmen were the cream of that race and the best qualified to rule over other peoples. But neither this conviction nor his own position as a government official prevented him from attacking what he regarded as the absurdities and the stupidities of his own government and the many defects he found in the English character. He believed hypocrisy to be one of the great faults of his countrymen: 'hypocrisy being the homage vice pays to virtue; a homage, I may observe, nowhere rendered more fulsomely than among the so-called Anglo-Saxon race'. One of his main complaints against the British Government was that it did not rule in as iron-fisted a manner as he thought necessary and he contrasted the attitude of his own government unfavourably with that of oriental nations: 'In the East men respect manly measures, not the hysterical, philanthropic pseudo-humanitarianism of modern government which is really cruellest of all.' Government in Eastern countries, he said, 'is a despotism tempered by assassination. And under no rule is a man socially freer and his condition contrasts strangely with the grinding social tyranny which characterizes every mode of democracy or constitutionalism, i.e., political equality.' Always in favour of hard measures, he said, 'There are indeed only two efficacious forms of punishment all the world over, corporal for the poor and fines for the rich, the latter being the severer form.'

East and West are often contrasted, always to the disadvantage of the latter, in religious matters. As he grew older, Burton became more and more anti-Christian. Isabel's missionary efforts were a complete failure. Burton thought that 'theologians . . . everywhere and at all times delight in burdening human nature'; that 'every race creates its own Deity after the fashion of itself'; and that 'the heaven of all faiths, including "Spiritualism", the latest development, is only an earth more or less glorified even as the Deity is humanity more or less perfected'. In Christianity he found the doctrine of original sin most distasteful to him and he called it 'a most sinful superstition'. He believed that the Bible had been 'hopelessly corrupted'. Of all faiths, he found that of Islam more to his taste. Islam was to him a 'religion of common sense' which, for example, would permit cannibalism when it was necessary to save human life and allowed polygamy where it was necessary to increase the population. He thought the Moslem call to prayer, 'beautiful and human', was far more pleasant than 'the brazen clang of the bell'. He would have strongly disapproved of the modern custom in Arabia of replacing the human muezzin with a loudspeaker that plays a record of the prayer call.

He also gave his views on morality in the footnotes. 'Morality is, like conscience, both geographical and chronological,' he said, adding, 'but strange and unpleasant truths progress slowly, especially in England.' He again put forward his theory that women are more passionate in low-lying lands and in hot damp climates and vice versa. His opinion of women in general was low. He believed 'women corrupt women more than men do' and he contended that only an ignorant girl could be seduced: 'A man of the world,' he said, 'may "seduce" an utterly innocent . . . girl. But to "seduce" a married woman! What a farce!'

Burton regarded himself as an expert on the subject of sex, with which a goodly portion of the *Nights* is concerned, and often makes authoritative statements that would lead one to believe that his experience was both vast and intimate: 'An uncircumcised woman,' he said, 'has the venereal orgasm much sooner and oftener than an uncircumcised man, and frequent coitus will injure her health.' How much of Burton's store of sexual lore was gleaned from first hand experience and how much from what he had heard and read is difficult to say, but he always presented his facts and theories in such a way as to lead his readers to assume that he was absolutely sure of his ground, although in many instances this was certainly not the case. But regardless of his sources or his methods of research, and in spite of the fact that many of his conclusions are certainly suspect, no man before him had ever taken his scientific interest in the subject. There are footnotes on drugs used to prolong coition, a lizard that acts as an aphrodisiac, modes of circumcision, and lust among lepers.

There was no subject too sacred or too profane for Burton to take up in his footnotes. Whether or not he ever actually wrote 'A History of Farting', he certainly had made a study of the subject and frequently makes reference to it in his footnotes. His excuse for this is the frequent use of the phenomenon in his text and that, in Arabic, 'even serious writers like Al-Hariri do not, as I have noted, despise the indecency'. He has only scorn for 'polite men' who translate by 'fled in haste' the Arabic expression 'farted for fear'. He himself does not hesitate to translate the Arabic nickname Abu Zirt as 'Father of Farts' and even tells a personal anecdote on the subject to illustrate the effectiveness of Egyptian beans:

I was once sitting in the Greek quarter of Cairo dressed as a Moslem when arose a prodigious hubbub of lads and boys, surrounding a couple of Fellahs. These men had been working in the fields about a mile east of Cairo; and, when returning home, one had said to the other, 'If thou wilt carry the hoes I will break wind once for every step we take.' He was as good as his word and when they were to part he cried, 'And now for thy bakhshish!' which consisted of a volley of fifty, greatly to the delight of the boys.

The footnotes in the *Nights* range far and wide, if seldom deep, covering the entire range of Burton's interests – swords and swordsmanship, the use of narcotics by American negroes, the necessity for removing body hairs in hot climates, a theory on laughter, points for judging the physical condition of a good slave and a 500-word essay on breeds of horses. It was a characteristic of Burton that once he acquired a theory or a prejudice, he never changed or relinquished it. So, at the end of his life, as when he had been a youth at Oxford, he is still protesting that English schools should teach their scholars to pronounce and write *y* instead of *j* in words of semitic origin.

Burton concluded his first series on *The Arabian Nights* with what is essentially one long footnote that covers 199 pages of Volume X. This is the famous 'Terminal Essay'. It consists of notes and comments on the origins of the stories, the translations that have been made in Europe, the manner and matter of the *Nights*, and the rhymed prose and poetry. But primarily this 'Essay' owes its fame to the section called 'Social Conditions as Shown in the Nights' which covers more than a third of the article. There are four subsections: A – Al-Islam, B – Women, C – Pornography, and D – Pederasty.

In the first of these subsections he states that from his own viewpoint, 'All the forms of "faith", that is, belief in things unseen, not subject to the senses, and therefore unknown and (in our present stage of development) unknowable, are temporary and transitory: no religion hitherto promulgated amongst men shows any prospect of being final or otherwise than finite.' He himself was an adherent of no religion. He appears to have believed in some sort of providence – which he usually referred as 'Provy' – but not the deity of any existing religion. 'The more I study religions,' he wrote, 'the more I am convinced that man never worshipped anything but himself.' But he makes it quite clear that he preferred Islam to Christianity. 'There is no more immoral work than the "Old Testament"', he said, 'Its deity is an ancient Hebrew of the worst type, who condones, permits or commands every sin in the Decalogue to a Jewish patriarch, *qua* patriarch.' He cites passages in the Bible of 'obscenity and impurity'; he lists other passages containing 'horrors forbidden to the Jews, who, therefore, must have practised them'; and still another series of Biblical passages are cited of which he says, 'For mere filth what can be fouler.' This part of the essay is an outright attack upon Christianity. While he does not accept wholeheartedly the teachings of Mohammed, he uses Islam to make comparisons with Christianity that are never to the credit of the latter. Beliefs aside, much of his argument is both illogical and unfair, as when he compares a Moslem saying ('cleanliness is next to godliness') with a purely local Christian practice ('even now English Catholic girls are at times forbidden by Italian priests a frequent use of the bath as a signpost to the sin of "luxury"').

'Women, all the world over, are what men make them,' Burton maintained in his section on women. Isabel would undoubtedly have agreed with him, although she would not have agreed with his views on sex education. Burton believed that young men should be taught 'the art and mystery of satisfying the physical woman' and cited the existence of a few of the many books to be found in all oriental countries designed to end all sexual mysteries.

He roundly condemned the practice of avoiding the subject of sex, saying, 'The mock virtue, the most immodest modesty of England and of the United States in the xix century, pronounces the subject foul and fulsome: "Society" sickens at all details; and hence it is said abroad that the English have the finest women in Europe and least know how to use them.'

After a short defence of the pornography to be found in the *Nights*, Burton moves, naturally enough, into the subject of pederasty:

There is another element in The Nights and that is one of absolute obscenity utterly repugnant to English readers, even the least prudish. It is chiefly connected with what our neighbours call *Le vice contre nature* – as if anything can be contrary to nature, which includes all things. Upon this subject I must offer details, as it does not enter into my plan to ignore any theme which is interesting to the Orientalist and the Anthropologist. And they, methinks, do abundant harm who, for shame or disgust, would suppress the very mention of such matters: in order to combat a great and growing evil deadly to the birth-rate – the mainstay of national prosperity – the first requisite is careful study.

Burton had made a careful study of *Le Vice*. In the course of his many travels he had not neglected to continue the study he had begun as a subaltern in Karachi. His conclusion was that the causes of pederasty were geographical and climatic rather than racial and that there was a 'Sotadic Zone' within which the offence was considered a mere peccadillo.

While there is no evidence that Burton took more than a scientific interest in this subject, he does relate several unscholarly anecdotes which obviously amused him. After telling how men caught in the harem are given to the grooms and slaves who force the opening with a sharpened tent peg, he relates with relish how a certain 'well-known missionary' with a 'conversion-mania' was once subjected to this indignity. With even less excuse he tells how a 'man cannon' was made by one Shaykh Nasr, Governor of Bushire:

A grey-beard slave was dragged in blaspheming and struggling with all his strength. He was presently placed on all fours and firmly held by the extremities; his bag-trousers were let down and a dozen peppercorns were inserted ano suo: the target was a sheet of paper held at a reasonable distance; the match was applied by a pinch of cayenne in the nostrils; the sneeze started the grapeshot and the number of hits on the butt decided the bet.

At the end of the 'Terminal Essay' Burton sounded a defiant note to all critics, maintaining that his free treatment of subjects normally considered taboo would be a national benefit and that men had been crowned for lesser services than he had here rendered. While admitting that the work as a whole contains errors, shortcomings and lapses, he quickly adds, 'Yet in justice to myself I must also notice that the maculae are few and far between.'

Burton sat back and awaited the criticisms and doubtless wondered how much his venture would cost him. To his surprise and pleasure, the ten-volume work was both a critical and a financial success. Sold by private subscription, the completed *Nights* realized £11,000 profit – more than all of his other books combined. The gold he had sought in Midian and West Africa was found buried in that literary work which he had used to escape the realities of his world. Burton believed it was the pornography in the *Nights* that made it a success, and he told his wife, 'Now that I know the tastes of England, we need never be without money.'

Chapter 25

The Coming of the Camel
1885 – 90

The Arabian Nights was not published all at once. The first ten volumes were published privately in 1885 – 6, and the six supplemental volumes between 1886 and 1888. Isabel, fearing that her husband's bold translation would injure his reputation, had at first strongly objected to the venture, but he convinced her that he was making a valuable contribution to the British Empire. The British ruled the greatest concentration of Moslems under a single ruler in the world, he said, and the ruling race was duty bound to know all of the facts, pleasant and unpleasant, about its Moslem subjects. On this basis, Isabel reluctantly agreed the work should be published and she set to work to make it a success, mailing no less than 34,000 circulars to potential subscribers from their home in Opicina. Strange to say, however, she never read this *magnum opus* of her husband. He made her promise not to and she kept her promise. It was only for oriental scholars, he told her.

In May 1885, the Burtons set out for London to see the first volumes through the press, he travelling by ship and she by land. Burton fully expected to be attacked for his freedom of language and thought it quite possible that he might be taken to court. 'I don't care a button about being prosecuted,' he is quoted as saying. 'I will walk into court with my Bible and my Shakespeare and my Rabelais under my arm, and prove to them that, before they condemn me, they must cut half of *them* out, and not allow them to be circulated to the public.' But when Volume I came off the press and was distributed, there was much praise for the work and less criticism than had been expected.

At about this same time there appeared an opportunity to rise on the official ladder. Sir John Drummond-Hay was about to retire from the post of minister to Morocco. Burton applied for the job, his letter of request mentioning that he had not received a promotion in the twenty-five years he had been in the service of the Foreign Office. He apparently had high expectations of receiving the appointment and one month later he set off for Tangier to inspect what he hoped would be his new sphere of activity.

Isabel was left behind to see Volumes IV to VII through the press, a difficult assignment since she was not allowed to read the proofs. She was still fearful of the reaction her husband's translation would make on the public, and she grew uncommonly suspicious: 'I was dreadfully spied upon by those who wished to get Richard into trouble about it, and once an unaccountable person came and took some rooms in the same lodgings with me after Richard left, but I settled with the landlord that either I should leave, or that person should not have the rooms; and of course he did not hesitate between the two, so I took the whole of his rooms for the remainder of my stay.'

She rushed through her work so as to be able to join her husband before 22 January 1886, their silver wedding anniversary. She met him at Gibraltar where she found him wearing a red fez and attempting to bargain with a man named Malford Campbell, who claimed to have secret knowledge of a sunken treasure ship in Vigo Bay in north-eastern Spain. Campbell refused to divulge his secret, but this disappointment was forgotten when, on 5 February, a telegram arrived addressed to 'Sir Richard Burton'. Trying to be casual, he tossed the telegram over to Isabel, saying, 'Some fellow is playing me a practical joke, or else it is not for me. I shall not open it, so you may as well ring the bell and give it back again.'

'Oh no!' said Isabel. 'I shall open it if you don't.'

She opened the telegram. It was from Lord Salisbury and stated that on his recommendation the Queen had made him a Knight Commander of the Order of St Michael and St George. From now on he was Sir Richard Burton, KCMG; he was honoured at last. Isabel was delighted, but he affected to be unimpressed. 'Oh, I shall not accept it,' he said.

'You had better accept it, Jemmy,' said Isabel, 'because it is a certain sign that they are going to give you the place' – meaning that of minister to Morocco.

The two posts that Burton had dreamed of some day obtaining were, first of all, Constantinople, and secondly, Tangier. Now that Morocco seemed almost assured, he took a critical look at the place and decided he did not like it. 'It is by no means a satisfactory place for an Englishman,' he wrote in his journal. Isabel too, was disappointed at this object of her husband's ambition:

We thought the Embassy [sic] a miserable little house, after the Palazzone at Trieste. . . . The streets were muddy and dirty, all uphill, and horribly stony. . . . After Damascus, and all the other Eastern places I had seen, I thought it horrid, and was sorely disappointed – I had heard it so raved about; but I would willingly have lived there, and put out all my best capabilities, if my husband could have got the place that he wanted, and for which I had employed every bit of interest we had on his side or mine to obtain.

For Burton, now nearly sixty-five years old, the present (February and March 1886) and the outlook for the future had never seemed so bright. His *Arabian Nights* was both a literary and a financial success; he had been knighted and soon expected a promotion that could lead to even greater honours. But this was the peak. The knighthood was not the promise of things to come but a consolation prize. The road ahead was all downhill.

Five months later he learned that the Moroccan post had been given to another man. Both he and Isabel felt the disappointment deeply, although at the same time they were a bit relieved. 'It was for the honour of the thing,' Isabel declared, but added, 'we saw for ourselves how uneasy a crown it would be.' One of their influential friends, a Cabinet Minister, wrote to them: 'We don't want to annex Marocco [*sic*], and we know that you two would be Emperor and Empress in about six months.'

Returning from Gibraltar to Trieste by ship, they encountered severe storms which washed away one of the ladders between the upper and lower decks. Isabel, sick already, apparently was not aware of the missing ladder and fell upon a pile of lumber. Burton, seeing her fall, at first thought it was a large feather pillow that had been thrown down. He was horrified to discover that it was his wife. Isabel, who did not want to frighten him, shook herself and said she was all right. But at Naples it was evident that she had hurt herself quite badly. All her married life Isabel had subordinated her own wishes to those of her husband. She had taken care of his business and of him. It was difficult for Burton to reverse this role, even temporarily. When it came time to leave Naples, he decided that she should leave the ship. 'I made her continue her journey by land,' he said, 'whilst I, who thoroughly enjoyed the sea, rejoined the ship.' He realized his wife was sick and hurt, but it never occurred to him that he should give up a bit of his own pleasure and convenience to stay with her. It was not that he loved her the less, but that the idea that she might now, after twenty-five years, need the same kind of care she had given him simply never occurred to him.

When Isabel, sick and aching, reached Trieste after a miserable train ride, she learned that her father was dead and buried. Burton was not at her side to give her comfort.

On 10 April 1886, Burton sent off Volume VIII of *The Arabian Nights* to the printer and began to write his Terminal Essay. Already he had conceived the idea of bringing out the supplemental volumes (he planned five and produced six). On 5 June the Burtons again went to England; he wanted to consult a particularly interesting manuscript containing *Arabian Nights* stories that was in the Bodleian Library at Oxford. His attempt to obtain the use of the Wortley Montagu manuscript at the Bodleian involved him in the last of the major angry disputes that punctuated his life.

Although there was no one at the university capable of reading this manuscript, the library had made a rule that they would not loan out books and manuscripts; they refused to make an exception for Burton. Unable to obtain satisfactory copyists and finding the cold walls of Oxford uncomfortable, he relieved his frustration by damning the curators. The problem was eventually solved by Isabel, who hit upon the idea of having the manuscript photographed. The university agreed to this novel solution and Burton was able to use the material, but he took his revenge in a most curious way.

Dedications of books, as everyone knows, are always made to honour friends, relations or distinguished persons. Burton's dedications of the various volumes of *The Arabian Nights* were to such old friends as Steinhaeuser, Lord Houghton, Arbuthnot, Dr Bird, John Larking, and that remarkable sadist, Fred Hankey. Volume IV of the *Supplemental Nights* honours a new friend, Professor William H. Chandler of Pembroke College, Oxford, who did everything in his power to assist Burton to obtain the Montague manuscript. But the dedication of Volume V of the *Supplemental Nights* is so unusual as to deserve quotation in full, since, instead of honouring someone, it attempts to hold two men up to ridicule and contempt. It was written in the Bodleian Library on 5 August 1888, and is in the form of a letter:

TO THE CURATORS OF THE BODLEIAN LIBRARY, OXFORD
Especially Revd. B. PRICE and Professor MAX MULLER

Gentlemen,

I take the liberty of placing your names at the head of this Volume which owes its rarest and raciest passages to your kindly refusing the temporary transfer of the Wortley Montague MS. from your pleasant library to the care of Dr. Rost, Chief Librarian, India Office. As a sop to 'bigotry and virtue', as a concession to the 'Scribes and Pharisees', I had undertaken, in case the loan were granted, not to translate tales and passages which might expose you, the Curators, to unfriendly comment. But possibly anticipating what injury would thereby accrue to the Volume and what sorrow to my subscribers, you were good enough not to sanction the transfer – indeed you refused it to me twice – and for this step my *clientèle* will be (or ought to be) truly thankful to you.

> I am, Gentlemen,
> Yours obediently,
>
> RICHARD F. BURTON

It was not long after writing this letter that Burton from Oxford wired Isabel in London: 'Gout in both feet. Come directly.' Isabel came, arranged for an ambulance to take him to London, and called in 'his gout doctor', one Dr Foakes, whose standard treatment was a diet of magnesia and rhubarb. Burton's feet were so sensitive to pain that he was afraid to have anyone come into the room for fear he would jar them and he swore that the noise of a person walking across the carpet was painful. After being confined to his room for six weeks without any appreciable relief, Burton decided to give up the rhubarb and switch to a Swedish doctor who had developed an athletic treatment for those suffering from gout. His method was to shampoo the feet, twisting them, pumping them up and down and then drive the patient around the room as though he were a wild animal in a cage. According to the Burtons, the gout temporarily improved.

While sitting in London with his gout, Burton made his last request of his government. It does not seem a very unreasonable request today. He wanted permission to retire on full pension at the age of sixty-five – that is, immediately – instead of at seventy. He cited his long service to his country and his many accomplishments, but in the main he based his request upon a statement that 'constant residence' in Trieste was undermining his health and had incapacitated him from work. The request was refused.

On 10 November 1886, the first volume of another edition of the Arabian Nights was published. This was *Lady Burton's Edition of her Husband's Arabian Nights*. The purpose of this expurgated version – in which a concubine is called 'an assistant wife' – was to enable Burton to copyright as much of his translation as possible and to provide a wider audience for his work. Isabel had very little to do with this edition.

Burton turned over to her his proof sheets with all the *risqué* words, phrases, notes and stories deleted and allowed her to substitute 'Society words'. The bulk of the work appears to have been done by a friend, Justin Huntley McCarthy. This edition was not a success; only 457 copies of the original printing of 1,000 were sold.

Before leaving London, the Burtons called on their old friend, Marie Louise de la Ramée, the cigar-smoking woman novelist better known as Ouida. She knew Isabel better than Burton, but it was he whom she admired. A romantic herself, she saw only the romantic side of Burton and could never understand why he remained in the Consular Service or why the British Government did not make better use of his talents. 'The beheading of Walter Raleigh was, I think, a kinder treatment than the imprisonment of Burton in Trieste,' she once said. Writing nearly twenty years after she last saw him, she said, 'Apparently, by all inheritance, he was a common-place Englishman of the middle classes; actually, he was a man who looked like Othello and lived like the Three Mousquetaires.' Such was the common impression of Burton during his lifetime even by those who claimed to know him. For Ouida he had only one defect:

In the eyes of women he had the unpardonable fault: he loved his wife. He would have been a happier and a greater man if he had had no wife; but his love for her was extreme; it was a source of weakness, as most warm emotions are in the lives of strong men. Their marriage was romantic and clandestine; a love-marriage in the most absolute sense of the words, not wise on either side, but on each impassioned. She adored him, and, like most women who adore, she was not always wise. . . . What made the one weakness in her character was the religious superstition which is the rift in the lute of so many a female soul. Like all her family, she was a devoted Catholic; this bigotry increased with years. . . .

On 4 January 1887, the Burtons left London for Folkestone to see Burton's sister, staying eight days. The following year they stayed an additional eleven days. Burton had never spent so much time with his sister since his marriage. Maria Stisted, like Ouida, resented Isabel and most particularly she resented her religious beliefs, for she was as strong a Protestant as Isabel was a Catholic. It is curious, this religious struggle over a man who cared as little for one sect as for the other.

On 12 January the Burtons crossed over to Paris, where a friend of Burton's claimed to have found an Arabic source for Aladdin, then down to Cannes for what Isabel described as 'our last little gleam of the gay world'. Unfortunately, the gay world of the Riviera was shaken by a series of bad earthquakes beginning on 23 February. The first shock occurred about six o'clock in the morning and Isabel thought it was an express train.

'By Jove! That's a good earthquake,' said Burton.

'All the people are rushing out in the garden undressed,' called Isabel. 'Shall we go too?'

'No, my girl, you and I have been in too many earthquakes to show the white feather at our age.'

'All right,' said Isabel, and went back to her toilette.

While the ground trembled and heaved and people were fleeing, the Burtons continued their usual business of writing, reading, paying calls and driving. They also enjoyed going to the station to see the terrified men and women, many scantily dressed, seeking a place on the crowded trains. Burton wrote, 'I enjoyed it as much as a schoolboy, for I took notes and caricatured them in their light costumes.'

The following day, however, Burton was seized by what Isabel called 'one of the most awful fits of epileptiform convulsions' and Isabel was panicked by the thought that he might not have been properly baptized. A doctor was visiting him when this occurred. Isabel asked if she might baptize her husband and the doctor said, 'You may do anything you like.' Isabel got some water, knelt beside him, and said some prayers as she sprinkled him. He was amused when she told him about this later.

His health was now very bad indeed and Isabel decided they should have a personal travelling doctor. He was very much against this, but she insisted and in a short time Dr Ralph Leslie arrived from England to stay with them. As soon as he arrived they started back to Trieste by slow stages.

It was a real Via Crucis, [said Burton] I had to be ambulanced the whole way, and being very weak, we were twenty-eight days accomplishing the twenty-eight hours by express train which lie between Cannes and Trieste, which was only varied by minor earthquakes till we reached Milan; at Genoa by the agitation of seeing Lord Gerard's death in the newspaper, and my wife having a large blood-cyst on her lip, which appeared soon after my fit, and which Dr. Leslie had to cut out at Milan. It was indeed a road of anguish and labour, and right thankful were we to find ourselves once more in our own home on the 5th of April, after being out ten months.

It was during this painful trip that Isabel wrote out and Burton signed the following statement:

Gorizia, 15 February, 1887

Should my husband, Richard Burton, be on *his* death-bed unable to speak – I perhaps already dead – and that he may wish and have the grace to retract and recant his former errors and join the Catholic Church and also receive the Sacraments of Penance, Extreme Unction and Holy Eucharist, he might perhaps be able to sign this paper or make the sign of the cross to show his need.

This document created a controversy after Burton's death as to whether he did indeed 'retract and recant his former errors' and become a Catholic. The most probable interpretation of this affair, however, is to assume that Burton, who had professed so many faiths for his own ends, did not quibble about signing this paper for his wife's peace of mind. It was indeed a great comfort to her.

On 19, 20, 21 June a gala was held by the consulate in Trieste, as it was in British consulates all over the world, in honour of the Golden Jubilee of Queen Victoria. Burton was helped by his doctor to the dinner at which he presided. It was the first and last time he wore his KCMG decoration and he proposed a long and moving toast, ending with these words:

May God's choicest blessings crown her good works! May she be spared for many long, happy, peaceful, and prosperous years to her loyal, devoted people! May her mantle descend upon her children and her children's children! And may the loving confidence between her Majesty and all English-speaking-peoples, throughout the world, ever strengthen and endure to all time!

Now let Trieste hear for once, with one heart and one voice, a true British cheer!

HER MAJESTY THE QUEEN!

However bitterly he complained of the neglect and abuses of her government, Burton remained a loyal subject of the Queen.

After a wandering tour of Austria in July and August, the Burtons again returned to Trieste, or rather Opicina. On 9 September the British squadron put in at Trieste with the Prince of Wales, the Duke of Edinburgh, Prince Louis of Battenberg and other grandees on board. On such occasions the Burtons liked to be in Trieste to give a party for the fleet, but Dr Leslie forbade them to participate. Burton reluctantly wrote excuses to the royal secretaries, but offered the use of their Trieste home. He sent for a major-domo from Vienna, ordered that their house be put in order, the flag to be hoisted, the house to be illuminated every night, and a cold buffet to be always laid. When they returned to Trieste they were hurt to find that no royalty had used the house and that not even the ships' officers had taken advantage of their hospitality.

The attraction of the Burton home was when Burton was in it. It cannot be said that he was forgotten by the world. There was a constant stream of visitors from all over the world to see and talk with him. Among the visitors at this time was Dr Heinrich Schliemann, the businessman turned archaeologist who discovered the ruins of Troy. Schliemann was always a great admirer of Burton and thought his pilgrimage to Mecca one of the greatest adventures since the Trojan War.

Burton enjoyed these visits. It did not seem to matter who called on him, he welcomed the opportunity to meet them. He seemed to have lost that selectivity he had always before shown in choosing his friends and acquaintances. He changed in many other ways too. He had always disliked cold weather and had frequently complained of being chilled, often insisting upon a fire even in summer; now he could not stand one even in the bitterest weather and said it made him sick to have a fire in the room. Now, too, he drank milk and ate sweets, which formerly he had never liked. He continued his habit of hiding things, but now he experienced greater difficulty in finding what he had hidden and frequently had to call upon his wife to help him look for them. Isabel had a particular prayer she always used when she was looking for something lost and Burton would often call, 'Come here, I want that prayer directly. I have lost some papers.' Isabel claimed to have seen Burton praying in secret, but, if so, no one knows to what god or gods he appealed.

In October, Dr Leslie was replaced by Dr Grenfell Baker and in December they were all off to Abbazia in Croatia, a place noted for its mild climate. They returned to Trieste on 5 March. Two weeks later, on his sixty-seventh birthday, Burton completed the sixteenth and last volume of *The Arabian Nights*; it was printed the following November.

In May 1888, the Burtons left Trieste for their last visit to England. It was a leisurely trip. They stopped off in Milan to visit the Emperor and Empress of Brazil and then went to Switzerland, where they spent a month at Aigle. Burton now often relaxed with a novel and at Aigle he read, of all things, *Little Lord Fauntleroy*. 'Richard was perfectly delighted with it,' according to Isabel.

Burton's insatiable curiosity, like his passion for travel, never dimmed. Wherever he went he insisted on seeing everything to be seen in the locality, whether it was a cave, mushroom-growing, a mine, a cigarette factory, an albino, or a university. Nor did he ever neglect to call on any famous man in the vicinity. The Burtons went to Geneva so that he could talk with Carl Vogt, the famous zoologist who worked with Agassiz in the preparation of his works on fishes. These two men, so dissimilar in temperament, became fast friends.

On 15 July they reached Paris and five days later crossed over to London. There was the last volume of the *Supplemental Nights* to be put through the press and friends to be seen. Many of his old friends, such as Lord Houghton, were dead now, but there were hosts of others, old and new: Arbuthnot, Du Chaillu, Henry Irving, Swinburne, Arthur Evans (long since freed from Austrian imprisonment) and Cameron. Of this period Cameron said that 'though then he was already an invalid, and the subject of loving and anxious care from his wife, his mighty intellect was still undimmed . . . and it was a pleasure to sit and listen to him unfolding somewhat of his vast store of experience and knowledge'.

It was during this visit that Burton was shown an Edison phonograph. He was delighted with it and thought it a scientific marvel with a great future. He offered to do the muezzin's prayer call into it, but somehow this was never done.

On 15 October he left London for the last time and, with Isabel, he paid a last visit to his sister at Folkestone. Maria's daughter has left a description of her uncle at this time:

His eyes wore that strained look which accompanies difficult respiration, his lips were bluish-white, his cheeks livid; the least exertion made him short of breath and sometimes even he would pant when quietly seated in his chair. The iron constitution which had borne so much pain and labour was almost exhausted, and heart disease, a hereditary malady, was making rapid strides. Still, his splendid pluck never forsook him, he seemed to live on by sheer force of will; and his wonderful faculty of concentrating his attention on outward objects . . . enabled him to keep at bay that distressing melancholy which is often bred by an incurable disorder.

From Folkestone the Burtons crossed over to Boulogne for a few days and then on to Paris and Geneva. He could not stay in one place. He had to go on and on and on, possessed with a pathological desire to be always moving. When he had been in one place for a few days he would anxiously ask Isabel, 'Do you think I shall live to get out of this and to see another place?'

She would regularly reassure him. 'Of course you will. Let us go today if you feel like that.'

'Oh no, say next Monday or Tuesday.'

The constant moving was hard on Isabel, who had to make all the arrangements for transport, baggage, rooms, and meals, and she was not well herself. In Geneva, on 19 November 1888, at the Hotel Nationale (today the Palais Wilson, containing the offices of a number of international organizations), the Burtons were almost killed by a chandelier falling on the dinner table. It was in Geneva too that Burton gave his last lecture; it was before Geneva's geographical society. Even this was a great effort for him now, and he was unable to remain standing. At the end he sat down and those who wished to ask him questions stood while he answered from his chair.

On 2 January 1889, they went to Montreux; in February to Lausanne and then to Bern; and in March to Lucerne, Milan, Venice and at last back to Trieste. Three months later they were again wandering about Austria. He was at Semmering in August when he received a letter from the Foreign Office demanding that he explain why he was taking so much leave. Isabel said the letter 'agitated him and hurt him'. Burton complained that Semmering did not agree with him and they left after twelve days, but Isabel said, 'The fact is, the Foreign Office letter had worried him, and made him anxious to get back to Trieste; so we went up to Vienna.'

In October he received another disturbing letter from the Foreign Office telling him that he was not giving his vice-consul enough money for doing all his work for him. This was followed by a third letter which accused him of having been in England. He was indignant. Why, he had not been in England for thirteen months. In November he set out with Isabel and Dr Baker for a four-month tour of Malta and North Africa, returning to Trieste on his sixty-ninth birthday.

Because he now found the climate in Trieste as unbearable in summer as in winter, they left again in July for another wandering tour around Austria and Switzerland. He was becoming increasingly irritable and found much to complain of wherever they went. He himself recognized this and said to Isabel, 'Do you know, I am in a very bad way; I have got to hate everybody except you and myself, and it frightens me, because I know perfectly well that next year I shall get to hate you and the year after that I shall get to hate myself, and then I don't know what will become of me. We are always wandering, and the places that delight *you* I say to myself, "Dry rot", and the next place I say, "Dry rotter", and the third place I say, "Dry rottest", and then *da capo*.'

In the Engadine the Burtons met Henry Morton Stanley and his wife who were there on their honeymoon. Stanley had followed roughly the route Burton had taken to Lake Tanganyika on his search for Dr Livingstone, but in his first book Stanley had said some rather hard things about his predecessor on the trail. Also, Stanley had shown that Burton's lake, the Tanganyika, was not a source of the Nile, and, by circumnavigating Lake Victoria, had proved Speke right and Burton wrong in the great controversy over the dimensions and importance of that lake. Nevertheless, Burton had developed a very high regard for Stanley and once called him 'the Prince of African travellers' – high praise indeed from Burton. One day when they were out taking photographs of each other Dorothy Stanley handed Burton a piece of folded paper and asked him for his autograph. Complying, he signed his name in English and in Arabic (Abdullah). Mrs Stanley then unfolded the paper and disclosed that he had signed a statement that said, 'I promise to put aside all other literature and, as soon as I return to Trieste, to write my own autobiography.' Everyone laughed and the rest of the party signed as witnesses.

That evening the Burtons and the Stanleys were again together and Stanley seriously urged Burton to write his reminiscences. Burton said he could not because he would have to speak of too many people in an unfavourable light. 'Be charitable to them, and write only of their best qualities,' Stanley advised him.

'I don't care a fig for charity,' Burton replied. 'If I write at all, I must write truthfully all I know.'

Some years earlier Burton had started to write his autobiography and had since worked at it off and on, but the work was never completed and only fragments have survived. He told Stanley he was currently engaged in writing a book called 'Anthropology of Men and Women', but that the title did not adequately describe its contents. In his journal that night Stanley wrote:

What a grand man! One of the real great ones of England he might have been, if he had not been cursed with cynicism. I have no idea to what his anthology refers, but I would lay great odds that it is only another means of relieving himself of a surcharge of spleen against the section of humanity who have excited his envy, dislike, or scorn. If he had a broad mind, he would curb these tendencies, and thus allow men to see more clearly his grander qualities.

The book on anthropology existed only in Burton's mind or, at best, in scattered notes. Telling Stanley he was working on this book was but another example of that curious tendency of his to speak of books he wanted to write or intended to write as though they were practically finished. In truth, he was at this time working on a translation of Catullus and other Latin poets in collaboration with Leonard C. Smithers. He did his work by writing directly on the pages of the Latin text. Sometimes in Switzerland he would take his Catullus to dinner with him and work on it at the table. One of these translations from the Latin appeared in this year (1890), although the names of the translators were not shown. The name of this book was *Priapeia, or the Sportive Epigrams of Divers Poets on Priapus*. Only 500 copies were printed and privately sold. In most copies there is a statement in the preface that says, 'The name of Sir Richard F. Burton, translator of "The Book of The Thousand Nights and a Night" has been inadvertently connected with the present work. It is, however, only fair to state that under the circumstances he distinctly disclaims having taken any part in the issue.' However, there exist at least two copies of this book in which quite different words appear at this point in the preface: 'English literary students have good reason to congratulate themselves on the collaboration of the talented translator of "The Book of The Thousand Nights and a Night", the mention of whose name is a sufficient guarantee for the quality of the work.' This version of the preface also mentions the proposed Catullus translation, saying that it will be in the same format as the present volume and 'It will suffice to say that Sir Richard Burton's metrical version will leave nothing for any future translator to accomplish, either on the score of poetical beauty or of fidelity to the original text.' Obviously, the version was printed before the translators changed their minds about attaching their names to the work. The *Priapeia* was the last book of Burton's printed in his lifetime.

The Burtons returned to Trieste on 8 September. Burton planned to start on another trip to Greece and Turkey on 15 November, but when that day arrived they were chanting in the church of his wife the last great dirge for the repose of his soul. The number of his days on earth was now forty-two.

During these last few days of life Burton worked hard translating erotic Latin poetry and annotating an Arabic book on sexual intercourse called *The Scented (or Perfumed) Garden*. He also pained Isabel by 'talking more than ever agnostically at the table'. Yet he felt the approach of death and talked more and more about it. He seemed somehow to connect his approaching end with the departure of the swallows. He would watch them for long periods with a sad look on his face. He said to Isabel, 'When the swallows form a dado round the house, when they are crowding on the windows, in thousands, preparatory to flight, call me.'

On 20 September, when he had exactly one month of life left, he wrote in his diary, 'I feel too well. . . . The house covered with swallows. . . . Sat on the balcony – perfect evening, perfect day.'

Early in October he complained much of his liver, but on 15 October he was well enough to pay an official call on the Austrian governor. There were five days left to him.

On 18 October – he would die the day after tomorrow – Dr Baker took a picture of the Burtons in their garden.

The next day he complained a bit of lumbago. How close now was Death. He must have heard the camel bell and felt the breath of the grave that would mark the beginning of his last pilgrimage. With Isabel he talked of 19 March, his seventieth birthday, when he would retire and they would live in a cottage or small apartment in England. The day before his death was Sunday and in the afternoon he took a walk alone in the garden. There he found a baby robin that had fallen into a tank of water. He called for Dr Baker to get it out, warmed the bird in his hands, put it inside his fur coat and fussed about it until assured it would get well. On this day too he worked on the last page of *The Scented Garden*, but he promised Isabel, 'Tomorrow I shall have finished this, and I promise you that I will never write another book on this subject. I will take to our biography.' And she replied, 'What happiness that will be!'

That night he went to bed about 9.30 and Isabel said prayers for him. While she was praying, a dog outside began a long howl.

When she had finished she gave her husband a novel to read, *The Martyrdom of Madeline* by Robert Buchanan. At midnight he complained of his gout. Isabel sat beside him and he dozed for a while. He awoke once and said, 'I dreamt I saw our little flat in London, and it had quite a nice large room in it.'

At four o'clock Isabel called Dr Baker, who came and gave him some medicine. A half-hour later he complained that he could not get air. Dr Baker came back and found him dying. Isabel frantically sent servants in all directions to find a priest.

Isabel held him in her arms and he cried out, 'Oh, Puss, chloroform – ether – or I am a dead man!'

Isabel sobbed, 'My darling, the doctor says it will kill you. He is doing all he knows.'

'My God, I am a dead man,' he cried.

And there came to him then the Destroyer of delights and the Sunderer of societies.

But Isabel refused to believe it. At her insistence, Dr. Baker attached an electric battery to his heart and she made him leave it there until seven o'clock in the morning. She knelt at the left side of the bed, feeling for a pulse that was not there and praying her heart out that his soul might remain within his body until a priest should arrive.

At last a country priest, Father Pietro Martelani, reached the house. He told Isabel he could not give extreme unction because Burton had not declared himself. Isabel promised to satisfy him on this point later and begged him to hurry. The priest looked at the body and then at Dr Baker, Isabel and the maid, and asked if he was dead. Isabel insisted that he was not, so he administered extreme unction.

All day long Isabel sat beside the body, watching it. She believed his brain lived after his heart had stopped. She believed he lived until sunset. At last she knelt down again with her broken heart and said her '*fiat voluntas tua*'. Then she stood up and said, 'Let the world rain fire and brimstone on me now!'

It did.

Chapter 26

Marble Tent and Burned Papers
1890 – 6

To be positively, absolutely sure beyond any doubt that her husband was indeed dead, Isabel ordered a strong charge of electricity to be applied in the left ulnar vein. But all life had fled. Even Isabel was at last convinced and she herself closed his eyes and bound up his jaw. The Visitatore dei Morti (a government official, usually a doctor) came and was persuaded to mark on his form under the question regarding religion: 'Catholic'. Then the embalmers came and injected their fluid into his veins and his body took on the appearance of white marble. Isabel said, 'He looked like in a peaceful sleep, with adorable dignity and repose – a very majesty in his death – every inch a man, a soldier, and a gentleman.'

So the god was dead. Nothing now remained but to preserve the myth, build the temple, promulgate the scriptures.

First came the funeral, or rather funerals, for there were, in effect, two funerals: one in Trieste and another in England. The first one, in Trieste, was the grandest. The bishop conceded to him all the great ceremonies of the Catholic Church and the Austrian authorities a splendid military funeral. 'They tell me,' said Isabel, 'that no funeral has been equal to it in the memory of any one living, not even Maria Theresa's, ex-Queen of Spain, in 1873.' Burton's friend, Attilio Hortis of Trieste, gave the funeral oration.

Then came what Dr F. Grenfell Baker described as 'the ruthless holocaust that followed his lamented death'. For sixteen days Isabel, Burton's literary executrix, remained closeted in her husband's room with at least twenty-seven years' accumulation of his notebooks, manuscripts, books and papers – sorting, classifying, packing – and burning. Because of her actions in this period, Isabel was pilloried in the press, old friends turned against her, and even today she is mainly known only as the woman who burned Burton's papers.

All his life Burton had kept journals and notebooks in which he recorded everything he had done and seen. Dr Grenfell Baker was most impressed with his meticulosity:

During his travels, and indeed always, he made it a daily practice to record every single occurrence of interest with which he became acquainted. If he were reading a book or other document of importance he would carefully resume the whole of its salient features that were previously unknown to him; if he himself were to write on any subject he would collect every detail bearing on it; if he talked with anyone he wrote down as soon as possible all that was novel or in any way striking that was uttered; and, in short, on each and every day he inscribed in his diary or elsewhere with meticulous care all that he considered worth while placing on permanent record.

There were at least two sets of journals: one was private and the other was simply a normal diary of daily events. Isabel burned all of the first and most of the second set. She also, apparently, burned many other private letters and papers, but Isabel's chief crime in the eyes of her critics was the burning of one particular manuscript: his translation of *The Perfumed Garden*, or *The Scented Garden*.

Burton always kept before him a number of literary pieces on which he worked when the fancy took him. When he died there were at least forty-one different books in various stages of completion (see Appendix). Of these, seven were complete, or nearly so. *The Scented Garden* was to have been finished on the day of his death. According to Dr Baker, Burton called this work his '*magnum opus*'; according to Isabel (after the storm broke), Burton called it simply 'a good potboiler'. In a letter to Leonard C. Smithers, with whom Burton was collaborating in the translation of *The Carmina of Caius Valerius Catullus*, Burton said of *The Scented Garden*, 'It will be a marvellous repertory of Eastern wisdom; how Eunuchs are made, and are married; what they do in marriage; female circumcision, the Fellahs copulating with crocodiles, etc. Mrs. Grundy will howl till she almost bursts, and will read every word with an intense enjoyment.'

It was Isabel herself who innocently let the cat out of the bag with a letter to the *Morning Post* on 19 January 1891, in which she confessed that she burned the manuscript. Here, she too called the book his '*magnum opus*'. Later she said, 'I shall never regret what I have done, but I shall regret all my life having confessed it.' The purpose of her letter was to give a general answer to those who had written to her since the death of her husband asking about posthumous works. Here she confessed her own doubts about destroying *The Scented Garden*: 'Was it sacrilege? It was his *magnum opus*, his last work he was so proud of, that was to have been finished on that awful morrow – that never came. Will he rise up to curse or bless me?' It was not Burton, but the great British public that rose up *en masse* to condemn her action in nearly every newspaper in the land. She also received a flood of letters, many anonymous, vilifying her for destroying her husband's work. Her sometime friend Ouida wrote years later, 'I never spoke or wrote to her after that irreparable act.'

Isabel was amazed. 'I never supposed for an instant that my action would excite any comment, one way or the other,' she said. On 31 October 1893, she wrote to Lady Guendolen Ramsden, daughter of her friends the Duke and Duchess of Somerset, 'My dear husband did it simply to fill our purse again. . . . My husband had no vicious motive in writing it. . . . I was so astonished to find myself either praised or blamed; it seemed to me the natural thing for a woman to do. . . . I know that he, being dead, would not have wished it published; if so, why did he leave it to me?'

Before Burton was in his tomb, Isabel was engaged in a tremendous controversy in which she, the greatest admirer of her husband's work, was blamed on all sides for destroying it. In her own defence she maintained that she had a right to destroy the manuscript (which she did), and that she had 'done infinitely more for his reputation and memory by burning it than by printing it. She also shifted her ground and maintained that it was not one of his important works: 'I was under some delusion which I have often bewailed, that I was responsible to, or owed some explanation to, the would-be buyers of that book, nor can I *now* think how I could have imagined that it was, or described it as, my husband's *magnum opus* – perhaps it was because it was the first work of the kind I had ever read – as it certainly was the *least* of his works.'

What exactly was *The Perfumed Garden*? Was it Burton's *magnum opus*? It is most doubtful if the loss to mankind or to world literature was great. The work was an expanded version of the translation he had made in 1886, the expansion probably taking the form of more lengthy annotation. While we can never know the precise contents of the 'anthropological notes', the nature of the work itself, a sixteenth-century manual of Arab erotology, said to have been written by one 'Sheikh Nefzawi', is not of the stuff from which great literature is made. The work has been, and is still, published in French and English by publishers in Paris, that capital of pornography for the Western world. Ostensibly it is a book of sexual advice and information, sprinkled with Arabic versions of old wives' tales. A listing of some of the chapter and section titles will illustrate the character of the work: 'Concerning the length of a virile member', 'Of the utility of scents in coition', 'Concerning the different postures of coition', 'Story of a man cuckolded by his donkey', 'How to develop the member and give it a superb appearance', 'How a woman may deodorize her armpits and vagina and how the latter may be shrunk', *et al.* In short, it was the sort of work Burton would enjoy annotating, but its literary merits were hardly comparable to *The Arabian Nights.* It is doubtful if many of those who criticized Isabel for burning it would have read the work; fewer still would have thought it worth reading. Still, the burning of dead authors' manuscripts is a bad business and those who damned Isabel doubtless felt themselves on safe ground.

Isabel was most bitter about the attacks made upon her and wondered why those who had neglected her husband and his works while alive should now take such a lively interest in his burned manuscripts now that he was dead. She saw all her years of devotion and work for her husband's interest put as nothing beside her few moments of trash burning after his death. She became quite melodramatic about this:

Who cheered him on in danger, toil, and heart-breaking sickness? Who, when he came back from Tanganyika (Africa) in 1859, coldly looked upon by the Government, bullied by the India House, rejected by the Geographical Society on account of the machinations of Captain Speke, so that he scarcely had ten friends to say good-morning to him, – who sought his side to comfort him? I did! ... Who copied and worked for and with him? Who fought for thirty years to raise his official position all she could and wept bitter tears over his being neglected? I did. ... Who rode or walked at his side through hunger, thirst, cold, and burning heat, with hardships and privations and danger, in all his travels? Who nursed him through seven long illnesses, before his last illness, some lasting two or three months, and never left his bed-head day or night, and did everything for him? I did! ... 'Burnt manuscript' readers! where were *you* all then? ... And do any of *you* pretend or wish to take *him* away from *me* in death? Oh, for shame, for shame!

After packing up Burton's books and personal effects in 204 cases and arranging for the body to be shipped, Isabel left for England, arriving on 7 February 1891. She at once went to inform Burton's sister and niece of the circumstances of her husband's death and of her intentions regarding his burial. Lady Stisted and her daughter Georgiana were not pleased. They had never liked Isabel and had always resented her religion. They were enraged at the account of Richard's death-bed conversion given them by Dr Baker and now the flames of anger were fanned by Isabel's plans for another funeral and a burial in a Catholic cemetery. 'Rome took formal possession of Richard Burton's corpse, and pretended, moreover, with insufferable insolence, to take under her protection his soul,' wrote Georgiana.

Isabel made some inquiries about the possibility of having her husband buried in Westminster Abbey, but she did not press the point and accepted the first excuse offered: the place was too crowded. What she really wanted was a Catholic burial in England, so she arranged for him to be buried in the Catholic cemetery at Mortlake in Surrey where they had bought a plot years before. She decided that his tomb should be something appropriate and extraordinary, and to create what she had in mind she collected £688 from friends. The result was an Arab tent twelve feet square and eighteen feet high made of dark Forest of Dean stone and Carrara marble with a nine-pointed gilt star on top and a crucifix over the door. Isabel described it as 'by far the most beautiful, most romantic, most undeathlike resting-place in the wide world'. It is indeed a curious mausoleum for a suburban English cemetery, but one which few people today have taken the trouble to find.

Georgiana Stisted, writing in 1896, said, 'Fifty years hence London's ever-advancing tide will have swept away every vestige of the shabby sectarian cemetery where Richard Burton lies.' Although it is now engulfed by Greater London, Miss Stisted's prediction has not proved quite correct. Covered with soot and grime, in an almost hidden churchyard tucked away in a working-class neighbourhood, the marble tent has suffered from neglect: the stained glass window is broken, memorial tablets have fallen off, the gilt star has rusted and the plot is overgrown with weeds. Because of a high wall around the cemetery, many of the people who live quite near do not even know of the tomb's existence.

It was several months after Isabel arrived in England before the marble tent was ready. Meanwhile, Burton's corpse arrived – though not in a piano case, as one unkind critic reported – and was stowed away in the crypt of St Mary Magdalen's church in Mortlake. Shortly afterwards, Isabel broke down. February, March and April were spent between bed and armchair in her sisters' care. 'The sense of desolation and loneliness and the longing for him was cruel,' she wrote.

At last, on 15 June, the marble tent was ready and Isabel prepared to lay her husband in it with another funeral. In spite of all entreaties, no member of the Burton family would attend except a cousin, Captain St George Burton. But nearly eight hundred people – Isabel's relations, friends, curious strangers – took the trains that left Waterloo Station at 10.20 a.m. for Mortlake.

The temple was built and Isabel, who was living in a house at 67 Baker Street, now also took a cottage at 2 North Worple Way in Mortlake, so she could continue her worship at the shrine and build the myth of Burton in an image of her own creation. In this she was not very successful. She had destroyed most of his papers, but Burton had written and published too much; besides, her own health was breaking down at an alarming rate and she was unequal to the task of recasting her husband in the mould of her own opinion. Nevertheless, she now began two ambitious projects: her own biography of Burton and a memorial edition of his complete works. Only seven volumes of the memorial edition were ever published, but she did manage to complete in 1893 her biography of her husband. It is a most curious affair. Its more than 1,200 pages appear to have been untouched by an editor's hand, and it contains numerous repetitious statements, contradictions and errors of fact and dates, many of which were copied by later biographers. Quotations and extracts from journals or publications were inserted, apparently without ever having been read. At one point, for example, she tells of descending the Morro Velho mine in Brazil, saying, 'I forget the positive depth of it, but am under the impression *now* that it was three-quarters of a mile straight down into the bowels of the earth.' On the very next page she quotes Burton's account of the mine descent in which he says that the mine was 1,134 feet deep. In some cases the same experience is described two and even three times. Rambling accounts such as this are no longer published today: the present-day reader's gain; the future biographer's loss.

Of the four posthumous books by Burton, only two were published during Isabel's lifetime. The first was a translation of *Il Pentamerone*, a collection of tales after the manner of the *Decameron*, published in 1893. The most remarkable aspect of this work is the fact that it was written in a rather difficult old Neapolitan dialect. Burton had probably learned the dialect as a young man but had had little occasion to use it since. Yet his remarkably retentive memory had enabled him to make this translation from the dialect nearly fifty years later.

The second posthumous work was a translation of *The Carmina of Catullus*, published in a limited edition of 750 copies in 1894. In a letter to Leonard Smithers, Burton's collaborator, Isabel said that Burton 'began his Catullus on Feb. 18th, 1890, at Hamman R'irha, in North Africa', yet by her own account in her biography of Burton, he began seriously working on this book at least as early as November 1889. It was Burton's idea that this work should be published in the original Latin – 'nude Roman poetry', he called it – but with each poem followed by an English metrical version by himself and a prose translation by Smithers. Burton and Smithers had corresponded on this work for some time, and the correspondence was continued by Isabel after her husband's death. She told Smithers that Burton had written in a margin, 'Work incomplete, but as soon as I receive Mr. Smithers' prose, I will fill in the words I now leave in stars, in order that we may not use the same expressions, and I will then make a third, fair, and complete copy.' It seems most improbable that Burton ever wrote such a marginal note. Certainly Smithers did not believe he did. Sir Richard had never before troubled himself in the least about using the same expressions as his collaborator, Smithers protested. Isabel refused all requests from Smithers to give him Burton's own manuscript. Instead, she sent a typewritten copy which she repeatedly assured him was a faithful transcription. Smithers complained that the typewritten copy was 'swarming with copyist's errors'. It seems quite obvious that Isabel was playing the role of censor and had eliminated all the words she felt were objectionable, leaving Smithers to supply them if he wished. Then it would not be her Burton who had written the naughty words but Smithers.

The remaining two posthumous works, *The Jew, the Gypsy and El Islam* and *Wanderings on Three Continents*, were published after Isabel's death and are simply compilations of various notes and incomplete manuscripts Burton had left. The first part of *The Jew, the Gypsy and El Islam*, an anti-semitic tract, had a rather curious history. It consists mainly of notes made between 1869 and 1871 when Burton was in Damascus. In its original form it included an appendix entitled 'Human Sacrifices amongst the Shepardim or Eastern Jews'. In 1873, when he was appointed consul at Trieste, he began to put the work into final form and in 1875 he took it with him to England to be published. Friends advised him not to publish the book because it would injure him in the eyes of prominent Jews, many of whom were in the government. Also, Isabel had just come out with her *Inner Life of Syria* in which she maintained that Burton was not anti-semitic but only disliked certain individual Jewish usurers he had encountered at Damascus. In 1886, after his failure to obtain the post at Tangier, Burton again took the manuscript from his drawer, worked on it, and had it recopied. Isabel persuaded him not to publish it at this time as she was then trying to obtain permission for him to retire on full pension at sixty-five and felt it would injure his chances. Burton again delayed publication, but he was determined to bring it out as soon as he retired. When Isabel died the manuscript was turned over to W. H. Wilkins by Isabel's sister. Wilkins published it in 1898, together with material Burton had written on gypsies and on Islam but without the appendix. The manuscript of the missing appendix was sold to Henry Frederick Walpole Manners Sutton who attempted to publish it in 1911. He was restrained from doing so by a court order, for Isabel's executors had, in 1909, reassigned the papers to D. L. Lawrence. It was Lawrence who obtained the court injunction and the manuscript has never been printed.

From her house in Baker Street Isabel continued her literary work with frequent stays at what she called 'our cottage' in Mortlake where she could be near the tomb of her husband. But her last years were neither easy nor comfortable. Sick and suffering, in reduced economic circumstances, uprooted from her beloved Trieste home, deprived of her god-husband by death, condemned by the Burton family for burying her husband as a Catholic, and reviled by press and public for burning his papers, her life was difficult and bitter.

The Baker Street house was a veritable Burton museum and she furnished it in oriental fashion: there were oriental curtains at the windows, Persian and Bedouin rugs on the floors and rooms stuffed with oriental curios, pictures, water-pipes and other Eastern bric-à-brac. In the living room was a life-sized portrait of Burton in Arabic dress. Burton's books – his own and those he had used – were everywhere, and in the attic were the remains of his notes and papers. Here she worked constantly on her husband's books and papers, intending to republish all his works in a grand series to be called 'The Labours and Wisdom of Sir Richard Burton'. Exactly what was to be included in this series is not known for it was never begun. She even started an autobiography, but it was never completed.

The main shrine of this one-woman cult was Burton's tomb. She used part of the money she received for his biography to embellish the mausoleum with 'festoons of camel bells'. She went there often, and on 22 January 1894, the thirty-third anniversary of her wedding, she spent the entire day in the tomb. It was even said, probably incorrectly, that she received visitors there. She did, however, often spend several months at a time at Mortlake. There was a strange sequel to Isabel's visits to the marble tent. For three years following Isabel's death there were séances held there by a woman who called herself 'Miss X' (she was a Miss Goodrich Freer). Then the cult died and the tomb was neglected.

There is no doubt that Burton attained a higher degree of popular fame immediately after his death than he enjoyed during his lifetime and it is ironical that this was mainly because of the furore created by Isabel's burning of his papers. No better indication of this sudden interest in Burton could be found than the decision of Madame Tussaud's wax museum to include his effigy in its collection. John Theodore Tussaud, grandson of the museum's founder, said 'When Sir Richard died his remarkable career became so much a subject of general comment in the press that the British public awakened to the fact that a great Englishman had just passed away.' Isabel was delighted by this recognition of her husband's greatness and she gave every assistance to the wax artists preparing the image. She personally dressed the figure with Burton's own clothes, those he had worn to Mecca, and she spent hours making sure that each detail of his costume was correct. She struck Tussaud as being a pathetic figure as her fingers lingered over the final touches of the robe, arranging the pleats and folds. One detail disturbed her, however: the original sandals Burton had worn to Mecca were unusable. She finally supplied this deficiency by sending Tussaud a pair of sandals she obtained from 'the Prior of the Franciscans'. For her, there was no incongruity.

Isabel at this time was described as 'handsome and stately', but she was also regarded by acquaintances and neighbours as a delightful eccentric. Although she had little money – the profits from *The Arabian Nights* had been spent on travelling and the private doctors – she never went out without giving away all the money she had with her to beggars. At Christmas she bought toys for poor children, buying them from street vendors rather than from stores and always attracting a crowd by haggling over the prices as though she were buying in the bazaar of Damascus. She was preyed upon by spiritualists and made attempts to commune with her dead husband. She was still concerned over cruelty to animals and engaged in vigorous controversies about vivisection; she never entered a cab without first inspecting the horse to see if it had been well treated, and even then she always kept the window down so as to keep a sharp eye on the driver: if he flicked his whip she would lunge at him with her umbrella, and if he protested she would shout, 'Yes, and how do you like it?'

But Isabel's health was fast failing. Cancer was consuming her and she had lost all real desire to live. She wanted to follow her husband into the new land into which she was sure he had gone. At the end of her biography of him she had written, 'Reader! I have paid, I have packed, I have suffered. I am waiting to join his caravan. I am waiting for a welcome sound – "the tinkling of his camel-bell".' She did not have long to wait.

On Passion Sunday, 21 March 1896, a priest came and administered extreme unction and the holy viaticum. When it was over she whispered, 'Thank God.' A few minutes later there came to her the Angel of Death and she went to join her 'earthly God and King'.

Appendix
Manuscript material left by Sir Richard Burton

In 1893 Isabel Burton compiled a list of her husband's unpublished works. The list was not complete and it would appear that it was simply written down from memory. Nevertheless, it gives some indication of the kinds of books Burton still planned to write. Much of the material he had been collecting over a period of many years. The first work listed was virtually complete; of the next three Isabel said, 'These are quite complete'; and of the 'Catullus' she notes that it was 'almost complete'. The others she described as 'In a semi-state of completion, or only materials and notes.'

'Uruguay'
'Ladislas Magyar's African Travels'
'Pentamerone'
A book on the Jews
'Catullus'
'More Notes on Paraguay'
'Personal Experiences in Syria'
'Lowlands of Brazil'
'North America'
'South America'
'Central America'
'A Book on Istria – more Castelleri'

According to Isabel, there were materials for another book of the sword, four more books on Camoens, books on Greek proverbs, gypsies, Slavonic proverbs, 'Dr. Wetstein's Hauràn', 'Apuleius, or the Golden Ass' and 'Ausonius (Epigrams)'.

In addition to this list, a Miss Plowman, who served for a time as a companion to Lady Burton, also compiled a list of manuscript material she claimed to have seen:

'A Study of the Wali'
'Akkas'
'A Trip up the Congo, 1863'
'Ober Ammergau'
'Vichy'
'Lectures and Poetry'
'The Eunuch Trade in Egypt'
'Akits as Mirza Ali'
'The Ashanti War'

Appendix

'Classics, Poetry and Scraps'
'Inscriptions'
'Sind – Karachi'
'The Adelsburg Caves'
'The Neapolitan Muses'
'Syrian Proverbs'
'Pilpay's Fables'
'An Essay on Islam'
'Four Cantos of Ariosto'

All of this material presumably escaped the flames of Isabel's paper burning shortly after Burton's death. There was, too, at least one small ($3'' \times 4\frac{1}{2}''$) notebook of Burton's that was saved. This was in the possession of N. M. Penzer, but was destroyed during World War II. As has been noted, *The Pentamerone*, *The Carmina of Catullus* and Burton's notes on *The Jew, the Gypsy and El Islam* were published after his death. Many of his travel notes were also collected and published posthumously in *Wanderings on Three Continents*. The manuscript for 'Uruguay', a translation by the two Burtons from the Portuguese, is now in the Huntington Library in San Marino, California, together with a collection of letters to and from the Burtons, including much correspondence between Isabel and Leonard C. Smithers regarding the *Catullus*. 'Pilpay's Fables' as well as most, if not all, of the material for further books on the sword is now with the remains of the Burton library at the Royal Anthropological Institute of Great Britain and Ireland in London.

Of the manuscript material seen by Miss Plowman, some had probably been published. 'Ober Ammergau' was perhaps the manuscript for *A Glance at the Passion Play* and the 'Syrian Proverbs' may have been 'Proverbia Communia Syriaca', originally published by the Royal Asiatic Society and printed as an appendix in *Unexplored Syria*. The material on the 'Ashantee War' was probably for a magazine article rather than a book. Many notes on a wide variety of subjects are still at the Royal Anthropological Institute, but there is not enough to make complete books.

The work listed as 'Ladislas Magyar's African Travels' by Isabel and which she said was 'quite complete', has been lost. It was probably a translation of Laszlo Magyar's *Reisen in Südafrika*, the first volume of which was published in 1859. The translation of *The Golden Ass* of Lucius Apuleius may still be extant. Penzer, although he had never seen the manuscript, reported that at one time it was in the hands of a bookseller in Paris.

Most of the other material listed as having been left by Burton when he died was presumably destroyed in the second burning of manuscripts and books that took place after the death of Isabel in 1896. Isabel's sister, Mrs Fitzgerald, sent much material to the flames in what Penzer called 'a mad fit of wantonness'.

Bibliography

THE formal bibliography given below is a simplified one, made possible by the fact that a very excellent and nearly complete bibliography of Burton already exists: *Annotated Bibliography of Sir Richard Burton*, by N. M. Penzer. This scholarly work has not only enabled me to simplify my own bibliography, but, more importantly, it has saved me months, probably years, of research. Knowing of the existence of a source is not everything – it is also necessary to find the material – but knowledge of its existence is certainly the all-important beginning. I am most grateful to Mr Penzer, and to Carl A. Malouf, who so kindly lent me his copy of this invaluable document for so many years.

Most of the facts of Burton's life were collected from his own voluminous writings and those of his wife; other facts were obtained from the writings of his friends and enemies, and from official and unofficial records. Locating the necessary material has involved a tremendous effort, although even now I cannot pretend to have found every scrap of paper. The greatest single task, however, has been to sort through the material available to learn the truth behind the many contradictions, inaccuracies and deliberate attempts to conceal information on the part of Burton or his wife. Even the usually simple matter of chronology – finding where Burton was when – has sometimes, as in the case of his terms on the west coast of Africa, been the work of many weeks. Unfortunately, I have not been aided much by the previous biographies of Burton, most of them written during his lifetime or shortly after his death. As Penzer rightly said, 'every single one was written for some particular object of a personal nature'.

The first bit of biography was published in 1880 by a man who called himself 'An Old Oxonian' and was entitled *A Short Sketch of the Career of Captain Richard F. Burton*. Old Oxonian was A. B. Richards who had attended Oxford with Burton. This sketch is notable for the number of errors it made which were copied by later biographers. For example, Old Oxonian listed among his references 'The whole of Vol. XXXIII of the Royal Geographical Society . . . 1860.' This particular volume, it turns out, was not published until three years after the date given and contains only a brief article by Burton. The volume obviously meant was Vol. XXIX, published in 1859, which was almost completely written by Burton. Yet this particular error was repeated in every subsequent biography that deigned to list references, including that of Burton's wife and Burton's niece (whose biography was written with the intention of contradicting Lady Burton's). Quite obviously, none of these people bothered to consult the reference.

It is astonishing how few, if any, of Burton's biographers even bothered to read all of his works. Many of the ancient mysteries have been cleared up through a close reading of Burton's own writings, most of which were hurriedly written and unedited. Information which he wanted to conceal at one period of his life he disclosed, intentionally or unintentionally, years later. Then, too, anyone who wrote as much about himself as Burton did was certain to sometimes say more than he wished. A comparison of statements in different books and articles at different times in his life has often been most illuminating.

In addition to printed source material, I have also, of course, made use of manuscript material. Most of this has come from the Royal Anthropological Institute of Great Britain and Ireland in London and the Huntington Library in San Marino, California. I have also consulted manuscript material from various agencies of the British Government, from my own collection, from private sources and from the Biblioteca Civica in Trieste. A fuller note on the manuscript material extant after Burton's death will be found in the Appendix.

Books by Sir Richard Burton

An almost complete list of the various editions of Burton's books and of the magazine articles by Burton is given by Norman M. Penzer in *An Annotated Bibliography of Sir Richard Francis Burton*, A. M. Philpot, London, 1923. The list that follows gives only the title, date and publisher of the first editions in chronological order, excluding translations.

Goa, and the Blue Mountains; or Six Months of Sick Leave. Richard Bentley, London, 1851.

Scinde: or The Unhappy Valley. 2 vols. Richard Bentley, London, 1851.

Sindh, and the Races that Inhabit the Valley of the Indus. William H. Allen, London, 1851.

Falconry in the Valley of the Indus. J. Van Voorst, London, 1852.

A Complete System of Bayonet Exercise. William Clowes & Sons, London, 1853.

Personal Narrative of a Pilgrimage to El-Medinah and Meccah. 3 vols. Longman, Brown, Green, & Longmans, 1855 – 6. (There have been a number of editions of this work, but the most complete is the 'Memorial Edition' published by Tylston & Edwards, London, 1893. It contains all eight appendices.)

First Footsteps in East Africa; or an Exploration of Harar. Longman, Brown, Green, & Longmans, London, 1856.

The Lake Regions of Central Africa. 2 vols. Longman, Green, Longman, & Roberts, London, 1860.

The City of the Saints and Across the Rocky Mountains to California. Longman, Green, Longman, & Roberts, London, 1861.

Abeokuta and the Camaroons Mountains. 2 vols. Tinsley Bros, London, 1863.

Wanderings in West Africa from Liverpool to Fernando Po. 2 vols. 'By a F.R.G.S.' Tinsley Bros, London, 1863.

A Mission to Gelele, King of Dahome. 2 vols. Tinsley Bros, London, 1864.

The Nile Basin. Part I, Burton and Part II by James M'Queen. Tinsley Bros, London, 1864.

The Guide Book. A Pictorial Pilgrimage to Mecca and Medina. William Clowes & Sons, London, 1865.

Stone Talk (ΛΙΘΟΦΩΝΗΜΑ): *Being Some of the Marvellous Sayings of a Petral Portion of Fleet Street.* 'By Frank Baker, D.O.N.' Robert Hardwicke, London, 1865.

The Highlands of Brazil. 2 vols. Tinsley Bros, London, 1869.

Letters from the Battle-fields of Paraguay. Tinsley Bros, London, 1870.

Unexplored Syria. 2 vols. With Charles F. Tyrwhitt-Drake. Tinsley Bros, London, 1872.

Zanzibar; City, Island, and Coast. 2 vols. Tinsley Bros, London, 1872.

Ultima Thule: or a Summer in Iceland. 2 vols. William P. Nimmo, London and Edinburgh, 1875.

Etruscan Bologne: A Study. Smith, Elder & Co., London, 1876.

A New System of Sword Exercise for Infantry. William Clowes & Sons, London, 1876.

Two Trips to Gorilla Land and the Cataracts of the Congo. 2 vols. Sampson Low, Marston, Low & Searle, London, 1876.

Scind Revisited. 2 vols. Richard Bentley & Son, London, 1877.

The Gold Mines of Midian and the Ruined Midianite Cities. C. Kegan Paul, London, 1878.

The Land of Midian (*revisited*). 2 vols. C. Kegan Paul, London, 1879.

The Kasîdah of Hâjî Abû El-Yezdî. 'Translated and annotated [*sic*] by His Friend and Pupil F. B.' Privately printed (Bernard Quaritch). London, 1880.

A Glance at the "Passion Play". W. H. Harrison, London, 1881.

To the Gold Coast for Gold. 2 vols. By Richard F. Burton and Verney Lovett Cameron. Chatto & Windus, London, 1883.

The Book of the Sword. Chatto & Windus, London, 1884.

Books translated by or edited and annotated by Burton and published in his lifetime.

The Prairie Traveller, a Handbook for Overland Expeditions. Randolph B. Marcy, edited (with notes) by Richard F. Burton. Trübner, London, 1863.

Wit and Wisdom from West Africa; or A Book of Proverbial Philosophy, Idioms, Enigmas, and Laconisms. Tinsley Bros, London, 1865.

Vikram and the Vampire or Tales of Hindu Devilry. Longmans, Green, London, 1870.

The Lands of Cazembe. The first part of this book (164 pp.): 'Lacerda's Journey to Cazembe in 1798' was translated (from the Portuguese) and annotated by Burton. Published by the Royal Geographical Society. John Murray, London, 1873.

The Captivity of Hans Stade of Hesse, in A.D. 1547 – 1555, Among the Wild Tribes of Eastern Brazil. Translated by Albert Tootal and annotated by Burton. Printed for the Hakluyt Society. London, 1874.

Os Lusiadas (The Lusiads). 'Englished by Richard Francis Burton (Edited by His Wife, Isabel Burton).' 2 vols. Bernard Quaritch, London, 1880.

Camoens: His Life and his Lusiads. 2 vols. Bernard Quaritch, London, 1881.

Camoens, The Lyricks. 2 vols. Bernard Quaritch, London, 1884.

The Book of the Thousand Nights and a Night. 10 vols. 'Printed for the Kamashastra Society for Private Subscribers Only.' Benares, 1885 – 8.

Iraçéma, The Honey-lips, By J. De Alencar, Translated by Isabel Burton and *Maluel De Moraes, A Chronicle of the Seventeenth Century,* By J. M. Pereira Da Silva, Translated by Richard F. and Isabel Burton. Bickers & Son, London, 1886. (These two works were published together in a paper cover.)

Priapeia, or the Sportive Epigrams of Divers Poets on Priapus. Printed by the translators for private subscribers only. Anonymous (Richard Burton and Leonard C. Smithers). 1890.

Posthumous works of Burton

Marocco and the Moors. By Arthur Leared. Second edition revised and edited by Sir Richard Burton. Sampson Low, Marston, Searle, & Rivington, London; Scribner & Welford, New York, 1891.

II Pentamerone ; or, the Tale of Tales. 2 vols. Translated by Burton. Henry, London, 1893.

The Carmina of Caius Valerius Catullus. Verses translated by Burton; prose, notes and introduction by Smithers. Printed for the translators for private subscribers only. London, 1894.

The Jew, the Gypsy and El Islam. By Burton with a preface and notes by W. H. Wilkins. Hutchinson, London, 1898.

Wanderings in Three Continents. By Burton but edited and with preface by W. H. Wilkins. Hutchinson, London, 1901.

Selected Papers on Anthropology, Travel & Exploration by Sir Richard Burton. Edited with an introduction by N. M. Penzer. A. M. Philpot, London, 1924.

Publications of the Hindu Kāma Shāstra Society

The Kāma Sūtra of Vatsyayana. 1883.
Ananga Ranga. 1873.
The Perfumed Garden of Cheikh Nefzaoui: A Manual of Arabian Erotology.
1886.
The Behāristān. 1887.
The Gulistān. 1888.

Some Books Relating to Burton

Blanch, Lesley. *The Wilder Shores of Love.* John Murray, London, 1954.

Blunt, Wilfrid Scawen. *My Diaries.* 2 vols. Martin Secker, London, 1919 – 20.

Bombay Government Records, No. xvii, New Series, Part II, pp. 613 – 36.

Burton, Isabel. *Arabia Egypt India.* William Mullan & Son, London and Belfast, 1879.

—*Inner Life of Syria, Palestine and the Holy Land.* Henry S. King, London, 1876.

—*The Life of Captain Sir Richard F. Burton.* 2. vols. Chapman & Hall, London, 1893.

Burton, Jean. *Sir Richard Burton's Wife.* George Harrap, London, 1942.

Cameron, Verney Lovett. *Across Africa.* Daldy, Isbister, London, 1877.

Dearden, Seaton. *The Arabian Knight: A Study of Sir Richard Burton.* Arthur Barker, London, 1936.

Dodge, W. Phelps. *The Real Sir Richard Burton.* T. Fisher Unwin, London, 1907.

Downey, Fairfax. *Burton: Arabian Nights Adventurer.* Charles Scribner's Sons, New York and London, 1931.

Gordon, C. G. *The Journals of Major-Gen. C. G. Gordon, C.B.* Edited by A. Egmont Hake. Kegan Paul, Trench, London, 1885.

Hennessy, James Pope. *Monckton Milnes: The Flight of Youth.* Constable, London, 1951.

Hitchman, Francis. *Richard F. Burton.* 2 vols. Sampson Low, Marston, Searle & Rivington, London, 1887.

Johnston, Sir Harry. *George Grenfell and the Congo.* 2 vols. Hutchinson, London, 1908.

—*The Nile Quest.* Lawrance & Bullen, London, 1903.

—*The Story of My Life.* Chatto & Windus, London, 1923.

Lafourcade, Georges. *Swinburne, a Literary Biography.* George Bell & Sons, London, 1932.

Life and Letters of Sir Joseph Dalton Hook. 2 vols. John Murray, London, 1918.

Moorehead, Alan. *The White Nile.* Hamish Hamilton, London, 1960.

Penzer, Norman M. *An Annotated Bibliography of Sir Richard Francis Burton.* Preface by F. Grenfell Baker. A. M. Philpot, London, 1923.

Ralli, Augustus. *Christians at Mecca.* William Heinemann, London, 1909.

Redesdale, Lord. *Memories.* 2 vols. Hutchinson, London, 1915.

Richards, Alfred Bates. *A Sketch of the Career of Richard F. Burton.* Andrew Wilson, and St Clair Baddeley. Waterlow & Sons, London, 1886.

Russell, Mrs Charles E. B. *General Rigby, Zanzibar and the Slave Trade.* Unwin Brothers, Woking, 1935.

Schiffers, Heinrich. *The Quest for Africa.* Translated by Diana Pyke. Odhams Press, London, 1957.

Schonfield, Hugh J. *Richard Burton: Explorer.* Herbert Joseph London, 1936.

A Short Sketch of the Career of Captain Richard F. Burton. By 'An Old Oxonian' (Alfred Bates Richards). William Mullan & Son, London, 1880.

Speke, John Hanning. *Journal of the Discovery of the Source of the Nile.* William Blackwood & Sons, London; Harper & Bros, New York, 1864.

—*What led to the Discovery of the Source of the Nile.* William Blackwood & Sons, London, 1863.

Stanley, Henry M. *The Autobiography of Sir Henry M. Stanley.* Edited by Dorothy Stanley. Sampson Low, Marston, London, 1909.

Stirling, Monica. *The Fine and the Wicked: The Life and Times of Ouida.* Victor Gollancz, London, 1958.

Stisted, Georgiana M. *The True Life of Capt. Sir Richard F. Burton.* H. S. Nicols, London, 1896.

Swinburne, Algernon Charles. *Poems and Ballads. Second Series.* Chatto & Windus, London, 1878.

Tussaud, John Theodore. *The Romance of Madame Tussaud's.* Odhams Press, London, 1919.

Wilkins, W. H. *The Romance of Isabel Lady Burton.* 2 vols. Told in Part by herself. Chapman & Hall, London, 1897.

Wright, Thomas. *The Life of Sir Richard Burton.* 2 vols. G. P. Putnam's Sons, New York; Everett, London, 1906.

Some additional background sources consulted

Blanch, Lesley. *The Sabres of Paradise.* John Murray, London, 1960.

Bombay Almanac & Directory. Printed at the Times Press, Bombay, 1842.

Camoens, Luis Vaz de. *The Lusiads.* Translated by William C. Atkinson. Penguin Books, Harmondsworth, 1952.

Crabitès, Pierre. *American in the Egyptian Army.* George Routledge & Sons, London, 1938.

Cromer, The Earl of. *Modern Egypt.* 2 vols. Macmillan, London, 1908.

Doughty, Charles M. *Travels in Arabia Deserta.* The Heritage Press, New York, 1953.

Gilbert, Michael. *The Claimant.* Constable, London, 1957.

Goncourt, Edmond and Jules. *Mémoires de la vie littéraire*. Flammarion and Fasquelle, Paris, 1896.

Gosse, Edmund. *The Life of Algernon Charles Swinburne*. Macmillan, London, 1917.

—*Books on the Table*. William Heinemann, London, 1921.

Grant, James Augustus. *A Walk Across Africa*. William Blackwood & Sons, London, 1864.

Guillaume, Alfred. *Islam*. Penguin Books, Edinburgh, 1954.

Lane, Edward William. *An Account of the Manners and Customs of the Modern Egyptians*. Alexander Gardner, London, 1895.

Lane, Edward William, (translator). *The Thousand and One Nights*. 3 vols. C. Knight, London, 1839 – 41.

Low, Sidney. *Egypt in Transition*. Smith, Elder, London, 1914.

Markman, Clements R. *The Fifty Years Work of the Royal Geographical Society*. John Murray, London, 1881.

Nefzawi, Sheikh. *The Perfumed Garden*. Editions de la Fontaine d'Or, Paris, n.d.

Reusch, Richard. *History of East Africa*. In Commission: Evang. Missionsverlag, Stuttgart, 1954.

Sale, George, (translator). *The Koran*. Frederick Warne, London and New York, 1887.

Smith, Cecil Woodham. *The Reason Why*. Constable, London, 1953.

Stanley, Henry M. *How I Found Livingstone*. Sampson Low, Marston, Searle & Rivington, London, 1872.

Stark, Freya. *The Southern Gates of Arabia*. John Murray, London, 1936.

Vatsyayana. *Kama-Soutra*. Pic, Paris, 1956.

Woodruff, Douglas. *The Tichborne Claimant*. Hollis & Carter, London, 1957.

Periodicals, Booklets and Papers
(Specific articles not included in Penzer are cited in full.)

Academy.

Annals and Magazines of Natural History, Ser. 9, Vol. ii, September 1918. Article by Oldfield Thomas: 'A Revised Classification of the *Otomyinae*, with Descriptions of new Genera and Species'. (Earlier articles included in Penzer.)

Anthropological Review.

Athenaeum.

The Bookman.

Cassell's Magazine.

Cornhill Magazine.

Correspondence with British Ministers and Agents in Foreign Countries and with Foreign Ministers in England Relating to the Slave Trade. Printed by

Harrison & Sons. Presented to both houses of Parliament by Command of Her Majesty, 1864.

Correspondence with his Excellency Riaz Pasha upon the Mines of Midian. Booklet 'Printed for Private Circulation only' by Burton. The Alexandrian Stationers & Booksellers Company Limited, Alexandria, Egypt, 1880.

Correspondence Respecting Captain Burton's Proceedings at Damascus. From the files of the British Public Record Office. Printed for the use of the Foreign Office. February 1872.

The English Historical Review, January 1944.

Fortnightly Review.

The Geographical Magazine.

The Impact of Islam on Christianity by Kenneth H. Crandall. American Friends of the Middle East, New York, 1952.

Journal of the Anthropological Institute of Great Britain and Ireland.

Journal of the Royal Asiatic Society of Great Britain and Ireland.

Journals of the Royal Geographical Society.

Macmillan's Magazine.

Man.

The Manchester Examiner and Times.

Mining World.

The New Review.

The Observer, 27 November 1960. Review by Sir Harold Nicolson of Alan Moorehead, *The White Nile.*

Occult Review.

Proceedings of the Linnean Society.

Proceedings of the Zoological Society of London.

Sir Richard F. Burton; a Footnote to History. A Christmas booklet by Richard Walder Hale. A. C. Getchell & Son, Boston, 1930.

The Spiritualist.

Tanganyika Notes and Records, No. 49, December 1957.

The Times.

Transactions of the Ethnological Society of London.

Transactions of the Royal Institute of British Architects.

Transactions of the Royal Society of Literature.

Transatlantic Review, March 1924.

Warwick Street Church, booklet by R. C. Fuller. Printed by Society of St Paul, Langley, Bucks., 1956.

Index

Aali Pasha, 277
Abbazia, 391
Abd el Kadir. *See* Kadir
Abdullah, Sheik, 89
Abeokuta, 208, 210, 237
Abokr, Abdi ('End of Time'), 106, 110, 111–12, 114, 118–19, 321
Abomey, 227, 228–9, 231; captured by French, 238
Accra, 207
Addah, Ali, Somali chief, 112
Addo-Kpon. *See* Gelele
Adelsberg. *See* Postojna
Aden, 104, 106, 121, 138, 174, 321, 326
Afa divination, 231
Agha, Ali, 70–2
Ahmad bin Abu Bakr, Amir of Harar, 115, 117, 118
Ahmed, Hasan, 321
Aigle, 391
Akbar, Mirza Ali, 321–2
Albert, Prince Consort, 213
Alchemy, 42
Alexandria, 62, 64, 208
Alford, Lady Marian, 296–7
Alfred, Prince, Duke of Edinburgh, 297, 390
Al-Hamra, 81
Al Hisma, 336
Ali, a Mecca pilgrim, 94
Ali, Ao, murderer of Stroyan, 125
Al-Ihram, ceremony of, 87–8
Allahdad, a Moslem servant, 39, 49
Alma, Battle of the, 127
Al-Muwailih, 98
Amir, Snay bin, Omani slaver, 156
Ampthill, Lord, 284
Ananga Ranga, 363
Ancobra River, 354
Andes, the, 251, 263
Andrade, Caetano, 141
Angola, 225
Antelope, HMSS, 227
Anthropologia, 316
Anthropological Review, 220
Anthropological Society of London, 220, 245, 248, 298, 313, 318
Apostleship of Prayer, 315
Aqaba, Gulf of, 78, 98

Aquila, 311
Arabian Nights (original), 4, 44, 86, 105, 107; Wortley Montagu MS., 386
Arafat, Mt, 92–3
Arbuthnot, Foster Fitzgerald, 102, 322, 363, 386, 392
Argentina, 251, 263; war against Paraguay, 259, 264
Arnold, Matthew, 22, 23
Arqua Petarca, 314
Arrogant, HMS, 208
Arrowsmith, John, 137
Arundell, Henry Raymond (Isabel's father), 135, 195, 298; death, 386
Arundell, Isabel. *See* Burton, Lady
Arundell, Jack (Isabel's brother), death, 304
Arundell of Wardour, Lord (Isabel's godfather), 57, 289, 295, 328, 340
Arundell, Mrs (Isabel's mother), 220; disapproval of daughter's marriage, 195, 199, 220; as Isabel's confidante, 252, 254, 257; death, 304
Arz Al-Aman, 104
Aspinwall. *See* Colón
Asunción, capture of, 264, 265
Athenaeum, the: reviews of Burton, 51, 55, 133
Aubertin, J. J., 269, 350
Austria, 328, 341
Axim, 354
Ayyal Shirdon tribe, the, 119

Bagdad caravan, 87
Bahawalpur, 36
Baker, Dr Grenfell, 391, 393, 396–7, 401; on Burton's notebooks, 398–9
Baker, Georgina (Burton's aunt), 9, 49
Baker, Martha. *See* Burton
Baker, Mrs (Burton's grandmother), 12, 14, 19, 24, 49
Baker, Richard (Burton's grandfather), 8
Baker, Richard (Burton's uncle), 8
Baker, Sir Samuel, 319
Baker, Sarah. *See* Burton (aunt)
Balaclava, 127
Ballantine, Mr Serjeant, 293
Bandar Gharra, 34

Baragu, 211

Baroda, 30

Barth, Heinrich, 137

Basyuni, Mohammed al-, 69–70, 73, 78, 79, 81, 83, 86, 89, 91, 92, 95–6, 97

Bathurst, 206, 356

Battaglia, 314

Beamer, John: *A Comparative Grammar of the Modern Aryan Languages of India*, 54

Beatson, General W. F., 128, 130; 'Beatson's Horse', 129; removed from command, 131; sues vice-consul, 131; loses case, 132

Bedingfield, Commander, 208, 210

Bedouins, attacks by, 81; tribal fights of, 85

Beecham, John, an interpreter, 228

Behāristān, 363

Beirut, 272, 287–8

Belo Horizonte, 254

Belém, 292

Beluchi tribe, the, 32, 34, 149, 151–2, 154, 165

Benin, Bight of, 208

Benin City, 217, 233

Berbera, 104, 118; attack on Burton at, 121–5; his gear and kit lost at, 133

Bergami, Bartolomeo, 7

Bernasko, Rev. Peter W., 227, 236

Bertoldsten, 333

Biafra, Bight of, 203, 204, 215

Binnie, George, and Co., 352

Bir Abbas, 81

Bird, Dr George, 198, 220, 305, 386

Blake, Dr Carter, 313

Blois, 13–14

Bloodhound, HMS, 211

Bludan, 273–4, 286

Blunt, Wilfrid Scawen: on Isabel, 257, 263; on Burton, 262–3; on the Tichborne Claimant, 293, 295

Bologna, 312

Bombay, 29 ff., 41, 138, 182, 321–2, 324

'Bombay' (Sidi Mubarak), 144, 146, 154, 157, 162, 163, 165, 167; appointed as headman, 170

Bombay Almanac and Directory (1843), 41

Bombay Geographical Society, 145

Bonny River, 211

Bovill, Sir William, 131

Brass River, 211

Brazil: discovery of rubies in, 251; war against Paraguay, 259, 264

Brazil, Emperor and Empress of, 252, 253, 391

British Association, 240

British National Association of Spiritualists, 341

Brock, Mr, vice-consul at Trieste, 350–1

Bube tribe, 203

Buchanan, James, 185

Buenos Aires, 261–5

Buko-no, Burton's host at Abomey, 229, 231, 237

Bulhar, 119–20

Bull Run, 207

Burckhart, John Ludwig, 61–2

Burke, Sir Bernard, 218

Burton, Edward Joseph Netterville (brother), 8, 13–14, 15–16, 17, 18–19; separated from Richard, 19; rejoins Richard, 24–5; to Cambridge, 25; sent down, 26; tragic accident, 50

Burton, Eliza (cousin), 19, 49

Burton, Francis (uncle), 218

Burton, Lady (wife): 57–60, 62, 102, 105–6, 127, 134, 160, 175; engagement, 134–5; left behind in England, 136; absence of letters from Burton, 139; greets him on his return from Lake Tanganyika, 176; loving sympathy for him, 178–9; letter to her mother on him, 179–80; hears he has gone to America, 183; meets him on his return, 194–5; her rules for guidance as a wife, 195–7; marriage, 198; presented at Court, 199; left behind while he is at Fernando Po, 204; sent to Paris to see Emperor and Empress, 218; accompanies Burton to Canary Islands, 223; returns home alone, 224; on Speke, 240; anxiety at publication of *Stone Talk*, 244; work for Burton's promotion, 245–6, 247; in Portugal, 248; returns to England alone, 249; convent retreat, 249; sails for Brazil, 249; meets Burton at Rio de Janeiro, 249; makes home at São Paulo, 250; constantly left alone, 251–2; confides

in her mother, 252; Burton hypno-
tizes her, 252; trips with Burton,
252–3, 254, 255; awaits him at Rio,
257; meets him and nurses him,
257–8; returns to England, 259, 266;
obtains Damascus post for Burton,
266–7; meets him on return to
England, 268; to Boulogne with
him and then ordered back to
London, 268; rebels and follows him
to Vichy, 269; arrives in Damascus,
272; happy social life, 273; accompanies him to Palmyra, 274; her
work for him, 274–5; Arab women
companions, 275–6; rushes to join
Burton at Beirut, 287–8; left behind
to clear up, 289; in England,
amasses evidence to clear Burton,
291–2; follows him to Trieste and
catches him up at Venice, 307–8;
arrival and home in Trieste, 308–10;
their marriage, 311; accompanies
him on his trips, 311–12; sent back
to England, 315; attempts to obtain
KCB for Burton, 319; sails with
him to India, 320; on the Mecca
pilgrims, 321; on the Hindu religion,
322; life back in Trieste, 327–8; at
Suez, 338; back in Trieste, 340–1;
publicly disagrees with Burton's
philosophy, 342; reactions to Oberammergau, 350; on her husband's
modesty, 352–3; defends him as
'Amateur Consul', 358; as a wife,
360–1; and the *Arabian Nights*, 383;
gets Burton to sign paper embracing
Catholic faith, 390; at his deathbed,
397; burns his MSS., 399–400; bitter
at attacks made on her, 401; creation
of his tomb, 402; difficult last years,
405; death, 406–7

Her illnesses and accidents, 249,
253, 254, 313, 340, 357, 385; her
work for animals, 275, 314–15, 322–
3; her superstitions and her religion,
249, 297, 314–15, 342, 390

Her writings: translation of *Iraçema*, 267; *The Inner Life of
Syria, Palestine and the Holy Land
from My Private Journal*, 281–2;
299, 317, 404; *Arabia Egypt India*,
325, 340; *Lady Burton's Edition of
her Husband's Arabian Nights*, 387–
8; her biography of Burton, 403

Burton, Lieutenant-Colonel Joseph
Netterville (father), 7–8; settles in
Tours, 8; returns to England, 11;
settles at Richmond, 12; again to
France, 12; at Blois, 13–14; in Italy,
14–16; returns to France, 17; again
in Italy, 18–19; roving life in Italy,
49–50

Burton, Maria Catherine Eliza (sister).
See Stisted, Lady

Burton, Martha (mother), 7–8, 17–18;
bringing up her children, 10, 14–15;
illness, 49; death, 121

Burton, Sir Richard Francis:
Biographical: Birth, 8; childhood
and early education, 9, 11–12; life
in France, 12–14, 17; in Italy, 14,
15–17, 18–19; takes cure in Switzerland, 19; separated from brother, 19;
life at Oxford, 21 ff.; vacations, 24–
5; sent down, 26; officer in Bombay
Native Infantry, 27; sails for India,
28; Bombay, 29; Baroda, 30; assigned to Sind Survey, 34; tour of
northern Sind, 35; rejoins regiment
for First Sikh War, 36; relations
with Napier, 37–8; attempt to abduct
nun, 38–40, 50–1; brawl on ship, 40;
returns to Sind Survey, 41; roams
country in disguise, 43 ff.; flirtation
with Persian girl, 43–5; his reports,
47; refused appointment as interpreter to army marching to Multan,
47–8; in England, 49; reunion with
parents, 49; meets Isabel, 57

Mecca and Medina: plan for
travelling to, 61, 63–4, 65, 68; in
Alexandria, 64; Cairo, 67; night in
jail, 69; departure, 70–2; Suez, 73–4;
voyage to Yenbo, 75–9; crosses
desert, 80–2; in Medina, 83; crosses
Nejd Desert, 86–9; reaches Mecca,
89; to Mt Arafat, 92–3; Muzdalifah,
94; ceremony of stoning the devil,
94–5; again in Mecca, 95, 96–7;
Muna, 96; applies for money at
Jidda, 97; Cairo, 98; Bombay, 99

Somali Peninsula: ambition to
reach Harar, 102; and to explore
Somali Peninsula, 103; preparations,

104 ff.; leaves Aden, 106; Zeila, 106–8; throws off disguise, 113–14; in Harar, 114–18; to Berbera, 118–20; prepares in Aden for new expedition, 121; attack on, outside Berbera, 121, 122–5; returns to England, 127

Volunteers for service in Crimea, 127; Chief of Staff to Beatson, 129; friction with Turkish officials, 129; his men in trouble, 130–1; resigns with Beatson, 131; tries to form company for helping pilgrims reach Mecca, 132

Lake Tanganyika: determined to discover fountain-head of Nile, 132; leaves for Africa, 136; ignores order to return as court-martial witness, 138; in Zanzibar, 139–41; preparations, 141; cruises down coast, 142; to Mombasa, Tanga, Pangani and Tongwe, 142–4; on Ugogo plains, 154–5; Unyamwezi, 155; Tabora, 156; finds Lake Tanganyika, 158; enters Ujiji, 159; to Uvira, 162; back to Tabora, 164–5; clam named after him, 164; Kunduchi, 172; Kilwa, 172; Zanzibar, 174; Aden, 174; returns to England, 176

Salt Lake City: leaves for America, 183; departs for Salt Lake City, 183; arrives, 188; San Francisco, 191, 192; signs of Indians, 191; Carson City, 191–2; Virginia City, 192; Panama, 192; Colón, 192; returns to England, 193; marriage, 198

Fernando Po: loses sinecure in Indian Army, 202; consulship of Fernando Po, 202–3; journey out, 206–8; arrival, 208; various trips, 208; to Cameroon Mts, 212–13; back in Fernando Po, 214–15; gorilla-hunting in the Gaboon, 215–16; second expedition, to study cannibalism, 217; Benin City, 217; on leave in England, 219–21; leave in Tenerife, 223–4; trip up the Congo River, 225; appointed Commissioner to Dahomey, 225; instructions from Foreign Office,

226–7; presented to King Gelele, 227–8; Abomey, 228–31; present at annual customs, 232–6; sends government's demands to king, 237–8; returns to Fernando Po, 238–9; home leave, 239

Santos: appointment as consul, 246; Ireland, 247; Portugal, 248; decides to live at São Paulo, 250; lead-mine concession, 251; to Rio de Janeiro and Petropolis, 252–3; Minas Gerais, 254; down São Francisco River on raft, 256–7; return to São Paulo, 257; applies for leave, 259; Montevideo, 260; Rosario, 260; Parana River, 261; Buenos Aires, 261; mysterious tour, 263; learns of appointment as consul at Damascus, 264; visits Paraguay battlefields again, 264; back in England, 268; Vichy, 268

Damascus: learns of objections to Damascus appointment, 270–1; arrives, 272; immediate trips, 272; Palmyra trip, 274; Palestine, 281; Nazareth incident, 283–4; disobeys order to remain in Damascus, 286; recalled, 287; returns to England, 288

Refuses small posts, 292; testimony in Tichborne case, 292–5; complaints on pay, 300–1; accepts private offer to explore sulphur-mining possibilities of Iceland, 301

Trieste: accepts consular post at Trieste, 304; journey out, 307–8; various trips, 311–12; in England again, 317–18; meeting with Gladstone, 318; second Icelandic trip, 318; France, 319; returns to Trieste, 319; Indian trip, 320–4; Goa, 324–5; Egypt, 326; suggests exploring for gold in Midian, 327; returns to Trieste, 327; gold project, 328–31; back in Trieste, 331; declines offer from General Gordon, 332–3; second Midian trip, 334–8; exhibition of results, 339; to Trieste and then back to England on leave, 339; Ireland, 339–40; returns to Trieste, 340; Austrian tour, 341; again in

Egypt, 344; returns to Trieste after Egyptian failure, 346; Oberammergau, 349–50; suggests himself as temporary Slave Commissioner in Red Sea, 351; abortive oil-mining schemes for Midian, 352; further trips, 353; at Geographical Congress in Venice, 353; prospecting on Gold Coast, 354–5; returns to England, 357; suggests himself as Governor of Gold Coast, 358; sent to Sinai to find Palmer, 359–60; fails to get post of Minister to Morocco, 383, 385; made KCMG, 384; returns to Trieste, 385–6; refused leave to retire at sixty-five, 387; stays with sister, 388; to Paris and Cannes, 388–9; earthquakes, 389; returns to Trieste, 389; proposes toast at Golden Jubilee dinner, 390; tours Austria, 390; Croatia, 391; final visit to England, 392; constant moving, 393; letter from Foreign Office complaining at excessive leave, 393; urged to write his autobiography, 394; death, 397; funerals, 398; great popularity after his death, 406

Personal: as a child, 9–11, 12; passion for languages, 23, 29, 30, 32–3, 41, 52; theories of, 23; the learning of, 23, 27, 29, 32, 34, 105, 111, 140, 187, 230–1; attitude to religion, 32, 90–1, 101–2, 245, 342, 378; fencing, 16, 22, 24, 60; affinity for gypsies, 22; impressions of Bombay, 29; of Karachi, 33–4; of the Dahomeans, 237; of the Paraguayans, 264–5; of Midian, 331; sports and pastimes, 31; his *bubu*, 31–2; report on pederasty for Napier, 35; monkey training, 37; his illnesses, 38, 41, 43, 111–12, 113, 142, 149–50, 156–7, 258, 313, 387, 389; studies: of Indian life, 35; of Islamic schools of thought, 42; of alchemy, 42; of oriental ways, 43; of Somali weapons, 107; of Arab life, 166; of American idiom, 184; of cannibalism, 217; of the Cici, 310; his writing, 50 ff., 274, 374, 375, 380; prejudices, 45–6, 50, 53, 377–8; superstitions, 53–4, 297; unsavoury

reputation, 56; financial difficulties and money-making schemes, 57, 296, 317–18; as 'Father of Moustaches', 87; sings to Bedouins, 87; disguises: oriental, 35, 43, 63–4; Afghan, 68; as Moslem merchant, 106, 108; and Isabel Arundell: their engagement, 134–5, 176; marriage, 198; as a husband, 199, 204–5, 218, 247, 252, 307–8, 360; careless in choosing personnel, 146–7; difficulties in handling men, 150; greater experience, 170, 171; relations with Speke, 166, 168, 182, 200, 201, 240–1, 242–3; interest in gold-mining, 254–5; relations with Rigby, 297–8; social and political outlook, 307; as an 'Amateur Consul', 358; eccentricities, 360–1; sense of failure, 362; opinions: on slavery and serfdom, 100, 351, 356; on polygamy, 101, 189, 211, 222–3; on mosquito as cause of malaria, 133; on inadequate defences of Red Sea ports, 138, 170–1; on whaling, 140; on German influence in East Africa, 140; on scalping, 186; on Mormon life, 188; on missionaries, 210; on the kola nut, 221; on women soldiers, 231; on a hermaphrodite, 248; on spiritualism, 341; on children, 356–7; on morality, 378–9; on sex, 379

Writings: Abeokuta and the Cameroons Mountains, 221, 244; Arabian Nights (translation), 250, 311, 317, 346, 361–82, 383, 386–7, 391, 392; 'Terminal Essay' in, 380–2; Battlefields of Paraguay, 258, 261–2, 274, 301; Book of the Sword, 346, 358; Camoens – his Life and his Lusiads, 248, 250, 347–8, 348–9; Captivity of Hans Stade (translation), 316; Carmina of Catullus (translation), 403–4; City of the Saints, 187, 188, 218; Complete System of Bayonet Exercise, 55; El Islam, or the Rank of Muhammadanism among the Religions of the World, 101; Etruscan Bologna, 321, 346; Falconry in the Valley of the Indus, 54–5; First Footsteps in East Africa,

133; *Glance at the 'Passion Play'*, 349; *Goa and the Blue Mountains*, 50; *Goldmines of Midian*, 334, 338; *Highlands of Brazil*, 254, 266–7, 325; *Iceland Revisited*, 318; *Il Pentamerone*, 403; *The Jew, the Gypsy and El Islam*, 404–5; *Kasîdah, the*, 342–4, 345; *Lake Regions of Central Africa*, 181, 222; *Land of Midian Revisited*, 340; *Lands of Cazembe*, 267, 315–16; *Lyricks*, 347, 349; *Manuel de Moraes* (translation with Isabel), 267–8; *Mission to Gelele, King of Dahome*, 244; *New System of Sword Exercise for Infantry*, 316; *Nile Basin, The*, 242, 346; *Personal Narrative of a Pilgrimage to Al-Madinah and Meccah*, 99–100, 267; *Priapeia*, (translation), 395; *Proverbia Communia Syriaca*, 274; *Scented Garden* (translation), 395, 396, 399, 400–1; *Scinde, or the Unhappy Valley*, 43–5, 51, 52; *Sind Revisited*, 323–4; *Sindh, and the Races that Inhabit the Valley of the Indus*, 47, 51, 54; *Stone Talk* (as by Frank Baker), 244–5; *To the Gold Coast for Gold*, 355, 357; *Two Trips to Gorilla Land*, 316; *Ultima Thule, or a Summer in Iceland*, 301–3, 316; *Unexplored Syria*, 274, 299, 304; *Uruguay*, 316; *Vikram and the Vampire*, 250, 274, 301, 317, 363; *Wanderings on Three Continents*, 404; *Wanderings in West Africa*, 221–2, 355; *Wit and Wisdom from West Africa*, 244, 317, 346; *Zanzibar*, 290–1. See also Appendix, pp. 411–14

Burton, Captain St George (cousin), 402

Burton, Sarah (aunt), 7, 24

Burton, Sarah (cousin), 19, 49

Cairo, 67–9, 80, 98, 145, 331, 338

Calicut, 41

Cameron, Captain Verney Lovett, RN, 181, 305, 353–5, 392

Cameroon Mts, 208, 211; names given to peaks, 212–13

Cameroon River, 212

Camoens, Luis Vaz de, 38, 172, 248, 347, 354

Camp Floyd, 190–1

Campbell, Malford, 384

Canary Islands, 52, 206, 223–4

Cannes, 388

Cannibal Club, 220–1, 300

Cardigan, 7th Earl of, 128

Caroline, Queen, 7

Carson City, 191–2

Castro, Thomas. See Tichborne

Cavalli, Signor, 16

Caza da Misericordia (convent), 38

Chamonix, 176

Chand, Him, 32

Chandler, Professor William H., 386

Charles X, King of France, 11

Charrington, Flag Lieutenant Harold, 359

Chatto, Andrew, 268

Chico, Isabel's servant, 250, 252, 255, 256

Chile, 251, 263

Church Missionary Society, 142

Chyudaton, Prince, a Dahomean noble, 229

Cici, the, 310

Clarence (Santa Isabel), 203, 217

Clarendon, 4th Earl of, 137, 269–70

Clarke, J., Charles J., 328, 339

Cleminshaw, C. G., 352

Cold Springs, 185

Cole, Charles, 97

Colón, 192

Congo River, 225

Constable, Sir Clifford, 193

Cooley, W. D.: Burton's attacks on, 222

Copal, 145

Cordoba, 263

Corrientes, 261

Corsellis, Colonel Henry, 36–7

Crimean War, 127–8, 245; end of, 132

Crooker, William, 251

Cruikshank, John, 227

Cunard, Samuel, 21

D'Aguilar, Mrs (Burton's aunt), 24

Dahomey, Kingdom of, 210, 225, 226; women warriors, 226; killings in, 226; declares war on Abeokuta, 237; defeated, 238; made French colony, 238

Daily Telegraph: Burton's article in, 320

Damascus, 264, 266 ff., 292

Damascus caravan, 77, 85, 86–7
Dana, Lieutenant James Jackson, 183, 187
Dana, Richard Henry, 21
Dana, Thesta, 183, 187
Dar es Salaam, 172
Darfur, 332
Darwin, Charles, 324
Delafosse, Rev. Charles, 11, 76
Denis (Gaboon), 215
Derby, 15th Earl of, 251, 264, 269, 296
Din, Haji Wali al-, 67–8, 71, 72, 327, 328, 330, 331, 334, 335
Drummond-Hay, Sir John, 383
Druze tribe, 285–6, 291
Dublin, 247, 339
Du Chaillu, Paul, 216, 217, 229, 392
Dunyazad, a cook, 109, 112, 321
Du Pre, H. R., 12–13, 16–19
Dwarka, the, 41, 97

East Africa, German influence in, 140
Edison phonograph, 392
Edward Prince of Wales (Edward VII), 297, 390
Egba tribe, 211
Egyptian caravan, 77
Eldridge, S. Jackson, 271, 273, 285–6
Elphinstone, Lord, 138
Ellenborough, Lord, 28
Elliot, Sir Henry, British Ambassador at Constantinople, 270, 271–2; attempts to get Burton recalled, 276–7, 279; makes trouble over Nazareth incident, 284 ff.
El Muwailih, 334, 336
Evans, Arthur, 357, 392
Examiner, the, on Burton's *Zanzibar*, 291
Exploration, in nineteenth century, 132

Faeroes, the, 304
Fan tribe, 217
Favre, Jules, 328
Fernando Po, 203, 208, 214–15; Burton finally falls in love with, 238–9
Fitzgerald, Edward, 200, 342
Florence, 15, 312
Floyd, John B., 185
Foakes, Dr, 387
Fon language, 231
Forbes, Duncan, 27
Forteune, a hunter, 216

Fort Kearny, 185
Fraser's Magazine for Town and Country, 250, 317
Freer, Miss Goodrich, 406
Friedenthal, Baron Pino de, 310
Fryston Hall, 219–20
Fuga, 144
Funchal, 223
Furious, HMS, 174

Gaboon, the (Gabon), 215
Gaboon River, 215
Galla tribe, 115
Galland, Antoine, 364, 366
Galton, Francis, 137
Gama, Vasco da, 38, 172
Gayangos y Arce, Pascual de, 23
Gelele, King of Dahomey, 226; Burton presented to, 227–8; ceremony at Abomey, 229–30; annual customs, 232–6; in his capacity as Addo-Kpon, 235–6
Geneva, 176, 392–3
Geography, physical, nineteenth century interest in, 132
Gezo, King of Dahomey, 226
Ghazni, fall of, 28
Ghana. *See* Gold Coast
Gilchrist, John, 9
Gill, Captain William John, 359
Girhi tribe, 108, 114
Gladstone, W. E., 318
Goa, 38, 40, 324–5
Golab, of the Yusuf tribe, 124
Gold Coast, 354–5, 358
Golden Age, the, 192
Gordon, General Charles, 'Chinese', 345, 351, 360; offers to Burton, 332–3, 338, 340
Gordon, Mrs, 255, 256
Gorilla-hunting, 215, 216–17
Grant, Colonel James A., 144, 166, 183, 243; his camp attacked and plundered, 207; probes connection between Lake Victoria and the Nile, 239
Granville, 2nd Earl, 276, 278, 279, 284, 291, 351–2; orders Burton to remain in Damascus, 286; offers him consular post in Trieste through Isabel, 304
Grebo War, the, 208
Grindlay, Captain Henry, 62

Index

Grove, Sir William Robert, 21
Guaicui (Guaicuhy), 256
Gudabirsi tribe, 108, 110
Guinea Coast Gold Mining Company, 354–5
Gulad, a policeman ('Long Gulad'), 106, 109, 114, 115, 118–19, 321
Gulistān, 363

Habr Awal tribe, 110, 113, 118, 119
Habr Girhajis tribe, 106, 119
Hajilik, The (Pilgrimage to Mecca Syndicate Ltd), 132
Hamerton, Lieutenant-Colonel Atkins, British Consul in Zanzibar, 139, 140–1, 145, 147, 163, 243
Hamid al-Samman. *See* Samman
Hammal, Al-. *See* Mahmud
Hamza of Isfahan (Arabic historian), 54
Hankey, Frederick, 181, 186, 217, 234, 386
Harar, 102, 106, 114–17; the people and customs, 117–18
Hare, Humphrey, 219
Harrison, W. H., 349
Hashim, Sheik, 42
Heidelberg, 24–5
Herne, Lieutenant G. E., 103, 104, 120, 121, 122–3, 124–5
Hogg, Sir James, 37, 61
Home News: description of Burton, 338
Honourable East India Company, 27, 102–3, 202; Burton's criticisms, 53; refuse compensation, 133; grant leave for Lake Tanganyika expedition, 137
Hooker, Sir Joseph Dalton, 212
Hortis, Attilio, 398
Houghton, Lord (Richard Monckton Milnes), 137, 180–1, 219, 233–4, 244, 268, 296, 340, 386, 392
Hughes, Tom, 22
Humaita, 261
Hunt, Dr James, 220
Hutaym tribe, 337
Hyderabad, 324; Battle of, 32

Iceland, 301–4, 315–6, 318
Idrisi, Al-: map and description of Central African Lakes, 137
Ignatius, St, 40–1

India Office: censure Burton, 201–2
Indian Mutiny, 163
Ionides, Luke, 263
Ipiranga lead mine, 266
Irvine, James, 354, 357
Irving, Henry, 392
Isa tribe, 108, 110
Islam: various schools of thought, 42; the fundamentals of, 77; sects, 80
Ismail I, Khedive of Egypt, 327, 328, 331, 334, 339
Istria, 310, 353
Italy, Burton family wanderings in, 14 ff., 49–50
Iturburu, Atilano Calvo, 212, 213

Jago, Thomas: takes over Damascus consulate, 287
Janeo, 32
Jats, the, as forerunners of gypsies, 54, 59
Jebel Abyab, 330, 335, 337
Jerusalem, 283, 313
Jidda, 97, 320; massacre at, 170, 171
Jinni, Sa'ad al-, 75, 76, 79, 81
Johnson, Rev. G. L., 353
Johnston, Sir Harry, 214
Journal of the Anthropological Society: Burton's articles in, 316
Journal of the Royal Geographical Society: Burton's articles in, 316
Journal of the Society of Arts: Burton's articles in, 316

Kaaba. *See* Mecca
Kadir, Abd el, 276, 278, 291
'Kalendar', the. *See* Yusuf
Kama Sūtra, 363
Kamashastra Society, 363
Kana (Kama), 227
Kannena, Chief, 159, 161, 162, 163
Kaol, 145
Karachi, 33–5, 41
Kars, Russian siege of, 130
Kaushan, Jirad Adan bin, 112–13
Kayf, pleasure of, 63
Kazeh. *See* Tabora
Kennedy, C. M.: investigates consular posts at Damascus, 278–9
Khamoor ('The Moon'), Isabel's maid, 275, 296–7
Khudabakhsh Namdar, Miyan, 67
Kidogo, of the 'Sons of Ramji', 155

Kilimanjaro, Mt, discovery of, 142
Kilwa Kisiwani, 167, 172
Kola nut, 221
Korogwe, 144
Krapf, Johann, 142
Kru language, 213
Krumen tribe, 212, 213
Kunduchi, 172

Ladha, a collector of customs, 148
Lagos, 207–8, 211
Lane, Edward William, 365, 376
Lane-Poole, Stanley, 100
Lang, Andrew, 376
Larkana, 35
Larking, John Wingfield, 64–5, 386
Lausanne, 176, 393
Lawrence, D. L., 405
Layard, Sir Austen Henry, 219
Leighton, Sir Frederick, 268; paints
    Burton, 300
Léon, Ponce de, 2
Lesseps, Ferdinand de, 339
Leslie, Dr Ralph, 389, 390–1
Lever, Charles James, 247, 304, 324
Libreville, 215
Light Brigade, Charge of, 127
Lima, 264
Lincoln, Abraham, 192
Lipizza, 311
Lisbon, 248, 354
Liverpool, 235, 339
Livingstone, Dr David, 144, 146,
    156, 159, 162, 166, 291, 394; ridiculed
    by Burton, 222; on sources of the
    Nile, 243
Loango, 225
Loretto, pilgrimage to, 312
Louis XIV of France, 7, 218
Louis, Prince, of Battenberg, 390
Lowe, Robert. *See* Sherbrooke, Lord
Luanda, 225
Lucan, 3rd Earl of, 128
Lucca, 19
Lucerne, 393
Lumsden, James Grant, 99, 103, 138

Mabruki, Muinyi, 146, 151, 154, 159,
    162, 164–5
McCarthy, Justin Huntley, 388
Maclaren, Archibald, 22
Macmillan's Magazine: Burton's arti-
    cles in, 316

M'Queen, James: criticisms of Speke,
    242–3
Madeira, 206, 354–5
Magellan Straits, 264
Maghribis, the, 75, 76
Mahabaleshwar, 324
Mahmud, Mohammed (Al-Hammal,
    'the Porter'), 106, 109, 112, 114,
    115, 118–19, 321
Maizan, Lieutenant, 139
Major, Mr, 325–6
Mann, Gustav, 211–14
Marar plains, the, 110
Marcy: *The Prairie Traveller*, 183, 223
Marie, George, 328, 329, 339, 340
Martelani, Fr Pietro, 397
Masai tribe, 142
Masqat, 61, 85
Mas'ud, Sheik, 86, 87, 92, 93, 94, 96
Matheran, 324
Maxwell, William Constable, 263, 297
Mazungera tribe, 139
Mbata, 215
Mecca, 61, 63; pilgrim caravans to, 77–
    8; the Kaaba, 61, 89–90, 91, 92, 95–
    6; the Black Stone, 61, 90, 91–2;
    Well of Zemzem, 91
Medina, 61, 63; pilgrimage to, 78–86;
    description of, 82; the Prophet's
    Mosque, 84
Mendoza, 263
Meydell, Baron de, 17
Mezrab, Jane Digby el (Lady Ellen-
    borough), 276
Mezrab, Medjuel el, 276
Miani, Battle of, 32
Midian, 327, 328–32, 334–7, 340, 352,
    393
Milan, 319
Milnes, Richard Monckton. *See*
    Houghton
Minas Gerais province, 251, 254
Mining Journal, The, 301, 304
Missionaries, dislike of Burton, 271
Mitford, Algernon Freeman-. *See*
    Redesdale
Mohammed al-Basyuni. *See* Basyuni
Mohammed, Jirad, Wazir of Harar,
    116, 117
Mohammed Khan Ka Tanda, 36
Mohammed the Prophet, 63
Mombasa, 141, 142
Montagu MS., 386

Montevideo, 260
Montreux, 393
Moore, Sir John, 7
Moore, 'Miss', 187-8
Mormons, 184, 188-90, 218
Morning Post: Isabel's letter to, confessing burning of MSS., 399-400
Morning Standard, the, 301
Morogoro. *See* Zungomero
Morro Velho, 254; disasters at, 255-6
Mortlake, 402-3
Mpombinda, 215
Muawiya, Caliph, 87
Mubarak, Sidi. *See* 'Bombay'
Mukhbir, the, 334, 336
Muller, Professor Max, 386
Multan, 47
Muna, 96
Murad, Ali, 75-6
Murchison, Sir Roderick, 137, 175, 268; death, 298
Murray, James, 270
Musurus Pasha, 297
Muzdalifah, 94

Napier, General Sir Charles, 32, 34-5, 245; his personality, 37-8
Naples, 15-17
Nassar, a camel driver, 72
Nazareth, incident at, 283-4
Neil, Brigadier T. G., 129-30
Nejd Desert, 86
Newman, Cardinal, 22
Nicolson, Sir Harold, 356-7
Niger River, delta, 208
Nigeria, 208, 217
Nightingale, Florence, 127
Nile River, 66-7, 121, 142; sources of, 132-3, 137, 145, 394; Speke and, 167-8, 239, 242-3
Nilgiri Hills, 38, 41
Noyce, Wilfred, 2
Numismatic Society, 318
Nur, an Indian servant, 66, 73, 80, 81, 83, 86, 89, 92, 96-7
Nyasa, Lake, 137, 164

Oberammergau, 349-50
Oil Rivers, the, 208, 238, 354
Oliphant, Lawrence, 240
Omar Effendi, 74, 78, 81, 86
Oomchanga, 332
Ootacamund, 41

Opicina, xi, 311, 340, 346, 390
Orton, Arthur. *See* Tichborne
Oshogbo, 226, 238
Ouida, 312, 388, 400; on the Burtons' marriage, 388
Ouidah, 227, 238
Outram, Colonel James, 104-5, 121

Palestine, 281
Palmer, Professor Edward Henry, 280-1, 359-60
Palmerston, 3rd Viscount, 199
Palmyra, 274
Panama, 192
Pangani, 144
Paraguay, 251; war in, 259, 261, 264
Parana River, 260-1
Paray-le-Monial, 319
Paris, 218, 388, 392
Pau, 17
Paul, a guide, 215
Pauletic, Fr, 353
Payne, John, 362, 365, 374, 376
Pedro, Don, Emperor of Brazil, 252, 253, 391
Pemba Island, 141
Perfumed Garden, The 363, 400-1. For translation see Scented Garden under Writings in Burton entry
Pernambuco. *See* Recife
Perrochel, Vicomte de, 274
Persians, unpopularity of among Moslems, 67-8, 80
Peru, 251, 263
Petermann, Augustus, 142
Petropolis, 252
Philby, H. St J., 85
Pigott, Blanche, 136, 175
Pinguete, 312
Pini, Antonia, 18
Pini, Caterina, 18
Pirapora, 256
Pisa, 14, 18-19, 49, 176
Pitts, Joseph, 61
Poichard de la Boulerie, M., 272
Postojna (Adelsberg), 333; caves, 312
Potts: *Die Zigeuner in Europa und Asien,* 54
Prevald, 311
Price, Rev. B., 386
Prometheus, HMS, 208
Provence, 17

Ptolemy: theory on sources of the Nile, 137
Punjab, the, 36

Radcliffe, Katherine, 295
Raghi, an Isa guide, 108, 109
Raglan, 1st Baron, 127–8; death, 128
Ramée, Marie Louise de la. *See* Ouida
Ramji, a customs clerk, 146, 148
Rashid Pasha, 271–2, 276–7, 299; attempts to have Burton murdered, 285; recall and murder, 292
Rassam, Hormuzd, 297
Rawlinson, Sir Henry, 299
Reade, Charles, 296
Rebmann, Johannes, 142, 144
Recife, 249
Recoaro, 314
Redesdale, 1st Baron, 204, 280
Red Sea ports, 138, 170
Rehatsek, Edward, 363
Reid, Winwood, 296
Reykjavik, 301, 304
Riaz, Pasha, 344–5, 351
Richards, Alfred Bates, 22, 308, 410
Richmond, Surrey, 11–12
Rickard, Major Ignacio, 263
Rigby, General Christopher Palmer, 33; British Consul in Zanzibar, 152; dislike of Burton, 174, 177, 201; work for Africa, 208; slave liberation, 239–40; argument with Burton at Royal Geographical Society, 297–8
Rio de Janeiro, 249, 252, 254, 257
Rodrigues, Valentine, 141, 149, 163
Rohri, 36
Rome, 15, 312
Rosario, 260
Rouen, 319
Royal Anthropological Institute of Great Britain and Ireland, 220, 298
Royal Asiatic Society, 47, 274, 290
Royal Geographical Society, 61, 62, 137, 138, 165, 169, 189, 267–8, 290, 291, 297–9, 316, 318; Burton reads paper to, 127; he reports on East African tour, 150; award of Gold Medal to Burton, 177
Ruhebo Mts, 153
Russell, 1st Earl (Lord John Russell), 202, 226; satisfaction at Burton's Dahomey mission, 238

Russell, Lady, 295
Russell, Odo. *See* Ampthill, Lord
Ruvu River, 144
Ruxton, Miss, governess, 12–13
Ruzizi River, 162
Ryan, Dr J. W. ('Paddy'), 29–30

Sa'ad al-Jinni. *See* Jinni
Sacramento, 192
Sagharrah, village of, 112–13
Said bin Salim. *See* Salim
Said el Muameri, Sayf bin, 146
Said, Sayid, Sultan of Zanzibar, 139
St Joseph, Mo., 183
Saker, Rev. Alfred, 212
Salahiyyeh, 272
Salim el Lamki, Said bin, 141, 154; dismissed as headman, 170, 171
Salisbury, 3rd Marquis of, 384
Salt Lake City, 183–4, 188–90
Salvador, 266
Salzburg, 353
Samman, Hamid al-, 74, 81, 83–6
San Bartolo, 311
San Canziano, caves of, 312
San Francisco, 191, 192
Santa Isabel. *See* Clarence
Santiago de Chili, 263
Santos, 246, 250, 252–3, 259
São Francisco River, 251, 254, 256–7
São Paulo, 250, 252, 257
Sartoris, Mrs (Adelaide Kemble), 268–9
Scalping, 186
Scarlett, General James, 128
Schinznach-Bad, 19
Schliemann, Dr Heinrich, 391
Scotsman: inaccurate report of Burton's death, 317
Scott, General Walter, 33, 34–5
Scott, William Bell, 269
Segrave, Louisa, 59, 133–4, 136
Selim Aga, a servant, 208, 212, 214, 215, 216
Selina, a gypsy girl, 22
Semmering, 393
Serpent, HMS, 248
Sevastopol, Battle of, 127
Shahrazad, a cook, 109, 112, 321
Shamyl, Caucasian leader, 130
Sharmarkay bin Ali Salih, Al-Hajj, 107, 113
Shaub al-Hajj, 81
Shaw, Dr Norton, 188, 189, 201, 290

Shepheard, Sam, 73
Sherbrooke, Lord, 219
Shi'ites, the, 67, 80
Shuldham, Arthur, 60
Siena, 14–15
Sierra Leone, 206
Sierra de San Luiz, 263
Sieveking, A. Forbes, 358
Sign language, 187, 212
Sikh War I, 36
Sikh War II, 47
Sikhism, 42
Sikujui, a slave, 153
Silk al-Zahab, voyage of, 74–80
Sinai desert, 359
Sind, acquired by British, 32
Sind Survey, 34 ff., 41 ff.
Sindhi, the, 45–6
Sinnar, the, 328, 336, 337
Slatin, Rudolf, 333
Smallpox, 151
Smith, Major-General Richard, 131
Smithers, Leonard C., 395, 399, 403–4
Sohrabji, Dosabhai, 29–30
Somali tribes, the, 110–11; attack on
    Burton's party at Berbera, 122–5
Somalia, 102; proposals for expeditions
    to, 102–3
Somerset, Duke and Duchess of, 296
South American Monthly, 260
Speke, John Hanning, 104, 121, 123,
    124–5, 144, 153–4, 165, 182; grudge
    against Burton, 126, 169, 177–8, 201;
    joins Burton for Lake Tanganyika
    expedition, 137–8, 141; illnesses,
    149, 153–4, 169–70; blindness, 157–
    8; ear trouble, 160–1; sub-expedition
    to Lake Ukerewe, 165–6; discovers
    Lake Victoria, 167–8; Rigby's
    support for, 174; leaves for Eng-
    land, 174; tells Royal Geographical
    Society of his discoveries, 175;
    reaches Cape of Good Hope, 189;
    in Usagara, 192; difficulties, 207;
    neglects western shores of Lake
    Victoria, 214, 243; proves link
    between Lake Victoria and Nile,
    239; meets Burton at British Asso-
    ciation meeting, 240–1; death, 241–2;
    Burton's criticisms of, 242, 290
Speke Gulf, 168
Spiritualist, The: Burton's articles in,
    316

Stanley, Henry M., 144, 146, 156, 159,
    162, 166, 181–2; *How I Found
    Livingstone*, 182; and sources of
    the Nile, 243; at home after finding
    Livingstone, 291; Burton's critic-
    ism of, 316; on Burton, 394, 395
Stanley, Dorothy, 394
Stanley, Lord. *See* Derby, 15th Earl of
Steinhaeuser, Dr John Frederick, 37,
    56, 105, 106, 138, 174, 313, 321,
    362–3, 386
Stisted, Elizabeth, 65
Stisted, Georgiana, 45, 392, 401–2
Stisted, General Sir Henry, 49
Stisted, Maria, Lady (Burton's sister),
    8, 45, 49, 388, 392, 401–2
Stocks, J. Ellerton, Assistant Surgeon
    Bombay Medical Establishment, 47,
    103–4
Stone, General Charles, 334
Strangford, Lord, 296
Stratford de Redcliffe, Lord, 130
Stroyan, Lieutenant William, 103–4,
    120, 121, 123; murdered, 125
Styria, 333
Suez, 73, 326, 337, 338
Suez desert, the, 72
Sufism, 42, 91
Sunnites, the, 80
Sutton, Henry Frederick Walpole
    Manners, 405
Swahili, 140
Swinburne, Algernon Charles, 200,
    219–20, 220–1, 392; to Vichy with
    Burton, 268, 269, 272; *Lesbia Bran-
    don*, 268; *Poems and Ballads, Second
    Series*, 269; on Burton's translation
    of Camoens, 348–9
Sykes, Colonel William Henry, 55, 137
Syrian caravan, 77

Tablet, the, 306
Tabora, 156, 164, 165
Tanganyika, Lake, 158–65, 394
Tangier, 384–5
Tenerife, 206, 223–4
Tewfik Pasha, 339, 344–5
Thierry, Baron de, 8
Thomas, Oldfield, 213
Thornton, Sir Edward, 251, 253
Thurburn, Hugh, 328
Thurburn, John, 64, 73
Thurburn, Robert, 208

Tichborne Claimant, 263, 281, 292–5
Times, The, 242; Burton's letters to, on spiritualism, 341
Times of India, The: Burton's articles in, 326
Tongwe, 144
Torch, HMS, 225
Torrens, Henry, 365, 376
Tours, 8, 11, 13, 319
Trieste, 304, 306, 308–11, 313, 319, 323, 339, 385–6, 390–1, 393, 398
Truth: on Burton, 352–3
Turin, 319
Tusker, Miss, criticized by Burton, 222
Tussaud, John Theodore, 406
Twain, Mark, 192
Tyrwhitt-Drake, Charles F., 280–1, 285, 286, 299, 312; death in Jerusalem, 313

Ugogo, 148; plains, 154–5
Ujiji, 159, 161–3; 'Sea of', 137, 148
Ukerewe Lake, 165
Umm Harb, 337
Umm el Karayat, 337
Unyamwezi, 145, 155
Unyamyembe, 153, 154
Uruguay: war against Paraguay, 239, 264
Usagara Hills, 150
Uspallata Pass, 263
Uvira, 162

Valparaiso, 263
Vanity Fair, on Burton, 358
Varley, John, 27
Venice, 176, 307, 312, 353–4, 393
Verona, 333
Vicenza, 314
Vichy, 268–9, 272, 319
Victoria (Nigeria), 211, 214
Victoria, Lake, 142, 167–8, 173, 175, 242–3, 394
Victoria, Queen, 21, 213, 281 f.

Vienna, 353; Great Exhibition at, 312
Villon Society, 365
Virginia City, 192
Vivian, General, 131
Vogt, Carl, 392

Wadi Nogai, 104, 133
Wahabi tribe, 87, 88–9
Wahumba tribe, 153
Wal, Said, an *abban*, 112
Wali al-Din, Haji: *see* Din
Wallin, George Augustus, 62, 95
Wanyamwezi tribe, 155
Warren, Captain Charles, 272, 359–60
Wasagara tribe, 154
Wejh, 79, 337
Wellington, 1st Duke of, 7
Wiesbaden, 24
Wilensi, village of, 112, 118
Wilkins, W. H., 405
Wilkinson, Sir John Gardner, 100
Williams, Charles, 266, 278
Wilson, Ellen, 275
Wilson, Frank, 241
Wiseman, Cardinal, 135, 195, 198
World, the: picture of Burton's house in Trieste, 308–10

Xavier, St Francis, 38, 324

Yaum Al-Tarwiyah, ceremonies of, 92
Yenbo, 80
Young, Brigham, 188; Burton's impressions of, 189–90
Yusuf ('The Kalendar'), a servant, 109, 112, 118, 321

Zagazig, 328, 334, 338
Zahle, 275
Zanzibar, 139–40, 144; turmoil in, 139, 174
Zanzibar, Sultan of, 174, 318
Zeila, 106–8
Zungomero, 150